Handbook of Race and Development in Mental Health

Edward C. Chang • Christina A. Downey
Editors

Handbook of Race and Development in Mental Health

Springer

Editors
Ph. D. Edward C. Chang
University of Michigan
Department of Psychology
2263 East Hall
530 Church St.
Ann Arbor Michigan 48109
USA
changec@umich.edu

Ph. D. Christina A. Downey
Indiana University Kokomo
Department of Psychology
2300 S. Washington St.
Kokomo Indiana 46904
USA
downeyca@iuk.edu

ISBN 978-1-4614-0423-1 e-ISBN 978-1-4614-0424-8
DOI 10.1007/978-1-4614-0424-8
Springer New York Dordrecht Heidelberg London

Library of Congress Control Number: 2011937055

Printed on acid-free paper

Springer is part of Springer Science+Business Media (www.springer.com)

I would like to dedicate this work to my parents, Tae Myung-Sook and Chang Suk-Choon. As immigrants, they sacrificed their life paths so that my journey to becoming a Korean American would be fruitful and bright. I will always keep close, in my heart and in my head, the pride I have of being their child, and make sure to offer my own path to my always remarkable child, Chang Olivia Dae.

E.C.C.

This volume is dedicated to every mental health researcher and practitioner who seeks to understand context, history, and the best qualities of each individual and culture. In addition, I offer sincere gratitude to my family, friends, colleagues, and mentors, for always showing me the best in myself and in you.

C. A. D.

Foreword

A systematic understanding of positive human development and behavior did not originate with Western psychology of the 20th and 21st centuries. A rich source of well-formulated positive psychology is found in Asian religions that go back more than 2500 yrs. Most major Asian religions have at their core a psychology little known to the millions of their followers, but articulated well by monks, gurus, yogis, erudite people, and health professionals (e.g., Nikhilananda, 1942). Two Asian psychological principles of virtuous ways of life are presented here briefly. First, a most complex laid-out psychology is classical Buddhism, called *Abhidharma* (Sanskrit word), which lays out the principle that every action is motivated by underlying mental factors that are positive and negative (Govinda, 1961); this system could be linked today to the stress-diathesis model of protective and risk factors (Benard, 1995). Second, in Hinduism, the notion of dependency in human development is viewed positively through the constructs of bond, bondship, and kinship (Sinha, 1968). Using Seligman's (2002) theory of positive psychology, the exercise of bonding may be interpreted as interpersonal and social signature strengths, leading to positive emotions, engagement, and meaning, and resulting in happiness and the promotion of well-being.

In Buddhism (Narada, 1968), factors in adulthood that interfere with meditation in spiritual practice or concentration in occupational work are unhealthy, while those that facilitate the mind's focus are healthy. This means that to attain a healthy mental state, unhealthy mental states are replaced with their corresponding polar opposites. In the hierarchy of healthy factors, **cognitive** factors come first. *Insight* is the central healthy state that suppresses *delusion*, the fundamental unhealthy factor. The essential partner of insight is *mindfulness*, and the presence of these two factors is sufficient to suppress all unhealthy factors. When there is a thought of a negative action, the twin factors of *modesty* (opposite of shamelessness) and *discretion* (opposite of remorselessness) act as preventative forces, both always connected with *good judgment* (called rectitude). *Confidence* is self-belief based on correct perception. The configuration of healthy cognitive factors of modesty, discretion, rectitude, and confidence together produce good behaviors, as judged by both personal and social standards.

The configuration of healthy **affective** factors of *nonattachment* (opposite of greed/egoism), *connectivity* (opposite of aversion), *impartiality* (opposite of envy), and *composure* (opposite of frustration) together replaces an acquisitive or rejecting attitude with an even-mindedness toward whatever object might arise in one's awareness. Another cluster of positive factors have both **physical and psychological** effects and are: *buoyancy* (opposite of pessimism), *pliancy* (opposite of inflexibility), *adaptability* (opposite of tightening/contraction), and *proficiency* (opposite of low mental and physical energy) prevent depression and make one adapt physically and mentally to changing conditions, meeting whatever challenges that may arise. Peterson and Seligman (2004) stated, "missing in the resilience literature is any discussion about which protective factors are relevant for whom, under what stressful circumstances, and with respect to what desirable outcomes" (pp. 79–80). It appears that *Abhidharma* of Gautama Buddha (536–438 B.C) identified the protective factors of resilience for common, everyday folks who are challenged by the limits of the body, senses, and mind that when overcome attain liberation from limits.

In Hinduism, another major Asian religion, the ideal of lifespan development emphasizes continuous dependency relations. In the extended/joint family, young children occupy a special status of spiritual innocence and are rarely exposed to prolonged frustration. They are continuously gratified bodily and reassured emotionally, especially by their mother. Through such parental dynamic, children are conditioned in the dependency relationship. The early permissiveness instills a foundation of belonging, self-worth, and safety. Subsequently, at the start of school, severe discipline follows to instill self-restraint, social harmony with siblings and classmates, and above all, commitment to the family. Discipline also teaches the control of anger and aggression. Particular social relations are observed with parents, aunts, uncles, grandparents, siblings, and cousins. Each relative is addressed with a respectful title based on the relative's birth order or kinship through marriage. Each stage of a person's development marks a new network of dependency relations. Each dependency relation is chracterized by a more or less rigid inherent relational status.

Old age prescribes dependency on children, who are morally obligated to pay back their parents. Filial piety is mutual exchange and ensures the full cycle of reciprocity. The goals of human development are satisfying and continuous dependency. Sons and daughters realize their social identity in a lifespan prolongation of their original state of dependency. Relationships among family members provide a model of positive interactions in all areas of life, work, and society, including leadership, as well as rationales with inherently religious meanings.

As these examples illustrate, positive psychology can be traced to the ancient religions of Buddhism and Hinduism, just as it can be located in the early 20th century existentialism and humanism, in counseling psychology's prevention approach, and in postmodernism, each with its own constructs of wellness. The credit, however, goes to Seligman in the 1990's and early 21st century for branding it and placing it within the American Psychological Association's (APA) policy (2006) of evidence-based practice. It's exciting to read psychologists in this book, influenced by Seligman, to be focusing on strengths of racial, ethnic, and other marginalized people, which make them resilient against challenges. The authors resist explanations of psychopathology related to "cultural deficits/disadvantages" and/or low environmental resources of minority children, adults, and the elderly. The universalistic assumption within American positive psychology is a sweeping generalization and has been corrected by the chapter authors with their understandings of group- and development-specific positive factors.

With regard to multicultural psychology, whose goal is the empowerment of racial, ethnic, and diversely identified minorities, Leong, Pickren, and Tang's chapter, *A History of Cross-Cultural Clinical Psychology* (in this book), brought to my mind Martin Luther King, Jr.'s Invited Distinguished Address at the 1967 Annual Convention of the American Psychological Associations. King said that psychologists who do individual therapy treat clients diagnosed with "Adjustment Disorder" (defined as the development of clinically significant emotional or behavioral symptoms in response to an identifiable psychosocial stressor or stressors [American Psychiatric Association, 2000]). However, King challenged that the goal of therapy is to help clients become "well-adjusted" to the social world around them. As King (1967) put it:

> You who are in the field of psychology have given us a great word. It is the word "maladjusted." This word is probably used more than any other word in psychology. It is a good word; certainly it is good that in dealing with what the word implies you are declaring that destructive maladjustment should be eradicated. You are saying that all must seek the well-adjusted life in order to avoid neurotic and schizophrenic personalities. But on the other hand, I am sure that we all recognize that there are some things in our society, some things in our world, to which we should never be adjusted....We must never adjust ourselves to racial discrimination and racial segregation. We must never adjust ourselves to religious bigotry. We must never adjust ourselves to economic conditions that take necessities from the many to give luxuries to the few. We must never adjust ourselves to the madness of militarism and the self-defeating effects of physical violence. (pp. 9–10)

King argued that for psychologists to make a meaningful contribution to people's mental health, they would have to find ways to help ordinary citizens develop their capacity for what King called "creative maladjustment nonconformity" (King as cited by Carson, 1995, p. 319). King's fundamental argument was that psychologists who are actively engaged in healing society are themselves creatively maladjusted, who model creative nonconforming behaviors to their clients to cope with racism.

Like King, Michael Lerner (1998) said, "Most therapists don't understand the social conditions which lead to so much pain in personal life, so they are unlikely to be able to uncover meaningful ways for individuals to deal with those social conditions" (p. 325). Clinical psychology is symptom-focused than etiologically-focused, which can discount the impact of context and social inequities on a client's life. While Lerner admits that therapy can help people be less self-destructive, he also points out that "these benefits mostly fit into the category of 'learning to cope with an oppressive reality'" (p. 329). Like King, Lerner argued that most psychologists unwittingly play a restraining/repressive role in society because they squander the opportunity to foster the strength of social justice advocacy in their clients, colleagues, and the organizations they serve. As Lerner put it:

> Lacking a sense of social causality, most therapists interpret the frustrations of family and personal life as individual failings. Instead of bringing their clients to an understanding of the larger social forces that shape their individual experiences, therapists implicitly suggest that the problems are individual in scope, and can be adequately solved by changes in individual psyches or through changes in their family systems. (p. 323)

In the present book, I found chapter authors refer to common strengths across American cultural minorities that are context-based, e.g., social network support, extended family composition, watchful parents and older relatives, religiousness or spiritual practice, guidance of cultural traditions and beliefs, and preference for racial, ethnic, or cultural identity. Group-specific strengths have also been identified by the authors.

Group specific strengths for African Americans include the enduring self-esteem and resilience of children and adolescents (see also APA, 2008) and the religious coping of the elderly. Respect for tribe/nation membership, spiritual practice, and cultural elements of healthcare are strengths of American Indian and Alaska Native adults. For Asian Americans, children's strengths include the maintenance of group harmony, parental engagement, educational values for achievement, and biculturalism that is inclusive of ethnic identity; adults abide by their collectivistic worldview, and the elderly feel secure in their family cohesion and peer support. For European Americans, children have a strong sense of purpose, an internal locus of control, social privilege, and the security of having membership in the dominant society; adults are cognitively involved, productive, and directed by positive help-seeking attitudes; the elderly are change-oriented, adaptable, educated, and engaged, and, therefore, have many resilience factors. For Latinos, their children's strengths are familismo values, bicultural competence that is inclusive of ethnic identification, and bilingualism; these strengths continue through adulthood, while for the elderly, who are first-generation immigrants, Hispanic cultural values and religion play important roles.

Both common and group-specific cultural strengths need to be utilized in treatments with racial, ethnic, and cultural groups to increase their general life satisfaction and mental health. The adaptation of mainstream therapies to specific cultural groups will increase the treatment efficacy of *particular* mental disorder presentations (e.g., Jackson et al. 2006; Shen et al. 2006). In a meta-analysis, Griner and Smith (2006) found that interventions that were based on a theory and on research of a specific culture were found to be almost twice as effective as interventions that did not consider race and/or culture.

The word "particular" in the previous paragraph is added emphasis because the individual, who varies in abiding by his or her culture owing to acculturation and/or personal temperament is given as much importance as the individual's universal humanity and membership in a race, ethnicity, culture, or local context. According to Sue (1998), clinicians who are multiculturally competent are scientifically minded and have skills in dynamic sizing. In other words, they are in the practice of making cultural hypotheses on the status of a particular client, including knowing when to generalize and when to exclude the experience of others in client case conceptualization and treatment. Thus clinicians are able to adopt treatment models to be sensible and acceptable to their individual minority clients.

Professor of Clinical Psychology
Director, Multicultural Center
for Research and Practice
Antioch University New England

Gargi Roysircar, EdD.

References

American Psychiatric Association (2000). *Diagnostic and statistical manual-IV-text revision (DSM-IV-TR)*. Washington: Author.

APA Presidential Task Force on Evidence-Based Practice (2006). Evidence-based practice in psychology. *American Psychologist, 61, 271–285.*

APATask Force on Resilience and Strength in Black Children and Adolescents (2008). *Resilience in African American children and adolescents: A vision for optimal development.* Retrieved July 1, 2011, from http://www.apa.org/pi/cyf/resilience.html.

Benard, B. (1995). *Fostering resilience in children*. Urbana, IL: ERIC Clearinghouse on Early Childhood Education. (ERIC Document Reproduction Service No. ED386327). Retrieved June 29, 2011, from http://chiron.valdosta.edu/whuitt/files/resilience.html.

Carson, C. (1995). Martin Luther King, Jr.: Charismatic leadership in a mass struggle. In J. T. Wren (Ed.), *Leader's companion: Insights on leadership through the ages* (pp. 318–324). New York: The Free Press.

Govinda, L. A. (1961). *The psychological attitude of early Buddhist philosophy*. London: Rider.

Griner, D., & Smith, T. (2006). Culturally adapted mental health interventions: A meta-analytic review. *Psychotherapy: Theory, Research, Practice, Training, 43,* 531–548.

Jackson, L. C., Schmutzer, P. A., Wenzel, A., & Tyler, J. D. (2006). Applicability of cognitive–behavior therapy with American Indian individuals. *Psychotherapy: Theory, Research, Training, 43*(4), 506–517. doi:10.1037/0033–3204.43.4.380.

Kakar, S. (1971). The theme of authority in social relations in India. *Journal of Social Psychology, 84,* 93–101.

King, M. L., Jr. (1967). *The role of the behavioral scientist in the Civil Rights Movement.* Invited Distinguished Address at the annual meeting of the American Psychological Association, Washington, DC. Retrieved July 12, 2011, from http://www.apa.org/monitor/jan99/king.html.

Lerner, M. (1998). *Surplus powerlessness: The psychodynamics of everyday life and the psychology of individual and social transformation.* Amherst: HB Publications.

Narada, M. (1968). *A manual of Abhidhamma*. Kandy, Sri Lanka: Buddhist Publication Society.

Peterson, C., & Seligman, M. E. P. (2004). *Character strengths and virtues: A handbook and classification.* New York: Oxford University Press.

Seligman, M. E. P. (2002). *Using the new positive psychology to realize your potential for lasting fulfillment: Authentic happiness.* New York: Free Press.

Shen, E. K., Alden, L. E., Söchting, I., & Tsang, P. (2006). Clinical observations of a Cantonese cognitive–behavioral treatment program for Chinese immigrants. *Psychotherapy: Theory, Research, Training, 43*(4), 518–530. doi:10.1037/0033–3204.43.4.380.

Sinha, J. B. P. (1968). The construct of dependence proneness. *Journal of Social Psychology, 76,* 129–131.
Sue, S. (1998). In search of cultural competence in psychotherapy and counseling. *American Psychologist, 53,* 440–448.
Nikhilananda, S. (1942). *The gospel of Sri Ramakrishna.* New York: Ramakrishna-Vivekananda Center.

Preface

We conceived the idea behind this book several years ago in the midst of growing interest in positive psychology. As researchers trained in clinical psychology, we were both excited by this movement; we believed that a balanced focus on both strengths and weaknesses represented a more constructive stance than the historically predominant view, which focused on pathology and illness. Yet, we noticed two key shortcomings. First, we noticed that much of the early positive psychology movement involved little appreciation for situating people's behaviors in the context of their sociocultural environment. That is, much of the work was spoken by, and for, mainstream whites. Perhaps it was because both of the current co-editors of the present work are of varying Korean backgrounds (and one of us raising a son whose other parent is African American), that this struck us as an obvious limitation if this movement was to be truly inclusive. Second, we did not feel that positive psychology took a complete view of being human across the full lifespan. Indeed, it again seemed too narrowly focused on addressing questions about how adults may seek and live a more purposeful life, with little attention at the time to children and older adults. It was from these concerns that we began discussing a need to offer a high-quality work that would address these shortcomings. Our aim was to offer readers an opportunity to appreciate the diverse richness and challenges of human behavior across the full lifespan, from childhood to late adulthood, across diverse racial/ethnic groups. The consequence of our discussions was a unique opportunity to join with a remarkable group of collaborators in putting together the present work. It is out of their collective passion and purposeful effort to expand and enrich our understanding of human potential that we hope readers of the present volume will be inspired, as we are, to take a more complex and nuanced view of themselves and others.

Ann Arbor, MI — Edward C. Chang
Kokomo, IN — Christina A. Downey

Contents

1 **Integrating Positive Psychology and Developmental Viewpoints into the Study of Mental Health Across Diverse Groups** ... 1
Edward C. Chang, Christina A. Downey and Jean M. Kim

2 **A History of Cross-Cultural Clinical Psychology, and Its Importance to Mental Health Today** ... 11
Frederick T. L. Leong, Wade E. Pickren and Lisa C. Tang

3 **Psychology of African American Children: Strengths and Challenges** ... 27
Richard Thompson, Ernestine C. Briggs and Sylvette A. LaTouche-Howard

4 **The Challenge of Understanding the Mental Health of African Americans: The Risks and Rewards of Segregation, Support, and John Henryism** ... 45
Harold W. Neighbors, Darrell L. Hudson and Kai McKeever Bullard

5 **Psychology of Older Adults: Exploring the Effects of Class and Culture on the Mental Health of African Americans** ... 67
Terry L. Mills and Susan Cody-Rydzewski

6 **More Than a Nice Thing to Do: A Practice-Based Evidence Approach to Outcome Evaluation in Native Youth and Family Programs** ... 87
Barbara J. Friesen, Terry L. Cross, Pauline R. Jivanjee, L. Kris Gowen, Abby Bandurraga, Sara Bastomski, Cori Matthew and Nichole June Maher

7 **Native American Adult Lifespan Perspectives: Where Power Moves** ... 107
Michael Tlanusta Garrett, Tarrell Awe Agahe Portman, Cyrus Williams, Lisa Grayshield, Edil Torres Rivera and Mark Parrish

8 **Psychology of Older American Indians and Alaska Natives: Strengths and Challenges to Maintaining Mental Health** ... 127
Sarah Poff Roman, Lori L. Jervis and Spero M. Manson

9 Psychology of Asian American Children: Contributions of Cultural Heritage and the Minority Experience 147
Lisa L. Liu, Shu-wen Wang, Joey Fung, Omar G. Gudiño, Annie Tao and Anna S. Lau

10 Psychology of Asian American Adults: Challenges and Strengths 169
Oanh Meyer, Manveen Dhindsa and Nolan Zane

11 Psychology of Asian American Older Adults: Status, Challenges, and Strengths 189
Ailee Moon and Inju Cho

12 Psychology of European American Children 207
Jean A. Baker, Alicia Fedewa and Sycarah Grant

13 Psychology of European American Adults: Challenges, Advantages, and the Push for Further Growth 223
Christina A. Downey and Wendy D'Andrea

14 Older White Adults and Mental Health 243
B. Jan McCulloch, Sara Lassig and Amanda Barnett

15 US Latino Youth 259
Nancy A. Gonzales, Miguelina Germán and Fairlee C. Fabrett

16 Psychology of Latino Adults: Challenges and an Agenda for Action 279
Margarita Alegría, Norah Mulvaney-Day, Meghan Woo and Edna A. Viruell-Fuentes

17 Psychology of Latino American Older Adults: Strengths and Challenges to Mental Health in a Shifting Society 307
Steven R. Applewhite and John M. Gonzales

18 Race, Age, and Mental Health: Expanding on the Transactional Model of Development to Include the Impact of Racial Group Membership 329
Christina A. Downey

19 Multidimensional Clinical Competence: Considering Racial Group, Development, and the Positive Psychology Movement in Clinical Practice 355
Christina A. Downey and Edward C. Chang

Erratum E1

Index 383

Contributors

Margarita Alegría Ph.D. Harvard Medical School and Center for Multicultural Mental Health Research, Cambridge Health Alliance, 120 Beacon Street, 4th floor, Somerville, MA 02143, USA
e-mail: malegria@charesearch.org

Steven R. Applewhite Ph.D. Graduate College of Social Work, 304 Social Work Building, Houston, TX 77204-4013, USA
e-mail: sapplewhite@uh.edu

Jean A. Baker Ph.D. (Deceased) Department of Counseling, Educational Psychology, and Special Education, Michigan State University, 447 Erickson Hall, East Lansing, MI 48824, USA

Abby Bandurraga Regional Research Institute, Portland State University, P.O. Box 751, Portland, OR 97207-0751, USA

Sara Bastomski Native American Youth and Family Center, 5135 Northeast Columbia Boulevard, Portland, OR 97218-1201, USA

Ernestine C. Briggs-King Ph.D. Center for Child and Family Health, Duke University Medical Center, 411 West Chapel Hill Street, Suite 908, Durham, NC 27701, USA
e-mail: ernestine.briggs@duke.edu

Edward C. Chang Ph.D. Department of Psychology, Asian/Pacific Islander American Studies, 2263 East Hall, University of Michigan, 530 Church Street, Ann Arbor, MI 48109-1043, USA
e-mail: changec@umich.edu

Inju Cho Ph.D. Division of Social Welfare and Public Health Administration, College of Social Science, Wonkwang University, 344-2 Shinyong-dong, Iksan, Jeonbuk, 570-749, South Korea
e-mail: injucho@wku.ac.kr

Susan Cody-Rydzewski Ph.D. Department of Cultural & Behavioral Sciences, Georgia Perimeter College, 2101 Womack Road, Dunwoody, GA 30338, USA
e-mail: Susan.Cody@gpc.edu

Terry L. Cross MSW, ACSW, LCSW National Indian Child Welfare Association, 5100 S.W. Macadam Avenue, Suite 300, Portland, OR 30338, USA

Wendy D'Andrea Ph.D. The New School, 80 Fifth Ave, 6th Floor, New York, NY 10011, USA
e-mail: dandreaw@newschool.edu

Manveen Dhindsa M.A. Department of Psychology, University of California Davis, One Shields Avenue, Davis, CA 95616, USA

Christina A. Downey Ph.D. Department of Psychology, Indiana University Kokomo, 2300 S. Washington St., Kokomo, IN 46904, USA
e-mail: downeyca@iuk.edu

Fairlee C. Fabrett M.A. Department of Psychiatry, McLean Hospital, Mail Stop 128, 115 Mill St., Belmont, MA 02478, USA

Alicia Fedewa Ph.D., NCSP Department of Educational, School, and Counseling Psychology, University of Kentucky, 170H Taylor Hall (Office), 238 Dickey Hall (Mail), Lexington, KY 40506-0017, USA
e-mail: alicia.fedewa@uky.edu

Barbara J. Friesen Ph.D. Research and Training Center on Family Support and Children's Mental Health, Regional Research Institute, Portland State University, P.O. Box 751, Portland, OR 97207-0751, USA
e-mail: friesenb@pdx.edu

Joey Fung M.A. Department of Psychology, University of California Los Angeles, 1285 Franz Hall, P.O. Box 951563, Los Angeles, CA 90095-1563, USA
e-mail: joeyfung@ucla.edu

Michael Tlanusta Garrett Ph.D. Department of Collaborative Support and Intervention, Education Center Annex, University of West Georgia, Carrollton, GA 30118, USA
e-mail: mgarrett@westga.edu

Miguelina Germán Ph.D. Department of Pediatrics, Department of Psychiatry and Behavioral Sciences, Albert Einstein College of Medicine of Yeshiva University, Montefiore Medical Center, 3444 Kossuth Avenue, Bronx, NY 10467, USA
e-mail: mgerman@montefiore.org

John M. Gonzales Ph.D. Department of English, The University of Texas at Austin, PAR 321, Mailcode B5000, Austin, TX 78712, USA
e-mail: jmgonzal@mail.utexas.edu

Nancy A. Gonzales Ph.D. Department of Psychology, Arizona State University, Box 871104, Tempe, AZ 85287-1104, USA
e-mail: nancy.gonzales@asu.edu

L. Kris Gowen Ph.D. Ed. M. Regional Research Institute, School of Social Work, Portland State University, P.O. Box 751, Portland, OR 97207-0751, USA
e-mail: gowen@pdx.edu

Sycarah Grant Fisher Ph.D. Ernest & Virginia Amos Campus (Amos 3), Dorothy I. Height Community Academy Public Charter Schools, 1400 First Street, Washington, DC, NW 20011, USA

Lisa Grayshield Ph.D. Department of Counseling and Educational Psychology, MSC 3 CEP, New Mexico State University, Las Cruces, NM 88003, USA
e-mail: llgray@nmsu.edu

Omar G. Gudiño Ph.D. NYU Child Study Center, 215 Lexington Ave., 16th Floor, New York, NY 10016, USA
e-mail: Omar.Gudino@nyumc.org

Darrell L. Hudson Ph.D., MPH George Warren Brown School of Social Work & Institute for Public Health, Washington University, Campus Box 1196, Brown Hall 211, One Brookings Drive, St. Louis, MO 63130, USA
e-mail: hudsond@fcm.ucsf.edu

Lori L. Jervis Ph.D. Center for Applied Social Research, University of Oklahoma, 2 Partners Place, 3100 Monitor Avenue, room 100, Norman, OK 73072-7805, USA
e-mail: lori.jervis@ou.edu

Pauline R. Jivanjee Ph.D. School of Social Work, Portland State University, P.O. Box 751, Portland, OR 97207-0751, USA
e-mail: jivanjeep@pdx.edu

Jean M. Kim Department of Psychology, University of Southern California, SGM 501, 3620 South McClintock Ave., Los Angeles, CA, 90089-2203, USA
e-mail: jeanmkim@usc.edu

Sylvette A. LaTouche-Howard M.A., NCC College Park School of Public Health, University of Maryland, 2387 SPH Bldg, College Park, MD 20742, USA

Anna S. Lau Ph.D. Department of Psychology, University of California Los Angeles, 1285 Franz Hall, P.O. Box 951563, Los Angeles, CA 90095-1563, USA
e-mail: alau@psych.ucla.edu

Sara Lassig MSW, Ph.D. Department of Family Social Science, Community Living Center Social Worker, University of Minnesota & VA Medical Center Minneapolis, 4824 E 53rd St. #205, Minneapolis, MN 55417, USA
e-mail: Sara.Lassig@va.gov

Oanh Le Meyer M.A. Department of Psychology, University of California Davis, One Shields Avenue, Davis, CA 95616, USA

Frederick T. L. Leong Ph.D. Department of Psychology, Consortium for Multicultural Psychology Research, Michigan State University, East Lansing, MI 48824, USA
e-mail: fleong@msu.edu

Lisa L. Liu Ph.D. Department of Psychology, University of California Los Angeles, 1285 Franz Hall, P.O. Box 951563, Los Angeles, CA 90095-1563, USA
e-mail: lisaliu@psych.ucla.edu

Nichole June Maher Native American Youth and Family Center, 5135 Northeast Columbia Boulevard, Portland, OR 97218-1201, USA

Spero M. Manson Ph.D. Department of Community and Behavioral Health, Colorado School of Public Health, Mail Stop F800, Nighthorse Campbell Native Health Building, 13055 E. 17th Ave., Aurora, CO 80045, USA
e-mail: Spero.Manson@ucdenver.edu

Cori Matthew Native American Youth and Family Center, 5135 Northeast Columbia Boulevard, Portland, OR 97218-1201, USA

Amanda E. Matzek Ph.D. Department of Family Social Science, University of Minnesota, 290 McNeal Hall, 1985 Buford Avenue, St. Paul, MN 55108, USA
e-mail: matze005@umn.edu

B. Jan McCulloch Ph.D. Department of Family Social Science, College of Education and Human Development, University of Minnesota, 290 D McNeal Hall, 1985 Buford Avenue, St. Paul, MN 55108, USA
e-mail: jmccullo@umn.edu

Kai McKeever Bullard Ph.D., MPH Division of Diabetes Translation Centers for Disease Control and Prevention, 4770 Buford Highway, NE Mailstop K-10, Atlanta, GA 30341, USA

Terry L. Mills Ph.D. Division of Humanities & Social Sciences, Morehouse College, Wheeler Hall, Room 201, Atlanta, GA, USA
e-mail: tmills@morehouse.edu

Ailee Moon Ph.D. Department of Social Welfare, University of California Los Angeles School of Public Affairs, 3250 Public Policy Building, Box 951656, Los Angeles, CA 90095-1656, USA
e-mail: aileem@ucla.edu

Norah Mulvaney-Day Ph.D. Center for Multicultural Mental Health Research, Cambridge Health Alliance and Harvard Medical School, 120 Beacon Street, 4th Floor, Somerville, MA 02143, USA
e-mail: nmulvaney-day@charesearch.org

Harold W. Neighbors Ph.D. Center for Research on Ethnicity, Culture and Health, School of Public Health and the Program for Research on Black Americans, Institute for Social Research, The University of Michigan, 109 South Observatory Drive, Ann Arbor, MI 48109-2029, USA
e-mail: woodyn@umich.edu

Wade E. Pickren Ph.D. Department of Psychology, Ryerson University, 350 Victoria Street, Toronto, ON M5B 2K3, Canada
e-mail: wpickren@psych.ryerson.ca

Sarah Poff Roman M. G. S. University of Colorado Denver, 13199 E. Montview Blvd., Suite 400, Aurora, CO 80045-7201, USA
e-mail: Sarah.Roman@ucdenver.edu

Tarrell Awe Agahe Portman Ph.D. N356 Lindquist Center, Department of Rehabilitation and Counselor Education, University of Iowa, Iowa City, IA 52242, USA
e-mail: tarrell-portman@uiowa.edu

Lisa C. Tang Ph.D. 91 W Neal St., Pleasanton, CA 94566, USA
e-mail: lisatangphd@gmail.com

Annie Tao M.A. Department of Psychology, University of California Berkeley, 125 Connemara Way #29, Sunnyvale, CA 94087, USA
e-mail: annietao@berkeley.edu

Richard Thompson Ph.D. Juvenile Protective Association, 1707 N Halsted, Chicago, IL 60614, USA
e-mail: RThompson@juvenile.org

Edna A. Viruell-Fuentes Ph.D., M.P.H. University of Illinois at Urbana-Champaign, 510 E. Chalmers, Champaign, IL 61820, USA
e-mail: eviruell@uiuc.edu

Shu-wen Wang M.A. Department of Psychology, University of California Los Angeles, 1285 Franz Hall, P.O. Box 951563, Los Angeles, CA 90095-1563, USA
e-mail: shuwenwang@ucla.edu

Cyrus Williams Ph.D. School of Psychology & Counseling, Regent University, 1000 Regent University Drive, CRB228, Virginia Beach, VA 23464-9800, USA
e-mail: cwilliams@regent.edu

Meghan Woo ScM Harvard University School of Public Health and Center for Multicultural Health Research, 120 Beacon Street, 4th Floor, Somerville, MA 02143, USA

Nolan Zane Ph.D. Department of Psychology, University of California Davis, 268B Young Hall, One Shields Avenue, Davis, CA 95616, USA
e-mail: nwzane@ucdavis.edu

About the Editors

Edward C. Chang is a Professor of Clinical Psychology and a Faculty Associate in Asian/Pacific Islander American Studies at the University of Michigan, Ann Arbor. He received his B.A. in Psychology and Philosophy from the State University of New York at Buffalo, and his M.A. and Ph.D. degrees from the State University of New York at Stony Brook. Dr. Chang completed his APA-accredited clinical internship at Bellevue Hospital Center-New York University Medical Center. He serves as a Program Evaluator for the Michigan Department of Community Health—Social Determinants of Health, working with the Asian Center Southeast Michigan. Dr. Chang also serves as an Associate Editor of *Cognitive Therapy and Research, the Asian American Journal of Psychology,* and the *Journal of Personality and Social Psychology*. He has published more than a hundred empirical and scholarly works focusing on optimism and pessimism, perfectionism, loneliness, social problem solving, and cultural influences on behavior. Dr. Chang is the editor of *Optimism and Pessimism: Implications for Theory, Research, and Practice* (2001), *Self-Criticism and Self-Enhancement: Theory, Research, and Clinical Implications* (2007), and *Handbook of Adult Psychopathology In Asians: Diagnosis, Etiology, and Treatment* (forthcoming), and is a co-editor of *Virtue, Vice, and Personality: The Complexity of Behavior* (2003), *Social Problem Solving: Theory, Research, and Training* (2004), and *Judgments Over Time: The Interplay of Thoughts, Feelings, and Behaviors* (2006).

Christina A. Downey is an Assistant Professor of Psychology at Indiana University Kokomo. She received her B.A. in Psychology from Purdue University, and her M.A. and Ph.D. degrees in Clinical Psychology from the University of Michigan, Ann Arbor. Her dissertation work focused on lay theories of health among community adults. Her research interests include mixed-method study of lay theories of health, understanding the relations between perfectionism and disturbed eating behaviors, college student attitudes about various aspects of diversity, and the outcomes of including service learning in college pedagogy. She has published articles in *Cognitive Therapy and Research and Eating Behaviors*, and has co-authored chapters in *Social Problem Solving: Theory, Research, and Training* (Chang et al. 2004) and *Judgments Over Time: The Interplay of Thoughts, Feelings, and Behav-*

iors (Sanna and Chang 2006). Her next chapter, on multicultural considerations in positive psychology (co-authored with Dr. Chang) will appear in the upcoming *APA Handbook of Multicultural Psychology*. She also maintains a strong commitment to excellent college teaching, and has presented on the value of incorporating service learning in the teaching of research methods in psychology.

Chapter 1
Integrating Positive Psychology and Developmental Viewpoints into the Study of Mental Health Across Diverse Groups

Edward C. Chang, Christina A. Downey and Jean M. Kim

In 1998, nearing the end of his presidential term at the American Psychological Association, Martin Seligman raised a public call for a new focus in psychology, what he referred to as a positive psychology (Seligman 1998). Then, in January of 1999, Martin Seligman invited several up and coming researchers to join him and a few senior colleagues to discuss what a positive psychology may look like in both theory and action. The first author was one of those fortunate to have been selected. We gathered in a small town in sunny Akumal, Mexico, and for several days and nights, we shared our thoughts and experiences of what a bold new psychology may look like. What was not questioned was the potential value of establishing such a psychology in the field. Now, nearly a decade later, the results of those early discussions have not only impacted the imagination of thousands of individuals, but they have also come to bear fruit in the form of hundreds of journal and book publications, confirming the interest and value of positive psychology in our world.

The Value of Positive Psychology: A More Balanced Approach to Understanding Ourselves

Positive psychology is both new and old. On the one hand, the formal emergence of positive psychology linked to Seligman's presidential call for a change in the way we have approached psychology is without a doubt a more recent event (Seligman and Csikszentmihalyi 2000). Early therapists like Sigmund Freud initially began not with the facilitation of positive functioning, but with the dampening of negative functioning, namely, reducing neuroses. On the other hand, positive psychology may be, as some have noted, an approach that has always been present in psychology (e.g., Bohart and Greening 2001; Jahoda 1958; McCullough and Snyder

E. C. Chang (✉)
Department of Psychology, 2263 East Hall, University of Michigan, 530 Church Street, Ann Arbor, MI 48109-1043, USA
e-mail: changec@umich.edu

E. C. Chang, C. A. Downey (eds.), *Handbook of Race and Development in Mental Health*, DOI 10.1007/978-1-4614-0424-8_1, © Springer Science+Business Media, LLC 2012

2000; Rathunde 2001). That is, a focus on the positive aspects of being human, including studies looking at self-actualization (Maslow 1962), creativity (Gardner 1988), intelligence (Sternberg 1985), positive regard (Rogers 1961), meaning/purpose (Frankl 1946/1962; Wong and Fry 1998), love (Sternberg and Grajek 1984), hope (Snyder et al. 1991), optimism (Scheier and Carver 1985), striving (Emmons 1986), and well-being (Diener 1984; Ryff and Keyes 1995), just to mention a few, have always been part of the psychological landscape. Additionally, within clinical psychology, one might argue that much of the driving force behind the development of prevention and treatment efforts in mental health over the past 63 years (Leahey 1997), itself, represents our basic appreciation of what positive psychology seeks to foster in practice, namely, more and better ways of living for all. Either way, what has been distinctly achieved by the positive psychology movement in recent years has been to push the field to develop more concerted and balanced efforts looking at both risk and resiliency factors in the study of human behavior. No longer is it sufficient to only look at the etiologies of weakness and dysfunction if we do not also consider etiologies of strength and well-being (Peterson and Seligman 2004; Ryff 1989, 1995). In that regard, the present volume is a product of this important and, perhaps, renewed initiative to gain a more inclusive understanding of human behavior.

Linking Positive Psychology and Race/Ethnicity Across the Lifespan

As researchers have recently discussed, notions of race and ethnicity is neither a simple nor easy task (Cokely 2007; Ponterotto and Park-Taylor 2007; Quintana 2007). Yet, the editors of this volume, as both researchers and clinicians who have long been concerned about issues of race and ethnicity in psychology, were both surprised and puzzled that the export of positive psychology to the study of mental health in diverse racial and ethnic groups has yet to form a substantive area of inquiry. To be fair, however, there are several reasons for the slow link-up between positive psychology and mental health among diverse groups. First, as noted earlier, those working with mental health issues have focused largely on studying psychopathology from the practical standpoint of treatment and intervention and thereby have concentrated on negative psychology, although often implicitly addressing some positive psychology issues (American Psychiatric Association 2000). Indeed, the goals of many interventions are to identify negative, maladaptive, and dysfunctional thoughts, feelings, and behaviors and replace them with positive, adaptive, and functional thoughts, feelings, and behaviors. In that regard, most interventions can be seen from the standpoint of a positive psychology framework. Second, it is quite common for researchers to be interested in bottom-up approaches that are so inclusive that they border on universalistic or biological models of human behavior. For example, models of personality that emerged in the USA, namely the Five-Factor Model (FFM) of personality, were assumed to be applicable to the understanding of all human behavior (McAdams 1992; Widiger 2005). Yet, there is not sufficient evidence that the FFM can be applied in other cultural contexts (Benet-Martínez and John 1998; Schmitt et al. 2008; Wu et al. 2000). Similarly, some researchers have used a more biological framework (Plomin et al. 2003) to explain personality and mental health. However, even then, biological factors are influenced by environmental contexts and experiences. Furthermore, even with models that appear to be contextual, they have at times been applied almost universally. As noted by Jensen and Hoagwood (1997), "most diagnostic constructs and their measures have been downwardly adapted from models of adult psychopathology. By and large, these models are descriptive, static, unidimensional, and provide relatively little context" (p. 231).

Third, and relatedly, because no single compelling model of positive psychology exists, it has been difficult for researchers to apply top–down strategies in a manner that would generate reliable and informative findings and implications for considering race/ethnicity. For example, different researchers have focused on different character strengths and virtues (Chang and Sanna 2003; Peterson et al. 2007; Snyder and McCullough 2000). Even when one considers a commonly assumed core virtue like optimism, different approaches to conceptualization and assessment have emerged in the literature (Chang 2001). Fourth, it has only been in recent years that we have seen an explosion in the accessibility and use of online surveys. No longer are researchers with limited funding support geographically paralyzed to only solicit and study individuals in their local environment. Lastly, given that positive psychology represents a relatively new emphasis, it may simply be a matter of being patient as it begins to naturally spread its influence across more and more domains. Again, our point is not to excuse the slow appreciation of race and ethnicity in positive psychology, as much as it is to energize and encourage it through the present volume.

Understanding Positive Psychology Across the Diverse Life Span

Beyond the import of positive psychology to the study of mental health among diverse racial and ethnic groups, another major disconnect that continues to exist is one involving development across the entire life span. Today, as it was true more than two decades ago (Sears 1986), much of psychological research and theory continues to be heavily drawn from studies of young adults. Indeed, even a quick scan of the Diagnostic and Statistical Manual of Mental Disorders, Fourth Edition, Text Revision (American Psychiatric Association 2000) makes clear its greater emphasis on adult disorders, over disorders found in children (e.g., conduct disorder) and in elderly (e.g., dementia). However, this does not imply that children and elderly are without challenges. Alternatively, the strengths children and elderly exhibit may be quite different in type and kind from those manifested during adulthood. Therefore, this volume highlights and details some of the basic challenges and strengths of different age groups across the lifespan.

However, even within a given age group, there is much diversity. Clearly, the challenges that face a young African American child may be dramatically different in quality and quantity from those faced by a European American child. But, perhaps, just as important for our understanding is an appreciation of how challenges faced by African American children look different from those of African American adults, and still more different from those of African American elderly. Similarly, although often overlooked, Asian Americans, Latino Americans, and Native Americans have their share of significant challenges and unique strengths. This is not to imply that similarities do not exist, but we wish to also highlight differences across the lifespan, which have historically been overlooked. Thus our goal was not to exclude but add to the extant literature by identifying possible points of important differences, which are important for theory, research, and practice.

Overview of the Present Volume

The present volume is organized into five major sections. In Sect. I, Leong, Pickren, and Tang take a very thoughtful and thorough look at the history of cross-cultural clinical and counseling psychology. The purpose of this chapter is to challenge universalistic assumptions about mental illness and treatment; to provide a brief historical overview of clinical psychology and the application of the field to minorities; and to discuss the progression of different models of mental health in minorities. By providing a history of how clinical psychology has approached the issues of culture, race, and ethnicity in the USA, the authors hope that the lessons learned from our collective past will guide psychologists toward a more enlightened science and practice, one not subjected to personal and cultural biases.

Sections II–VI discuss positive psychology and mental health challenges in various racial/ethnic groups (presented alphabetically). Section II presents information on positive psychology and African Americans. In Chap. 3, Thompson, Briggs-King, and LaTouche-Howard look at African American children. They provide insight on challenges for this group, such as exposure to violence, maltreatment/punitive parenting, and limited access to mental health services in African American children. Perhaps less noted are the strengths of this group, including extended social supports, appropriately restrictive parents, and robust self-esteem. Often, we do not necessarily pay attention to both the challenges and strengths and only focus on one or the other, but the authors of this chapter provide a comprehensive overview of this cohort. The authors also discuss the need to recognize the diversity among African American children while identifying and addressing the needs of those children most at risk. Chapter 4, authored by Neighbors, Hudson, and McKeever Bullard, highlights African American adults and mental health. The writers discuss racial segregation, social support, and John Henryism as both challenges and assets. Their discussion integrates culture and context in an exploration of the coping mechanisms African Americans use to alleviate the harmful effects of racial discrimination on mental health. Additional recommendations are also detailed, including a need to further examine the association between socioeconomic status and depression and African Americans' unique cost of mobility in their endeavors for higher socioeconomic status. Lastly, in Chap. 5, Mills and Cody-Rydzewski present information on mental health issues among African American elderly. They note social inequality and racial discrimination as major challenges to the maintenance of mental health in this group; and extended family, social support, and religiosity as strengths contributing to resiliency. Finally, the authors discuss directions for future research and practice, including an examination of over diagnosis and under diagnosis in older African American adults, the prescription of antipsychotic medications, admission and attrition rates, and implications for mental health practitioners.

Section III focuses on mental health in American Indians and Alaskan Natives. In Chap. 6, Friesen et al. describe the application of Practice-Based Evidence (PBE) to understanding outcomes of strengths-building programming in American Indian/Alaska Native youth. This chapter describes the strong current emphasis on Evidence-Based Practice (EBP) in community programming as positive, but limited, particularly when little research has been done on the efficacy of particular program components for specific groups. The authors argue for greater recognition of PBE among, for example, funding agencies which support programs for culturally diverse youth. They describe the development of their PBE approach, the principles that guided the effort, and some findings resulting from their work. In Chap. 7, Garrett, Portman, Williams, and Grayshield discuss how issues such as widespread health problems, low education, economic disparity, and intergenerational grief and trauma challenge the maintenance of mental health among American Indian (AI) and Alaska Native (AN) adults. These authors also identify social factors, such as acculturation, that make AI/AN adult populations vulnerable to mental health problems. The authors emphasize how cultural traditions and beliefs, particularly regarding respect for tribe/nation membership, family membership, and spiritual practice, serve to preserve wellness in this group. These authors make a number of recommendations, including enhancing research on how cultural beliefs may promote positive functioning, particularly among AI/ANs living in rural areas (such as on reservations). In Chap. 8, Roman, Jervis, and Manson present information on psychological issues among older AI and AN adults. Major challenges in this group include sociohistorical factors, environmental factors, and barriers to help-seeking, while several significant strengths for Native American and Alaskan Native elders consist of support systems, ethnic and cultural identity, and spirituality. In this chapter, Roman, Jervis, and Mansonalso provide recommendations for capitalizing upon these strengths in order to address the challenges faced by Native elders, including the importance of engaging community networks in the research process and incorporating Native cultural elements into biomedical mental healthcare. The chapter then concludes with recommendations for future research, including the need to develop culturally relevant instrumentation and methods specific to this population.

Section IV highlights the integration of positive psychology and race in Asian Americans. Chapter 9 by Liu and his colleague's present information on mental health issues in Asian American children, focusing on cultural orientation and minority-related experiences as challenges toward the maintenance of mental health, as well as strengths contributing to resilience in this group. Specifically, interdependence concerns, maladaptive perfectionism, acculturative stress, heightened family conflict, discrimination, and the model minority stereotype are discussed as major challenges; and temperament related to maintaining group harmony, parenting behavior, values bolstering academic success, biculturalism/integration, and ethnic identity are mentioned as Asian American children's strengths. The authors of this chapter then recommend ways through which we can draw upon the assets of Asian American youth to encourage resiliency and overcome vulnerabilities in adjustment. In Chap. 10, Meyer, Dhindsa, and Zane elaborate upon mental health issues in Asian American adults, focusing on challenges and strengths that impact members of this group. The authors address challenges first, describing research findings on the relations between mental health on the one hand, and prejudice and discrimination, migration and acculturative stress, and family conflict (particularly conflicts perpetuated by intergenerational differences in acculturation) on the other. Strengths which serve to bolster Asian American adult resilience include collectivistic cultural values, social networks such as family and community institutions, and ethnic identity. These authors make recommendations for greatly increased research on the relations between these phenomena and mental health among Asian Americans, with particular attention needed to how these factors impact help-seeking for mental health issues. Chapter 11, authored by Moon and Cho, extends the discussion of mental health among Asian Americans into the older adult stage of life. These authors present detailed background information on what is known about the most prevalent mental health problems in this population, and identify widespread stigmatization of mental health problems, lack of knowledge about these diagnoses, and underutilization of available mental health services as major challenges to the maintenance of positive mental health in this group. Personal and social strengths such as family cohesion and companionship, religion and spirituality, and investment in strong peer support are key strengths that these authors feel buttress mental and emotional wellness among older Asian Americans. These authors make a number of research and practice recommendations, but draw particular attention to the need to understand better how members of this group fundamentally conceptualize mental health.

Section V looks at the integration of positive psychology and mental health for understanding European Americans. First, in Chap. 12, Baker, Crowl, and Grant examine European American children and provide a review of their history. They discuss the group's challenges of limited familial support systems, media exposure, and internalized feelings of racial superiority but also bring to discussion their strengths of sense of purpose, familiarity with the dominant culture, socioeconomic status, internal locus of control, and authoritative parenting style. The authors additionally make future recommendations to garner a more comprehensive picture of European American children's experience. Because of European Americans' status as the privileged majority, they have primarily been used as a comparison group for other racial groups, leaving the specific needs of European American children to have been underrepresented in the mental health literature. Next, Chap. 13 by Downey and D'Andrea concentrates on European American adults. The authors focus on poverty, traumatic experience, and alcohol abuse as major challenges to the maintenance of mental health in this group; and access to health care, willingness to seek assistance for mental health issues, and selected cognitive factors as strengths contributing to resilience. Given our racially pluralistic society, the authors make recommendations for the continuation of research on European American racial identity and its relation with mental health and disorder, which is frequently understudied. Finally, in Chap. 14 McCulloch, Lassig, and Matzek outline mental health issues for older adults and provision specific information where appropriate concerning older European Americans. They detail issues such as dementia, depression, suicide, and anxiety but also cover resilience factors including stable intellectual functioning, capacity for change, productive engagement, education, resilience, and adaptability. These authors discuss our general lack of awareness for "Whiteness" and how being European American affects aging and mental health, and the authors recommend an increase in awareness of the positive outcomes for mental illness treatment among elders.

Section VI focuses on Latino American mental health and positive psychology. In Chap. 15, Gonzales, Germán, and Fabrett discuss Latino youth in America, examining challenges such as family and community poverty, immigration and cultural adaptation, minority status, and discrimination. They also detail important cultural strengths, including traditional Latino familism values, ethnic identity, and bicultural competence. Finally, the authors make recommendations for more diverse and sensitive services that focus on the central role of family, strong ethnic identity, and bicultural competence. Next, Chap. 16, written by Alegría, Mulvaney-Day, Woo, and Viruell-Fuentes, presents information on mental health topics in Latino adults. Major challenges for this group include socioeconomic status, mental health service use, and access to mental health care. In contrast, important strengths contributing to resilience include family support, biculturalism, bilingualism, and nativity. Unique to this chapter, the authors examine data from the National Latino and Asian American Study (NLAAS) to describe in detail what is known about Latino adults' mental health and to highlight key themes on resilience factors. The authors then compare the rates of mental health disorders of NLAAS Latinos with non-Latino Whites from the National Comorbidity Survey Replication using a combined dataset of the two studies to illustrate these themes. Then in Chap. 17, Applewhite and Gonzales discuss mental health issues in Latino American older adults, highlighting communication difficulties, acculturative stress, and service utilization as major challenges to the maintenance of mental health in this group. They then discuss family, cultural values, and religion as strengths contributing to resilience in this group. Finally, these authors detail ways in which Latin American older adults' cultural strengths can be engendered more effectively toward increasing overall mental health.

Finally, Sect. VIII presents a conclusion, where in Chap. 18, Downey presents a model of developmental mental health called the Expanded Transactional Model, which attempts to argue that racial group membership can be significant in biological, cognitive, and affective development over the lifespan. The model has been shown to have potential for identifying individuals at risk for pathology and for making culturally appropriate, positive, individual or systemic interventions to alter the trajectory of development. In this chapter, research techniques and examples are described, and recommendations for future recommendations and policy are made. This chapter seeks to motivate researchers and practitioners to consider their work within the larger theoretical context of development and to inspire further work in this regard.

Concluding Thoughts

In summary, this volume presents current knowledge of mental health issues in different racial, ethnic, and age cohorts. Each chapter vividly illustrates the verity that individuals from different groups have different needs, as well as different strengths. It additionally provides a succinct overview of the history of clinical and counseling psychology and presents a thoughtful and integrative model of developmental health.

The purpose of this work is to provide a unique integration of several emerging foci in the literature we have seen, namely an appreciation for the etiology and course of mental health and illness and the identification and facilitation of positive aspects and desired outcomes that may look different for different groups. It is no longer sufficient to examine the etiologies of illness alone, but we must also consider the etiologies of well-being. Therefore, our hope is to inspire and stimulate further research in multicultural and multiracial mental health, with particular hopes that we will see the emergence of new approaches and models representing the synergy of mental health, positive psychology, and development. Indeed, we are hopeful that the byproduct of this future research involving the synergy of developmental, positive, and multicultural/multiracial psychology will lead to more useful interventions that are more sensitive and match the contexts and conditions of authentic people living in a diverse society with differing resources and vulnerabilities (Paul 1969). Indeed, we hope that this work will be of use to clinicians, researchers, students, and others who wish to garner a more inclusive understanding of the diversity of human behavior across the lifespan.

References

American Psychiatric Association. (2000). *Diagnostic and statistical manual of mental disorders* (Revised 4th ed.). Washington, DC: American Psychiatric Association.

Benet-Martínez, V., & John, O. P. (1998). Los cincograndes across cultures and ethnic groups: Multitrait-multimethod analyses of the big five in Spanish and English. *Journal of Personality and Social Psychology, 75*, 729–750.

Bohart, A. C., & Greening, T. (2001). Humanistic psychology and positive psychology. *American Psychologist, 56,* 81–82.
Chang, E. C. (Ed.). (2001). *Optimism and pessimism: Implications for theory, research, and practice*. Washington, DC: American Psychological Association.
Chang, E. C., & Sanna, L. J. (Eds.). (2003). *Virtue, vice, and personality: The complexity of behavior*. Washington, DC: American Psychological Association.
Cokely, K. (2007). Critical issues in the measurement of ethnic and racial identity: A referendum on the state of the field. *Journal of Counseling Psychology, 54,* 224–234.
Diener, E. (1984). Subjective well-being. *Psychological Bulletin, 95,* 542–575.
Emmons, R. A. (1986). Personal strivings: An approach to personality and subjective well-being. *Journal of Personality and Social Psychology, 51,* 1058–1068.
Frankl, V. E. (1946/1962). *Man's search for meaning: Introduction to logotherapy* (trans: I. Lasch). Boston: Beacon. (Original work published in 1946).
Gardner, H. (1988). Creativity: An interdisciplinary perspective. *Creativity Research Journal, 1,* 8–26.
Jahoda, M. (1958). *Current concepts of positive mental health.* New York: Basic Books.
Jensen, P., & Hoagwood, K. (1997). The book of names: DSM-IV in context. *Development and Psychopathology, 9,* 231–249.
Leahey, T. H. (1997). *A history of psychology: Main currents in psychological thought.* Upper Saddle River: Prentice Hall.
Maslow, A. (1962). *Toward a psychology of being*. New York: Van Nostrand.
McAdams, D. P. (1992). The five-factor model in personality: A critical appraisal. *Journal of Personality, 60,* 329–361.
McCullough, M. E., & Snyder, C. R. (2000). Classical sources of human strength: Revisiting an old home and building a new one. *Journal of Social and Clinical Psychology, 19,* 1–10.
Paul, G. L. (1969). Outcome of systematic desensitization: I. Background procedures and uncontrolled reports of individual treatment. In C. M. Franks (Ed.), *Behavioral therapy: Appraisal and status* (pp. 63–104). New York: McGraw-Hill.
Peterson, C., & Seligman, M. E. P. (2004). *Character strengths and virtues: A handbook and classification*. New York: Oxford University Press.
Peterson, C., Ruch, W., Beermann, U., Park, N., & Seligman, M. E. P. (2007). Strengths of character, orientations to happiness, and life satisfaction. *Journal of Positive Psychology, 2,* 149–156.
Plomin, R., DeFries, J. C., Craig, I. W., & McGuffin, P. (2003). *Behavioral genetics in the postgenomic era*. Washington, DC: American Psychological Association.
Ponterotto, J. G., & Park-Taylor, J. (2007). Racial and ethnic identity theory, measurement, and research in counseling psychology: Present status and future directions. *Journal of Counseling Psychology, 54,* 282–294.
Quintana, S. M. (2007). Racial and ethnic identity: Developmental perspectives and research. *Journal of Counseling Psychology, 54,* 259–270.
Rathunde, K. (2001). Toward a psychology of optimal human functioning: What positive psychology can learn from the 'experimental turns' of James, Dewey, and Maslow. *Journal of Humanistic Psychology, 41,* 135–153.
Rogers, C. (1961). *On becoming a person*. Boston: Houghton Mifflin.
Ryff, C. D. (1989). Happiness is everything, or is it? Explorations on the meaning of psychological well-being. *Journal of Personality and Social Psychology, 57,* 1069–1081.
Ryff, C. D. (1995). Psychological well-being in adult life. *Current Directions in Psychological Science, 4,* 99–104.
Ryff, C. D., & Keyes, C. L. M. (1995). The structure of psychological well-being revisited. *Journal of Personality and Social Psychology, 69,* 719–727.
Scheier, M. F., & Carver, C. S. (1985). Optimism, coping, and health: Assessment and implications of generalized outcome expectancies. *Health Psychology, 4,* 219–247.
Schmitt, D. P., Realo, A., Voracek, M., & Allik, J. (2008). Why can't a man be more like a woman? Sex differences in big five personality traits. *Journal of Personality and Social Psychology, 94,* 168–182.

Sears, D. O. (1986). College sophomores in the laboratory: Influences of a narrow data base on social psychology's view of human nature. *Journal of Personality and Social Psychology, 51,* 515–530.

Seligman, M. E. P. (1998). Presidential statement. APA Monitor, May, 11–12.

Seligman, M. E. P., & Csikszentmihalyi, M. (2000). Positive psychology: An introduction. *American Psychologist, 55,* 5–14.

Snyder, C. R., & McCullough, M. E. (2000). A positive psychology field of dreams: 'If you build it, they will come …'. *Journal of Social and Clinical Psychology, 19,* 151–160.

Snyder, C. R., Harris, C., Anderson, J. R., Holleran, S. A., Irving, L. M., Sigmon, S. T., Yoshinobu, L., Gibb, J., Langelle, C., & Harney, P. (1991). The will and the ways: Development and validation of an individual-differences measure of hope. *Journal of Personality and Social Psychology, 60,* 570–585.

Sternberg, R. J. (1985). Implicit theories of intelligence, creativity, and wisdom. *Journal of Personality and Social Psychology, 49,* 607–627.

Sternberg, R. J., & Grajek, S. (1984). The nature of love. *Journal of Personality and Social Psychology, 47,* 312–329.

Widiger, T. A. (2005). Five-factor model of personality disorder: Integrating science and practice. *Journal of Research in Personality, 39,* 66–83.

Wong, P. T. P., & Fry, P. S. (Eds). (1998). *The human quest for meaning: A handbook of psychological research and clinical applications*. Mahwah: Lawrence Erlbaum Associates.

Wu, Y., Wang, W., Du, W., Li, J., Jiang, X., & Wang, Y. (2000). Development of a Chinese version of the Zuckerman-Kulman personality questionnaire: Reliabilities and gender/age effects. *Social Behavior and Personality, 28,* 241–249.

Chapter 2
A History of Cross-Cultural Clinical Psychology, and Its Importance to Mental Health Today

Frederick T. L. Leong, Wade E. Pickren and Lisa C. Tang

In American Samoa, a person may be said to be suffering from *ma'ipopole* or worry sickness if he/she becomes involved in a conflict that seems intractable to solution or, conversely, becomes very happy about an impending event. This worry sickness, which can take many forms, reflects the deep social interrelatedness of Samoan culture (Clement 1982).

The "cure" for *ma'ipopole* usually comes from the passage of time or when a new situation arises that demands attention, though in some cases the sufferer may talk his worry over with his pastor, family, or close friends. This simple example illustrates two truths about mental health and culture. One, we cannot assume that the nosology of mental disorders found in DSM-IV is sensitive to issues of culture, despite the inclusion of a category of "culture-bound syndromes." (This term, culture-bound syndromes, is evidence of a deep privileging of Western norms about what constitutes mental disorder and begs the question of whether all disorders or, at least, nosologies of mental disorders, are not culture-bound.) Two, treatment of individuals suffering from mental illness may take many different forms and may not involve a therapeutic session with a professional. Yet, a historical perspective on the development of clinical psychology in North America reveals a science-based profession predicated upon universalist assumptions about both illness and treatment. To what extent this now applies in other cultures and places is an open and important question. In our age of globalization and migration, there are active efforts to export the North American approach to diagnoses and treatment worldwide.

In this chapter, we trace the development of clinical psychology in the twentieth century. We first offer a brief overview of the field, then discuss the application of the field with racial and ethnic minorities prior to the 1960s in the United States. We then offer an account and analysis of the dynamic era of encounter, challenge, and change that began to emerge by the mid-1960s. In this era, models of mental health and illness about racial and ethnic minorities were articulated by mainstream clinical and developmental psychologists. These models were challenged by a growing

---

F. T. L. Leong (✉)
Department of Psychology, Consortium for Multicultural Psychology Research,
Michigan State University, East Lansing, MI 48824, USA
e-mail: fleong@msu.edu

E. C. Chang, C. A. Downey (eds.), Handbook of Race and Development in Mental Health,
DOI 10.1007/978-1-4614-0424-8_2, © Springer Science+Business Media, LLC 2012

cohort of psychologists who were members of racial and ethnic minority groups. These psychologists countered with models predicated on a different view of human beings. We recount how out of these encounters and challenges, organizational, institutional, and personal transformations occurred. We review the evolution of different dominant models so that by the end of the twentieth century in North America, there were new practices and scholarship related to mental health that were based on multidimensional and multicultural notions.

Clinical Psychology in North America: Even the Patient was White

As is so often the case in American psychology, the name of William James is linked to the early development of abnormal psychology and its treatment in America. Along with other first generation pioneers (1890–1920) in the medico-psychological field, James was fascinated by what he termed exceptional mental states and what they indicated about human consciousness and functioning. James was a member of the Boston School of Abnormal Psychology, which, along with other psychotherapeutic efforts, such as the Emmanuel Movement, represented an indigenous American approach to theory and treatment (Caplan 1998). The Emmanuel Movement grew out of a collaboration between clergy at Boston's Emmanuel Church and Boston physicians to provide therapy and counseling services based upon both science and religion. The movement had a brief period of success between 1906 and 1910 and laid the foundation for the later development of pastoral counseling. So when Sigmund Freud's methods of psychoanalysis began to circulate in America, there was already a tradition of direct psychological treatment; some American practitioners simply incorporated aspects of Freud's approach (Taylor 1999).

By the late 1930s, the meaning of the term "clinical psychology" had begun to move from its initial primary reference to school-based problems to its more contemporary meanings. As America entered World War II, psychologists were using helping skills in a variety of settings, including school guidance offices, homes for the mentally retarded, psychiatric settings, and psychotherapy offices (Benjamin 1997; Finch and Odoroff 1939; Napoli 1981). For the purposes of this chapter, what and where were the applications of psychology in settings where race or ethnicity was a factor?

Guthrie (1998), in his now classic study, *Even the Rat Was White,* pointed out that psychology was quite popular in Historically Black Colleges and Universities (HBCUs). Black college students typically did not have access to mainstream, predominantly White graduate programs in this era, and only a few HBCUs had graduate programs in psychology. As Guthrie pointed out, the practical needs of Black communities and schools often dictated that college graduates return home and apply their skills to these needs. So, African American graduates, with either the BA or MA, did use psychology to address mental health, counseling, and guidance needs of Black students and Black community members. But, given that the doctoral degree was adopted very early as the standard credential of the American psychologist (not the norm in other countries then or now), these Black practitioners have been left out of the mainstream historical narrative. It was in this era that the first dominant model of cultural differences was formulated: the deficit model.

The Deficit or Inferiority Model

Supported by Darwin's (1859) work on the heritability of traits and hierarchical perspective on diversity and Gobineau's (1915) writings on the superiority of the Aryan race, both psychiatry and psychology developed in a cultural and professional context that assumed that the White male was at the apex of the evolutionary ladder by way of its' perceived dominance in culture and intelligence. Non-White races were believed to be in the relatively immature adolescent stages of development, and thus were considered to be inferior.

The assumption of inferiority initially precluded consideration of the so-called "primitive" people (non-Whites) from the insanity designation. During the early ninetieth century, insanity was viewed as resulting from the demands that civilization put on the person. Thus, insanity was thought to be rare in countries where civilization was believed to be not yet fully developed, such as China, Turkey, Spain, and Mexico (Esquirol 1938). The "primitive societies" were considered to be without culture or ethics, thereby placing no demands on their citizens. The "advanced" European civilization, in contrast, demanded organization and mental production from its citizens (Krafft-Ebing 1879). The insane were believed to be those who had a mental weakness that made the demands of civilization overwhelming for them. With the spread of colonization, it was observed that rates of mental illness, as well as infectious diseases, tended to increase among the native "primitive people." The proliferation of disease represented support for the beliefs that civilization was harmful to the "primitive man." When "madness" was detected among non-White civilizations, it was understood as reflective of cultural depravity (Raimundo Oda et al. 2005). Moreau de Tours (1843) observed that eastern Mediterranean people tended to only confine the aggressive and dangerous patients while the remaining mentally disturbed were cared for by family within their home. Moreau interpreted this culturally different behavior as evidence for insanity being a "sacred evil" among Eastern cultures.

During the turn of the century when neurological theories of human functioning gained popularity, Western science again used its science to justify racism and asserted that African Americans had smaller frontal lobes, resulting in "more developed inferior mental faculties such as smell, sight, manual ability, corporeal sense and melody, while whites, on the other hand, would have developed higher mental faculties such as self-control, ambition, ethical and aesthetic sense and reason" (Bean 1906 as summarized by Raimundo Oda et al. 2005, p. 163). After the abolition of slavery in the USA, some American authors wrote that rates of mental illness among African Americans had increased due to the lack of mental preparation of these "primitive" peoples for life in a free society (Jarvis 1844, 1852). Nina-Rodrigues (1903) wrote that "civilized life would be prejudicial to Africans and their descendants, 'a race accustomed to centuries of life in African jungles'" (Raimundo Oda et al. 2005, p. 164).

The inferiority model was expressed in the ethnocentric conceptualization of suicide, as well. In a recently completed special issue devoted to ethnicity and suicide (Leong and Leach 2007), the review of suicide among African Americans by Utsey et al. (2007) contains a disturbing but representative example of this deficit conceptualization. Utsey et al. (2007) identify the first known major work in this area by Prudhomme (1938), who characterized the "American Negro" as too ignorant to consider suicide: "The Negro of uneducated ancestry, who has become a scholar by severe study, is less liable to suicide dependent upon education than the White man whose ancestors have felt the effect of education for generations" (Prudhomme 1938, p. 373 cited in Utsey et al. 2007).

Francis Galton, a pioneer of mental testing in the late nineteenth century and Charles Darwin's first cousin, was a believer in the heritability of intelligence (Galton 1883). He interpreted differential performance on his tests by people of color as proof of their racial inferiority. Referring to those of African descent, Galton (1870) wrote:

> The number among the negroes of those whom we should call half-witted men is very large…. The mistakes the negroes make in their own matters were so childish, stupid, and simpleton-like as frequently to make me ashamed of my own species. (p. 339)

This notion of racially based differences was widely held among the early developers of intelligence tests in the United States. Henry Goddard, a psychologist trained at Clark University under G. Stanley Hall, brought the Binet-Simon test (1905) to the United States in 1908. It soon sparked research that intended to "scientifically" show intellectual differences among the races (e.g., Strong 1913). For much of the next two decades, this was the major use of intelligence tests, a period that Guthrie (1998) termed the era of psychometric racism. For example, when the Binet-Simon scales were standardized and revised (Terman 1916; Terman and Merrill 1937, 1960), deliberate attempts were made to exclude children of color from the normative sample. Terman's views of people of color were evident in his description of two Portuguese boys with borderline intelligence:

> No amount of school instruction will ever make them intelligent voters or capable citizens in the true sense of the word…their dullness seems to be racial, or at least inherent in the family stocks from which they come. The fact that one meets this type with such extraordinary frequency among Indians, Mexicans, and Negroes suggests quite forcibly that the whole question of racial differences in mental traits will have to be taken up anew and by experimental methods. The writer predicts that when this is done, there will be discovered enormously significant racial differences in general intelligence, differences that cannot be wiped out by any scheme of mental culture. (pp. 91–92 as quoted by Valencia and Suzuki 2001)

As psychologists in this era moved into a social management role, the technology of the intelligence test was used to legitimize racial hierarchies and became part of scientific racism (Jackson and Weidman 2006; Richards 1997). By the time of America's entry in to the World War I (1917), the development of American mental testing technology had advanced significantly from the failed efforts of James McKeen Cattell's program of mental testing at Columbia University in the 1890s (Sokal 1987).

The widespread use of the Stanford-Binet scales popularized the ratio "IQ" as a measurable and immutable human property. The following decades saw a rise in cross-cultural psychological research, termed "race psychology." This new psychology was primarily concerned with comparing the intellectual abilities of White children versus non-White children. In his review of race psychology research, Garth (1925) identified 45 studies of 19 racial groups and concluded "These studies taken all together seem to indicate the mental superiority of the white race" (p. 359, as quoted by Valencia and Suzuki 2001). To his credit, Garth later recanted this position of racial inequality in IQ to support an idea of racial equality that emerged by 1930 (Valencia and Suzuki 2001).

Intelligence tests proved particularly useful as tools to sort a society that was becoming increasingly heterogenous due to the mass immigration that took place in the late nineteenth and early twentieth centuries. Many of the immigrants were from southern and eastern Europe and were generally considered inferior to the dominant stock of earlier immigrants from England and northern Europe (Fass 1980). Concerns about this massive influx of immigrants played into eugenics fears of a number of leading psychologists and led to an inferiority model of non-White citizens, as detailed below. The recently freed slaves of African descent, many of whom had moved into northern states, were thought to be a threat to racial purity (Grant 1916). Intelligence tests were one way to "prove" the inferiority of these immigrants and African Americans (Fass 1980; Richards 1997).

World War I was the proving ground for such racism. Robert Yerkes, as American Psychological Association (APA) President when the United States entered World War I, viewed the war as an opportunity to advance psychology as a science by proving its usefulness to the military (Reed 1987). What ensued was a massive testing effort, in which nearly 1.7 million recruits had their mental ability tested by specially developed Army Alpha and Beta (non-verbal) tests.

Yerkes and others also used the test results to argue for innate racial differences. That is, there were significant and meaningful racial differences in mental ability. Those of northern European and Anglo-Saxon descent were the high scorers, while those who were descended from slaves of African descent were the lowest scorers. The military men who were of eastern or southern European descent were ranged in the middle. African American recruits and draftees could be further subdivided by skin color. According to psychologist Ferguson (1919), those African American recruits with a greater proportion of White blood were more likely to score higher. Yerkes (1921) incorporated Ferguson's analysis into his own major report for the National Academy of Sciences. Here is an excerpt from his report:

> An interesting attempt was made at [Camp] Lee to further distinguish within the negro group on the basis of skin color. Two battalions were classified as lighter or darker on the basis of offhand inspection. Two other battalions were classified as black, brown, and yellow on the basis of skin color. The median score of the 'black' negroes in a was 39, that of the 'yellow' was 59; while that of the 'brown' negroes fell between these values. (Yerkes 1921, p. 531)

This kind of thinking about race was not problematic for most White Americans at this time. It simply reflected what seemed to be the order of nature. It justified this era as one dominated by a deficit or inferiority model of difference.

Undermining the Deficit Model

By the mid-1920s, a backlash had begun among some psychologists against the notion of racial hierarchies and racial differences in intelligence (e.g., Garth 1930; Klineberg 1928; Richards 1998). Otto Klineberg, a recent Columbia University PhD, was a key player in this reconfiguration of social psychology toward studies of race prejudice. Historians of psychology have tended to focus on the work of mainstream psychologists like Klineberg in these efforts (e.g., Samelson 1978). However, psychologists of color were also doing important work to counter the invidious notions of psychometric and scientific racism.

In the 1930s in New Mexico, psychologist George Sanchez, a Chicano, addressed the use of psychological tests with Mexican American schoolchildren. Sanchez found that tests standardized with White children were not valid for use with Chicano children. He argued that because Chicano children did not have the same cultural and language experiences as White middle-class children, the tests were inappropriate (Sanchez 1932, 1934; Padilla and Olmedo 2009).

African American psychologist, Howard Hale Long, a Harvard PhD (1933), worked in the Washington, DC, public schools for much of his career. Long argued, based on his experience, that it was not intellectual inferiority but problems of inequality in educational resources that led to inequality in test scores and lower academic achievement for African American students (Guthrie 1998; Long 1935). Among other minority psychologists who made important contributions to refuting ideas of racial inferiority were Albert S. Beckham and Herman G. Canady. Beckham, a NYU PhD (1930), addressed questions of the impact of urban environments on intelligence scores of Black children (Beckham 1933). Much of his career was spent with the Chicago Board of Education Bureau of Child Study. Through the Bureau, Beckham was able to establish guidance counseling clinics at many Chicago schools that served large minority populations. Canady succeeded Francis Sumner, the first African American to earn a doctorate in psychology, at West Virginia State College in 1928 as president. According to Guthrie (1998), Canady made West Virginia State into the most productive HBCU psychology department of its time. It was Canady who first questioned the role that racial differences between the examiner and examinee may play in obtaining accurate results on intelligence tests. He showed the importance of establishing rapport with minority children in order to gain the most accurate assessment of intelligence (Canady 1936). He also contributed research that highlighted the difficulty in obtaining the same testing environment for Black and White participants. This necessitated, Canady argued, great care in making any comparisons between races on test results (Canady 1943). By the time America entered World War II, then, psychologists of color were successfully challenging the results of scientific and psychometric racism. It was after the war that a new environment developed and through a confluence of factors, new voices emerged that challenged the old racist notions of inferiority and then rose to the challenge of the new racism of cultural deprivation. Out of this struggle, a new positive emphasis on identity grounded in the lived experiences of racial and ethnic minority psychologists emerged.

Postwar Challenges and Postmodern Identities

African American psychologists Canady, Beckham, Ruth Howard, and Martin David Jenkins, among others, played important roles in the 1930s and 1940s to establish psychological clinics and counseling centers to serve communities of color (Guthrie 1998). After World War II, policymakers' concerns about the mental health of Americans fuelled the rapid development of clinical psychology through the infusion of millions of dollars into new training initiatives set up by the Veterans Administration and the National Institute of Mental Health (Baker and Pickren 2007; Pickren and Schneider 2005). It has been in this postwar era that the delivery of psychological services (e.g., clinical and counseling psychology) has become dominant within American psychology.

Psychological issues related to the American urban context had begun to be explored prior to the war (e.g., Beckham 1933). After the war, some metropolitan-based psychologists began applying their science to issues of social justice (Cherry and Borshuk 1998). In New York City a bold new venture was undertaken by the African American psychologists, Mamie Phipps Clark and her husband, Kenneth Bancroft Clark.

Mamie Phipps Clark had begun her work on racial identity and preference at Howard University in 1937, not long after she and Kenneth were secretly married. The research served as the basis of her master's thesis and was elaborated in several other studies in which Kenneth Clark was her collaborator (Clark and Clark 1939, 1940). In the words of Kenneth Clark:

> It was a terribly disturbing bit of research for us. I did the actual field work on it and I was disturbed by that. And Mamie did the tabulation. When we looked at the results we left those data in our files for about two years because we were so disturbed. ...[the data] demonstrated so clearly the damage to self-awareness, to self-esteem which racial rejection was doing to human beings at such an early age. (Clark in Nyman (1976), pp. 108–109)

Out of this disturbing experience, Mamie Clark decided to act. She persuaded Kenneth to work with her to open the Northside Center for Child Development. Initially using their own money to fund the Center, they were able to get private foundation support. What Mamie Clark wanted to do was "give children security" (Lal 2002). The approach at Northside Center at first used an approach that focused on the individual child and even, at times, used a psychoanalytical framework. However, that was soon discarded as being culturally irrelevant to the experience of these children and their families (Markowitz and Rosner 1996). Mamie was the Director of the Center, while Kenneth headed the research team. A major focus of the Center was the inappropriate placement of minority children in classes for the retarded. The Clarks and their staff tested the children and found that many of the children were above average in intelligence. This led to a long battle with New York Board of Education in which they fought for change in the school board policies (Pickren 2006). The problem of inappropriate placement has been fought many times since the Clarks encountered it in New York. Their work provided a model for how to address the problem. A specific example was the suit brought against the state of California in the 1970s in the case of *Larry P.* Members of the Bay Area Association of Black Psychologists (ABPsi), provided data and testified against the use of standardized intelligence test with minority children and won. It is still not permissible in the state of California to use such tests for academic placement.

While the Clarks were working through the Northside Center to effect positive social change, the Supreme Court handed down its landmark decision in May 1954, *Brown v Board of Education of Topeka Kansas*. The Court ruled that segregation in public schools by race was unconstitutional. Of course, segregation did not end just because of the ruling, nor did discrimination or the inappropriate use of psychological technologies with racial and ethnic minorities end. But, it was a momentous decision and one that gave added impetus to the growing Civil Rights movement.

The Civil Rights movement in the United States was part of a worldwide struggle against colonialism and racial and economic oppression (e.g., Fanon 1963; Sandoval 2000). By the mid-1960s, this struggle began to impinge on American psychology and the leaders of the APA (Pickren and Tomes 2002). One response was to turn to Kenneth B. Clark for leadership, which was a critical moment for change in American psychology, as Clark articulated a way to fairly address some of the pressing social problems that psychology could impact. A new challenge that emerged was the liberal notion of the minority family and minority children as suffering from cultural deprivation.

The Disadvantaged and Culturally Deprived Model

Intending to improve the condition of ethnic minorities, Reissman (1962) proposed a cultural deprivation model where poor test performance and presumed life failures among ethnic minorities were attributed to deficiencies in culture and personality. Samuda (1975) described several ways that ethnic minorities were at a disadvantage to Whites in school and in society, including a deteriorating living environment, psychological problems (poor motivation, lower self-concept), malnutrition, language factors, and living within a context of "slum and ghetto values" (cited in Sue and Sue 2003). Contrary to previously held ideas of genetic transmission of inferiority in the races, the current view was that deficiency in culture and personality among non-Whites was transmitted across generations via socialization by parents who reared their children under "conditions adverse to good mental health" and the internalization of parental pathology during the adolescent years (Stein 1971, p. 255).

What these beliefs assumed was that the prototypical model of healthy culture was the White middle-class. Well-meaning psychologists sought to bring Blacks and other minorities "up" to their standards. No credit was given to the cultural strengths of minority communities; little attention was paid to the successes of ethnic minorities in raising their children successfully despite the often grinding oppression fostered by the mainstream society. A cogent response to this disrespect of the strengths and virtues of racial and ethnic minorities was given by Joseph L. White. White was one of the founders of ABPsi and was the first to use the term Black Psychology in print. Here is an excerpt from his very powerful article, "Toward a Black Psychology:"

> Most psychologists take the liberal point of view which in essence states that black people are culturally deprived and psychological maladjusted because the environment in which they were reared as children lacks the necessary early experiences to prepare them for excellence in school, appropriate sex-role behavior, and, generally speaking, achievement within an Anglo middle-class frame of reference.... Possibly, if social scientists, psychologists, and educators would stop trying to compensate for the so-called weaknesses of the black child and try to develop a theory that capitalizes on his strengths, programs could be designed which from the get-go might be more productive and successful. The black family represents another arena in which the use of traditional white psychological models leads us to an essentially inappropriate and unsound analysis. Maybe people who want to make the Black a case for national action should stop talking about making the black family into a white family and instead devote their energies into removing the obvious oppression of the black community which is responsible for us catchin' so much hell. (White 1970/1972, pp. 43–45)

It was this kind of pushback that was necessary to continue the process of change. Racial and ethnic minorities were to be defined on their own terms, with an identity that was developed in the community of origin, not imposed on them by Whites, however well-meaning.

Although well intentioned, the concept of cultural depravity continued to perpetuate the Eurocentric view of diversity as inferiority and further insulted the cultural integrity of non-White groups. The adoption of the cultural deprivation model engendered social policies and legislation that would have controversial implications for the role of ethnic minorities in the United States. These policies were aimed at rectifying the deficiencies in culture among non-White groups by attempting to indoctrinate them with White middle-class family values. Although many ethnic minorities have benefited from affirmative action programs adopted to equalize the playing field for disadvantaged minorities, the expectation in these programs was still that the culturally different had to conform to the dominant White middle-class ideals. Head Start programs were implemented to give low-income children additional educational supports to help boost their chances to do well academically.

These programs lacked cultural sensitivity and cultural competence in that no attempts were made to alter the Eurocentric educational system or accommodate the cultural values of non-White employees.

In this context, research on social class and mental health indicated that even when partialling out age, sex, race, religion, and marital status, social class remained linked to mental illness such that mental illness was more common in the lower classes than in higher classes (Hollingshead and Redlich 1958). Inequality in treatment was also found such that lower class patients were more likely to be continuous institutional residents, were less likely to see a professional, and were less likely to receive psychotherapy, presumed by the authors to be a universally effective treatment for mental health patients (Hollingshead and Redlich 1958). Rosenthal and Jacobson's (1968) research highlighted the impact of labeling and expectation on performance of school children on IQ tests. Although not fully researched until Steele and colleagues' work on stereotype threat (Steele 1997; Steele and Aronson 1995), there was increasing recognition that negative labeling of ethnic minorities could cause a self-fulfilling prophecy and limit their academic and job success.

In this era, the increased organization of minority groups since the civil rights movement and integration of ethnic minorities into positions of power within organized psychology (see Trickett et al. 1994) focused attention on the harmful effects of oppression on ethnic minorities (Grier and Cobb 1968). By 1968, there was a younger generation of African American psychologists for whom being Black was a marker of positive identity. Influenced by militant writers such as Malcolm X, these younger psychologists grew tired of waiting for APA to act on their concerns about social justice and minority communities. At the September 1968 meeting of the APA, a small group of Black psychologists formed the ABPsi. They immediately challenged the leadership of APA to begin to dismantle the legacy of racism in testing and the failure to develop appropriate psychological services or admit minority students to graduate programs in psychology (Pickren 2004; White 2004; Williams 1997; Williams 1974).

The concrete and specific demands of ABPsi along with concomitant pressure from a strong women's movement among psychologists provided a model for the organizational development of Asian Americans (Leong 1995; Leong and Okazaki 2009), Latino/as (Padilla and Olmedo 2009), and American Indians (Trimble and Clearing-Sky 2009) in psychology. By the late 1970s, with the meeting of the now famed "Dulles Conference," racial and ethnic minority psychologists had reached a critical mass of numbers and the pace of change toward a multicultural psychology was strong enough to begin the next phase of the struggle: developing culturally appropriate psychological services with concurrent training in the appropriate delivery of those services by all professional psychologists.

The Culturally Different Model

Also known as the culturally pluralistic model, the culturally different model (Katz 1985; Sue 1981) abandons the value judgments of diversity as inferiority or deprived that plagued its predecessors and embraces the idea that cultural differences must be celebrated as naturally occurring variation among human species. The normative frame of reference for health was shifted away from the Anglo-Saxon middle-class male to a contextually bound framework. Additionally, the historically universalistic application of ethnocentric psychological theories and methods were challenged. Population specific psychologies arose out of assertions that it was impossible for White psychologists to step outside of their cultural context to adequately understand and promote the psychologies of culturally different groups:

> dominant methods of psychological research, the problems selected as important to pursue, and the demographics of the data gatherers have conspired against developing a psychology of individuals that emerges from the experiences and perspectives of those who occupy different places in the social order. (Trickett et al. 1994, pp. 20–21)

Thus arose Black Psychology, Chicano Psychology, Asian American Psychology, and others that pursued to understanding of the unique psychologies of these groups within culture-specific paradigms. This culturally different model also allowed for recognition of a White cultural identity that could now be decisively researched as different from other cultural identities. Concepts of oppression, prejudice, and racism were also studied within the experience of diversity and it was recognized that ethnic minorities within the dominant culture are actually bicultural and function in multiple cultural contexts (Sue et al. 1992).

Many psychologists now accepted that the Western conception of intelligence was culture-bound and ethnocentric, with questionable external validity to culturally diverse groups. Culturally different conceptions of intelligence were also investigated from a value-free perspective (see Butcher et al. 1998). To counteract the universalistic application of intelligence tests to all cultural groups despite known biases, Berry (1974) proposed an extreme perspective that specific intellectual assessments should be developed for each cultural group to prevent cultural biases in testing (as cited in Butcher et al. 1998). Psychologists did not embark on the establishment of culture-specific intellectual assessments. However, other efforts were made to limit culturally biased psychological assessment, including the inclusion of ethnic minorities in the norming process, use of non-verbal assessments, efforts to develop culturally universal items, and use of group specific norms.

The Positive Psychology Model

Positive psychology is defined as the "science of positive subjective experience, positive individual traits, and positive institutions" (Seligman and Csikszentmihalyi 2000, p. 5). The positive psychology movement has risen in the past decade in an effort to counterbalance the deficit perspective on human functioning that took over the field of psychology in the aftermath of World War II. Positive psychology is a study of human strengths and virtues and conceptualizes mental health as consisting of positive aspects of functioning, as opposed to the deficit perspective that leaves health to be defined as devoid of negativity.

Spearheaded by Martin Seligman, positive clinical psychology is the study of human strengths. During his presidency of the APA in 1998, Seligman launched the field of positive psychology by noting that the field of psychology had focused mainly on deficits and dysfunctions and mental disorders and ignored optimal human functioning and human strengths and assets. As a counterpart to the Diagnostic and Statistical Manual of Mental Disorders (DSM) published by the American Psychiatric Association which drives much of clinical psychology's focus on human psychopathology, Seligman and his colleagues began to create a classification of human strengths. This classification was labeled the Values in Action (VIA) Classification of Strengths and published in the book *Character Strengths and Virtues* co-authored by Peterson and Seligman (2004). The following character strengths were identified in the VIA: Wisdom and Knowledge, Courage, Humanity and Love, Justice, Temperance, and Transcendence. Measures were developed to assess these character strengths and their antecedents and consequences are being explored by researchers around the country. Recent formulations of these human strengths were classified as cognitive strengths (curiosity, rationality, intelligence), emotional strengths (zest, hope, wonder), strengths of will (courage, perseverance), relational and civic strengths (kindness, humor, social responsibility), and strengths of coherence (honesty, self-control, prudence, spirituality) (Seligman and Peterson 2002).

Taking lesson from the mistakes of preceding models, the positive clinical psychology model recognizes the conception of "strength" as being culturally constructed (Lopez et al. 2002) whereby some cultural behaviors can be adaptive in one cultural context but maladaptive in another. While not progressing as fast as the global positive psychology movement, cross-cultural research in positive clinical psychology has begun to compare levels of attributes between cultures and examined them for adaptiveness. Findings indicate differential predictability of health status of a variety of factors specific to culture. For example, religiosity has been found to serve as a protective method of coping among African Americans, but not among Caucasians (Blaine and Crocker 1995; Rosen 1982 as cited in Lopez et al. 2002).

Summary

By providing a historical review of how clinical psychology has approached the issues of culture, race and ethnicity in this country, we hope that the lessons identified in this chapter from our collective past will guide us to use a more enlightened science and practice in the decades ahead. Like many before us, we cannot escape the conclusion that good science in clinical psychology, as in any field of psychology, should be a complete science—it cannot be a science for some people, not others, and still remain science. Furthermore, good science should always be accurate and not subjected to personal and cultural biases as well as preconceptions.

References

Baker, R. R., & Pickren, W. E. (2007). *Psychology and the Department of Veterans Affairs: A historical analysis of training, research, practice, and advocacy*. Washington, DC: APA Books.

Bean, R. B. (1906). Some racial peculiarities of the Negro brain. *American Journal of Anatomy, 5,* 353–415.

Beckham, A. S. (1933). A study of the intelligence of colored adolescents of differing social-economic status in typical metropolitan areas. *Journal of Social Psychology, 4,* 70–91.

Benjamin, L. T., Jr. (1997). Organized industrial psychology before Division 14: The ACP and the AAAP. *Journal of Applied Psychology, 82,* 459–466.

Berry, J. W. (1974). Radical cultural relativism and concept of intelligence. In J. Berry & P. Dasen (Eds.), *Culture and cognition: Readings in cross-cultural psychology*. London: Methuen.

Blaine, B., & Crocker, J. (1995). Religiousness, race, and psychological well-being: Exploring social psychological mediators. *Personality and Social Psychology Bulletin, 21,* 1031–1041.

Butcher, J. N., Nezami, E., & Exner, J. (1998). Psychological assessment of people in diverse cultures. In S. S. Kazarian & D. R. Evans (Eds.), *Cultural clinical psychology: Theory, research, and practice* (pp. 61–105). New York: Oxford University Press.

Canady, H. G. (1936). The effect of rapport on the 'IQ'. *Journal of Negro Education, 5,* 209–219.

Canady, H. G. (1943). The problem of equating the environment of Negro-White groups for intelligence testing in comparative studies. *Journal of Social Psychology, 17,* 3–15.

Caplan, E. (1998). *Mind games: American culture and the birth of psychotherapy*. Berkeley: University of California Press.

Cherry, F., & Borshuk, C. (1998). Social action research and the commission on community interrelations. *Journal of Social Issues, 54,* 119–142.

Clark, K. B., & Clark, M. K. (1939). The development of consciousness of self and the emergence of racial identification in negro preschool children. *Journal of Social Psychology, S.P.S.S.I. Bulletin, 10,* 591–599.

Clark, K. B., & Clark, M. K. (1940). Skin color as a factor in racial identification of Negro preschool children. *Journal of Social Psychology, S.P.S.S.I. Bulletin, 11,* 159–169.

Clement, D. (1982). Samoan folk knowledge of mental disorder. In A. J. Marsella & G. White (Eds.), *Cultural conceptions of mental health and therapy* (pp.193–213). Boston: Reidel.

Darwin, C. (1859). *The origin of species by means of natural selection*. London: Murray.

Esquirol, J. E. D. (1938). *Die Geisteskrankheiten in BeziehungzurMedizin und Staatsarzneikunde*. Berlin: Verlag der Voss'schen Buchhandlung.

Fanon, F. (1963).*The wretched of the earth*. New York: Grove.

Fass, P. (1980). The IQ: A cultural and historical framework. *American Journal of Education, 88,* 431–458.

Ferguson, G. O. (1919). The intelligence of Negroes at Camp Lee, Virginia. *School and Society, 9,* 721–726.

Finch, F. H., & Odoroff, M. E. (1939). Employment trends in applied psychology. *Journal of Consulting Psychology, 3,* 118–122.

Galton, F. (1883). *Inquiries into the human faculty*. London: MacMillan.

Galton, S. F. (1870). *Hereditary genius: An inquiry into its laws and consequences*. New York: Appleton.

Garth, T. R. (1925). A review of race psychology. *Psychological Bulletin, 22,* 343–364.

Garth, T. R. (1930). A review of race psychology. *Psychological Bulletin, 27,* 329–356.

Gobineau, de. (1915). *Essay on the inequality of the human races*. New York: Putnam.

Grant, M. (1916). *The passing of the great race*. New York: Scribners.

Grier, W. H., & Cobb, P. M. (1968). *Black rage*. New York: Bantam Books.

Guthrie, R. V. (1998). *Even the rat was white: A historical view of psychology*. Boston: Allyn & Bacon.

Hollingshead, A. B., & Redlich, G. C. (1958). *Social class and mental illness: A community study*. New York: Wiley.

Jackson, J. P., Jr. & Weidman, N. M. (2006). *Race, racism, and science: Social impact and interaction*. New Brunswick: Rutgers University Press.
Jarvis, E. (1844). Insanity among the colored population of the free states I. *American Journal of Medical Science, 7,* 71–83.
Jarvis, E. (1852). Insanity among the colored population of the free states II. *American Journal of Insanity, 8,* 268–282.
Katz, J. (1985). The sociopolitical nature of counseling. *The Counseling Psychologist, 13,* 615–624.
Klineberg, O. (1928). An experimental study of speed and other factors in 'racial' differences. *Archives of Psychology, 93.*
Krafft-Ebing, R. V. (1879). *Lehrbuch der Psychiatrie auf klinischer Grundlage für practische Ärzte und Studirende*. Stuttgart: Ferdinand Enke.
Lal, S. (2002). Giving children security: Mamie Phipps Clark and the racialization of child psychology. *American Psychologist, 57,* 20–28.
Leong, F. T. L. (1995). History of Asian American psychology. *AAPA Monographs, 1,* 1–54.
Leong, F. T. L., & Leach, M. M. (2007). Ethnicity and suicide in the United States: Guest editors' introduction. *Death Studies, 31,* 393–398.
Leong, F. T. L., & Okazaki, S. (2009). History of Asian American psychology. *Cultural Diversity and Ethnic Minority Psychology, 15,* 352–362.
Long, H. H. (1935). Some psychogenic hazards of segregated education of Negroes. *Journal of Negro Education, 4,* 336–350.
Lopez, S. J., Prosser, E. C., Edwards, L. M., Magyar-Moe, J. L., Neufeld, J. E., & Rasmussen, H. N. (2002). Putting positive psychology in a multicultural context. In C. R. Snyder & S. J. Lopez (Eds.), *Handbook of positive psychology* (pp. 700–714). Oxford: Oxford University Press.
Markowitz, G., & Rosner, D. (1996). *Children, race, and power: Kenneth and Mamie Clark's northside center*. Charlottesville: University of Virginia Press.
McReynolds, P. (1997). *Lightner Witmer: His life and times.* Washington, DC: American Psychological Association.
Moreau de Tours, J. (1843). Recherches sur les aliénés en orient: Notes sur les établissements qui leur sont consacrés a Malte (Ile de), au Caire (Égypte), a Smyrne (Asie-Mineure), a Constantinople (Turquie). *Annales médico-psychologiques, 1,* 103–132.
Napoli, D. S. (1981). *Architects of adjustment: The history of the psychological profession in the United States*. Port Washington: Kennikat.
Nina-Rodrigues, R. (1903). La paranoïa chez les nègres. *Archives d'anthropologiecriminelle, de criminologieet de psychologienormale et pathologieque, 118,* 609–655, 689–714.
Nyman, L. (1976). *Recollections: An oral history of the psychology department of the City College of the City University of New York*. New York: Author.
Padilla, A. M., & Olmedo, E. (2009). Synopsis of key persons, events, and associations in the history of Latino Psychology. *Cultural Diversity and Ethnic Minority Psychology, 15,* 363–373.
Peterson, C., & Seligman, M. (2004). *Character strengths and virtues: A handbook and classification*. New York: Oxford University Press.
Pickren, W. E. (2004). Between the cup of principle and the lip of practice: Ethnic minorities and American psychology, 1966–1980. *History of Psychology, 7,* 45–64.
Pickren, W. E. (2006). Social justice and psychological science in New York City, 1945–1965. Invited address to the New York Academy of Sciences, New York, NY.
Pickren, W. E., & Schneider, S. F. (2005). *Psychology and the National Institute of Mental Health: A historical analysis of science, practice, and policy*. Washington, DC: APA Books.
Prudhomme, C. (1938). The problem of suicide in the American Negro. *Psychoanalytic Review, 25,* 372–391.
Pickren, W. E., & Tomes, H. (2002). The legacy of Kenneth B. Clark to the APA: The board of social and ethical responsibility in psychology. *American Psychologist, 57,* 51–59.
Raimundo Oda, A. M. G., Banzato, C. E. M., & Dalgalarrondo, P. (2005). Some origins of cross-cultural psychiatry. *History of Psychiatry, 16*(2), 155–169.

Reed, J. (1987). Robert M. Yerkes and the mental testing movement. In M. M. Sokal (Ed.), *Psychological testing and American society* (pp. 75–94). New Brunswick: Rutgers University Press.
Reissman, F. (1962). *The culturally deprived child and his education*. New York: Harper and Brothers.
Richards, G. (1997). *Race, racism, and psychology*. London: Routledge.
Richards, G. (1998). Reconceptualizing the history of race psychology: Thomas Russell Garth (1872–1939) and how he changed his mind. *Journal of the History of the Behavioral Sciences, 34*, 15–32.
Rosen, C. E. (1982). Ethnic differences among impoverished rural elderly in use of religion as a coping mechanism. *Journal of Rural Community Psychology, 3*, 27–34.
Rosenthal, R., & Jacobson, L. (1968). *Pygmalion in the classroom*. New York: Holt, Rinehart, & Winston.
Samelson, F. (1978). From race psychology to studies of prejudice. *Journal of the History of the Behavioral Sciences, 14*, 265–278.
Samuda, R. J. (1975). From ethnocentrism to a multicultural perspective in educational testing. *Journal of Afro-American Issues, 3*, 4–18.
Sanchez, G. I. (1932). Scores of Spanish-speaking children on repeated tests. *Journal of Genetic Psychology, 40*, 223–231.
Sanchez, G. I. (1934). Bilingualism and mental measures. *Journal of Applied Psychology, 18*, 765–772.
Sandoval, C. (2000). *Methodology of the oppressed*. Minneapolis: University of Minnesota Press.
Seligman, M. E. P., & Csikszentmihalyi, M. (2000). Positive psychology: An introduction. *American Psychologist 55*, 5–14.
Seligman, M. E. P., & Peterson, C. (2002). Positive clinical psychology. In L. G. Aspinwall & U. M. Staudinger (Eds.), *A psychology of human strengths: Perspectives on an emerging field*. Washington, DC: American Psychological Association.
Sokal, M. M. (1987). James McKeen Cattell and mental anthropometry: Nineteenth-century science and reform and the origins of psychological testing. In M. Sokal (Ed.), *Psychological testing and American society,* 1890–1930 (pp. 21–45). New Brunswick: Rutgers University Press.
Steele, C. M. (1997). A threat in the air: How stereotypes shape intellectual identity and performance. *American Psychologist, 52*, 613–629.
Steele, C. M., & Aronson, J. (1995). Stereotype threat and the intellectual test performance of African Americans. *Journal of Personality and Social Psychology, 69*, 797–811.
Stein, R. F. (1971). *Disturbed youth and ethnic family patterns*. Albany: State University of New York Press.
Strong, A. C. (1913). Three hundred fifty white and colored children measured by the Binet-Simon measuring scale of intelligence. *Pedagogical Seminary, 20*, 485–515.
Sue, D. W. (1981). *Counseling the culturally different: Theory and practice*. New York: Wiley.
Sue, D. W., Arredondo, P., & McDavis, R. J. (1992). Multicultural counseling competencies and standards: A call to the profession. *Journal of Counseling and Development, 70*, 477–486
Sue, D.W., & Sue, D. (2003). *Counseling the culturally-different: Theory and practice*. (4th ed.). New York: Wiley.
Taylor, E. I. (1999). *Shadow culture: Psychology and spirituality in America*. Washington, DC: Counterpoint.
Terman, L. (1916). *The measurement of intelligence: An explanation of and a complete guide for the use of the Stanford revision and extension of the Binet-Simon scales*. Boston: Houghton Mifflin.
Terman, L., & Merrill, M. A. (1937). *Measuring intelligence*. Boston: Houghton Mifflin.
Terman, L., & Merrill, M. A. (1960). *Stanford-Binet Intelligence Scale: 1960 norms edition*. Boston: Houghton Mifflin.
Trickett, E. J., Watts, R. J., & Birman, D. (1994). Toward an overarching framework for diversity. In E. J. Trickett, R. J. Watts, & D. Birman (Eds.), *Human diversity: Perspectives on people in context*. San Francisco: Jossey-Bass.

Trimble, J. E., & Clearing-Sky M. (2009). An historical profile of American Indians and Alaska Natives in psychology. *Cultural Diversity and Ethnic Minority Psychology, 15*, 338–351.

Utsey, S. O., Hook, J. N., & Stanard, P. (2007). A re-examination of the cultural factors in relation to risk, resilience, and African American suicide: A review of the literature and recommendations for future research. *Death Studies, 31*, 399–416.

Valencia, R. R., & Suzuki, L. A. (2001). *Intelligence testing and minority students: Foundations, performance factors, and assessment issues*. Thousand Oaks: Sage.

White, J. L. (1970/1972). Toward a black psychology. In R. L. Jones (Ed.), *Black psychology* (pp. 43–50). New York: Harper & Row. [An early version appeared in the Black Scholar with a popular version in Ebony magazine, 1970.]

White, J. L. (2004). *Oral history interview with Wade E. Pickren, Irvine, CA, October*. Washington, DC: APA Archives.

Williams, B. H. (1997). Coming together: The founding the association of Black psychologists (Doctoral dissertation, University of Michigan, 1997). *Dissertation Abstracts International* (UMI Number: 9822882).Williams, R. (1974). A history of the association of Black psychologists: Early formation and development. *Journal of Black Psychology, 1*, 9–24.

Yerkes, R. M. (1921). *Psychological examining in the U. S. Army. Memoirs of the National Academy of Sciences, No. 15*. Washington, DC: National Academy of Sciences.

Chapter 3
Psychology of African American Children: Strengths and Challenges

Richard Thompson, Ernestine C. Briggs and Sylvette A. LaTouche-Howard

Chapter Focus

This chapter presents information on mental health issues in African American children, focusing on exposure to violence, maltreatment/punitive parenting, and limited access to mental health services as major challenges to the maintenance of mental health in this group; extended social supports, firm, appropriately restrictive parents, and robust self-esteem as strengths contributing to resilience this group; and the need to recognize the diversity among African American children while identifying and addressing the needs of those children most at risk.

Demographic Characteristics of African American Children

African Americans make up roughly 13% of the American population, and their proportion of the American population is growing (U.S. Census 2001). The proportion of African Americans under 18 is greater than would be predicted by national statistics. Specifically, 31.4% of African Americans are under the age of 18, compared with 25.7% of all Americans (U.S. Census 2001). African American children and youth are also more likely to be living in poverty; more than 30% of African American children and youth live in poverty, compared with less than 20% of American children overall (U.S. Census 2001). Although the majority of African Americans still live in the American South, most research on African American children has been conducted on those living in Northeast or Midwest cities.

R. Thompson (✉)
Juvenile Protective Association, 1707 N Halsted, Chicago, IL 60614, USA
e-mail: RThompson@juvenile.org

E. C. Chang, C. A. Downey (eds.), *Handbook of Race and Development in Mental Health*,
DOI 10.1007/978-1-4614-0424-8_3, © Springer Science+Business Media, LLC 2012

Challenges to Maintaining Mental Health

Exposure to Violence

African American children are exposed to an inordinate amount of violence. The literature on African American youth suggests that they are at greater risk for exposure to violence, due largely to the concentrated violence in urban African American communities (Tolan and Gorman-Smith 2002). Exposure to violence may occur within the family or in the neighborhood/community (O'Donnell et al. 2006).

Regardless of setting, exposure to violence has been associated with a myriad of consequences. In addition to disruptions in developmental tasks, African American youth may exhibit several internalizing and externalizing behavioral problems (Hill and Madhere 1996). The sequelae associated with violence exposure includes: higher rates of anxiety, depression, delinquency, and substance use, poorer self-esteem and physical health, increased risk for relationship difficulties, and teen pregnancy (Cooley-Quille et al. 2001). Many of these symptoms may be compounded by the additional stress associated with living in urban environments (housing difficulties), poverty, and/or racism. Additionally, children's level of functioning appears to decline as the number and frequency of stressors increases (Rutter 1987).

Other research has focused primarily on anxiety-related symptoms with most of this work examining posttraumatic stress disorder (PTSD). Numerous empirical studies have examined PTSD which includes an array of arousal, avoidance, and re-experiencing symptoms. PTSD has been linked with exposure to violence and other traumatic events including maltreatment and other victimization experiences (Overstreet et al. 1999). For example, Overstreet and colleagues (1999) found that a third of children in their sample displayed a symptom pattern consistent with PTSD. Similarly, Rich and Grey (2005) suggest that African American young men may feel particularly vulnerable to violence and unprotected by the justice system, which increases risk of trauma symptoms and risk-taking and/or violent behavior.

Many studies have examined externalizing behaviors associated with trauma exposure. These include the general categories of "aggressive acting out" (Cooley-Quille et al. 2001). In addition, exposure to violence in urban youth has also been linked to poor school functioning (Kennedy and Bennett 2006), increased self-reported aggression in school, and worsened teacher-reported school-related competencies (Ozer 2005). In sum, African American children are at increased risk of exposure to violence, and this exposure places them at risk for several challenges to psychosocial functioning.

Maltreatment/Punitive Parenting

Child maltreatment is a serious public health problem (Rovi et al. 2002), and a source of both immediate and long-term dysfunction (Edwards et al. 2003; Johnson et al. 2002). Maltreatment is associated with significant risk for poor mental health outcomes for children, in many domains of functioning: depression (Kim and Cicchetti 2006), suicidality (Finzi et al. 2001), aggressive behavior (Johnson et al. 2002), and conduct disorder (Paz et al. 2005). Heightened difficulties in peer relationships and self-esteem have also been reported as being associated with greater severity and chronicity of maltreatment (Bolger et al. 1998). These outcomes of maltreatment are likely to persist into adulthood (Edwards et al. 2003).

Given the fact that maltreatment also has an impact on the development of personality (Rogosch and Cicchetti 2004) and cognition (Jean-Giles and Crittenden 1990), the effects of maltreatment are likely to impact emotional health in ways other than a formal mental health diagnosis. Emotional maltreatment, including shaming, is often more difficult to verify in the lives of African American children. Such maltreatment can have an impact on socialization, giving children a distorted view for self-appraisal (Loader 1998). Parents frequently fail to see such behavior as abusive (Butler and Williamson 1999), and may fail to contemplate the effects of such behavior on children's outcomes. The use of strategies to help parents recognize its impact on child development is needed to minimize the effects.

African American children are more likely than other children to be identified as maltreated (Fluke et al. 2003), and are disproportionately represented in the foster-care system (Lau et al. 2003; Lu et al. 2004). After a first report to child protective services (CPS), African American children are more likely than other children to be reported to CPS a second time (Fuller and Wells 2003). It would seem, then, that African American children are at increased risk for maltreatment and the associated problems. This conclusion, however, remains controversial. First, there is evidence of bias in the CPS system at all levels (e.g., Lau et al. 2003) in terms of: which families get reported to the system, which reports are investigated, and which families have children removed. Moreover, once removed, African American children are less likely to be reunited with their families than are other children (Lu et al. 2004). The prevention of neglect and abuse must be a top priority for African American families. It is also essential to recognize that separation of children from their parents can also be a disruptive and painful experience for children, to be implemented only when necessary (Simons et al. 2002).

Given the apparent biases in the system and the disruption that CPS involvement often means for families, it has been argued that the disproportionate involvement of CPS in the lives of African American families represents a civil rights issue (Roberts 2003). Several of the biases regarding evaluations of the parenting of African Americans will be reviewed below, in the section on protective factors. In short, some parenting behavior that might be seen by an unbiased observer as firm or authoritative may be seen as harsh or abusive when the parents are African American (Berger et al. 2005).

There is some evidence, however, that the disparity is not simply due to bias. African American parents are more likely to report using corporal punishment (Giles-Sims et al. 1995), a finding that is echoed by observational research (Bradley et al. 2001). African American parents also are somewhat more likely to engage in forms of punishment that are unambiguously physical or verbal abuse (Ferrari 2002), and

African American children are at elevated risk to experience severe violence at the hands of their parents (Wolfner and Gelles 1993). These differences are much less pronounced, however, than the differences in rates of CPS involvement (Lau et al. 2003). Therefore, much of the real differences in punitive parenting may be due to differences in rates of poverty (Bradley et al. 2001; Giles-Sims et al. 1995). The concentration of poverty may be particularly important. Poor families that also reside in impoverished communities may face multiple challenges, associated not just with their own poverty but with community factors as well. Rates of child maltreatment among African Americans are strongly associated with the proportion of African American female-headed families living in poverty (Schuck 2005). African American children are also less likely to spend time interacting with their fathers, leaving mothers more likely to be overwhelmed by the task of parenting alone (Bradley et al. 2001).

Taken together, this research suggests that African American children are at somewhat higher risks of being maltreated and much higher risks of being involved with the child welfare system. Both outcomes (maltreatment and child welfare involvement) have profound and well-established links with poor child outcomes (Edwards et al. 2003; Johnson et al. 2002; Roberts 2003). These risk factors are related, and both are associated with a host of negative outcomes.

Limited Access to Mental Health Services

Although most youth with mental health needs do not receive needed services, this problem is especially profound for African American children (Flisher et al. 1997). In general, most research finds that African American children are roughly half as likely to receive mental health services as are White children (Angold et al. 2002). This disparity is not simply a function of differences in mental health needs. Specifically, African American children are more likely than White children to have mental health needs that go unmet (Flisher et al. 1997). Indeed, this disparity persists among children with identified mental health needs (Kodjo and Auinger 2004), and with specific mental health issues, such as depression (Wu et al. 2001) or violent crime victimization (Guterman et al. 2002). A recent report by the US Surgeon General (U.S. Public Health Service 2000) has identified this disparity for African Americans as a key area of focus for practice and research.

This disparity also does not appear to be due solely to African American parents' failure to recognize their children's mental health needs. Indeed, African American parents are as likely as other parents to recognize their children's mental health needs, yet the disparity persists among children identified by their parents as needing services. (Thompson 2005; Thompson and May 2006). In foster care and child welfare settings, where parental decision-making has less influence, this disparity remains (Burns et al. 2004).

Systemic economic factors appear to play some part in the ethnic disparity in services utilization. Gyamfi (2004) found that poverty appeared to explain some of the disparity. More specific socioeconomic factors have been noted as associated with failure to meet children's mental health needs, including: lack of insurance (Flisher et al. 1997) or Medicaid (Angold et al. 2002), being on public assistance (Flisher et al. 1997), and the location of the neighborhood (Kodjo and Auinger 2004). However, although poverty predicts mental health use in general, research indicates that it either fails to explain ethnic differences in mental health utilization or only partially explains them (e.g., Angold et al. 2002; Flisher et al. 1997).

Another set of structural explanations for the disparity in mental health services centers around racism or bias in the mental health system. Mental health services are often not designed to address the specific needs or utilize the unique strengths of African American youth (Borum 2005). Undoubtedly, the limitations of the mental health system reinforce some of the negative attitudes about treatment held by African American youth and their parents (Lindsey et al. 2006). It is possible that African American children typically access mental health services through criminal justice or social service avenues, whereas White children are usually referred by family or friends (Chow et al. 2003). Other systemic barriers to mental health services, like lack of proximity to services, have been proposed, but these have typically failed to explain the disparity when empirically tested (Kodjo and Auinger 2004).

Aside from factors external to African American youth and their families, the other class of explanations for this disparity focuses on cultural or attitudinal factors. One consistent finding is that African Americans tend to be less likely to expect mental health services to be helpful (Cooper et al. 2003). This may be because of past negative experiences with social services (Thompson 2005) or general mistrust of mental health service providers (Thompson et al. 2004). African American parents may worry that service providers are likely to impose foreign mores (Borum 2005), fail to understand African American concerns (Drauker 2005), or simply be racist (Borum 2005). These concerns are also held by African American youth (Lindsey et al. 2006). These perceptions of the inadequacy of the mental health services system may be reinforced by past negative experiences with these systems (Kerkorian et al. 2006).

There is some evidence that African Americans are more likely to see the treatment of mental health problems as stigmatizing (Ayalon and Young 2005; Thompson et al. 2004), or to view mental health problems as "luxuries" that African Americans cannot "afford" (Borum 2005). As well, it is often proposed that African Americans are more likely to use alternative approaches to such problems, like services through church or extended family (Thompson et al. 2004). However, there is little evidence that these alternate approaches to mental health needs are used widely by African Americans (Ayalon and Young 2005).

The diminished use of mental health services by African American children represents an important challenge to their maintenance of mental health and well-being. Although most children do not require formal mental health services, these services have been demonstrated to be useful for the minority of children who have serious mental health problems (Greenbaum et al. 1996). Because African American children are overrepresented in settings where mental health services are frequently needed (such as foster care and the juvenile justice system), those with the most pressing needs are also likely to go untreated.

Strengths Contributing to Mental Health

Historically, most research on ethnic minorities in general has examined pathology, rather than normative development (Quintana et al. 2006). This has led to a focus on differences between ethnic minorities and "majority" children, and on weaknesses, especially in the case of African American children (Winfield 1995). Part of the problem may be an attempt to "universalize" the mainstream experience, and to assume that it is normative (Ungar 2004). Recent efforts have examined the normative development of African American children (Quintana et al. 2006) and their particular strengths (Hopps et al. 2002).

The implicit "assumption of deficit" has also led some African American strengths to be understood as weaknesses. Several examples are described below. This list of strengths is not exhaustive; these are examples of some of the strongest positive influences on the mental health of African American children. They may be as important as vulnerabilities in thinking about interventions; some of the most promising approaches to working with African Americans focus on building on the strengths of young people and families (e.g., Hopps et al. 2002).

Extended Social Supports

A strength often cited in the literature on African American families is the social support network. In particular, participation in extended kinship networks offers both guidance and support (Taylor et al. 1996). These elaborate social support networks may include relatives, older siblings, neighbors, and friends and provide a variety of functions, ranging from financial assistance to emotional support (Bell-Scott and Mckenry 1986). Multiple dimensions of social support networks have been examined including extent and size of social networks, social embeddedness, stability, and perceptions of support (Barrow et al. 2007), as well as tangible and emotional support (Barrera 1986).

Reliance on informal networks as a practical source of support among African Americans has been attributed to a number of social, economic, and cultural factors (Billingsley 1992; Taylor et al. 1997). Regardless of the precipitating factors (i.e., poverty, traditional beliefs regarding collectivism and cooperation), informal networks have demonstrated their utility in providing various forms of assistance to cope with stressful life events (Bost et al. 2004). Indeed, the findings from several studies suggest that informal support is one of the most common coping resources identified by African Americans as valuable in helping them deal with a myriad of stressful situations including economic difficulties, housing needs, and interpersonal problems (Taylor et al. 1993).

The literature on social support indicates that social support, particularly family support, acts as a protective factor, attenuating the effects of a host of internalizing and externalizing behavioral problems. Moreover, the support provided by social network members positively influences coping strategies, mental health outcomes, and health-related behaviors (Barrow et al. 2007). Numerous studies have identified social support as a potent influence in the lives of African American parents (Ceballo and McLoyd 2002) and youth (Barbarin 1993; McCabe et al. 1999). Social networks and support systems may moderate the effects of negative or stressful life events by enhancing adults' psychological well-being (e.g., reducing depression) and thus parenting capacity (Dressler 1985; McLoyd 1998; Taylor et al. 1993). In particular, such support may increase parental sensitivity in response to children's needs (Crnic et al. 1984). Additionally, extended social networks increase the number of adults that are involved in children's lives (Levitt et al. 1993). Thus, involvement in extended social networks appears to be an important protective factor for African American children. Aside from the benefits of social support, it may also provide a positive source of identity.

For African American children, racial identity formation is a complex process involving an attempt to integrate values of the larger "mainstream" culture and of African American culture, while grappling with barriers such as prejudice and discrimination (Tatum 1997; Sellers et al. 2006). These barriers have been linked to increased levels of behavior problems, lower self-esteem, and reliance on externalizing coping strategies (Clark et al. 2004; Simons et al. 2002). However, there is emerging empirical support for the important role that racial identity plays in African American adolescents' behavioral functioning (Sellers et al. 2006; Wong et al. 2003), suggesting that a healthy racial identity, fostered by the broader social network, can play an important protective function. Belonging to a religious community also appears to be protective. This protective function may stem in part from the benefits of social support networks. There is emerging empirical evidence that suggests that religiosity is a protective factor against violence (Wallace and Forman 1998), promotes behavioral and emotional self-regulation (Stevenson 1997), and decreases the likelihood of antisocial activity (Cook 2000).

Thus, overall, there is a growing body of research highlighting the protective influence of the extended social networks that are a part of the lives of many African American children. Membership in such networks provides a valuable source of identity as well as the positive influence of caring adults, beyond the immediate "nuclear" family.

Firm, Appropriately Restrictive Parents

In addition to the general benefits of an extended family network, African American children are also likely to benefit from the parenting styles frequently used by their caregivers. In particular, the style of parenting exercised by many African Americans appear to promote autonomy, while at the same time providing structure and safety, particularly for children living in dangerous communities.

Early on, it was thought that African American parents were uniformly deficient, relative to White parents (Moynihan 1965). The pioneering work of Baumrind (1972), however, demonstrated that the "authoritarian" parenting style employed by Black parents (although not the normatively desired parenting style) promoted the development of autonomy and maturity, especially in girls. Other research has demonstrated that parenting styles seen as harmful in the mainstream culture may be neutral or even beneficial for African American children. Although parental intrusiveness is associated with a host of negative outcomes in mainstream families, it is only related to poor child outcomes for African American children when it appears along with low parental warmth (Ispa et al. 2004). Similarly, although the use of corporal punishment is typically associated with negative outcomes for children, there appears to be an absence of negative effects of it for African American children (Deater-Deckard et al. 1996).

On the other hand, research has also found that African American children fare best when treated in an authoritative (rather than authoritarian) manner (Querido et al. 2002). Moreover, many of the parenting factors found to be positive in other communities are also helpful for African American children. For example, fathers' involvement and nurturance predicts a host of positive outcomes for African American children (Black et al. 1999). Parental warmth is also associated with positive outcomes for African American children (Ispa et al. 2004). Several studies find that African American parents are more supportive and assertive than other parents, and that they more actively promote child autonomy (Bartz and Levine 1978). Taken together, the research suggests that the "strict" behavior of many African American parents promotes positive outcomes in their children (Black et al. 1999). It also raises the possibility that some mainstream metrics may not apply to African American parents.

The assessment of parental behavior may include some biases. In one study, it was found that raters tended to perceive African American parents as more rigid and controlling than other parents, independent of any differences in actual parental behavior (Gonzales et al. 1996). Given this tendency, it is not hard to imagine that parental behavior that is appropriately authoritative may be interpreted as authoritarian, overly restrictive, cold, or overly punitive. Similarly, self-report measures may also detect African American parents who engage in normative parental behavior as "bad parents." However, because their behavior is normative, it will be associated with positive child outcomes. It is hard to apply this explanation to the findings for the use of physical punishment, which seems less subject to reporter or observer biases.

A second related possibility is that there are simply superficial cultural differences in normative parental behavior, and that what is important for child outcomes is not the particular form that parental behavior takes, but how normative it is. From this perspective, African American parents may be more "no-nonsense" (Brody and Flor 1998) than other parents, but such parental behavior is normative, and thus associated with good child outcomes. Similarly, parental intrusiveness (Ispa et al. 2004) may not be associated with negative outcomes for African American children because it is normative for African American parents. Finally, this explanation may apply to the use of corporal punishment as well (Deater-Deckard et al. 1996).

Although this explanation is appealing, it begs an important question: Why are parental restrictiveness, "authoritarianism," intrusiveness, and the use of physical punishment normative for African American parents? Baumrind (1972) proposed that the parenting styles employed by African American parents were designed to promote autonomy in their children. This has also been supported by other research, which notes that the parenting behavior of African Americans works to promote self-regulation (Brody and Flor 1998) and to prevent behavioral problems (Lau et al. 2006). Another perspective suggests that these parental behaviors are needed to counteract the influence of community violence and poverty, which place African American children at risk for negative outcomes. For example, Mason et al. (1996) proposed that the relatively strict parenting behavior of African American parents serves to protect children from the dangers posed by violent communities. Indeed, in relatively dangerous environments, parents have a simultaneous need to be restrictive (to limit exposure to risk factors) while at the same time promoting independence earlier (to ensure that children can deal with risk factors when they are present). Thus, parenting in such communities is often characterized by restrictiveness (Letiecq and Koblinsky 2004) and the promotion of autonomy (Brody and Flor 1998).

Regardless of the particular reasons for this parenting style, it apparently serves to promote the well-being of African American children. By promoting child safety and autonomy, African American parents ensure that their children will have some measure of protection against many of the dangers and risks they face. Such parenting is also likely to reduce the likelihood of externalizing (violent and risk-taking) behavioral problems. Thus, the firm and relatively restrictive parenting behavior described here works in an opposing direction to the challenges described elsewhere in this chapter.

Robust Self-Esteem

Although early work suggested that African American children had deficits in self-esteem, this appears to have either been inaccurate or based on an historical artifact (Gray-Little and Hafdahl 2000). The bulk of recent research suggests that African American children actually tend to have higher self-esteem than White children, as demonstrated by a recent meta-analysis by Gray-Little and Hafdahl (2000). This advantage in self-esteem is especially pronounced for African American girls (Biro et al. 2006). The implications of this advantage for mental health issues are unclear. There are, however, two particular domains in which self-esteem is likely to be important and where African American children have some advantages: eating disorders/body dysmorphic disorders, and suicide risk.

There is a growing body of literature that demonstrates that African American girls and women are at reduced risk for eating disorders, relative to others (Bisaga et al. 2005; Grabe and Hyde 2006). One key reason for this disparity is probably the fact that African American girls and women tend to have relatively positive body image, and this is a unique advantage among "ethnic minority" women in America (Grabe and Hyde 2006). In turn, this healthy body image is related to more general self-esteem (Young-Hyman et al. 2003). Thus, it is not simply that African American girls and women engage in less negative behavior around problem eating, but they are more likely to have an actively positive body image (Kelly et al. 2005).

There may be limits to this advantage. Recent reports suggest that the prevalence of body dissatisfaction and eating disorders is increasing in the African American community (Grabe and Hyde 2006). African American children are as likely to be teased for being overweight as are other children, and are not immune to the effects of such teasing on body image (Young-Hyman et al. 2003). Finally, it is important to note that mainstream definitions of positive body image focus almost exclusively on weight (Grogan 2006). African American women may not have an advantage in terms of body image issues other than weight (like skin tone, hair texture, or falling *below* the cultural weight standard). Indeed, some recent research finds that skin tone and self-esteem are correlated in African American children (Kerr 2005; Young-Hyman et al. 2003).

A second area where advantages in self-esteem appear to result in clear advantages for mental health is in the domain of suicidality. In particular, African American youth are roughly half as likely as White youth to commit suicide (Committee on Adolescents 2000; Snyder and Swann 2004). Not only is there an advantage in risk of actual suicide, but African American youth tend to report lower rates of suicidal ideation (Thompson et al. 2005) and to report more reasons for living and more negative attitudes about suicide (Morrison and Downey 2000). There is a well-established link between self-esteem and various forms of suicidal ideation and behavior (Beautrais et al. 1999; Palmer et al. 2003); thus, it is likely that the advantages in self-esteem explain at least part of this finding.

Recent trends also suggest that this advantage may not be as great as it once was. Recent trends also suggest that this advantage may not be as great as it once was mostly because of a general trend downward in suicide rates for youth overall. The difference between African American and White youths in suicide risk has diminished. The rate of suicide for young African American men has increased recently (Joe 2006). Possible explanations include reduced cohesion in impoverished African American communities where there is concentrated social disadvantage (Kubrin et al. 2006), diminished influence of religion, and the perception that Black youth are responsible for their own problems (which were in the past more widely attributable to racism; Joe 2006).

The recent negative trends for suicidality and eating disorders should not overshadow the very stable and high rates of self-esteem in African American children (Gray-Little and Hafdahl 2000). What is the source of the advantage for African American youth in self-esteem? This question is particularly important in light of the challenges faced by African American youth, in terms of ongoing racial prejudice and social disadvantage. Some of this advantage is probably due to the fact that, for many African Americans, racial identity is a positive factor and an important source of meaning, whereas it is not usually for Whites (Judd et al. 1995). This notion is supported by the fact that the strength of ethnic identity predicts self-esteem in African Americans, but not in Whites (Phinney et al. 1997). Another possibility is that African Americans use a different reference group than do Whites (Gray-Little and Hafdahl 2000). As noted earlier, stronger community institutions may also be protective (Ball et al. 2003), as may a tendency for African American youth to be more individualistic than White youth (Twenge and Crocker 2002). Finally, because racism is widely known and expected among African Americans, it is possible that African American youth "adjust" for such external factors in estimating their achievements and worth (Constantine and Blackmon 2002).

Discussion

Future Recommendations

The above table summarizes the challenges and strengths of African American children discussed here. Any consideration of the protective and risk factors associated with a particular cultural or ethnic group is necessarily an arbitrary exercise. Chil-

African American Children: A Summary

Demographics	Challenges	Strengths
4% of general population Growing more quickly than the general population	Exposure to violence • High levels of community violence • Associated with externalizing behavior	Extended social supports • Informal and extended family networks are important • Racial identity may provide an additional sense of belonging
	Maltreatment/punitive parenting • At much greater likelihood to be identified as maltreated • Associated with myriad behavioral problems • Identification processes may be biased	Firm, appropriately restrictive parents • Restrictive parenting may be particularly important in dangerous communities • Normative African American styles of parenting promote independence
	Limited access to mental health services • Even when identified with needs, unlikely to receive services • Explanations for disparity remain largely untested	Robust self-esteem • Elevated in self-esteem relative to other groups • May be particularly protective in terms of eating disorders and suicide risk • Protective advantage may be diminishing

dren and their families come with a complex mixture of risk and resiliency factors. Further complicating the consideration of ethnic groups is the fact that there is not necessarily a facile connection between ethnicity and culture (Gjerde and Onishi 2000). African American children, in particular, vary greatly in the degree to which they are acculturated to the mainstream, and in the degree to which they participate in African American culture.

Future research would do well to take a more integrative approach to the mental health of African American children, and to develop a richer, more qualitative understanding of the experiences of African American children and their families. For example, we have provided some plausible explanations for the advantage African American children enjoy, in terms of suicide risk, and for the diminishment of this advantage. However, these explanations have been largely untested, except for some recent innovative work by Joe and colleagues (e.g., Joe et al. 2007). Future qualitative work should examine the links between self-esteem, religiosity, and suicidality in African American youth. Similarly, a variety of explanations have been offered for the disparity between African American and White children in use of mental health services, including factors external to African American families and those internal to them. Qualitative research could examine the interplay between these influences: The degree to which perceived racism and other practical barriers interact with expectations and stigma in decision-making about seeking mental health services for these children.

In terms of developing interventions, a particularly promising approach will involve the development of interventions that simultaneously build on the strengths of families while acknowledging the important problems that families deal with. Simplistic approaches, whether strengths-based or deficits-based, are equally unlikely to be effective if they do not address the real-life experiences of the families seen.

References

Angold, A. (2002). Psychiatric disorder, impairment, and service use in rural African American and White youth. *Archives of General Psychiatry, 59,* 893–901.

Ayalon, L., & Young, M. A. (2005). Racial group differences in help-seeking behaviors. *Journal of Social Psychology, 145,* 391–403.

Barbarin, O. A. (1993). Coping and resilience: Exploring the inner lives of African American children. *Journal of Black Psychology, 19,* 478–492.

Barrera, M. (1986). Distinctions between social support concepts, measures, and models. *American Journal of Community Psychology, 14,* 413–445.

Barrow, F. H., Armstrong, M. I., Vargo, A., & Boothroyd, R. A. (2007). Understanding the findings of resilience-related research for fostering the development of African American adolescents. *Child and Adolescent Psychiatric Clinics of North America, 16,* 393–413.

Bartz, K. W., & Levine, E. S. (1978). Child-rearing by Black parents: A description and comparison to Anglo and Chicano parents. *Journal of Marriage and the Family, 40,* 709–719.

Baumrind, D. (1972). An exploratory study of socialization effects on Black children: Some Black–White comparisons. *Child Development, 43,* 261–267.

Beautrais, A. L., Joyce, P. R., & Mulder, R. T. (1999). Personality traits and cognitive styles as risk factors for serious suicide attempts among young people. *Suicide and Life-Threatening Behaviors, 29,* 37–47.

Bell-Scott, P., & Mckenry, P. C. (1986). Black adolescents and their families. In G. K. Leigh & G. W. Peterson (Eds.), *Adolescents in families* (pp. 410–432). Cincinnati: South Western.

Berger, L. M., McDaniel, M., & Paxson, C. (2005). Assessing parenting behaviors across racial groups: Implications for the child welfare system. *Social Service Review, 79,* 653–688.

Billingsley, A. (1992).Climbing Jacob's ladder: The enduring legacy of African-American families. New York: Simon & Schuster.

Biro, F. M., Striegel-Moore, R. H., Franko, D. L., Padgett, J., & Bean, J. A. (2006). Self-esteem in adolescent females. *Journal of Adolescent Health, 39,* 501–507.

Bisaga, K., Whitaker, A., Davies, M., Chuang, S., Feldman, J., & Walsh, B. T. (2005). Eating disorder and depressive symptoms in urban high school girls from different ethnic backgrounds. *Journal of Developmental and Behavioral Pediatrics, 26,* 257–266.

Black, M., Dubowitz, H., & Starr, R. H. (1999). African American fathers in low-income, urban families: Development, behavior, and home environment of their three-year-old children. *Child Development, 70,* 967–978.

Bolger, K. E., Patterson, C. J., & Kupersmidt, J. B. (1998). Peer relationships and self-esteem among children who have been maltreated. *Child Development, 69,* 1171–1197.

Borum, V. (2005). An Afrocentric perspective in working with African American families. In E. Congress, & M. Gonzalez (Eds.), *A multicultural perspective in working with families* (2nd ed., pp. 242–266). New York: Springer.

Bost, K. K., Vaughn, B. E., Boston, A. L., Kazura, K. L., & O'Neal, C. (2004). Social support networks of African-American children attending Head Start: a longitudinal investigation of structural and supportive network characteristics. *Social Development, 13,* 393–412.

Bradley, R. H., Corwyn, R. F., McAdoo, H. P., & Garcia Coll, C. (2001). The home environments of children in the United States part I: Variations by age, ethnicity, and poverty status. *Child Development, 72,* 1844–1867.

Brody, G. H., & Flor, D. L. (1998). Maternal resources, parenting practices, and child competence in rural, single-parent African American families. *Child Development, 69,* 803–816.

Burns, B. J. (2004). Mental health need and access to mental health services by youths involved with child welfare: A national survey. *Journal of the American Academy of Child and Adolescent Psychiatry, 43,* 960–970.

Butler, I., & Willamson, H. (1999). Children's view of their involvement. In D. Shemmings (Ed.), *Involving children in family support and child protection* (pp. 9–14). London: The Stationary Office.

Ceballo, R., & McLoyd, V. C. (2002). Social support and parenting in poor, dangerous neighborhoods. *Child Development, 73,* 1310–1321.

Clark, R., Coleman, A. P., & Novak, J. D. (2004). Brief report: Initial psychometric properties of the everyday discrimination scale in Black adolescents. *Journal of Adolescence, 27,* 363–368.

Committee on Adolescents, American Academy of Pediatrics. (2000). Suicide and suicide attempts inadolescents. *Pediatrics, 105,* 871–874.

Constantine, M. G., & Blackmon, S. M. (2002). Black adolescents' racial socialization experiences: Their relations to home, school, and peer self-esteem. *Journal of Black Studies, 32,* 322–335.

Cook, K. (2000). "You have to have somebody watching your back, and if that's God, then that's might big": The church's role in the resilience of inner-city youth. *Adolescence, 35,* 717–730.

Cooley-Quille, M. R., Boyd, R. C., Frantz, E., & Walsh, J. (2001). Emotional and behavioral impact of exposure to community violence in inner-city adolescents. *Journal of Clinical Child Psychology, 30,* 199–206.

Cooper, L. A. (2003). The acceptability of treatment for depression among African-American, Hispanic, and White primary care patients. *Medical Care, 41,* 479–489.

Crnic, K. A., Greenberg, M. T., Robinson, N. M., & Ragozin, A. S. (1984). Material stress and social support: Effects on the mother–infant relationship from birth to 18 months. *American Journal of Orthopsychiatry, 54,* 224–235.

Deater-Deckard, K., Dodge, K., Bates, J., & Pettit, G. (1996). Physical discipline among African American and European American mothers: Links to children's externalizing behavior. *Developmental Psychology, 32,* 1065–1072.

Dressler, W. (1985). Extended family relationships, social support, and mental health in a southern black community. *Journal of Health and Social Behavior, 26,* 296–318.

Edwards, V. J. et al. (2003). Relationship between multiple forms of childhood maltreatment and adult mental health in community respondents: Results from the adverse childhood experiences study. *American Journal of Psychiatry, 160,* 1453–1460.

Ferrari, A. M. (2002). The impact of culture upon child rearing practices and definitions of maltreatment. *Child Abuse and Neglect, 26,* 793–813.

Finzi, R. et al. (2001). Depressive symptoms and suicidality in physically abused children. *American Journal of Orthopsychiatry, 71,* 98–107.

Flisher, A. J. et al. (1997). Correlates of unmet need for mental health services by children and adolescents. *Psychological Medicine, 27,* 1145–1154.

Fluke, J. D., Yuan, Y. -Y. T., Hedderson, J., & Curtis, P. A. (2003). Disproportionate representation of race and ethnicity in child maltreatment: investigation and victimization. *Children and Youth Services Review, 25,* 359–373.

Fuller, T. L., & Wells, S. J. (2003). Predicting maltreatment recurrence among CPS cases with alcohol and other drug involvement. *Children and Youth Services Review, 25,* 553–569.

Giles-Sims, J., Strauss, M. A., & Sugarman, D. B. (1995). Child, maternal, and family characteristics associated with spanking. *Family Relations, 44,* 170–176.

Gjerde, P. F., & Onishi, M. (2000). In search of theory: The study of "ethnic groups" in developmental psychology. *Journal of Research on Adolescence, 10,* 289–297.

Gonzales, N. A., Cauce, A. M., & Mason, C. A. (1996). Interobserver agreement in the assessment of parental behavior and parent-adolescent conflict: African American mothers, daughters, and independent observers. *Child Development, 67,* 1483–1498.

Grabe, S., & Hyde, J. S. (2006). Ethnicity and body dissatisfaction among women in the United States: A meta-analysis. *Psychological Bulletin, 132,* 622–640.

Gray-Little, B., & Hafdahl, A. R. (2000). Factors influencing racial comparisons of self-esteem: A quantitative review. *Psychological Bulletin, 126,* 26–54.

Greenbaum, P. E., Dedrick, R. F., Friedman, R. M. et al. (1996). National Adolescent and Child Treatment Study (NACTS): Outcomes for children with serious emotional and behavioral disturbance. *Journal of Emotional and Behavioral Disorders, 4,* 130–146.

Grogan, S. (2006). Body image and health: Contemporary perspectives. *Journal of Health Psychology, 11,* 523–530.

Guterman, N. B., Hahm, H. C., & Cameron, M. (2002). Adolescent victimization and subsequent use of mental health counseling services. *Journal of Adolescent Health, 30,* 336–345.

Gyamfi, P. (2004). Children with serious emotional disturbance: the impact of poverty and receipt of public assistance on behavior, functioning, and service use. *Children and Youth Services Review, 26,* 1129–1139.

Hill, H., & Madhere, S. (1996). Exposure to community violence and African American children: A multidimensional model of risks and resources. *Journal of Community Psychology, 24,* 26–43.

Hopps, J. G., Tourse, R. W. C., & Christian, O. (2002). From problems to personal resilience: Challenges and opportunities in practice with African American youth. *Journal of Ethnic and Cultural Diversity in Social Work, 11,* 55–77.

Ispa, J. M., Fine, M. A., Halgunseth, L. C. et al. (2004). Maternal intrusiveness, maternal warmth, and mother-toddler relationship outcomes: Variations across low-income ethnic and acculturation groups. *Child Development, 75,* 1613–1631.

Jean-Giles, M., & Crittenden, P. M. (1990). Maltreating families: A look at siblings. *Family Relations, 39,* 323–329.

Joe, S. (2006). Explaining changes in the patterns of Black suicide in the United States from 1981 to 2002: An age, cohort, and period analysis. *Journal of Black Psychology, 32,* 362–384.
Joe, S., Romer, D., & Jamieson, P. E. (2007). Suicide acceptability is related to suicide planning in U.S. adolescents and young adults. *Suicide and Life-Threatening Behavior, 37,* 165–178.
Johnson, R. M., Kotch, J. B., Catellier, D. J. et al. (2002). Adverse behavioral and emotional outcomes from child abuse and witnessed violence. *Child Maltreatment, 7,* 179–187.
Judd, C. M., Park, B., Ryan, C. S., Brauer, M., & Kraus, S. (1995). Stereotypes and ethnocentrism: Diverging interethnic perceptions of African American and White American youth. *Journal of Personality and Social Psychology, 69,* 460–481.
Kelly, A. M., Wall, M., Eisenberg, M. E., Story, M., & Neumark-Sztainer, D. (2005). Adolescent girls with high body satisfaction: Who are they and what can they teach us? *Journal of Adolescent Health, 37,* 391–396.
Kerkorian, D., McKay, M., & Bannon, W. M. (2006). Seeking help a second time: Parents'/Caregivers' characterizations of previous experiences with mental health services for their children and perceptions of barriers to future use. *American Journal of Orthopsychiatry, 76,* 161–166.
Kerr, A. E. (2005). The paper bag principle: Of the myth and the motion of colorism. *Journal of American Folklore, 118,* 271–289.
Kim, J., & Cicchetti, D. (2006). Longitudinal trajectories of self-system processes and depressive symptoms among maltreated and nonmaltreated children. *Child Development, 77,* 624–639.
Kodjo, C. M., & Auinger, P. (2004). Predictors for emotionally distressed adolescents to receive mental health care. *Journal of Adolescent Health, 35,* 368–373.
Kubrin, C. E., Wadsworth, T., & DiPietro, S. (2006). Deindustrialization, disadvantage and suicide among young black males. *Social Forces, 84,* 1559–1579.
Lau, A. S., Litrownik, A. J., Newton, R. R., Black, M. M., & Everson, M. D. (2006). Factors affecting the link between physical discipline and child externalizing problems in Black and White families. *Journal of Community Psychology, 34,* 89–103.
Lau, A. S., McCabe, K. M., Yeh, M. et al. (2003). Race/ethnicity and rates of self-reported maltreatment among high-risk youth in public sectors of care. *Child Maltreatment, 8,* 183–194.
Letiecq, B. L., & Koblinsky, S. A. (2004). Parenting in violent neighborhoods: African American fathers share strategies for keeping children safe. *Journal of Family Issues, 25,* 715–734.
Levitt, M. J., Guacci-Franco, N., & Levitt, J. L. (1993). Convoys of social support in childhood and early adolescence: Structure and function. *Developmental Psychology, 29,* 811–818.
Lindsey, M. A., Korr, W. S., Broitman, M., Bone, L., Green, A., & Leaf, P. J. (2006). Help-seeking behaviors and depression among African American adolescent boys. *Social Work, 51,* 49–58.
Loader, P. (1998). Such a shame-a consideration of shame and shaming mechanisms in families. *Child Abuse Review, 7,* 44–57.
Lu, Y. E., Landsverk, J., Ellis-Macleod, E. et al. (2004). Race, ethnicity, and case outcomes in child protective services. *Children and Youth Services Review, 26,* 447–461.
Mason, C., Cauce, A., Gonzales, N., & Hiraga, Y. (1996). Neither too sweet nor too sour: Problem peers, maternal control, and problem behavior in African American adolescents. *Child Development, 67,* 2115–2130.
McCabe, K., Clark, R., & Barnett, D. (1999). Family protective factors among urban African American youth. *Journal of Clinical Child Psychologist, 28,* 137–150.
McLoyd, V. C. (1998). Socioeconomic disadvantage and child development. *American Psychologist, 53,* 185–204.
Morrison, L. L., & Downey, D. L. (2000). Racial differences in self-disclosure of suicidal ideation and reasons for living: Implications for training. *Cultural Diversity and Ethnic Minority Psychology, 6,* 374–386.
Moynihan, D. (1965). *The Negro family: The case for national action*. Washington, DC: Department of Labor, Office of Planning and Research.
O'Donnell, D. A., Schwab-Stone, M. E., & Ruchkin, V. (2006). The mediating role of alienation in the development of maladjustment in youth exposed to community violence. *Development and Psychopathology, 18,* 215–232.

Overstreet, S., et al. (1999). Availability of family support as a moderator of exposure to community violence. *Journal of Clinical Child Psychology, 28,* 151–158.

Palmer, C., Rysiew, M., & Koob, J. J. (2003). Self-esteem, locus of control, and suicide risk: A comparison between clinically depressed White and African American females on an inpatient psychiatric unit. *Journal of Ethnic and Cultural Diversity in Social Work, 12,* 49–63.

Paz, I., Jones, D., & Byrne, G. (2005). Child maltreatment, child protection and mental health. *Current Opinion in Psychiatry, 18,* 411–421.

Phinney, J. S., Cantu, C. L., & Kurtz, D. A. (1997). Ethnic and American identity as predictors of self-esteem among African American, Latino, and White adolescents. *Journal of Youth and Adolescence, 26,* 165–185.

Querido, J. G., Warner, T. D., & Eyberg, S. M. (2002). Parenting styles and child behavior in African American families of preschool children. *Journal of Clinical Child and Adolescent Psychology, 31,* 272–277.

Quintana, S. M., Aboud, F. E., Chao, R. K. et al. (2006). Race, ethnicity, and culture in child development: Contemporary research and future directions. *Child Development, 77,* 1129–1141.

Rutter, M. (1987). Psychosocial resilience and protective mechanisms. *American Journal of Orthopsychiatry, 57,* 316–331.

Rich, J. A., & Grey, C. M. (2005). Pathways to recurrent trauma among young Black Men: Traumatic stress, substance use, and the "Code of the Street". *American Journal of Public Health, 95,* 816–824.

Roberts, D. E. (2003). Child welfare and civil rights. *University of Illinois Law Review, 1,* 171–182

Rovi, S., Chen, P.-H., & Johnson, M. S. (2004). The economic burden of hospitalizations associated with child abuse and neglect. *American Journal of Public Health, 94,* 586–590.

Schuck, A. M. (2005). Explaining Black-White disparity in maltreatment: Poverty, female-headed families, and urbanization. *Journal of Marriage and Family, 67,* 543–551.

Sellers, R. M., Copeland-Linder, N., Martin, P. P., & Lewis, R. L. (2006). Racial identity matters: The relationship between racial discrimination and psychological functioning in African American adolescents. *Journal of Research on Adolescence, 16*(2), 187–216.

Simons, R. L., Lin, K. H., Gordon, L. C., Brody, G. H., Murry, V., & Conger, R. D. (2002). Community differences in the association between parenting practices and child conduct problems. *Journal of Marriage and Family, 64,* 331–345.

Snyder, H. N., & Swahn, M. H. (2004). Juvenile suicides, 1981–1998. *Youth Violence Research Bulletin, 196978.* https://www.ncjrs.gov/html/ojjdp/196978/contents.html

Stevenson, H. (1997). Managing anger: Protective, proactive, or adaptive racial socialization identity profiles and African American manhood development. *Journal of Prevention and Intervention in the Community, 16,* 35–61.

Tatum, B. D. (1997). *Why are all the black kids sitting together in the cafeteria*? New York: Basic Books.

Taylor, R. D., Casten, R., & Flickinger, S. (1993). The influence of kinship social support on the parenting experiences and psychological adjustment of African American adolescents. *Developmental Psychology, 29,* 382–388.

Taylor, R. J., Chatters, L. M., & Jackson, J. S. (1997). Changes over time in support network involvement among Black Americans. In R. J. Taylor, J. S. Jackson, & L. M. Chatters (Eds.), *Mental health in Black America* (pp. 293–316). Thousand Oaks: Sage.

Taylor, R. J., Hardison, C. B., & Chatters, L. M. (1996). Kin and non-kin as sources of informal assistance. In H. W. Neighbors, & J. S. Jackson (Eds.), *Mental health in black America* (pp. 130–145). Thousand Oaks: Sage.

Thompson, R. (2005). The course and correlates of mental health care received by young children: Descriptive data from a longitudinal urban high-risk sample. *Children and Youth Services Review, 27,* 39–50.

Thompson, R., Briggs, E., English, D. J. et al. (2005). Suicidal ideation among maltreated and at-risk 8-year-olds: Findings from the LONGSCAN studies. *Child Maltreatment, 10,* 26–36.

Thompson, R., & May, M. A. (2006). Caregivers' perceptions of child mental health needs and service utilization: An urban 8-year-old sample. *Journal of Behavioral Health Services and Research, 33*(4), 474–482.

Thompson, V. L. S., Bazile, A., & Akbar, M. (2004). African Americans' perceptions of psychotherapy and psychotherapists. *Professional Psychology: Research and Practice, 35,* 19–26.

Tolan, P. H., & Gorman-Smith, D. (2002). What violence prevention research can tell us about developmental psychopathology. *Development and Psychopathology, 14,* 713–729.

Twenge, J. M., & Crocker, J. (2002). Race and self-esteem: Meta-analyses comparing Whites, Blacks, Hispanics, Asians, and American Indians and comment on Gray-Little and Hafdahl (2000). *Psychological Bulletin, 128,* 371–408.

Ungar, M. (2004). A constructionist discourse on resilience: Multiple contexts, multiple realities among at-risk children and youth. *Youth and Society, 35,* 341–365.

U.S. Census. (2001). *United States Census Briefs and Special Reports.* Washington, DC: United States Census. http://www.census.gov/population/www/cen2000/briefs.html. Accessed 9 Oct 2006.

U.S. Public Health Service. (2000). *Report of the surgeon general's conference on children's mental health: A national action agenda.* Washington, DC: Department of Health and Human Services.

Wallace Jr., J. M., & Forman, T. A. (1998). Religion's role in promoting health and reducing risk among American youth. *Health Education & Behavior, 25,* 721–741.

Winfield, L. F. (1995). The knowledge base on resilience in African-American adolescents. In L. J. Crockett, & A. C. Crouter (Eds.), *Pathways through adolescence: Individual development in relation to social contexts* (pp. 87–118). Mahwah: Erlbaum.

Wolfner, G. D., & Gelles, R. J. (1993). A profile of violence toward children: A national study. *Child Abuse and Neglect, 17,* 197–212.

Wong, C. A., Eccles, J. S., & Sameroff, A. (2003). The influence of ethnic discrimination and ethnic identification on African American adolescents' school and socioemotional adjustment. *Journal of Personality, 71,* 1197–1232.

Wu, P., Hoven, C. W., Cohen, P., Liu, X. H., Moore, R. E., Tiet, Q., Okezie, N., Wicks, J., & Bird, H. R. (2001). Factors associated with use of mental health services for depression by children and adolescents. Psychiatric Services, *52,* 189–195.

Young-Hyman, D., Schlundt, D. G., Herman-Wenderoth, L., & Bozylinski, K. (2003). Obesity, appearance, and psychosocial adaptation in young African American children. *Journal of Pediatric Psychology, 28,* 463–472.

Chapter 4
The Challenge of Understanding the Mental Health of African Americans: The Risks and Rewards of Segregation, Support, and John Henryism

Harold W. Neighbors, Darrell L. Hudson and Kai McKeever Bullard

Demographic Characteristics of African Americans

The educational, employment, and financial status of African Americans differs from that of other US race/ethnic groups, particularly White Americans. For example, in July 2006, it was estimated that 23.8 million Americans aged between 18 and 64 years, or 12.6% of the total US population, were African American. Of the African American noninstitutionalized, civilian population, 11.3 million (47.5%) were male, and 12.5 million (52.5%) were female (US Census Bureau 2006d). According to the 2004 Current Population Survey, the majority of African American adults (54%) reside in the South. In 2006, 8.2 million African American adults aged 18–64 years (36.1%) earned a high school diploma, while 2.7 million (11.9%) earned a bachelor's degree compared to 30.3 and 20.4% of non-Hispanic White Americans who earned a high school diploma or bachelor's degree, respectively (US Census Bureau 2006b). The average African-American family median income in 2006 was US$ 32,372 in comparison to US$ 52,375 for non-Hispanic White families (US Census Bureau 2006a). In 2006, the US Census Bureau reported that 25.3% of African Americans were living at or below the poverty level, compared to 9.3% for White Americans. Forty-eight percent of African Americans owned their own home, while over three-quarters of White Americans were homeowners in 2006 (US Census Bureau 2006c). As of July 2007, the unemployment rate for African Americans (8%) was twice that of White Americans (4%) (Bureau of Labor Statistics, Current Employment Statistics Survey 2007). One-third (33%) of African-

Dr. Kai McKeever Bullard's contribution was made while completing a postdoctoral fellowship at the University of Michigan.

H. W. Neighbors (✉)
Center for Research on Ethnicity, Culture and Health, School of Public Health
and the Program for Research on Black Americans, Institute for Social Research,
The University of Michigan, 109 South Observatory Drive, Ann Arbor, MI 48109-2029,
USA
e-mail: woodyn@umich.edu

E. C. Chang, C. A. Downey (eds.), *Handbook of Race and Development in Mental Health*,
DOI 10.1007/978-1-4614-0424-8_4, © Springer Science+Business Media, LLC 2012

American adults aged 19–64 years were uninsured or experiencing a gap in coverage during 2005 compared to 20% for their White American counterparts(Doty and Holmgren 2006). It is not difficult to conclude that many of the benefits derived from improved socioeconomic standing vary by racial group membership (Conley 1999; Krieger et al. 1997; Oliver and Shapiro 1995; Shapiro 2004; Williams and Collins 1995).

As this brief introduction indicates, most of these demographic comparisons place African Americans at a relative *disadvantage*. Such relative disadvantage can be stressful and worse, psychologically painful. Most scholars interested in gaining a deeper understanding of the lives of African Americans, like academicians, researchers, clinicians and policymakers, grapple with the classic question asked by Mildred Cannon and Ben Locke over 30 years ago: "Is being Black detrimental to one's mental health?" (Cannon and Locke 1977). To those familiar with the kind of racial disparities described in the opening paragraph, the answer seems so obvious that the question appears rhetorical. It is safe to say that most people *assume* that the level of mental illness among African Americans is notably higher than levels found among White Americans because they also assume that the life of the average African American is more stressful than that of the typical White American. Given that stress leads to various negative outcomes, including hypertension and poor mental health (Krieger and Sidney 1996; Williams and Williams-Morris 2000; Williams et al. 2003), this conclusion makes sense. However, in reality, the model of African American mental health is not as simple as the stress-exposure argument implies. For instance, psychiatric epidemiologic data show that the prevalence of such mental disorders as depression is lower for African Americans compared to White Americans (Kessler et al. 2005; Williams et al. 2007). This raises another simple yet profound question: *Why*?

Depression is the leading cause of disability for Americans aged 15–44 (WHO World Mental Health Survey Consortium 2004). Kessler et al. (2005) estimate that depression affects over 14 million Americans each year, nearly 7% of the US population. Epidemiologic studies such as the Epidemiologic Catchment Area (ECA) Program, the National Comorbidity Study (NCS), and the National Survey of American Life (NSAL) have consistently found that White Americans report higher rates of depression than African Americans (Blazer et al. 1994; Kessler et al. 2005). Williams et al. (2007) used the NSAL data to estimate the prevalence and distribution of major depression among a nationally representative sample of African Americans, Caribbean Blacks, and non-Hispanic Whites (N=6,082) aged 18 years and older. They found that although White Americans had higher rates of lifetime depression prevalence, African Americans rated their depression as more severe and disabling. Despite a higher risk of persistence of depression, African Americans were more likely to remain untreated. Essentially, Williams and colleagues suggest that African Americans suffer more severe forms of depression and are less likely to receive adequate treatment for depression. Researchers note that while African Americans usually report lower rates of depression diagnosis than White Americans, they report higher levels of psychological distress and greater amounts of depressive symptoms than White Americans (Jackson and Knight 2006; Williams et al. 2007).

There is considerable debate in the depression literature as to why African Americans report lower rates of depression than White Americans. There are complicated methodological challenges of measuring mental disorders within the context of race (Neighbors et al. 2003). Research suggests that depression may be inadequately assessed in African Americans because of group differences in the expression of depressive symptoms and the difficulty clinicians have in taking such diversity into account in their diagnostic procedures (Neighborset al. 1989; Snowden 2003; United States Department of Health and Human Services (USDHHS) 2001). This issue is further complicated by the fact that current epidemiologic approaches to the identification of mental disorder leave little room for clinical judgment and, as a result, bear only a modest relationship to a clinical diagnosis. Thus, it is not clear whether the relatively lower rate of depression observed in African Americans is the result of under-reporting, misdiagnosis, or superior coping capacity. In this chapter, we address the latter portion of the previous sentence by focusing on the concept of resilience. Resilience is defined as "a process of adapting well in the face of adversity, trauma, tragedy, threats or even significant sources of stress—such as family and relationship problems, serious health problems, or workplace and financial stressors" (American Psychological Association (APA) 2004). Resilience refers to protective factors, such as social support and individual assets, which offset or mitigate exposure to risk and promote successful adaptation (Garmezy 1991; Masten 1994). We submit that African Americans as a group have been able to draw upon a number of psychological strengths, as well as social and interpersonal resources. In the following discussion, we attempt to provide a deeper understanding of and appreciation for how a group of people subjected to one of the harshest socio-political legacies imaginable has nevertheless been able to maintain a relative advantage in terms of mental disorder in the face of adversity.

This chapter presents information on mental health issues in African American adults, focusing on residential segregation, social support, and the concept of John Henryism (James et al. 1983) as having aspects which are both challenges to the maintenance of mental health and strengths which contribute to resilience in this group. Recognizing that most coping strategies and resources are not uniformly positive or uniformly negative, each of these three factors is examined as both a *strength* and as a *challenge* to African American mental health. While it is more typical to think of psychosocial factors as either "good" or "bad," our more nuanced approach rejects the somewhat artificial bifurcation that permeates the stress and coping literature. The judgment that these constructs have definitive positive or negative psychological effects is complex and cannot be made without explicit acknowledgment of mental health outcomes. Therefore, our review draws upon statistical data with an emphasis on major depression. Specifically, we address the processes and mechanisms whereby African Americans adapt to such stressful exposures as prejudice, discrimination, and racism. Given that racial discrimination plays a significant etiologic role in African American mental health, we begin by exploring several coping strategies used to protect against racial discrimination (Fischer and Shaw 1999; Williams and Williams-Morris 2000; Williams et al. 2003).

Racism and Racial Discrimination

Racial discrimination is a unique contextual issue that African Americans face, more so than any other racial/ethnic minority group in the United States (Charles 2003). Clark et al. (2002) highlight the importance of recognizing perceived discrimination as a unique stressor that African Americans encounter. At the micro level of analysis, a plethora of journalistic and anecdotal accounts captured by scholars have illustrated the distress African Americans derive from incidents of discrimination they encounter in their careers, in their neighborhoods, and in their travels (Cole and Omari 2003; Cose 1993; Fulwood 1996; Hochschild 1995). These regular, everyday types of slights threaten the mental health of African Americans. Kessler et al. (1999) report that the experience of racial discrimination is highly stressful, ranking in significance with other major stressful life events such as job loss, divorce, and death of a loved one. Indeed, researchers have found empirical associations between discrimination and psychological well-being, self-esteem, and depression (Karlsen and Nazroo 2002; Williams et al. 2003). For instance, in a study of middle-class African American men, Sellers et al. (2006) reported a statistically significant negative relationship between racial discrimination and mental health. There is also ample evidence provided in the literature supporting a relationship between experiences of discrimination and heightened blood pressure and hypertension (Bonham et al. 2004; Din-Dziethan et al. 2004; Krieger and Sidney 1996).

At the macro level of analysis, racial discrimination is manifest in structural factors which are embedded in the historical, economic, political, and ideological framework of society (Farmer et al. 2006; Geronimus 2001; Geronimus and Thompson 2004). One tangible demonstration of racism is the significant racial segregation that exists in this country (Massey and Denton 1993). Racial residential segregation is responsible for much of the inequitable distribution of resources in society and is a significant factor in the production of racial differences in health (Geronimus and Thompson 2004). In fact, researchers have described racial residential segregation as the "structural lynchpin" of racial relations in the United States (Bobo 1989; Farley and Frey 1994). The next section discusses various aspects of how segregation affects the lives of African Americans.

Aspects of Residential Segregation Which Challenge African Americans

Racial residential segregation is typically thought of in uniformly negative terms, which is understandable considering its link to US racial political oppression strategies and/. However, as stated in the introduction, we take the position that no one social factor is uniformly positive or negative. Thus, while the negative implications of segregation may be easier to appreciate, we will identify some of the protective aspects that racialized residential segregation may offer. Several researchers have argued that some of the racial separatism experienced by African Americans, particularly those in the middle and upper middle income levels who have the financial resources to live in more integrated neighborhoods, is voluntary and, as a result, a desired and therefore "desirable" situation (Darden and Kamel 2000; Farley and Frey 1994; Feagin and McKinney 2003).

While levels of racial residential segregation have declined in some areas of the southern and western United States (Charles 2003; Farley and Frey 1994; Ross and Turner 2005), data from the 2000 US Census indicate that racial residential segregation is still widespread throughout the country (Farley and Frey 1994; Ondrich et al. 2003; Williams and Collins 2001). The index of dissimilarity is a commonly used measure of segregation. In 2000, it was 0.66 for African Americans, which suggests that 66% of African Americans would have to move in order to eliminate segregation. Although African Americans are the most supportive of racially integrated neighborhoods of any other racial/ethnic minority group in the United States, the 2000 census indicates that the residential exclusion of African Americans remains higher and more distinctive than that of any other racial/ethnic minority group in the United States (Glaeser and Vigdor 2001; Williams and Collins 2001). Researchers have argued that White Americans have more financial resources to buy homes of higher financial value that are located in more attractive neighborhoods (Conley 1999; Landry 1987). Charles (2003) contends that African American homeowners are actually penalized financially for owning a home, since their homes are more likely to be located in less affluent, segregated neighborhoods compared to White neighborhoods; neighborhoods where housing values are unlikely to increase at the same rate at those in better neighborhoods, if they increase at all. Williams and Collins (2001) argue that residential segregation shapes socioeconomic mobility and socioeconomic conditions across multiple levels, including individual, household, neighborhood, and community. Even African Americans who can afford homes in integrated neighborhoods may still encounter discriminatory practices, such as residential steering, a practice in which real-estate agents show home buyers houses that are located in different neighborhoods according to the race of the home buyer (Ondrich et al. 2003) and discriminatory loan practices (Farley and Frey 1994; Yinger 1986). Furthermore, researchers have discussed the idea of a racialized "tipping point," or the point at which the number of African Americans in a neighborhood undergoing racial integration rises to the point where White Americans decide to move out in favor of living in more racially homogenous neighborhoods (Conley 1999; Massey and Denton 1993).

Researchers suggest that racial residential segregation negatively affects the physical and mental health of African Americans through several mechanisms. First, community and neighborhood level socioeconomic position (SEP) can be even more important in regard to health than individual level SEP. Baum et al. (1999) found that community-level SEP predicted individual health above and beyond the effects of individual education and income. This suggests that a broader environmental context for SEP effects on health and well-being must be taken into account. Diez Roux et al. (2001) found that people who live in neighborhoods where residents report less wealth and lower levels of income were more likely to have coronary heart disease than those who lived in more advantaged neighborhoods. Szreter and Woolcock (2004) assert that poor health outcomes are the result of systematic exclusion from material resources.

The second way in which residential segregation could affect the physical and mental health of African Americans is that predominantly African American neighborhoods are comparatively poorer than White neighborhoods, as many African American communities do not have comparable resources or access to services (Williams and Collins 2001). Racial residential segregation is largely responsible for many African Americans residing in neighborhoods that have reduced access to services and institutions, ranging from full service grocery stores to quality public schools and libraries (LaVeist 2002; Massey and Denton 1993; Williams and Collins 1995, 2004).

Third, racial residential segregation significantly affects possibilities for social capital accumulation among African American communities across various levels of SEP (Conley 1999; Massey and Denton 1993; Williams and Collins 2001). Szreter and Woolcock (2004) assert that one component of social capital—inequality—can help explain growing and persisting economic disparities between African Americans and Whites, resulting in social isolation, increased anxiety, and diminished health among certain disadvantaged communities. Various researchers have emphasized the role of segregation in creating dense pockets of extreme poverty and despair (Massey and Denton 1993; Wilson 1978, 1996). Because of this social isolation, African Americans lack access to mechanisms to create social capital, which in turn leads to more favorable employment opportunities.

Upwardly mobile African Americans are also affected by residential segregation. As discussed earlier, African Americans who wish to live in integrated communities may encounter residential steering or may not be able to obtain home loans. Researchers have found African American middle-class neighborhoods are comparatively poorer than White middle-class neighborhoods (Adelman 2004). For instance, researchers argue that middle-class African Americans usually live in much closer proximity to poorer neighborhoods than their White middle-class counterparts (Massey and Denton 1993; Patillo-McCoy 1999). Adelman (2004) found that the rate of poverty in Black middle-class neighborhoods is two times higher than in White middle-class neighborhoods, and there is significantly more boarded up, dilapidated housing in African American middle-class neighborhoods. Large Black–

White differences in wealth, unequal financial compensation on the job for similar levels of experience, and education in concert with lower property values due to persisting levels of racial residential segregation could suggest that middle-class African Americans are qualitatively and quantitatively different from their White middle-class counterparts. Nonetheless, Lacy (2004) finds that some African Americans who can afford to live in racially integrated neighborhoods still choose to live in predominantly African American neighborhoods. Below we explore some of the more positive aspects of racial residential segregation in more detail.

Aspects of Residential Segregation Which Serve African Americans Positively

African Americans and White Americans have a different tolerance for a neighborhood's racial composition. African Americans are more likely to prefer to live in a neighborhood where the racial composition is closer to 50% African American and 50% White (Cashin 2004; Charles 2003; Conley 1999). On the other hand, they may consciously choose to live in predominantly Black neighborhoods because they feel more comfortable in racially homogenous neighborhoods, and residing in certain types of predominantly Black neighborhoods can be protective of mental health by promoting certain cultural assets (Cashin 2004; Feagin and McKinney 2003; Lacy 2004). One such cultural adaptation is the kin network originally described by Stack (1974). Stack argues that kin networks offer a way to pool resources and risk such that families within kin networks can rely upon one another for resources such as money and child care. This kin network is illustrated in numerous studies such as Catherine Newman's *No Shame in My Game* (1999), which chronicles her ethnographic account of participants who work minimum wage jobs at fast food restaurants in New York City. Indeed, participants who had more extensive, reliable support networks had much more success in finding reliable, trustworthy childcare which allowed them to work minimum wage jobs and complete school in some cases.

These networks contrast with what Geronimus and Thompson (2004) criticize as the prevailing ideology of "developmentalism," which strongly emphasizes the endorsement of independent nuclear families in the United States. Geronimus and Thompson argue that because many African Americans value collectivism over individualism, an extended and multigenerational family structure is more adaptive than strict adherence to the nuclear family model. Stack (1974) maintains that kin networks are weakened or destroyed when a family is removed from it and placed elsewhere, such as residential mobility programs like the Movement to Opportunity Program (Kling et al. 2004). While Stack's study applies to low-income African American families, it may also be relevant to middle-class African Americans. More recently, Lacy (2004) discusses how African Americans maintain connections to their communities and how these connections influence their racial identity construction. For African Americans who have the financial means to live in integrated neighborhoods, some choose to live in predominantly African American neighborhoods as a way to reduce interaction with White colleagues and acquaintances. In other words, voluntary racial residential segregation may reinforce the cultural aspects of predominantly African American neighborhoods. Even African Americans who live in predominantly White neighborhoods attempt to increase the exposure of their children to African American culture by involving them in social clubs and organizations.

African Americans may choose to live in segregated neighborhoods because they feel more comfortable in residential settings with other African Americans (Cashin 2004). Feagin and McKinney (2003) argue that African Americans seek refuge in their home environments due to their frequent encounters with racial discrimination and cultural adaptation, such as changing hairstyles or vernacular, required in integrated occupational settings. For instance, Claude Steele discusses the concept of stereotype threat, described as the underachievement of minorities and women due to fears of failure, living up to negative stereotypes about their racial minority group or gender (Steele 1998). Perhaps overwhelming feelings of responsibility for representing all African Americans may encourage African Americans to live in racially homogeneous neighborhoods. This may be even more relevant to middle-class African Americans since they are more likely to encounter racial discrimination from White Americans in occupational settings where they sometimes take on the uncomfortable cloak of White workplace norms and "cannot really be themselves until they get home" (Feagin and McKinney 2003; Forman et al. 1997; Patillo-McCoy 1999; Steele 1991,1998).

Aspects of Social Support Which Challenge African Americans

Feagin and McKinney (2003) argue that when African Americans experience racial discrimination, it is not just the individual who is affected; the entire family suffers from these encounters. There are certain contextual realities associated with social support as a coping resource employed to defend against racial discrimination. For example, as one draws upon support from social network members, the fact that family and friends may hold *different* views regarding particular incidents of unfair treatment may compromise the quality of support offered and how it is received. In fact, it is possible that these interpersonal transactions may become *sources* of stress. Disagreements among friends and family who differ in their racial ideologies about ambiguous forms of unfair treatment may result in arguments or worse.

Researchers have also reported negative associations between mental health and social support. For instance, researchers have documented the increased amount of psychological distress, depression, and other mental health problems that is associated with people who are primary caregivers for elderly or disabled friends and family (Schulz et al. 1995). There are also several unique challenges that may strongly influence social support among African Americans. Feagin and McKinney (2003) argue that individuals who encounter instances of racial discrimination share this burden with their families and friends. Such instances of racial discrimination have a cumulative impact on individual health and the health of their entire social support networks. There are a number of rich studies that have investigated social support among African Americans (Heflin and Patillo 2002; Higginbotham and Weber 1992; McAdoo 1978). For instance, Higginbotham and Weber (1992) interviewed a sample of 200 working and middle-class Black and White women to investigate the levels of responsibility and obligation these women felt toward members of their social networks. Specifically, Higginbotham and Weber asked women the following: "Generally, do you feel you owe a lot for the help given to you by your family and relatives?" The authors reported that while the question perplexed many White women, most Black women responded affirmatively to it. Higginbotham and Weber also demonstrated that African Americans of higher SEP maintain strong links to their social support networks. Importantly, Heflin and Patillo (2002) found that middle-class African Americans are highly likely to have low-income siblings, and that they incorporate the SEP of their extended families into their own conceptions of class standing, corroborating Geronimus and Thompson's argument (Geronimus and Thompson 2004) that African Americans often incorporate extended and multigenerational family members into their concept of family. Additionally, Charles et al. (2004) argue that African American college students at integrated colleges and universities who are from segregated backgrounds experience greater levels of family-related stress than students from more integrated backgrounds and that the grades of students from segregated backgrounds may be negatively impacted due to their devotion of more time to familial issues.

Another challenge that African Americans may face is the declining density of and proximity to social support networks among African Americans as they become upwardly mobile, both economically and socially. For instance, Lareau (2003) reports in an ethnographic study that middle-class African Americans have less-frequent contact with members of their extended family and live farther away from them. Colen et al. (2006) found that as Black women begin to achieve upward social mobility, they may be less likely to rely on their mothers for support during their pregnancy or for assistance with child-rearing responsibilities after their child is born. These findings suggest that as African Americans become upwardly mobile, they may have diminished access to social support networks that can help navigate certain stressful situations, partly because they may live farther away from their social support networks (Colen et al. 2006; Lareau 2003).

Aspects of Social Support Which Serve African Americans Positively

There are various conceptualizations of social support. One conceptualization is social networks, which are defined as structures of social connections between in-

Fig. 4.1 Conceptual model

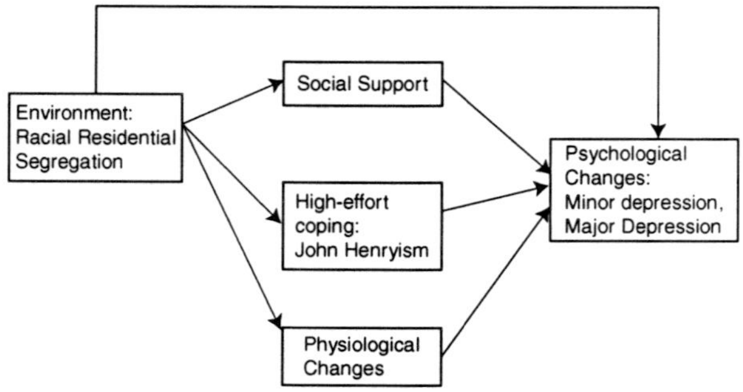

dividual members within a network (Cohen and Wills 1985; Pearlin and Schooler 1978; Thoits 1995). Israel et al. (2002) conceptualize social support as instrumental and emotional support offered by individuals in respondents' social networks. Emotional support is described as a measure of the availability of people within respondents' social networks to rely upon for advice or to share worries with. Instrumental support is described as the availability of people within respondents' social networks who can help them with material support such as money, transportation, or childcare (Fig. 4.1).

Researchers have argued that social support can mitigate the impact of stress on health (House et al. 1988; Wenzel et al. 2002) and have highlighted the importance of social support in coping with stressors, particularly in buffering against psychological distress (Wheaton 1985; Thoits 1995). From a stress and coping framework, Cassel (1976) concluded that "the most feasible and promising interventions to reduce disease will be to improve and strengthen the social supports rather than reduce the exposure to stressors." Social support has also been described as a buffer against race-related stress (Geronimus and Thompson 2004; Williams 1999).

Some of the best information on social support among African Americans comes from the National Survey of Black Americans (Jackson 1991). One of the most comprehensive reviews of the social support literature for African Americans comes from the work of Taylor and Chatters (e.g., Taylor et al. 1997; Chatters 1989; Taylor et al. 1996; Lincoln et al. 2003a; Taylor and Chatters 1991; Taylor et al. 1993). Chatters and Taylor draw two basic conclusions on the basis of this research. First, social support networks of African Americans are critical in coping with serious stressful episodes and serious health problems Chatters 1989. Second, the composition of informal social support networks reflect a diverse group of individuals such as extended family members, best friends, fictive kin, and church members (Chatters 1989; Taylor 1986; Taylor and Chatters 1986; Taylor, et al. 1997; Chatters et al. 2002). Church members, in particular, are a critical, yet seldom examined source of informal assistance among Black Americans.

Using data from the NSBA, Neighbors and LaVeist (1989) found that among Black Americans, material social support in the form of financial assistance significantly reduced the negative impact of economic stress on psychological distress. Neighbors (1997) showed that African American informal support networks typically provide the "first line of defense" against stress but that at the same time, the provision of such support takes it toll on network members. Lincoln et al. (2003a) found that older African found that contrary to Neighbors and Laveist (1989), social support did not mediate the effects of financial strain or traumatic events on distress among older African Americans. By examining the role of social networks in the lives of African Americans, future studies can gain important insights into how social networks contribute to mental health.

In summary, surprisingly little research has focused on the more specific stress-buffering hypothesis for African Americans. Unfortunately, not enough studies focus on social support or negative interactions within representative samples of African Americans (Lincoln et al. 2005; Lincoln 2000). The lack of studies on this topic in African American samples fosters an assumption of racial homogeneity because too many authors are willing to extrapolate from studies of White Americans. The few studies examining the association among stress, social support, and mental health among African Americans have produced equivocal findings. Despite the prominence of extended families as an important support resource, continued and prolonged reliance on family members can be burdensome. While much useful information exists regarding the form, function, and utility of support networks within African American communities, not enough of this work addresses the hypothesis that social support buffers the impact of stress on the mental health of African Americans; and practically no one has addressed this within the racial disparities context. The next section describes John Henryism as a vehicle through which we explore the advantages and disadvantages of direct action as a coping strategy for African Americans.

Aspects of John Henryism Which Challenge African Americans

The mental health of African Americans has much to do with how individuals respond to racially based obstacles against advancement and the manner in which African Americans balance the upward pull of advancement and the downward pressures of discrimination (Neighbors and Lumpkin 1990; Neighbors and Williams 2001; Parker and Kleiner 1966). Direct action involves a direct verbal or behavioral act that confronts the perpetrator of discrimination, removing oneself from the immediate environment, or contacting the appropriate authorities (Cohen 1987). It is instructive to briefly revisit the origins and development of John Henryism, which is defined as an active, high-effort behavioral response to race-based obstacles characterized by persistent, prolonged efforts to cope with the blocked opportunities put in place by racism and buttressed by acts of discrimination (James 1994). James (2002) described John Henryism as "a cultural adaptation on the part of newly freed people faced with the daunting task of creating for themselves an American identity." To be authentic, that identity had to make possible a coherent expression of core American values such as hard work, self-reliance, and freedom. John Henryism may represent an empirical example of one aspect of African American culture that is relevant to mental health (Neighbors et al. 1996).

Investing heavily in John Henryism can mean taking a strategic *risk* for African Americans. Prolonged engagement in an unsuccessful struggle for upward social mobility can lead to either salubrious or deleterious outcomes; it literally depends on the amount of success that one is able to achieve. On the other hand, there are important implications for those who are successful as well. Success, in some cases, leads to more responsibility and conceivably more stress. It may not just exclusively be prolonged engagement in an *unsuccessful* struggle but prolonged engagement in a struggle, period. Bonham et al. (2004) suggest that John Henryism is a protective coping strategy, while others argue that such high-effort coping strategies are deleterious to health (Geronimus and Thompson 2004). Multiple studies have found significant associations between John Henryism and elevated blood pressure and hypertension (Dressler et al. 1998; James et al. 1992; James 1994). Bennett et al. (2004) argue that a strong commitment to John Henryism and the continuous and active engagement of chronic stressors lead to elevated physiological reactions such as elevated blood pressure and increased cardiovascular reactivity, which in turn lead to hypertension. Findings such as these raise questions about the benefits of John Henryism such as these, one must wonder what the benefits of John Henryism are. While James et al. (1983) conceptualized John Henryism as a risk *and* protective factor for hypertension, there may be important implications for major depressive disorder and depressive symptoms (Neighbors and Lumpkin 1990; Neighbors et al. 1996). Unfortunately, very little research has explored the relationship of John Henryism to depression. Neighbors et al. found that the relationship of John Henryism to depressive symptoms varied both by race/ethnicity and by attitudes about social stratification and social dominance. African Americans were higher on John Henryism than White Americans. However, multivariate analyses revealed higher levels of John Henryism decreased depressive symptoms for White Americans only; African Americans did not show a significant relationship between John Henryism and depressive symptoms. This remains an area that that deserves more empirical investigation.

Aspects of John Henryism Which Serve African Americans Positively

We propose that the benefits of John Henryism for depression in African Americans are best understood within the following framework: First, as SEP increases, depression decreases. Second, in spite of racism, prejudice, and discrimination, significant numbers of African Americans have been and continue to be successful in their upward mobility struggles. Third, the success of the African American middle and upper middle class tends to receive less attention than the stories of lower-income (e.g., impoverished) African Americans. We do not understand enough about how African Americans have "overcome" race-based obstacles designed to impede progress.

Williams and Collins (1995) argue that SEP indicators are not equivalent across race and this inequality could be one potential explanation for the persistence of racial differences in health. Researchers have argued that beyond some level of SEP, usually around the median for income, additional increases in SEP have little or a greatly diminished effect in reducing mortality and morbidity rates (Williams and Collins 1995). When we look closer at successful African Americans, we see that cultural *values* such as a strong work-ethic, personal responsibility, and those reflected in the construct of John Henryism (i.e., individual persistence) have been instrumental in the overall success of African Americans in the United States. These are the values upon which we argue that successful African Americans have drawn for the strength to "push back" against racial oppression (Neighbors et al. 1990, 1995; Patterson 1997; Wilson 1978, 1996). If upward mobility reduces the prevalence of depression and the values incorporated within John Henryism contribute to upward social mobility, it follows that we must promote those values across all segments of African Americans communities.

It is important to note the gender of John Henry because scholars have raised the question of the representativeness of this construct within the context of male–female differences in coping (Williams and Lawler 2001). The legend of John Henry notes that he was a "steel-drivin' man." Feminist scholars ask whether John Henryism is gendered in such a way as to make it inapplicable as a meaningful way of understanding the mental health of African American women. For example, some have argued that John Henryism should incorporate the combined effects of racism and sexism into this cultural narrative of the African American struggle (Bennett et al. 2004; Mullings 2002; Williams and Lawle 2001). Questioning the applicability of high-effort coping to African American women because the origin of the concept was based on the legend of a mythic *male* figure may be unfounded since it does not follow necessarily that John Henryism is irrelevant for African American women. For example, Geronimus et al. (1996, 2006) emphasize that persistent high-effort coping is used by African American women to contend with factors such as discrimination and unequal access to economic opportunities. In order to capture a more "gendered" aspect of high-effort persistent coping, Mullings (2001) coined the term "Sojourner Syndrome" to characterize the lived realities of African American women and to capture the joint influence of race *and* being female on health. The implication is that by virtue of being female, Black women in particular must confront hardships that are not only different from those of Black men, but also more difficult as a result of the additional burden of sexism.

Undoubtedly, Black women have been instrumental in the class advancement of African Americans in the United States (Mullings 2002). It is also true that there has been a lack of information about the gender-specific health effects of persistent high-effort coping for African Americans women. The Sojourner Syndrome provides a theoretical perspective for emphasizing that these social processes operate for Black women as well as Black men (Mullings and Wali 2001). Female gender provides another important link to the "down side" of social support mentioned earlier—the stress of being obligated in the role of *care-giver* as opposed to being the recipient of support (Mattlin et al. 1990). The stress of care giving along with occupational experiences of racism and sexism play a role in eroding African American women's health over time (Geronimus et al. 1996; Newman 1999). While the Sojourner Syndrome asserts that differential exposure to stress leads to the deterioration of health in Black women, the relevant question for this chapter is how African American women cope with these multiple stressors and whether or not their coping repertoire increases or decreases the risk for depression. When it comes to gendered health disparities, African American women typically fare better than Black men (Airhihenbuwa and Liburd 2006). On the other hand, the prevalence of major depression is higher for African American women than men. Nolen-Hoeksema (2001) suggests that women's lack of social power as well as the social roles that women carry increases their risk of depression. More specifically, she states that because women are more likely to experience certain stressors than men, women are more vulnerable to developing depression.

Conclusions

The discussion presented integrates culture and context in order to explore the coping mechanisms African Americans use to mitigate the negative effects of racial discrimination on mental health. These coping mechanisms double as both challenges and assets for African American mental health. We have discussed the fact that racial residential segregation continues to persist throughout the United States and plays a significant role in the allocation of financial resources and services to African American communities. Conversely, we have highlighted some of the potential protective factors that may lead some African Americans to self-segregate. We have also illustrated the critical role of social support in coping with stress among African Americans. Yet, due to the unique social position of many African Americans, social support can also be interpreted as a challenge to African American mental health. As African Americans experience upward social mobility, they may find themselves separated from their social support networks. Additionally, they may be exposed to stress from feelings of accountability and responsibility for helping less successful members of their former communities. Finally, we illustrated how high-effort coping, operationally defined as John Henryism, could be responsible for motivating African Americans to achieve upward social mobility, which in turn could be protective of mental health. Such complicated findings certainly suggest that more research on John Henryism and its possible female counterpoint, the Sojourner Syndrome is necessary.

There are numerous areas of future research this chapter could have addressed. Nonetheless, we have focused on just a few major areas of inquiry. First, depression is an important health outcome to investigate because of its magnitude and its links to physical health problems such as heart disease and diabetes as well as its well established link to suicide. Second, there is a paucity of research focused on the "unique costs of mobility" that upper status African Americans may pay in their acquisition of higher SES. To date, most researchers note a higher prevalence of depression among people of lower SEP (Dohrenwend et al. 1992; Muntaner et al. 1998; Murphy et al. 1991). However, Williams et al. (1992) note the complexity in the mental health literature as to whether SEP is a protective factor against depression, citing studies that have found associations between low SEP and depression as well as studies that have found that SEP has no effect on depression. Other researchers have found that low childhood SEP is predictive of adult depression (Gilman et al. 2002; Kessler et al. 1993; Sadowski et al. 1999). Accordingly, Colen et al. (2006) argue that many African Americans, even those of higher SEP, are much more likely to have grown up in poverty, which would increase their risk for depression as adults. As noted before, SEP is not equivalent across race because of differences in wealth (Conley 1999; Oliver and Shapiro 1995; Shapiro 2004; Williams and Collins 1995), and researchers have noted that the health benefits associated with higher SEP among African Americans are marginal (Geronimus 2001). The possible costs associated with social mobility, such as increased exposure to racial discrimination and the use of high-effort coping may diminish the mental health protective benefits that increased SEP offers. The relationship between SEP and depression is an area that needs further exploration (Williams et al. 1992).

More comprehensive examinations of the protective aspects of African American neighborhoods are necessary in order to determine if residential segregation is uniformly stressful or whether some aspects of voluntary segregation, particularly among middle- and upper-income African Americans, are protective of mental health. Additionally, there have not been enough systematic examinations of the mental health effects of John Henryism among African Americans, nor have there been enough examinations of the intersection between John Henryism (or the Sojourner Syndrome), exposure to racial discrimination, and depression.

While discussions of racial and ethnic differences in depression invoke notions of culture, it is important to note that neither race nor ethnicity is synonymous with culture. Although race and culture are certainly related, the latter is rarely measured in mental health research on racial differences. Race is more typically defined by respondent self-report. As a result, there is an important need for research that measures race and ethnicity as well as the various forms of subjective experience assumed to be indicators of culture. This is the only way the field will be able to identify the psychological and social factors that link race/ethnicity to depression and other mental disorders. More importantly, this is our only chance for demonstrating whether or not various social constructs of interest (e.g., identity, social relations, neighborhood structure) are risk or protective factors for depression among African Americans. For example, social support can lead to active coping behaviors in the face of discrimination (Wenzel et al. 2002). Krieger and Sidney (1996) found that African American women who used passive coping strategies in response to discrimination were more likely to be hypertensive than African American women who utilized active coping techniques behaviors. This body of research must move beyond the tendency to do no more than make demographic comparisons (e.g., Black–White, male–female) in psychiatric morbidity. Continuing to generate reams of descriptive publications will not lead to the kinds of intellectual insights necessary to explain, understand, and ultimately improve upon racial and ethnic differ-

Table 4.1 Summary of factors that potentially offer challenges and strengths to the mental health of African Americans

Demographics	Challenges	Strengths	Recommendations
• African Americans are 12.6% of the total US population • Median household income is US$ 32,372 • 8% national unemployment rate • 25.3% living at or below the poverty level • 33% of adults aged 19 to 64 years are uninsured	*Racial Segregation* • Residential segregation shapes socioeconomic mobility and socioeconomic conditions • African American neighborhoods are comparatively poorer than White neighborhoods *Social Support* • Interpersonal transactions may become *sources* of stress • Decreasing proximity to social networks • Feelings of responsibility and obligation *John Henryism* • High-effort coping strategies maybe deleterious to mental health	*Racial Segregation* • African Americans may feel more comfortable in racially homogenous neighborhoods • Residing in predominantly Black neighborhoods is protective to their mental health • Black neighborhoods promote Black culture *Social Support* • Social support can mitigate effects of stress on mental health • Social support serves as a buffer against race-related stress *John Henryism* • John Henryism could be a protective, cultural coping strategy • May lead to social mobility among African Americans	• Depression is an important mental health outcome to investigate because of the magnitude of related disability and its link to physical health problems such as heart disease and diabetes as well as suicide • There is a paucity of research focused on the "unique costs of mobility" that upper status African Americans may pay in their acquisition of higher SES. More research is needed in this area • SES is not equivalent across race because of differences in wealth, thus the relationship between SEP and depression needs further exploration

ences in major depression. It is only by incorporating *into our empirical analyses* those psychosocial measures hypothesized to link race/ethnicity to depression that we will be able to move the field forward toward a deeper understanding of race, culture, and mental health (Table 4.1).

References

Adelman, R. (2004). Neighborhood opportunities, race, and class: The Black middle class and residential segregation. *City and Community, 3*, 43–63.

Airhihenbuwa, C. O., & Liburd, L. (2006). Eliminating health disparities in the African American population: The interface of culture, gender, and power. *Health Education & Behavior, 33*(4), 488–501.

American Psychological Association (APA). (2004), *The Road to Resilience,* American Psychological Association, Arlington, VA. http://apahelpcenter.org/featuredtopics/feature.php?id=6&ch=2. Accessed Oct 1 2007.

Baum, A., Garofalo, J. P., & Yali, A. M. (1999). Socioeconomic status and chronic stress. Does stress account for SES effects on health? *Annals of the New York Academy of Sciences, 896,* 131–144.

Bennett, G. G., Merritt, M. M., Sollers, J. J., Edwards, C. L., Whitfield, K. E., Brandon, D. T., & Tucker, R. D. (2004). Stress, coping, and health outcomes among African Americans: A review of the John Henryism hypothesis, *Psychology & Health, 19*(3), 369–383.

Blazer, D. G., Kessler, R. C., McGonagle, K. A., & Swartz, M. S. (1994). The prevalence and distribution of major depression in a national community sample: The national comorbidity survey. *The American Journal of Psychiatry, 151*(7), 979–986.

Bonham, V. L., Sellers, S. L., & Neighbors, H. W. (2004). John Henryism and self-reported physical health among high-socioeconomic status African American men. *American Journal of Public Health, 94*(5), 737–738.

Bureau of Labor Statistics. (2007). Current Employment Statistics Survey. http://www.bls.gov/news.release/pdf/empsit.pdf. Accessed Oct 1 2007.

Cannon, M. S., & Locke, B. Z. (1977). Being Black is detrimental to one's mental health: Myth or reality? *Phylon, 38*(4), 408–428.

Cashin, S. (2004). *The failures of integration: How race and class are undermining the American dream*. New York: Public Affairs.

Cassel, J. (1976). The contribution of the social environment to host resistance. *American Journal of Epidemiology, 104*(2), 107–123.

Charles, C. Z. (2003). The dynamics of racial residential segregation. *Annual Review of Sociology, 29,* 167–207.

Charles, C. Z., Dinwiddie, G., & Massey, D. S. (2004). The continuing consequences of segregation: Family stress and college academic performance. *Social Science Quarterly, 85*(5), 1353–1373.

Chatters, L. M. (1989). Subjective well-being among older Black adults: Past trends and current perspectives. In J. S. Jackson (Ed.), *Aging research on Black populations.* New York: Springer.

Chatters, L. M, Taylor, R. J., Lincoln, K. D., & Schroepfer, T. (2002). Patterns of informal support from family and church members among African Americans, *Journal of Black Studies, 33*(1), 66–85.

Clark, R., Anderson, N. B., Clark, V. R., & Williams, D. R. (2002). Racism as a stressor for African Americans: A biopsychosocial model. In T. LaVeist (Ed.), *Race, ethnicity, and health.* San Francisco: Jossey-Bass.

Cohen, F. (1987). Measurement of coping. In S. V. Kasl & C. L. Cooper (Eds.), *Stress and health: Issues in research methodology*. Chichester: Wiley.

Cohen, S., & Wills, T. A. (1985). Stress, social support, and the buffering hypothesis. *Psychological Bulletin, 98*(2), 310–357.

Cole, E. R., & Omari, S. R. (2003). Race, class and the dilemmas of upward mobility for African Americans. *Journal of Social Issues, 59*(4), 785–802.

Colen, C. G., Geronimus, A. T., & Phipps, M. G. (2006). Getting a piece of the pie? The economic boom of the 1990s and declining teen birth rates in the United States. *Social Science & Medicine, 63*(6), 1531–1545.

Conley, D. (1999). *Being Black, living in the Red.* Berkeley: University of California Press.

Cose, E. (Ed.). (1993). *Rage of a privileged class*. New York: Harper Perennial.

Darden, J. T. & Kamel, S. M. (2000). Black residential segregation in the city and suburbs of Detroit: Does socioeconomic status matter? *Journal of Urban Affairs, 22*(1), 1–13.

Diez Roux, A. V., Stein Merkin, S., Arnett, D., Chambless, L., Massing, M., Nieto, F. J., et al. (2001). Neighborhood of residence and incidence of coronary heart disease. *New England Journal of Medicine, 345,* 99–106.

Din-Dzietham, R., Nembhard, W. N., Collins, R., & Davis, S. K. (2004). Perceived stress following race-based discrimination at work is associated with hypertension in African-Americans. The Metro Atlanta Heart Disease Study, 1999–2001. *Social Science & Medicine, 58*(3), 449–461.

Dohrenwend, B. P., Levav, I., Shrout, P. E., et al. (1992). Socioeconomic status and psychiatric disorders: The causation-selection issue. *Science, 255*, 946–952.

Doty, M. M., & Holmgren, A. L. (2006). Health Care Disconnect: Gaps in Coverage and Care for Minority Adults, The Commonwealth Fund, August 2006.

Dressler, W. W., Bindon, J. R., & Neggers, Y. H. (1998). John Henryism, gender, and arterial blood pressure in an African American community. *Psychosomatic Medicine, 60*(5), 620–624.

Farley, R., & Frey, W. H. (1994). Changes in the segregation of Whites from Blacks during the 1980s: Small steps toward a more integrated society. *American Sociological Review, 59*, 23–45.

Feagin, J. R., & McKinney, K. D. (2003). *The many costs of racism*. Lanham: Rowman & Littlefield.

Fischer A. R. & Shaw C. M. (1999). African Americans' mental health and perceptions of racist discrimination: the moderating effects of racial socialization experiences and self-esteem. *Journal of Counseling Psychology, 46*, 395–407.

Forman, T. A., Williams, D. R., & Jackson, J. S. (1997). Race, place, and discrimination. In C. Gardner (Ed.), *Perspectives on social problems* (pp. 9, 231–261). New York: JAI Press.

Fulwood, Sam. (1996). *Waking from the dream*. New York: Anchor Books.

Garmezy, N. (1991). Resiliency and vulnerability to adverse developmental outcomes associated with poverty. *American Behavioral Scientist 34*(4), 416–430.

Geronimus, A. T. (2001). Understanding and eliminating racial inequalities in women's health in the United States: The role of the weathering conceptual framework. *Journal of the American Medical Women's Association, 56*(4), 133–136, 149–150.

Geronimus, A. T., & Thompson, J. P. (2004). To denigrate, ignore, or disrupt: Racial inequality in health and the impact of a policy-induced breakdown of African American communities. *Du Bois Review, 1*(2), 247–279.

Geronimus, A. T., Bound, J., Waidmann, T. A., Hillemeier, M. M., & Burns, P. B. (1996). Excess mortality among Blacks and Whites in the United States. *The New England Journal of Medicine, 335*(21), 1552–1558.

Geronimus, A. T., Hicken, M., Keene, D., & Bound, J. (2006). "Weathering" and age patterns of allostatic load scores among Blacks and Whites in the United States. *American Journal of Public Health, 96*(5), 826–833.

Gilman, S. E., Kawachi, I., Fitzmaurice, G. M., & Buka, S. L. (2002). Socioeconomic status in childhood and the lifetime risk of major depression. *International Journal of Epidemiology, 31*, 359–367.

Glaeser, Edward L., & Vigdor, J. L. (2001). *Racial segregation in the 2000 census: Promising news. Census 2000 series*. Washington, DC: Brookings Institution, Center on Urban and Metropolitan Policy.

Heflin, C. M., & Patillo, M. (2002). *Crossing class boundaries: Race, siblings, and socioeconomic heterogeneity*. Northwestern University/University of Chicago: Chicago: Joint Center for Poverty Research.

Higginbotham, E., & Weber, L. (1992). Moving up with kin and community: Upward social mobility for Black and White women. *Gender and Society, 6*(3), 416–440.

Hochschild, J. L. (1995). *Facing up to the American dream: Race, class, and the soul of the nation*. Princeton: Princeton University Press.

House, J. S., Landis, K. R., & Umberson, D. (1988). Social relationships and health. *Science, 241*(4865), 540–545.

Israel, B. A., Farquhar, S. A., Schulz, A. J., James, S. A., & Parker, E. A. (2002). The relationship between social support, stress, and health among women on Detroit's East Side. *Health Education and Behavior, 29*(3), 342–360.

Jackson, J. S. (1991). *Life in Black America*. Newbury Park: Sage.

Jackson, J. S., & Knight, K. M. (2006). Race and self-regulatory health behaviors: The role of the stress response and the HPA axis in physical and mental health disparities. In L. L. Cartensen

& K. W. Schaie (Eds.). *Social structure, aging and self-regulation in the elderly*. New York: Springer.

James, S. A. (1994). John Henryism and the health of African-Americans. *Culture, Medicine and Psychiatry, 18*(2), 163–182.

James, S. A. (2002). John Henryism and the health of African Americans. In T. A. LaVeist (Ed.), *Race, ethnicity, and health*. San Francisco: Jossey-Bass.

James, S. A., Hartnett, S. A., & Kalsbeek, W. D. (1983). John Henryism and blood pressure differences among Black men. *Journal of Behavioral Medicine, 6*(3), 259–278.

James, S. A., Keenan, N. L., Strogatz, D. S., Browning, S. R., & Garrett, J. M. (1992). Socioeconomic status, John Henryism, and blood pressure in Black adults. The Pitt County study. *American Journal of Epidemiology, 135*(1), 59–67.

Karlsen, S., & Nazroo, J. Y. (2002). Relation between racial discrimination, social class, and health among ethnic minority groups. *American Journal of Public Health, 92(4)*, 624–631.

Kessler, R. C., Chiu, W. T., Demler, O., & Walters, E. E. (2005). Prevalence, severity, and of 12 month DSM-IV disorders in the national comorbidity survey replication. *Archives of General Psychiatry, 62,* 617–627.

Kessler, R. C., McGonagle, K. A., Swartz, M., Blazer, D. G., & Nelson, C. B. (1993). Sex and depression in the national comorbidity survey I: Lifetime prevalence, chronicity, and recurrence. *Journal of Affective Disorders, 29,* 85–96.

Kessler, R. C., Mickelson, K., & Williams, D. (1999). The prevalence, distribution, and mental health correlates of perceived discrimination in the United States. *Journal of Health and Social Behavior, 40,* 208–230.

Kling, J. R., Liebman, J. B., Katz, L. F., & Sanbonmatsu, L. (2004). Moving to opportunity and tranquility: Neighborhood effects on adult economic self-sufficiency and health from a randomized housing voucher experiment. http://www.wws.princeton.edu/~kling/mto/481.pdf. Accessed Oct 1 2007.

Krieger, N., & Sidney, S. (1996). Racial discrimination and blood pressure: The CARDIA study of young Black and White adults. *American Journal of Public Health, 86*(10), 1370–1378.

Krieger, N., Williams, D. R., & Moss, N. E. (1997). Measuring social class in US public health research: Concepts, methodologies, and guidelines. *Annual Review of Public Health, 18,* 341–378.

Lacy, K. R. (2004). Black spaces, black places: Strategic assimilation and identity construction in middle-class suburbia. *Ethnic and Racial Studies 27*(6), 908–930.

Landry, B. (1987). *The new Black middle class*. Berkeley: University of California Press.

Lareau, A. (2003). *Unequal childhoods: Class, race, and family life*. Berkeley: University of California Press.

LaVeist, T. A. (Ed.). (2002). *Race, ethnicity, and health*. San Francisco: Jossey-Bass.

Lazarus, R. S., & Folkman, S. (1984). *Stress, appraisal, and coping*. New York: Springer.

Lincoln, K. D. (2000). Social support, negative social interactions and psychological well-being. *Social Service Review, 74*(2), 231–252.

Lincoln, K. D., Chatters, L. M., & Taylor, R. J. (2005). Social support, traumatic events and depressive symptoms among African Americans. *Journal of Marriage and Family, 67*(3), 754–766.

Lincoln, K. D., Taylor, R. J., & Chatters, L. M. (2003a). Correlates of emotional support and negative interaction among Black Americans. *Journals of Gerontology: Social Sciences 58B*(4), S225–S233.

Lincoln, K. D., Chatters, L. M., & Taylor, R. J. (2003b). Psychological distress among Black and White Americans: Differential effects of social support, negative interaction and personal control. *Journal of Health and Social Behavior 44*(3), 390–407.

Massey, D., & Denton. N. (1993). *American apartheid, segregation and the making of the underclass*. Cambridge: The President and Fellows of the Harvard College.

Masten, A. S. (1994). Resilience in individual development: Successful adaptation despite risk and adversity. In M. Wang & E. Gordon (Eds.), *Risk and resilience in inner city America: Challenges and prospects*. (pp. 3–25). Hillsdale: Erlbaum.

Mattlin, J. A., Wethington, E., & Kessler, R. C. (1990). Situational determinants of coping effectiveness. *Journal of Health and Social Behavior, 31,* 103–122.
McAdoo, H. P. (1978). Factors related to stability in upwardly mobile Black families. *Journal of Marriage and the Family, 40,* 226–236.
Mullings, L. (2002). The Sojourner syndrome: Race, class, and gender in health and illness. *Voices, 6*(1), 32–36.
Mullings, L., & Wali, A. (2001). *Stress and resilience: The social context of reproduction in central Harlem*. New York: Plenum.
Muntaner, C., Eaton, W. W., Diala, C., Kessler, R. C., & Sorlie, P. D. (1998). Social class, assets, organizational control and the prevalence of common groups of psychiatric disorders. *Social Science & Medicine, 47,* 2043–2053.
Murphy J. M., Olivier D. C., Monson R. R., Sobol A. M., Federman E. B., & Leighton A. H. (1991). Depression and anxiety in relation to social status. *Archives of General Psychiatry, 48,* 223–229.
Neighbors, H. W. (1997). Husbands, wives, family, and friends: Sources of stress, sources of support. In R. J. Taylor, J. S. Jackson, L. M. Chatters (Eds.), *Family life in Black America* (pp. 277–299). Thousand Oaks: Sage.
Neighbors, H. W., & LaVeist, T. A. (1989). Socioeconomic status and psychological distress: The impact of financial aid on economic problem severity. *Journal of Primary Prevention, 10*(2), 149–165.
Neighbors, H. W., & Williams, D. R. (2001). The epidemiology of mental disorder. In R. L. Braithwaite & S. E. Taylor (Eds.), *Health issues in the Black community* (pp. 99–128). San Francisco: Jossey-Bass.
Neighbors, H., Braithwaite, R., & Thompson, E. (1995). Health promotion and African Americans: From personal empowerment to community action. *American Journal of Health Promotion, 9*(4), 281–287.
Neighbors, H. W., Elliott, K. A., & Gant, L. M. (1990). Self-help and Black Americans: A strategy for empowerment. In T. J. Powell (Ed.), *Working with self-help* (pp. 189–217). Silver Spring: National Association of Social Workers.
Neighbors, H. W., Jackson, J. S., Campbell, L., & Williams, D. (1989). Racial influences on psychiatricdiagnosis: A review and suggestions for research. *Community Mental Health Journal, 25*(4), 301–311.
Neighbors, H. W., & Lumpkin, S. (1990). The epidemiology of mental disorder in the Black population. In D. S. Ruiz & J. P. Comer (Eds.), *Handbook of mental health and mental disorder among Black Americans* (pp. 55–70). New York: Greenwood.
Neighbors, H. W., Jackson, J. S., Broman, C., & Thompson, E. L. (1996). Racism and the mental health of African Americans: The role of self and system blame. *Ethnicity and Disease, 6,* 167–175.
Neighbors, H. W., Njai, R., & Jackson, J. S. (2007). *Research in Human Development, 4*(1–2), 71–87.
Neighbors, H. W., Trierweiler, S. J., Ford, B. C., & Muroff, J. R. (2003). Racial differences in DSM diagnosis using a semi-structured instrument: The importance of clinical judgment in the diagnosis of African Americans. *Journal of Health & Social Behavior, 44,* 237–256.
Newman, K. S. (1999). *No shame in my game*. New York: Sage.
Nolen-Hoeksema, S. (2001). Gender differences in depression. *Current Directions in Psychological Science, 10*(5), 173–176.
Oliver, M., & Shapiro. T. (1995). *Black wealth/White wealth*. London: Routledge.
Ondrich, J., Ross, S., & Yinger, J. (2003). Now you sSee It, Now you don't: Why do real estate agents withhold available houses from Black customers? *The Review of Economics and Statistics, 85*(4), 854–873.
Parker, S., & Kleiner, R. J. (1966). *Mental illness in the urban Negro community.* New York: Free Press.
Patillo-McCoy, M. (1999). *Black Picket Fences: Privilege and Peril Among the Black Middle Class*. Chicago: The University of Chicago Press.

Patterson, O. (1997). *The ordeal of integration: Progress and resentment in America's "Racial"crisis.* Washington, DC: Counterpoint/Civitas.
Pearlin, L. I., & Schooler, C. (1978). The structure of coping. *Journal of Health and Social Behavior, 19*(1), 2–21.
Ross, S. L., & Turner M. A. (2005). Housing discrimination in metropolitan America: Explaining changes between 1989 and 2000. *Social Problems, 52*(2), 152–180.
Sadowski, H., Ugarte, B., Kolvin, I., Kaplan, C., & Barnes, J. (1999). Early life family disadvantages and major depression in adulthood. *British Journal of Psychiatry, 174,* 112–120.
Schulz R., O'Brien A. T., Bookwala J., & Fleissner K. (1995). Psychiatric and physical morbidity effects of dementia caregiving: Prevalence, correlates, and causes. *Gerontologist, 35,* 771–791.
Sellers, S. L., Bonham, V., Neighbors, H. W., & Amell, J. W. (2006). Effects of racial discrimination and health behaviors on mental and physical health of middle-class African American men. *Health Education & Behavior.*
Shapiro, T. M. (2004). *The hidden cost of being African American: How wealth perpetuates inequality.* New York: Oxford University Press.
Snowden, L. R. (2003). Bias in mental health assessment and intervention: Theory and evidence. *American Journal of Public Health, 93*(2), 239–243.
Stack, C. (1974). *All our kin: Strategies for survival in a black community.* New York: Harper & Row.
Steele, S. (1991). *The Content of our character: A new vision of Race in America.* New York: HarperPerennial.
Steele, S. (1998). *A dream deferred.* New York: Harper Collins.
Szreter, S., & Woolcock, M. (2004). Health by association? Social capital, social theory, and the political economy of public health. *International Journal of Epidemiology, 33*(4), 650–667.
Taylor, R. J. (1986). Receipt of support from family among Black Americans: Demographic and familial differences. *Journal of Marriage and the Family, 48,* 67–77.
Taylor, R. J., & Chatters, L. M. (1986). Patterns of informal support to elderly Black adults: Family, friends, and church members. *Social Work, 31*(6), 432–438.
Taylor, R., & Chatters, L. (1991). Religious life. In J. Jackson (Ed.), *Life in Black America* (pp. 105–123). Newbury: Sage.
Taylor, R. J., Chatters, L. M., & Jackson, J. S. (1993). A profile of familial relations among three-generation Black families. *Family Relations, 42*(3), 332–341.
Taylor, R. J., Chatters, L. M., & Jackson, J. S. (1997). 'Changes over time in support network involvement among Black Americans.' In R. J. Taylor, J. S. Jackson, & L. M. Chatters (Eds.), Family life in Black America (pp. 293–316). Thousand Oaks: Sage.
Taylor, R. J., Chatters, L. M., Jayakody, R., & Levin, J. S. (1996). Black and White differences in religious participation: A multi-sample comparison. *Journal for the Scientific Study of Religion, 35*(4), 403–410.
Thoits, P. A. (1995). Stress, coping, and social support processes: Where are we? What next? *Journal of Health and Social Behavior, Spec No,* 53–79.
US Census Bureau (2006a). American Community Study. http://factfinder.census.gov/servlet/DTSubjectShowTablesServlet?_ts=209417510212. http://factfinder.census.gov/servlet/STTable?_bm=y&-geo_id=01000US&-qr_name=ACS_2006_EST_G00_S1701&-ds_name=ACS_2006_EST_G00_&-redoLog=false. Accessed Oct 1 2007.
US Census Bureau. (2006b). Current Population Survey. http://www.census.gov/population/www/socdemo/education/cps2006/tab01-03.xls. http://www.census.gov/population/www/socdemo/education/cps2006/tab01-04.xls. Accessed Oct 1 2007.
US Census Bureau. (2006c). Housing and Household Economic Statistics Division. Housing Vacancies and Homeownership Annual Statistics. http://www.census.gov/hhes/www/housing/hvs/annual06/ann06t20.html. Accessed Oct 1 2007.
US Census Bureau. (2006d). Population Division. http://www.census.gov/popest/national/asrh/NC-EST2006/NC-EST2006-04-BA.xls. Accessed Oct 1 2007.
United States Department of Health and Human Services (USDHHS). (2001). *Mental health: Culture, race, and ethnicity: A supplement to mental health: A report of the surgeon general-*

executive summary. Rockville: US Department of Health and Human Services, Public Health Service, Office of the Surgeon General.

Wenzel, L., Glanz, K., & Lerman, C. (2002). Stress, coping and health behavior. In K. Glanz, B. K. Rimer, & F. M. Lewis (Eds.), *Health behavior and health education: Theory research and practice* (3rd ed). San Francisco: Jossey-Bass.

Wheaton, B. (1985). Models for the stress-buffering functions of coping resources. *Journal of Health and Social Behavior, 26*(4), 352–364.

WHO World Mental Health Survey Consortium. (2004). Prevalence, severity, and unmet need for treatment of mental disorders in the World Health Organization world mental health surveys. *Journal of the American Medical Association, 291*(21), 2581–2590.

Williams, D. R. (1999). Race, socioeconomic status, and health. The added effects of racism and discrimination. *Annals of the New York Academy of Sciences, 896*, 173–188.

Williams, D. R., & Collins, C. (1995). US socioeconomic and racial differences in health: Patterns and explanations. *Annual Review of Sociology, 21*, 349–386.

Williams, D. R., & Collins, C. (2001). Racial residential segregation: A fundamental cause of racial disparities in health. *Public Health Reports, 116(5)*, 404–416.

Williams, D. R., & Collins, C. (2004). Reparations: A viable strategy to address the enigma of African American health. *American Behavioral Scientist, 47*(7), 977–1000.

Williams, D. R., & Lawler, K. A. (2001). Stress and illness in low-income women: The roles of hardiness, John Henryism, and race. *Women & Health, 32*(4), 61–75.

Williams, D. R., & Williams-Morris, R. (2000). Racism and mental health: the African American experience. *Ethnicity and Health, 5*, 243–268.

Williams, D. R., Gonzalez, H. M., Neighbors, H., Nesse, R., Abelson, J. M., Sweetman, J., et al. (2007). Prevalence and distribution of major depressive disorder in African Americans, Caribbean Blacks, and non-Hispanic Whites: Results from the National Survey of American Life. *Archives of General Psychiatry, 64*(3), 305–315.

Williams, D. R., Neighbors, H. W., & Jackson, J. S. (2003). Racial/ethnic discrimination and health: Findings from community studies. *American Journal of Public Health, 93(2)*, 200–208.

Williams, D. R., Takeuchi, D., & Adair, R. (1992). Socioeconomic status and psychiatric disorder and African Americans and Whites. *Social Forces, 71*(1), 179–194.

Williams, D. R., Yu, Y., Jackson, J. S., & Anderson, N. B. (1997). Racial differences in physical and mental health: Socioeconomic status, stress and discrimination. *Journal of Health Psychology, 2*, 335–351.

Wilson, W. J. (1978). *The declining significance of race*. Chicago: The University of Chicago Press.

Wilson, W. J. (1996). *When work disappears: The world of the new urban poor*. New York: Knopf.

Yinger, J. (1986). Measuring discrimination with fair housing tests: Caught in the act. *American Economic Review, 76*, 881–893.

Chapter 5
Psychology of Older Adults: Exploring the Effects of Class and Culture on the Mental Health of African Americans

Terry L. Mills and Susan Cody-Rydzewski

Chapter Focus

This chapter presents information on mental health issues among older African Americans, focusing on social inequality and racial discrimination as major challenges to the maintenance of mental health in this group; and extended family ties, social support, and religiosity as strengths contributing to resilience. In our discussion, we provide an overview of demographic changes in the age, race, and ethnic composition of the American population, followed by a brief review of physical and psychological health disparities between African Americans and Whites. We then explore strengths and challenges facing African Americans as they confront the possibility of mental health problems in old age as well as the results of a study of self-rated health and perceptions of depression among community-dwelling older African Americans. Finally, we discuss directions for future research and implications for mental health practitioners.

Demographic Characteristics of Older African Americans

The growth of the older population of the United States is quite remarkable. In 1900, only 4.1% of Americans were 65 and older. By the year 2000, that number had risen to over 12%. By 2030, it will increase to 20% (Quadagno 2005). However, perhaps more than the "graying" of America, the most dramatic shift in the demographic composition of the United States is the graying of the minority population (Angel and Angel 2006). By 2030, African Americans aged 65 and older will comprise about 10% of the population. The proportion of older adults who are non-Hispanic

T. L. Mills (✉)
Division of Humanities & Social Sciences, Morehouse College,
Wheeler Hall, Room 201, Atlanta, GA, USA
e-mail: tmills@morehouse.edu

E. C. Chang, C. A. Downey (eds.), *Handbook of Race and Development in Mental Health*,
DOI 10.1007/978-1-4614-0424-8_5, © Springer Science+Business Media, LLC 2012

White will decline from 83% in 2003 to 72% in 2030 (Centers for Disease Control and Prevention and the Merck Company Foundation 2007).

While the medical and sociological literature is replete with studies of physical health concerns for older adults (Braithwaite and Taylor 1992; Hayward et al. 2000; Hildreth and Saunders 1992; Link and Phelan 1995; Preston and Taubman 1994; Robert and House 2000; Ross and Mirowsky 2001; Schoenbaum and Waidmann 1997; Williams and Collins 1995), more attention to the psychological health needs of this population is needed. A consistent finding in health research is that African Americans experience higher rates of disease and disability than do Whites (Anderson 2002; Williams et al. 1997), as well as shorter life expectancies (Howard et al. 2000; Williams et al. 1997). Furthermore, African Americans experience more psychological distress (Cockerham 2006; Williams et al. 1997). It is known that persons with chronic health conditions are more likely to suffer from depression (Mills et al. 2004). African Americans experience a higher rate of life-threatening diseases and chronic conditions such as cancer (DeLeeuw et al. 2000; Walker et al. 1999; Wilkinson and Kitzinger 2000), hypertension (Clark and Harrell 1992; Cooper and Rotimi 1997; Cooper et al. 1999; Hayward and Heron 1999), heart disease (Belgrave 1992; Carney et al. 1999; Murrell et al. 1983), and AIDS (Belgrave 1992). Therefore, older adults, and older African Americans in particular, are likely to be at higher risk for depression than other groups (Mills 2001; Mills et al. 2004). In general, the risk for psychological distress increases with the number of chronic diseases and level of functional disability (Mills 2001). The link between depression and chronic illness is especially concerning since elderly may not seek treatment for chronic illness if they believe it is a normal part of aging (Mills 2001). Furthermore, depression worsens the effects and the outcomes of comorbid medical conditions (Mills et al. 2004), for which African Americans also have greater risk than their White counterparts.

Challenges to Maintaining Mental Health

Socioeconomic Status

It has been shown that socioeconomic status (SES) is a strong predictor of psychological well-being (Cockerham 2004; Kessler et al. 1994; McLeod and Nonnemaker 2000) and that there is a strong connection between economic inequality and health (Hirschfeld and Cross 1982; Link and Phelan 1995; Raphael 2000; Tennstedt and Chang 1998; Williams and Harris-Reid 1999). In the most comprehensive study of mental health in the United States, the relationship between mental health and race disappeared when social class variables were held constant (Cockerham 2006; Williams and Collins 1995). In addition, studies of "subjective well-being" find that racial differences are not significant when controlling for SES (Brown 1988; Krause 1993).

Although it would seem that race relations have improved and that substantial progress toward racial equality has been made, the economic disparities between Whites and African Americans are persistent and large (Raajpoot 2000). In fact, according to some economic and health indicators, African Americans have *lost* ground in recent years (Williams et al. 1997). SES negatively impacts health through a variety of channels, including lack of access to health insurance (Blendon et al. 1995; Seccombe et al. 1994), residence in high crime and/or polluted areas (LeClere and Soobader 2000), and employment in dangerous occupations (Clarke and Gerlak 1998; Pinderhughes 1996). Even employed African Americans have lower rates of insurance coverage than their White counterparts (Seccombe et al. 1994). These factors would predict less regular access to care and/or not having a stable, consistent source of care (Cornelius 1991).

African Americans have lower household incomes, lower rates of home ownership, higher poverty rates, and higher unemployment rates than do Whites (Williams et al. 1997), with unemployment being a strong predictor of depressive symptoms. More specifically, among Southern Blacks, unemployment correlates with depressive symptoms regardless of other demographic factors (Jenkins et al. 1991). Lower levels of education and lower lifetime earnings negatively affect African Americans across the life course (Angel and Angel 2006; Shea et al. 1996). Financial strain, including lack of home ownership, is a common source of marital dissatisfaction and a predictor of divorce (White 1990; White and Rogers 2000). Perhaps due to more intense and more persistent financial difficulties, African Americans experience greater strain and more unhappiness in marriage than do Whites (Broman 1993).

Socioeconomic position not only affects one's health, diet, and access to health care, but also one's sense of control in life (Hayward et al. 2000). Those who are better able to tap into valuable resources, such as discretionary income, health insurance benefits, or strong social networks, during times of adversity are more likely to feel more secure, confident, and empowered in their lives (Hendricks and Hatch 2006). Studies reveal that African Americans are less hopeful, less talkative, more likely to feel disliked by others, and more likely to perceive others as unfriendly. These differences generally disappear, however, when controlling for income, education, and physical health (Blazer et al. 1998). Even in the case of hypertension among blacks, there is a strong possibility that stress exaggerates this condition (Clark and Harrell 1992).

In understanding the mental health of African Americans (or any population), it is important to first distinguish between psychological distress and mental illness. Mental illness refers to "clinically diagnosable conditions," while psychological distress involves negative or problematic responses, such as anxiety or headaches, to environmental stimuli (Mills and Edwards 2002). Mental health research is also complicated by the fact that no single definition of mental health or mental disorder is agreed upon (Cockerham 2006). Old age is often viewed negatively in our society. Consequently, the symptoms of depression among older persons may go undetected or ignored (Mills 2000). Depressive symptoms in older adults may also be misdiagnosed as symptoms of some type of physical illness (Koenig 1999).

Although lower SES Blacks may have higher levels of psychological distress than lower SES Whites, they may not have higher rates of mental disorder (Williams et al. 1992). In one study, Blacks experienced a higher rate of depressive symptoms but a lower rate of lifetime major depression (Vega and Rumbaut 1991). On the other hand, some studies indicate that older African Americans may have *lower* rates of depressive symptoms (Blazer et al. 1991). The Epidemiological Catchment Area studies of the 1980s found that rates of lifetime major depressive disorder were very similar for Blacks and for Whites (Cockerham 2006; Vega and Rumbaut 1991). Some community-based mental health studies have found that African Americans do not report a higher prevalence of mental disorder (Lindsey and Cuellar 2000).

A few studies, however, find that racial differences in health status remain even after controlling for the effects of SES (Lillie-Blanton et al. 1996). This finding necessitates a consideration of noneconomic factors as well. Unlike poor Whites, poor Blacks confront the combined effects of economic deprivation and race discrimination. In addition to structural racism, African Americans are subject to a dominant ideology of White superiority and its subtle yet pervasive influence in all areas of social life (Feagin et al. 2001; Essed 1991). Blacks are much more likely than Whites to report having experienced multiple instances of discrimination (Williams et al. 1997). Feeling a lack of control over one's life is linked to an increased risk of psychological distress (Mirowsky and Ross 1989).

Structural Contributors to Mental Health Challenges

Since African Americans represent the second largest racial minority group in the United States after Hispanics (Seccombe 2007), it is important to understand how social, cultural, and economic factors affect the psychological health of older African-Americans. Rather than rely on a medical perspective, a sociological perspective requires attention to the effects of a historical legacy of slavery as well as contemporary and persistent patterns of racial prejudice and discrimination on the psychological health of African Americans (Mills and Edwards 2002). Gerontologist Kenneth Ferraro has described the cultural, historical, and sociological understanding of old age and older adults as the "gerontological imagination" (Mills and Edwards 2002).

Admission rates to psychiatric hospitals as well as to community mental health centers have been higher for African Americans than for European Americans (Lindsey and Cuellar 2000). There is an overdiagnosis of schizophrenia and an underdiagnosis of mood disorders in the African-American population (Bell and Mehta 1980; Strakowski et al. 1995; Baker and Bell 1999). Antipsychotic medications are disproportionately prescribed to African-American patients (Strakowski et al. 1993). When African Americans pursue treatment for mental health, they are more likely to wait until the illness has progressed. Additionally, they have higher attrition rates from mental health services than do Whites (Lindsey and Cuellar

2000). Furthermore, African Americans with similar symptoms are less likely than Whites to be referred for mental health treatment (Leo et al. 1997).

Problems of diagnosis are at least partially attributable to racial prejudice (Coleman and Baker 1994) or to cultural variations in the presentation of symptoms (Whaley 1997). Variations in dialect may also be to blame for misdiagnosis (Lindsey and Cuellar 2000). It is entirely possible that African Americans experience mental health problems which are unique to, and result from, the experience of being African American in a Eurocentric culture (Lindsey and Cuellar 2000). Most measures of psychological well-being rely on universal symptom checklists which do not account for social, economic, or cultural variations in psychological health or in the presentation of symptoms (Vega and Rumbaut 1991). Until recently, African Americans have been largely ignored in epidemiological studies (Mills 2000). Screening instruments are typically based upon studies of Whites and/or health assumptions associated with a White European framework (Baldwin 1992). Cultural background may shape views and expressions of various emotions (Mills et al. 2004). Because most measures of depression have evolved from a European framework, it is likely that persons of other cultural backgrounds are at a disadvantage in the diagnosis and treatment of mental health problems. It is, therefore, important to recognize that understandings of depression may vary across cultures and subcultures (Jenkins et al. 1991).

A significant proportion of African Americans associate depression with weak or poor character and a majority indicate that they would rely on prayer and religious faith to cope with depression (Mills et al. 2004; Mills 2000; National Mental Health Association Survey 1996; Steffens et al. 1997). On the other hand, there is some evidence that African Americans are more likely to engage in somatization; that is, they attribute emotional or psychological health problems to physical sources (Kleinman 1989). Somatization of depressive symptoms has been shown to delay or prevent the pursuit of professional treatment for mental health problems (Katon et al. 1982).

Service Use Among African Americans

Several factors have been found to be predictive of service use among older adults. Gender, age, and educational level are perhaps the strongest predictors, with women, older adults, and those with higher levels of education relying on health care services more often. In terms of psychological health care services, women, those who are Jewish, those who are not particularly religious, those with higher levels of education and higher incomes, and those who live in urban or suburban areas seek outside assistance more often (Cockerham 2006; Greenley and Mechanic 1976). Poverty is often linked to social and psychological isolation. Thus, the poor are less likely to talk to others about emotional and psychological difficulties (Veroff et al. 1981). Regardless of social status, most people initially seek informal assistance through family, friends, or clergy (Cockerham 2006; Grusky and Pollner 1981; Veroff et al. 1981).

Studies indicate that social factors such as social class, race, ethnicity, and region influence the likelihood that professional help for mental health problems will be sought (Alegria et al. 2002). Whites are more likely than African Americans or Latinos to receive mental health care by a psychiatrist, psychologist, or psychotherapist (Alegria et al. 2002; Neighbors et al. 1998). Furthermore, this difference is not necessarily due to income, residence, or geographic location (Alegria et al. 2002). In one study, African Americans who were not poor had lower rates of mental health service use than Whites who were poor (Alegria et al. 2002). Lower rates of mental health service use among African Americans may be partially explained by sociocultural factors, in addition to economic factors. African Americans may be less trusting of the medical establishment due to past mistreatment at the hands of major social institutions (Lillie-Blanton et al. 2000).

In a study of community-dwelling older adults, Mills et al. (2004) explored the self-rated psychological health of older adults through a telephone survey, which included an oversampling of African Americans. Tracts which met the race requirement of at least 50% African American and the age requirement of age 60 or older were selected. The final sample consisted of 404 participants, aged 60 to 95. About three-quarters of the sample were women and 55% were African American. About 30% of the sample graduated from high school, while another third had less than a high school education. About 19% had some college education and 11% completed college.

The primary dependent variable in this study is the subjective definition of depression to older adults. The goal of the study was to explore the meanings associated with psychological distress and whether or not these meanings are influenced by the medical model. Psychological health was measured using the Center for Epidemiological Studies Depression Scale (CES-D), a short, self-report scale designed to measure depressive symptoms in the general population. Respondents are asked to indicate how often they have experienced each of ten behavioral or affective symptoms during the past week. The number of reported depressive symptoms ranged from 0 to 8. Scores at or above 4 suggest a clinically significant level of depressive symptoms that are highly indicative of a risk for major depression. The overall sample mean for CES-D score was 1.98 suggesting that the older adults in this study were moderately symptomatic, but significant enough to indicate minor depression or an early or residual form of major depression.

The primary control variables in this study are age, gender, race, education level, and income level. Measures of physical and subjective health were taken. Participants were asked if they viewed depression as a personal weakness, whether they viewed depression as a medical condition, and whether they would ever take medication for depression. Participants were also asked whether they felt depressed, and if the way they felt over the past week was different from the way they usually feel. In addition, a measure of social context variables was taken. Participants were asked about their caregiving responsibilities. Finally, to assess social network contact, participants were asked whether or not there was someone else besides their primary care doctor with whom they would discuss their feelings.

Descriptive analyses and hierarchical multivariate regression analyses were used to examine the association between the mean level of CES-D scores and the various risk factors. The sample was stratified by race to examine whether there was racial variance in the correlates of overall self-reported depression. Racial group differences in the response rates for the eight CES-D categories were also explored. In summary, the authors tested four hypotheses:

1. As compared with African Americans, for Caucasians the level of education and income will be associated with lower levels of self-reported depressive symptoms.
2. As compared with African Americans, Caucasians will report fewer doctor-diagnosed chronic medical conditions and better overall self-assessed physical health. Consequently, Caucasians will report lower levels of depressive symptoms.
3. As compared with African Americans, Caucasians are more likely to perceive of depression as a medical condition, and consequently report lower scores on the CES-D scale.
4. As compared to Caucasians, African Americans are more likely to report somatic complaints associated with depressive symptoms; and also are more likely to report feeling that everything was an effort.

As expected, compared to older African Americans, Caucasians had a higher level of education and higher incomes. There also was a significant difference in subjective self-assessment of health, with Whites reporting better overall health. There was a significant difference between groups on whether participants had ever taken medication for depression. Older Whites were more likely than their African American counterparts to report having ever taken medication for depression. In addition, Caucasian older adults were more likely than older African Americans to see depression as a medical condition. African Americans, on the other hand, were more likely to view depression as a personal weakness. This difference may be due to the strong influence of religion in the lives of many African Americans and the tendency to explain personal problems in terms of spiritual weakness or struggle (Mills et al. 2004). African Americans were more likely to discuss their feelings with a friend. No differences were found in the caregiving responsibilities of Whites and African Americans (Mills et al. 2004).

The relationship between level of education and CES-D scores was found to be negative. However, when controlling for sociodemographic factors, doctor-diagnosed chronic conditions, and self-assessed physical health, the relationship between education level and CES-D score remained only for African Americans. There were no significant differences in CES-D scores for the factors of age, income, gender, and race. No significant differences between African Americans and Caucasians were found in the total number of doctor-diagnosed illnesses. However, African Americans with self-reported "poor" health had higher mean CES-D scores than those with health described as "fair," "good," or "excellent." For Caucasians, being in either "poor" or "fair" health was associated with higher mean levels of self-reported depressive symptoms.

In examining perceptions of depression, no differences in mean CES-D scores were found for older adults who perceive depression as being neither a medical condition or a personal weakness, nor only a medical condition or only a personal weakness. However, older African Americans who believe that depression is both a medical condition *and* a personal weakness had higher mean CES-D scores than those who only see it as a personal weakness. Older Whites who viewed depression as a medical condition had significantly lower CES-D scores than those who did not (Mills et al. 2004). In the analysis of individual CES-D items, responses to one item differed significantly by race. Nearly one-third of all African Americans reported that "everything was an effort," compared to just over 20% of Whites (Mills et al. 2004).

In the multivariate analysis, higher levels of education were associated with lower CES-D scores. Furthermore, this relationship was stronger for African Americans. Older Caucasians who believe that depression is a medical condition had lower CES-D scores on average. Older Whites who had ever taken medication for depression had higher CES-D scores, as expected. However, these relationships were not found among older African Americans. Also, having a belief that depression is a personal weakness was not associated with depressive symptoms for African Americans or Caucasians.

Strengths Contributing to Mental Health

Social Support

Despite economic disadvantage, African Americans possess some protective mental health factors. While social supports are generally weaker and less present among lower socioeconomic persons (Jenkins et al. 1991), familial and extrafamilial support is considered to be an enduring feature of African-American culture. In general, White Americans are more likely to express highly individualistic and independent attitudes, and this may be even more common among older Whites (Pyke and Bengston 1996). Conversely, African Americans maintain a more collective or communal perspective (Triandis 2001). The existence of large, supportive social networks may serve to mitigate the symptoms or severity of depression (Penninx et al. 1997, 1998).

African-American families have been described as "cohesive" (Luckey 1994), and this cohesiveness may offset some of the effects of economic strain. While the organization of Black families has been lamented for several decades (Rainwater and Yancey 1967; Moynihan 1965), more recently strengths-based approaches have noted the resiliency of such families (Ladner 1998; Hill 2005; St. Jean and Feagin 1997). To be precise, the existence of extended family support networks is applauded as an innovative and effective response to social isolation and economic hardship.

Older African Americans are more likely than Whites to live in larger, multigenerational households and/or households involving fictive kin (Burton et al. 1995; Delgado and Humm-Delgado 1982). They are more likely to care for older adult family members informally and less likely to institutionalize family members who need assistance (Damon-Rodriguez et al. 1994; Salive et al. 1993; Tennstedt and Chang 1998; Wallace et al. 1998). It has been shown that older African Americans experiencing disability receive more informal care than do older White persons (Tennstedt and Chang 1998). Adams and Jackson (2000) report that contact with friends and family members promotes subjective well-being among African Americans. There is evidence that family support is more important than other types of support to Black individuals (Raymond et al. 1980) and that the home is a vital source of support and livelihood for African Americans (Clark 1993; hooks 1990). Furthermore, African-American caregivers are less likely to be stressed than other caregivers and have stronger beliefs about the necessity for family support networks (Connell and Gibson 1997). Extended family ties, and the expectation for support that accompanies them, may also be a source of psychological distress, however. Older adult caregivers, for example, may experience negative affect and decreased positive feelings if their health is poor and if they feel burdened by the caregiving role (Pruchno and McKinney 2002).

Many studies demonstrate that married people have better mental health, on average, than unmarried people (Gove et al. 1983; Engram and Lockery 1993; Kim and McKenry 2002; Waite 1995; Waite and Gallagher 2000). While African Americans have lower rates of marriage than do other groups (McKinnon 2003), satisfying marriages have been shown to boost mental health (Ross 1995; Wickrama et al. 1997). Thus, encouraging healthy marriage partnerships among African Americans is potentially an avenue toward improving their mental health.

Religiosity

In addition to extended family support, religiosity has been shown to be an important protective mental health factor for older adults, especially African Americans (Black 1999; Ellison 1991, 1994; Levin et al. 1995; Smith et al. 2003). Most studies of religious commitment and participation find that women, lower income persons, and African Americans have higher levels of religious participation and stronger religious beliefs (Idler 2006; Lincoln and Mamiya 1990; Neighbors et al. 1983; Taylor and Chatters 1991). In one national study of Black Americans, prayer was cited as the single most important coping response (Neighbors et al. 1983).

Religiosity has been shown to alleviate stress, to reduce the risk of depression, and to improve self-esteem among caregivers (Moen et al. 1995; Picot et al. 1997). Among those experiencing stressful life events, such as illness or loss of a loved one, religiously active persons are better insulated from depression than are other persons (Idler and Kasl 1992; Koenig et al. 1992; Mattlin et al. 1990; Smith et al. 2003). Furthermore, among older adults who are dying, those who are religious are less depressed and experience less suicidal ideation (Van Ness and Larson 2002). Ellison et al. (2001) found that having a belief in the afterlife correlates with higher subjective well-being. Other studies have shown that religious participation lowered the risk of death among older African Americans (Bryant and Rakowski 1992). Qualitative studies of African-American women reveal that religion is often a source of reassurance and comfort during times of adversity (Black 1999). Overall, religiosity seems to promote a unique set of coping mechanisms, including prayer or conversing with churchgoers or clergy (Ellison et al. 2001).

There is less agreement, however, as to the reasons for religion's boost to mental and physical health. There are multiple causal pathways (Idler 2006). Religious involvement may lower the likelihood of participation in risky or antisocial behaviors, such as drinking or promiscuity (Cochran et al. 1988). Other theories suggest that religious involvement increases social resources and opportunities for social support (Black 1999; Williams et al. 1997). Those who attend religious services frequently often have larger support networks than those who do not (Ellison and George 1994). Having a sense of meaning or purpose in one's life may very well increase subjective well-being (George 2006). Religiously based belief systems, such as beliefs in the afterlife and the intrinsic value of human life contribute to better psychological health (Ellison 1991; Pollner 1989). In addition, adherence to religious beliefs may allow individuals to redefine stressful situations as positive or self-strengthening (Ellison et al. 2001).

Future Recommendations and Concluding Remarks

The costs of mental health problems are far more than economic. Mental disorder and psychological distress exact a toll on a number of life outcomes, including professional productivity and family obligations (Lopez 2002). As the proportion of older African Americans continues to grow, it is imperative that social scientists and medical practitioners focus their attention on the unique concerns and mental health needs of this population. It has already been shown that older adults, in general, are at increased risk for mental health problems, especially depression. While there is conflicting evidence on the comparative prevalence of depression among Whites and African Americans, older African Americans are at higher risk for depressive symptoms and symptoms of psychological distress. This is consistent with other studies linking depression and depressive symptoms to lower SES. What is most compelling, however, is the finding that lower class Blacks may be at higher risk for depressive symptoms when compared to lower class Whites. This finding is suggestive of the dual or overlapping effects of economic deprivation and racial prejudice. While economic disparity can be quantifiably measured, racial prejudice often operates more informally. Rather than conceptualize racism as intentional, exclusionary actions, it may be necessary to reframe it in terms of omission and invisibility. One of the consequences of being underrepresented and socially invisible is that dominant group members continue to use a White, middle-class measurement of mental health. It is critical that practitioners re-educate themselves regarding the pervasiveness of racial bias in the medical community, historically and today.

Part of the challenge for social scientists and mental health practitioners is to increase awareness of cultural bias and to recognize that the medical profession has a long history of racial bias. Clinical and nonclinical studies have relied on White samples. Diagnostic instruments have been designed with these study results in mind. Consequently, psychologists, psychiatrists, and general practitioners may inadvertently or unintentionally either misdiagnose or fail to diagnose mental illness in non-White populations. It is highly probable that economic disparity, together with social isolation, may produce a different psychological outcome than economic disparity alone. Poor Whites, while separated from the mainstream of society via economic resources, are aligned with the mainstream on matters of cultural values, language, history, social prestige, and representation across major social institutions.

Most studies indicate a lower rate of medical service use among African Americans, especially in the area of mental health treatment. The reasons for this are complex. First, lower wages, higher rates of unemployment, and lower rates of health insurance coverage preclude many lower income persons from seeking professional help for health concerns. Secondly, it has been shown that the poor are generally less trusting of major social institutions. Trust is gradually eroded when valuable, social resources are differentially distributed on the basis of ascriptive traits, such as race. Furthermore, faith in the credibility of social institutions is undermined when representatives of these institutions engage in unjustifiable, negative sanctioning of minority group members while simultaneously failing to protect or safeguard them (Feagin et al. 2001). Thirdly, the African-American community has expressed a preference for informal social supports, such as extended family, fictive kin and/or friends, and religion. The organization of African-American families has been discussed and researched rather extensively. The preference for extended family structures and for a looser definition of "family" has been attributed to the enslavement of Blacks.

In general, African-American families are more likely than White families to maintain extended family connections and to engage in patterns of mutual assistance with secondary family members as well as with fictive kin (Boyd-Franklin 1989). This pattern is found among both working- and middle-class African-American families (McAdoo 1988). It is not clear, however, whether reliance on informal support systems, as well as rejection of formal support, is the result of economic or subcultural factors (Wallace et al. 1998).

In the past several years, there has been a sharp increase in the number of grandparent/grandchild households, especially among African Americans (Mills 2001; Mills et al. 2005). Studies indicate that grandparents who are directly involved in parenting are less satisfied with their health and are at higher risk for depression than grandparents who are not involved in direct parenting (Minkler and Fuller-Thompson 1999). Being married seems to lessen psychological distress among grandmothers who give primary care to grandchildren (Mills et al. 2005).

Table. 5.1 Key research findings associated with psychosocial well-being among older African Americans

Category of research:	Significant challenges facing older African Americans:	Factors associated with strength and resilience among African Americans:	Mental health services use challenges for African Americans:
Key finding:	Chronic illness associated with depressive symptoms	Familial and extra-familial support is enduring aspect of African-American culture	Over diagnosis of schizophrenia, and under diagnosis of affective disorders, such as depression
	African Americans experience more chronic illness that Whites	Older African Americans more likely to live in multigenerational household than Whites	Antipsychotic medications disproportionately prescribed to African-American patients
	African Americans have shorter life expectancy	Contact with friends and family members promotes subjective well-being among African Americans	African Americans experience higher admission rates to formal mental health facilities
	Health disparities more likely are due to SES, not race	Religiosity shown to be important protective mental health factor among older African Americans	African Americans have higher attrition rates from mental health services than Whites
	SES is a strong predictor or psychological well-being		
	African Americans are less likely to have private insurance and lower rates of insurance coverage than Whites		
	Racial differences in health outcomes often persist, even after control for SES		

African-American grandmothers are more active than White grandmothers in the lives of their grandchildren and are more likely to live in the home with grandchildren (Pearson et al. 1990). There is some indication that African-American grandmothers experience higher levels of life satisfaction than do other grandmothers (Goodman and Silverstein 2001). Older African-American women report fewer depressive symptoms than do older White women (Mui and Burnette 1996). African-American parents and siblings who are engaged in caregiving report similar or higher levels of caregiving duties yet report feeling less burdened than their White counterparts (Horwitz and Reinhard 1995). Future studies should continue to explore the experiences of grandparent caregivers and the implications of this role for psychological well-being.

Education about mental health issues has been increasing in recent years. Several "high profile" individuals, including former Presidential candidate Al Gore's wife, Tipper Gore, have made their struggles with mental health very public (CBS News 2000; Epstein 1999). Still, segments of the population who are at greatest risk for mental health problems are often those least likely to receive or be exposed to this information. Physicians, particularly family doctors, general practitioners, or those working in public health settings, must be proactive in their efforts to educate the local community, through information-disseminating and social outreach. In addition, since it is known that older African Americans place a considerable amount of emphasis on religious life (Table. 5.1); ministers and other church support staff are vital participants in this effort as well. It is important that the matter is approached with cultural sensitivity, however. While professional treatment is to be encouraged, mental health workers must remain open to the possibility of informal support from family, friends, and religion as well.

References

Adams, V. H., & Jackson, J. S. (2000). The contribution of hope to the quality of life among African Americans, 1980–1992. *International Journal of Aging and Human Development, 50,* 279–295.

Alegria, M., Glorisa, C., Rios, R., Vera, M., Calderon, J., Rusch, D., & Ortega, A. N. (2002). Inequalities in use of specialty mental health services among Latinos, African Americans, and Non-Latino Whites. *Psychiatric Services, 53*(12), 1547–1555.

Anderson, R. N. (2002). Deaths: Leading causes for 2000. *National vital statistics reports, 50*(16), Table 1. Washington, DC: National Center for Health Statistics.

Angel, R. J., & Angel, J. L. (2006). Diversity and aging in the United States. In R. H. Binstock & L. K. George (Eds.), *Handbook of aging and the social sciences* (pp. 94–110). Burlington: Academic.

Baker, F. M., & Bell, C. C. (1999). Issues in the psychiatric treatment of African Americans. *Psychiatric Services, 50*(3), 362–368.

Baldwin, J. A. (1992). The role of Black psychologists in Black liberation. In K. H. Burlew, W. C. Banks, H. P. McAdoo, & D. Ajani ya Azibo (Eds.), *African American psychology: Theory, research, and practice*. Thousand Oaks: Sage.

Belgrave, F. Z. (1992). Improving health outcomes of African Americans: A challenge for African American psychologists. In K. H. Burlew, W. C. Banks, H. P. McAdoo, & D. Ajani ya Azibo (Eds.), *African American psychology: Theory, research, and practice* (pp. 356–358). Thousand Oaks: Sage.

Bell, C. C., & Mehta, H. (1980). The misdiagnosis of Black patients with manic depressive illness. *Journal of the National Medical Association, 72,* 141–145.

Black, H. K. (1999). Life as gift: Spiritual narratives of elderly African-American women living in poverty. *Journal of Aging Studies, 13,* 441–455.

Blazer, D. G., Burchett, B., Service, C., & George, L. K. (1991). The association of age and depression among the elderly: An epidemiologic exploration. *The Journals of Gerontology: Series A46*(6), M210–M215.
Blazer, D. G., Landerman, L. R., Hays, J. C., Simonsick, E. M., & Saunders, W. B. (1998). Symptoms of depression among community-dwelling elderly African American and White older adults. *Psychological Medicine, 28,* 1311–1320.
Blendon, R. J., Scheck, A. C., Donelan, K., Hill, C. A., Smith, M., Beatrice, D., & Altman, D. (1995). How White and African Americans view their health and social problems: Different experiences, different expectations. *Journal of the American Medical Association, 273*(4), 341–346.
Boyd-Franklin, N. (1989). *Black families in therapy: A multisystems approach.* New York: Guilford.
Braithwaite, R. L., & Taylor, S. E. (1992). *Health issues in the Black community.* San Francisco: Jossey-Bass.
Broman, C. L. (1993). Race differences in marital well-being. *Journal of Marriage and Family, 55,* 724–732.
Brown, D. (1988). Socio-demographic vs. domain predictors of perceived stress: Racial differences among American women. *Social Indicators Research, 20,* 517–532.
Bryant, S., & Rakowski, W. (1992). Predictors of mortality among elderly African Americans. *Research on Aging, 14,* 50–67.
Burton, L., Kasper, J., Shore, A., Cagney, K., LaVesit, T., Cubbin, C., & German, P. (1995). The structure of informal care: Are there differences by race? *The Gerontologist, 35,* 744–752.
Carney, R. M., Freedland, K. E., Veith, R. C., Cryer, P. E., Skala, J. A., Lynch, T., & Jaffe, A. S. (1999). Major depression, heart rate, and plasma norepinephrine in patients with coronary heart disease. *Biological Psychiatry, 45,* 458–463.
CBS News. (2000). The black dog: Tipper Gore talks about her battle with depression. http://www.cbsnews.com/stories/2000/10/09/60II/main239704.shtml. Accessed 26 July 2011.
Centers for Disease Control and Prevention and the Merck Company Foundation. (2007). *The state of aging and health in America 2007.* Whitehouse Station: The Merck Company Foundation.
Clark, H. (1993). Sites of resistance: Place, "race," and gender as sources of empowerment. In P. E. Jackson & J. Penrose (Eds.), *Constructions of race, place, and nation* (pp. 121–142). London: UCL.
Clarke, J. N., & Gerlak, A. K. (1998). Environmental racism in the sunbelt? A cross-cultural analysis. *Environmental Management, 22*(6), 857–867.
Clark, V. R., & Harrell, J. P. (1992). The relationship among type A behavior, styles used in coping with racism, and blood pressure. In K. H. Burlew, W. C. Banks, H. P. McAdoo, & D. Ajani ya Azibo (Eds.), *African American psychology: Theory, research, and practice* (pp. 359–369). Newbury Park: Sage.
Cochran, J. K., Beeghley, L., & Bock, W. (1988). Religiosity and alcohol behavior: An exploration of reference group theory. *Sociological Forum, 3*(2), 256–276.
Cockerham, W. C. (2004). *Medical sociology.* Upper Saddle River: Prentice Hall.
Cockerham, W. C. (2006). *Sociology of mental disorder.* Upper Saddle River: Prentice Hall.
Coleman, D., & Baker, F. M. (1994). Misdiagnosis of Schizophrenia among older Black Veterans. *Journal of Nervous and Mental Disease, 182,* 527–528.
Connell, C. M., & Gibson, G. D. (1997). Racial, ethnic, and cultural differences in dementia caregiving: Review and analysis. *The Gerontologist, 37,* 355–364.
Cooper, R. S., & Rotimi, C. N. (1997). Hypertension in Blacks. *American Journal of Hypertension, 10*(7 pt 1), 804–816.
Cooper, R. S., Rotimi, C. N., & Ward, R. (1999). The puzzle of hypertension in African Americans. *Scientific American, 280*(2), 56–62.
Cornelius, L. J. (1991). Access to medical care for Black Americans with an episode of illness. *Journal of the National Medical Association, 83,* 617–626.

Damon-Rodriguez, J., Wallace, S., & Kington, R. (1994). Service utilization and minority elderly: Appropriateness, accessibility and acceptability. *Gerontology and Geriatrics Education, 15*(1), 45–63.
DeLeeuw, J. R., DeGraeff, A., Ros, W. J., Hordijk, G. J., Blijham, G. H., & Winnubst, J. A. (2000). Negative and positive influences of social support on depression in patients with head and neck cancer: A prospective study. *Psychooncology, 9*(1), 20–28.
Delgado, M., & Humm-Delgado, D. (1982). Natural support systems: Source of strength in Hispanic communities. *Social Work, 27,* 83–89.
Ellison, C. G. (1991). Religious involvement and subjective well-being. *Journal of Health and Social Behavior, 32,* 80–99.
Ellison, C. G. (1994). Religion, the life stress paradigm, and the study of depression. In J. S. Levin (Ed.), *Religion in aging and health: Theoretical foundations and methodological frontiers* (pp. 78–121). Thousand Oaks: Sage.
Ellison, C. G., & L. K. George. (1994). Religious involvement, social ties, and social support in a Southeastern community. *Journal for the Scientific Study of Religion, 33,* 46–61.
Ellison, C. G., Boardman, J. D., Williams, D. R., & Jackson, J. S. (2001). Religious involvement, stress, and mental health. *Social Forces, 80,* 215–249.
Engram, E., & Lockery S. A. (1993). Intimate partnerships. In J. S. Jackson, L. M. Chatters, & R. J. Taylor (Eds.), *Aging in Black America* (pp. 84–97). Newbury Park: Sage.
Epstein, R. (1999). Tipper Gore and Rosalynn Carter: America's mental health crisis. *The 1999 White House Conference on Mental Health.* http://www.psychologytoday.com/articles/pto-19990901-000032.html. Accessed 26 July 2011.
Essed, P. (1991). *Understanding everyday racism: An interdisciplinary theory.* Newbury Park: Sage.
Feagin, J., Vera, H., & Batur, P. (2001). *White racism.* New York: Routledge.
George, L. K. (2006). Perceived quality of life. In R. H. Binstock & L. K. George (Eds.), *Handbook of aging and the social sciences* (pp. 320–336). Amsterdam: Elsevier.
Goodman, C. C., & Silverstein, M. (2001). Grandmothers who parent their grandchildren: An exploratory study of close relations across three generations. *Journal of Family Issues, 22,* 557–578.
Gove, W., Hughes, M., & Style, C. (1983). Does marriage have positive effects on the well-being of the individual? *Journal of Health and Social Behavior, 24,* 122–131.
Greenley, J. R., & Mechanic, D. (1976). Patterns of seeking care for psychological problems. In D. Mechanic (Ed.), *The growth of bureaucratic medicine* (pp. 177–196). New York: Wiley.
Grusky, O., & Pollner, M. (1981). *The sociology of mental illness: Basic studies.* New York: Holt, Rinehart & Winston.
Hayward, M. D., & Heron, M. (1999). Racial inequality in active life among adult Americans. *Demography, 36*(1), 77–91.
Hayward, M. D., Crimmins, E. M., Miles, T., & Yang, Y. (2000). The significance of socioeconomic status in explaining the racial gap in chronic health conditions. *American Sociological Review, 65,* 910–930.
Hendricks, J., & Hatch, L. R. (2006). Lifestyle and aging. In R. H. Binstock & L. K. George (Eds.), *Handbook of aging and social sciences* (pp. 303–320). Burlington: Academic.
Hildreth and Saunders. (1992). John Henryism and the health of African Americans. *Culture, Medicine, and Psychiatry, 18*(2), 163–182.
Hill, S. A. (2005). *Black intimacies: A gender perspective on families and relationships.* Rowman Altamira.
Hirschfeld, R. M., & Cross, C. K. (1982). Epidemiology of affective disorders. *Archives of General Psychiatry, 39*(1), 35–46.
hooks, bell. (1990). *Yearning: Race, gender, and cultural politics.* Boston: South End.
Horwitz, A. V., & Reinhard, S. C. (1995). Ethnic differences in care giving duties and burdens among parents and siblings of persons with severe mental illnesses. *Journal of Health and Social Behavior, 36,* 138–150.

Howard, G., Anderson, R. T., Russell, G., Howard, V. L., & Burke, G. L. (2000). Race, Socioeconomic status and cause-specific mortality. *Annals of Epidemiology, 10*(4), 214–223.
Idler, E. L. (2006). Religion and aging. In R. H. Binstock & L. K. George (Eds.), *Handbook of aging and the social sciences* (pp. 277–300). Amsterdam: Elsevier.
Idler, E. L., & Kasl, S. V. (1992). Religion, disability, depression, and the timing of death. *American Journal of Sociology, 97,* 1052–1079.
Jenkins, J. H., Kleinman, A., & Good, B. J. (1991). Cross-cultural studies of depression. In J. Becker & A. Kleinman (Eds.), *Psychosocial aspects of depression* (pp. 67–99). Hillsdale: Lawrence Erlbaum.
Katon, W., Kleinman, A., & Rosen, G. (1982). The prevalence of somatization in primary care. *Comprehensive Psychiatry, 25*(2), 208–215.
Kessler, R. C., McGonagle, K. A., Zhao, S., Nelson, C. B., Hughes, M., Eshleman, S., Wittchen, H. U., & Kendler, K. S. (1994). Lifetime and 12-month prevalence of DSM-III-R psychiatric disorders in the United States: Results from the national comorbidity survey. *Archives of General Psychiatry, 51,* 8–19.
Kleinman, A. (1989). *The illness narratives: Suffering, healing, and the human condition.* New York: Basic Books.
Kim, K. H., & McKenry, P. C. (2002). The relationship between marriage and psychological well-being. *Journal of Family Issues, 23*(8), 885–911.
Koenig, H. G. (1999). Late-life depression: How to treat patients with comorbid chronic illness. *Geriatrics, 54,* 56–61.
Koenig, H. G., Meador, K. G., Goli, V., Shelp, F., Cohen, H. J., & Blazer, D. G. (1992). Self-rated depressive symptoms in medical inpatients: Age and racial differences. *International Journal of Psychiatry in Medicine, 22*(1), 11–31.
Krause, N. (1993). Race differences in the life satisfaction among aged men and women. *The Journals of Gerontology, 48,* S235–S244.
Ladner, J. A. (1998). *The ties that bind: Timeless values for African American families.* New York: Wiley.
LeClere, F. B., & Soobader, M. J. (2000). The effect of income inequality on the health of selected U. S. demographic groups. *American Journal of Public Health, 90*(12), 1892–1897.
Leo, R. J., Narayan, D. A., Sherry, C., Michalek, C. & Pollock, D. (1997). Geropsychiatric consultation for African American and Caucasian patients. *General Hospital Psychiatry, 19,* 216–222.
Levin, J. S., Chatters, L. M., & Taylor, R. J. (1995). Religious effects on health status and life satisfaction among Black Americans. *The Journals of Gerontology: Series B, Psychological Sciences and Social Sciences, 50*(3), S154–S163.
Lillie-Blanton, M., Parsons, P. E., Gayle, H., & Dievler, A. (1996). Racial differences in health: Not just Black and White, but shades of gray. *Annual Review of Public Health, 17,* 411–448.
Lillie-Blanton, M., Brody, M., Rowland, D., Altman, D., & McIntosh, M. (2000). Race, Ethnicity, and the Health Care System: Public Perceptions and Experiences. *Medical Care Research and Review, 57*(1), 218–235.
Lincoln, C. E., & Mamiya, L. (1990). *The Black church in the African American experience.* Durham: Duke.
Lindsey, M. L., & Cuellar, I. (2000). Mental health assessment and treatment of African Americans: A multicultural perspective. In I. Cuellar & F. A. Paniagua (Eds.), *Handbook of multicultural health: Assessment and treatment of diverse populations.* San Diego: Academic.
Link, B. G., & Phelan, J. (1995). Social conditions as fundamental causes of disease. *Journal of Health and Social Behavior, 35,* 80–94.
Lopez, S. R. (2002). A research agenda to improve the accessibility and quality of mental health care for Latinos. *Psychiatric Services, 53*(12), 1569–1573.
Luckey, I. (1994). African-American elders: The support network of generational kin. *Families in Society, 75*(2), 82–89.
Mattlin, J. A., Wethington, E., & Kessler, R. (1990). Situational determinants of coping and coping effectiveness. *Journal of Health and Social Behavior, 31,* 103–122.

McAdoo, H. P. (1988). Transgenerational patterns of upward mobility in African-American families. In H. P. McAdoo (Ed.), *Black families* (pp. 148–168). Newbury Park: Sage.

McKinnon, J. (2003). The Black population of the United States. *Current Population Reports*, P-20-541.

McLeod, J. D., & Nonnemaker, J. M. (2000). Poverty and child emotional and behavioral problems: Racial/ethnic differences in processes and effects. *Journal of Health and Social Behavior, 41*, 137–161.

Mills, T. L. (2000). Depression, mental health, and psychological well-being among older African Americans. *African-American Research Perspectives, 6*, 93–104.

Mills, T. L. (2001). Comorbid depressive symptomatology: Isolating the effects of chronic medical conditions on self-reported depressive symptoms among community-dwelling older adults. *Social Science & Medicine, 53*, 569–578.

Mills, T. L., & Edwards, C. A. (2002). A critical review of research on the mental health status of older African Americans. *Ageing & Society, 22*, 273–304.

Mills, T. L., Alea, N. L., & Cheong, J. A. (2004). Differences in the indicators of depressive symptoms among a community sample of African-American and Caucasian older adults. *Community Mental Health Journal, 40*(4), 309–331.

Mills, T. L., Gomez-Smith, Z., & De Leon, J. M. (2005). Skipped generation families: Sources of psychological distress among grandmothers of grandchildren who live in homes where neither parent is present. In R. K. Caputo (Ed.), *Challenges of aging on U.S. families: policy and practice implications* (pp. 172–191). Binghamton: Haworth Press.

Minkler, M., & Fuller-Thompson, E. (1999). The health of grandparents raising grandchildren: Results of a national study. *American Journal of Public Health, 89*, 1384–1389.

Mirowsky, J., & Ross, C. E. (1989). *The social causes of psychological distress*. New York: Aldine de Gruyter.

Moen, P., Robison, J., & Dempster-McClain, D. (1995). Caregiving and women's well-being: A life course approach. *Journal of Health and Social Behavior, 36*, 259–273.

Moynihan, D. P. (1965). *The Negro family: The case for national action*. Washington, DC: Government Printing Office.

Mui, A. C., & Burnette, D. (1996). Coping resources and self-reported depressive symptoms among frail older ethnic women. *Journal of Social Science Research, 21*, 19–37.

Murrell, S. A., Himmelfarb, S., & Wright, K. (1983). Prevalence of depression and its correlates in older adults. *American Journal of Epidemiology, 117*, 173–185.

National Mental Health Association Survey. (1996). American attitudes about clinical depression and its treatment: Clinical depression and African Americans. http://www.nmha.org/ccd/support/africanamericanfact.cfm.

Neighbors, H. W., Jackson, J. S., Bowman, P. J., & Gurin, G. (1983). Stress, coping, and black mental health: Preliminary findings from a national study. *Prev Human Services, 2*(3), 5–29.

Neighbors, H. W., Musick, M. A., & Williams, D. R. (1998). The African American minister as a source of help for serious personal crises: Bridge or barrier to mental health care? *Health Education & Behavior, 25*(6), 759–777.

Pearson, J., Hunter, A., Ensminger, M., & Kellum, S. (1990). Black grandmothers in multigenerational households: Diversity in family structure and parenting involvement in the Woodlawn Community. *Child Development, 161*(2), 434–442.

Penninx, B. W. H. J., van Tilburg, T., Boeke, A. J. P., Deeg, D. J. H., Kriegsman, D. M. W., & Eijk, J. Th. M. (1998). Effects of social support and personal coping resources on depressive symptoms: Different for various chronic diseases? *Health Psychology, 17*(6), 551–558.

Penninx, B. W. H. J., van Tilburg, T., Deeg, D. J. H., Kriegsman, D. M. W., Boeke, A. J. P., & Eijk, J. T. M. (1997). Direct and buffer effects of social support and personal coping resources in individuals with arthritis. *Social Science & Medicine, 44*, 393–402.

Picot, S. J., Dehanne, S. M., Namazi, K. H., & Wykle, M. L. (1997). Religiosity and perceived rewards of Black and White caregivers. *The Gerontologist, 37*(1), 89–101.

Pinderhughes, R. (1996). The impact of race on environmental quality: An empirical and theoretical discussion. *Sociological Perspectives, 39*(2), 231–248.

Pollner, M. (1989). Divine relations, social relations, and well-being. *Journal of Health and Social Behavior, 30*, 92–104.

Preston, S. H., & Taubman, P. (1994). Socioeconomic differences in adult mortality and health status. In L. Martin & S. Preston (Eds.), *Demography of aging* (pp. 279–318). Washington, DC: National Academy.

Pruchno, R., & McKinney, D. (2002). Psychological well-being of Black and White grandmothers raising grandchildren: Examination of a two-factor model. *The Journals of Gerontology, Series B: Psychological Sciences and Social Sciences, 57*, 444–452.

Pyke, K. D., & Bengston, V. L. (1996). Caring more or less: Individualistic and collectivistic systems of family eldercare. *Journal of Marriage and the Family, 58*, 379–392.

Quadagno, J. (2005). *Aging and the life course: An introduction to social gerontology*. Boston: McGraw Hill.

Raajpoot, U. A. (2000). Multicultural demographic developments: Current and future trends. In I. Cuellar & F. A. Paniagua (Eds.), *Handbook of multicultural mental health: Assessment and treatment of diverse populations* (pp. 79–94). San Diego: Academic.

Rainwater, L., & Yancey, W. L. (1967). *The Moynihan report and the politics of controversy*. Cambridge: MIT.

Raphael, D. (2000). Health inequities in the United States: Prospects and solutions. *Journal of Public Health Policy, 21*(4), 394–427.

Raymond, J. S., Rhoads, D. L., & Raymond, R. I. (1980). The relative impact of family and social involvement on Chicano mental health. *American Journal of Community Psychology, 8*(5), 557–569.

Robert, S. A., & House, J. S. (2000). Socioeconomic inequalities in health: Integrating individual-, community-, and societal-level theory and research. In G. L. Albrecht, R. Fitzpatrick, & S. C. Scrimshaw (Eds.), *The handbook of social studies in health and medicine* (pp. 115–135). Thousand Oaks: Sage.

Ross, C. E. (1995). Reconceptualizing marital status as a continuum of social attachment. *Journal of Marriage and Family, 57*(1), 129–140.

Ross, C. E., & Mirowsky, J. (2001). Neighborhood disadvantage, disorder, and health. *Journal of Health and Social Behavior, 42*(3), 258–276.

Salive, M. E., Collins, K. S., Foley, D. J., & George, L. K. (1993). Predictors of nursing home admission in a biracial population. *American Journal of Public Health, 83*(12), 1765–1767.

Schoenbaum, M., & Waidmann, T. (1997). Race, socioeconomic status, and health: Accounting for race differences in health. *The Journals of Gerontology: Series B, Psychological Sciences and Social Sciences, 52*, 61–73.

Seccombe, K. (2007). *Families in poverty*. New York: Allyn and Bacon.

Seccombe, K., Clarke, L. L., & Coward, R. T. (1994). Discrepancies in employer-sponsored health insurance among Hispanics, Blacks, and Whites: The effects of sociodemographic and employment factors. *Inquiry, 31*, 221–229.

Shea, D. G., Miles, T., & Hayward, M. (1996). The health-wealth connection: Racial differences. *The Gerontologist, 36*, 342–349.

Smith, T. B., McCullough, M. E., & Poll, J. (2003). Religiousness and depression: Evidence for a main effect and the moderating influence of stressful life events. *Psychological Bulletin, 129*, 614–636.

St. Jean, Y., & Feagin, J. (1997). *Double burden: Black women and everyday racism*. Armonk: M.E. Sharpe.

Steffens, D. C., Artigues, D. L., Ornstein, K. A., & Krishnan, K. R. R. (1997). A review of racial differences in geriatric depression: Implications for care and clinical research. *Journal of the National Medical Association, 89*, 731–736.

Strakowski, S. M., Lonczak, H. S., Sax, K. W., West, S. A., Crist, A., Mehtar, R., & Thienhaus, O. J. (1995). The effects of race on diagnosis and disposition from a psychiatric emergency service. *Journal of Clinical Psychology, 56*, 101–107.

Strakowski, S. M., Shelton, R. C., & Kolbrener, M. L. (1993). The effects of race and comorbidity on clinical diagnosis in patients with psychosis. *Journal of Clinical Psychiatry, 54*, 96–102.

Taylor, R. J., & Chatters, L. (1991). *Religious life of Black Americans*. In J. S. Jackson (Ed.), *Life in Black America* (pp. 105–123). Newbury Park: Sage.
Tennstedt, S., & Chang, B. H. (1998). The relative contribution of ethnicity versus socioeconomic status in explaining differences in disability and receipt of informal care. *The Journals of Gerontology: Series B, 53*(2), S61–S71.
Triandis, H. (2001). Individualism and collectivism: Past, present, and future. In D. Matsumoto (Ed.), *Handbook of culture and psychology* (pp. 35–50). New York: Oxford University Press.
Van Ness, P. H., & Larson D. B. (2002). Religion, senescence, and mental health: The end of life is not the end of hope. *American Journal of Geriatric Psychiatry, 10,* 386–397.
Vega, W. A., & Rumbaut, R. G. (1991). Ethnic minorities and mental health. *Annual Review of Sociology, 17,* 351–383.
Veroff, J., Kulka, R. A., & Douvan, E. (1981). *Mental health in America*. New York: Basic Books.
Waite, L. J. (1995). Does marriage matter? *Demography, 32*(4), 483–507.
Waite, L. J., & Gallagher, M. (2000).*The case for marriage: Why married people are happier, healthier, and better off financially*. New York: Doubleday.
Walker, L. G., Heys, S. D., Walker, M. B., Ogston, K., Miller, I. D., Hutcheon, A. W., Sarkar, T. K., Ah-See, A. K., & Eremin, O. (1999). Psychological factors can predict the response to primary chemotherapy in patients with locally advanced breast cancer. *European Journal of Cancer, 35*(13), 1783–1788.
Wallace, S. P., Levy-Storms, L., Kington, R. S., & Andersen, R. M. (1998). The persistence of race and ethnicity in the use of long-term care. *The Journals of Gerontology: Series B, 53*(2), S104–S113.
Whaley, A. L. (1997). Ethnicity/race, paranoia, and psychiatric diagnoses: Clinician bias versus sociocultural differences. *Journal of Psychopathology and Behavioral Assessment, 19*(1), 1–20.
White, L. K. (1990). Determinants of divorce: A review of research in the eighties. *Journal of Marriage and Family, 52,* 904–912.
White, L. K., & Rogers, S. J. (2000). Economic circumstances and family outcomes: A review of the 1990s. *Journal of Marriage and Family, 62,* 1035–1051.
Wickrama, K. A. S., Lorenz, F. O., Conger, R. D., & Elder, G. H. (1997). Marital quality and physical illness: A latent growth curve analysis. *Journal of Marriage and Family, 59*(1), 143–155.
Wilkinson, S., & Kitzinger, C. (2000). Thinking differently about thinking positive: A discursive approach to cancer patients' talk. *Social Science and Medicine, 50*(6), 797–811.
Williams, D. R., & Collins, C. (1995). Socioeconomic and racial differences in health. *Annual Review of Sociology, 21,* 349–386.
Williams, D. R., & Harris-Reid, M. (1999). Race and mental health: Emerging patterns and promising approaches. In A. V. Horwitz & T. L. Scheid, *A handbook for the study of mental health: Social contexts, theories, and systems* (pp. 295–314). New York: Cambridge University Press.
Williams, D. R., Takeuchi, D.T., & Adair, R. K. (1992). Marital status and psychiatric disorders among Blacks and Whites. *Journal of Health and Social Behavior, 33,* 140–157.
Williams, D. R., Yu, Y., Jackson, J. S., & Anderson, N. B. (1997). Racial differences in physical and mental health: Socio-economic status, stress and discrimination. *Journal of Health Psychology, 2*(3), 335–351.

Chapter 6
More Than a Nice Thing to Do: A Practice-Based Evidence Approach to Outcome Evaluation in Native Youth and Family Programs

Barbara J. Friesen, Terry L. Cross, Pauline R. Jivanjee, L. Kris Gowen, Abby Bandurraga, Sara Bastomski, Cori Matthew and Nichole June Maher

Introduction

This chapter describes the activities and results of a practice-based evidence (PBE) project designed to develop a framework for culturally responsive effectiveness evaluation within a community agency serving urban American Indian and Alaska Native (AI/AN) youth and families.

US Census statistics for 2000 show that AI/AN people account for 1.5% of the population. Of these, nearly 67% of AI/AN people live in urban areas (Urban Indian Health Institute 2009). The AI/AN population experiences disparities in social, economic, and health areas relative to other ethnic groups. Suicide rates are 1.8 times higher for Native youth than the national average, and suicide is the second leading cause of death for AI/AN young people (Centers for Disease Control and Prevention 2009). In addition, Native youth live in poverty, experience higher high school dropout rates, lower employment attainment, higher rates of substance abuse relative to their White peers (Urban Indian Health Institute 2009), and are at greater risk for serious mental health problems (Gone 2004). Although urban Native youth experience risk factors at similar rates as their tribal peers, they do so without the supports and provisions (e.g., access to grants for tribes to improve health and mental health outcomes or tribal programs and services specific to the community) that exist in tribal communities to address these disparities (Fox et al. 2005).

Recognizing the need to identify effective interventions for working with AI/AN youth, and in response to mandates for evidence-based services, members of the PBE team engaged in a community-based participatory research process (CBPR), first to identify community-defined indicators of success (outcomes) and then to develop an online youth self-assessment tool that reflects these outcomes, generates

B. J. Friesen (✉)
Research and Training Center on Family Support and Children's Mental Health, Regional Research Institute, Portland State University, P. O. Box 751, Portland, OR 97207-0751, USA
e-mail: friesenb@pdx.edu

E. C. Chang, C. A. Downey (eds.), *Handbook of Race and Development in Mental Health*, DOI 10.1007/978-1-4614-0424-8_6,

information for service planning, and provides a baseline against which to measure progress over time.

Although the emergence of evidence-based practice (EBP) has been welcomed in the field of child and family services because it has directed attention and resources to interventions of proven effectiveness (Hoagwood et al. 2002; Singh and Oswald 2004), critical reviews have highlighted the inappropriateness of many EBPs, as they are currently developed and implemented, for culturally specific communities. The use of randomized clinical trials (RCTs) as the "gold standard" for reaching judgments of efficacy has also been criticized because of the lack of representation of culturally diverse youth and families and those with complex needs and/or co-occurring disorders. These families are typically served by community agencies, but are not usually included in RCT study samples (Brannan 2003; Espiritu 2003). There is growing discomfort with the conceptualization of EBP as comprising lists of practices approved for use in addressing specific disorders based on findings of specific types of research methods, primarily RCTs and quasi-experimental designs. Concerns have also been expressed about the restricted definitions of what constitutes evidence—and who decides which evidence counts, and about the imposition of interventions that are judged by members of cultural communities to be inappropriate for their members because of their narrow rather than holistic approaches. According to Scheyett (2006), dominant discourse on EBP privileges the voice of the researcher and neglects the dynamics of power and the potential for oppression, by silencing the voices of youth and families who use services and subjugating community knowledge. Furthermore, EBP is described as a "regime of truth," which "(re)produces the exclusion of certain forms of knowledge production" and which researchers are called upon to deconstruct (Holmes et al. 2006, p. 185).

The Challenge: The Demand for Linearity in a Relational World View

In their enthusiasm for "evidence-based practice," federal, state, and private funding agencies have required that community agencies adopt evidence-based interventions regardless of whether appropriate EBPs exist for the populations that they are serving (in this case, American Indian/Alaska Native; AI/AN youth) (Espiritu 2003). With some notable exceptions (e.g., Bigfoot and Braden 2007; Gone and Alcántara 2007), the EBP researchers who developed these mental health and social service interventions have been from the dominant culture, and generally have reflected a Western, linear view. These researchers built their work on previous empirical studies and usually did not include AI/AN consultants in the conceptualization and implementation of their studies. Thus the interventions are typically not culturally based, and may seem "foreign" to AI/AN youth and families, who are more likely to embrace a holistic, nonlinear, and relational world view (Cross 1995).

In Oregon, these concerns have gained a level of urgency because of the implementation of legislation (Oregon Senate Bill 267 2003, O.R.S. 182.525), that required an increasing percentage of public funds allocated to adult and youth corrections, child welfare, and addictions and mental health services, be spent on EBPs (2005: 25%; 2007: 50%; 2009 and thereafter: 75%). This requirement posed a major challenge to many community agencies, including those providing culturally based services, stimulating efforts to find alternative strategies to demonstrate the effectiveness of their interventions. In addition to questions about the appropriateness of EBPs for the youth and families that they served, agency staff and leaders also worried that a requirement that the adoption of "off the shelf" evidence-based interventions would result in their having to abandon existing programs and practices that they believe are effective.

Culturally- and community-based agencies have over the years developed practices and interventions that are highly valued, but are largely not tested through mainstream research. Although many of these practices and services may be associated with good outcomes, they are usually not considered to have a strong enough evidence base to support service providers' assertions of effectiveness. These practices are often not amenable to study using RCTs because of small numbers of participants or because cultural and spiritual dimensions of the interventions are such that the community would not permit a study that includes withholding treatment from a control group or randomizing community members to treatments seen as unequal. As a result, culturally- and community-based programs are challenged to preserve funding support for their programs without abandoning the practices and services that they and their clients value in favor of EBPs that appear on one or more lists of "proven practices." In response to these requirements, agencies providing culturally specific services for AI/AN communities have been faced with four difficult options: (1) to comply and adopt EBPs; (2) to adapt EBPs to be more culturally appropriate; (3) to seek exemptions for their populations; or (4) to attempt to use research to demonstrate that the services they provide are effective for the youth and families served. This last strategy was selected as the preferred approach in the case of the project featured in this chapter.

A Response: Practice-Based Evidence

Designed in response to the dilemma faced by the Native American Youth and Family Center (NAYA) and other community-based agencies, a collaborative research and evaluation team was formed to develop and implement a PBE approach that culturally- and community-based programs could use to address the demand for EBP.

The approach to PBE that we used was a research strategy in which knowledge is co-created by service providers, service recipients, and families. It incorporates the subjective experiences of receiving services and takes account of social and cultural contexts (Evans et al. 2003). Practice-based research is designed to identify practices that "work" in natural settings and with diverse populations (Evans et al. 2003). PBE is appropriate in practice settings in which culturally shaped perspectives are incompatible with RCTs or where sample sizes are not adequate for traditional research studies. The development of a PBE model can involve both qualitative and quantitative research methods to create a cyclical model in which PBE and EBP can inform one another to create a basis for assessing service outcomes and building evidence of effectiveness (Barkham and Mellor-Clark 2003).

The PBE project was developed in 2004 as one of several projects within the Research and Training Center on Family Support and Children's Mental Health (RTC). The RTC was funded by the National Institute of Disability and Rehabilitation of Research (U.S. Department of Education), and the Center for Mental Health Services, Substance Abuse and Mental Health Services Administration (SAMHSA), HHS.

The PBE team comprised representatives from NAYA, an agency serving urban Indian children and youth and their families, the National Indian Child Welfare Association (NICWA), and the RTC at the Regional Research Institute for Human Services, Portland State University. NAYA was identified as the study site, with one project goal being to develop an evaluation model that documented and built on the successes that NAYA had demonstrated with the youth and families that participated in its various programs and activities. Some good outcomes achieved by enrolled NAYA youth included:

- High school graduation rates five times that of all Indian children within the Portland Public Schools (PPS);
- NAYA students who participated in the tutoring center completed and exceeded state benchmarks in math, science, and reading at more than twice the rate of all PPS students;
- Students who participate in culture, arts, and sports programs have significant increases in daily school attendance rates and benchmark achievement rates, as well as decreases in behavioral incidents or referrals. (Cross et al. 2007, p. 13).

The second related goal was to develop a PBE model that could be adapted by other culturally- and community-based agencies to evaluate program effectiveness, building on evidence of program success.

NAYA's infrastructure, program philosophy, and approach to providing services posed a number of issues related to undertaking effectiveness research. First, NAYA is committed to holistic, comprehensive programming. Although NAYA is organized into departments, expectations for growth and change in the young people and family members who attend the program are not tightly tied to a particular program or department. Rather, young people voluntarily enroll in one or more programs or sets of activities (e.g., sports, culture and arts, and/or the tutoring center), according to their interests and needs. They may enter service through any one activity, moving or adding services as desired or advised. The NAYA youth who are a part of the Youth Services Program are usually referred because they are seen as "high risk" (not NAYA's term) and in need of guidance and intervention or intercession by a youth advocate (care manager). However, all aspects of NAYA's programming are available to all youth, and an operating assumption is that positive growth and development will result from being in an environment where Native culture is fully integrated, that is accepting, structured, and safe, and provides resources, opportunities, and guidance from adults who serve as role models and mentors. Another programming principle is that young people will profit from learning about their history and their cultural and spiritual traditions and practices, and that growth and healing will occur as they develop a positive cultural identity. NAYA is also committed to offering services that are individualized and dynamic, changing with the needs and circumstances of young people and their families.

Taken together, these characteristics of NAYA, while clearly appropriate for NAYA's philosophy and purposes, meant that a "program by program" approach to evaluation was not appropriate, and that isolating crucial services and discrete interventions that accounted for change would be very difficult. Thus, the PBE research team had many challenges as we worked to develop an approach to outcome evaluation that would be acceptable to the NAYA community, useful to other culturally- and community-based organizations, and seen as credible by the larger research community.

PBE project operating principles included:

- *Use of a relational world view model (Cross* 1995, 2003*) as the project framework.* In this model, often associated with the medicine wheel, health and well-being are understood to depend on the balance between four aspects of life: mind, body, spirit, and context. In this culturally based model, usually depicted as a four-quadrant circle, the purpose of services is to help individuals restore equilibrium and promote harmony among these quadrants. Through addressing the whole person, services support, heal, and comfort the person while fostering a culturally based understanding of self in relationship to the environment.
- *A commitment to using strength-based approaches,* and to build on existing good outcomes.
- *Collaboration between the three partners, across disparate cultures, and agendas*, with the expectation that each partner would bring and contribute its own strengths and resources.
- *Implementation of a CBPR approach.*
- *Production of work and products seen as credible by both Native constituents and by the mainstream research community.*

Project Phases

Building Relationships and Refining Plans

A crucial first step was building relationships among the three partners in order to develop trust and understanding, and with the broader NAYA community to refine research goals and methods. The history of multigenerational trauma and misuse of research findings has led AI/AN communities to be reluctant to engage in research, especially with non-Indian researchers (Weaver 1997). A CBPR approach was believed to be an appropriate approach for studying "what works" because it "allows for the inclusion of community values, cultural heritage, and historical perspective" (Fisher and Ball 2005, p. iii46). Further, participatory approaches are based on the idea that people can benefit from research conducted with their communities if there is community control over the research (Davis and Keemer 2002). A CBPR goal is for communities to become empowered to assume ownership of the research process and to use research findings to improve the lives of their people. Research codes of ethics and principles to guide research with AI/AN communities have been developed by several organizations, with key elements in common: research focused on issues of concern to the community, taking account of traditional holistic Native knowledge systems, with community oversight built on long-term relationships with community members, using culturally appropriate research methods, with research resources shared, and with dissemination of findings to benefit the community (American Indian Law Center 1999; Fisher and Ball 2005; McDonald 2002).

Relationship building began with research team members' spending several months meeting—to learn about each other, and to refine preliminary project goals. One mechanism for getting acquainted involved rotating the meeting place among the research team partners (NAYA, NICWA, and Portland State University). Research team members also explored the challenges and opportunities associated with conducting evaluation that would be recognized as sufficient evidence of effectiveness in the Oregon and national EBP policy context.

The project was designed to employ a participatory approach that involved community members' shaping project goals and practices. Team members met individually and as a group with stakeholders, including elders, NAYA staff, program participants, families, and other NAYA community partners. Through dialogue with these stakeholders, the research purposes and methodology were refined so that they were meaningful and reduced the potential for harm to the NAYA community. This process resulted in agreement among the research partners that the first question that needed to be addressed in thinking about effectiveness was, "What is the definition of success?" that is, "What does success look like for Native youth?" When the project began, NAYA operated in a context typical of most community agencies, in that it was accountable to multiple funding sources, each of which required reporting, usually on the process and/or amount of service provided, and each with a set of particular purposes, or outcomes in mind. Because this reporting was a condition of receiving funding, NAYA had very little say about the goals, measures, or reporting methods associated with its various funded programs. Team members agreed that defining valued outcomes for Native American youth was the right and responsibility of the NAYA community, and turned attention to developing an approach to defining "success" for Native youth. Considering both AI/AN cultures and the cultural milieu at NAYA, research team members chose focus groups

Fig. 6.1 Outcomes sorted according to relational world view (RWV)

as the most appropriate methodology for determining which youth outcomes were most important to the NAYA community.

Focus groups were held with several subgroups of the NAYA community in order to hear from community members about their views of what "success" looks like for urban Native youth served by NAYA and what NAYA services they viewed as integral to helping youth develop in positive, successful ways. Separate focus groups were conducted with middle school youth ($n=6$), high school youth ($n=6$), youth in foster care who participate in NAYA's programs ($n=7$), and families of youth ($n=7$). Additional focus groups included elders from Portland's Native communities ($n=11$), NAYA's board of directors ($n=7$), community partners ($n=11$), and staff and management at NAYA ($n=43$), for a total of 98 participants. Consent forms were collected from all participants, but no demographic data were collected. This process is described in depth in Cross et al. (2011).

Following the guidance of project partners and stakeholders, responses were not audio taped. Rather, a note-taker recorded responses on newsprint charts as people spoke, with frequent check-ins to assure that information was captured correctly. Member checking occurred both prior to data analysis and afterward to assist with interpreting the results. Results from the focus groups provided the research team with a long list of qualities, characteristics, and behaviors associated with success for Native youth (see Fig. 6.1). The conceptualization of success consisted of both the absence of risk factors as well as the presence of protective factors. Identified indicators of success were sorted into the four quadrants of the RWV model in order to create a culturally relevant evaluation and case management tool that addressed all life domains.

Project partners reviewed findings from the focus groups and input from NAYA staff and community members and determined that, initially, the best approach to program evaluation for NAYA was to look at effectiveness at the level of youth outcomes and changes in the measures over time. To address the multiple outcomes that were identified, it was necessary to locate or create measures that integrated both separate indicators of success and balance among the RWV areas.

Central to measuring the success of NAYA youth was the development of an online youth self-assessment tool (NAYA Assessment Tool, or NAT) which was aligned with the outcomes identified through the focus group process. This tool is now used by youth and their youth advocates as the basis for service planning, and as a periodic measure of progress toward planned outcomes.

Identifying Culturally Appropriate Outcome Measures

The development of the NAT began with an extensive literature review to link NAYA identified outcomes with research findings on these outcomes and to locate preexisting, strength-based measures for assessing youth that: (1) resonated with the NAYA community; (2) assessed the concepts of success articulated in the focus groups; (3) were reliable and valid; and (4) had been developed or used in previous research with Native communities. The NAT assessment tool includes questions that relate to all four quadrants of the RWV model.

Given the dearth of research conducted with Native American youth, measures that had not been tested on Native youth were also considered if they reflected the meanings of success articulated in the focus groups. Where there were important concepts to assess, but no measure, the research team developed new measures in a collaborative process; this was necessary in only a few instances. Both existing and newly developed measures were taken to NAYA youth advocates to review for cultural appropriateness and to ensure that they resonated with the NAYA community. The NAT consists of 22 measures. Four resilience scales (Ungar et al. 2008) encompass all four quadrants of the RWV (cultural resilience, individual resilience, community resilience, relational resilience). The remaining measures are located within the four RWV quadrants: **Body**: financial status, housing, drug and alcohol use, access to health care, exercise, and sexual health; **Mind**: depression, suicidality, feeling calm and peaceful, hope, perceived discrimination, conflict management, and coping; **Spirit**: traditional spiritual involvement, and participation in traditional activities; and **Context**: community mindedness, school belongingness, and neighborhood safety.

Strength-based/protective measures and health outcomes that are associated with mainstream EBPs were of particular interest for this project. Strength-based measures for the NAYA Assessment Tool (NAT) include:

- A scale measuring four types of resilience—cultural, community, individual, and relational—that was developed by the International Resilience Project and has been used with youth around the world, including First Nations youth in Canada (International Resilience Project n.d.).

- Feeling calm and peaceful, one item from *Oregon Healthy Teens (OHT*; Oregon Department of Humans Services 2007).
- The Children's Hope Scale (Snyder et al. 1997), a six-item measurement tool relating to a participant's outlook on life.
- A community mindedness scale (*Voices of Indian Teens Project,* Manson et al. n.d.) relating to a participant's behavior in the community away from school.
- Participation in traditional activities, a measure developed from the existing literature and expanded with NAYA elders. Participants' involvement is measured in eight categories of traditional Native culture: games and sports; ceremony, rituals, and ways of acting; history, cultural knowledge, and cultural skills; traditional forms of living; subsistence, food, and medicines; music and dance; kinship, family, and gender roles; and tribal crafts.

Health outcomes are measured in areas relating to drug and alcohol use, sexual health, depression, and suicidality. All of these measures, with the exception of the depression scale, were taken from Youth Risk Behavior Surveillance System (YRBSS; Centers for Disease Control and Prevention 2007). Depression is measured using the seven-item Center for Epidemiological Studies Depression Scale (CES-D; Radloff 1977) which has been used with tribal youth (Manson et al. n.d.).

Piloting the NAT Self-assessment Instrument

After measures were approved by the members of the research team and the community, they were combined to create the NAT which was prepiloted with two groups—NAYA middle school and high school students. Approval for both the prepilot and pilot testing of the NAT was obtained from the Institutional Review Board at Portland State University.

Results of the user testing indicated that all youth liked the online administration of the self-assessment tool and found the online format easy to navigate. Participants reported that most of the measures seemed relevant and comprehensible, but indicated that some items should be changed. These changes related to general comprehension, the use of outdated language, and cultural sensitivity. For example, there was wide consensus among the high school students that phrases like "down in the dumps" and "shake off the blues" were outdated and distracting. Additionally, middle school students reported that they would prefer a selection option of "Not interested in learning this activity" (as well as "interested") in the measure relating to cultural activities. All responses were honored and several changes were made to the NAT to both update language and add additional choices for youth to select.

Following the prepilot, adjustments were made based on youth feedback described above. The revised NAT was piloted with 126 youth who took the NAT as a part of their preparation for case planning between August 2008 and May 2009.

Table 6.1 Scale reliabilities of strength-based measures

Scale	Number of items	Cronbach's alpha
Depression	7	0.88
Hope	6	0.86
Community mindedness	6	0.78
Resilience: cultural	6	0.74
Resilience: relational	6	0.73
Resilience: community	8	0.67
Resilience: individual	8	0.65

Findings

Data analysis was conducted to:

1. Determine the validity and reliability of the strength-based and health measures used in the NAT;
2. Measure the protective factors of urban-based AI/AN youth that are "high risk" (i.e., receiving case management services);
3. Assess the health behaviors of high-risk urban AI/AN youth;
4. Examine the associations among the strength-based measures and health behaviors in our sample of high-risk AI/AN youth.

Of the 126 youth that took the NAT, 114 self-identified as American Indian, Alaska Native, and/or First Nation; their responses are used in all subsequent analyses. Demographic characteristics of the youth are as follows: 53% male, 46% female, 1% two-spirit; 48% 12–14 years old, 40% 15–17 years old, and 12% over 18. Most participants (77.2%) stated that they currently lived with their parents; however, over one-fourth (27%) of the youth reported changing living situations in the past 12 months.

Internal reliability of the strength-based measures was assessed using Cronbach's alpha (Table 6.1). The seven scales showed adequate to strong reliability, ranging from 0.65 (Individual Resilience) to 0.88 (Depression).

Correlations among the eight strength-based measures were computed (Table 6.2). Most intercorrelations were significant, but moderate with some notable exceptions; two resilience subscales—community and individual—correlated strongly at 0.71 ($p < 0.01$). In addition, participation in traditional activities, scored as the total number of activities engaged in was correlated with only two other strength measures—Community Mindedness (0.24, $p < 0.01$) and Cultural Resilience (0.23, $p < 0.05$). Generally, it appears that each measure assesses different aspects of youth strength that were associated with other strengths measures, but was not identical to any.

Table 6.2 Intercorrelations of strength-based measures

	Resilience: community	Resilience: individual	Resilience: cultural	Feeling calm and peaceful	Hope	Community mindedness	Participation in traditional activities
Resilience: relational	0.67**	0.53**	0.53**	0.49**	0.47**	0.31**	0.13
Resilience: community	X	0.71**	0.55**	0.40**	0.48**	0.34**	0.09
Resilience: individual		X	0.42**	0.31**	0.54**	0.29**	0.10
Resilience: cultural			X	0.39**	0.53**	0.34**	0.23*
Feeling calm and peaceful				X	0.50**	0.27**	0.02
Hope					X	0.39**	0.02
Community mindedness						X	0.24**
Participation in traditional activities							X

*$p<0.05$, **$p<0.01$, ***$p<0.001$

Table 6.3 Strength-based measure scores (means)

Measure	Mean (*SD*)	Maximum score
Resilience: community	4.0 (0.60)	5
Resilience: cultural	3.9 (0.83)	5
Resilience: individual	4.2 (0.55)	5
Resilience: relational	3.8 (0.79)	5
Community mindedness	2.3 (0.65)	4
Hope	4.2 (1.1)	6
Feeling calm and peaceful	4.1 (1.1)	6
Participation in traditional activities	3.7 (2.6)	8

Strengths and Health Behaviors of Youth

Relationship of Strength-Based Measure Scores and Participant Characteristics As illustrated in Table 6.3, despite being assigned to case management and experiencing other "at-risk" circumstances (such as unstable housing), these youth score high on most strength-based assessments.

In contrast, youth scored relatively low on many negative health behaviors.

Substance Use Less than half (44%) of participants reported ever drinking alcohol. Of those, about half (53%) reported drinking alcohol in the past 30 days. One-third (33%) of participants reported ever using drugs. Of those who reported ever using drugs, half (51%) reported using drugs in the past 30 days. Compared to those in stable living situations, those under unstable living conditions were more likely to have ever used drugs ($X^2=4.3$, $p<0.05$), but there were no significant differences in reported alcohol or drug use in the past 30 days between those under less stable and more stable living conditions.

Mental Health Overall, youth reported low levels of depression (mean = 1.5 (0.65) on a four-point scale); 8% ($n=10$) seriously contemplated suicide during the past 12 months; 8 of the 10 had attempted suicide at least once during that time frame. Compared to youth in stable living situations, those under unstable living conditions were more likely to have seriously considered suicide in the last 12 months ($X^2=4.0$, $p<0.05$).

Sexual Behavior About one-third (36%) of youth reported ever having sexual intercourse. Of those, 71% used a condom the last time they had sex, and 75% did not drink and/or use drugs during their last sexual encounter.

Finally, the relationships among strength-based measures and health behaviors were assessed using Pearson two-tailed correlations and independent *t*-tests for mean comparisons (Table 6.4). Overall, higher scores on strength-based measures were associated with healthier behaviors. Relational Resilience and Hope were associated with the highest number of positive health behaviors. Community mindedness was not significantly associated with any health measures.

These pilot data provide promising evidence of the reliability and validity of the NAT, a community-generated, strength-based assessment tool that can be used to evaluate youth programming at an urban-based AI/AN community center. Re-

Table 6.4 Relationships among strengths and health behaviors

Strength measures	Alcohol use: ever	Alcohol use: past 30 days	Drug use	Depression	Suicidality	Condom use at last intercourse	Substance use at last intercourse
Resilience: relational			$t=-3.1$**	$r=-0.37$**	$t=-4.8$***	$t=2.4$*	$t=-2.2$*
Resilience: community			$t=-2.5$*		$t=-2.6$**	$t=2.4$*	$t=-3.0$**
Resilience: individual			$t=-2.6$*		$t=-2.1$*	$t=2.4$*	$t=-3.4$**
Resilience: cultural					$t=-2.5$*		
Hope	$t=-2.5$*	$t=-1.9$*	$t=-2.7$**	$r=-.18$*	$t=-2.5$*	$t=2.7$**	$t=-3.1$**
Feeling calm	$t=-2.3$*		$t=-2.3$*	$r=-.35$**	$t=-4.7$***		
Participation traditional activities					$t=-2.3$*		

*$p<0.05$, **$p<0.01$, ***$p<0.001$

sults of from this pilot study also show that these AI/AN youth report having many strengths such as high resilience and low levels of depression, and most report not engaging in many unhealthy behaviors, despite belonging to a "higher risk" population in that they were participating in case management, and more than one-quarter experienced unstable housing in the past 12 months. One notable exception is that youth who reported suicide contemplation also reported high levels of attempts (80% of those contemplating suicide have also attempted); this finding parallels others that highlight suicide as a health disparity among AI/AN youth (Urban Indian Health Institute 2009). Nevertheless, such findings support already established treatment approaches that emphasize the importance of focusing on the strengths of young people, especially AI/AN youth, when developing programs to improve their well-being (Crooks et al. 2010; Kurtines et al. 2008). However, interpretation of these results should be made with caution as this study analyzed data from a self-report measure (see Brener et al. 2003 for an assessment of the limitations of relying on self-report of adolescent behavior) that was conducted in a single setting, with a small sample size. In addition, youth who participate at NAYA do so voluntarily, so it is possible that self-selection into the program could bias findings. As more data become available, future analyses will consider age and gender differences in the strength characteristics of these youth; additionally, longitudinal study will help assess the effectiveness of NAYA's programs in increasing the well-being of the youth that it serves.

Examination of the NAYA-Derived Outcomes in Relation to Mainstream Outcome Research

The process of identifying community-defined indicators of success for urban Native youth yielded many outcomes, such as lower depression, lower alcohol use, and increased school belongingness that are also identified as important outcomes by the mainstream research community. In addition to these, focus group members also identified eight indicators of success that were highly valued by this urban Indian community, but are not widely acknowledged in research and policies addressing EBPs. Outcomes in this category were: community mindedness, conflict resolution, cultural identity, hope, perceived discrimination, a positive relationship with an adult, school belongingness, and spirituality. In order to build an evidence base for NAYA's work, it was important to examine the relationships of these variables, many of which might be considered to be mediators or moderators, with mainstream outcomes so that the evaluation results would be meaningful for both the cultural community and members of mainstream research, funding, and policy groups.

Members of the research team conducted an extensive literature review designed to explore the relationship between community-identified variables relating to well-being for AI/AN youth and outcomes that are associated with evidence-based programs, or are widely accepted as desirable distal outcomes (Friesen et al. 2010). Overall, we found that many outcome variables in the mainstream research literature were associated with the NAYA-defined outcomes. For example, positive cultural identity, an outcome that is central to NAYA's programming, has been associated with reduced suicide, increased school belongingness and school success, antidrug adherence, higher self-esteem, higher social functioning, increased resilience, and better physical and psychological health (Friesen et al. 2010). This synthesis of research provides support for the importance and relevance of the NAYA-derived outcomes to both the cultural community and the body of mainstream research.

Linking PBE Work to NAYA's Needs and Goals

According to feedback from NAYA staff and management, the agency's involvement in this project has benefited the agency in a number of ways. First, it has required that staff apply a deliberate, highly coordinated approach to the planning and provision of services. Predictably, the requirement that all youth entering the Youth Services program complete the NAT self-assessment, and the expectation that service plans be guided by individual NAT results has resulted in many implementation challenges. However, the NAT has been built into the agency's client management database, and agency evaluation staff can now easily create reports at the individual and program levels that are useful to staff in working with individual youth and in managing their caseloads. Staff investment in the NAT and the evaluation process has also been heightened by the CBPR process that encourages questions and feedback. NAYA staff are more engaged because their perspectives are not only heard, but acted upon.

NAYA's participation as a partner in this project has also increased staff and management's ability to clearly define Native American-specific programs and services, and to relate services to community-defined measures of youth success. The project work has provided ways to clearly communicate the agency purposes, programs, and outcomes to mainstream providers and funding agencies.

Project participation has also increased NAYA's influence over the reporting and evaluation expectations that accompany funding from public and private sources. For example, NAYA recently secured a major contract that states that NAYA will "improve self-esteem, cultural identity, and connection to culture of origin for its youth participants." The NAT allows NAYA staff to concretely demonstrate these changes in clients.

Next steps include the further development and testing of a case planning protocol that is tied to individual scores on the NAT. This will provide a direct way for staff to link case plans, youth and staff activities, and changes in individual NAT scores and progress. When this case level information is aggregated, it will produce information to evaluate the effectiveness of particular service strategies, and it will begin to address the question of overall program effectiveness for Native youth.

Lessons Learned

There was much to learn as this project unfolded and developed. Some of what was learned may be identified as "positive wisdom gained"; other lessons address areas where considerable adjustment was necessary.

Perhaps the most important lesson that we learned was about communication and collaboration across multiple cultures. Although probably the most obvious cultural divide is that between the Indian and non-Indian members of the research team, we encountered many other cultural differences along the way. These included the gap that often exists between research and practice, the different "rhythms" and requirements of the university and community organizations, and different expectations from our respective funders, which included ideas about the primary purpose of our work.

As the Indian and non-Indian members of the research team began to work together, many differences in values, communication styles, standards of courtesy, and understanding of each others' background and context were apparent. Although all team members were alert to these issues, we still struggled to understand, to be understood, or often, not to feel misunderstood. Non-Indian members of the team were particularly concerned about giving offense, but direct mistakes were probably less common than differences in behavior and expressed or unexpressed values that affected group dynamics, comfort, mutual trust and understanding, and the ability to move steadily forward. An example of contrasts in behavior is the communication styles of the non-Indian members (generally more assertive, willing to interrupt, and speaking in louder tones) compared to the Indian members of the team (generally more reticent, do not interrupt, and speaking more softly) that sometimes made for tension, or at least, awkward moments. Differences in cultural beliefs and values were also apparent as we threaded our way among topics such as what might be open to study, and what was not.

Issues related to the research-practice and the university-community divide continue to be very important. In many ways, our experience was probably similar to that of any effort to conduct research in a community setting. The ongoing dynamic, adaptive, and service-oriented nature of NAYA, the community agency, was compounded by rapid growth, staff turnover, and physical relocation of the agency. The central concerns of direct line staff lie in providing good service and ongoing support to youth and their families, helping them grow and flourish, and troubleshooting negative events (e.g., discriminatory behavior on the part of teachers or students at school), and not in meeting data collection deadlines or other research needs. One approach to addressing this challenge was to try to increase the extent to which direct service staff felt invested in and could see the value of the process and products of the project.

The two major project purposes (to help NAYA measure service effectiveness, and to develop a framework that other organizations can use) are not incompatible, but the degree to which one is emphasized over the other has been a source of ongoing questions. For example, the NAT was developed from the ground up through a series of steps that involved multiple constituencies, and was rooted in the assumption that the NAYA community should be in charge of identifying what "effectiveness" means for them, that is, the definition of success for Native youth should emerge from the context, culture, and community in which they live. NAYA staff feel great ownership of the NAT because of the way it was developed and its utility as an assessment and planning tool. We have transitioned from the data from the NAT being viewed as research data, with ultimate control resting with the university, including the University IRB, to the data being seen as belonging to NAYA, with the university researchers seeking NAYA and IRB approval to do secondary data analysis using the aggregated de-identified NAYA data.

There is a clear and direct mandate from the federal funding agency that the main purpose of the grant is to support research and the creation of knowledge. Any benefit to NAYA would be considered secondary. We believe that we have achieved a reasonable balance between creating useful knowledge, and helping NAYA further its goals, but the dual purposes remain a source of complexity and confusion, at times.

One of the main objectives of this project has been to develop methodology to produce PBE to document the effectiveness of NAYA's services, as an alternative to EBP. We knew that the nature of the project could put this research at odds with the EBP research world. Our goal was not to discount EBP. In fact, we believe in the science to practice paradigm and value rigorous inquiry in pursuit of knowledge. We do, however, recognize a dilemma inherent in EBPs. For small community-based, culturally, specific organizations, EBPs are not feasible and sometimes not advisable. Additionally, only a handful of EBPs are available for Native populations (Gone and Alcántara 2007). Because we value the work of those who are leaders in EBP we invited several to advise our project, to critique our work, and to suggest strategies for maintaining appropriate rigor. The advice we received was invaluable. We learned that our fellow researchers recognized the limits of EBPs and were intrigued by our approach. In the words of one advisor, "If you can successfully pull this off, it will be a great contribution to the field." Our careful attention to methods and our frequent presentations at research conferences have been important elements of keeping our work open to our colleagues who can watch it unfold and provide feedback on what they see, thus helping us sharpen our approach.

Discussion

This chapter describes the development of a culturally appropriate self-assessment tool for AI/AN youth as one step in developing a method for effectiveness evaluation using CBPR methods. Next steps include further testing of this approach, and this tool, in other AI/AN settings. We hope that other organizations will find our approach and this tool useful, but the work is time and labor intensive, and we recognize that many community-based organizations do not have research and evaluation capacity or links to university-based evaluation resources. Next steps clearly need to address feasibility issues associated with this approach.

Our work to develop the NAT demonstrates that the AI/AN community represented by NAYA members emphasizes strengths, not just the absence of risk, in defining success for Native youth. Additionally, the indicators of success defined through our focus group process overlap considerably with many mainstream outcomes, but are at the same time qualitatively different from many of the outcomes found in the research literature.

The more culturally specific outcome indicators (strengths) identified by the NAYA community were found to be tied to many health outcomes of critical importance, such as alcohol and drug use, depression, suicidality, and healthy sexual behavior. The results of our work so far lead us to suggest that this approach to the assessment of effectiveness, beginning with community-identified indicators of success, and building data-based approaches to strength-based practice, is "more than a nice thing to do." Rather, the PBE approach described here has been critical to improving programming and practice at NAYA, giving NAYA the tools to gather data to demonstrate to researchers, funders, and the wider community the effectiveness of NAYA programs, and to laying the foundation for helping other community- and culturally-based organizations improve the lives of Native youth and their families.

References

American Indian Law Center. (1999). *Model tribal research code* (3rd ed.). Albuquerque: American Indian Law Center.

Barkham, M., & Mellor-Clark, J. (2003). Bridging evidence-based practice and practice-based evidence: Developing a rigorous and relevant knowledge for the psychological therapies. *Clinical Psychology and Psychotherapy, 10,* 319–327.

Bigfoot, D. S., & Braden, J. (2007). Adapting evidence-based treatments for use with American Indian and Native Alaskan children and youth. *Focal Point, 1*(21), 19–22.

Brannan, A. M. (2003). Ensuring effective mental health treatment in real-world settings and the critical role of families. *Journal of Child and Family Studies, 12*(1), 1–10.

Brener, N. D., Billy, J. O. G., & Grady, W. R. (2003). Assessment of factors affecting the validity of self-reported health-risk behavior among adolescents: Evidence from the scientific literature. *Journal of Adolescent Health, 33,* 436–457.

Centers for Disease Control and Prevention. (2007). Youth risk behavior survey. www.cdc.gov/yrbss. Accessed 4 June 2007.

Centers for Disease Control and Prevention. (2009). Suicide: facts at a glance. http://www.cdc.gov/violenceprevention/pdf/Suicide-DataSheet-a.pdf. Accessed 19 August 2010.

Crooks, C. V., Chiodo, D., Thomas, D., & Hughes, R. (2010). Strengths-based programming for First Nations youth in schools: Building engagement through healthy relationships and leadership skills. *International Journal of Mental Health and Addiction, 8,* 160–173.

Cross, T. L. (1995). Understanding family resiliency from a relational view. In H. I. McCubbin, E. A. Thompson, A. I. Thompson, & J. E. Fromer (Eds.), *Resiliency in ethnic minority families: Vol. I. Native and immigrant American families*. Madison: University of Wisconsin.

Cross, T. L. (2003). Culture as a resource for mental health. *Cultural Diversity and Ethnic Minority Psychology, 9*(4), 354–359.

Cross, T. L., Friesen, B. J., & Maher, N. (2007). Successful strategies for improving the lives of American Indian and Alaska Native youth and families. *Focal point: Research, policy & practice in children's mental health, 21*(7), 10–13.

Cross, T., Friesen, B. J., Jivanjee, P., Gowen, L. K., Bandurraga, A., Mathew, C., & Maher, N. (2011). Defining youth success using culturally appropriate community-based participatory research methods. *Best Practices in Mental Health, 7*(1), 94–114.

Davis, J. D., & Keemer, K. (2002). A brief history and future considerations for research in American Indian and Alaska Native communities. In J. D. Davis, J. S. Erickson, S. R. Johnson, C. A. Marshall, P. Running Wolf, & R. Santiago (Eds.), *Workgroup on American Indian research and program evaluation methodology (AIRPEM), Symposium on research and evaluation methodology: Lifespan issues related to American Indians/Alaska Natives with disabilities* (pp. 9–18). Flagstaff: Northern Arizona University, Institute for Human Development, Arizona University Center on Disabilities, American Indian Rehabilitation Research and Training Center.

Espiritu, R. C. (2003). What about promotoras, shamans, and Kru Khmers? *Data Matters, 6*(Spring/Summer), 19–20.

Evans, C., Connell, J., Barkham, M., Marshall, C., & Mellor-Clark, J. (2003). Practice-based evidence: Benchmarking NHS primary care counseling services at national and local levels. *Clinical Psychology and Psychotherapy, 10,* 374–388.

Fisher, P. A., & Ball, T. J. (2005). Balancing empiricism and local cultural knowledge in the design of prevention research. *Journal of Urban Health: Bulletin of the New York Academy of Medicine, 82*(2), iii44–iii55.

Fox, K., Becker-Green, J., Gault, J., & Simmons, D. (2005). *Native American youth in transition: The path from adolescence to adulthood in two Native American communities.* Portland: National Indian Child Welfare Association. http://www.hewlett.org/download?guid=5fad634f-49c4-102c-ab7e. Accessed 19 August 2010.

Friesen, B. J., Gowen, L. K., Lo, P., Bandurraga, A., Cross, T. L., & Matthew, C. (2010). *Literature support for outcomes in evaluating culturally- and community-based programs. Indicators of success for urban American Indian/Alaska Native youth: An agency example.* Portland: Practice-Based Evidence Project, Research & Training Center on Family Support & Children's Mental Health, Portland State University.

Gone, J. P. (2004). Mental health services for Native Americans in the 21st century United States. *Professional Psychology: Research and Practice, 35*(1), 10–18.

Gone, J. P., & Alcántara, C. (2007). Identifying effective mental health interventions for American Indians and Alaska Natives: A review of the literature. *Cultural Diversity and Ethnic Minority Psychology, 13*(4), 356–363.

Hoagwood, K., Burns, B. J., & Weisz, J. R. (2002). A profitable conjunction: From science to service in children's mental health. In B. J. Burns & K. Hoagwood (Eds.), *Community treatment for youth: Evidence-based interventions for severe emotional and behavioral disorders* (pp. 327–338). New York: Oxford University Press.

Holmes, D., Murray, S. J., Perron, A., & Rail, G. (2006). Deconstructing the evidence-based discourse in health sciences: Truth, power, and fascism. *International Journal of Evidence Based Health, 4,* 180–186.

International Resilience Project. (n.d.). *The Child and Youth Resilience Measure (CYRM)-28: User Manual.*

Kurtines, W. M., Ferrer-Wreder, L., Berman, S. L., Lorente, C. C., Silverman, W. K., & Montgomery, M. J. (2008). Promoting positive youth development: New directions in development theory, methods, and research. *Journal of Adolescent Research, 23,* 233–244.

Manson, S., Mitchell, C., Fleming, C., Baron, A., Keane, E., Shangreaux, D., & Martin, R. (n.d.). *Voices of Indian Teens Project: Scales documentation.* Unpublished manuscript. National Center for American Indian and Alaska Native Mental Health Research. http://aianp.uchsc.edu/ncaianmhr/research/pdf_files/vcscales.pdf. Accessed 20 November 2007.

McDonald, J. D. (2002). A model for conducting research with American Indian participants. In J. D. Davis, J. S. Erickson, S. R. Johnson, C. A. Marshall, P. Running Wolf, R. Santiago, et al. (Eds.), *Workgroup on American Indian research and program evaluation methodology (AIR-*

PEM), Symposium on research and evaluation methodology: Lifespan issues related to American Indians/Alaska Natives with disabilities (Appendix D, pp. 176–178). Flagstaff: Northern Arizona University, Institute for Human Development, Arizona University Center on Disabilities, American Indian Rehabilitation Research and Training Center. (Reprinted with permission of the author.)

Oregon Department of Human Services. (2007). Center for health statistics. Oregon Healthy Teens–Youth Surveys, Salem, Oregon. http://www.dhs.state.or.us/dhs/ph/chs/youthsurvey/ohteens/2007/oht8th2007.pdf. Accessed 26 April 2007.

Oregon Senate Bill 267. (2003). http://pub.das.state.or.us/LEG_BILLS/PDFs/ESB267.pdf. Accessed 5 May 2009.

Radloff, L. S. (1977). The CES-D scale: A self-report depression scale for research in the general population. *Applied Psychological Measurement, 1*, 385–401.

Scheyett, A. (2006). Silence and surveillance: Mental illness, evidence-based practice, and a Foucaultian lens. *Journal of Progressive Human Services, 17*(1), 71–92.

Singh, N. N., & Oswald, D. P. (2004). Evidence-based practice. Part I: General methodology. *Journal of Child and Family Studies, 13*(20), 129–142.

Snyder, C. R., Hoza, B., Pelham, W., Rapoff, M., Ware, L., Danovsky, M., & Stahl, K. J. (1997). The development and validation of the Children's Hope Scale. *Journal of Pediatric Psychology, 22*(3), 399–421.

Urban Indian Health Institute. (2009). *Urban Native American and Alaska Native youth: An analysis of select national data sources.* Seattle: Seattle Indian Health Board.

Ungar, M., Liebenberg, L., Boothroyd, R., Kwong, W. M., Lee, T. Y., Leblanc, J., Duque, L., & Makhnach, A. (2008). The study of youth resilience across cultures: Lessons from a pilot study of measurement development. *Research in Human Development, 5*(3), 166–180.

Weaver, H. N. (1997). The challenges of research in Native American communities. *Journal of Social Service Research, 23*(2), 1–15.

Chapter 7
Native American Adult Lifespan Perspectives: Where Power Moves

Michael Tlanusta Garrett, Tarrell Awe Agahe Portman, Cyrus Williams, Lisa Grayshield, Edil Torres Rivera and Mark Parrish

> *"Ah, I see my reflection," I responded proudly. "That's good," he replied confidently. "What you see is your whole life ahead of you. Know that the Great One has a plan for you to be the keeper of everything you see with your eyes, "cause every living thing is your brother and sister." "Even the rocks?" I questioned. "Yes, even the rocks," he answered, "because they have elements of Mother Earth and Father Sky, just as we do."*
>
> *"Remember to give thanks every day for all things that make up the Universe," said my Grandfather. "Always remember to walk the path of Good Medicine and see the good reflected in everything that occurs in life. Life is a lesson, and you must learn the lesson well to see your true reflection in the water."*
>
> J. T. Garrett, Eastern Band of Cherokee (in Garrett 1996b, p. 12)

Demographics: Understanding "the People"

Native Americans—a generalized term referring to American Indian and Alaska Native peoples of this continent—consist of approximately 2.4 million self-identified people with a population that is steadily growing. Although this number represents only 1% of the total population of the United States (US Bureau of the Census 2001), Native people have been described as representing "fifty percent of the diversity" in our country (Hodgkinson 1990, p. 1). Of that total 2.4 million self-identified persons according to the US census, 1.7 million are enrolled tribal members, meaning that, by contrast, there are at least 770,000 nonenrolled people who consider themselves Native. Across the United States, there are more than 563

M. T. Garrett (✉)
Department of Collaborative Support and Intervention, 237 Education Center Annex
University of West Georgia, Carrollton, GA 30118, USA
e-mail: mgarrett@westga.edu

E. C. Chang, C. A. Downey (eds.), *Handbook of Race and Development in Mental Health*,
DOI 10.1007/978-1-4614-0424-8_7, © Springer Science+Business Media, LLC 2012

federally recognized tribes/nations, 228 of which are located in Alaska, and several hundred state-recognized tribes (Russell 2004). In addition, there are approximately 245 tribes in various stages of petitioning the government for federal recognition. Furthermore, there are more than 200 tribes that have become extinct. Of the total population of Native people, 78% exist in urban areas, while the remaining 22% live in rural areas or on any of the 314 federally recognized reservations and 46 state-recognized reservations; and represent a wide-ranging diversity illustrated, for example, by approximately 252 different languages. Overall, Native people come from different tribal groups with different customs, traditions, and beliefs; they live in a variety of settings meaning that the degree of traditionalism versus the degree of acculturation to mainstream American values and cultural standards for behavior is an important consideration in understanding and working with this population (Garrett and Pichette 2000).

Given the wide-ranging diversity of this population, it is important to understand that the term "Native American" encompasses the vastness and essence of tribal traditions represented by hundreds of sovereign nations. The term Native American or Native people (and sometimes, Indian) will be used here to refer generally to those Native people indigenous to the United States, who self-identify as Native American, and maintain cultural identification as a Native person through membership in a Native American tribe recognized by the state or Federal government or through other tribal affiliation and community recognition.

The purpose of this chapter is to present information summarizing research findings on strengths and challenges to mental health in Native adult populations. This will be accomplished by offering a comprehensive overview and understanding of this population through discussion of (a) basic demographic information, (b) strengths that contribute to the resilience of Native adults, and (c) significant challenges Native adults face in maintaining mental health. Finally, a discussion linking strengths and challenges at the level of research and/or policy will be offered in order to better understand how the strengths and resilience of Native adults can be used for the betterment of this population.

Strengths and Resilience: Native Ways

A resilience framework is based on the notion that people have the capacity to overcome adverse life experiences. Masten et al. (1990) define resilience, as "the process of, capacity for or outcome of, successful adaptation despite challenging or threatening circumstances" (p. 426). Operationally, resilience is the result of multiple factors. Kitano and Lewis wrote there are four dynamics often discussed in resilience theory, including risk factors, vulnerability areas, compensatory strategies, and protective factors. Risk factors are the characteristics of individuals and families, social contexts, and the interactions between individuals and their environments these factors are associated with poor developmental outcomes (Glantz and Johnson 1999). Examples of risk factors may include inferior schools, a culture of violence, and/or a lack of parental attention. Protective factors are the attributes of individuals and environments that serve as a buffer between the person and a stressful situation (Glantz and Johnson 1999). These factors can be internal and external, for example, intelligence, self-efficacy, emotional self-regulation, mentorship, and peer support. Vulnerability areas and compensatory strategies are important aspects of resilience. Vulnerability areas are specific aspects of a person that may manifest itself as problematic in a particular situation. Example of vulnerability areas includes gender, socio–economic status, and race/ethnicity. Compensatory strategies are tactics that individuals develop to protect themselves from being vulnerable and that contribute to positive outcomes.

Any of the resiliency factors can be a risk or protective factor depending on the presence or absence of another factor. In other words, risk factors can shape outcomes; however, the individual, family, or community has the ability to ultimately influence the impact of the risk factor through the use of internal and external protective factors (Carlson 2001). An individual's ability to manage the interaction between risk and protective factors, vulnerability areas, and compensatory strategies may be the difference between them overcoming or succumbing to their environmental and situational conditions. By using a resilience theory along with a strengths-based perspective may provide researchers and practitioners with the opportunity to focus more on health promotion and building on and augmenting individual strengths (McShane 1988).

There is a rich history of resilience research that is aligns well with the cultural focus of Native American customs and traditions. Native people have always believed and encouraged the gifts and potential of their people, so in a way they have believed in the concept of resiliency long before it was named resilience (HeavyRunner and Morris 1997). The authors of this chapter assert the idea that resilience theory with a strength-based perspective may be a good match for researchers and helping professionals to adopt when endeavoring to understand and work with this population to reach their potential. A strength-based perspective is not a model or theory, but rather, a collection of principles, ideas and techniques that are evolving (Saleebey 1992, 1997). This perspective honors the power of the self to heal and right itself with the help of the environment, and the need for an alliance with the hope that life can get better (Saleebey 1997). By considering the prevalence of generational poverty and other risk factors to be discussed in a subsequent section, there is a need to identify the strengths and resources of this client population. HeavyRunner and Morris (1997) agree with this assertion saying:

> Cultural resilience is a relatively new term, but it is a concept that predates the so-called 'discovery' of our people. The elders teach us that our children are gifts from the Creator and it is the family, community, school and tribe's responsibility to nurture, protect and guide them. This traditional process is what contemporary researchers, educators and social service providers are now calling resilience. Thus resilience is not new in our people; it is a concept that has been taught for centuries. The word is true but the meaning is old. (p. 28)

Though limited research on resilience of adult Native Americans exists and even less data on identifying the strengths of this high-risk population, several authors have described common core values that characterize Native traditionalism across tribal nations as a source of strengths and protective resources identified in the literature. Some of these Native traditional values (see Table 7.1) include the importance of community contribution, sharing, acceptance, cooperation, harmony and balance, noninterference, extended family, attention to nature, immediacy of time, awareness of the relationship, and a deep respect for elders (Garrett 2001; Garrett and Garrett 1996, 2003; Garrett 1996b, 1998, 1999b; Heinrich et al. 1990; Herring 1999). All in all, these traditional values show the importance of honoring, through harmony and balance, what Native people believe to be a very sacred connection with the energy of life; this is the basis for a traditional Native worldview and spirituality across tribal nations that has served as the foundation for strength and resilience in the face of adversity of all kinds over generations.

Tribe/Nation

Traditional Native people experience a unique relationship between themselves and the tribe. In a very real sense, Native American individuals are extensions of their tribal nation—socially, emotionally, historically, and politically. For many Indian people, cultural identity is rooted in tribal membership, community, and heritage. Many Native nations are matriarchal/matrilineal or matriarchal/patrilineal, but there are those that follow patriarchal/patrilineal ways too (or other variations of gender dominance and tracing of family heritage). This, in turn, affects not only communal and social structure and functioning, but also family/clan structure and functioning. The extended family (at least three generations) and tribal group take precedence over all else. The tribe is an interdependent system of people who perceive themselves as parts of the greater whole rather than a whole consisting of individual parts. Likewise, traditional Native people judge themselves and their actions according to whether or not they are benefiting the tribal community and its continued harmonious functioning.

In mainstream American society, worth and status are based on "what you do" or "what you have achieved." For Native Americans, "who you are is where you come from." Native Americans essentially believe that, "If you know my family, clan, tribe, then you know me." As a result, traditional Native people might be likely to describe some aspect of their family or tribal heritage when asked to talk about themselves.

Family

It has been said that "about the most unfavorable moral judgment an Indian can pass on another person is to say "he acts as if he didn't have any relatives" (DuBray

Table 7.1 Comparison of cultural values and expectations. (Adapted from Garrett and Pichette 2000)

Traditional Native American	Contemporary Mainstream American
Harmony with nature	Power over nature
Cooperation	Competition
Group needs more important than individual needs	Personal goals considered important
Privacy and noninterference; try to control self, not others	Need to control and affect others
Self-discipline both in body and mind	Self-expression and self-disclosure
Participation after observation (only when certain of ability)	Trial and error learning, new skills practiced until they are mastered
Explanation according to nature	Scientific explanation for everything
Reliance on extended family	Reliance on experts
Emotional relationships valued	Concerned mostly with facts
Patience encouraged (allow others to go first)	Aggressive and competitive
Humility	Fame and recognition; winning
Win once, let others win also	Win first prize all of the time
Follow the old ways	Climb the ladder of success; importance of progress and change
Discipline distributed among many; no one person takes blame	Blame one person at cost to others
Physical punishment rare	Physical punishment accepted
Present-time focus	Future-time focus
Time is always with us, things happen in their own time	Clock-watching
Present goals considered important; future accepted as it comes	Plan for future and how to get ahead
Encourage sharing freely and keeping only enough to satisfy present needs	Private property; encourage acquisition of material comfort and saving for the future
Speak softly, at a slower rate	Speak louder and faster
Avoid singling out the listener	Address listener directly (by name)
Interject less	Interrupt frequently
Use less "encouraging signs"	Use verbal encouragement (uh-huh, head nodding)
Delayed response to auditory messages	Use immediate response
Nonverbal communication	Verbal skills highly prized

1985, p. 36). Upon meeting for the first time, many Indian people ask, "Where do you come from? Who's your family? Who do you belong to? Who's your people?" The intent is to find out where they stand in relation to this new person, and what commonality exists. In fact, this is a simple way of building bridges...or recognizing bridges that already exist, but are as yet unknown. Family may or may not consist of blood relations. It is common practice in the Indian way, for instance, to claim another as a relative, thereby welcoming him or her as real family (Red Horse 1980). From that point on, that person is a relative, and that is that. After all, family is a matter of blood, and of spirit.

Wisdom Keepers

Native elders are the keepers of the sacred ways. They are protectors, mentors, teachers, and support-givers, regardless of their "social status." Native communities honor their Indian elders, the "Keepers of the Wisdom," for their lifetime's worth of knowledge and experience. Elders have always played an important part in the continuance of the tribal community by functioning in the role of parent, teacher, community leader, and spiritual guide (Garrett and Garrett 1996). To refer to an elder as grandmother, grandfather, uncle, aunt, "old woman," or "old man" is to refer to a very special relationship that exists with that elder characterized by deep respect and admiration.

In the traditional way, the prevalence of cooperation and sharing in the spirit of community is essential for harmony and balance. It is not unusual for a Native child to be raised in several different households over time. This is generally not due to a lack of caring or responsibility, but because it is an obligation and a pleasure to share in raising and caring for the children in one's family. Grandparents, aunts, uncles, and other members of the community are all responsible for the raising of children, and they take this responsibility very seriously.

There is a very special kind of relationship based on mutual respect and caring between Indian elders and Indian children as one moves through the life circle from "being cared for" to "caring for," as Red Horse (1997) puts it. With an increase in age comes an increase in the sacred obligation to family, clan, and tribe. Native American elders pass down to the children the tradition that their life force carries the spirits of their ancestors. With such an emphasis on connectedness, Native traditions revere children, not only as ones who will carry on the wisdom and traditions, but also as "little people" who are still very close to the spirit world and from whom we have much to learn. Brendtro et al. (1990) relate a story shared with them by Eddie Belleroe, a Cree elder from Alberta, Canada:

> In a conversation with his aging grandfather, a young Indian man asked, "Grandfather, what is the purpose of life?" After a long time in thought, the old man looked up and said, "Grandson, children are the purpose of life. We were once children and someone cared for us, and now it is our time to care". (p. 45)

Harmony and Balance

Different tribal languages have different words or ways of referring to the idea of honoring one's sense of connection, but the meaning is similar across nations in referring to the belief that human beings exist on Mother Earth to be helpers and protectors of life. In Native communities, it is not uncommon, as an example, to hear people use the term "caretaker." Therefore, from the perspective of a traditionalist, to see one's purpose as that of caretaker is to accept responsibility for the gift of life by taking good care of that gift, the gift of life that others have received, and the surrounding beauty of the world in which we live (Garrett 2001).

More or less, the essence of Native American spirituality is about "feeling" (Wilbur 1999a, b). The feeling of connection is something that is available to all of us, though experienced in differing ways. It is important to note that the spiritual beliefs of Native Americans depends on a number of factors including level of acculturation (traditional, marginal, bicultural, assimilated, pan-traditional); geographic region; family structure; religious influences; and tribally specific traditions (Garrett and Pichette 2000; LaFromboise et al. 1993). However, it is possible to generalize, to some extent, about a number of basic beliefs characterizing Native American traditionalism and spirituality across tribal nations. The following, adapted from Locust (1988, pp. 317–318), elaborates on a number of basic Native American spiritual and traditional beliefs:

1. There is a single higher power known as Creator, Great Creator, Great Spirit, or Great One, among other names (this being is sometimes referred to in gender form, but does not necessarily exist as one particular gender or another). There are also lesser beings known as spirit beings or spirit helpers.
2. Plants and animals, like humans, are part of the spirit world. The spirit world exists side by side with, and intermingles with, the physical world. Moreover, the spirit existed in the spirit world before it came into a physical body and will exist after the body dies.
3. Human beings are made up of a spirit, mind, and body. The mind, body, and spirit are all interconnected (see Fig. 7.1); therefore, illness affects the mind and spirit, as well as the body.
4. Wellness is harmony in body, mind, and spirit; unwellness is disharmony in mind, body, and spirit.
5. Natural unwellness is caused by the violation of a sacred social or natural law of creation (e.g., participating in a sacred ceremony while under the influence of alcohol, drugs, or having had sex within four days of the ceremony).
6. Unnatural unwellness is caused by conjuring (witchcraft) from those with destructive intentions.
7. Each of us is responsible for our own wellness by keeping ourselves attuned to self, relations, environment, and universe.

This list of beliefs in Native American spirituality crosses tribal boundaries, but is, by no means, a comprehensive list. It does, however, provide a great deal of insight

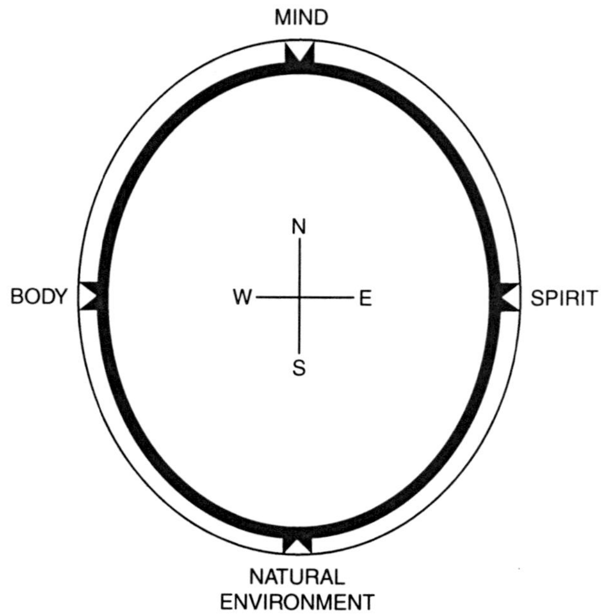

Fig. 7.1 Medicine circle representing the four directions. (From Garrett and Myers 1996)

into some of the assumptions that may be held by a "traditional" Native client with what it means to "walk in step" according to Native American spirituality as a way of seeking harmony and balance in life (Garrett and Wilbur 1999).

Challenges: Facing the Winds

Effective multicultural helping professionals know the importance of understanding diverse cultures from the culture's perspective within the context of oppressive structures, and seeking to work from a strength-based, culturally-sensitive approach. Native Americans, however, have been continually described in the literature as a group of persons facing enormous problems, as illustrated by demographic information (Heinrich et al. 1990; Russell 2004, pp. 101–104) related to issues around health, education, and economic disparity:

Health

- Alcohol mortality is 770% greater than for all other races combined.
- The rate of alcoholism for Native Americans is two times that of the general population.
- Fetal alcohol syndrome (FAS) is 33 times higher than other Americans.

- Homicide is 210% greater than all other Americans.
- Accidental deaths are 280% higher than all other Americans.
- Suicides are 190% higher than all other Americans.
- One in six adolescents has attempted suicide which is four times more often than all other teenagers.

Education

- 52% finish high school.
- 17% attend college.
- 4% graduate from college.
- 2% attend graduate school.

Economic Disparity

- 75% of the Native work force earns less than US$ 7,000 per year.
- Native people show a median income half that of the majority population.
- 45% of Native people live below the poverty level.
- The average unemployment rate among Native people is 45%, a rate that is 3–11 times greater than that of the general population.
- Unemployment on some reservations is as high as 90%.
- In many areas, arrest rates for Native Americans are three times those for African Americans.
- Most housing is inadequate and substandard; on the Navajo reservation, for example:
  - 46% have no electricity
  - 54% have no indoor plumbing
  - 82% live without a telephone.

Some of the possible challenges that Native people bring with them to the counseling process are evident when one absorbs the implications of the statistics described above. Keeping this information in mind to help provide a specific context for the struggle that many Native people face in day-to-day living, it is also important to understand the historical context and stories that are involved in this struggle for survival for many.

Surviving "History": Intergenerational Grief and Trauma

In order to better understand issues related to mental health for Native people, it is important to begin with the influence of the historical context from which Native individuals and their families come. As such, it is important to consider the powerful influence of what many Native people refer to as generational grief and trauma, and the effect it has had on Native worldview. Many authors have described the deliberate attempts throughout United States history by mainstream American institutions, such as government agencies, schools, and churches to destroy the Native American institutions of family, clan, and tribal structure, religious belief systems and practices, customs, and traditional way of life (Deloria 1988; Heinrich et al. 1990; Locust 1988; Reyhner and Eder 1992). Deloria (1988, p. 166) commented, "When questioned by an anthropologist about what the Indians called America before the White man came, an Indian said simply, Ours." Characterized by institutional racism and discrimination, dominant culture has a long history of opposition to Native cultures and the attempts to assimilate Native people, having a long-lasting effect on the cultures and Native people's way of life (Deloria 1988; Locust 1988).

It was not until 1924 that the US government recognized the citizenship of Native Americans—no longer a threat to national expansion—through passage of the Citizenship Act (Deloria 1988). In addition, Native Americans were not granted religious freedom until 1978 when the American Indian Religious Freedom Act was passed, overturning the Indian Religious Crimes Code of 1889, and guaranteeing Native people the constitutional right to exercise their traditional religious practices for the first time in a century (Deloria 1988; Loftin 1989). In more recent times, massive efforts to "civilize" Native people through government supported, religiously run boarding schools and the Relocation Programs of the 1950s have created an historical context of generational trauma and cultural discontinuity (Hirschfelder and Kreipe de Montano 1993). These events have affected Native Americans psychologically, economically, and socially for generations. From a historical and contemporary perspective, oppression is and continues to be a very real experience for Native people.

Acculturation

Although many of the core traditional values permeate the lives of Native Americans across tribal groups (see Table 7.1), Native Americans are not a completely homogeneous group, differing greatly in their level of acceptance of and commitment to specific tribal values, beliefs, and practices (Garrett and Garrett 1996). Native individuals differ in terms of their level of acculturation, geographic setting (urban, rural, or reservation), and socioeconomic status (Choney et al. 1995; Garrett and Pichette 2000; Herring 1999). The following levels of acculturation, defined as "the cultural change that occurs when two or more cultures are in persistent contact" (Garcia and Ahler 1992, p. 24), have been identified for Native Americans:

1. *Traditional*—May or may not speak English, but generally speak and think in their native language; hold only traditional values and beliefs and practice only traditional tribal customs and methods of worship.
2. *Marginal*—May speak both the native language and English; may not, however, fully accept the cultural heritage and practices of their tribal group nor fully identify with mainstream cultural values and behaviors.
3. *Bicultural*—Generally accepted by dominant society and tribal society/nation; simultaneously able to know, accept, and practice both mainstream values/behaviors and the traditional values and beliefs of their cultural heritage.
4. *Assimilated*—Accepted by dominant society; embrace only mainstream cultural values, behaviors, and expectations.
5. *Pantraditional*—Assimilated Native Americans who have made a conscious choice to return to the "old ways." They are generally accepted by dominant society, but seek to embrace previously lost traditional cultural values, beliefs, and practices of their tribal heritage. Therefore, they may speak both English and their native tribal language. (Garrett and Pichette 2000)

These five levels represent a continuum along which any given Native American individual may fall. Regardless of blood quantum, the most popular and most deceiving means of determining a person's "Indianness" and degree of traditionalism comes not only from ethnic heritage, but also from his or her life experiences and life choices (Garrett and Garrett 1994). Acculturation for Native Americans is not a positive aspect, because it is a reminder of forced assimilation, and the loss of traditions and values (Atkinson et al. 1998). It means conforming to the dominant culture, which goes against many Native American values and traditions. This conforming leaves many Native Americans living in two worlds separated between their own ethnic communities and mainstream society, which creates an even bigger problem when seeking help (Moran 1999). Having to live in two worlds causes Native people to be bicultural, which can be difficult. Although it can be helpful in some aspects such as education, it may cause confusion and rejection, because of the fear of leaving behind certain aspects of the Native American culture (Atkinson et al. 1998; Weaver 1999). Therefore, geographic contextual issues may take on heightened importance for counselors and researchers due to cultural incongruity.

Discussion: Native Strengths and Challenges in Context

Although Native Americans face obstacles, this ethnic group also possesses many strengths that have helped them to survive incredible adversity over generations of being the target of racism, forced relocation, and genocide (Brave Heart and DeBruyn 1998). Today, this population is not just surviving, but thriving in many areas as evidenced by statistics that indicate nearly 55% of all Native Americans own their own home, 75% age 25 and older have at least a high school diploma, and 14% have a bachelor's degree (Goodluck 2002). In 2003, Goodluck conducted a meta-analysis of research articles that focused on identifying the strengths of Native Americans. The goal of the study was to identify strengths, as well as present a more holistic and balanced view of Native Americans. Results of the analysis yielded 42 specific strengths of Native Americans that were combined into three categories: extended family, spirituality, and social connections (see Table 7.2). These are significant to acknowledge within an entire body of literature about Native people that tends to focus on implicit struggles and obstacles rather than cultural strength and resilience.

Much of the literature on Native Americans emphasizes the high-risk behaviors and the negative consequences that these behaviors have on the physical and mental health of this population. Likewise, various practitioners, such as counselors and social workers who work with this population often times focus on "fixing" the maladaptive behaviors their Native clients struggle to overcome rather than considering a more holistic perspective that might include cultural, environmental, and historical influences. It is suggested that new theories and perspectives be adopted in order to facilitate a shift from addressing the negative aspects of Native Americans, to a theory that is consistent with this populations traditions and has a more hopeful viewpoint (Neumann et al. 1991). Nonetheless, the struggles Native adults endure continue and the need for appropriate, effective, culturally-responsive help is pervasive.

Help-seeking behaviors related to health care of Native people include seeking counseling services, such as mental health, rehabilitation, substance abuse, and school counseling. Native American health care still falls well below all other US racial groups (Provan and Carson 2000). These health care needs from US governmental statistics indicate mortality rates due to behavioral health concerns of alcoholism, accidents, suicide, and homicide are greater than the 1993 age-adjusted all race US population statistics (Indian Health Services 1997). Mental health issues are the fourth leading cause of hospitalization among American Indians 15–44 years of age and the fifth leading cause for ambulatory visits for indigenous peoples 25–44 years of age (Provan and Carson 2000, p. 17).

Originally, the federal government established a program to provide health services to Native American peoples through a treaty. However, today these Indian Health Service (IHS) facilities are located primarily near recognized Native American Indian communities in states with large Native American populations. The IHS is responsible for assuring access to high quality care depending on need; to assist tribes in developing more control over services offered through training and management, assist Native American tribes in accessing entitled programs. In addition, IHS is responsible for inpatient and ambulatory clinical services, community and preventative medicine, manpower development programs, and health facility construction. Prevention, treatment, and rehabilitation services are offered on a more comprehensive level, which includes optometry, dental, drug and alcohol, mental health, and referral service (Pfefferbaum et al. 1998). The services provided through

Table 7.2 Summary of information

Demographics	Strengths	Challenges	Recommendations
Total population • Approximately 2.4 million self-identified Native Americans (1.7 million enrolled tribal members; 770,000 nonenrolled people) • Represents roughly 1% of the total US population of the United	Extended Family • Group belonging • Relational focus • Personal relationships • Honoring and caring for elders • Sense of community and common history together	Health, Education, and Economic disparities • Alcoholism rate two times that of general population • 52% finish high school • 75% of the Native work force earns less than US$7,000 per year	Develop new theories • Literature tends to emphasize high risk behaviors and negative consequences on physical and mental health • Practitioners often focus on "fixing" maladaptive behaviors rather than considering more holistic perspective including cultural, environmental, and historical influences • New theories can be adopted to shift from negative aspects to perspective consistent with Native culture and traditions
Nations • More than 563 federally recognized tribes/nations • 228 of these are located in Alaska, • Several hundred state-recognized tribes/nations	Social connections • Helping each other • Artistic behaviors and valuing of creative expression • Sharing work • Caring for each other	Intergenerational grief and trauma • United States did not recognize citizenship of Native Americans until 1924 • Not granted religious freedom until 1978 through American Indian Religious Freedom Act • Government supported, religiously-run boarding schools and Relocation Programs of 1950s	Understand help-seeking behaviors • Studies have revealed perception of help-seeking outside of the native communities as sign of weakness • Many native Americans seek help through traditional healing practices if available • Acculturation and tribal affiliation must be understood as context; more insight into acculturation is needed when considering Native Americans living in rural, urban, or suburban geographic contexts

Table 7.2 (continued)

Demographics	Strengths	Challenges	Recommendations
Location/Language • 78% of total Native population live in urban areas • 22% live in rural areas or on any of the 314 federally recognized reservations and 46 state-recognized reservations; • Approximately 252 different languages	Spirituality • Emphasis on harmony and balance • Tribal affiliation • Kinship • Tribal identity • Traditions	Current social and Political issues • Identity/blood quantum • Natural resources/treaty rights • Religious freedom • Mascot issues and cultural perception • Gaming • Cultural/language preservation	Explore systemic, Environmental, and other contextual factors • Historical factors • Isolation • Generational splits • Sociodemographics • Physiology and health • Social facilitation • Coping mechanisms • Noninterference and respect

IHS focus on treaty lands not general geographic living areas, thus pushing Native Americans to live on or near such areas to receive health care services.

Current Conditions

According to LaFromboise (1993), mental health providers lack recognition of the special needs of ethnic minorities. Cultural ignorance is the number one reason for dropout rates and underutilization of help-seeking behaviors (LaFromboise 1993). Awareness of issues is an important aspect that is often overlooked by health providers. Identifying issues unique to Native American cultures and understanding that all tribes are diverse with respect to geographic area, language, customs, religions, and family structures is important (Brucker and Perry 1998). An examination of research related to Native Americans is necessary to support the need for more diversified descriptive information in publications related to this population—especially geographic context and tribal affiliation.

Weaver (1999) reported on a 1995–1996 needs assessment conducted by Native American researchers with participants from a Native American reservation. Data were gathered from 13 focus groups that consisted of 3–25 participants and 23 individual interviews. The groups were asked about the agency services that were offered and how helpful they were. The result indicated 25% of the community including staff where unfamiliar with these services. Yet the number of people that stated the programs were helpful had never even used the services. While other members of the community stated that some programs were not helpful at all because of alienation, political divisions, and cultural insensitivity. Other reasons included lack of training and service delivery because of a limited number of qualified people. The lack of outreach and communication made helpful programs ineffective. This study presented the perspective of Native Americans in a set geographic context (reservation) and found services need to be addressed by proactively seeking funding to meet these needs and not to offer services based on the most available types of funding (Weaver 1999).

Another study by Earle (1998) included 45 American Indian recipients of mental health services (neither tribal affiliations nor geographic contexts were provided) and 6,064 White participants. This study revealed that Native Americans differed greatly from their White counterparts. Demographic characteristics, attitudes, and differences within response rates of Native Americans and Whites differed. It is interesting to note findings from this study point out the definition of "who is Indian" has a great impact when seeking help, because of federal recognition. However, the study had only 45 Native Americans participating which was less than 1% of the entire sample. The author concluding that blood quantum was a significant indicator of help-seeking behaviors appears to be far reaching. A study with more equally distributed population groups compared mental health by using a questionnaire of 66 Native Americans and 93 White undergraduate students. White students were found more likely to associate with poor mental health rather than Native American students when having visions, communicating with spirits, guiding one's life accordingly, and seeing and hearing things that others do not see or hear were present. Because of the spiritual, cultural, and traditional contexts, Native Americans are more likely to be wrongfully diagnosed; this may affect help-seeking behaviors (Earle 1998). However, again tribal affiliations of the Native students are not provided or their geographic context is not supplied. This study ignores the spirituality differences found between tribal affiliations.

Another study was done to explore help-seeking behaviors of Native American high school students. A total of 139 Native American students were surveyed (Gates et al. 1996). Results show Native American boys and girls differed in that boys tended to seek help from their family (parent, friend, or relative), outside resources (teachers, counselors, and school staff), or no one (most often reported). Girls chose to seek help from a parent (most often reported), a friend, no one, and a teacher. Most of the students turned to outside sources of help for academic and career rather than personal reasons. Only one person reported by using community resources such as IHS. High self-esteem was found to be a barrier to seeking help from community and other helping professionals and was a factor in reduced help-seeking behaviors. These findings may be related to perceiving help-seeking outside of the native communities as a sign of weakness. An indication that many Native Americans are seeking help either through traditional healing practices, such as medicine men or women or spiritual healing through various ceremonies was also given (Nadler 1983; Gates et al. 1996). This reference provides insight into the cultural behaviors of Native Americans. Culture includes those values, beliefs, perceptions, and traditions that are learned or socially acquired. Processes of thinking, feeling, or acting, which is patterned or repetitive, are also included (Harris 1987; Haviland 1989). This study relied on context and tribal affiliation as an underlying premise but calls for more insight into acculturation.

Revisiting the Spirit: A Call for Research Related to Rural Native Americans

The research on multiculturalism has focused on Native American (all tribal affiliations and Nations) as one homogeneous population. This approach has failed to consider "within group" differences by affiliation and geographic context. For example, Native American children who live and grow up in rural areas may be involved in many cultural activities, such as pow wows, dances, ceremonial events, health fairs, and family cultural gatherings. This rural "Indianness" or manner of embracing cultural heritage may be far removed from the life ways of Native Americans living on reservations or in urban areas. This difference may also manifest in the care and consideration of elders within rural Native American communities. How are elders treated differently by families or tribal administration centers based on their living in rural contexts? What are the helping seeking behaviors of Native American in various geographic contexts or by various tribal affiliations?

Helping professionals as well as other community caregivers tend to view Native American populations from a stereotypical, homogeneous population rather than recognizing that within the modern context of rural, urban, suburban, and reservation settings are a varied mix of people from different nations and tribal affiliations, each with their own unique sets of problems and needs. This not only stymies the delivery of needed services, it sends a message that fails to support diversity in research or a focus on "within group" differences based on both affiliation and geographic realities. It is time to put forth a call for research related to how Native Americans face cultural issues within public institutions in rural contexts, such as schools, health care facilities, and community/rehabilitation counseling agencies. The following questions although not inclusive may begin the discussion or encourage researchers to conduct further investigations:

- What is the social justice role of health professionals in promoting research and counseling services that are contextually relevant (rural, suburban, urban, and reservation) to Native Americans?
- Does the public health profession including mental health professionals maintain an obligation to advocate for American Indian children and elders? If so why does the research focus primarily on young to middle adulthood in the lifespan?
- Are Native American elders receiving appropriate counseling and health care services across all living contexts?
- How are differences between socio–economic status, poverty and class being addressed among various groups of Native American living in rural, suburban, and urban contexts?

Summary and Conclusion: The Gift of Stories

The overall purpose of this chapter was to present information summarizing research findings on strengths and challenges to mental health in Native adult populations. A comprehensive overview and understanding of this population was offered through (a) basic demographic information, (b) strengths that contribute to the resilience of Native adults, (c) significant challenges Native adults face in maintaining mental health, and (d) a discussion linking strengths and challenges at the level of research and/or policy in order to better understand how the strengths and resilience of Native adults can be used for the betterment of this population.

Through culturally-sensitive forms of intervention, as we examine the overall state of research and policy as it relates to Native adults, we turn to an approach that is more congruent with traditional Native worldviews, we listen to the life-stories of Native elders, adults, and youngsters alike, and begin to understand where power moves. With this, we discover a better sense of where Native people have come from and where they are going. We see the powerful influences of history, social and political issues, acculturation, values and beliefs, spirituality, cultural symbolism and practices, and communication style. We see the continuity of the Circle in stories of images and experiences that flow from the heart, and we begin to arrive at a better understanding of where we stand in relation to everything around us, and in relation to our clients. We begin to understand the importance of attending to the stories—the meanings, language, experiences, images, and themes—of our Native clients. And we begin to learn, as it has traditionally been taught by so many Native elders, that true learning is a life-long process, just as a story unfolds, and offers the gift of its life to us. Stories carry the words, ghosts, dreams, and spirit of Native life. The following quote from a Native elder is illustrative of the power of tradition and community to many American Indians. He was asked to describe who he was as a Native person:

> Well, I think the stories probably gave me a sense of connection with the Indian side more than anything else. What I remember most of all is everything that my grandfather ever said because to me, he must have been the tallest man in the world. I was such a little boy, and I'd look up at him, and he was tall, tall and slender. Boy, I thought he was such a fine man. The first thing he'd say every time I'd see him was 'CeoTsayoga', in other words, hello there little bird, how you doing. The first thing he would always do is he'd put me up on his shoulders, I remember that, and take me down to the creek bank. He'd say, 'Come on, let's go to the creek bank...gonna do some fishin'. I never fished. I never got a chance to fish. I don't know that he ever fished. It's like if he had a chance to take me fishing, that was a chance to tell me stories, teach me values. And one that I do remember very much was when we'd look in the water because I really enjoyed as a little kid just looking at the little minnows, seeing the fish in the water. And he'd let me look for hours, and I don't know whether he was fishing or not, I think he was. We never brought home any fish. I think he would always put the fish back, even if he caught one. (J. T. Garrett, Eastern Band of Cherokee, in Garrett 1996a)

References

Atkinson D. R., Morten G, & Sue D. W. (1998). American Indian Mental Health Policy. In Teresa LaFromboise (Ed.), *Counseling American Minorities*, (pp. 137–158). United States: A Times Mirror Higher Education Group Inc.

Brave Heart, M. Y. & DeBruyn, L. M. (1998). The American Indian holocausts: Healing historical unresolved grief. *American Indian and Alaska Native Mental Health Research, 8* (2), 55–78.

Brendtro, L. K., Brokenleg, M., & Van Bockern, S. (1990). *Reclaiming youth at risk: Our hope for the future*. Bloomington: National Education Service.

Brucker P. S., & Perry B. J., (1998). American Indians: Presenting concerns and consideration for family therapists. *The American Journal of Family Therapy,* 26(4), 307–319.

Carlson D. J. (2001). *Development and Validation of a College Resilience Questionnaire. Dissertation Abstracts International, A (Humanities and Social Sciences), 62*, 2025.

Choney, S. K., Berryhill-Paapke, E., & Robbins, R. R. (1995). The acculturation of American Indians:Developing frameworks for research and practice. In J. G. Ponterotto, J. M. Casas, L. A. Suzuki, & C. M. Alexander (Eds.), *Handbook of multicultural counseling,* (pp. 73–92). Thousand Oaks: Sage.

Deloria, V. Jr. (1988). *Custer died for your sins: An Indian manifesto*. Norman: University of Oklahoma Press.

DuBray, W. H. (1985). American Indian values: Critical factor in casework. *Social Casework: The Journal of Contemporary Social Work, 66,* 30–37.

Earle K. A., (1998). Cultural diversity and mental health: The Haudenosaunee of New York State. *Social Work Research, 22*(2), 89–99.

Garcia, R. L., & Ahler, J. G. (1992). Indian education: Assumptions, ideologies, strategies. In J. Reyhner (Ed.), *Teaching American Indian students,* (pp. 13–32). Norman: University of Oklahoma Press.

Garrett, J. T. (2001). *Meditations with the Cherokee: Prayers, songs, and stories of healing and harmony.* Rochester: Bear & Company.

Garrett, J. T., & Garrett, M. T. (1994). The path of good medicine: Understanding and counseling Native Americans. *Journal of Multicultural Counseling and Development, 22,* 134–144.

Garrett, J. T., & Garrett, M. T. (1996). *Medicine of the Cherokee: The way of right relationship.* Santa Fe: Bear & Company.

Garrett, M. T. (1996a). "Two people": An American Indian narrative of bicultural identity. *Journal of American Indian Education, 36,* 1–21.

Garrett, M. T. (1996b). Reflection by the riverside: The traditional education of Native American children. *Journal of Humanistic Education and Development, 35,* 12–28.

Garrett, M. T. (1998). *Walking on the wind: Cherokee teachings for harmony and balance.* Santa Fe: Bear & Company.

Garrett, M. T. (1999a). Soaring on the wings of the eagle: Wellness of Native American high school students. *Professional School Counseling, 3,* 57–64.

Garrett, M. T. (1999b). Understanding the "Medicine" of Native American traditional values: An integrative review. *Counseling and Values, 43,* 84–98.

Garrett, M. T., & Garrett, J. T. (2003). *Native American faith in America.* New York: Facts on File.

Garrett, M. T., Garrett, J. T., & Brotherton, D. (2001). Inner circle/outer circle: Native American group technique. *Journal for Specialists in Group Work, 26,* 17–30.

Garrett, M. T., Garrett, J. T., Wilbur, M., Roberts-Wilbur, J., & Torres-Rivera, E. (2005). Native American humor as spiritual tradition: Implications for counseling. *Journal of Multicultural Counseling and Development, 33,* 194–204.

Garrett, M. T., & Pichette, E. F. (2000). Red as an apple: Native American acculturation and counseling with or without reservation. *Journal of Counseling and Development, 78,* 3–13.

Garrett, M. T., & Wilbur, M. P. (1999). Does the worm live in the ground? Reflections on Native American spirituality. *Journal of Multicultural Counseling and Development, 27,* 193–206.

Gates D. B., Howard-Pitney B., LaFromboise T. (1996). Help-seeking behavior of Native American indian high school students. *Professional Psychology: Research and Practice,* 27(5), 495–499.

Goodluck, C. (2002, December). Native American children and youth well-being indicators: A strengths perspective. Portland: National Indian Child Welfare Association. http://www.casey.org/NR/rdonlyres/F8D88BB3-CF5B-4317-B147C9E1CA138725/119/casey_nicwa_wellbeing_indicators.pdf

Glantz, M. D., & Johnson, J. L. (1999). *Resilience and development: Positive life adaptations.* New York, : Kluwer Academic/Plenum Publishers.

Harris, B. J. (1987). *Cultural Anthropology.* (2nd ed.). New York: Harper Row.

Haviland, W. A. (1989). *Anthropology.* (5th ed.). Orlando: Holt, Rinehart and Winston.

HeavyRunner, I. & Morris, J. S. (1997). Traditional Native culture and resilience. *Research and Practice, 5*(1), 28–33.

Heinrich, R. K., Corbine, J. L., & Thomas, K. R. (1990). Counseling Native Americans. *Journal of Counseling and Development, 69,* 128–133.

Herring, R. D. (1999). *Counseling with Native American Indians and Alaska Natives: Strategies for helping professionals.* Thousand Oaks: Sage.

Hirschfelder, A., & Kreipe de Montano, M. (1993). *The Native American almanac: A portrait of Native America today.* New York: Macmillan.

Hodgkinson, H. L. (1990). *The demographics of American Indians: One percent of the people; fifty percent of the diversity.* Washington, DC: Institute for Educational Leadership.

Indian Health Service (1997). Trends in Indian Health 1997; General Mortality Statistics. [on-line]. http://www.ihs.gov/publicinfo/publications/trends97/tds97pt3.pdf. Accessed 5 Dec 2003.

LaFromboise T. D. (1993). American Indian Mental Health Policy. In D. R. Atkinson, A. Morten, & D. W. Sue (Eds.), *Counseling American Indian Minorities*, (p. 123–144). New York: Wiley.
LaFromboise, T. D., Coleman, H. L. K., & Gerton, J. (1993). Psychological impact of biculturalism: Evidence and theory. *Psychological Bulletin, 114,* 395–412.
Locust, C. (1988). Wounding the spirit: Discrimination and traditional American Indian belief systems. *Harvard Educational Review, 58,* 315–330.
Loftin, J. D. (1989). Anglo-American jurisprudence and the Native American tribal quest for religious freedom. *American Indian Culture and Research Journal, 13,* 1–52.
Masten, A. S., Best, K. M., Garmezy, N. (1990). Resilience and development: Contributions from the study of children who overcome adversity. *Development and Psychopathology, 2,* 425–444.
McShane, D. (1988). An analysis of mental health research with American Indian youth. *Journal of Adolescence, 11,* 87–116.
Moran, J. R. (1999). Measuring Ethnic Identity among American Indian Adolescents: A factor analytic study. *Journal of Adolescent Research, 14*(4), 405–426.
Nadler, A. (1983). Personal Characteristics and Help Seeking. *New Directions in Helping.* In B. M. Depaulo, A. Nadler, & J. D. Fisher (Eds.), (p. 303–340). New York: Academic Press.
Neumann, A. K., Mason, V., Chase, E., & Albaugh, B. (1991). Factors associated with success among southern Cheyenne and Arapaho Indians. *Journal of Community Health, 16*(2), 103–115.
Pfefferbaum, R. L., Pfefferum B., Rhoades E. R., Strickland R. J. (1998). Providing health care needs of Native Americans: Policy, programs, procedures, and practices. *American Indian Law Review, 21*(2), 211–258.
Provan, K. G., & Carson, L. M. P. (2000). Behavioral health funding for Native Americans in Arizona: Policy implications for states and tribes. *The Journal of Behavioral Health Services & Research, 27,* 17–28.
Red Horse, J. G. (1980). Indian elders: Unifiers of families. *Social Casework, 61,* 490–493.
Red Horse, J. G. (1997). Traditional American Indian family systems. *Families, Systems, & Health, 15,* 243–250.
Reyhner, J., & Eder, J. (1992). A history of Indian education. In J. Reyhner (Ed.), *Teaching American Indian students* (pp. 33–58). Norman: University of Oklahoma Press.
Russell, G. (2004). *American Indian facts of life: A profile of today's tribes and reservations.* Phoenix: Native Data Network.
Saleebey, D. (1992). The strengths perspective in social work practice: Extensions and cautions. *Social Work, 41*(3), 296–304.
Saleebey, D. (1997). *The strengths perspective in social work practice*. White Plains: Longman Publishers.
United States Bureau of the Census. (2001). *2000 census counts of American Indians, Eskimos, or Aleuts and American Indian and Alaska Native areas*. Washington: Author.
Weaver, H. N. (1999). Assessing the needs of Native American communities: A north eastern example. *Evaluation and Program Planning, 22*(2), 155–161.
Wilbur, M. P. (1999a). The rivers of a wounded heart. *Journal of Counseling and Development, 77,* 47–50.
Wilbur, M. P. (1999b). Finding balance in the winds. *Journal for Specialists in Group Work, 24,* 342–353.

Chapter 8
Psychology of Older American Indians and Alaska Natives: Strengths and Challenges to Maintaining Mental Health

Sarah Poff Roman, Lori L. Jervis and Spero M. Manson

Introduction

Relatively little is known about mental health among American Indians and Alaska Natives (AI/ANs) of any age, and even less about the mental health status of older AI/ANs. Manson (1995b, p. 140) observed more than a decade ago that "… our recognition and understanding of health and mental health problems of older Indians have been slow to mature in spite of evidence of extensive need"; unfortunately, this statement remains true today. Much of the extant literature on Native elder mental health is based on small studies with those living in rural and reservation settings, and the bulk of this work is increasingly dated. Ageism is likely at least partially responsible for continuing knowledge gaps in the area of Native elder mental health, as are assumptions that AI/AN mental health needs are sufficiently met through the Indian Health Service (IHS). Neglect of this area could also be due, in part, to the complexity of conducting research with a population that is extremely diverse and who, accordingly, may have varied processes for obtaining approvals to conduct research. Likewise, relatively small numbers of elders within the overall Native population makes drawing a sufficient sample for larger scale quantitative studies challenging. Regardless of the myriad reasons why the mental health of older AI/ANs has drawn little attention compared to research conducted with many other populations, as well as Native youth and adults, this chapter describes a number of issues unique to AI/ANs that illustrate why more attention to this line of research is crucial.

S. P. Roman (✉)
University of Colorado Denver, 13199 E. Montview Blvd., Suite 400,
Aurora, CO 80045-7201, USA
e-mail: Sarah.Roman@ucdenver.edu

E. C. Chang, C. A. Downey (eds.), *Handbook of Race and Development in Mental Health*,
DOI 10.1007/978-1-4614-0424-8_8,

Chapter Focus

This chapter presents information on mental health issues among older American Indian and Alaska Native (AI/AN) adults, focusing on sociohistorical factors, environmental factors, and barriers to help-seeking as major challenges to the maintenance of mental health in this group. We also describe several strengths that contribute to resilience among Native elders, including support systems, ethnic and cultural identity, and spirituality. We provide recommendations for capitalizing upon these strengths in order to address the challenges faced by Native elders, including the importance of engaging community networks in the research process and incorporating Native cultural elements into biomedical mental health care. The chapter concludes with recommendations for future research, including the need to develop culturally relevant instrumentation and methods specific to this population.

Demographic Characteristics of Older AI/AN Adults

The AI/AN population, totaling 4.1 million people (or 1.5% of the US population), arguably comprises the most diverse group to be assigned to one ethnic category (U.S. Census Bureau 2002). There are currently 561 federally recognized tribes (Bureau of Indian Affairs 2005), several of which are comprised of multiple culturally distinct bands or subgroups. AI/AN tribes vary in terms of culture, language, religion, family/community structure, and degree of acculturation. The AI/AN population is younger than the general population, with only 5.6% over the age of 65, compared to 12.4% of the total US population (U.S. Department of Commerce & U.S. Census Bureau 2006). AI/ANs over the age of 65 comprise 0.4% of the total US population, a number which is projected to increase to 0.6% by 2050 (Administration on Aging 2000). With regard to educational attainment, 29.1% of the adult AI/AN population (age 25+) has less than 12 years of formal education, and only 11.5% holds a bachelor's degree or higher (U.S. Department of Commerce & U.S. Census Bureau 2006). In comparison, 19.6% of the US total adult population has less than a high school degree, and 24.4% holds postsecondary degrees (U.S. Department of Commerce & U.S. Census Bureau 2006).

The percentage of AI/ANs living below the poverty level (25.7%) is more than twice the rate for the general population (12.4%) (U.S. Department of Commerce & U.S. Census Bureau 2006). Among older AI/AN adults (65+) in 2000, 23.5% were below the poverty level compared to 8.2% of older whites (U.S. Census Bureau 2005). These conditions have a significant impact on older generations, who often find themselves responsible for raising grandchildren and contributing to the financial survival of extended families (Jervis and Manson 2006).

As will be discussed, there are significant challenges to collecting mental health data specific to older AI/ANs; these include language barriers, socioeconomic factors, historical factors, geography, and culturally specific conceptions of mental health and aging. As a result, much of what we know about the mental health of

Table 8.1 AI-SUPERPFP DSM-IV lifetime prevalence rates for oldest age cohort (45–54) (weighted)

	Overall number with disorder (unweighted)	NP males (%)	NP females (%)	SW males (%)	SW females (%)	Total both sites and genders (%)
Alcohol abuse/dependence	227	47.2	32.5	41.7	11.0	32.7
Post-traumatic stress disorder	138	13.3	24.4	13.6	23.6	19.0
Major depressive disorder/dysthymia	76	8.8	12.1	4.6	12.8	9.8
Generalized anxiety disorder/panic disorder	62	6.0	6.5	8.0	10.2	7.9
Drug abuse/dependence	34	7.4	5.2	7.2	1.5	5.2
Any disorder	741	53.2	45.7	46.8	36.7	45.4

older AI/ANs comes from service utilization data rather than community-based empirical studies (see Moss et al. 2004). This introduces a new level of complexity, as these populations appear to use mental health services at a much lower rate than the prevalence of disorders would portend (Manson 2000).

Psychiatric Epidemiology. While attention to AI/AN mental health issues in general has increased, the majority of studies have been small-scale, community-based, and targeted to youth and substance-abuse issues. One exception to this rule, although not focused on elders, was the American Indian Service Utilization, Psychiatric Epidemiology, Risk, and Protective Factors Project (AI-SUPERPFP). With a relatively large, population-representative adult sample (N=3,046), this study investigated the prevalence of several psychiatric disorders among two tribal groups: one in the Northern Plains and the other in the Southwest, as well as help-seeking behaviors and protective factors (Beals et al. 2006).

One of AI-SUPERPFP's most significant findings was that alcohol disorders and post-traumatic stress disorder are more common among AIs than other populations and that comorbidity between depressive and/or anxiety disorders and substance disorders is especially prevalent (Beals et al. 2005). Among the oldest age cohort (ages 45–54 at the time of sampling), as in the study as a whole, alcohol disorders predominated, followed by PTSD and depressive disorders (Table 8.1). While limited to middle-aged adults, these findings provide some indication of the extent of psychiatric disorders among older AIs.

No large-scale, population-based psychiatric epidemiological studies have specifically focused on AI elders. Some smaller prevalence studies have been conducted, although many of these date to the 1980s–early 1990s and focus on depression. For instance, over 30% of Native elder outpatients at an urban IHS clinic were found to have significant depressive symptoms (Manson 1992). Additionally, among a sample of 309 Great Lakes Native elders, 18% were depressed by using a traditional cut-off score for the Center for Epidemiological Studies Depression Scale (CES-D); these depressive symptoms were associated with impaired function (Curyto et al. 1999, 1998). However, closer scrutiny of the factor structure of the CES-D when administered to this sample raised questions of how accurately the measure assessed depression among older AIs (Chapleski et al. 1997).

Little is known about the prevalence of psychiatric disorders other than depression among older AIs, although significant psychiatric symptoms were found among 20% of older Natives at a primary care clinic on the Navajo Reservation (Goldwasser and Badger 1989). Almost nothing is known about the prevalence of mental health issues among ANs, young or old.

There are indications that, at least in some Native communities, cognitive impairment may play a significant role among older AI/ANs. In a study of cognitive function among 140 Community-dwelling Northern Plains Native elders, nearly 11% scored more than two standard deviations below performance expectations (a conservative standard for possible cognitive impairment) on the Mini-Mental State Exam; 28% did so on the Mattis Dementia Rating Scale (Jervis et al. 2007a). Cognitive impairment was found to be comorbid with other psychiatric conditions, with 35.7% of elders in this study reporting lifetime alcohol problems; 30.0% reporting past-year depressive and 9.3% past-year anxiety symptoms.

Considerable cognitive, psychiatric, and behavioral morbidity was found in a study of a Northern Plains tribal nursing home (Jervis and Manson 2007); non-Alzheimer's disease dementia, cognitive impairment, anxious symptomatology, and resistance to care were highly prevalent. Moreover, tribal nursing home residents appeared to be underdiagnosed for dementia and anxiety and undertreated for depressive and psychotic/agitated symptoms (Jervis et al. 2007b).

In summary, the extant literature suggests that considerable psychiatric morbidity may exist among some older Natives, but our knowledge base in this area remains quite undeveloped.

Challenges to Maintaining Mental Health

While a number of factors contribute positively to the mental health of Native elders, the challenges faced by this population are numerous and severe. Studies, although limited in scope and number, suggest that older Natives are at higher risk for mental disorders than other ethnic minority groups in the United States (Nelson et al. 1992). The Native population, as a whole, suffers disproportionately from mental health issues. According to the National Health Interview Survey (1999–2003), 8.2% of all AI/AN adults reported experiencing serious psychological distress over the past 30 days, compared to only 2.8% of White adults (Barnes et al. 2005). From a provider perspective, 10 out of 12 IHS Service Areas identified mental health as the top health priority among their populations in 2001 (Johnson and Cameron 2001).

Sociohistorical Factors

> … I feel like I've been carrying a weight around that I've inherited. If I knew how to let it go, I would … I think we're all inhibited by the sense of responsibility and the sense of guilt … we blame ourselves for our loss of tradition. I feel a sense of responsibility to undo the pain of the past. I can't separate myself from the past, the history and the trauma. It has been paralyzing to us as a group (the American Indian people). (Yellow Horse Brave Heart and DeBruyn 1998, p. 72)

As is true of any population, the current experiences and circumstances of Native elders cannot be understood without consideration of historical factors, at the individual and cohort level (Somervell et al. 1995). Many of the oldest cohorts of AI/ANs are survivors of forced acculturation into the dominant society and a subsequent loss of culture, language, religion, and identity (Johnson and Cameron 2001). Many of these elders lived through the boarding school era, which stripped AI children of their cultural identities and traditions by removing them from their families (Johnson and Cameron 2001). In these settings, some children were subjected to abuse (physical, emotional, and/or sexual), forbidden from speaking Native languages, and dressed in government-issued uniforms (Jackson and Chapleski 2000). These historical traumas are thought to have significantly impacted the mental health of older AI/ANs, as well as subsequent generations (Gone and Alcàntara 2005).

Yellow Horse Brave Heart and DeBruyn (1998) coined the term *historical unresolved grief* to explain these lasting effects on AI communities, families, and individuals. Their model proposes that unresolved intergenerational grief and trauma is at the root of numerous social problems that deteriorate the collective mental and physical health of Native communities (Yellow Horse Brave Heart and DeBruyn 1998). Despite its popularity and sense of the experience of some Native people, very few rigorous empirical studies of historical trauma among AIs have been conducted to date (Jervis et al. 2006). As an exception, one study of 132 AI and Canadian aboriginal adults found that at least 25% thought daily about the loss of Native language, culture, spirituality, and loss of respect for elders or for traditional ways (Whitbeck et al. 2004). Many of these elders experienced negative emotional responses when having these thoughts; for instance, 16% were often or always sad or depressed, 9% anxious, and 9% felt like "it is happening again" when thinking about these losses.

Environmental Challenges

Place of Residence. Less than half of AI/AN elders live in rural settings; most of those who do live primarily on reservations, where the challenges inherent in rural life are magnified manyfold (Indian Health Service 2002). Many live in extremely remote areas, isolated from basic services, such as health care, treated water, waste disposal, electricity, and plumbing (Nelson et al. 1992). The limitations imposed by this environment are even more severe for the older population, who are further isolated due to limited physical mobility and access to transportation. Based on 1990 Census data, per capita income among rural AI/AN elders was roughly 70% of that of urban elders (Manson 1992) and nearly one-half lived at or below the poverty level (Manson 1995a). Rural extended family households with members over the age of 65 were twice as likely to be below the poverty line as urban families with the same makeup (Manson 1995a). In an analysis of the 2000 Census Public Use Microdata Sample, Goins et al. (2007) found that 31.5% of AI/ANs age 55+ had annual household incomes less than $15,000, compared to 17.4% of whites in the same age group. The challenges posed by extreme rurality and economic disadvantage may have a further devastating effect, namely the out-migration of much of the younger generation (Rodenhauser 1994). This relocation of many AI/AN youth has contributed to culture loss, in addition to leaving the older generations with fewer options as to informal caregivers.

While rural environments pose significant challenges to older Natives, urban-dwelling elders face a unique set of obstacles related to maintaining mental health. Based on 2000 Census data, an estimated 60–70% of older AI/ANs live in urban areas (Indian Health Service 2002). Some of these elders find themselves largely isolated from their Native communities, traditional ways, and IHS services. Urban Native elders have been referred to as "invisible Indians," because they often fall through the cracks of the fragmented services available in urban areas (Hendrix 2003). Isolation from others who share their cultural background has the potential to significantly impact the mental health of urban elders as well. Moreover, health care providers from the dominant culture are unlikely to be knowledgeable about Native spirituality, traditional medicine, Native languages, and customs surrounding health and illness (National Indian Health Board 2006). Urban elders have been largely ignored in the literature (Kramer 1991), underlining the assumption that these individuals are more acculturated and thus more self-sufficient.

Family Issues. Among many AI communities, there is a cultural expectation to care for "one's own," which—in "the Indian way"—can include a vast network of family, metaphoric kin, and other community members (Manson 1992). In particular, it is a matter of respect and obligation to look after elders financially and in terms of health care. While this sense of family security can undoubtedly have positive effects, it can also have severe consequences. The pressure to care for elders at home combined with the realities of living in extreme poverty can in some cases open the door to elder abuse, including psychological, verbal, financial, and physical abuse (National Indian Council on Aging 2004). In a medical chart review of 550 AI/AN patients (age 50+) served by the Seattle Indian Health Board, Buchwald et al. (2000) found physical abuse reported among 10% of the sample. Significant correlates of physical abuse ($P < 0.001$) included female gender, current depression and dependence on others for food (Buchwald et al. 2000).

Among some groups, cultural norms may also discourage families from seeking professional help for significant health events (Manson 1992). Because families feel responsible for providing elder care, seeking help outside of the Native community can be perceived as a failure. Families are further burdened by the structure and limitations of services available to them. Because the IHS offers largely acute outpatient care, most facilities are not equipped to provide long-term or specialized services, and reservation communities often lack other facilities that can meet these needs. As a result, older patients with significant physical or mental health needs are frequently discharged from IHS hospitals into the care of family members who lack the resources and the knowledge to address mental health issues (Manson 1992).

Barriers to Help Seeking

The rate at which older AI/ANs seek and receive treatment for mental health issues is incongruent with the estimates of psychiatric disorders among this population (Manson 2000; Somervell et al. 1995). One of the few studies of mental health and social service utilization by older AIs found that those 65 years of age and older made far fewer visits to a clinic than did younger people, and that many presented with "social" problems rather than "mental" problems per se (Rhoades et al. 1980). In a study of reservation-dwelling Native elders, self-perceived need was the strongest predictor of mental health service use (Barney 1994). Clinicians have observed that Native elders rarely present to the IHS mental health service directly, but are typically referred by Community Health Representatives (paraprofessional health workers), community nurses, or primary care physicians, some of whom may not always accurately identify psychiatric issues (Neligh and Scully 1990). Moreover, nonspecific physical complaints may be emphasized over psychological/psychiatric symptoms due to the perceived unacceptability of the latter (Neligh and Scully 1990). There are several factors which may contribute to these disparities, including financial barriers, limited availability of services, cultural conceptualizations of mental health and illness, and cultural differences between clients and providers (Manson 2000).

Structure and Funding. The availability and scope of mental health services available to older AI/ANs varies by location. For those living on reservations and AI statistical areas (state-designated areas for federally recognized tribes lacking an official land base) (U. S. Census Bureau 2000), the IHS provides fairly comprehensive (although some would say rudimentary) health services, including mental health and referral (Somervell et al. 1995). Services offered by the IHS tend to be acute in nature, and have historically been skewed in the favor of child and family care (Manson 1992). While considerable effort has been made to develop and improve IHS mental health services over the past several decades, there are a number of factors that limit the accessibility, effectiveness, and cultural relevance of these efforts. A comprehensive review of these issues can be found in Dixon and Roubideaux's (Eds.) (Dixon and Roubideaux 2001) volume on public health policy related to AI/ANs (see Chaps. 3, 7, and 12 by M. Dixon, S. M. Manson, and M. Dixon and Y. Joseph-Fox, respectively).

As of recently, mental health programs can be found in the majority (80%) of IHS service areas (Gone 2004). Most of these programs provide on-call mental health services, which are largely outpatient, crisis-oriented, and underfunded (Johnson and Cameron 2001). The operating budget for IHS in general is considered inadequate by many, and of that, only 7% goes toward mental health services, including substance abuse programs (Gone 2004). In response to the President's FY 2006 proposed budget for the IHS, which allocated $59.2 million for mental health programs, the American Psychological Association advised congress that an additional $30 million would be needed for IHS mental health programs to keep pace with documented need in their communities (American Psychological Association 2005). With limited funding and noncompetitive salary levels, qualified staff are difficult to recruit and retain in remote areas, which further promotes the crisis model of mental health care (Nelson et al. 1992).

For urban elders without private health insurance, mental health care is even more challenging to obtain. In terms of government programs available through Medicare, many older AI/ANs do not participate or are not eligible for these services (Dixon and Joseph-Fox 2001). While the issue has not received much research attention, there is concern among health care providers serving this population that many do not qualify for coverage because of punctuated work histories; others struggle with premium, deductible and co-pay policies (Dixon and Joseph-Fox 2001). While these financial obligations do not exist with Indian health organizations (funded through IHS grants, private sources, and local government funds), such organizations can only be found in 41 urban sites across the country, making these services inaccessible to the majority of urban elders (National Council of Urban Indian Health, unknown; Somervell et al. 1995). US Census data from 2000 suggests that up to 29% of AI/ANs have no health care insurance at all, IHS or otherwise (DeNavas-Walt et al. 2005). An additional threat to the health of urban elders is the proposed elimination of Urban Indian Health Program funding which, despite being rejected by Congress for the FY07 budget, was included again in the President's FY08 budgetary recommendations (National Council of Urban Indian Health 2007; National Indian Health Board 2006).

Cultural Relevance. Another considerable deterrent to seeking and obtaining mental health care is the contrasting cultural notions of mental illness between the dominant and Native cultures. The cultural mismatch between western mental health care and some Native elders' belief systems has been identified as a significant barrier to help-seeking behavior among this population (Johnson and Cameron 2001).

The notion that different cultures have different ways of understanding, expressing, and dealing with psychiatric distress has been well established by the fields of medical and psychological anthropology. Cultural variations in the phenomenology of depressive experience, for example, may involve: (1) how the self is understood, (2) indigenous categories of emotions, (3) emphases on particular aspects of emotional life, (4) the patterning of relationships between emotions, (5) the social contexts that precipitate emotions, and (6) the ethnophysiology of bodily experiences of emotions (Jenkins et al. 1990). As is true among other cultural groups, AI/ANs have distinct ways of conceptualizing mental health problems and interventions for these problems. There are numerous psychiatric conditions included in the health lexicon of Native cultures, each associated with specific symptoms, diagnostic criteria, and treatments (See Manson 1994, 1997, 2000).

As the meaning and conceptualization of illness are culturally constructed, efforts at cross-cultural translation of mental health terminology are problematic (Manson 2000). It is not as simple as mere translation, since semantic equivalents for western categories of illness often do not exist in Native cultures. Moreover, indigenous illness categories often lack a 1:1 correspondence with Diagnostic and Statistical Manual of Mental Disorders (DSM) criteria (American Psychiatric Association 1994; Manson et al. 1985). Some tribal languages do not even possess a word equivalent to, for example, the English word "depressed" (Manson et al. 1985; Storck et al. 2000; Terminsen and Ryan 1970). Some of these differences persist despite acculturation. For instance, even in an AI tribe with a high rate of intermarriage with Whites, depressive experience differed in its attributions and phenomenology (O'Nell 1996). O'Nell (1996) found that depressive experience among the Flathead tended to be expressed through the idiom of loneliness, which was itself differentiated into three categories: "feeling bereaved," "feeling aggrieved," and "feeling worthless." Further complicating the matter, somatic and emotional distress tends not to be well differentiated for some AIs (Ackerson et al. 1990; Manson et al. 1990; Somervell et al. 1993).

While physical manifestations of psychiatric disorders may be recognizable across cultures, it is the idiomatic expression of such distress that complicates diagnosis and subsequently treatment (Manson 2000). Although not universally accepted, AIs have often been argued to have "sociocentric" (the person is seen in relational and interdependent terms) rather than "egocentric" (the person is seen as independent and autonomous) cultural systems (Schweder and Bourne 1984). Given this presumed sociocentric orientation, diagnostic criteria that rely exclusively on ego-oriented, decontextualized statements such as "*I* feel blue" or "*I* fear things that *I* do not normally fear" impose constraints on discovering other ways of experiencing and expressing depressive or anxious affect (Manson 1995a). To the extent this sociocentric orientation is applicable, it may explain the tendency to express depressive experiences through the idiom of loneliness rather than in more individual terms for some AIs.

Across cultures, the way psychiatric symptoms are grouped may vary considerably (Kleinman 1980; Manson et al. 1985; Storck et al. 2000). Some AI tribes express their distress in configurations of symptoms that have sometimes (and controversially) been labeled "culture-bound syndromes" (Simmons and Hughes 1985)–conditions that only appear within a particular cultural milieu (Hahn 1995). For instance, *soul loss* or similar syndromes appear in the anthropological records of numerous Plains tribes and include symptoms, such as an orientation to the past, feeling blocked or hopeless, thoughts of death, preoccupation with ghosts and spirits, "losing one's mind" to the dwelling (or ghost camp) of dead relatives, and facilitating the process of sending one's spirit to the ghost camp through self-destructive behavior (Johnson and Johnson 1965; Trimble et al. 1984) (see Trimble et al. 1984, for a comprehensive review of North American indigenous concepts of mental disorders). At first glance, these symptoms sound like biomedically defined depression with a "cultural twist." However, such an interpretation raises the question of whether psychiatric nosology better defines the phenomenology of this experience than does *soul loss*, as well as the question of what treatments would be most efficacious for someone suffering from this condition. An indigenous Lakota illness category, the "downhearted" variant of *Wac'ink'o* ("pouting"), also bears some similarity to depression (Lewis 1990). *Wac'ink'o* is believed to occur "when people don't get what they want," and includes symptoms, such as anger, withdrawal, mutism, and self-destructiveness (in some cases resulting in suicide) (Lewis 1990).

This mismatch between emic (Native) and etic (western) explanatory models for mental health and aging significantly complicates our understanding and treatment of AI/AN mental health issues (Manson and Shore 1981). As explored below, this discord introduces great potential for misdiagnosis, distrust of providers, and culturally irrelevant patient outreach and treatment regimens.

Compelling insights on Native perspectives of mental health come from Gone's work (Gone 2004, 2008; Gone and Alcàntara 2005), which highlights the difficulties that arise when AI/AN populations are viewed through the lens of contemporary (western) psychology. This disconnect extends beyond the theoretical foundation of western psychology to the physical setting in which mental health services are provided. In the traditional Native way of life for many tribes, health and wellness are community issues that are addressed in familial and congregative settings. Adherence to rigid schedules, pharmacological interventions, and isolation from family and community members make Western approaches to mental health care seem oppressive to many Natives. "The culture of the mental health clinic is *not* the culture of the reservation or urban Indian community" (Gone and Alcàntara 2005, p. 124). Furthermore, treating the mind as an entity separate from the body, the soul, the individual's ancestral history, and familial and community roles is a western imposition (Trimble et al. 1984). Gone (2004) states that some Native people even consider clinical psychology to be yet another plot of the "White man" to strip them of their cultural identity.

Likewise, for some Native elders, a mismatch may exist between their own conceptualizations of their psychological distress and the approaches that are available to them via a biomedical framework. In a study of long-term care service availability for older AIs, Jervis et al. (2002) found that distrust/fear of services, bureaucratic requirements, belief that the services will not help, minimization of the need for help, and fear of stigma were identified by providers from 108 tribal communities as significant barriers to elders seeking mental health services. As a whole, alcohol, drug, and mental health services were found to have a greater number of barriers to utilization than any other service category (e.g., primary health care, social services, spiritual services, etc.) (Jervis et al. 2002).

In summary, the major challenges to maintaining mental health among older AI/ANs include sociohistorical factors, including historical grief and trauma;

environmental factors, such as geographic isolation and poverty; family issues, such as extended family pressures and the culture of caring for elders at home; and barriers to help seeking, including the structure and funding of mental health services, and the cultural relevance of biomedical mental health services, nomenclature and diagnostic measures.

Strengths Contributing to Mental Health

Support Systems

AI/AN communities characteristically place a premium on extended family and community support networks. Particularly in rural settings, Native elders often co-reside with children, grandchildren, or extended and metaphorical kin. In a study of 1,039 AI elders aged 60 and older, John et al. (2003) found that 82.6% lived in households with others (21% lived with a spouse, 28.1% lived with a spouse and others, and 33.5% lived with others). Though drawing from a very different data source, US Census data indicates that 69.2% of all adults age 65+ lived with others in 2003 (US Department of Health and Human Services 2005). This social structure can provide a significant source of strength and security, especially to elders affected by poverty, illness, and mobility issues. While caring for elders is common among many Native cultures, it bears noting that significant differences exist in the perception and treatment of older adults from culture to culture. The Apache, for example, historically abandoned elders who had become infirm and dependent (Kramer 1991).

In contemporary Native communities, many elders assume a prominent role in their households, contributing childcare and financial resources, as well as serving as cultural mentors (Jervis and Manson 2006). However, this extended family structure may be as much a product of financial necessity as an observance of cultural expectations for some, which in some cases can over ride the potentially positive effects of such support (Manson 1992, 1995a). This is especially true in cases where elders find themselves psychologically and financially stretched by the need to provide care to grandchildren or to share housing with numerous family members (Jervis and Manson 1999).

AI/AN Ethnic and Cultural Identity

> For the elderly, ethnicity can provide a broad spectrum of social, cultural, and psychological resources. Regardless of what liabilities such identity may entail, it can provide a reservoir of shared values, potential relationships, mutual support, activities, skills, and common experience. (Simić 1993, p. 10)

While the suppression and destruction of Native cultures has a long history in the United States, many Native peoples and communities have responded with resilience and adaptability. Various elements of traditional cultures, such as language, religion, and social structures, have been maintained and/or revitalized (Nelson et al. 1992; Somervell et al. 1995). A sense of Native identity and a connection to the past is a source of strength for many elders, who are often responsible for preserving and passing on traditional ways to subsequent generations.

An important element of some AI/AN traditional cultures is the revered status of elders. Elder status has been argued to be an earned position of respect that marks a certain level of accomplishment, rather than chronological age per se (Weibel-Orlando 1989). In many Native groups, honoring elders is an integral part of traditional culture; elders are considered wise and connected to the spirit world, are valued as the head of families and communities, and are consulted for advice and guidance (Morgan et al. 1997; Weibel-Orlando 1988). Having a sense of worth and importance has been identified as contributing to mental health in older adults in general, and possibly has a protective effect with respect to depression (Attico 1997). In a study reviewing medical communication in older AIs, Garroutte et al. (2006) found that individuals with strong Native identities had much more positive attitudes and higher levels of optimism regarding their overall health. Unfortunately, there is the perception in some Native communities that respect for elders is on the decline.

While some elders are torch bearers for traditional Native culture, others are relatively acculturated to the dominant US culture. Perhaps due to the history of forced acculturation experienced by this cohort, of which boarding school was a major component (Pickering 2000), many of these Natives at least partially identify with Western worldviews and traditions. In a study of Native elders among several Great Lakes tribes, Jackson and Chapleski (2000) found that 41% of respondents over the age of 55 never participated in traditional activities and identified more strongly with mainstream culture. Although this may be interpreted by some in negative terms, these findings also point to a strength of Native elders–*adaptability*. The ability to adapt to change and face stress with resiliency has been documented in the gerontological literature as a contributing factor to mental health in later years (Rowe and Kahn 1997; Simić 1993). This adaptability has also led to the development of a national or "Pan-Indian" identity, where common cultural elements have been used to unify these diverse groups and strengthen their visibility on the political front (Kramer 1991; Weibel-Orlando 1988). One element of Pan-Indianism is the spread of cultural practices to tribes in which these practices were not previously present (e.g., the pow wow) (Howard 1955). This may be especially beneficial to urban elders who may be isolated from Native communities.

Spirituality

As has been demonstrated with various religious faiths and practices, there is a positive relationship between mental health and spirituality in advanced age (Meisenhelder and Chandler 2000; Moberg 1997). In very general terms, traditional AI spirituality involves faith in the interconnectedness of a higher being (e.g., the "Great Spirit") and harmony with the natural world (Meisenhelder and Chandler 2000). Traditionally, AI/AN cultures attribute health problems to an imbalance between the spiritual and natural worlds (Meisenhelder and Chandler 2000). In a survey examining the importance of faith and health outcomes in a sample of AIs over the age of 65, Meisenhelder and Chandler (2000) found that respondents who considered faith to be an important part of their lives scored higher on the mental health subscale.

Spirituality also appears to be positively related to help-seeking behavior for mental health issues. In the aforementioned AI-SUPERPFP project, respondents who sought help for substance abuse problems identified spirituality and Native traditions as highly important to them (Beals et al. 2006). The higher the degree of general spirituality reported, the more likely the individual was to seek help from multiple sources, incorporating both Native and biomedical approaches to their care (Beals et al. 2006). Although AI-SUPERPFP data is not specific to older AI/AN adults, there is reason to believe that these findings may extend to elders.

Discussion

Applying Strengths to Meet Challenges

As has been discussed, the challenges that jeopardize the mental health of older AI/ANs are culturally, historically, and socially based. While there are no easy solutions, our exploration of these issues points to several attributes which may be harnessed to diminish the impact of these forces. Table 8.2 includes a description of both strengths and challenges to mental health that Native elders possess.

Community Networks. Because Native communities traditionally consider health and well-being to be larger than the individual–that is, a harmonious balance among community members, the natural world, and the spirit world–community-level initiatives hold promise for addressing mental health needs among Native elders. As suggested by Yellow Horse Brave Heart and DeBruyn (1998), healing initiatives at the community level are vital to healing historical unresolved grief.

In terms of research, involvement of community members and organizations is crucial (Salois et al. 2006). As demonstrated through the AI-SUPERPFP project, nurturing relationships with community stakeholders, health professionals, and traditional healers was essential to the effort to initiate and carry out a study of this magnitude on a topic (mental health) which some would regard as potentially stigmatizing (Beals 2006). In addition to promoting cultural relevance, the involvement of community members has the potential to diminish the deep-seated mistrust of western medical and research practices.

Table 8.2 Summary table—older AI/ANs: strengths and challenges to maintaining mental health

Demographics	Challenges	Strengths	Recommendations
AI/AN population age 65+ comprises 0.4% of total US population	*Sociohistorical factors*	*Support systems*	Engage community networks in research and MH initiatives
AI/AN population age 65+ projected to increase to 0.6% of total US population by 2050	• Historical trauma, forced acculturation	• AI/AN family structure	Incorporate Native culture into biomedical MH care
23.5% of AI/ANs over 65 live below poverty level	• Loss of culture, language, and religion	• Community networks	Additional research needed on AI/AN MH issues
29.1% of AI/ANs over 25 have less than 12 years of formal education	• Mistrust of research and biomedicine		Develop culturally relevant instrumentation and methods
11.5% of AI/ANs over 25 have a bachelor's degree or higher	*Environmental challenges*	*AI/AN ethnic and cultural identity*	
	• Place of residence (urban vs. rural)	• Tradition of caring for older adults at home	
	• Family issues (tradition of caring for older adults at home)	• Traditional respect for elders	
	• Poverty	• Native cultural traditions	
	Barriers to help seeking	*Spirituality*	
	• Structure and funding	• Positive impact on mental health	
	• Cultural relevance	• Positive impact on help-seeking	

Incorporating Native Culture into Biomedical Mental Health Care. The incorporation of Native cultural elements into biomedical mental health care may counter some of the challenges faced by elders. As identified by Gone (2008), many Native people consider a return to traditional ways to be the answer to solving mental health crises facing contemporary Native communities. Traditional cultural elements identified as important to mental health maintenance included the use of traditional ritual spaces, religious and ceremonial practices, and involvement of traditional healers. Specific examples of incorporating traditional healing into care regimens include using a talking circle format to conduct group therapy and using the sweat lodge for healing and cleansing (Manson 1986; Somervell et al. 1995).

Future Recommendations

Research. More research on Native elder mental health is sorely needed. Requests for increases in funding or culturally relevant program/policy development stand a much greater chance to succeed if backed by scientific data (Gone 2004). In a review of population-based studies on the health of older Americans (Rhoades 2006), only 13% of studies included a sizeable sample of Native elders ($N \geq 100$). In another inventory of publications related to AI/AN mental health released between 1980 and 1995, Manson (2000) found that 69% had no empirical foundation. The majority of these publications (76%) argued for the importance of culturally competent care without presenting supporting data (Manson 2000). Furthermore, the scant literature that exists on AI mental health issues focuses almost exclusively on substance abuse disorders, often with youth or young adults (Manson 2000; Somervell et al. 1995).

Another substantial need in the field of AI/AN mental health research is the development of culturally relevant instrumentation and research methods. Standardized assessment instruments, frameworks, and psychiatric nomenclature may have limited applicability to AI/ANs (Manson 2000; Somervell et al. 1995), a problem that may even be more pronounced among older generations. While some researchers seem eager to critique the utility of established measures, few have offered empirically tested alternatives (Gone and Alcàntara 2005; Manson 1986).

Additionally, though significant obstacles to mental health maintenance have been identified, little is known about potential protective factors. Research is needed to understand the role that spirituality, Native identity, involvement in traditional practices, and social structures (e.g., the extended family) may play in maintaining or improving mental health among this population.

At the heart of any research initiative should be an overarching respect for historical and contemporary forces impacting the health of Native elders. This includes acknowledging the history of exploitative research to which AI/ANs have been subjected (Beals et al. 2003; Somervell et al. 1995). Tribes, as well as individuals, may be hesitant to participate in research projects, and efforts should be made to ensure that there is a direct benefit for those involved whenever possible (Beals et al. 2003).

Concluding Comments

A final consideration when conducting research with Native elders are the cultural biases inherent in western psychology and psychiatry. Acknowledging the linkages between biomedical conceptions of mental health and western cultural assumptions is an important step toward understanding diverse conceptualizations of pathology and treatment (Gone 2004). To be truly culturally competent, researchers and professionals working with Native populations need to move beyond translating categories of distress to understanding the cultural foundations that underlie definitions of mental illness (Gone 2004). This is admittedly a very tall order and one that is not likely to be accomplished overnight. Nonetheless, with this approach, researchers and clinicians will be better equipped to develop culturally relevant approaches, resulting in a better understanding and better treatment of the mental health needs of Native elders.

References

Ackerson, L. M., Dick, R. W., Manson, S. M., & Baron, A. E. (1990). Depression among American Indian adolescents: Psychometric characteristics of the inventory to diagnose depression. *Journal of the American Academy of Child and Adolescent Psychiatry, 29,* 601–607.

Administration on Aging. (2000). Facts and figures: Statistics on minority aging in the U.S. http://www.aoa.gov/prof/statistics/minority_aging/facts_minority_aging.asp#PopulationbyRace. Accessed November 16, 2007.

American Psychiatric Association. (1994). *Diagnostic and statistical manual of mental disorders, fourth edition (DSM-IV).* Washington, DC: American Psychiatric Association.

American Psychological Association. (2005). Briefing sheet on Indian health service mental health/alcohol and substance abuse programs. http://www.apa.org/ppo/funding/ihsbriefingsheet.html. Accessed June 1, 2006.

Attico, N. B. (1997). The elder female: A preventative care plan and health watch. *The IHS Primary Care Provider, 22*(5), 80–87.

Barnes, P. M., Adams, P. F., & Powell-Griner, E. (2005). *Health Characteristics of the American Indian and Alaska Native Adult Population: United States, 1999–2003.* Rockville: U.S. Department of Health and Human Services, National Center for Health Statistics.

Barney, D. D. (1994). Use of mental health services by American Indian & Alaska Native elders. *American Indian & Alaska Native Mental Health Research, 5*(3), 1–14.

Beals, J., Manson, S. M., Mitchell, C. M., Spicer, P., & the AI-SUPERPFP Team. (2003). Cultural specificity and comparison in psychiatric epidemiology: Walking the tightrope in American Indian research. *Culture, Medicine and Psychiatry, 27,* 259–289.

Beals, J., Manson, S. M., Whitesell, N. R., Spicer, P., Novins, D. K., Mitchell, C. M., et al. (2005). Prevalence of DSM-IV disorders and attendant help-seeking in two American Indian reservation populations. *Archives of General Psychiatry, 62,* 99–108.

Beals, J., Novins, D. K., Spicer, P., Whitesell, N. R., Mitchell, C. M., Manson, S. M., & the American Indian Service Utilization, Psychiatric Epidemiology, Risk, and Protective Factors Project Team, (2006). Help seeking for substance use problems in two American Indian reservation populations. *Psychiatric Services, 57*(4), 512–520.

Buchwald, D. S., Tomita, S., Ashton, S., Furman, R., & Manson, S. M. (2000). Physical abuse of urban Native Americans. *Journal of General Internal Medicine, 15,* 562–564.

Bureau of Indian Affairs. (2005). Indian entities recognized and eligible to receive services from the United States Bureau of Indian Affairs. *Federal Register, 70*(226), 71194–71198.

Chapleski, E. E., Lamphere, J. K., Kaczynski, R., Lichtenberg, P. A., & Dwyer, J. W. (1997). Structure of a depression measure among American Indian elders: Confirmatory factor analysis of the CES-D Scale. *Research on Aging, 19,* 462–485.

Curyto, K. J., Chapleski, E. E., & Lichtenberg, P. A. (1999). Prediction of the presence and stability of depression in the Great Lakes Native American elders. *Journal of Mental Health and Aging, 5,* 323–340.

Curyto, K. J., Chapleski, E. E., & Lichtenberg, P. A., Hodges, E., Kaczynski, R., & Sobect, J. (1998). Prevalence and prediction of depression in American Indian Elderly. *Clinical Gerontologist, 18,* 19–37.

DeNavas-Walt, C., Proctor, B. D., & Lee, C. H., U.S. Census Bureau. (2005). Income, poverty, and health insurance coverage in the United States: 2004. http://www.ncuih.org/about/index.html. Accessed December 13, 2006.

Dixon, M., & Joseph-Fox, Y. (2001). Federal and state policy to strengthen Indian health. In M. Dixon & Y. Roubideaux (Eds.), *Promises to keep: Public health policy for American Indians and Alaska natives in the 21st century* (pp. 275–295). Washington, DC: United Book.

Dixon, M., & Roubideaux, Y. (Eds.). (2001). *Promises to keep: Public health policy for American Indians and Alaska Natives in the 21st century.* Washington, DC: United Book.

Garroutte, E. M., Kunovich, R. M., Buchwald, D., & Goldberg, J. (2006). Medical communication in older American Indians: Variations by ethnic identity. *The Journal of Applied Gerontology, 25*(10), 27S–43S.

Goldwasser, H. D., & Badger, L. W. (1989). Utility of the psychiatric screen among the Navajo of Chinle: A fourth-year clerkship experience. *American Indian & Alaska Native Mental Health Research, 3,* 6–15.

Gone, J. P. (2004). Mental health services for Native Americans in the 21st Century United States. *Professional Psychology: Research and Practice, 35*(1), 10–18.

Gone, J. P. (2008). So I can be like a white man: The cultural psychology of space and place in American Indian mental health. *Culture and Psychology, 14*(3), 369–399.

Gone, J. P., & Alcàntara, C. (2005). Practice makes perfect? Identifying effective psychological treatments for mental health problems in Indian country. In E. H. Hawkins & R. D. Walker (Eds.), *Best practices in behavioral health services for American Indians and Alaska Natives.* Portland: One Sky National Resources Center for American Indian and Alaska Native Substance Abuse Prevention and Treatment Services.

Hahn, R. A. (1995). *Sickness and healing: An anthropological perspective.* New Haven: Yale University Press.

Hendrix, L. R. (2003). Intercultural collaboration: An approach to long term care for urban American Indians. *Care Management Journals, 4*(1), 46–52.

Howard, J. H. (1955). Pan-Indian culture of Oklahoma. *The Scientific Monthly* (November), 215–220.

Indian Health Service. (2002). American Indian and Alaska Native roundtable on long term care: Final report 2002. http://www.ihs.gov/PublicInfo/PublicAffairs/PressReleases/Press_Release2002/Final_LTC_Report_ALL.pdf. Accessed January 10, 2007.

Jackson, D. D., & Chapleski, E. E. (2000). Not traditional, not assimilated: Elderly American Indians and the notion of 'cohort'. *Journal of Cross-Cultural Gerontology, 15,* 229–259.

Jenkins, J., Kleinman, A., & Good, B. (1990). Cross-cultural studies of depression. In J. Becker & A. Kleinman (Eds.), *Advances in Mood Disorders* (pp. 67–99). New York: Erlbaum.

Jervis, L. L., & Manson, S. M. (1999). Native elder component - Major themes and emerging questions. In *Redefining Retirement: Research directions for successful aging among America's diverse seniors* (pp. 17–22). Washington, DC: SPRY Foundation.

Jervis, L. L., & Manson, S. M. (2006). Native American elders. In R. Schulz (Ed.), *Encyclopedia of Aging*: Springer Publishing Company.

Jervis, L. L., & Manson, S. M. (2007). Cognitive impairment, psychiatric disorders, and problematic behaviors in a tribal nursing home. *Journal of Aging and Health, 19*(2), 260–274.

Jervis, L. L., Beals, J., Croy, C. D., Klein, S. A., Manson, S. M., & The AI-SUPERPFP Team. (2006). Historical consciousness among two American Indian tribes. *American Behavioral Scientist, 50*(4), 526–549.

Jervis, L. L., Beals, J., Fickenscher, A., & Arciniegas, D. B. (2007a). Performance on the Mini-Mental State Examination and Mattis Dementia Rating scale among older American Indians. *Journal of Neuropsychiatry and Clinical Neuroscience, 19*(2), 173–178.

Jervis, L. L., Jackson, M. Y., & Manson, S. M. (2002). Need for, availability of, and barriers to the provision of long-term care services for older American Indians. *Journal of Cross-Cultural Gerontology, 17,* 295–311.

Jervis, L. L., Shore, J., Hutt, E., & Manson, S. (2007b). Suboptimal pharmacotherapy in a tribal nursing home. *Journal of the American Medical Directors Association, 8,* 1–7.

John, R., Kerby, D. S., & Hennessy, C. H. (2003). Patterns and impact of comorbidity and multimorbidity among community-resident American Indian elders. *The Gerontologist, 43*(5), 649–660.

Johnson, J. L., & Cameron, M. C. (2001). Barriers to providing effective mental health services to American Indians. *Mental Health Services Research, 3*(4), 215–223.

Johnson, D. L., & Johnson, C. A. (1965). Totally discouraged: A depression syndrome of the Dakota Sioux. *Transcultural Psychiatric Research, 1,* 141–143.

Kleinman, A. (1980). *Patients and healers in the context of culture: An exploration of the borderland between anthropology, medicine, and psychiatry.* Berkeley: University of California Press.

Kramer, J. B. (1991). Urban American Indian aging. *Journal of Cross-Cultural Gerontology, 6*(2), 205–217.

Lewis, T. H. (1990). *The medicine men: Oglala Sioux ceremony and healing.* Lincoln: University of Nebraska Press.

Manson, S. M. (1986). Recent advances in American Indian mental health research: Implications for clinical research and training. In N. I. o. M. Health (Ed.), *Mental Health Research and Practice in Minority Communities: Development of Culturally Sensitive Training Programs*

Manson, S. M. (1992). Long-term care of older American Indians: Challenges in the development of institutional services. In C. Barresi & D. E. Stull (Eds.), *Ethnicity and long-term care* (pp. 130–143). New York: Springer.

Manson, S. M. (1994). Culture and depression: Discovering variations in the experience of illness. In W. J. Lonner & R. S. Malpass (Eds.), *Psychology and culture* (pp. 285–290). Needham: Allyn and Bacon.

Manson, S. M. (1995a). Culture and major depression: Current challenges in the diagnosis of mood disorders. *Psychiatric Clinics of North America, 18*(3), 487–501.

Manson, S. M. (1995b). Mental health status and needs of the American Indian and Alaska Native elderly. In P. D. (Ed.), *Handbook on ethnicity, aging and mental health.* Westport, CT: Greenwood Press.

Manson, S. M. (1997). Ethnographic methods, cultural context, and mental illness: Bridging different ways of knowing and experience. *Ethos, 25*(2), 249–258.

Manson, S. (2000). Mental Health Services for American Indians and Alaska Natives: Need, use, and barriers to effective care. *Canadian Journal of Psychiatry, 45*(7), 617–626.

Manson, S. M., Ackerson, L. M., Dick, R. W., Baron, A. E., & Fleming, C. M. (1990). Depressive symptoms among American Indian adolescents: Psychometric characteristics of the the Center for Epidemiological Studies Depression Scale (CES-D). *Psychological Assessment, 2,* 231–237.

Manson, S. M., Shore, J. H., & Bloom, J. D. (1985). The depressive experience in American Indian communities: A challenge for psychiatric theory and diagnosis. In A. Kleinman & B. Good (Eds.), *Culture and depression* (pp. 331–368). Berkeley: University of California Press.

Meisenhelder, J. B., & Chandler, E. N. (2000). Faith, prayer, and health outcomes in elderly Native Americans. *Clinical Nursing Research, 9*(2), 191–203.

Moberg, D. O. (1997). Religion and aging. In K. F. Ferraro (Ed.), *Gerontology perspectives and issues, second edition* (2nd ed., pp. 193–220). New York: Springer.

Morgan, W. L., Hooper, E.Y., & Saari, J. F. (1997). Earthstar project, Inc. *The IHS Primary Care Provider, 22*(5), 75.

Moss, M. P., Roubideaux, Y. D., Jacobsen, C., Buchwald, D., & Manson, S. (2004). Functional disability and associated factors among older Zuni Indians. *Journal of Cross Cultural Gerontology, 19,* 1–12.

National Council of Urban Indian Health. (2007). Administration proposes elimination of urban Indian health program again. http://www.ncuih.org/. Accessed February 13, 2007.

National Council of Urban Indian Health. (unknown). http://www.ncuih.org. Accessed Dec. 13, 2006. National Indian Council on Aging. (2004). Preventing and responding to abuse of elders in Indian country. http://www.elderabusecenter.org/pdf/whatnew/abuseindian040707.pdf. Accessed December 13, 2006.

National Indian Health Board. (2006). Testimony of the national Indian health board presented to the Senate committee on Indian affairs by Kathy Kitcheyan chairwoman–San Carols Apache Tribe and board member national Indian health board on the President's fiscal year 2007 (FY07) budget for American Indian and Alaska Native health programs. http://www.nihb.org/docs/budget_fy07_testimony_nihb.pdf. Accessed Oct. 10, 2006.

Neligh, G., & Scully, J. (1990). *Differential diagnosis of major mental disorders among American Indian elderly* (No. DHHS publication no. HRS-P-DV-90). Washington, DC: US Government Printing Office.

Nelson, S. H., McCoy, G.F., Stetter, M., & Vanderwagen, W.C. (1992). An overview of mental health services for American Indians and Alaska Natives in the 1990s. *Hospital and Community Psychiatry, 43*(3), 257–262.

O'Nell, T. (1996). *Disciplined hearts: History, identity, and depression in an American Indian community*. Berkeley: University of California.

Pickering, K. A. (2000). *Lakota culture, world economy*. Lincoln: University of Nebraska Press.

Rhoades, D. A. (2006). National health data and older American Indians and Alaska Natives. *Journal of Applied Gerontology, 25*(1 Suppl), 9S–26S.

Rhoades, E. R., Marshall, M., Attneave, C., Echohawk, M., Bjork, J., & Beiser, M. (1980). Impact of mental disorders upon elderly American Indians as reflected in visits to ambulatory care facilities.

Rodenhauser, P. (1994). Cultural barriers to mental health care delivery in Alaska. *The Journal of Mental Health Administration, 21*(1), 60–70.

Rowe, J. W., & Kahn, R. L. (1997). Successful aging. *The Gerontologist, 37*(4), 433–440.

Salois, E. M., Holkup, P. A., Tripp-Reimer, T., & Weinert, C. (2006). Research as spiritual covenant. *Western Journal of Nursing Research, 28*(5), 505–524.

Schweder, R., & Bourne, E. (1984). Does the concept of the person vary cross-culturally? In R. Schweder & R. LeVine (Eds.), *Culture theory: Essays on mind, self, and emotion* (pp. 158–199). Cambridge: Cambridge University Press.

Simić, A. (1993). Aging and ethnic identity: A refutation of the double-jeopardy theory. *Journal of Case Management, 2*(1), 9–13.

Simmons, R. C., & Hughes, C. C. (1985). *The culture-bound syndromes*. Boston: D. Reidel.

Somervell, P. D., Beals, J., Kinzie, J. D., Leung, P., Boehnlein, J., Matsunga, D., et al. (1993). Use of the CES-D in an American Indian village. *Culture, Medicine and Psychiatry, 16,* 503–517.

Somervell, P. D., Manson, S.M., & Shore, J. H. (1995). Mental illness among American Indians and Alaska Natives. In I. Al-Issa (Ed.), *Handbook of culture and mental illness: An international perspective* Madison: International Universities Press, Inc.

Storck, M., Csordas, T. J., & Strauss, M. (2000). Depressive illness and Navajo healing. *Medical Anthropology Quarterly, 14*(4), 571–597.

Terminsen, J., & Ryan, J. (1970). Health and disease in a British Columbian community. *Canadian Psychiatric Association Journal, 15,* 121–127.

Trimble, J. E., Manson, S. M., Dinges, N. G., & Medicine, B. (1984). American Indian concepts of mental health: Reflections and directions. In P. B. Pedersen, N. Sartorius, & A. J. Marsella (Eds.), *Mental health services: The Cross-cultural context* (pp. 199–220). Beverly Hills: Sage.

U.S. Census Bureau. (2000). American Indian and Alaska Native areas geographic program for census 2000: Notice. *Federal Register, 65*(121), 39062–39069.

U.S. Census Bureau. (2002). *The American Indian and Alaska Native population: 2000. Census 2000 Brief.* Washington, DC: U.S. Department of Commerce, U.S. Census Bureau.

U.S. Census Bureau. (2005). American Indian, Alaska Native tables from the statistical abstract of the United States 2004–2005. http://www.census.gov/statab/www/sa04aian.pdf. Accessed 16 November 16, 2007.

U.S. Department of Commerce, & U.S. Census Bureau. (2006). *We the people: American Indians and Alaska Natives in the United States*. Washington, DC.

U.S. Department of Health and Human Services. (2005). Current population reports–65+ in the United States: 2005. http://www.census.gov/prod/2006pubs/p23-209.pdf. Accessed November 26, 2007.

Weibel-Orlando, J. (1988). Indians, ethnicity as a resource and aging: You can go home again. *Journal of Cross-Cultural Gerontology, 3,* 323–348.

Weibel-Orlando, J. (1989). Elders and elderlies: Well-being in Indian old age. *American Indian Culture and Research Journal, 13*(3 & 4), 149–170.

Whitbeck, L. B., Adams, G. W., Hoyt, D. R., & Chen, X. (2004). Conceptualizing and measuring historical trauma among American Indian people. *American Journal of Community Psychology, 33*(3/4), 119–130.

Yellow Horse Brave Heart, M., & DeBruyn, L. M. (1998). The American Indian holocaust: Healing historical unresolved grief. *American Indian and Alaska Native Mental Health Research, 8*(2), 60–82.

Chapter 9
Psychology of Asian American Children: Contributions of Cultural Heritage and the Minority Experience

Lisa L. Liu, Shu-wen Wang, Joey Fung, Omar G. Gudiño, Annie Tao and Anna S. Lau

Introduction

Chapter Focus

This chapter presents information on mental health issues in Asian American children, focusing on cultural orientation and minority-related experiences as posing challenges to the maintenance of mental health, as well as providing strengths which contribute to resilience in this group. We then recommend some ways through which we may draw upon the strengths of Asian American youth to promote resiliency and overcome vulnerabilities in adjustment.

Demographics

In 2000, there were 11.9 million Asian Americans, with approximately one quarter (3.3 million) being children under 18 years of age. This highly diverse population originates from over 20 different countries. Due to an Asian American immigration history that largely began with a small, early influx of laborers in the nineteenth century followed by longstanding exclusionary immigration policies, some Asian American children today are now well into the 7th generation, while larger proportions of Asian American children are 3rd and 4th generation descended from post-1965 immigrants. Of course with significant continuing immigration, over 60% of all Asian Americans are 1st generation. As such, any two Asian American children may share little in common, having different immigration histories, heritage cultures, languages, and living conditions in the United States.

L. L. Liu (✉)
Department of Psychology, University of California Los Angeles,
1285 Franz Hall, P.O. Box 951563, Los Angeles, CA 90095-1563, USA
e-mail: lisaliu@psych.ucla.edu

E. C. Chang, C. A. Downey (eds.), *Handbook of Race and Development in Mental Health*,
DOI 10.1007/978-1-4614-0424-8_9, © Springer Science+Business Media, LLC 2012

Though there is representation in all 50 states, almost half of all Asian American children reside in only three: California, New York, and Hawaii. Remarkably, over half of all Asian Americans live in one of seven metropolitan areas, including Los Angeles, New York, San Francisco, Honolulu, Washington D.C., Baltimore, and Chicago. Clearly then, most Asian American children grow up within dense coethnic enclaves. However, in most towns and cities in the interior of the country, the Asian American population falls well below the national average of 4.2%. This tells us that Asian American children are a heterogeneous group who grow up in a range of socialization settings. Much of what we know about Asian American children is based on research with 1st and 2nd generation youth of East Asian and Southeast Asian descent living in urban areas with notable coethnic density. Thus, the experiences of many Asian American children are likely not well understood.

With this important caveat in mind, we examine the development of Asian American children and youth through an integrative framework that considers heritage cultural influences, adaptation processes in migration and acculturation, as well as the unique contextual demands associated with minority group status (Garcia Coll et al. 1996). We begin by introducing a broad cultural theme with specific implications for familial values that have developmental significance across many Asian American ethnic groups. Next, we diverge toward themes focused less on heritage cultural influences and more on experiences attributable to ethnic minority status. We examine developmental issues involving ethnic identity formation and cultural socialization with the goal of understanding the essential processes involved in navigating what it means to be Asian American.

Heritage Cultural Influences in Broad Strokes: Interdependence

It is an impossible task to summarize the rich cultural teachings and morés of over 20 originating Asian countries. As such we will rely instead on heuristically helpful conceptual models of cultural orientation that have been thought to broadly account for differences in emotions, behaviors, and beliefs about personhood between Western and non-Western cultures (e.g., Hofstede 1980; Triandis et al. 1988). Briefly, in this tradition, Asian cultures have been broadly viewed as interdependent, where individuals see themselves as fundamentally connected with others. Subsequently, social relationships, roles, norms, and group harmony affect one's behavior more than personal beliefs and needs (e.g., Markus and Kitayama 1991; Triandis 1989). In order to maintain harmonious relations, Asian values emphasize the control and regulation of personal attributes and desires so that individuals may align themselves within the roles and demands of their social contexts (e.g., Markus and Kitayama 1991; Weisz et al.1984). Similarly, the emphasis on interpersonal connectedness and fitting in with others is also associated with concerns about saving face, or maintaining one's public image (e.g., Ting-Toomey 1994). Thus, Asian cultural values tend to underscore social and relational priorities, such as reciprocity, conformity, politeness and humility, hierarchy, respect for authority, honor, and family duty.

We contend that socialization within an interdependent tradition and internalization of these values has a variety of implications for Asian American child development, serving as both sources of competency and vulnerability. First, we review how a cultural emphasis on personal restraint, moderation, and self-control appears to also have positive implications for temperament, behavior regulation patterns, and coping strategies among Asian American youth. Additionally, we explore how the interdependent nature of Asian cultural values essentially shapes the family structure and the socialization experiences of youth. These influences are illustrated through an examination of parent–child relations, the importance of filial piety, and parenting styles and practices used in Asian American families. In these ways, we discuss how the interdependent cultural script can often lead to positive outcomes for Asian American youth.

Heritage Culture and Sources of Strength for Asian American Children

Culture and Child Temperament In examining sources of strength for Asian American children, we commence with a consideration of temperament, which refers to biologically based individual differences in reactivity and self-regulation that are present early in life (Rothbart and Bates 1998; Rothbart and Derryberry 1981). Evidence from cross-national research on temperament suggests that Asian infants and toddlers are generally less active, more reserved, and quicker to calm in stressful situations (e.g., Caudill and Weinstein 1969; Kagan et al. 1994; Chen et al. 1998) than their Western counterparts. In terms of self-regulation, Chinese toddlers were also more likely to display mature self-control behavior compared to Canadian children (e.g., self-generated control; Chen et al. 2003). In addition, Zhou et al. (2004) reported that high levels of effortful control—an ability to sustain attention and inhibit inappropriate behavior—among Chinese children predicted positive adjustment in terms of decreased behavioral problems and increased social competence. Such temperamental differences in arousal, activity, and self-regulatory processes may promote calm dispositions and a capacity for self-restraint in children of Asian descent.

Although the biological underpinnings of temperament are often emphasized, an alternative view posits that temperament is a product of culture, such that enculturative socialization practices result in differences in temperament (Matsumoto 2006). Scholars note that behavioral inhibition and low reactivity may be adaptive within an interdependent cultural script as these dispositions may be essential for maintaining harmony (Chen 2000). Consideration of the impact of one's actions and behaviors on others is highly emphasized in Asian culture (Chen et al. 2003) while lack of self-control is strongly discouraged (Zhou et al. 2004). Thus, children may be socialized to inhibit the expression of strong emotions because they may be detrimental to interpersonal relationships.

While European American children display more emotional expressivity compared to Chinese and Chinese American children, there is evidence that cultural differences in family environment determine levels of expressivity. Maternal strictness discouraging the expression of strong affect results in lower levels of expressivity in Chinese American children relative to Chinese children adopted by European American parents. In terms of affect valuation, Tsai et al. (2007) noted that Chinese American and Taiwanese preschoolers tend to prefer calmer facial expressions and story elements over excited expressions and elements in storybooks compared to European American children, with evidence suggesting that cultural differences in ideal affect are evident in socialization influences such as storybooks. Thus, both familial and cultural socialization forces may converge to promote restraint of activity level, affective expression, and pursuit of individual desires, thereby heightening capacity for self-control and inhibition in children of Asian descent.

Culture and Parenting It has been argued that psychological models of parenting have largely been ensconced within an independent cultural worldview (e.g., Chao 1994; Rothbaum et al. 2000). Given that parenting styles have predominantly been studied in Western cultural contexts, autonomy, expressiveness, and assertiveness are emphasized as desired endpoints of child development. However, interdependent cultures are often typified by socialization goals that involve interpersonal accommodation, deference to authority, and group harmony (Markus and Kitayama 1991; Rothbaum et al. 2000). Accordingly, researchers have described Asian childrearing traditions as strategies that cultivate parental authority (Chao and Tseng 2002). Compared to European Americans, Asian American parents report establishing more strict rules and limits on child conduct, granting less autonomy, and expecting more obedience (e.g., Wu 1996). These parental strategies seem motivated by the goal of maintaining order and organization in the family (Rohner and Pettengill 1985).

Evidence suggests strategies emphasizing parental control and authority may be adaptive in Asian and Asian American familial contexts in ways not observed among European American families. While forms of restrictive parental control have been associated with perceived parental hostility and rejection in European American families, these strategies have been associated with perceived parental warmth and acceptance in Japan (Kornadt 1991; Trommsdorff 1985) and Korea (Rohner and Pettengill 1985). Similarly, while parental control is negatively related to family cohesion in European American families (Nomura et al. 1995), it is positively associated with warmth, cohesion, and lower levels of conflict in Asian American families (e.g., Lau and Cheung 1987). Furthermore, parental control is linked to developmental benefits including self-regulation, confidence, positive relationship attitudes, and frustration tolerance among Chinese children (Xu et al. 1991).

These findings can be understood through a consideration of Confucian roots that provide the foundation for parenting and parent-child relationships in many Asian cultures. According to the Confucian doctrine of filial piety, children are taught to respect and obey their elders with specific obligations to defer to the wishes of their parents (e.g., Ho 1986). Parents, in turn, are responsible for governing, teaching, and disciplining their children. As such, Asian American parents have been found to emphasize control, obedience, and obligation to family (Leung et al. 1998; Lin and Fu 1990). While these parenting characteristics may be construed as restrictive or demanding in Western independent cultural contexts, they embody parental care, concern, and love for children among families of Chinese descent (Chao 1994).

Given that Western concepts of parental control do not capture the salient features of Asian American parenting, investigators have identified parenting constructs that are indigenous to Asian cultures. Chao (1994) described training ideologies which emphasize parental responsibility to teach children appropriate behaviors which motivate high levels of parental involvement and concern. This involvement may take the form of setting clear expectations, close monitoring of child's behavior, and prioritizing caretaking and education of the child (Chao 2000). Research indicates that training is positively associated with health and life satisfaction (Stewart et al. 1998), relationship harmony (Stewart et al. 1999), and academic achievement (e.g., Chao 2000) among Asian and Asian American adolescents.

Another indigenous construct of parenting behavior involves the socialization of shame. In line with the emphasis on maintaining group harmony in interdependent cultures, shame is a central emotion that can help guide behavior within interactions across social settings (Fung 1999). Shaming may involve evoking shameful feelings in children through explicit disapproval of misbehavior or social comparison against more well-behaved children. Although the practice of shaming children is sometimes viewed as hostile or punitive, some research indicates that shame socialization appears distinct from other measures of harsh or authoritarian parenting in Chinese samples (Wu et al. 2002). Fung (1999) suggests that shaming serves to foster the development of children's awareness and sensitivity to moral values and social rules, an important socialization goal given the interdependent orientation of Asian cultures. As such, Asian children understand and demonstrate a sense of shame earlier than children in Western nations (Fung et al. 2003). Additional research is needed to determine the developmental outcomes of shame socialization among Asian American children, and to evaluate potential links to interpersonal attunement skills, such as empathy or perspective-taking.

Academic Achievement The phenomenon of Asian American academic achievement has been widely noted. As of 2004, 48.9% of Asian Americans had a bachelor's degree or higher, a proportion well above that of any other group (US Census Bureau 2004). It is a statistic made much more likely due to the fact that on the road to college, Asian American students have higher GPAs, better scores on achievement tests, and lower drop-out rates than other ethnic groups (Aldous 2006; Chen and Stevenson 1995; Goyette and Xie 1999). Although high rates of educational attainment are evident, there are competing explanations for this performance. Though commonly invoked, the explanatory value of cultural upbringing remains a subject of debate. In their consideration of the phenomenon, Sue and Okazaki (1990) reviewed several hypotheses, the most controversial of which points to heritable differences in intelligence. Evidence in support of this position indicated IQ advantages among Asians compared to European Americans (Lynn 1977; Sowell 1978); however, these studies were riddled with methodological flaws leading most scholars to dismiss a purely biogenetic explanation (Sue and Okazaki 1990). Other research points to structural differences in the home environments of Asian American youth that may account for their academic advantage (e.g., Goyette and Xie 1999; Peng and Wright 1994). For instance, Asian American children are more likely to reside in an intact family with two parents, and to have parents with advanced college degrees. The average household incomes of Chinese, Japanese, Filipino, and South Asian Americans are higher than that of European Americans. Yet these characteristics also fail to account for ethnic group differences in educational attainment (Sue and Okazaki 1990). Furthermore, these demographic findings merely beg the question of how Asian American families have come to enjoy these conditions that facilitate academic success.

A variety of research findings have been discussed as evidence supporting the notion that aspects of Asian American culture and parenting explain high levels of educational attainment. For example, studies have suggested that Asian American home environments structure key-learning opportunities (Peng and Wright 1994), Asian cultural values cheer educational success (Kim and Chun 1994), and indigenous parenting practices support academic motivation (Chao 2001). Fuligni et al. (1999) identified family obligation values as central in promoting academic values, studying, and educational aspirations among Asian American adolescents. However, the burdens of assisting the family on a daily basis can actually interfere with academic performance (Tseng 2004). These findings serve as an important reminder that the associations between cultural values and academic achievement are likely complex.

Research on the cultural socialization of beliefs and expectations about achievement supports a social cognitive approach to understand Asian American school success. There is a strong correlation between student achievement and high academic expectations held by Asian American parents (e.g., Goyette and Xie 1999). High parental expectations appear to derive from an emphasis on effort (Stevenson and Stigler 1992) leading Asian American parents to teach their children to believe that internal and controllable factors lead to success, especially in educational attainment (Kim and Chun 1994). Beliefs that effort and time-on-task are more important than native ability may explain why Asian American parents exert more control over children's time outside of the classroom (e.g., Peng and Wright 1994), structuring free time with extra homework and tutoring lessons. Accordingly, Chinese American mothers cite pushing their children to work hard as the number one reason for their children's school success (Chao 1996).

Asian American students appear to internalize these messages, tending to attribute success to effort more so than ability, and studying more hours per week compared to their European American peers (Chen and Stevenson 1995; Sue and Zane 1985). Some evidence indicates that the temperamental characteristic of effortful control in sustaining attention and inhibiting impulsive behavior may also contribute to academic success among Chinese children (Zhou et al. 2007). Asian American parents also appear to adopt an internal locus regarding their ability to support their children's achievement. Studies indicate that Asian American parents are more likely than other groups to be involved in their children's schooling (Schneider and Lee 1990), especially during the early school years (Choi et al. 1994; Shoho 1994). In the elementary grades, parents support learning through direct methods, such as teaching math and reading or assigning extra homework (Chao and Tseng 2002). However, as Asian American children reach adolescence this advantage seems to expire and Asian American parents actually appear less involved in children's schooling than parents from other groups (Chao and Tseng 2002). It is possible that this reversal may be an artifact of how parental involvement is measured. As children enter high school, Asian American parents shift their focus to college admittance, thereby also shifting to indirect methods of involvement, such as providing resources for SAT preparation.

While the findings reviewed here have generally been cited as evidence of heritage cultural influence on achievement, an alternative explanation focuses on constraints in the attainment of social mobility faced by Asian Americans as a minority group. Sue and Okazaki (1990) discuss the importance of the relative functionalism of academic achievement for socioeconomic advancement among groups. They argue that Asian American youth may be steered toward educational achievement for upward mobility because other avenues toward advancement are blocked to minorities. Therefore, Asian Americans tend to enter fields which require high levels of education (e.g., engineering, medicine), where hiring and promotion depend largely on academic credentials and are less likely to be affected by discrimination. The emphasis on minority status as an important contextual factor in the relative functionalism hypothesis serves as an important counterpoint to a purely cultural thesis in explaining Asian American achievement. The notion of adaptive culture may be invoked to integrate the two positions. According to Garcia Coll et al. (1996), "adaptive culture is the product of [a] group's prior collective history (cultural, political, and economic) and the contextual demands placed by the promoting and inhibiting environments" of the host culture. The inhibitory environment limiting social mobility opportunities for Asian American youth highlighted by Sue and Okazaki (1990) may potentiate existing cultural values about family obligation, effort, and achievement. The interaction of the contextual constraints and heritage socialization traditions may culminate in the adaptive cultural response of Asian American investment in higher education, highlighting the important roles of both the relative functionalism and heritage cultural influences.

Heritage Culture and Sources of Vulnerability for Asian American Children

Avoidant Coping Building further upon our discussion of cultural orientation, we identify areas of challenge that are manifested in particular mental health concerns relevant to Asian American youth. Traditional Asian cultural values and the interdependent tradition may at times present challenges for the development and well-being of Asian American youth and their families. For example, the restraint of self-expression (e.g., Kim and Sherman 2007) and use of indirect coping strategies (Weisz et al. 1984) demonstrated by many Asian American youth can result in avoidant forms of coping that may negatively impact well-being. Asian American college students report using avoidant coping strategies, such as problem avoidance and social withdrawal, more than their European American counterparts (Chang 1996). While indirect coping strategies can be adaptive in some situations, they may also be associated with more depressive symptoms in Asian American youth (Chang 1996), thus, posing concerns for their well-being.

Given the interdependent and relational focus of traditional Asian cultural values, one might infer that Asian American youth would turn to loved ones, and actively seek out social support to cope with stressful events. A large body of research concludes that being socially integrated with access to support confers a wealth of beneficial mental and physical health effects (Seeman 1996). However, recent evidence indicates that the importance given to harmonious relationships in traditional Asian values may actually deter support-seeking behaviors in Asian American youth. Asian American college students seek social support less often and find support-seeking to be less helpful compared to European American college students (Kim et al. 2006; Taylor et al. 2004). Findings suggest that Asian American students are less willing to actively seek out social support primarily because of interdependence concerns about disrupting the harmony of the group, unduly worrying others, and losing face (Taylor et al. 2004). Similarly, cross-national research has indicated that mobilizing social support actually caused more stress for students in China in ways not seen among American students (Liang and Bogat 1994). Recent research suggests that Asian American students may benefit more from implicit forms of social support that are relationally less "risky" (Taylor et al. 2007). Thus, any potential benefits of receiving support may be outweighed by concerns about burdening others with one's problems, or losing face in the eyes of loved ones. These interdependence concerns appear to provide social disincentives for Asian American youth to seek help from others in times of trouble.

Perfectionism and Distress Interdependence concerns may also contribute to psychological challenges for Asian American youth through their link to perfectionist tendencies, which have been found to be higher in Asian American students relative to their peers (e.g., Peng and Wright 1994). Researchers have often attributed perfectionism among Asian American students to a cultural focus on achievement to fulfill family obligation and avoid loss of face (Stevenson and Lee 1996; Sue and Okazaki 1990). While some aspects of perfectionism promote adaptation by inspiring individuals to strive for excellence, researchers have identified "maladaptive perfectionism" as being motivated by a fear of failure (Slade and Owens 1998) and characterized by self-doubt and excessive concern over mistakes (Bieling et al. 2004). Maladaptive perfectionism has been linked to depression and suicidality among Asian Americans (Beevers and Miller 2004; Castro and Rice 2003), with recent findings that Asian American college students are more vulnerable to maladaptive perfectionism and associated depressive symptoms when they hold more interdependence values (Yoon and Lau 2008). Thus, the same interdependent cultural traditions that promote achievement may also confer some burdens borne by Asian American youngsters.

In sum, the literature suggests that being oriented toward interdependence may confer some psychological costs. Interdependence concerns may increase the risk for psychological distress in Asian American youth and young adults because of tendencies toward avoidant coping, maladaptive perfectionism, and a decreased willingness to seek support from others. Furthermore, these challenges related to interdependence are also compounded by hardships that Asian American youth may encounter owing to their minority status in the United States.

The Minority Experience

The Minority Experience and Sources of Vulnerability for Asian American Children

The Model Minority Stereotype In addition to the challenges engendered through cultural influences, Asian American youth also encounter and respond to a variety of prevailing racial stereotypes. One of the most common stereotypes attributed to Asian American youth is the "model minority" stereotype, a widely shared belief that Asian Americans have successfully overcome discrimination to become a uniformly successful minority group worthy of admiration by other minorities (Chun 1995). On the surface, the model minority stereotype appears to ascribe a positive image to Asian Americans, but critics point to its divisive effect on race relations and the many inaccuracies in interpretation of evidence used to propagate a myth of success (Chun 1995). Touting the model minority stereotype effectively conceals the wide diversity that exists within the Asian American community, allowing for the needs of Asian American children and youth with problem behaviors to go unrecognized and untreated (Tsunokai 2005). Given the widespread acceptance of the model minority stereotype, Asian American students who drop out of school are often overlooked and do not receive the resources needed to achieve academically (Lew 2003). Barriers to college achievement faced by Asian Americans also go unrecognized. For example, in 2005, Asian American freshmen were more likely than the national freshman population to come from poor or low-income families, require remedial work in English, and seek employment to help pay for college (Chang et al. 2007).

Furthermore, despite higher aggregate levels of academic achievement, Asian American students tend to experience the world as less comprehensible, manageable and meaningful (Ying et al. 2001a), and are more likely to have negative or ambivalent attitudes toward pursuing academic achievement (Lee and Ying 2001). Moreover, there is also evidence that the model minority stereotype leads to peer harassment as children from other ethnic groups perceive Asian American children as receiving preferential treatment by teachers (Rosenbloom and Way 2004). The stereotype of Asian Americans as being gifted academically has also been linked to the segregation of Asian American youth from other peer groups (Kao 2000). Furthermore, the salience of the model minority stereotype to Asian American students has ironically been shown under some circumstances to undermine their performance in achievement contexts. Although some studies have demonstrated that subtly priming Asian ethnic identity can boost performance on math achievement tasks (Shih et al. 1999), Cheryan and Bodenhausen (2000) demonstrated that making public expectations of the model minority stereotype salient can cause Asian American students to "choke under pressure." Hence, propagation of what may seem to be a benign or positive stereotype about Asian Americans can be racially divisive, interfere with recognition of genuine mental health or educational needs, and be detrimental at an individual level for interpersonal functioning, academic performance, and psychological well-being.

Acculturative Stress and Acculturation Gaps Another challenge that Asian American children face in growing up in the United States involves the acculturative process, or the process by which attitudes and/or behaviors of persons from one cultural group are modified as a result of contact with a different culture (Moyerman and Forman 1992). Studies indicate that individuals who feel marginalized and separated from ethnic and dominant cultural groups tend to experience the highest levels of "acculturative stress," the psychological difficulties originating from adjusting to a new environment, which involves loss of social support, experiencing discrimination and stereotyping, overcoming linguistic barriers, and having to adapt to changes in political and economic contexts (e.g., Berry and Kim 1988). For Asian American immigrants, studies have found that higher levels of acculturative stress are related to mental health problems, including anxiety and somatic symptoms (Williams and Berry 1991), depressive symptoms (Shin 1994), and maladaptive eating patterns (Furukawa 1994).

One source of acculturative stress among Asian American immigrant families is related to the different rates of acculturation between immigrant parents and their children, since children in immigrant families tend to acculturate to American traditions and values more quickly than their parents (Okagaki and Bojczyk 2002; Ying and Chao 1996). Research with Asian American samples has shown that perceived acculturation gaps are associated with intergenerational family conflict (Ying et al. 2004, 2001b), a proposed mechanism of action in the relationship between acculturation gaps and youth maladjustment (e.g., Lee et al. 2000; Ying 1999). The clashing nature of the differences between the host and heritage culture exacerbates this problem for Asian American families, as presses for autonomy are likely met by increasingly controlling parental responses, with both sides becoming more polarized by repeated conflicts.

Especially within the interdependent tradition of Asian cultures, acculturation gaps and conflict or estrangement between parents and children may place Asian American youth at heightened risk of detrimental outcomes (Lau et al. 2002). Indeed, several studies among Asian American adolescents have indicated that higher levels of family conflict are associated with low self-esteem, depression, and lower educational achievement (Rumbaut 1994, 1997). Similarly, studies among Asian American college students have found that family conflicts are related to lower family satisfaction, negative affect, and somatic symptoms of distress (Lee et al. 2005). Hence, the literature suggests that Asian American immigrant youth are at heightened risk for maladaptive adjustment and intergenerational conflict which may accompany the rigors of acculturation.

The Minority Experience and Sources of Strength for Asian American Children

Biculturalism and Positive Ethnic Identity Development While some processes encountered during acculturation may pose significant challenges, other forms of adaptation to acculturative demands lead to healthy development for Asian American youth. Multidimensional theories of acculturation take into account not only how one relates to other ethnic groups in society, but also one's sense of ethnic belonging (Berry 1980). Research on acculturation styles indicate that a strong sense of belonging to both one's ethnic group and to the dominant culture is associated with healthy psychosocial outcomes, including greater academic achievement, stronger ethnic pride, higher levels of self-esteem, and perceived social support (Berry and Kim 1988; Kim and Omizo 2005; Phinney et al. 1992). These findings suggest that biculturalism, accomplished through the facile integration of oneself into the social worlds of both the heritage and mainstream American cultures, permits the flexible navigation of the many adaptational demands faced by Asian American youngsters.

The importance of one's ethnic group and heritage culture is further highlighted by research that points to the protective and adaptive role of ethnic identity, a sense of identification or belonging as a member of a minority ethnic group (Phinney 1990). Ethnic identity development is thought to be facilitated by two socialization processes. First, enculturation processes expose children to cultural opportunities that promote ethnic awareness and pride. Second, racialization processes promote awareness of the social reality of discrimination and aid children in developing strategies to manage these experiences. Studies of Asian American youth have found that ethnic pride, involvement, and ethnic identity achievement are related to positive adjustment as evidenced by increased happiness, self-esteem, and goal directedness, and lower levels of internalizing and externalizing behavior problems (Kiang et al. 2006; Martinez and Dukes 1997; Shrake and Rhee 2004). In addition, having a well-developed sense of ethnic identity has been found to protect Asian American youth from the negative psychological effects of discrimination by facilitating the employment of more adaptive coping skills such as problem-solving strategies (Yoo and Lee 2005). Lastly, Kiang et al. (2006) have also suggested that a sense of ethnic belonging may relate to the construction of solid social support networks, and feelings of positive ethnic regard may evolve into a broader sense of well-being that supports healthy social and emotional development.

Discussion

Applying Strengths to Meet Challenges

In this chapter, we reviewed literature asserting that an interdependent cultural orientation serves as a foundation for competencies and resilience for Asian American youth by shaping contexts of family and community. The strengths described in this chapter are rooted in priorities emphasizing group harmony, nurturing relationships, and duty to family which often converge to drive positive adaptation. More importantly, we contend that this interdependent view of the world can serve as an important resource in addressing the challenges Asian American youth encounter in their adjustment and growth. Thus, we believe that a key strategy for harnessing the strengths of these children in order to promote resiliency is to capitalize upon the interdependence values that broadly characterize their cultural heritage (see Table 1).

One essential avenue to promote youth resiliency would be to support Asian American parents to leverage naturally occurring strategies that promote optimal child development. In order to capitalize on the cultural importance given to interconnectedness and group solidarity, encouraging parents to participate in parenting enrichment programs within the Asian American community can cultivate well-being in their children. Research has suggested that traditional Western psychological treatments and services may present multiple cultural and practical barriers to participation by Asian Americans (e.g., Leong and Lau 2001). Thus, embedding supportive parenting programs within well-accepted Asian American community institutions (e.g., heritage language schools, faith-based organizations, health and wellness clinics, and community schools) would make them more welcoming and better attended. Programs that are collaborative with respected community leaders and offered in group format may appeal most to Asian American families with interdependent sensibilities. Emphasizing valued socialization goals (e.g., promoting values of educational attainment, strengthening family cohesion and integrity) and the modern day relevance of heritage cultural practices (e.g., training) within these programs would also increase their relevance.

Table 1 Summary of demographics, challenges, strengths, and recommendations

Demographics	Challenges	Strengths	Recommendations
1.2% of the general population	Challenges related to cultural orientation	Strengths related to cultural orientation	Capitalizing on strengths to promote resiliency
Over 60% of all Asian Americans are 1st generation	• Interdependence concerns about disrupting group harmony may lead to less social support seeking behaviors	• Characteristics of temperament, such as self-control and inhibition may be related to cultural emphasis on maintaining group harmony	• Given importance of family, encourage parent participation in parenting programs with emphasis on valued socialization goals
Over 75% of all Asian Americans reside in large metropolitan areas	• Maladaptive perfectionism may stem from a cultural focus on academic achievement, family obligation, and loss of face	• Indigenous parenting behaviors, such as parental control and socialization of shame may be related to positive developmental outcomes	• Psychoeducation regarding maladaptive perfectionism, intergenerational acculturation conflicts, etc. would be important given tendencies not to mobilize support to cope with common stressors
Heterogeneous group includes more than 20 different cultures		• Values such as deference for teachers, high academic expectations and belief in hard work may bolster academic success	• Encourage positive ethnic identity development in youth through participation in mentoring programs and cultural activities
	Challenges related to the minority experience	Strengths related to the minority experience	
	• Acculturation processes may lead to acculturative stress and heightened family conflict	• Biculturalism or integration allows one to navigate demands of both heritage and mainstream cultures	
	• Youth encounter discrimination and stereotypes, such as the model minority stereotype	• Ethnic identity and parental cultural socialization have been found to be related to positive youth adjustment	

Parenting programs can be instrumental in educating Asian American parents about how to identify and address potential adjustment difficulties for their children. Psychoeducation regarding concerns of particular relevance for Asian American youth (e.g., maladaptive perfectionism, intergenerational acculturation conflicts) would be important, given the concern that Asian American youngsters tend not to mobilize support to cope with common stressors. These groups could also provide a venue through which Asian American parents can connect with other parents who are likely to be encountering similar struggles with their children, providing a safe and culturally responsive forum where parents can share, compare, support, and normalize each other's experiences. In a nonevaluative group setting, an appreciation of mental health issues for Asian American youth can be fostered, potentially leading to decreased feelings of stigma regarding concerns about psychological wellness. Therefore, providing resources and information, as well as empathetic connections with other Asian Americans, can promote a sense of community and the spirit of collaboration among parents of Asian American youth.

A specific example of a supportive community-based program for Asian American parents would focus on how to best encourage academic success in children, since this appears to be of paramount importance in the community. Group leaders can provide much sought after practical information regarding the American school system, how to collaborate with teachers, and how to overcome possible language and cultural barriers in supporting children's learning. Parents can be educated about how academic pressure and demands for perfection may negatively impact youth, and acquire skills for promoting resilience in academically demanding settings. Group leaders must be trained to facilitate supportive group process which fosters interdependence through encouraging parents to rely on and help each other, instead of struggling in isolation due to concerns about losing face or burdening others.

In addition to supporting parents to promote resilience in their children, special efforts should also be made to directly reach Asian American youth to help them overcome developmental challenges. Given the established research finding that achieved ethnic identity is related to psychological well-being, it would be advisable to promote resiliency in Asian American youth by encouraging positive ethnic identity development. While there is a dearth of intervention studies for Asian American youth, studies conducted with other ethnic minority samples have indicated that programs which expose minority youth to cultural beliefs, values, and practices, and minority role models, strengthen ethnic identity and self-esteem (e.g., Belgrave et al. 2000). Programs of this type might foster resiliency among Asian American youth by ensuring that they feel cared for and embedded within a distinctive and worthwhile community. This may include participation in heritage language schools, after school enrichment programs, religious communities, and cultural activities such as martial arts, calligraphy, and folk dancing. Participation in these activities can expose Asian American children to their peers in positive, identity-building settings, and to create stronger support networks. Mentoring programs where Asian American children can benefit from relationships with older

Asian Americans may prove especially beneficial in providing guidance to youth who may not actively mobilize support from others.

Future Recommendations

While we believe the strengths and challenges proposed in our review may apply to many Asian American children, they cannot be generalized to the entire population given the tremendous heterogeneity within this group. Hence, a general direction for future research is to distinguish the factors influencing development across Asian subgroups with special attention to the historical context of their immigration histories and the specific ecological demands of their local social contexts. Since research has largely focused on Asian American youth in ethnically dense cities, more attention is needed to understand the development of Asian American children growing up in relative ethnic isolation.

Gaps in the extant literature also suggest specific areas for future research. First, recent findings identifying reticence among Asian American young adults in seeking social support warrant further investigation. These findings are alarming given that previous researchers have suggested that Asian Americans are reluctant to seek mental health services and instead rely on informal social support. Taken together, these findings imply that we should be doubly concerned about the health behaviors of Asian Americans in distress. Second, we have noted that previous research has not examined the intersection of cultural influences and minority status concerns in jointly explaining Asian American academic achievement. Third, research on the beneficial effects of Asian American parenting have largely been focused on school performance outcomes and more research is needed to examine whether benefits may extend to other developmental outcomes (e.g., emotion regulation, social competence). Fourth, it would be helpful for intervention development to identify the mechanisms by which ethnic identity promotes healthy adjustment and protects against the ill-effects of discrimination. Finally, we hope to see work begin on the development and evaluation of programs and interventions that cultivate ties within the community, raise awareness of mental health issues, and promote ethnic identity formation among Asian American children to encourage healthy bicultural adaptation.

Concluding Comments

Our review of the literature demonstrates that Asian American children and youth exhibit many strengths that extend across a number of domains, including dispositional characteristics that promote self-regulation, family systems marked by parental involvement, and positive developmental outcomes including academic achievement. Yet, while the presence of these strengths suggests that Asian American youth should have the resources to maintain psychological well-being, some evidence suggests that this group is vulnerable to certain developmental challenges. We conclude that Asian American youth are uniquely faced with the rather difficult task of residing at the intersection of two disparate cultural traditions. On the one hand, Asian American children are socialized by their families and ethnic communities to embody interdependent values and norms, and on the other hand, they are expected to function in an independently oriented society that demands assertion and expression of individuality. Individuals who are able to successfully negotiate the demands of these two worlds may be best described as bicultural—possessing a well-developed sense of achieved ethnic identity while also integrating toward the expectations of the dominant American culture. Asian American youth must develop the skills to successfully navigate the dualities in their local social world by adjusting themselves to operate under differing cultural frameworks from one context to the next.

This flexibility is particularly important given that some of the purported strengths of Asian American youth can contribute to maladjustment under certain conditions. For example, behavioral inhibition and shy temperament among Chinese youth may be seen as desirable and adaptive within interdependent cultural contexts because they may aid in maintaining group harmony. However, these same dispositions are associated with increased psychological distress in Western societies (Chen et al. 2005). Similarly, parenting practices that involve high levels of control may be associated with positive school adjustment when applied in traditional Asian American families and communities, but may have negative consequences in contexts where the prevailing norms for family relations differ.

Thus, we contend that resilience among Asian American youth can be optimized in two ways: through the strengthening of ties within the community and by cultivating positive ethnic identity development. We propose that encouraging Asian American parents and youth to participate in supportive programs in the community not only allows for them to acquire knowledge and learn new skills, but also helps to create a local social world in which cultural vitality can thrive. Community institutions could be instrumental in promoting networks within the Asian American community that bring together children and families who share similar histories and traditions. In these settings, the strengths of Asian American youth can be fostered through the cultural socialization practices of enculturation and racialization. Fostering ethnic identity development may promote successful transitions between dual cultural contexts by enabling Asian American youth to flourish both within heritage cultural contexts and by buffering them from occasional negative interactions within dominant cultural contexts.

References

Aldous, J. (2006). Family, ethnicity, and immigrant youths' educational achievements. *Journal of Family Issues, 27,* 1633–1667.

Beevers, C. G., & Miller, I. W. (2004). Perfectionism, cognitive bias, and hopelessness as prospective predictors of suicidal ideation. *Suicide and Life-Threatening Behavior, 34,* 126–137.

Belgrave, F. Z., Chase-Vaughn, G., Gray, F., Addison, J. D., & Cherry, V. R. (2000). The effectiveness of a culture- and gender-specific intervention for increasing resiliency among African American preadolescent females. *Journal of Black Psychology, 26,* 133–147.

Berry, J. W. (1980). Acculturation as varieties of adaptation. In A. M. Padilla (Ed.), *Acculturation: Theory, model, and some new findings* (pp. 9–25). Boulder: Westview.

Berry, J. W., & Kim, U. (1988). Acculturation and mental health. In P. R. Dasen, J. W. Berry, & N. Sartorius (Eds.), *Health and cross-cultural psychology.* Beverly Hills: Sage.

Bieling, P. J., Israeli, A. L., & Antony, M. M. (2004). Is perfectionism good, bad or both? Examining models of the perfectionism construct. *Personality and Individual Differences, 26,* 1373–1385.

Castro, J. R., & Rice, K. G. (2003). Perfectionism and ethnicity: Implications for depressive symptoms and self-reported academic achievement. *Cultural Diversity & Ethnic Minority Psychology, 9,* 64–78.

Caudill, W., & Weinstein, H. (1969). Maternal care and infant behavior in Japan and America. *Psychiatry: Journal for the Study of Interpersonal Processes, 32,* 12–43.

Chang, E. C. (1996). Cultural differences in optimism, pessimism, and coping: Predictors of subsequent adjustment in Asian American and Caucasian American college students. *Journal of Counseling Psychology, 43,* 113–123.

Chang, M. J., Park, J. J., Lin, M. H., Poon, O. A., & Nakanishi, D. T. (2007). *Beyond myths: The growth and diversity of Asian American college freshmen: 1971–2005.* **Los Angeles:** Higher Education Research Institute.

Chao, R. K. (1994). Beyond parental control and authoritarian parenting style: Understanding Chinese parenting through the cultural notion of training. *Child Development, 65,* 1111–1119.

Chao, R. K. (1996). Chinese and European American mothers' beliefs about the role of parenting in children's school success. *Journal of Cross-cultural Psychology, 27,* 403–423.

Chao, R. K. (2000). Cultural explanations for the role of parenting in the school success of Asian American children. In R. W. Taylor & M. C. Wang (Eds.), *Resilience across contexts: Family, work, culture, and community* (pp. 333–363). Mahwah: Erlbaum.

Chao, R. K. (2001). Extending research on the consequences of parenting style for Chinese Americans and European Americans. *Child Development, 72,* 1832–1843.

Chao, R., & Tseng, V. (2002). Parenting of Asians. In M. H. Bornstein (Ed.), *Handbook of parenting* (pp. 59–93). Mahwah: Erlbaum.

Chen, C., & Stevenson, H. W. (1995). Motivation and mathematics achievement: A comparative study of Asian-American, Caucasian-American, and East Asian high school students. *Child Development, 66,* 1215–1234.

Chen, X. (2000). Social and emotional development in Chinese children and adolescents: A contextual cross-cultural perspective. In F. Columbus (Ed.), *Advances in psychology research* (Vol. I, pp. 229–251). Commack: Nova Science.

Chen, X., Cen, G., Li, D., & He, Y. (2005). Social functioning and adjustment in Chinese children: The imprint of historical time. *Child Development, 76,* 182–195.

Chen, X., Hastings, P. D., Rubin, K. H., Chen, H., Cen, G., & Stewart, S. L. (1998). Child rearing attitudes and behavioral inhibition in Chinese and Canadian toddlers: A cross-cultural study. *Developmental Psychology, 34,* 677–686.

Chen, X., Rubin, K. H., Liu, M., Chen, H., Wang, L., Li, D., et al. (2003). Compliance in Chinese and Canadian toddlers. *International Journal of Behavioral Development, 27,* 428–436.

Cheryan, S., & Bodenhausen, G. V. (2000). When positive stereotypes threaten intellectual performance: The psychological hazards of "model minority" status. *Psychological Science, 11,* 399–402.

Choi, Y. E., Bempechat, J., & Ginsburg, H. P. (1994). Educational socialization in Korean American children: A longitudinal study. *Journal of Applied Developmental Psychology, 15,* 313–318.

Chun, K. T. (1995). The myth of Asian American success and its educational ramifications. *IRCD Bulletin, 15*(1 and 2), 1–12. (Reprinted in D. T. Nakanishi & T. Y. Nishida (Eds.), *The Asian American educational experience: A source book for teachers and students.* New York: Routledge).

Fuligni, A. J., Tseng, V., & Lam, M. (1999). Attitudes toward family obligations among American adolescents from Asian, Latin American, and European backgrounds. *Child Development, 70,* 1030–1044.

Fung, H. (1999). Becoming a moral child: The socialization of shame among young Chinese children. *Ethos, 27,* 180–209.

Fung, H., Leiber, E., & Leung, P. W. L. (2003). Parental beliefs on shame and moral socialization in Taiwan, Hong Kong, and the United States. In K. S. Yang, K. K. Hwang, P. B. Pedersen, & I. Daibo (Eds.), *Progress in Asian social psychology: Conceptual and empirical contributions* (pp. 83–109). Westport: Praeger.

Furukawa, T. (1994). Weight change sand eating attitudes of Japanese adolescents under acculturative stress: A prospective study. *International Journal of Eating Disorder, 15,* 71–79.

Garcia Coll, C., Crnic, K., Lamberty, G., Wasik, B. H., Jenkins, R., Garcia, H. V., & McAdoo, H. P. (1996). An integrative model for the study of developmental competencies in minority children. *Child Development, 67,* 1891–1914.

Goyette, K., & Xie, Y. (1999). Educational expectations of Asian American youths: Determinants and ethnic differences. *Sociology of Education, 72,* 22–36.

Ho, D. Y. F. (1986). Chinese patterns of socialization: A critical review. In M. H. Bond (Ed.), *The psychology of the Chinese people*. Hong Kong: Oxford University Press.

Hofstede, G. (1980). *Culture's consequences.* Beverly Hill: Sage.

Kagan, J., Arcus, D., Snidman, N., & Feng, W. Y. (1994). Reactivity in infants: A cross-national comparison. *Developmental Psychology, 30,* 342–345.

Kao, G. (2000). Group images and possible selves among adolescents: Linking stereotypes to expectations by race and ethnicity. *Sociological Forum, 15,* 407–430.

Kiang, L., Yip, T., Gonzales-Backen, M., Witkow, M., & Fuligni, A. J. (2006). Ethnic identity and the daily psychological well-being of adolescents from Mexican and Chinese backgrounds. *Child Development, 77,* 1338–1350.

Kim, B. S. K., & Omizo, M. M. (2005). Asian and European American cultural values, collective self-esteem, acculturative stress, cognitive flexibility, and general self-efficacy among Asian American college students. *Journal of Counseling Psychology, 52,* 412–419.

Kim, H. S., & Sherman, D. K. (2007). "Express yourself": Culture and the effect of self-expression on choice. *Journal of Personality and Social Psychology, 92*(1), 1–11.

Kim, H. S., Sherman, D. K., Ko, D., & Taylor, S. E. (2006). Pursuit of comfort and pursuit of harmony: Culture, relationships, and social support seeking. *Personality and Social Psychology Bulletin, 32,* 1595–1607.

Kim, U., & Chun, M. (1994). Educational "success" of Asian Americans: An indigenous perspective. *Journal of Applied Developmental Psychology, 15,* 329–339.

Kornadt, H. J. (1991). Aggressive motive and its developmental conditions in Eastern and Western cultures. In N. Bleichrodt & J. D. Pieter (Eds.), *Contemporary issues in cross-cultural psychology* (pp. 155–167). Amsterdam: Swets & Zeitlinger.

Lau, A. S., Jernewall, N. M., Zane, N., & Myers, H. (2002). Correlates of suicidal behaviors among Asian American outpatient youths. *Cultural diversity & Ethnic Minority Psychology, 8,* 199–213.

Lau, S., & Cheung, P. C. (1987). Relations between Chinese adolescents' perception of parental control and organization and their perception of parental warmth. *Developmental Psychology, 23,* 726–729.

Lee, P. A., & Ying, Y.-W. (2001). Asian American adolescents' academic achievement: A look behind the model minority image. *Journal of Human Behavior in the Social Environment, 3,* 35–48.

Lee, R. M., Choe, J., Kim, G., & Ngo, V. (2000). The construction of the Asian American family conflict scale. *Journal of Counseling Psychology, 47,* 211–222.

Lee, R. M., Su, J., & Yoshida, E. (2005). Coping with intergenerational family conflict among Asian American college students. *Journal of Counseling Psychology, 52,* 389–399.

Leong, F. T. L., & Lau, A. S. (2001). Barriers to providing effective mental health services to Asian Americans. *Mental Health Services Research, 3,* 201–214.

Leung, K., Lau, S., & Lam, W. L. (1998). Parenting styles and academic achievement: A cross-cultural study. *Merrill-Palmer Quarterly, 44*, 157–169.

Lew, J. (2003). Korean American high school dropouts: A case study of their experiences and negotiations of schooling, family, and communities. In S. Books (Ed.), *Invisible children in the society and its schools* (2nd ed., pp. 53-66). Mahwah: Erlbaum.

Liang, B., & Bogat, G. A. (1994). Culture, control, and coping: New perspectives on social support. *American Journal of Community Psychology, 22,* 123–147.

Lin, C. Y. C., & Fu, V. R. (1990). A comparison of child-rearing practices among Chinese, Immigrant Chinese, and Caucasian-American Parents. *Child Development, 61,* 429–433.

Lynn, R. (1977). The intelligence of the Japanese. *Bulletin of the British Psychological Society, 40*, 464–468.

Markus, H. R., & Kitayama, S. (1991). Culture and the self: Implications for cognition, emotion, and motivation. *Psychological Review, 98,* 224–253.

Martinez, R. O., & Dukes, R. L. (1997). The effects of ethnic identity, ethnicity, and gender on adolescent well-being. *Journal of Youth and Adolescence, 26,* 503–516.

Matsumoto, D. (2006). Are cultural differences in emotion regulation mediated by personality traits? *Journal of Cross-Cultural Psychology, 37,* 421–437.

Moyerman, D. R., & Forman, B. D. (1992). Acculturation and adjustment: A meta-analytic study. *Hispanic Journal of Behavioral Sciences, 14,* 163–200.

Nomura, J., Noguchi, Y., Saito, S., & Tezuka, I. (1995). Family characteristics and dynamics in Japan and the United States. *International Journal of Intercultural Relations, 19*, 59–86.

Okagaki, L., & Bojczyk, K. E. (2002). Perspectives on Asian American development. In G. C. Nagayama Hall & S. Okazaki (Eds.), *Asian American psychology: The science of lives in context* (pp. 67–104). Washington, DC: American Psychological Association.

Peng, S. S., & Wright, D. (1994). Explanation of academic achievement of Asian American students. *The Journal of Educational Research, 87,* 346–352.

Phinney, J. S. (1990). Ethnic identity in adolescents and adults: Review of research. *Psychological Bulletin, 108,* 499–514.

Phinney, J., Chavira, V., & Williamson, L. (1992). Acculturation attitudes and self-esteem among high school and college students. *Youth and Society, 23,* 299–312.

Rohner, R. P., & Pettengill, S. M. (1985). Perceived parental acceptance-rejection and parental control among Korean adolescents. *Child Development, 56*, 524–528.

Rosenbloom, S. R., & Way, N. (2004). Experiences of discrimination among African American, Asian American, and Latino adolescents in an urban high school. *Youth and Society, 35*, 420–451.

Rothbart, M. K., & Bates, J. E. (1998). Temperament. In W. Damon (Ed.) & N. Eisenberg (Vol. Ed.), *Handbook of child psychology: Social, emotional, and personality development, Vol. 3*, (5th ed., pp. 105–176). New York: Wiley.

Rothbart, M. K., & Derryberry, D. (1981). Development of individual differences in temperament. In M. E. Lamb & A. L. Brown (Eds.), *Advances in developmental psychology* (Vol. 1, pp. 37–86), Hillsdale: Erlbaum.

Rothbaum, F., Weisz, J., Pott, M., Kazuo, M., & Morelli, G. (2000). Attachment and culture: Security in the United States and Japan. *American Psychologist, 55*, 1093–1104.

Rumbaut, R. G. (1994). The crucible within: Ethnic identity, self-esteem, and segmented assimilation among children of immigrants. *International Migration Review, 28*, 748–794.

Rumbaut, R. G. (1997). Assimilation and its discontents: Between rhetoric and reality. *International Migration Review, 31*, 923–960.

Schneider, B., & Lee, Y. (1990). A model for academic success: The school and home environment of East Asian students. *Anthropology and Education Quarterly, 21,* 358–377.

Seeman, T. E. (1996). Social ties and health: The benefits of social integration. *Annals of Epidemiology, 6,* 442–451.

Shih, M., Pittinsky, T. L., & Ambady, N. (1999). Stereotype susceptibility: Identity salience and shifts in quantitative performance. *Psychological Science, 10,* 80–83.

Shin, K. S. (1994). Psychosocial predictors of depressive symptoms in Korean-American women in New York city. *Women & Health, 2*, 73–82.
Shoho, A. R. (1994). A historical comparison of parental involvement of three generations of Japanese Americans (Isseis, Niseis, Sanseis) in the education of their children. *Journal of Applied Developmental Psychology, 15*, 305–311.
Shrake, E. K., & Rhee, S. (2004). Ethnic identity as a predictor of problem behaviors among Korean American adolescents. *Adolescence, 39*, 601–622.
Slade, P. D., & Owens, R. G. (1998). A dual process model of perfectionism based on reinforcement theory. *Behavior Modification, 22*, 372–390.
Sowell, T. (Ed.). (1978). *Essay and data on American ethnic groups.* Washington, D. C.: Urban Institute.
Stevenson, H. W., & Lee, S. (1996). The academic achievement of Chinese students. In M. H. Bond (Ed.). *The handbook of Chinese psychology* (pp. 124–142). Hong Kong: Oxford University Press.
Stevenson, H. W., & Stigler, J. W. (1992). *The learning gap: Why our schools are failing and what we can learn from Japanese and Chinese education.* New York: Summit Books.
Stewart, S. M., Bond, M. H., Zaman, R. M., McBride-Chang, C., Rao, N., Ho, L. M., & Fielding, R. (1999). Functional parenting in Pakistan. *International Journal of Behavioral Development, 23*, 747–770.
Stewart, S. M., Rao, N., Bond, M. H., McBride-Chang, C., Fielding, R., & Kennard, B. D. (1998). Chinese dimensions of parenting: Broadening Western predictors and outcomes. *International Journal of Psychology, 33*, 345–358.
Sue, S., & Okazaki, S. (1990). Asian-American educational achievements: A phenomenon in search of an explanation. *The American Psychologist, 45*, 913–920.
Sue, S., & Zane, N. (1985). Academic achievement and socioemotional adjustment among Chinese university students. *Journal of Counseling Psychology, 32*, 570–579.
Taylor, S. E., Sherman, D. K., Kim, H. S., Jarcho, J., Takagi, K., & Dunagan, M. S. (2004). Culture and social support: Who seeks it and why? *Journal of Personality and Social Psychology, 87*, 354–362.
Taylor, S. E., Welch, W. T., Kim. H. S., & Sherman, D. K. (2007). Cultural differences in the impact of social support on psychological and biological stress responses. *Psychological Science, 18*, 831–837.
Ting-Toomey, S. (1994). *The challenge of facework: Cross-cultural and interpersonal issues.* Albany: State University of New York Press.
Triandis, H. C. (1989). The self and social behavior in differing cultural contexts. *Psychological Review, 96*, 506–520.
Triandis, H. C., Bontempo, R., Villareal, M. J., Asai, M., & Lucca, N. (1988). Individualism and collectivism: Cross-cultural perspectives on self-ingroup relationships. *Journal of Personality and Social Psychology, 54*, 323–338.
Trommsdorff, G. (1985). Some comparative aspects of socialization in Japan and Germany. In I. R. Lagunes & Y. H. Pootinga (Eds.), *From a different perspective: Studies of behavior across cultures* (pp. 231–240). Lisse: Swets & Zeitlinger.
Tsai, J. L., Louie, J. Y., Chen, E. E., & Uchida, Y. (2007). Learning what feelings to desire: Socialization of ideal affect through children's storybooks. *Personality and Social Psychology Bulletin, 33*, 17–30.
Tseng, V. (2004). Family interdependence and academic adjustment in college: Youth from immigrant and U.S. born families. *Child Development, 75*, 966–983.
Tsunokai, G. T. (2005). Beyond the lenses of the 'model' minority myth: A descriptive portrait of Asian gang members. *Journal of Gang Research, 12*, 37–58.
US Census Bureau.(2004). *The Asian alone or in combination population in the United States: 2004* (PPL-184). http://www.census.gov/population/socdemo/race/api/ppl-184/tab7ic.pdf. Accessed 15 April 2007.
Weisz, J. R., Rothbaum, F. M., & Blackburn, T. C. (1984). Standing out and standing in: The psychology of control in America and Japan. *American Psychologist, 39*, 955–969.

Williams, C. L., & Berry, J. W. (1991). Primary prevention of acculturative stress among refugees: Application of psychological theory and practice. *American Psychologist, 46*, 632–641.
Wu, D. Y. H. (1996). Chinese childhood socialization. In M. H. Bond (Ed.), *The handbook of Chinese psychology* (pp. 143–154). Hong Kong: Oxford University Press.
Wu, P., Robinson, C. C., Yang, C., Hart, C. H., Olsen, S. F., Porter, C. L., Jin, S., Wo, J., & Wu, X. (2002). Similarities and differences in mothers' parenting of preschoolers in China and in the United States. *International Journal of Behavioral Development, 26*, 481–491.
Xu, Z., Wan, C. W., Mussen, P. H., & Shen, J. X. (1991). Family socialization and children's behavior and personality development in China. *Journal of Genetic Psychology, 152*, 239–253.
Ying, Y. (1999). Strengthening intergenerational/intercultural ties in migrant families: A new intervention for parents. *Journal of Community Psychology, 27*, 89–96.
Ying, Y., & Chao, C. (1996). Intergenerational relationship in Iu Mien American families. *Amerasia Journal, 22*, 47–64.
Ying, Y., Lee, P. A., & Tsai, J. L. (2004). Psychometric properties of the intergenerational congruence in immigrant families—child scale in Chinese Americans. *Journal of Comparative Family Studies, 35*, 91–103.
Ying, Y., Lee, P. A., Tsai, J. L., Hung, Y., Lin, M., & Wan, C. T. (2001a). Asian American college students as model minorities: An examination of their overall competence. *Cultural Diversity & Ethnic Minority Psychology, 7*, 59–74.
Ying, Y., Lee, P. A., Tsai, J. L., Lee, Y. J., & Tsang, M. (2001b). Relationship of young adult Chinese Americans with their parents: Variation by migratory status and cultural orientation. *American Journal of Orthopsychiatry, 71*, 342–349.
Yoo, H. C., & Lee, R. M. (2005). Ethnic identity and approach-type coping as moderators of the racial discrimination/well-being relation in Asian Americans. *Journal of Counseling Psychology, 52*, 497–506.
Yoon, J., & Lau, A. S. (2008). Maladaptive perfectionism and depressive symptoms among Asian American college students: Contributions of interdependence and parental relations. *Cultural Diversity and Ethnic Minority Psychology, 14*, 92–101.
Zhou, Q., Eisenberg, N., Wang, Y., & Reiser, M. (2004). Chinese children's effortful control and dispositional Anger/Frustration: Relations to parenting styles and children's social functioning. *Developmental Psychology, 40*, 352–366.
Zhou, Q., Main, A., & Wang, Y. (2007). *The relations of temperamental effortful control and anger/frustration to Chinese children's academic achievement: A longitudinal study.* Paper presented at the meeting of the American Psychological Association, San Francisco, CA.

Chapter 10
Psychology of Asian American Adults: Challenges and Strengths

Oanh Meyer, Manveen Dhindsa and Nolan Zane

Chapter Focus

This chapter examines the mental health issues of Asian American adults from two perspectives. First, there is a focus on prejudice and discrimination, acculturative stress, and family conflict as major challenges to psychological adjustment and mental health. Second, psychosocial factors that contribute to resilience in Asian American adults are discussed, specifically, cultural values, family, religious and community institutions, and ethnic identity.

Demographic Characteristics of Asian American Adults

An examination of Asian American health issues must be placed in the context of the nature of the population. The Asian American/Pacific Islander population is the fastest growing group in the United States and is quite diverse. By 2050, the Asian American population is expected to increase by 213% to 33.4 million (U.S. Census Bureau 2000). The Asian population increased faster than the total U.S. population between 1990 and 2000 (48% vs. 13%). Native Hawaiians and other Pacific Islanders numbered 0.3% of the U.S. population. Another important characteristic of the Asian population is its diversity. More than 50 Asian American groups have been identified. The largest subgroups are Chinese Americans (2.4 million), Filipino Americans (1.9 million), Asian Indians (1.7 million), Vietnamese Americans (1.1 million), Korean Americans (1.1 million), and Japanese Americans (0.8 million). Native Hawaiians are the largest Pacific Islander group, followed by Samoans. More than half of Pacific Islanders live in two states: Hawaii and California (U.S. Census Bureau 2000). The diverse nature of the Asian population is also revealed

O. Meyer (✉)
Department of Psychology, University of California Davis,
One Shields Avenue, 95616, Davis, CA, USA
e-mail: olmeyer@ucdavis.edu

E. C. Chang, C. A. Downey (eds.), *Handbook of Race and Development in Mental Health*, 169
DOI 10.1007/978-1-4614-0424-8_10, © Springer Science+Business Media, LLC 2012

by the proportion of the population born in other countries. The vast [1]majority of Chinese, Filipino, Vietnamese, Koreans, and Thai are foreign-born (U.S. Census Bureau 2000).

Other demographic characteristics revealed by the 2006 American Community Survey are important to note (U.S. Census Bureau 2000). The Asian American population and the general population do not markedly differ in gender composition (percent of females: AAs—52%, PIs—49%, National—51%) or in marital status (percent of married-couple families: AAs—60%, PIs—51%, National—50%). However, there are substantial differences in college graduation rates (AAs—30%, PIs—10%, National—17%), median household income (AAs—$ 63,000, PIs—$ 49,000, National—$ 48,000), and per capita income (AAs—$ 27,000, PIs—$ 18,000, National—$ 25,000). Poverty levels are quite similar for Asian Americans and the U.S. population, but a larger percentage of Pacific Islanders fall below the poverty line (AAs—11%, PIs—16%, National—13%).Again, important inter-Asian differences are found in educational attainment. For example, the percentage of Asian Indians with a bachelor's degree (64%) was much higher than that of Hmong Americans (8%).

Challenges to Maintaining Mental Health

Many Asian Americans face significant challenges to their mental health. These challenges result from daily stressors that can create problems for individuals' mental health and well-being. Daily life stress can occur in various forms—financial stress, family stress, etc., and stress has long been associated with psychological well-being (Kessler 1997). In this section, three challenges are discussed in terms of their influence on Asian American mental health: prejudice and discrimination, acculturative stress, and family conflict.

Prejudice and Discrimination

The Surgeon General's Report (U.S. Department of Health and Human Services (USDHHS) 2001) listed racial discrimination as a serious risk factor for mental disorders. Jones (2000) defined discrimination as actions from individuals and institutions that negatively and systematically impact groups with less power. Asian Americans have faced a long history of discrimination in the United States (Fong 2002). Although they have been in the United States since the 1500's, Asian Americans have faced discrimination in issues of citizenship, land ownership, and due process under the law (Fong 2002). Earlier, discrimination was institutionalized

[1] Work on this chapter was supported by the Asian American Center on Disparities Research (National Institute of Mental Health grant: 1P50MH073511-01A2).

through the Chinese Exclusion Act of 1882, Executive Order 9066, the Gentleman's Agreement, as well as by means of miscegenation and other anti-Asian laws. Many of these actions resulted from fears of the "yellow peril," that multitudes of ruthless and sneaky Asians would threaten the "American" way of life and eliminate scarce jobs and resources for White Americans (Mok 1998). Even today, Asian immigrants may face racism and discrimination because of concerns that they are monopolizing resources, services, and jobs that would otherwise be available to Americans (Young and Takeuchi 1998). Although explicit prejudice is not as prevalent today, a sizable number of "racial microaggressions" against Asian Americans continue to occur (Sue et al. 2007b). Microaggressions are "brief, everyday exchanges that send denigrating messages to people of color because they belong to a racial minority group" (Sue et al. 2007b, p. 273). These microaggressions may be intentional or unintentional, and are so subtle that they often leave individuals wondering if they truly were the object of discrimination. Asian Americans describe strong and lasting negative reactions (e.g., anger, rage, frustration, sense of being invalidated) to the racial microaggressions they encounter (Sue et al. 2007a). Covert types of discrimination may be more harmful than overt behaviors because individuals may be less able to detect and cope with these more subtle forms of racism.

Discrimination is associated with various mental health outcomes, including mental health adjustment, self-esteem, happiness, depression, and generalized anxiety disorder among Blacks, Latinos, and Whites (Kessler et al. 1999). Similarly, for Asian Americans, discrimination is associated with depressive symptoms (Mossakowski 2003), substance use (Gee et al. 2007a) among Filipino Americans, and poor mental health (Gee 2002). Discrimination has also been related to depressive symptoms among gay Asian Americans (Yoshikawa et al. 2004). Japanese American college students who perceive more racial prejudice and inequality are also more likely to have lower self-concept (i.e., lower self-worth or self-satisfaction) than those who perceive less racial prejudice (Asamen and Berry 1987).

Using a nationally representative sample of Asian Americans, Gee et al. (2007b) examined the relationship between self-reported discrimination and mental disorders. Results demonstrated that after controlling for poverty, family cohesion, and acculturative stress, discrimination was associated with mental disorders (e.g., depressive, anxiety, or any DSM-IV disorder). Even among immigrants, discrimination appeared to be a more important predictor of mental disorders than acculturative stress or years in the United States. Therefore, contrary to the notion that Asian Americans do not face discrimination, findings from various studies highlight the fact that not only do Asian Americans continue to perceive discrimination, but that it is related to poorer mental health. Studies have shown that expecting to be the target of prejudice is cognitively depleting and exhausting, and perhaps this effect eventually contributes to poorer mental health (e.g., Richeson et al. 2005).

Stereotypes also can have a harmful effect on the mental health of Asian Americans. In the early 1900s, common stereotypes of Asian Americans were that the men were sneaky and corrupt while the women were exotic and servile (Mok 1998; Sue and Kitano 1973). In the latter part of this century, Asian Americans have been viewed as the "model minority" (Sue and Morishima 1982; Uba 1994). This stereotype of Asian Americans encompasses the notion that Asian Americans represent the "American Dream" since they are hardworking, high-achieving individuals with few psychological problems. This image portrays Asian Americans as having achieved economic parity with Whites, despite language and other cultural barriers (Hune and Chan 1997). However, the perception that Asian Americans are the model minority appears to be a myth for several reasons. One, the myth fails to take into account the heterogeneity of the Asian population. While some Asian American groups may have achieved success in certain areas, other groups (e.g., Southeast Asians) have not thrived socially or economically (Rumbaut and Cornelius 1995). Two, even for those groups who appear to be succeeding, their success may occur in only one domain, such as academic performance. In terms of mental health, prevalence rates of depression, somatization, and post-traumatic stress disorder among Asian Americans are at least as high as those for White Americans, and, in many cases, higher (Lee et al. 2001). In addition, research highlighting the economic success of Asian Americans has focused only on household income. When adjusting for working hours and number of workers in the household, the individual earnings ratio for Asian Americans is actually lower than for Whites (Hurh and Kim 1989). Moreover, the model minority stereotype denies the reality that Asian Americans continue to encounter racism and discrimination. Finally, it may create a significant amount of pressure by making Asian American students believe that unless they are excelling academically, they are not normal. Cheryan and Bodenhausen (2000) found that Asian American students performed significantly worse on a math test when they were made to think about their ethnic group identity compared to those in a control group. Cheryan and Bodenhausen attributed this decrement in performance to the fear of failing to confirm a positive stereotype, or not living up to the expectation. This type of pressure has the possibility of leading to considerable negative outcomes for Asian Americans. Thus, not only do stereotypes affect self-esteem and general well-being, they have the power to affect performance in important domains, like school and work (Leong 1998; Shih et al. 2006; Steele and Aronson 1995).

Stress Associated with Migration and Acculturation

A major source of stress involves the circumstances under which Asian immigrants leave their native country. Premigration trauma has been found to be a major predictor of psychological distress for Southeast Asian refugees (Chung and Kagawa-Singer 1993; Hinton et al. 1997; Mollica et al. 1987). For many individuals, such as Southeast Asians, the conditions that forced them to immigrate to the United States were traumatic. Many studies have demonstrated the relationship between premigration trauma experiences and the level of adjustment and adaptation to the United States (Chung and Bemak 2006; Chung and Kagawa-Singer 1993). Traumatic experiences that Southeast Asian refugees faced included food and shelter deprivation, physical injury and torture, incarceration and reeducation camps, and witnessing killing, experiencing torture, or both (Mollica et al. 1985). Because of their premigration experiences and possible postmigration obstacles, some groups have been identified to be at high risk for developing serious mental health problems (Chung and Bemak 2007).

Another significant source of stress for Asian Americans stems from the challenges associated with acculturation. Acculturation is a process in which members of one cultural group adopt the beliefs and behaviors of another group. It involves acquiring the language, attitudes, values, and roles of the dominant society, and the process of adjusting to these changes (Berry 1980; Organista et al. 2003). Acculturative stress involves the strains of adjustment and adaptation among immigrants, including the demands of learning a new culture, worries about legal status, and potential guilt for leaving behind loved ones (Berry and Annis 1974; Berry et al. 1987).

Acculturative stress has been associated with depression, anxiety, and other negative health outcomes (Noh and Kaspar 2003). Vega et al. (2004) found that stressors due to adjustment in a new culture were associated with poorer mental health for immigrants. Acculturative stress can impact people by narrowing the range of options that they perceive as feasible. As daily pressures increase, people with more acculturative stress start having "tunnel vision" and experience a decrease in the ability to make and execute decisions effectively (Smart and Smart 1995). As their perception of viable choices is narrowed, individuals with greater levels of acculturative stress may start feeling hopeless (Kim 2007). A meta-analysis of 49 studies on acculturation and adjustment indicated that greater acculturative stress was positively correlated with psychosocial and health problems (Moyerman and Forman 1992).

Family Conflict

Certain characteristics within Asian American families may serve as protective factors against mental health problems. However, other characteristics may put individuals at risk for developing mental health problems. Family conflict may act as a compelling stressor resulting in substantive distress (Abe-Kim et al. 2002). First, a disruption in traditional gender roles that differ from Asian Americans' native country can generate family conflict. In the United States, men typically experience economic and social loss while women become either coproviders or the sole providers for their families (Espiritu 2001). Because of the traditional patriarchal family structure in many Asian American families, conflicts with gender roles can cause much stress for the family. Second, Asian American children may want to date and/or intermarry individuals from other ethnicities, and this also can cause major disagreements within families (Chung 2001). Third, Asian American children may be more skilled with the English language and mainstream social norms, thrusting them into the role of cultural and language brokers for their parents. Consequently, parents may feel inadequate and ashamed because they have to depend on their children. These changes in family dynamics can serve as major sources of stress and conflict in the family. Fourth, the experience of Asian American parents and children may differ in terms of majority and minority status. That is, parents who immigrate to the United States were raised in a culture and environment where they were most likely the ethnic majority, while their children living in the United States tend to make up the minority. Therefore, they may not understand their children when they express their feelings of prejudice and discrimination because of their minority status. Because parents do not have the same experience, they may ignore their children's complaints (e.g., that their teachers are discriminating against them because they are Asian American), and this can lead to greater family conflict. Finally, another significant source of stress in Asian American families may be the clash of valuing certain emotions over others. Due to the value placed on emotional restraint in many Asian cultures, parents may be less likely to express their emotions toward their children, be they positive or negative emotions. In contrast, more acculturated children may start to value being praised and shown physical affection. Thus, the suppression of positive emotions in the family can serve as a significant source of stress in Asian American families (Yee et al. 2007). However, it may be that less acculturated parents and their more acculturated children place similar value on certain emotions, but these emotions may be expressed differently. For Asian American children, expressing care and love may be achieved through physical and verbal affection. For Asian American parents however, care may be communicated through gestures and behavioral actions—like cooking dinner for their children or doing their laundry. Thus, the "language of emotion" may vary between more acculturated and less acculturated family members, and this communication difference may be an additional stressor.

Intergenerational conflicts stemming from acculturation differences between parents and children can negatively influence family cohesion (Tseng and Fuligni 2000). Family cohesion reflects the degree to which family members are connected and involved with one another (Crane et al. 2005). Individuals from low cohesion families are often at higher risk for depression, suicidal ideation, anxiety, and social avoidance (Harris and Molock 2000; Reinherz et al. 2003). The mental health consequences of intergenerational conflict for both Asian American parents and children have been well documented. Southeast Asian parents have reported feeling betrayed and dismayed by this conflict (Kibria 1993; Ying and Chao 1996). The greater the differences in acculturation level between parents and children, the greater the likelihood that parents and children may make choices that can lead to significant intergenerational conflicts (Uba 1994).

In summary, it is evident that Asian Americans may encounter many difficulties related to prejudice and discrimination, acculturative stress, and family conflict that may pose significant challenges to their mental health and well-being. However, some Asian Americans have thrived in spite of such hardships and stressors, and this is evident from their success in certain areas (e.g., academics). It appears that there are various resources and coping strategies used by Asian Americans that may make them more resilient to these stressors.

Strengths Contributing to Mental Health

Resiliency is characterized as a process in which one faces risks and challenges but is able to draw on resources to yield positive outcomes (Yee et al. 2007). In this section, resources such as cultural values, family, religious and community institutions, and a sense of ethnic identity will be discussed as these protective factors may help Asian Americans cope with the stressors in their environment.

Cultural Values

Cultures may influence how one perceives and manages stressful life events. The collectivistic cultures of East Asia espouse a set of values and beliefs that may promote resiliency in a different manner than what is found in individualistic societies. In particular, the value of harmonizing oneself with the environment can impact one's control orientation. This value can lead to the use of secondary control, in which case an individual gains control by aligning oneself with the existing conditions and altering one's psychological response to the situation (Rothbaum et al. 1982; Weisz et al. 1996). Principles underlying secondary control such as accommodating to and accepting a situation may be conducive to well-being, especially under circumstances that are directly outside of one's influence (Cross and Markus 1999). Secondary control tends to be emphasized more in collectivistic societies than in individualistic ones (Heine 2008; Lam and Zane 2004; McCarty et al. 1999; Morling 2000; Morling and Evered 2006; Morling et al. 2002). While primary control is the preferred mode for handling stressful situations, recognition that certain situations do not lend themselves to personal control may lead to the use of secondary control (Rothbaum et al. 1982).

Sastry and Ross (1998) investigated the relationship between sense of personal control, or lack thereof, and depression and anxiety among Asians (in Asia and in the United States) and non-Asians. Asians and Asian Americans reported having significantly less personal control than non-Asians, and while lack of personal control was positively related to depression for non-Asians, it was not significantly related to depression for Asians or Asian Americans. Sastry and Ross suggested that the relationship between personal control and well-being may not be as strong for Asians in general because well-being may not result from pursuing self-interests via primary control but rather, from fulfilling cultural norms, which may be related to secondary control.

Similarly, Chang's work illustrates how certain cultural values may influence the degree of optimism and pessimism among Asian Americans. An orientation toward maintaining harmony and interconnectedness may lead some to adopt a more pessimistic outlook. By anticipating incidents that may result in negative consequences for the group, one may be more inclined to initiate preventive actions (Chang 2001). In a series of studies (Chang 2002 1996a, b), Asian Americans were similar to Caucasians in levels of optimism, but Asian Americans were significantly higher in levels of pessimism. Despite Asian Americans tendency to be more pessimistic, it was the lack of optimism that best predicted their depressive symptoms, whereas pessimism emerged as a good predictor of maladjustment for Caucasians (Chang 1996a). Asian Americans employed more *problem avoidance* strategies when dealing with stress, but there were no ethnic differences in depressive and physical symptoms. This research highlights that well-being may not be solely affected by proactive strategies directed at the stressor, as is the view in many Western cultures, but also by alternative strategies that emphasize regulating one's emotional response to stressful events.

In a similar vein, Heine's work (e.g., Heine et al. 1999; Ross et al. 2005) on self-enhancement among Asians reveals much the same in that well-being is tied to being interdependent and in harmony with the group. One feels good about himself/herself when one strives for accord with others and honors the obligations that one has as a member of the group. Influenced by the teachings of Confucius which suggest that one should respect relationships and strive to fulfill the roles and duties associated with these relationships, research has shown that Asians are more inclined to focus on their shortcomings as that indicates that they are making efforts to improve themselves (Heine 2001). Such a self-critical outlook serves as a face maintenance strategy for many Asian Americans as it facilitates a positive reputation, and as a result, enhances their self-esteem (Heine 2004).

In summary, resiliency and well-being appear to be influenced by cultural norms and value orientations to a great degree. Cultural norms that promote interconnectedness and harmony seem to shape Asian Americans' behaviors and coping methods. By acknowledging that primary control sometimes may be unattainable, secondary control may afford one the endurance to overcome adversity. Additionally, research illustrates that coping methods influenced by collectivistic and interdependent values may also contribute to one's well-being. A defensive pessimistic outlook may, at times, help better prepare Asian Americans for disappointments and failures. Self-critical efforts aimed as self-improvement also may result in greater persistence on tasks in the face of stressors, increasing the likelihood that these efforts will result in success or effective coping. Moreover, defensive pessimism, self-criticism, and avoidance problem solving were positively related to the mental and physical health of Asian Americans but not White Americans. These interesting ethnic differences in what constitutes protective factors underscore the relative nature of adaptive behavior across cultures.

Familial, Religious, and Community Institutions

Family, religious, and community institutions serve as important sources of social support for many Asian Americans. Such networks have the ability to protect against the adverse effects of life and acculturative stress. Research has generally found a positive relationship between social support and mental health (e.g., Krause and Liang 1993; Li and Liang 2007; Okabayashi et al. 2004), and the research reviewed below illustrates the positive effects that family, religious, and community institutions may have on Asian Americans.

In East Asian cultures, the family is the essential unit for self-definition, support, and well-being. Principles emphasized by Confucianism situate the family as the fundamental unit in a person's life (Park and Chesla 2007). The interdependent nature of Asian American families tends to generate intergenerational support in which the welfare and integrity of the collective is prioritized over the personal needs of the individual. In Western cultures typically centrality is placed on the nuclear unit of the family whereas in many Asian American families, multiple generations tend to reside in the same household and thus are able to contribute to its welfare (Yee et al. 2007). The connectedness promoted in Asian American families can offer many psychological benefits. Hsu (1971) argued that Asian Americans have a better sense of who they are because the family provides a person with a stable and consistent reference for one's identity. Further, DeVos (1978) has noted that the structure of Asian American families, in particular Japanese American families, may make the members more resistant to stress due to the nature of the relationships. Specifically, clearly defined roles and a hierarchical structure make relationships predictable and less stressful (DeVos 1978).The structure of Asian American families often provides a supportive environment that can buffer individuals against stressors associated with deviance and acculturative pressures (Choi 1997; Jang 2002; Thomas and Choi06; Vartanian et al. 2007). The communal nature of these families coupled with the interdependent tendencies emphasized in Asian cultures may foster a shared understanding in which family members collectively work to support a member in distress. Distress may be assuaged with the knowledge that others are there to help (DeVos 1978). Taylor et al.'s (Taylor et al. 2007) found that implicit support (i.e., being in the company of others without disclosing or sharing one's problems) produced psychologically and physiologically beneficial outcomes for Asian Americans over explicit support (i.e., soliciting advice and emotional comfort from one's social support network), whereas the opposite was found for European Americans. Thus, for Asian Americans, well-being seems to be enhanced by the mere presence of others and the recognition of their availability to help (Taylor et al. 2007).

While the family plays a crucial role in providing support to its members, religious institutions also assume a major role in the lives of Asian Americans. Participation in religious activities has a positive effect on psychological health (e.g., Ellison 1993; Krause 1995). In particular, religious communities offer companionship through the fellowships available at churches or temples, which have been found to reduce psychological and physical stressors (Seybold and Hill 2001); moreover, religious beliefs may help one to develop an optimistic explanatory style to understand the negative events in one's life, which may facilitate beneficial resolution of such events (Seybold and Hill 2001). For Korean Americans, churches strengthen cultural ties and identification and offer emotional support in times of crisis (Hurh and Kim 1990). Religious institutions also are actively involved in providing assistance to recent Asian immigrants by offering services that help them adjust to the new culture (Bankston and Zhou 1995; Min 2000). These services may reduce the experience of acculturative stress and help to maintain positive mental health.

Lastly, community institutions and organizations often serve as sources of social and economic support for Asian Americans. Ethnic communities provide a variety of services to their constituents that enhance upward mobility and ease adjustment problems (Vartanian et al. 2007). These local institutions provide social capital to help many Asian Americans succeed in business and other careers. They also provide a social support system, a sense of belonging, and a sense of personal identity. For example, Zhou (2000) documented how an ethnic enclave, like New York City's Chinatown, provided great economic and social support for Chinese Americans residing in that area so that they could integrate and become successful members of society.

Ethnic Identity

As an ethnic minority group, Asian Americans have the highest percentage of ethnic immigrants (Yee et al. 2007). As such, ethnic identity issues often play a major role in the social and psychological adjustment of this group. Ethnic identity has been positively linked to academic achievement as well as a number of favorable psychological outcomes such as self-esteem and well-being (Cheryan and Tsai 2007; Crocker et al. 1994; Fuligni et al. 2005; Lee and Yoo 2004; Phinney 1992; St. Loius and Liem 2005; Tsai et al. 2001). In a study examining Asian American college students, Lee and Yoo (2004) found that ethnic identity was related to self-esteem. A sense of belonging and a rich understanding of one's ethnic group can contribute to a positive identity which, in turn, can help to maintain a positive sense of well-being.

Ethnic identity also may foster resilience in coping with discrimination. Some studies have found that ethnic identity can serve as a buffer to discrimination (e.g., Phinney et al. 1998), while others have not (e.g., Lee 2003). Lee (2003) found that ethnic identity was positively correlated with well-being. However, the results did not support the prediction that ethnic identity would protect against the effects of discrimination. Yoo and Lee (2005) found that Asian Americans with strong ethnic identities were less adversely affected by discrimination when discrimination was perceived to be low but not when it was perceived to be high.

The previous research suggests that the salutary effects of ethnic identity for Asian Americans may be limited depending on the social context in which the discrimination is experienced. The findings seemed to vary depending on the region in which the research was conducted. Incidents of and experiences with discrimination and tokenism may be greater in Midwestern and Southern states (Lee 2003; Yoo and Lee 2005) than in the Western coastal states due to the greater concentration of ethnic minority individuals in the latter region. In the former, more frequent discrimination combined with fewer social support resources may result in minority individuals feeling more threatened compared to those who reside in areas with greater ethnic minority populations. Under these conditions, even a strong sense of ethnic identity may not be sufficient to buffer minority individuals against the negative consequences of discrimination and racism-related stressors.

Discussion

Applying Strengths to Meet Challenges

The psychosocial strengths found among Asian Americans include certain cultural value orientations, family, religious, and community institutions, and ethnic identity. These culturally based psychological resources and resiliencies can be activated through a number of means to address the challenges involved in coping with prejudice and discrimination, acculturative stress, and family intergenerational conflict. First, social institutions or organizations in Asian American communities that are especially effective in affirming one's cultural heritage may foster those very orientations and values that have been found to enhance one's resistance to stress. Second, on a more personal level, certain cultural orientations, such as the emphasis placed on secondary control, may mitigate the effects of acculturative stress among Asian Americans. If stress-inducing situations cannot be or are difficult to change, by accommodating oneself to the situation, Asian Americans may be more able to emotionally cope and adapt rather than engaging in futile efforts to affect immutable conditions (Cross and Markus 1999). Third, mastery and empowerment experiences may be optimized by social institutions, family practices, and community activities that foster greater ethnic identification with one's culture. The social activities and processes found in these community units often enhance ethnic identification through the process of being around similar others (Hammond 1988). Ethnic and collective identity serve as major sources of psychological well-being for ethnic minorities (Crocker et al. 1994; Oetting and Beauvais 1991). Ethnic identification involves psychological stake in which individuals systematically engage and participate in a certain cultural lifestyle with the expectation of receiving some psychological benefits (e.g., social support, self-definition, cultural rules for success, sense of belonging). As such, the process of ethnic identification often leads to developing competencies and mastery experiences instrumental for adjustment and well-being (Oetting and Beauvais 1991). Moreover, as Rappaport (1981) has noted, these empowerment experiences can increase the likelihood that individuals will make greater efforts to change inequitable social conditions that often cause life stress for individuals. Essentially, this empowering process of ethnic identification constitutes another pathway in which ethnic identification may work to offset the deleterious effects accruing from prejudice and discrimination, acculturative stress, and family conflict.

Future Recommendations

A number of recommendations can be made to enhance future research on factors that optimize mental health among Asian Americans (see Table 1). This review highlighted the benefits of family, religious, and community institutions, but most of the supporting evidence was anecdotal in nature. Due to the lack of empirical

Table 1 The Asian American population: Challenges and Strengths

Demographics	Challenges	Strengths	Recommendations
Asian American (AA) population has increased by 48% from 6.9 million in 1990 to 10.2 million in 2000. This group is expected to grow 213% to 33.4 million by the year 2050 Native Hawaiians and other Pacific Islanders (PI) comprise 0.3% of the US population	Prejudice and discrimination • Perceived discrimination is associated with poorer mental health for Asian Americans because discrimination serves as a stressor • Research has shown discrimination to be negatively associated with psychological well-being and positively associated with distress	Cultural values • By voluntarily relinquishing control, especially in situations impermeable to change, secondary control may afford one endurance during hardships • Harmonizing oneself with the group may also promote well-being. By being a dutiful member of a group, one may receive validation from others and this may lead to greater well-being	• Empirically test mediating influences of community and religious institutions on Asian American mental health • Examine individuals who are resilient and hardy • Integrate cultural features into mental health treatment
Largest nationalities represented include Chinese (2.4 million); Filipino (1.9 million); Asian Indians (1.7 million); Vietnamese(1.1 million); Korean (1.1 million); Japanese (0.8 million) Native Hawaiians are the largest Pacific Islander group	Acculturative stress • Stressors associated with the adjustment in a new culture may contribute to poorer mental health because of the perception that viable options are limited and this can create hopelessness for some immigrants • For particular immigrant groups (i.e., Southeast Asians), premigration trauma coupled with possible postmigration obstacles may put some at risk for developing serious mental health problems	Family, religious, and community institutions • The structure and the interdependent nature of Asian American families foster intergenerational support and the good of the collective • Religious and community institutions may offer services that may facilitate adjustment for recent immigrants. These institutions may also foster a sense of belonging among its constituents	• Include biracial individuals into study of Asian American mental health

Table 1 (Continued)

Demographics	Challenges	Strengths	Recommendations
Asian Americans are highly concentrated in California, New York, and Hawaii. More than half of the Pacific Islanders live in Hawaii and California Education: 30% of AA and 10% of PI have a college degree vs. 17% national rate) Median household income: AA: $ 27,000; PI: $ 18,000; National: $ 25,000	Family conflict • Changes in roles may create conflict. Men may experience economic loss while women may play a greater role in being a provider for the family. • Some Asian American children may outmarry and this may create problems within the family • Parents may feel embarrassed for depending on their children to serve as cultural brokers	Ethnic identity • Ethnic identity may be related to positive mental health outcomes. Knowledge of one's ethnic group may produce a positive self identity. This, in turn, may contribute to positive well-being • Some have found ethnic identity to protect against discrimination. Ethnic identity has been found to be a protective factor when discrimination is perceived to be low, but not when it is perceived to be high (Yoo and Lee 2005)	

investigations, it is unclear whether the roles of these institutions are equivalent or if one institution may be more effective or efficient at promoting well-being than another. Possible mediating factors that may explain the relationship between such institutions and mental health also are unknown. Another promising approach would be to shift the focus in research from those who succumbed to the adverse influences of their sociocultural environment to also include those people who may have been exposed to these negative elements but, were able to resist these stressors or even develop greater strengths in response to them. For example, examining those who may have experienced discrimination but were able to deflect the negative consequences of such experiences may offer insights into hardy Asian American personalities, which may offer valuable information about mental well-being. It also is highly advisable to pursue research that systematically integrates cultural strengths into current health and mental health care practices for Asian Americans. Capitalizing on a group's cultural strengths may be a very promising alternative and more efficient way of developing culturally competent interventions. By its nature, the cultural strength approach guarantees that the approach will be culturally relevant and appropriate. Culturally competent care continues to be a major issue in heath and mental health sectors (Zane 2005). To date, few interventions have systematically used the cultural orientations discussed here as the basis for changing behaviors and attitudes of Asian American clients. The approach would need to withstand the usual empirical tests, but it appears to be a viable and potentially useful strategy to providing culturally informed or culturally nuanced health and mental health services and treatment. Lastly, given the rising numbers of interracial unions among Asian Americans, it is important to engage in more research on biracial individuals for several reasons. Research is needed to enhance understanding of adaptive functioning of and the mental health of this rapidly growing population in the United States. More importantly, biracial individuals are excellent exemplars of multicultural functioning so the study of Asian American biracial mental health can provide major insights into how individuals vary in their efforts to negotiate between and/or integrate their experiences and learning from diverse cultural frames. In view of the increasing complexity in the United States as a multicultural society, such processes need to be better understood.

Concluding Comments

Asian Americans encounter a significant number of challenges to their mental health and well-being, but they also possess resources, internal and external, that could potentially help them overcome these challenges. Clearly, some of these strengths (e.g., ethnic identity, social supports) have similar effects across cultures but the mediators or moderators of effects may differ among cultures. More examination of the strengths of Asian Americans as a group, particularly those individuals who seem to be quite proficient in these adaptive capacities, might shed some interesting information on how to overcome various psychosocial challenges as well as how to develop more culturally syntonic interventions and services.

References

Abe-Kim, J., Takeuchi, D., & Hwang, W. (2002). Predictors of help seeking for emotional distress among Chinese Americans: Family matters. *Journal of Consulting and Clinical Psychology, 70,* 1186–1190.

Asamen, J. K., & Berry, G. L. (1987). Self-concept, alienation, and perceived prejudice: Implications for counseling Asian Americans. *Journal of Multicultural Counseling and Development, 15,* 146–160.

Bankston, C. L., & Zhou, M. (1995). Religious participation, ethnic identification, and adaptation of Vietnamese adolescents in an immigrant community. *Sociological Quarterly, 36,* 523–534.

Berry, J. W. (1980). Acculturation as varieties of adaptation. In A. M. Padilla (Ed.), *Acculturation: Theory, models and some new findings* (pp. 9–25). Boulder: Westview.

Berry, J. W., & Annis, R. C. (1974). Acculturative stress: The role of ecology, culture and differentiation. *Journal of Cross-Cultural Psychology, 5,* 382–406.

Berry, J. W., Kim, U., Minde, T., & Mok, D. (1987). Comparative studies of acculturative stress. *International Migration Review, 21,* 491–511.

Chang, E. C. (1996a). Cultural differences in optimism, pessimism, and coping: Predictors of subsequent adjustment in Asian American and Caucasian American college students. *Journal of Counseling Psychology, 43,* 113–123.

Chang, E. C. (1996b). Evidence for the cultural specificity of pessimism in Asians vs. Caucasians: A test of a general negativity hypothesis. *Personality and Individual Differences, 21,* 819–822.

Chang, E. C. (2001). Cultural influences on optimism and pessimism: Differences in Western and Eastern construals of the self. In E. C. Change (Ed.), *Optimism and Pessimism: Implication for theory, research, and practice* (pp. 257–280). Washington: American Psychological Association.

Chang, E. C. (2002). Cultural differences in psychological distress in Asian and Caucasian American college students: Examining the role of cognitive and affective concomitants. *Journal of Counseling Psychology, 49,* 47–59.

Cheryan, S., & Bodenhausen, G. V. (2000). When positive stereotypes threaten intellectual performance: The psychological hazards of "model minority" status. *Psychological Science, 11,* 399–402.

Cheryan, S., & Tsai, J. L. (2007). Ethnic identity. In F. T. L. Leong, A. Ebreo, L. Kinoshita, A. G. Inman, L. H. Yang, & M. Fu (Eds.), *Handbook of Asian American psychology* (2nd ed., pp. 125–139). Thousand Oaks: Sage.

Choi, G. (1997). Acculturative stress, social support, and depression in Korean American families. *Journal of Family Social Work, 2,* 81–97.

Chung, R. H. G. (2001). Gender, ethnicity, and acculturation in intergenerational conflict of Asian American college students. *Cultural Diversity and Ethnic Minority Psychology, 7,* 376–386.

Chung, R. C., & Bemak, F. (2006). Counseling Americans of Southeast Asian descent: The impact of the refugee experience. In C. C. Lee (Ed.), *Multicultural issues in counseling: New approaches to diversity* (3rd ed., pp. 151–170). Alexandria: American Counseling Association.

Chung, R. C., & Bemak, F. (2007). *Asian immigrants and refugees.* Thousand Oaks: Sage.

Chung, R. C., & Kagawa-Singer, M. (1993). Predictors of psychological distress among Southeast Asian refugees. *Social Science and Medicine, 36,* 631–639.

Crane, D. R., Ngai, S. W., Larson, J. H., & Hafen, M., Jr. (2005). The influence of family functioning and parent-adolescent acculturation on North American Chinese adolescent outcomes. *Family Relations, 54,* 400–410.

Crocker, J., Luhtanen, R., Blaine, B., & Broadnax, S. (1994). Collective self-esteem and psychological well-being among White, Black, and Asian college students. *Personality and Social Psychology Bulletin, 20,* 503–513.

Cross, S. E., & Markus, H. R. (1999). The cultural constitution of personality. In L. A. Pervin and O. P. John (Eds.), *Handbook of personality: Theory and research,* 2nd ed. (pp. 378–396). New York: Guilford Press.

DeVos, G. A. (1978). Selective permeability and reference group sanctioning: Psychocultural continuities in role degradation. In M. Yinger & S. Cutler (Eds.), *Major Social Issues* (pp. 9–24). New York: Macmillan.
Ellison, C. G. (1993). Religious involvement and self perception among Black Americans. *Social Forces, 71,* 1027–1055.
Espiritu, Y. L. (2001). "We don't sleep around like white girls do": Family, culture and gender in Filipina American lives. *Signs, 26,* 415–440.
Fong, T. P. (2002). The history of Asians in America. In *The contemporary Asian American experience: Beyond the model minority* (2nd ed.). Upper Saddle River: Pearson Education.
Fuligni, A. J., Witkow, M., & Garcia, C. (2005). Ethnic identity and the academic adjustment of adolescents from Mexican, Chinese, and European backgrounds. *Developmental Psychology, 41,* 799–811.
Gee, G. C. (2002). A multilevel analysis of the relationship between institutional racial discrimination and health status. *American Journal of Public Health, 92,* 615–623.
Gee, G. C., Delva, J., & Takeuchi, D. T. (2007a). Relationships between self-reported unfair treatment and prescription medication use, illicit drug use, and alcohol dependence among Filipino Americans. *American Journal of Public Health, 97,* 933–940.
Gee, G. C., Spencer, M., Chen, J., Yip, T., & Takeuchi, D. T. (2007b). The association between self-reported racial discrimination and 12-month DSM-IV mental disorders among Asian Americans nationwide. *Social Science and Medicine, 64,* 1984–1996.
Hammond, O. W. (1988). Needs assessment and policy development: Native Hawaiians as Native Americans. *American Psychologist, 43,* 383–387.
Harris, T. L., & Molock, S. D. (2000). Cultural orientation, family cohesion and family support in suicide ideation and depression among African American college students. *Suicide and Life-Threatening Behavior, 30,* 341–353.
Heine, S. J. (2001). Self as cultural product: An examination of East Asian and North American selves. *Journal of Personality, 69,* 881–906.
Heine, S. J. (2004). Positive self views: Understanding universals and variability across cultures. *Journal of Cultural and Evolutionary Psychology, 2,* 109–122.
Heine, S. J. (2008). Motivation. In *Cultural psychology* (pp. 227–272). New York: Norton.
Heine, S. J., Lehman, D. R., Markus, H. R., & Kitayama, S. (1999). Is there a universal need for positive self-regard? *Psychological Review, 106,* 766–794.
Hinton, W. L., Tiet, Q., Tran, C. G., & Chesney, M. (1997). Predictors of depression among refugees from Vietnam: A longitudinal study of new arrivals. *Journal of Nervous and Mental Disease, 185,* 39–45.
Hsu, F. (1971). Psychosocial homeostasis and Jen: Conceptual tools for advancing psychological anthropology. *American Anthropologist, 73,* 23–44.
Hune, S., & Chan, K. S. (1997). Special focus: Asian Pacific American demographic and educational trends. In D. J. Carter & R. Wilson (Eds.), *Minorities in higher education: Fifteenth annual status report* (pp. 39–67). Washington: American Council on Education.
Hurh, W. M., & Kim, K. C. (1989). The "success" image of Asian Americans: Its validity and its practical and theoretical implications. *Ethnic and Racial Studies, 12,* 514–561.
Hurh, W. M., & Kim, K. C. (1990). Religious participation of Korean immigrants in the United States. *Journal for the Scientific Study of Religion, 29,* 19–34.
Jang, S. J. (2002). Race, ethnicity, and deviance: A study of Asian and non-Asian adolescents in America. *Sociological Forum, 17,* 647–680.
Jones, C. (2000). Levels of racism: A theoretical framework and a gardener's tale. *American Journal of Public Health, 90,* 1212–1215.
Kessler, R. C. (1997). The effects of stressful life events on depression. *Annual Review of Psychology, 48,* 191–214.
Kessler, R. C., Mickelson, K. D., & Williams, D. R. (1999). The prevalence, distribution, and mental health correlates of perceived discrimination in the United States. *Journal of Health and Social Behavior, 40,* 208–230.

Kibria, N. (1993). *Family tightrope: The changing lives of Vietnamese Americans*. Princeton: Princeton University Press.
Kim, B. S. K. (2007). Acculturation and enculturation. In F. T. L. Leong, A. Ebreo, L. Kinoshita, A. G. Inman, L. H. Yang, & M. Fu (Eds.), *Handbook of Asian American psychology* (2nd ed., pp. 141–158). Thousand Oaks: Sage.
Krause, N. (1995). Religiosity and self-esteem among older adults. *Journals of Gerontology: Series B: Psychological Sciences and Social Sciences, 50,* 236–246.
Krause, N., & Liang, J. (1993). Stress, social support, and psychological distress among the Chinese elderly. *Journals of Gerontology, 48,* 282–291.
Lam, A. G., & Zane, N. W. S. (2004). Ethnic differences in coping with interpersonal stressors: A test of self-construals as cultural mediators. *Journal of Cross-Cultural Psychology, 35,* 446–459.
Lee, R. M. (2003). Do ethnic identity and other-group orientation protect against discrimination for Asian Americans? *Journal of Counseling Psychology, 50,* 133–141.
Lee, R. M., & Yoo, H. C. (2004). Structure and measurement of ethnic identity for Asian American college students. *Journal of Counseling Psychology, 51,* 263–269.
Lee, J., Lei, A., & Sue, S. (2001). The current state of mental health research on Asian Americans. *Journal of Human Behavior in the Social Environment, 3,* 159–178.
Leong, F. T. L. (1998). Career development and vocational behaviors. In L. C. Lee & N. W. S. Zane (Eds.), *Handbook of Asian American psychology* (pp. 359–398). Thousand Oaks: Sage.
Li, L. W., & Liang, J. (2007). Social exchanges and subjective well-being among older Chinese: Does age make a difference? *Psychology and Aging, 22,* 386–391.
McCarty, C. A., Weisz, J. R., Wanitromanee, K., Eastman, K. L., Suwanlert, S., & Chaiyasit, W. et al. (1999). Culture, coping, and context: Primary and secondary control among Thai and American youth. *Journal of Child Psychology and Psychiatry, 40,* 809–818.
Min, P. G. (2000). The structure and social functions of Korean immigrant churches in the United States. In M. Zhou & J. V. Gatewood (Eds.), *Contemporary Asian America: A multidisciplinary reader* (pp. 372–391). New York: New York University Press.
Mok, T. A. (1998). Getting the message: Media images and stereotypes and their effect on Asian Americans. *Cultural Diversity and Mental Health, 4,* 185–202.
Mollica, R. F., Lavelle, J., & Khoun, F. (1985). *Widows at highest risk*. Paper presented at the Cambodian Mental Health Conference, "A Day to Explore Issues and Alternative Approaches to Care," New York.
Mollica, R. F., Wyshak, G., & Lavelle, J. (1987). The psychosocial impact of war trauma and torture on Southeast Asian refugees. *American Journal of Psychiatry, 144,* 1567–1572.
Morling, B. (2000). "Taking" an aerobics class in the U.S. and "entering" an aerobics class in Japan: Primary and secondary control in a fitness context. *Asian Journal of Social Psychology, 3,* 73–85.
Morling, B., Evered, S. (2006). Secondary control reviewed and defined. *Psychological Bulletin, 132,* 269–296.
Morling, B., Kitayama, S., Miyamoto, Y. (2002). Cultural practices emphasize influence in the United States and adjustment in Japan. *Personality and Social Psychology Bulletin, 28,* 311–323.
Mossakowski, K. N. (2003). Coping with perceived discrimination: Does ethnic identity protect mental health? *Journal of Health and Social Behavior, 44* (Special Issue: Race, ethnicity and mental health), 318–331.
Moyerman, D. R., & Forman, B. D. (1992). Acculturation and adjustment: A meta-analytic study. *Hispanic Journal of Behavioral Sciences, 14,* 163–200.
Noh, S., & Kaspar, V. (2003). Perceived discrimination and depression: Moderating effects of coping, acculturation, and ethnic support. *American Journal of Public Health, 93,* 232–238.
Oetting, E. R., & Beauvais, F. (1991). Orthogonal cultural identification theory: The cultural identification of minority adolescents. *International Journal of the Addictions, 25,* 655–685.

Okabayashi, H., Liang, J., Krause, N., Akiyama, H., & Sugisawa, H. (2004). Mental health among older adults in Japan: Do sources of social support and negative interaction make a difference? *Social Science and Medicine, 59,* 2259–2270.

Organista, P. B., Organista, K. C., & Kurasaki, K. (2003). The relationship between acculturation and ethnic minority health. Washington: American Psychological Association.

Park, M., & Chesla, C. (2007). Revisiting Confucianism as a conceptual framework for Asian family study. *Journal of Family Nursing, 13,* 293–311.

Phinney, J. S. (1992). The multigroup ethnic identity measure: A new scale for use with diverse groups. *Journal of Adolescent Research, 7,* 156–176.

Phinney, J. S., Madden, T., & Santos, L. J. (1998). Psychological variables as predictors of perceived ethnic discrimination among minority and immigrant adolescents. *Journal of Applied Social Psychology, 28,* 937–953.

Rappaport, J. (1981). In praise of paradox: A social policy of empowerment over prevention. *American Journal of Community Psychology, 9,* 1–25.

Reinherz, H. Z., Paradis, A. D., Giaconia, R. M., Stashwick, C. K., & Fitzmaurice, G. (2003). Childhood and adolescent predictors of major depression in the transition to adulthood. *American Journal of Psychiatry, 160,* 2141–2147.

Richeson, J. A., Trawalter, S., & Shelton, J. N. (2005). African American's implicit racial attitudes and the depletion of executive function after interracial interactions. *Social Cognition, 23,* 336–352.

Ross, M., Heine, S. J., Wilson, A. E., & Sugimori, S. (2005). Cross-cultural discrepancies in self-appraisals. *Personality and Social Psychology Bulletin, 31,* 1175–1188.

Rothbaum, F., Weisz, J. R., Snyder, S. S. (1982). Changing the world and changing the self: A two-process model of perceived control. *Journal of Personality and Social Psychology, 42,* 5–37.

Rumbaut, R. G., & Cornelius, W. A. (1995). *California immigrant children.* La Jolla: Center for U.S. Mexican Studies, University of California.

Sastry, J., & Ross, C. E. (1998). Asian ethnicity and the sense of personal control. *Social Psychology Quarterly, 61,* 101–120.

Seybold, K. S., & Hill, P. C. (2001). The role of religion and spirituality in mental and physical health. *Current Directions in Psychological Science, 10,* 21–24.

Shih, M., Pittinsky, T. L., & Trahan, A. (2006). Domain-specific effects of stereotypes on performance. *Self and Identity, 5,* 1–14.

Smart, J. F., & Smart, D. W. (1995). Acculturative stress: The experience of the Hispanic immigrant. *Counseling Psychologist, 23,* 25–42.

St. Loius, G. R., & Liem, J. H. (2005). Ego identity and ethnic identity, and the psychosocial well-being of ethnic minority and majority college students. *Identity: An International Journal of Theory and Research, 5,* 227–246.

Steele, C. M. & Aronson, J. (1995). Stereotype threat and the intellectual test performance of African Americans. *Journal of Personality and Social Psychology, 69,* 797–811.

Sue, S., & Kitano, H. H. (1973). Stereotypes as a measure of success. *Journal of Social Issues, 29,* 83–98.

Sue, S., & Morishima, J. (1982). *The mental health of Asian Americans.* San Francisco: Jossey–Bass.

Sue, D. W., Bucceri, J., Lin, A. I., Nadal, K. L., & Torino, G. C. (2007a). Racial microaggressions and the Asian American experience. *Cultural Diversity and Ethnic Minority Psychology, 13,* 72–81.

Sue, D. W., Capodilupo, C. M., Torino, G. C., Bucceri, J. M., Holder, A. M. B., & Nadal, K. L. et al. (2007b). Racial microaggressions in everyday life: Implications for clinical practice. *American Psychologist, 62,* 271–286.

Taylor, S. E., Welch, W. T., Kim, H. S., & Sherman, D. K. (2007). Cultural differences in the impact of social support on psychological and biological stress responses. *Psychological Science, 18,* 831–837.

Thomas, M., & Choi, J. B. (2006). Acculturative stress and social support among Korean and Indian immigrant adolescents in the United States. *Journal of Sociology & Social Welfare, 33,* 123–143.

Tsai, J. L., Ying, Y., & Lee, P. A. (2001). Cultural predictors of self-esteem: A study of Chinese American female and male young adults. *Cultural Diversity & Ethnic Minority Psychology, 7*, 284–297.

Tseng, V., & Fuligni, A. J. (2000). Parent-adolescent language use and relationships among immigrant families with East Asian, Filipino and Latin American backgrounds. *Journal of Marriage & the Family, 62*, 465–476.

Uba, L. (1994). Asian Americans: Personality patterns, identity, and mental health. New York: Guilford.

U.S. Census Bureau (2000). *We the people: Asians in the United States (Census 2000 special reports)*. Washington: U.S. Government Printing Office.

U.S. Department of Health and Human Services (USDHHS). (2001). *Mental Health: Culture, race, and ethnicity—a supplement to mental health: A report of the Surgeon General*. Rockville: U.S. Department of Health and Human Services, Public Health Service, Office of the Surgeon General.

Vartanian, T. P., Karen, D., Buck, P. W., & Cadge, W. (2007). Early factors leading to college graduation for Asians and non-Asians in the United States. *Sociological Quarterly, 48*, 165–197.

Vega, W. A., Sribney, W. M., Aguilar-Gaxiola, S., & Kolody, B. (2004). 12-month prevalence of DSM-III-R psychiatric disorders among Mexican Americans: Nativity, social assimilation, and age determinants. *Journal of Nervous and Mental Disease, 192*, 532–541.

Weisz, J. R., Eastman, K. L., McCarty, C. A. (1996). Primary and secondary control in East Asia: Comments on Oerter et al. *Culture & Psychology, 2*, 63–76.

Yee, B. W. K., DeBaryshe, B. D., Yuen, S., Kim, S. Y., & McCubbin, H. I. (2007). Asian American and Pacific Islander families: Resiliency and life-span socialization in a cultural context. In F. T. L. Leong, A. Ebreo, L. Kinoshita, A. G. Inman, L. H. Yang, & M. Fu (Eds.), *Handbook of Asian American psychology* (2nd ed., pp. 69–86). Thousand Oaks: Sage.

Ying, Y., & Chao, C. (1996). Intergenerational relationship in Iu Mien American families. *Amerasia Journal, 22*, 47–64.

Yoo, H. C., & Lee, R. M. (2005). Ethnic identity and approach-type coping as moderators of the racial discrimination/well-being relation in Asian Americans. *Journal of Counseling Psychology, 52*, 497–506.

Yoshikawa, H., Wilson, P. A., Chae, D. H., & Cheng, J. (2004). Do family and friendship networks protect against the influence of discrimination on mental health and HIV risk among Asian and Pacific Islander gay men? *AIDS Education and Prevention, 16*, 84–100.

Young, K., & Takeuchi, D. T. (1998). Racism. In L. C. Lee & N. W. S. Zane (Eds.), *Handbook of Asian American psychology* (pp. 401–432). Thousand Oaks: Sage.

Zane, N. (2005). Evidence-based practice in psychology: Challenges for effectively serving ethnic minority populations. *The California Psychologist, 38*, 15–16.

Zhou, M. (2000). Social capital in Chinatown: The role of community-based organizations and families in the adaptation of the younger generation. In M. Zhou & J. V. Gatewood (Eds.), *Contemporary Asian America: A multidisciplinary reader* (pp. 315–335). New York: New York University Press.

Chapter 11
Psychology of Asian American Older Adults: Status, Challenges, and Strengths

Ailee Moon and Inju Cho

Introduction

This chapter discusses the major challenges to the maintenance of mental health in the Asian American older adult population. Major points of discussion focus on the stigmatization of and lack of knowledge about mental health disorders and the underutilization of mental health services. Familial support, religion/spirituality, and peer support and social networks are also presented as major strengths, which contribute to the resilience exhibited by older Asian Americans. It begins with an overview of the demographic characteristics of the population and followed by the prevalence rates of mental disorders most commonly found in several older Asian American groups.

Demographic Characteristics of Asian American Older Adults

The US Census 2000 identified at least 24 Asian American groups, excluding Pacific Islanders. Accordingly, it counted 11.9 million Asian Americans in 2000 (4.2% of the total US population) and recorded a 72% increase from 1990, which is significantly higher than the 13% growth in the total population (U.S. Census Bureau 2002). By 2050, the Asian American population is projected to grow 213%, constituting about 8% of the total population (Mui et al. 2006).

There were 843,543 Asian Americans ages 65 and older in 2000, representing 7.1% of the Asian American population and 2.3% of the total older adult population (U.S. Census Bureau 2002). The older Asian American population grew at a whirlwind rate of 92% between 1990 and 2000, compared to modest a 12% increase in the total older adult population. Using the Census 2000 "Asian alone" data, Chinese

A. Moon (✉)
Department of Social Welfare, University of California Los Angeles School of Public Affairs
3250 Public Policy Building, Los Angeles, 951656, 90095-1656, CA, USA
e-mail: aileem@ucla.edu

E. C. Chang, C. A. Downey (eds.), *Handbook of Race and Development in Mental Health*,
DOI 10.1007/978-1-4614-0424-8_11, © Springer Science+Business Media, LLC 2012

Americans constituted almost 30% of all older Asian Americans, followed by Filipino—(20.8%), Japanese—(20.8%), Korean—(8.5%), and Asian Indian—(7.9%) Americans.

The continued influx of older adult immigrants from different Asian countries, together with the aging American-born Asian descents and earlier immigrants from the past decades, highlight the increasing diversity found between the older Asian American ethnic groups. This diversity is reflected in the distinct cultures, languages, and histories of each ethnic group's country-of-origin, as well as in their immigration backgrounds, religious affiliations, socioeconomic statuses, acculturation levels, English proficiencies, health beliefs, and life experiences in the United States, all of which influence their well-being. (Moon and Rhee 2006; Min and Moon 2006). For example, while 78% of the total older Asian American population was foreign-born in 2000, only 29% of older Japanese Americans were foreign-born, suggesting that many older Japanese Americans are more English proficient and highly acculturated. Whereas over 80% of Hmong, Cambodian, and Laotian American older adults had less than a high school education, over 40% of older Filipino, Malaysian, and Indonesian Americans had some college or more. Older Asian Americans also differ in religious affiliations. While many Filipino and Korean Americans are predominantly Christian, most Cambodians and Laotians are Buddhist, Asian Indians are Hindu, and Indonesians are Muslim.

The growing variation in life experiences, challenges, needs, and resources between and within older Asian American ethnic groups makes it increasingly difficult to generalize the overall status of mental health and other related issues. Indeed, the lack of comprehensive, comparative, and empirical knowledge of the diversity in mental health issues between these distinct ethnic minority populations poses a major challenge to developing evidence-based mental health programs for them. However, older Asian Americans, who have life-long experiences as members of an ethnic minority group, share common encounters with subtle forms of racism, discriminatory treatment, and prejudiced attitudes. Demeaning experiences such as these may be internalized and have negative consequences on their mental health (Iwamasa and Hilliard 1999).

Prevalence of Mental Disorders

Although no national estimates on the prevalence rates of mental health disorders for older Asian Americans exists, growing evidence suggests that a considerable proportion of this population suffers from mental health disorders (Browne et al. 1994; Diwan et al. 2004; Han et al. 2007; Mui 1998; Harada and Kim 1995; Iwamasa and Hilliard 1999; Jang et al. 2006; Kang and Kang 1995; Kuo 1984; Lee et al. 1996, 2004; Min et al. 2005; Mui and Kang 2006; Shibusawa and Mui 2001; Soonthornchaiya and Dancy 2006; Stokes et al. 2001; Wong et al. 2007). From the array of mental health disorders, depression is the most studied amongst Asian American elders. Based on the Center for Epidemiological Scale of Depression, an earlier study of depression drawing from 499 older Chinese, Japanese, Filipino, and Korean Americans in Seattle found that Koreans had the highest rates of depression and all Asian American groups were significantly more depressed than Whites (Kuo 1984). Similar findings were reported in older Chinese immigrants in Canada who were found to have lower levels of psychological well-being than their European Canadian counterparts (Wong and Reker 1985).

A study of older Japanese Americans found that the combined prevalence of depression and depressive symptoms was 30% among the 44 respondents living in a retirement home, while the rate significantly drops to 5% among 78 respondents in the community group (Yamamoto et al. 1985). The study also reported that, although anxiety was not as prevalent as depression, 9% of the older Japanese American respondents were diagnosed with panic disorder.

A recent study of depression among six older Asian immigrant groups in New York found that 40% of the 407 respondents were depressed based on the Geriatric Depression Scale (Mui and Kang 2006). Among the six groups, depression was the highest for the Japanese (76%), followed by the Vietnamese (64%), Indian (50%), Chinese (46%), Korean (24%), and Filipino (15%) immigrants.

Using a probability sampling method, a two-wave panel study of depression, measured by the Center for Epidemiologic Scale of Depression scale, between 172 older Korean immigrants and 157 older Whites in Los Angeles found that the Korean respondents on average reported significantly higher levels of depression at both time points (12.9 and 11.9 vs. 7.6 and 7.1, respectively) (Min et al. 2005). Notably, while the changes in self-rated health and Instrumental Activities of Daily Living (IADL) were significant factors for improvement or deterioration of psychological distress over time, social and familial factors, like social support, were found to be the most significant factors in accounting for decreases in psychological distress for Korean immigrant respondents, but not for the older White respondents (Min et al. 2005). Another study of 95 older Korean immigrants in Los Angeles found that 39% of them were clinically depressed (Lee et al. 2004).

In light of the data found on depression, limited data on the suicide rates for some Asian American older adult populations raises serious concerns. In a comparative study of suicide rates between 1987 and 1996 among several Asian and other ethnic minority female cohorts in San Francisco, Barron (2000) found that immigrant Chinese older adults accounted for 89% of all older Chinese suicides and that Chinese women had a higher suicide rate than women in all other racial-ethnic groups, including Filipino, Japanese, African, Latino, and Native Americans. Yu (1986) discovered that the suicide rate for older Chinese immigrants was almost three times higher than the rate for their American-born Chinese counterparts. Furthermore, Asian women over the age of 85 had the highest rates of suicide across both groups and gender during the period between 1987 and 1994 in San Francisco, California (Shiang et al. 1997).

For many older Southeast Asian refugees, the impact of pre-migration experiences are long lasting even many years after they resettle in the United States. They suffer from post-traumatic stress disorder as a consequence of traumatic premigration experiences, such as the torture and loss of significant others, and various postmigration stress and adjustment problems, including the loss of personal autonomy, language and social isolation, and unfamiliarity with the American system (Abueg and Chun 1996; Ngo et al. 2001).

According to Abueg and Chun (1996), the Cambodian, Hmong, and Mien refugees, who arrived in the United States more recently, represent the three most traumatized subgroups among the Southeast Asian refugee groups. A study on the psychosocial adaptation of three generations of Vietnamese immigrants found that the two older generations (older adults, middle-aged) were experiencing significantly greater difficulties with adaptation to life in the United States than the young adult group (Shapiro et al. 1999). In general, recent refugee and immigrant older adults are more likely to experience mental health problems and less likely to seek treatment compared to younger Asian Americans, American-born or long-time Asian immigrants and to their European American counterparts (Iwamasa and Hilliard 1999; Moon and Rhee 2006).

A study of adult Vietnamese refugees stressed the significant effects of acculturation on depression. Of the Vietnamese with shared traumatic pre-immigration experiences, depression had a stronger effect on those with lower levels of acculturation than those who were highly acculturated (Ngo et al. 2001). In fact, a number of studies identified significant correlates of psychological constructs, such as depression, isolation, and low morale among older Asian Americans. They include low levels of acculturation, shorter length of residency in the United States, poor self-rated health, functional limitation, living alone, and lack of family support and quality relationships (Casado and Leung 2001; Chung et al. 2000; Moon and Pearl 1991; Lee et al. 1996, 2004; Moon 1996; Min et al., 2005; Mui 1998; Mui and Kang 2006; Shibusawa and Mui 2001).

Challenges to Maintaining Mental Health

Stigmatization of Mental Health Disorders

Cultural perceptions of mental health disorders influence symptom manifestations and responses to the illness. Conceptualization of mental health problems varies among and within Asian American communities and is associated with the subpopulation's cultural beliefs and acculturation levels (Iwamasa and Sorocco 2007). Despite such distinctions, the majority of older Asian Americans—especially among less-acculturated, recent immigrants, and refugees who maintain the belief systems of their countries-of-origin—tend to attribute the causes of mental health problems to one's emotional weakness or lack of willpower, social relational problems, unexplainable supernatural forces, religious and spiritual forces, and consequences of past deeds (Abueg and Chun 1996; Min and Moon 2006).

Many older Asian Indians who practice Hinduism or Sikhism believe in reincarnation and *karma*, which regard dementia as the manifestation of bad *karma* from past lives and render many to feel that the problems are unsolvable as the result of *karma* (Periyakoil 2006). Similarly, many Chinese and Vietnamese American older adults may view dementia as one's fate, the retribution for the sins of the family or of one's ancestors, or the imbalance between the body's complementary forms of energy (*yin* and *yang*) (Nguyen and Anderson 2005; Wang et al. 2006). In fact, fatalism, which is also a cultural and religious belief among Buddhist Asian American older adults, suggests that one's mental illness is either a fate or consequence of past deeds (Abueg and Chun 1996). However, it has been suggested that there has been a departure from such attitudes.

Moon (2006) indicated that most Koreans and Korean Americans, like the Chinese, used to regard dementia and mental illness as a consequence of "bad blood," evil spirits, past deeds, or the improper alignment of an ancestor's grave. However, growing evidence suggests that Korean immigrants are departing from such traditional beliefs. A survey of 78 Korean immigrants, including 54 older adults, found only 4% of the respondents related dementia to the improper alignment of a house or grave of an ancestor, while 8% viewed it as retribution for the sins of an ancestor or a family misdeed (Moon 2005). Another study found that only 7% of the Korean American respondents viewed "old age" as the cause of Alzheimer's disease and 10% attributed it to "senility," while almost one-half correctly indicated the cause as "unknown" (Watari and Gatz 2004). In this regard, Moon (2006) suggested that increased exposure to biomedical explanations of dementia and the high rate of the Christian religion (70–80%) in Korean Americans may explain what appears to be a denouncement of traditionally superstitious and non-Christian beliefs.

In general, the traditional, religious, or spiritual beliefs about the causes of mental or physical illness, such as the punishment for sins committed in one' s past life, fail to adhere to the principles of one's religion; and belief in the possession by evil spirits still prevail in many Asian American communities. Such perceptions may be, in part, reinforced by the beliefs that no physiological or medical explanations for the causes or cures of mental illness exist. These beliefs, in turn, may reflect the tendency to narrowly define or identify mental illnesses based on the most apparent behavioral problems (excluding the more subtle state of one's mind or feelings). However, there seems to be a growing recognition among older Asian Americans that some mental disorders can be cured. For example, most of the English-speaking older Japanese American respondents ($n=23$) in a study thought that depression was a preventable and treatable mental condition (Iwamasa et al. 1998).

Unlike physical illnesses, mental disorders carry a strong stigma and disgrace the family in most Asian American communities, especially among older adults (Iwamasa et al. 1998). People who manifest symptoms, such as withdrawal, depression, thought disorder, and bizarre behavior, were and, to a lesser extent, still are often labeled as lazy or crazy (Iwamasa and Sorocco 2007). People with mental disorders are also generally characterized as strange, unpredic, and even dangerous. As such, it is no surprise that among most Asian Americans, dementia is stigmatized and defined as a mental illness. In this situation, mental health problems in the family are hardly ever revealed to outsiders.

Stigmatization of mental health disorders and the cultural value of shame among older Asian Americans have thus contributed to the denial of having a mental disorder, the failure to appropriately recognize symptoms or behaviors, and delayed treatment. Such negative responses consequently exacerbate the problem, where help is not sought until the problems are no longer manageable without outside help and the symptomology is severe. Chinese Americans, for example, have identified stigmatization of Alzheimer's disease as a barrier in seeking treatment (Zhan 2004). Thus, these cultural beliefs and perceptions must be recognized by the Western and medical concepts of and interventions to mental illness in the Asian American communities, especially with respect to immigrant populations.

Psychosocial problems in older Asian Americans, especially among less acculturated recent immigrants, often present as somatic symptoms or complaints. Rather than seeking mental health services for such problems, older Asian Americans preferentially seek medical care for their physical symptoms. In part, this preference may be attributed to the view and experience of the mind and body as a unitary system (Browne et al. 1994; Pang 2000). In large, the expression of physical symptoms is more acceptable than the expression of emotional difficulties or behavioral problems, which perpetuates the stigma attached to mental disorders and the cultural value of avoiding shame.

However, the somatization of psychological and emotional problems may be the result of a lack of experience in labeling, describing, and communicating about such issues (Douglas and Fujimoto 1995). For example, typical somatic symptoms commonly expressed by immigrant Chinese older adults include difficulty falling asleep, loss of appetite, headaches, feeling weak, shortness of breath, and pain all over their bodies (Douglas and Fujimoto 1995; Hong et al. 1995). A study on older Korean immigrants found a significant relationship between somatization and symptom expression, where those who met the criteria for depression on the Brief Symptom Inventory (BSI) had the highest mean score on the BSI somatization dimension (Pang 2000). In a separate study on older Korean immigrants ($n=674$), Pang (1995) noted that even those who were not clinically depressed reported feelings of sadness, loneliness, and somatic symptoms. Iwamasa et al. (1998) also found some conceptual overlap between depression and anxiety as some respondents described symptoms of depression using those of anxiety, such as worrying.

These findings raise serious questions about whether and the extent to which currently available and well-known measures that have been standardized on nonminority groups may also be valid for specific older Asian American populations (Iwamasa and Hilliard 1999). Indeed, more systematic and large scale research is needed in order to increase current understandings of how major mental health disorders, including depression and anxiety, are conceptualized by older adults in specific Asian American communities. Only through the direct expressions or descriptions of symptoms experienced by older adults will it be possible to develop culturally valid and clinically reliable assessment tools that will accurately identify the symptoms and measure the severity of mental disorders in specific older Asian American communities.

Notably, however, some Asian American older adults also believe that developing a mental disorder later in life, such as depression and anxiety, as well as dementia, is a natural part of aging. This perspective on aging underestimates an illness or condition that requires or can be improved with appropriate formal or informal help. This high level of tolerance of mental disorder associated with age, among many factors, seems to contribute to a relatively high prevalence of mental disturbances among older Asian Americans. Therefore, underlying cultural perceptions of mental problems and their causes need to be addressed in order to maintain and improve the mental health status of older Asian Americans.

Lack of Information and Knowledge about Mental Health Disorders

Like physical illness, prevention, early diagnosis, and the appropriate treatment of mental disorders are crucial for maintaining and re-establishing mental health. Unlike physical illnesses, however, mental health problems receive little attention from the ethnic media and are rarely a topic for public education seminars or community health fairs in most Asian American communities. While information about the causes and symptoms of various physical health problems (i.e., how to prevent them, what should be done for effective remedies) is widely available in several Asian ethnic languages, such information about mental health disorders is hard to find outside mental health facilities in these communities.

This phenomenon is largely attributed to the social stigma attached to mental health disorders and the tendency to narrowly define it to include only severe types of mental illness, which affect a very small number of the population. This assumes that mental health is not a high priority or a major problem in the Asian American community. Older Asian Americans, especially those immigrants with limited English proficiency, who rely primarily on ethnic media and organizations for most of their news and information, rarely have the opportunity to learn about different types of mental health problems, including symptoms, possible causes, coping strategies, treatment options, and possible consequences if not treated, as well as available mental health services. The lack of information and knowledge about mental disorders indeed is a major factor contributing to the perpetuation of stigmatization, the somatization of mental disorders, the inability to recognize and describe psychological symptoms, and the prolonged or unnecessary suffering and deterioration of the situation as a result of delayed treatment.

In fact, few studies have demonstrated that with proper assessment processes, which devote sufficient time and attention to the issues, Asian American older adults acknowledge and express psychological symptoms, as well as somatic symptoms (Iwamasa and Sorocco 2007). For example, Japanese American older adults in a study defined anxiety and depression by describing primarily psychological symptoms (Iwamasa et al. 1998).

It is also interesting to note culturally unique psychiatric conditions, such as *Hwa-Byung* among older Korean women. It refers to the prolonged suppression of unbearable pain, suffering, loss, anger, or resentment, which develops into clinical depression, anxiety, and somatic symptoms (Lin et al. 1992; Pang 1990). The most unique aspect of *Hwa-Byung* is that Koreans label themselves as having this "illness" (or *byung* in Korean) with little fear of stigma, and it is a commonly used and accepted expression for one's psychological and physiological status.

On an individual level, a host of factors serve as major barriers to maintaining mental health among Asian American older adults, especially those first-generation immigrants and refugees from non-English speaking countries. Factors include a lack of understanding about the various types of mental disorder and how to maintain mental health, the inability to label and describe psychological symptoms, the reluctance to seek outside help, and the inability to identify appropriate mental health treatment. However, these seemingly individual barriers are, in fact, the collective responsibility of Asian American communities working together with mental health organizations and the media to educate their community members. These joint efforts must address relevant mental health issues, including cultural stigma, somatic and psychological symptoms, biomedical, psychosocial, and other treatment approaches to recovery, coping strategies, and possible consequences if not treated, as well as the availability, or lack of linguistically and culturally tailored mental health services, in specific Asian American communities.

Knowledge about mental health disorders also increases the ability to address the lack of information and public resources and programs to assess, prevent and treat mental health problems. Unfortunately, mental health issues among Asian American older adults will continue to be undervalued or overlooked as long as other issues such as underemployment, crowed living conditions, language problems, discrimination, and intergenerational cultural gaps and conflicts are regarded as pressing issues deserving more public attention and resources (Braun et al. 1995).

Underutilization of Mental Health Services

Many Asian American older adults, at first, tend to internalize, deny or cope with psychological problems on their own, believing that they should handle the problems independently and that nobody else can solve or help them with their internal emotional problems. When their attempt to solve the problems alone fails, some may seek help and keep the problems within the family. Indeed, family has been the primary source of support for dealing with mental illnesses in Asian American communities (Min and Moon 2006; Inman and Yeh 2007). Also, family can play an important role in encouraging or discouraging elderly relatives with mental illnesses to seek outside professional help (Snowden 1998; Snowden et al. 2006).

As Asian American older adults often present physical and somatic symptoms for psychosocial problems, some may seek Western medical treatment and/or traditional healers or herbal doctors, who are often used in Asian cultures to treat the physical disorders believed to be the patient's major problem (Inman and Yeh 2007; Pourat et al. 1999). In addition, Asian immigrant older adults may seek help from folk healers because they speak the same language, share the same cultural perceptions on the causes of mental problems, apply the cure methods only the cultural folk healers can perform, and sometimes make use of family members and religion (Cheung and Snowden 1990).

On the other hand, many older adults in most Asian American communities view seeking formal help as the last resort, since it is a shameful act of weakness to disclose one's psychological distresses and emotional problems to a stranger, even a professional mental health specialist, bringing disgrace to the family (Casado and Leung 2001; Uba 1994). A study found that delays in mental health service use among Asian Americans with mental illness were positively related to their relatives' higher levels of stigma about the mental illness (Okazaki 2000).

Perhaps the lack of knowledge about the mental health system delivered at the agency level may also serve as a barrier to seeking mental health services and treatment. Many older adults, especially immigrants, may not be familiar with or know the professional ethic of confidentiality. Some may worry that their specialists may not honor their confidentiality and tell others about their emotional and personal problems. Because mental disorders carry a stigma, Asian American older adults are most likely to maintain modesty in their expression and less willing to describe extreme feelings or serious behavioral symptoms to mental health professionals until a strong sense of trust is established (Min and Moon 2006).

Considering the cultural values and preferences for self-help and informal support in dealing with mental health problems, it is not surprising that *underutilization* is a common theme that emerges from many studies on the use of formal mental health services among older Asian Americans. (Abe-Kim et al. 2007; Browne et al. 1994; Harada and Kim 1995; Matsuoka et al. 1997; Moon et al. 1998). Asian Americans, especially first-generation older adults, tend to seek mental health services when the conditions are severe and disrupt the lives of the individuals and their surroundings (Kung 2003; Wynaden et al. 2005).

An analysis of national survey data found that the percentage of Asian American and Pacific Islanders who utilized mental health services at public and private facilities was a third of the proportion of European Americans. The older adult population was even less likely use mental health services (Matsuoka et al. 1997). A comparative study of Korean immigrant and non-Hispanic White older adults in Los Angeles found that only 1.3% of Korean respondents, compared to 41.3% of their counterparts, were aware of mental health services available in the community. Although the Korean group was also far less aware than the Whites of the other 14 community-based services available, it is no that among those respondents aware of services the group differences in service usage were much smaller. This finding suggests that the lack of knowledge of mental health services may be an important barrier to the utilization of mental health services (Moon et al. 1998).

In addition to cultural issues, there is a great need to address the various institutional and socio-structural barriers to mental health service use, especially for those culturally and linguistically isolated older adults. These barriers include a lack of awareness of and unfamiliarity with the mental health service systems and supportive home-and community-based services; geographic locations in proximity to services; lack of transportation service; financial constraints; the stereotype that Asian American older adults are taken care of by their families; and lack of culturally appropriate services and bilingual staffs (Leong and Lau 2001; Snowden et al. 2006).

Strengths Contributing to Mental Health

Familial Support

Most traditional Asian cultures emphasize family solidarity, filial piety, and respect for older adults as the governing principles for family life and relations (Min and Moon 2006). Although many Asian American families may not perform filial piety in a traditional sense, such as living together with older parents, the family is the vital source of support and care for Asian American older adults, regardless of the living arrangement. Studies have shown that Asian American adult children provide a considerable amount of emotional and instrumental support to their elderly parents (National Alliance for Caregiving and American Association for Retired People 2004; Mui 2001; Mui and Kang 2006; Shibusawa and Mui 2001).

For example, a study of caregivers conducted by the National Alliance for Caregiving and American Association for Retired People (2004) estimated that although the proportion of older adults is significantly smaller among Asian Americans than Whites, 15% of Asian Americans, compared with 17% of Whites, provided unpaid care to someone 50 or older in the last 12 months. The same study also found that Asian American caregivers were far more likely to indicate "old age" or "being old" as the main problem or illness of the person they were caring for (23%, as compared with 12% White, 10% African American, and 9% Hispanic caregivers). A study of six Asian American groups reported that older Indian, Japanese, and Filipino respondents received more emotional and instrumental support from their adult children than the Chinese, Korean, and Vietnamese respondents, although all six groups received a considerable amount of support from their adult children (Mui and Kang 2006). A recent study on older Korean Americans found that adult children were the most common source of support, regardless of the type of need and even when the respondent had a living spouse (Han et al. 2007).

The research further suggests that the perceived relationship between adult children and filial satisfaction are important correlates or predictors of psychological well-being (Jang et al. 2006; Moon 1996; Mui 1998). In a study of older Chinese immigrants living alone, the levels of their depressive symptoms were correlated to the perceived satisfaction of family help and not to the size of family network (Mui 1998). In a study of six older Asian American groups, the number of children living in proximity (within two hours driving distance) was a significant predictor of lower levels of depressive symptoms (Mui and Kang 2006). Perceived closeness or a good relationship with their adult children was a significant predictor of higher levels of morale among older Korean immigrants living alone or with their spouse only (Moon 1996). Similarly, filial satisfaction was found to be an important factor in the mental health of older Korean Americans (Jang et al. 2006).

It is interesting to note, however, that a study on older Chinese and Korean immigrants reported that those who lived with their spouse and adult children had lower overall psychological well-being and lower positive affect compared to those who lived alone (Wong et al. 2007). The study also found that having more emotional and companionship support significantly contributed to higher psychological well-being, lower depression, and higher positive affect. These findings perhaps suggest that living with their spouse and adult children for some respondents could mean living with intergenerational conflicts, being a provider rather than a receiver of instrumental support and other help to adult children, higher levels of social isolation and having limited opportunities for social activities outside the home. Indeed, one's living arrangement appears to have become a weak indicator of whether adult children provide care or emotional and instrumental support for their parents in Asian American families.

Religion and Spirituality

Religious and spiritual connections have been an important means of coping with daily stressors, such as health and adjustment problems, loneliness, and interpersonal issues, and also provide a source of informal supports and networks for older Asian American populations. Thai immigrant older adults, for example, identified practicing Buddhist teachings and meditations, going to the temple, and participating in social activities offered by the temple as coping strategies for their depressive symptoms (Soonthornchaiya and Dancy 2006). In addition, talking to faith leaders, including monks, priests, pastors and nuns, about personal and family problems is a more common coping and help-seeking behavior than seeking help from mental health professionals among religious Asian American older adults, especially first-generation immigrants (Min and Kim 2002).

Research, in general, has supported the important role of religion as a coping resource and an effective protective factor against loss and depressive symptoms for Asian Americans (Inman and Yeh 2007). Using multidimensional aspects of religion (religious support, coping, and forgiveness), spirituality, and well-being, Lee (2007), in her study on Chinese and Korean American older adults, found that religious support was associated with lower depression and higher life satisfaction, utilization of religious coping skills with higher life satisfaction and greater practice of forgiveness. Mui and Kang (2006) in their study of six Asian American older groups also found that higher religiosity, measured by respondents' perceptions about the importance of religion in their lives, was a significant predictor of lower depression. A study of older Asian Indian immigrants also found that greater religiosity, along with increased mastery, was associated with less negative affect (Diwan et al. 2004).

In addition to religious training and practice, religious congregations in ethnic Asian American communities, especially for newcomers and linguistically isolated older adults, also provide vital social support by functioning as ethnic community recreational and information centers. They often organize ethnic, cultural, and educational activities and programs and offer useful information and connections to resources that are helpful for adjustment and resettlement, including employment, housing, and social services. These activities and services are likely to have a positive impact on the mental health of congregation members, particularly recent older immigrants.

Peer Support and Social Networks

In addition to family supports and religion, a number of studies support that culturally or ethnically similar peers and support networks have been important factors contributing to the promotion of mental health in the older Asian American population, especially linguistically isolated immigrants (Diwan et al. 2004; Han et al. 2007; Min et al. 2005; Mui 1998; Shibusawa and Mui 2001; Wong et al. 2007).

Research on Japanese American older adults who lacked emotional support, had fewer close friends, reported having poorer health, and feared dependency on family reported more depressive symptoms (Shibusawa and Mui 2001). Similarly, findings from a study on older Asian Indian immigrants indicated that satisfaction with friendships was a significant predictor of greater positive affect (Diwan et al. 2004). Research on older Chinese and Korean immigrants reported that, while Koreans were more depressed than the Chinese, greater availability of emotional support and companionship was a significant contributor to better overall psychological well-being, lower depression and higher positive affect for both groups (Wong et al. 2007). In fact, an earlier study by Mui (2001) concluded that the number of good friends one had was the strongest factor contributing to the improved mental health of older Korean Americans. This suggests that good friends are a vital source of emotional and instrumental support, preventing loneliness and isolation, particularly during the period of adjustment in a new country.

A study on older Korean immigrants found that higher acculturative stress and lower social support were associated with higher depression levels, even after demographics and health status were controlled for, while the size of social network was not (Han et al. 2007). In a two-wave panel study of older Korean immigrants and non-Hispanic Whites, increased social support was a significant predictor of decreased psychological distress over time for Koreans (Min et al. 2005).

Discussion and Conclusion

Attempts to generalize the mental health status and related issues of the older Asian American population, as shown in Table 1, poses a great challenge to the formulation of appropriate approaches, interventions, and treatments. Such assumptions on the homogeneity of Asian Americans ignore the growing diversity of the older Asian American population and the distinct ethnic and cultural groups captured by the socially constructed umbrella term. This difficulty is, in part, attributed to the lack of a large, comprehensive, ethnic-and age-specific group data set, or disaggregated data, collected by using a representative sample and valid measures for each distinct ethnic group at the national level. In fact, research over the past two decades has produced useful information about various aspects of mental health issues on the more visible Asian American ethnic groups, primarily Chinese, Korean, Japanese, and Vietnamese older adults in several regions of the country, while other groups, including the Hmong, Laotian, and Samoans, have received far less attention from researchers. The disparities in research and information dissemination efforts need to address the knowledge gap in the understudied older Asian American populations.

Although there has been some effort to examine well-known measures of mental health disorders, developed primarily on the European American population, to determine their appropriateness for specific older Asian American groups, a more fundamental approach is needed. Acknowledging that older Asian Americans may conceptualize mental health disorders differently, both qualitative and quantitative approaches are needed to investigate how they express, describe, and show their feelings, thoughts, and behaviors. These findings would then provide integral information on the conceptualization and development of culturally valid and ethnic-specific measures of mental health disorders.

Needless to say, untreated mental health problems can seriously and detrimentally affect morbidity, functional ability, and quality of life. Existing evidence indicates that a considerable proportion of the older Asian American population suffers from various types of mental health disorders. Furthermore, this population generally has high levels of tolerance for mental illness and strongly denies its actual affects. This is due to a combination of cultural perceptions of and stigma toward mental illness and a lack of knowledge about the current state of medical and psychosocial treatments, community efforts, and public resources devoted to education, information dissemination, and the provision of ethnic-specific culturally and linguistically effective mental health services. Therefore, neglecting to address specific barriers to the mental health status of Asian Americans at large seriously disservices the larger community. This justifiably calls for more resources to be devoted to intervention research on existing and newly emerging mental health services, assessing their effectiveness on ethnic-specific older Asian American groups, and generating evidence-based information for improving services.

Informal supports from family, friends, religion, spirituality, and other sources, such as indigenous healers, contribute to the mental health of older Asian American

Table 1 A Summary of Challenges, Strengths, and Recommendations

Demographics	Challenges	Strengths	Recommendations
(1) *All Asian Americans* in 2000: 4.2% of the general population (2) *Older Asian Americans:* 7.1% of All Asian Americans; 2.3% of the total older adult population (65 years and older) (3) *By 2050* , the Asian American population is projected to grow 213%, constitute about 8% of the total population	(1) *Stigmatization of mental health disorders (MHD):* – Attribute MHD to one's emotional weakness, fate, religious and spiritual forces, consequences of past deeds, etc – MHD bring shame to the family, denial of having a MHD and delay treatment – Somatization of MHD (2) *Lack of knowledge about MHD:* – MHD is a rarely topic for ethnic media coverage, public education seminars or health fairs – Perpetuation of stigmatization, inability to recognize MHD symptoms, lack of awareness of formal treatment options (3) *Underutilization of MH services:* – Dominant view of formal MH services from specialists as a last resort – Lack of willingness to reveal personal and MH problems to strangers, lack of trust or confidence in curability of MHD – Lack of knowledge about available MH services in the community as a barrier to seeking treatment	(1) Familial support: – The family is a vital source of support and care, regardless of living arrangement – Perceived closeness and filial satisfaction, and living in proximity all contribute to psychological well-being of older Asian Americans (2) Religion and spirituality: – Religious and spiritual connections serve as an important means of coping with daily stressors – Religious congregations provide vital social support as ethnic community recreational centers and also offer useful information and connections to resources for adjustment and resettlement, contribution to MH of congregation members (3) Peer support and social network: – Good friends provide emotional and instrumental support – Availability of companionship prevents loneliness and isolation, particularly during the period of adjustment among immigrant older adults	(1) A greater effort is needed to reduce the knowledge gap in the understudied older Asian American populations (2) Both qualitative and quantitative approaches are needed to investigate how older adults in each Asian American population express, describe, and show their feelings, thoughts, and behaviors in order to conceptualize and develop culturally valid and ethnic-specific measures of mental health disorders (3) Increase community efforts and public resources for education, information dissemination, and the provision of ethnic-specific culturally and linguistically effective mental health services (4) Address cultural stigma and the shame associated with mental health disorders and the use of formal mental health services among family members, religious leaders, indigenous healers, other community leaders

populations. This means that the provision of additional supports and disseminating information to family members, including their adult children, religious leaders, and indigenous healers about various aspects of aging specifically related to physical and mental health, will contribute to the overall health and well-being of older Asian American adults by educating them to prevent, detect, and treat mental health problems early on.

On the other hand, it is equally important to recognize and address the effects of acculturation on the declining traditional practice of filial piety in some Asian American families. Changing cultural and familial practices may result in intergenerational conflicts and the consequential negative impact on the mental health of older adults in these families. Asian Americans can make a significant contribution to the overall quality of life for both older and younger members in their respective ethnic community by increasing cultural, social, recreational, and intergenerational programs and activities for all family members to participate. Finally, cultural stigma and the shame associated with mental health disorders and the use of formal mental health services among family members, religious leaders, indigenous healers, other community leaders must be addressed in order to connect older adults with mental health disorders to formal resources for support and treatment, in addition to those informal sources available to them.

References

Abe-Kim, J., Takeuchi, D. T., Hong, S., Zane, N., Sue, S., & Spencer, M. S. (2007). Use of mental health-related services among immigrant and US-born Asian Americans: Results from the National Latino and Asian American study. *American Journal of Public Health, 97*(1), 91–98.

Abueg, R. R., & Chun, K. M. (1996). Traumatization stress among Asian and Asian Americans. In A. J. Marsella, M. J. Friedman, E. T. Gerrity, & R. M. Scurfield (Eds.), *Ethnocultural aspects of posttraumatic stress disorder: Issues, research, and clinical applications* (pp. 285–299). Washington, DC: American Psychological Association.

Barron, S. L. (2000). Suicide in context: Elderly Chinese female suicide in San Francisco from 1987 through 1996 (Doctoral dissertation, Pacific Graduate School of Psychology, 2000). *Dissertation Abstract International, 61*(03B), 1624.

Braun, K. L., Takamura, J. C., Forman, S. M., & Sasaki, P. A. (1995). Developing and testing outreach materials on Alzheimer's disease for Asian and Pacific Islander Americans. *Gerontologist, 35,* 122–126.

Browne, C., Fong, R., & Mokuau, N. (1994). The mental health of Asian and Pacific Islander elders: Implications for mental health administrators. *Journal of Mental Health Administration, 21*(1), 52–59.

Casado, B. L., & Leung, P. (2001). Migratory grief and depression among elderly Chinese American immigrants. *Journal of Gerontological Social Work, 36*(1/2), 5–26.

Cheung, F. K., & Snowden, L. R. (1990). Community mental health and ethnic minority populations. *Community Mental Health Journal, 20,* 277–291.

Chung, R. C.-Y., Bemak, F., & Wong, S. (2000). Vietnamese refugees' levels of distress, social support and acculturation: Implications for mental health counseling. [Peer Reviewed]. *Journal of Mental Health Counseling, 22*(2), 150–161.

Diwan, S., Jonnalagadda, S. S., & Balaswamy, S. (2004). Resources predicting positive and negative affect during the experience of stress: A study of older Asian Indian immigrants in the United States. *The Gerontologist, 44* (5), 605–614.
Douglas, K. C., & Fujimoto, D. (1995). Asian Pacific Islanders: Implications for health care providers. *Clinics in Geriatric Medicine, 11*(1), 69–82.
Han, H. R., Kim, M., Lee, H. B., Pistulka, G., & Kim, K. B. (2007). Correlates of depression in the Korean American elderly: Focusing on personal resources of social support. *Journal of Cultural Gerontology, 22*(1), 115–27.
Harada, N. D., & Kim, L. S. (1995). Use of mental health services by older Asian and Pacific Islander Americans. In D. K. Padgett (Ed.), *Handbook on ethnicity aging and mental health* (pp. 185–202). Westport: Greenwood.
Hong, G. K., Lee, B. S., & Lorenzo, M. K. (1995). Somatization in Chinese American clients: Implications for psychotherapeutic services. *Journal of Contemporary Psychotherapy, 25*(2), 105–118.
Inman, A. G., & Yeh, C. J. (2007). Asian American stress and coping. In F. T. Leong, A. Ebreo, L. Kinoshita, A. G. Inman, L. H. Yang, & M. Fu (Eds.), *Handbook of Asian American psychology* (2nd ed., pp. 323–338). London: Sage.
Iwamasa, G. Y., & Hilliard, K. M. (1999). Depression and anxiety among Asian American elders: A review of literature. *Clinical Psychology Review, 19*(3), 343–357.
Iwamasa, G. Y., & Sorocco, K. H. (2007). The psychology of Asian American older adults. In F. T. L. Leong, A. G. Inman, A. Ebreo, L. H. Yang, L. Kinoshita, & M. Fu (Eds.), *Handbook of Asian American psychology* (2nd ed., pp. 213–226). London: Sage.
Iwamasa, G. Y., Hilliard, K. M., & Osato, S. S. (1998). Conceptualizing anxiety and depression: The Japanese American older adults perspectives. *Clinical Gerontologist, 19,* 77–93.
Jang, Y., Kim, G., & Chiriboga, D. A. (2006). Health perception and depressive symptoms among older Korean Americans. *Journal of Cross-Cultural Gerontology, 21*(3/4), 91–102.
Kang, T. S., & Kang, G. E. (1995). Mental health status and needs of the Asian American elderly. In D. K. Padgett (Ed.), *Handbook on ethnicity, aging, and mental health* (pp. 113–131). Westport: Greenwood.
Kung, W. (2003). Chinese Americans' help seeking for emotional distress. *The Social Service Review, 77*(1), 110–134.
Kuo, W. H. (1984). Prevalence of depression among Asian Americans. *Journal of Nervous and Mental Disease, 172,* 449–457.
Lee, E. O. (2007). Religion and spirituality as predictors of well-being among Chinese American and Korean Americano older adults. *Journal of Religion, Spirituality & Aging, 19*(3), 77–100.
Lee, M. S., Crittenden, K. S., & Yu, E. (1996). Social support and depression among elderly Korean immigrants in the United States. *International Journal of Aging and Human Development, 42*(4), 313–327.
Lee, H. Y., Moon, A., & Knight., B. (2004). Depression among Elderly Korean immigrants: Exploring socio-cultural factors. *Journal of Ethnic and Cultural Diversity in Social Work, 13*(4), 1–26.
Leong, F. T. L., & Lau, A. S. L. (2001). Barriers to providing effective mental health services to Asian Americans. *Mental Health Services Research. Special Issue: Barriers to providing effective mental health services to racial and ethnic minorities in the United States, 3*(4), 201–214.
Lin, K., Lau, J. K., Yamamoto, J., Zheng, Y., Kim, H., Cho, K., & Nakasaki, G. (1992). Hwa-byung: A community study of Korean Americans. *Journal of Nervous and Mental Illness, 180,* 386–391.
Matsuoka, J. K., Breaus, C., & Ryujin, D. H. (1997). National utilization of mental health services by Asian Americans/Pacific Islanders. *Journal of Community Psychology, 25*(2), 141–145.
Min, P. G., & Kim, J. H. (Eds.). (2002). *Religion in Asian America: Building faith communities.* Lanham: AltaMira.
Min, J. W., & Moon, A. (2006). Social work practice with Asian American elders. In B. Berkman (Ed.), *Handbook on aging* (pp. 257–271). Oxford: Oxford University Press.

Min, J. W., Moon, A., & Lubben. J. E. (2005). Determinants of psychological distress over time among older Korean Americans and non-Hispanic White elders: evidence from a two-wave panel study. *Journal of Aging and Mental Health, 9*(3), 210–222.
Moon, A. (1996). Predictors of morale among Korean immigrant elderly in the USA. *Journal of Cross-Cultural Gerontology, 11,* 351–367.
Moon, A. (2005). Perception and knowledge about dementia and related services: A survey of Korean Americans. Unpublished data.
Moon, A. (2006). Working with Korean American families. In G. Yeo & D. Gallagher-Thompson (Eds.), *Ethnicity and the dementias* (2nd ed., pp. 245–261). New York: Routledge.
Moon, J. H., & Pearl, J. H. (1991). Alienation of elderly Korean American immigrants as related to place of residence, gender, age, years of education, time in the U.S., living with or without a spouse. *International Journal of Aging and Human Development, 32,* 115–124.
Moon, A., & Rhee, S. (2006). Social work practice with immigrant and refugee elders. In B. Berkman (Ed.), *Handbook on aging* (pp. 205–217). Oxford: Oxford University Press.
Moon, A., Lubben, J. E., & Villa, V. (1998). Awareness and utilization of community long-term care services by elderly Koreans and non-Hispanic White Americans. *The Gerontologist, 38*(3), 309–316.
Mui, A. C. (1998). Living along and depression among older Chinese immigrants. *Journal of Gerontological Social Work, 30*(3/4), 147–166.
Mui, A.C. (2001). Stress, coping and depression among elderly Korean immigrant. *Journal of Human Behavior in the Social Environment, 3*(3/4), 281–299.
Mui, A. C., & Kang, S. (2006). Acculturation stress and depression among Asian immigrant elders. *Social Work, 51*(3), 243–255.
Mui, A. C., Kang, D., Nguyen, D. D., & Domanski, M. D. (2006). Demographic profiles of Asian immigrant elderly residing in metropolitan ethnic enclave communities. *Journal of Ethnic and Cultural Diversity in Social Work, 15*(1/2), 193–214.
National Alliance for Caregiving and American Association for Retired People. (2004). Caregiving in the U.S. http://research.aarp.org/il/us_caregiving.html. Accessed 23 Aug 2004.
Ngo, D., Tran, T. V., Gibbons, J. L., & Oliver, J. M. (2001). Acculturation, premigration traumatic experiences, and depression among Vietnamese Americans. *Journal of Human Behavior in the Social Environment, 3*(3/4), 225–242.
Nguyen, Q. C. X., & Anderson, L. P. (2005). Vietnamese Americans' attitudes toward seeking mental health services: Relation to cultural variables. *Journal of Community Psychology, 33*(2), 213–231.
Okazaki, S. (2000). Treatment delay among Asian-American patients with severe mental illness. *American Journal of Orthopsychiatry, 70*(1), 58–64.
Pang, K. Y. (1990). Hwabyung: The construction of a Korean popular illness among Korean elderly immigrant women in the United States. *Culture, Medicine, and Psychiatry, 14,* 495–512.
Pang, N. Y. C. (1995). A cross-cultural understanding of depression among elderly Korean immigrants: Prevalence, symptoms and diagnosis. *Clinical Gerontologist, 15*(4), 3–20.
Pang, N. Y. C. (2000). Symptom expression and somatization among elderly Korean immigrants. *Journal of Clinical Geropsychology, 6*(3), 199–212.
Periyakoil, V. S. (2006). Working with Asian Indian American families. In G. Yeo & D. Gallagher-Thompson (Eds.), *Ethnicity and the Dementias* (2nd ed., pp. 165–172). New York: Routledge.
Pourat, N., Lubben, J., Wallace, S., & Moon, A. (1999). Predictors of use of traditional Korean healers among elderly Koreans in Los Angeles. *The Gerontologist, 39*(6), 711–719.
Shapiro, J., Douglas, K., de la Rocha, O., Radecki, S., Vu, C., & Dinh, T. (1999). Generational differences in psychosocial adaptation and predictors of psychological distress in a population of recent Vietnamese immigrants. *Journal of Community Health, 24*(2), 95–113.
Shiang, J., Blinn, R., Bongar, B., Stephens, B., Allison, D., & Schatzberg, A. (1997). A comparison of Caucasian and Asian groups 1987–1994. In A. Leenaars, R. Moris, & Y. Takahashi (Eds.), *Suicide: Individual, culture, international perspectives* (pp. 80–91). New York: Guilford Press.

Shibusawa, T., & Mui, A. C. (2001). Stress, coping, depression among Japanese American elders—sample of 131 Japanese American elders aged 60 years or older. *Journal of Gerontological Social Work, 36*(1/2), 63–81.

Snowden, L. R. (1998). Racial differences in informal help seeking for mental health problems. *Journal of Community Psychology, 26*(5), 429–438.

Snowden, L., Masland, M., Ma, Y., & Ciemens, E. (2006). Strategies to improve minority access to public mental health services in California: Description and preliminary evaluation. *Journal of Community Psychology. Special Issue: Addressing mental health disparities through culturally competent research and community-based practice, 34*(2), 225–235.

Soonthornchaiya, R., & Dancy, B. L. (2006). Perceptions of depression among elderly Thai immigrants. *Issues in Mental Health Nursing, 27*(6), 681–698.

Stokes, S. C., Thompson, L. W., Murphy, S., & Gallagher-Thompson, D. (2001). Screening for depression in immigrant Chinese-American elders: Results of a pilot study. *Journal of Gerontological Social Work, 36,* 27–44.

Uba, L. (1994). *Asian Americans: Personality patterns, identity, and mental health.* New York: Guilford Press.

U.S. Census Bureau. (2002). The Asian population: 2000 [Census 2000 brief]. http://www.census.gov/prod/2002pubs/c2kbr01-16.pdf. Accessed 2 May 2004.

Wang, P., Tong, H., Liu, W., Long, S., Leung, L. Y. L., Yau, E., & Gallagher-Thompson, D. (2006). Working with Chinese American families. In G. Yeo & D. Gallagher-Thompson (Eds.), *Ethnicity and the dementias* (2nd ed., p. 176). New York: Routledge.

Watari, K., & Gatz, M. (2004). Pathways to care for Alzheimer's disease among Korean Americans. *Cultural Diversity and Ethnic minority Psychology, 10*(1), 23–38.

Wong, P., & Reker, G. (1985). Stress, coping, and well-being in Anglo and Chinese elderly. *Canadian Journal of Aging, 4,* 29–37.

Wong, S. T., Yoo, G. J., & Stewart, A. L. (2007). An empirical evaluation of social support and psychological well-being in older Chinese and Korean immigrants: Sample of 200 Chinese and Koreans aged 65 years and older. *Ethnic Health, 12*(1), 43–67.

Wynaden, D., Chapman, R., Orb, A., McGowan, S., Zeeman, Z., & Yeak, S. (2005). Factors that influence Asian communities' access to mental health care. *International Journal of Mental Health Nursing, 14*(2), 88–95.

Yamamoto, J., Machizawa, S., Araki, F., Reece, S., Steinberg, A., Leung, J., & Cater, C. (1985). Mental health of elderly Asian Americans in Los Angeles. *The American Journal of Social Psychiatric Research, 17,* 37–49.

Yu, E. S. (1986). Health of the Chinese elderly in America. *Research on Aging, 8*(1), 84–109.

Zhan, L. (2004). Caring for family members with Alzheimer's disease: Perspectives from Chinese American caregivers. *Journal of Gerontological Nursing, 30*(8), 19–29.

Chapter 12
Psychology of European American Children

Jean A. Baker, Alicia Fedewa and Sycarah Grant

Psychological well-being is the foundation for all children's developmental competence and school success. Despite recommendations that socializing institutions, such as schools, devote more resources to children's mental health (United States Department of Health and Human Services (USDHHS) 1999a), relatively little is known about the needs and resources of some groups of children. In this chapter, we will focus on European American children and adolescents. Despite their majority status, they have been relatively understudied as a racial group per se, with most information deriving from their role as a comparison for other racial or ethnic groups. We will review their history, mental health status, mental health needs and resources, and make recommendations for future research and practice.

Demographic Characteristics

The term "European American" connotes the race category that the National Institute of Health (National Institute of Health (NIH) 2001) specifies as "White." The NIH definition is "A person having origins in any of the original peoples of Europe, the Middle East, or North Africa." We will use European American and White interchangeably.

White immigration to the North American continent began in the late sixteenth and early seventeenth centuries with the first European permanent settlements. The European American population grew steadily with expanded colonization until the late 1700s when immigration slowed. An influx of economic refugees fleeing crop failures in Europe bolstered the numbers of immigrants from Ireland, Germany, and Eastern European nations into the mid-nineteenth century. Industrialization and its associated increased economic opportunities at the turn of the twentieth century brought the largest influx of immigrants from Europe. Scandinavian farmers settled

A. Fedewa (✉)
Department of Educational, School, and Counseling Psychology, University of Kentucky, 170H Taylor Hall (Office), 238 Dickey Hall (Mail), 40506-0017, Lexington, KY, USA
e-mail: alicia.fedewa@uky.edu

E. C. Chang, C. A. Downey (eds.), *Handbook of Race and Development in Mental Health*, DOI 10.1007/978-1-4614-0424-8_12, © Springer Science+Business Media, LLC 2012

the Midwestern region of the US beginning in about 1840 and continuing through the World War I. Following both World Wars, waves of economic and political refugees from Europe contributed to a growth in White immigration to this country (Webb et al. 2003).

Currently, European Americans comprise 77% of the US population according to the most recent census data (U.S. Census Bureau 2002). There is regional and state variation in this statistic, with Wyoming having a 94% White population and Mississippi having a 62% one. European American youth (ages 5–17 years) comprise approximately 60% of the total school-age population in the United States (Statistical Abstracts of the United States 2005). This percentage equates to approximately 31,000,000 non-Hispanic European American school-aged youth. Of this population, close to 98% are enrolled in either public or private schools. Within US schools, European American youth continue to make up the majority of school-aged children, representing 3 out of 4 students in public schools, and close to 8 of 10 students in private schools (Statistical Abstracts of the United States 2004).

The Well-Being of European American Children and Youth

The well-being of European American children and youth is difficult to ascertain, because they are not often profiled according to their racial status. As with any group characterized only by their racial or ethnic identity, there is a risk of stereotyping their needs, assets, and resources. There is tremendous intragroup variability that is not accounted for in group statistics. However, status indicators such as economic and educational outcomes can provide an insight into the material or social well-being of this group.

Related to economic well-being, 17% of all children lived in families with incomes below the poverty thresholds in 2004 (Federal Interagency Forum on Child and Family Statistics 2006). European American children had a poverty rate of 10%, whereas other racial/ethnic groups experienced significantly more poverty (33% and 29% for African American and Hispanic children, respectively). In 2006, 76% of White children lived with two married parents, compared to 35% for Black children and 65% for Hispanic children (Federal Interagency Forum on Child and Family Statistics 2006).

Educational statistics tell a similar story of relative advantage for White children. Racial disparities are evident in every marker of educational well-being, with European American and Asian children out-pacing Hispanic and African American children (Federal Interagency Forum on Child and Family Statistics 2006). They are more likely to have preliteracy activities taken place in their homes as preschoolers and to achieve better on standardized educational tests in 4th and 8th grades. Asian and European American students complete high school (95% and 92%, respectively) at a higher rate than do African American (83%) or Hispanic (70%) peers. Moreover, Asian and European American students are advantaged in all indicators of school success relative to these other two racial/ethnic groups.

Behavioral patterns suggesting risk and resiliency permit additional glimpses into the well-being of European American children. In our recent population-based studies of normal behavioral variability in American public schools, about 55% of elementary aged students show typical development, with no significant behavior problems and some or many behavioral strengths (such as good social skills or leadership), 21% show moderate levels of problems and few strengths, and 16% show clinically significant levels of behavior and emotional problems coupled with few developmental assets and significant academic problems. Of the children showing good developmental profiles, 80% were White, 12.7% were African American, and 7.2% were Hispanic. Of those in the poorest category of mental health outcomes, 63% were White, 33% were African American, and 2% were of Hispanic origin (Kamphaus et al. 1997). In schools serving children living in poverty, these distributions are skewed toward more problems, even though European American children retained their developmental advantage (Baker et al. 2006). However, active risk-taking behavior, such as patterns of heavy drinking, shows that European American children may be more vulnerable than some other groups. In 2005, 11% of 8th-graders, 21% of 10th-graders, and 28% of 12th-graders self-reported binge drinking. This pattern was more prevalent among European American and Hispanic students than among African Americans in all ages (Federal Interagency Forum on Child and Family Statistics 2006).

It is clear that biological, psychosocial, and situational factors interact to predict mental health outcomes in children (Bronfenbrenner and Ceci 1994). Thus, ethnic or racial differences in mental health status are difficult to ascertain. Possible differences may be attributed to disproportionate exposure to psychosocial conditions (such as poverty, maltreatment, or inadequate parenting) or biological events (such as low-birth weight or genetic factors) by some groups rather than race or ethnicity per se. For example, African American infants are more likely than babies of other races to be of low birth weight. In 2005, 14.0% of Black infants were of low birth weight, compared with 8% of Asians/Pacific Islanders, 7.4% of American Indians/Alaska Natives, 7.3% of Whites, and 6.9% of Hispanic infants (Child Trends Data Bank 2007). Additionally, racial or ethnic disparities in access to mental health care services likely skew the statistics regarding prevalence rates between groups. The status of African American or Hispanic children may be inaccurately reported because they do not use health care services at the same rate as do European Americans. Finally, cultural differences in problem conceptualization, help-seeking, and service utilization may contribute to difficulties ascertaining prevalence rates for mental health problems between groups.

However, several studies have attempted to directly compare the mental health status of racial groups. One epidemiological study indicated that African Americans have a lower lifetime occurrence of internalizing disorders than Whites. Even controlling for demographic or socioeconomic status, 11.6% of African Americans had been diagnosed with major depression, compared to 17.7% of Whites (United States Department of Health and Human Services (USDHHS) 1999b). Again, it is difficult to know if these are true prevalence rates or reflect underreporting issues. Very little epidemiological data exist for children and youth. One study notes disparities in how much mental health care was received by children for whom it was needed (defined as having a functional impairment but no care in the previous 6 months), finding that African American children were much more likely to have unmet mental health needs than Whites (United States Department of Health and Human Services (USDHHS) 1999a). Although caution should be exercised when interpreting mental health statistics, it does appear that European American students show some advantages in this area relative to other racial groups.

Challenges to Maintaining Mental Health

Challenge 1: Family Support

Although European American youth hold a number of privileges relative to other ethnic and racial groups (Hughes and Hertel 1990), they also have several unique challenges that may be detrimental to their mental health. The most notable challenge is reflected in the limited number of familial social support systems for European American youth when compared to their African American, Asian, or Hispanic counterparts (Williams and Fenton 1994). Research has consistently documented the positive effects of having strong social support networks (Hirsch and DuBois 1992; Rhodes et al. 1994). Thus, possible adverse effects may stem from the lack of these networks to buffer economic, social, and other environmental stressors. Particularly, research has found that few familial social support networks for Whites most likely explains the strong SES relationships found with such health factors as adolescent smoking and obesity. In other words, researchers have identified low parental education and income as stronger correlates of poor general health outcomes for Whites than they are for Asians or Hispanics, and have hypothesized that fewer support networks for European American youth may account for this finding (Chen et al. 2006). Additionally, fewer social support networks for European American youth are associated with lower resiliency to such stressors as family poverty and community adversity (Chase-Lansdale et al. 1997; McLeod and Nonnemaker 2000). Using the National Longitudinal Survey of Youth (NLSY) data, McLeod and Nonnemaker (2000) found that White children had significantly more behavioral problems than black children when faced with chronic poverty. The differentially stronger impact of family poverty on European American's has been confirmed in recent studies and suggest the importance of building resilience and protective factors to facilitate positive mental health among youth embedded in disadvantaged neighborhoods (Wickrama et al. 2005).

Challenge 2: Media Exposure

Another challenge unique to European Americans is with respect to the media. Socialization through the media has become an integral process in children's development, as children spend their waking time watching television more than doing any other activity (Bang and Reece 2003). Thus, many children are frequently presented with media messages through which they are constructing meaning. As Denevi (2001) writes, one of the ways in which the notion of "whiteness" is created is through the media. The media consistently conveys messages through attractive, wealthy, and powerful European American figures. Thus, children are socialized into a culture of White superiority (Denevi 2001). The effect of media socialization on European American youth's mental health is particularly salient when it comes to the prevalence of eating disorders, depression, and low self-esteem. Specifically, when asked to explicitly identify which factors most affected their ideal body size, European American females' ideal body image has been found to be more influenced by the media than are African American girls (Parnell et al. 1996). The media—including television programs, music videos, magazines, advertisements, sports photography, and advertisements—exerts its influence on women's body image through the objectification of female bodies. This influence is particularly detrimental to the mental health outcomes of European American females given that the ideal standard for beauty appeals to the dominant White male culture. The unrealistic expectations portrayed through predominately slim European American female figures is thought to significantly influence the high rates of eating disorders, depression, and low self-esteem among European American females. In particular, prevalence of these mental health risks is higher among adolescents than any other age group, with rates of depression across the lifespan approximately twice as high in European Americans as they are for African American or Hispanic groups (see Fredrickson and Roberts 1997). Further, several researchers have found that eating disorders are mainly a White, middle-class phenomenon (Abrams et al. 1993; Akan and Grillo 1995; Molloy and Herzberger 1998; Parker et al. 1995; Rucker and Cash 1992).

Challenge 3: Power and Privilege

Finally, what is commonly understood as privilege and power for European American youth can also reflect disadvantage when it comes to European American's mental health. Thus, White power and privilege can serve as a double-edged sword for many European American youth (Denevi 2001). One pertinent example of this stems from previous research findings documenting White youth's experience of social alienation when embedded in racially diverse communities, as community characteristics may be more salient for European Americans than for other racial groups (Halpern-Felsher et al. 1997; Welch et al. 2001; Williams and Fenton 1994). For example, European American youth may experience feelings of powerlessness, fear, and anxiety when living in communities where they are not the majority race. These negative feelings can in turn have an adverse effect on European American youth's mental health.

European American privilege and superiority is constructed early in children's lives. White children become "socialized into racism" as early as four years of age (Van Ausdale and Feagin 2001). Many White children can accurately identify themselves as White and associate Whiteness with something positive or normal, while identifying characteristics of other racial groups as abnormal (Derman-Sparks and Ramsey 2006). Van Ausdale and Feagin (2001) share a scenario in which four-year-old Renee repeatedly asks her teacher for reassurance that she is still White despite her recent tan. She then goes back to inform the other two White girls that even though she's tan, she is still White. The researchers remark that, two weeks later, they continue to observe her reassuring other students that she is still White.

Renee's case clearly illustrates children's ability to think of themselves as racial beings in addition to placing a value on that categorization. This recognition of race and difference is a part of racial identity development. The development of White racial identity is the process of coming to terms with one's dominant place in society and determining how one wishes to use that status. Individuals progress through a series of stages of identity development leading toward the integration of a healthy sense of one's own race and the place of race in society. However, European American youth, who progress through these stages with internalized feelings of racial superiority and power, can experience detrimental effects including: hindered critical thinking ability; unrealistic perceptions of themselves based on a false sense of superiority; and internal guilt and moral conflict (see Derman-Sparks and Ramsey 2006). This latter effect, that of "White Guilt," has been addressed by researchers interested in European American youth's racial identity development and has consequences for children's mental health. Denevi (2001) reflects on how European American youth, when faced with the full implications of their racial identity, will feel not only guilt, but embarrassment and shame.

Strengths Contributing to Mental Health

Strength 1: Allegiance to the American Dream

An asset that European Americans share is their allegiance to the American dream. The idea that individual effort is responsible for success yields benefits for those who ascribe to it (Hochschild 1996). These include optimism, a sense of self-determination, ambition, trust in oneself and the availability of opportunities, and a work ethic that is likely to be rewarded by the dominant societal structure. The "rags to riches" idea is a uniquely American one, popularized during the time of the Industrial Revolution and the opening of the west to European settlers. These economic opportunities, and their widespread availability, fostered a notion that wealth and material success was attainable for those who sought them. This idea faded during the Great Depression of the 1930s but experienced a resurrection in the affluent period following World War II. There are class and racial distinctions in this belief, with middle-class Whites ascribing more to it than middle-class African Americans (Hochschild 1996). Although a belief in the American dream belies fundamental inequities in society, its power as a fundamental belief is in its guiding optimism and sense of purpose for those who ascribe to it.

Strength 2: Cultural Familiarity

Another strength that Whites hold that contribute to their resilience date back to the days of American colonization. White settlers constructed societies that reflected their beliefs and cultures. These became codified into laws that continue to influence contemporary society. This cultural backdrop is "invisible" to many Whites who see it as normative. This ease and familiarity with the dominant culture is an asset for Whites who more readily access services and resources than those from minority cultures. This familiarity with the dominant culture can lead to White privilege, or set of advantages that individuals who are White or are perceived to be White benefit from because the dominant societal framework extends advantages to them. McIntosh (1989) describes White privilege as, "…an invisible package of unearned assets which I can count on cashing in each day, but about which I was 'meant' to remain oblivious" (p. 10). An example of this privilege is cultural capital. Whites fit into the mainstream or dominant culture by virtue of subscribing to the European culture passed down by their families. Delpit (1995) discusses the cultural capital that White children gain through their families as "codes of power" that replicate the dominant social structures in society. Therefore, European American children fit more readily into mainstream social institutions, such as schools, that share their backgrounds and cultural perspectives. Because of their comfort within these institutions, Whites can leverage resources that enhance their adaptation and well-being.

Whites also can access greater human and social capital because of their dominant place in society. Human capital includes skills and capabilities that an individual obtains (i.e., educational degrees). Because Whites have more access to schooling opportunities, and remain in school longer than some other groups, they are more likely to acquire this form of societal advantage. Social capital, another benefit to individuals who are White, is the relationships between people; trust between individuals is one such example of social capital (Coleman and Hoffer 1987). White middle-class families have more trust or social capital with school personnel than do other minorities (Purcell-Gates 2002). This allows for ease of communication and increased parental involvement that have been proven to increase school achievement, and reduce drop-out rates (Astone and McLanahan 1991; Sui-Chu and Williams 1996).

Strength 3: Socioeconomic Status

Other areas of resilience that stem from White privilege include socioeconomic status and locus of control. A study done by Dornbusch et al. (1991) found that parental education and family structure is more predictive of school achievement for Whites than African Americans. This is important because it indicates that European American children who come from middle class, two-parent households, gain more benefits than African Americans in the same SES and family structure. In addition, family status, level of parental education, and coming from two-parent households were consistently positively correlated to high school grades for White children. Research has also documented that White students hold less of an external locus of control relative to other groups. Whites are less likely to attribute things that happen to chance or to believe that things happen because of the control of powerful others. Instead, they feel more in charge of themselves and their futures. An internal locus of control orientation has been found to be associated with higher mental health outcomes (Malcarne et al. 2005). This finding is consistent with research that indicates that White students have high educational aspirations and that their aspirations stay fairly constant throughout their schooling (Kao and Tienda 1998).

Strength 4: Parenting Style

A form of family structure that is beneficial for European American children is parenting style. Popular conceptualizations of the different variations of parenting styles stem from the work of Diana Baumrind (1971). Baumrind initially conceptualized three different types of parenting: authoritarian, permissive, and authoritative. The authoritarian parent is often directive and often uses punishment as a means of parenting. The permissive parent is one who allows the child to determine their own activities and rarely issues any structure or punishment for behavior.The most widely culturally supported parent style for European American children is the Authoritative parenting style. This parenting style is characterized by relationship closeness, high standards, clear and direct communication, and appropriate levels of autonomy (Darling and Steinberg 1993). This parenting style has been associated with independence, maturity, and academic success (Chao 2001). These findings have not been consistent across ethnic groups and are therefore unique for European American children. Chao (2001) indicates that these outcomes for European American children may be due to the nature of the close relationship that is inherent with authoritative parents. Other researchers suggest that outcomes are due to the child's increased ability to be receptive to parenting, the enabling of effective socialization, and the development of self-regulatory skills that accompany this style of parenting, all of which enhance the child's functioning when not in the home environment (Steinberg 2001).

As children move into adolescence, research suggests that the authoritative parenting style, particularly by a father figure, plays a protective role in the prevention of depression and/or alcohol use (Patock-Peckam and Morgan-Lopez 2007). The extension of the research on children to adolescents also indicates that adolescents receive some of the same benefits as children from authoritative parenting such as better attendance in school, fewer mental health problems, higher self-esteem and less drug use (Steinberg 2001).

Discussion

Promoting Mental Health Among European American Children and Youth

Our perspective on promoting mental health in children and youth uses the framework of ecological-systems theory (Bronfenbrenner 1979; Bronfenbrenner and Ceci 1994). This model posits that children are embedded within multiple, mutually influencing systems with which they interact to affect their development. As children move through time, they become better or less well adapted to the various environmental contexts in which their development unfolds. The developmental capacities of children, the adequacy of naturally occurring environment to optimally support development, and the interaction of these dynamic systems together shape adjustment. Thus, prevention and intervention efforts must attend to these overlapping foci: the child's competencies and coping resources, as well as the adequacy of the environment to promote positive development.

The promotion of children's mental health must include enhancing the natural environments with which children interact so that their development is optimized. One such environment is the school. The World Health Organization (WHO) (2003) defined a healthy school environment as one that encourages active learning and creativity in a climate of warmth, equity, safety, cooperation, and open communication. Healthy schools link to students' home communities, include parents, and permit authentic participation in democratic or decision-making processes by stakeholders. This type of environment promotes well-being by fostering children's fundamental psychological needs for autonomy, competence, and connectedness to others (Deci and Ryan 2002; Baker et al. 2003). All children's mental health is likely to be promoted by improving schooling so that the environment supports children's developmental trajectories.

A key step to promoting children's well-being is universal screening of mental health in schools. Although about 1 in 10 adolescents experiences a social or emotional problem significant enough to impair functioning (United States Department of Health and Human Services (USDHHS) 1999a), only 2% of American high schools screen all their students, and only 7% screen most of their students for mental health issues (Romer and McIntosh 2005). Recent population-based screening in under-resourced, urban elementary schools indicated that 17% of the children in the first through fifth grades had pervasive, severe externalizing behavior problems, coupled with significant learning problems, and poor prosocial competencies. Yet, only a third of these children were being served with specialized educational programs. Although there are ethical and pragmatic concerns with universal screening approaches (see Baker in press), they may be the only way to uncover students' needs in a specific school context.

School-based primary and secondary prevention efforts have been directed toward promoting children's mental health. For example, Adelman and Taylor (2006) provide strategies for mapping, analyzing, and enhancing school resources to address mental health and learning problems, and additional strategies are available online at the Center for Mental Health in Schools website (UCLA School Mental Health Project 2006). Similarly, the Collaborative for Academic, Social and Emotional Learning provides both web-based and print resources. Their resource, *Safe & Sound* (CASEL 2006), describes and reviews the evidence-base for many specific school-based intervention programs. For this review, we could not identify any programs designed specifically for European American children. However, programs that are designed to promote empowerment, equity, and social justice may target issues of power, privilege, and moral decision-making and may help more privileged students gain a perspective on the sociocultural aspects of racism. Because of the social isolation experienced by many European American youth, programs that bolster naturally occurring kinship networks, or provide compensatory ones, may be especially efficacious.

One specific area of intervention in promoting European American children's mental health involves the use of media education. Given the pervasiveness of unrealistic, unattainable, and powerful European American images in society's media, White children are at risk for developing a number of mental health problems. Thus, prevention efforts must be directed at helping children become critical consumers of the media. Media literacy programs are a promising means to this end, as they teach children to be analytical and challenge the messages embedded throughout the material to which they are so frequently exposed. Growing evidence suggests that a number of these mental health risks can be lessened through the use of media literacy education (see Kline et al. 2006; Watson and Vaughn 2006). Teaching children to think critically about the media therefore not only benefits mental health outcomes, but also leaves children better informed of the biases inherent in the messages they receive. Media education programs thus provide the tools European American children need to challenge the all-too accepted norms of the dominant culture and to become active proponents of change with respect to the White power and privilege so pervasively represented in the media.

Future Recommendations and Concluding Comments

The specific needs and assets of European American children have been underrepresented in the mental health literature. Because of their status as the privileged

Table 12.1 Summary table for characteristics of European American children and youth

Demographics	Challenges	Strengths	Recommendations
77% of US population 60% of school-age population 10% live in poverty 76% from two parent homes 92% high school completion rate Fewer problem behaviors and more developmental assets as reported by teachers More likely to have access to mental health services	Limited familial social support systems • Relative to some other groups • Health outcomes differentially moderated by SES for Whites Media socialization to unrealistic and racist images • Socialized into a culture of White superiority • Unrealistic portrayal of body image for girls White privilege can lead to feelings of racial superiority, guilt or shame • Socialized into culture of racism early • Racist beliefs associated with lower critical thinking skills	Opportunity and optimism embedded in cultural aspirations • Belief in the American dream provides inspiration Historical, cultural, social capital; White privilege • Share the dominant "covert" power structure and agenda • Share expectations/beliefs with societal institutions Internal locus of control • Belief in own ability • Belief in the power to affect change in one's world Parenting consistent with school attainment and cultural norms • Authoritative pattern promotes school achievement • Authoritative pattern is consistent with school and other cultural norms	Specific attention to needs and resources Universal (school-based) screening Primary prevention programs, especially relating to social justice and media education Research on White identity development Research on interventions to promote social justice

majority, their needs have been primarily considered either as a starting point for epidemiological studies or as a comparison point for other racial and ethnic groups. Although Whites were the exclusive subject of research in the past, contemporary perspectives recognize the importance of acknowledging the interaction of race, racial identity, and mental health outcomes in research (Diener et al. 2003). Further, basic research is needed that includes racial identity as a mediating or moderating influence on the well-being of White children. Applied research on interventions designed to help White students acknowledge their privileged status and move toward greater conceptualizations of social justice are needed as well. To date, most of this research has been conducted with minority students. Practitioners and researchers alike would benefit from gaining a better understanding of the strengths and challenges of European American youth that intersect with intervention efforts to promote mental health. Ultimately, research aimed at garnering a more comprehensive picture of White children's experiences will allow for services that better meet the mental health needs of this particular population (Table 12.1).

References

Abrams, K. K, Allen, L. R., & Gray, J. J. (1993). Disordered eating attitudes and behaviors, psychological adjustment, and ethnic identity: A comparison of Black and White female college students. *International Journal of Eating Disorders, 14,* 49–57.

Adelman, H. S., & Taylor, L. (2006). Student learning supports: New directions for addressing barriers to learning. Thousand Oaks: Corwin.

Akan, G. E., & Grilo, C. M. (1995). Sociocultural influences on eating attitudes and behavior, body image and psychological functioning: A comparison of African American, Asian American, and Caucasian college women. *International Journal of Eating Disorders, 18,* 181–187.

Astone, N. M., & McLanahan, S. S. (1991). Family structure, parental practices and high school completion. *American Sociological Review, 56,* 309–320.

Baker, J. A. (in press). Assessing school risk and protective factors. In B. Doll & J. Cummings (Eds.), *Population-based approaches to preventing mental health problems in children.* Bethesda: National Association of School Psychologists.

Baker, J. A., Dilly, L., Aupperlee, J., & Patil, S. (2003). The developmental context of school satisfaction: Schools as psychologically healthy environments. *School Psychology Quarterly, 18,* 206–222.

Baker, J. A., Kamphaus, R. W., Horne, A. M., & Winsor, A. (2006). Evidence for population-based perspectives on children's behavioral adjustment and needs for service delivery in schools. *School Psychology Review, 35,* 31–46.

Bang, H. K., & Reece, B. B. (2003). Minorities in children's television commercials: New, improved, and stereotyped. *The Journal of Consumer Affairs, 37*(1), 42–67.

Baumrind, D. (1971). Current patterns of parental authority. *Developmental Psychology Monographs, 4,* 1–103.

Bronfenbrenner, U. (1979). The ecology of human development: Experiments by nature and design. Cambridge: Harvard University Press.

Bronfenbrenner, U., & Ceci, S. J. (1994). Nature-nurture reconceptualized: A bio-ecological model. *Psychological Review, 101,* 568–586.

CASEL. (2006). Introduction to SEL: SEL competencies. http://www.casel.org/about_sel/SELskills.php. Accessed 6 March 2006.

Chao, R. K. (2001). Extending research on the consequences of parenting style for Chinese Americans and European Americans. *Child Development, 72,* 1832–1843.

Chase-Lansdale, L., Gordon, R., Brooks-Gunn, J., & Klebanov, P. (1997). Neighborhood and family influences on the intellectual and behavioral competence of preschool and early school-age children. In J. Brooks-Gunn, G. Duncan, & J. L. Aber (Eds.), *Neighborhood poverty: Context and consequences for children* (pp. 79–118). New York: Sage.

Chen, E., Martin, A. D., & Matthews, K. A. (2006). Understanding health disparities: The role of race and socioeconomic status in children's health. *American Journal of Public Health, 96*(4), 702–708.

Child Trends Data Bank. (2007). *Low and very low birth weight infants.* http://www.childtrendsbank.org/indicators/57LowBirthweight.cfm. Accessed 13 May 2007.

Coleman, J., & Hoffer, T. (1987). *Human capital and social capital. Public and private high schools: Schools, families, and communities* (pp. 221–233). New york: Basic Books.
Darling, N., & Steinberg, L. (1993). Parenting style as context: An integrative model. *Psychological Bulletin, 113*, 487–496.
Deci, E. L., & Ryan, R. M. (2002). *Handbook of self-determination research.* Rochester: University of Rochester Press.
Delpit, L. (1995). The silenced dialogue: Power and pedagogy in educating other people's children. In L. Delpit (Ed.), *Other people's children: Cultural conflict in the classroom* (pp. 21–47). New York: New Press.
Denevi, E. (2001). Whiteness: Helping White students and educators understand their role in a multicultural society. *Independent School, 61*(1), 101–108.
Derman-Sparks, L., & Ramsey, P. G. (2006). *How children construct White identities: Fostering children's identities. What if all the kids are White? Anti-bias multicultural education with young children and families* (pp. 39–65). New York: Teachers College Press.
Diener, E., Oishi, S., & Lucas, R. (2003). Personality, culture and subjective well-being: Emotional and cognitive evaluations of life. *Annual Review of Psychology, 54,* 403–425.
Dornbusch, S. M., Ritter, P. L., & Steinberg, L. (1991). Community influences on the relation of family statuses to adolescent school performance: Differences between African Americans and non-Hispanic Whites. *American Journal of Education, 99*(4), 543–567.
Federal Interagency Forum on Child and Family Statistics. (2006). *America's children in brief: Key national indicators of well-being 2006.* http:www.childstats.gov/pubs.asp. Accessed 26 March 2007.
Fredrickson, B., & Roberts, T. (1997). Objectification theory: Toward understanding women's lived experiences and mental health risks. *Psychology of Women Quarterly, 21,* 173–206.
Halpern-Felsher, B. L., Connell, J. P., Spencer, M. B., Aber, J. L., Duncan, G. J., Clifford, E., et al. (1997). Neighborhood and family factors predicting educational risk and attainment in African American and White children and adolescents. In J. Brooks-Gunn, G. J., Duncan, & J. L. Aber (Eds.), *Neighborhood poverty: Vol. 1. Context and consequences for children* (pp. 146–173). New York: Sage.
Hirsch, B.,& DuBois, D. (1992). The relation of peer social support and psychological symptomatology during the transition to junior high school: A two-year longitudinal analysis. *American Journal of Community Psychology, 20,* 333–347.
Hochschild, J. L. (1996). Facing up to the American dream: Race, class, and the soul of the nation. Princeton: Princeton University Press.
Hughes, M., & Hertel, B. R. (1990). The significance of color remains: A study of life chances, mate selection, and ethnic consciousness among Black Americans. *Social Forces, 68*(4), 1105–1120.
Kamphaus, R. W., Huberty, C. J., Distefano, C., & Petosky, M. J. (1997). A typology of teacher-rated child behavior for a national U.S. sample. *Journal of Abnormal Psychology, 25,* 453–463.
Kao, G., & Tienda, M. (1998). Educational aspirations of minority youth. *American Journal of Education, 106,* 349–384.
Kline, S., Stewart, K., & Murphy, D. (2006). Media literacy in the risk society: Toward a risk reduction society. *Canadian Journal of Education, 29*(1), 131–153.
Malcarne, V. L., Drahota, A., & Hamilton, N. A. (2005). Children's health-related locus of control beliefs: Ethnicity, gender, and family income. *Children's Health Care, 34*(1), 47–59.
McIntosh, P. (1989). White privilege: Unpacking the invisible knapsack. *Peace and Freedom, 1989*(July/August), 10–12.
McLeod, J. D., & Nonnemaker, J. M. (2000). Poverty and child emotional and behavioral problems: Racial/ethnic differences in processes and effects. *Journal of Health and Social Behavior, 41,* 137–161.
Molloy, B. L., & Herzberger, S. D. (1998). Body image and self esteem: a comparison of African American and Caucasian women. *Sex Roles, 38,* 631–643.

National Institute of Health (NIH). (2001). NIH policy on reporting race and ethnicity data: Subjects in clinical research. http://grants.nih.gov/grants/guide/notice-files/NOT-OD-01-053.html. Accessed 15 April 2007.

Parnell, K., Sargent, R., Thompson, S. H., Duhe, S. F., Valois, R. F., & Kemper, R. C. (1996). Black and White adolescent females' perceptions of ideal body size. *Journal of School Health, 66*(3), 112–118.

Parker, S., Nichter, M., Nicther, M., & Vuckovic, N. (1995). Body image and weight concerns among African American and Caucasian adolescent females: Differences that make a difference. *Human Organization Sum, 54,* 103–114.

Patock-Peckam, J. A., & Morgan-Lopez A. A. (2007). College drinking behaviors: Mediational links between parenting styles, parental bonds, depression, and alcohol problems. *Psychology of Addictive Behaviors, 21,* 297–306.

Purcell-Gates, V. (2002). "¼ As soon as she opened her mouth!" In L. Delpit & J. K. Dowdy (Eds.), *The skin that we speak: An anthology of essays on language, culture and power*. Vancouver: CPLS Publication.

Rhodes, J., Contreras, J., & Mangelsdorf, S. (1994). Natural mentors' relationships among Latina adolescent mothers: Psychological adjustment, moderating processes, and the role of early parental acceptance. *American Journal of Community Psychology, 22,* 211–227.

Romer, D., & McIntosh, M. (2005). The roles and perspectives of school mental health professionals in promoting adolescent mental health. In D. L. Evans, E. B. Foa, R. E. Gur, H. Hendin, C. P. O'Brien, M. E. P. Seligman, & B. T. Walsh (Eds.), *Treating and preventing adolescent mental health disorders: What we know and what we don't know, A research agenda for improving the mental health of our youth* (pp. 597–616). Oxford: Oxford University Press.

Rucker, C. E., & Cash, T. F. (1992). Body images, body size perceptions and eating behaviors among African American and White college women. *International Journal of Eating Disorders, 12,* 291–299.

Statistical Abstracts of the United States. 2004. U.S. Census Bureau. http://www.census.gov/compendia/statab/population/estimatesandprojectionsbyagesexraceethnicity/. Accessed 30 June 2007.

Statistical Abstracts of the United States. 2005. U.S. Census Bureau. http://www.census.gov/compendia/statab/population/estimatesandprojectionsbyagesexraceethnicity/. Accessed 30 June 2007.

Steinberg, L. (2001). We know some things: Parent-adolescent relationship in retrospect and prospect. *Journal of Research on Adolescence, 11,* 1–19.

Sui-Chu, E. H., & Willms, J. D. (1996). Effects of parental involvement on eight grade achievement. *Sociology of Education, 69*(2), 126–141.

UCLA School Mental Health Project. (2006). Center for Mental Health in the Schools. http://smhp.psych.ucla.edu/. Accessed 6 September 2006.

United States Department of Health and Human Services (USDHHS). (1999a). *Mental health: A report of the surgeon general.* Rockville: U.S. Department of Health and Human Services, Substance Abuse and Mental Health Services Administration, Center for Mental Health Services, National Institute of Health, National Institute of Mental Health. http://www.surgeongeneral.gov/library/mentalhealth/summary.html. Accessed 15 Sept 2003.

United States Department of Health and Human Services (USDHHS). (1999b). *Mental health: A report of the surgeon general: Culture, race, ethnicity supplement.* Rockville: U.S. Department of Health and Human Services, Substance Abuse and Mental Health Services Administration, Center for Mental Health Services, National Institutes of Health, National Institute of Mental Health. http://mentalhealth.samhsa.gov/cre/default.asp. Accessed 15 Sept 2003.

US Census Bureau. (2002). *US Census 2000 demographic profiles*. http://censtats.census.gov/pub/Profiles.shtml. Accessed 16 April 2007.

Van Ausdale, D., & Feagin, J. (2001) *The first R: How children learn race and racism.* Lanham: Rowman & Littlefield.

Watson, R., & Vaughn, L. M. (2006). Limiting the effects of the media on body image: Does the length of a media literacy intervention make a difference? *Eating Disorders, 14*(5), 385–400.

Webb, L. D., Metha, A., & Jornda, K. F. (2003). *Foundations of American education*. Upper Saddle River: Merrill/Prentice Hall.

Welch, S., Sigelman, L., Bledsoe, T., & Combs, M. (2001). *Race and place: Race relations in an American city*. New York: Cambridge University Press.

Wickrama, K. A. S., Noh, S., & Bryant, C. M. (2005). Racial differences in adolescent distress: Differential effects of the family and community for Blacks and Whites. *Journal of Community Psychology, 33*(3), 261–282.

Williams, D. R., & Fenton, B. (1994). The mental health of African Americans: Findings, questions, and directions. In I. L. Livingston (Ed.), *Handbook of Black American health: The mosaic of conditions, issues, policies, and prospects* (pp. 253–268). Westport: Greenwood.

World Health Organization (WHO). (2006). Resources and tools for advocacy. http://www.who.int/school_youth_health/resources/en/. Accessed 6 Sept 2006.

Chapter 13
Psychology of European American Adults: Challenges, Advantages, and the Push for Further Growth

Christina A. Downey and Wendy D'Andrea

Introduction

Chapter Focus

This chapter presents information on mental health issues in European American (White) adults, focusing on poverty, traumatic experience, and alcohol abuse as major challenges to the maintenance of mental health in this group; access to health care, willingness to seek assistance for mental health issues, and selected cognitive factors as strengths contributing to resilience in this group; and how some of the advantages enjoyed by Whites in the United States can be furthered to strengthen the overall mental health of this group.

Demographic Characteristics of White American Adults

According to the US Census Bureau, non-Hispanic Whites comprise approximately 66.9% of the total population of the United States. Of these, approximately 126.1 million people (41.9%) fall into the adult age cohort (18–64 years of age) (United States Census Bureau 2007a). In terms of race/age groupings, this cohort currently represents the largest segment of American society by a wide margin. Regarding the educational status of individuals in this group, 41.6% of non-Hispanic Whites have attained high-school level education, another 26.5% have achieved up to the Bachelor's degree, and 31.8% have achieved a Bachelor's degree or higher (United States Census Bureau 2007b). Median income in this group is approximately $ 52,400 per year, less than the median income of Asian Americans ($ 64,200 per year) but considerably greater than annual incomes of Black ($ 32,000 per year) or

C. A. Downey (✉)
Department of Psychology, Indiana University Kokomo, 2300 S. Washington St., Kokomo, IN 46904, USA
e-mail: downeyca@iuk.edu

E. C. Chang, C. A. Downey (eds.), *Handbook of Race and Development in Mental Health*, DOI 10.1007/978-1-4614-0424-8_13, © Springer Science+Business Media, LLC 2012

Latino ($ 37,800 per year) households (DeNavas-Walt et al. 2007). Still, the real impact on society of the variability in individual earnings within this group is not always apparent from popularized statistics. For example, the rate of poverty among non-Hispanic Whites was the lowest of the racial groups assessed in the DeNavas-Walt et al. (2007) study, at 8.2% (compared to an astonishing 24.3% for Blacks, 20.6% for Hispanics, and 10.3% for Asians). However, due to the sheer size of this demographic group, non-Hispanic Whites accounted for the greatest proportion of individuals and families in poverty, at 43.9% (approximately 16.9 million people, compared to 9 million Blacks, and 9.2 million people of Hispanic origin).

We do not present these numbers to diminish the relevance of poverty as a major challenge to the mental health of individuals of African American, Latino American, or any other racial minority group membership. Clearly higher rates of overall poverty in minority groups is a significant challenge to the psychological functioning of individuals in these groups, and has been identified as such in much research (some of which is presented elsewhere in the present volume). Likewise, we recognize that identifying poverty as an important "independent" variable in the mental health of Whites is problematic, as socioeconomic status is a multifaceted variable that involves (among other things) education, employment, and possibly even family structure (Bratter and Eschbach 2005). However, our task in the present chapter is to outline significant challenges to the mental health of European Americans as a racial group. We argue that the experience of poverty is one of those major challenges, which has vivid negative effects on the lives of millions of European Americans; the fact that a relatively smaller proportion of Whites experience poverty does not mean that this group is immune from these effects.

Challenges to Maintaining Mental Health

Poverty

Rates of significant psychological dysfunction tend to appear at higher rates among people of impoverished socioeconomic status than among the general population (Adler et al. 2000; Boothroid et al. 2006). For example, research has shown that people living at the lowest end of the income continuum are significantly more likely (1.24 times in one study) to experience a first depressive episode than people at the top of the income scale. In addition, the poor were 2.04 times more likely than the wealthy to remain depressed than the rich were (Lorant et al. 2003). Findings such as these have been consistent in the literature over several decades (e.g., Dohrenwend and Dohrenwend 1974; Haring et al. 1984). In examining how poverty specifically impacts the mental health of European Americans, we will review a subset of studies which have identified Whites (or non-Hispanic Whites, in some cases) as a group of interest. While these studies have, by and large, examined White adults as a "baseline" group with which to contrast the experiences of minority individuals, their findings still provide valuable information about the mental health experiences of Whites as a racial group in a changing society.

For example, a study conducted in the late 1980s of a nationally representative survey sample (over sampled for minorities) by Amato and Zuo (1992) found that on the whole, Americans of lower SES showed significantly higher levels of depressive symptoms, lower levels of reported happiness, and lower levels of perceived health than Americans of higher SES. When urban vs. rural residence was investigated as a possible factor in this phenomenon, it was found that the rural poor reported significantly lower levels of psychological health than the urban poor. In addition, and significant to the mental health status of White American adults, Whites who lived in urban areas were found to report higher levels of happiness and lower levels of depression than Whites who lived in rural areas (while the inverse was found to be true for Black Americans in this study). The authors ventured the explanation that Whites, who tend to see themselves as a higher-status group than Black Americans, may feel they have "relatively more to lose by being poor, unemployed, and on public assistance … [and] may be especially likely to see their poverty as deviant or shameful and to experience condemnation from others" (p. 238). Other studies which have compared rates of mental disorders among poor Whites and other ethnic groups have revealed similarly interesting findings. For example, Bassuk et al. (1998) found overall rates of mental disorders to be significantly higher among poor White single mothers than among poor Puerto Rican single mothers, though the overall rates of disorders in both groups was considerably higher than in the general population. Bratter and Eschbach (2005) found in a large-scale study of ten different racial groups in the United States (the National Health Interview Study, with $N > 160{,}000$) that non-Hispanic Whites experienced less psychological distress than Native Americans, Puerto Ricans, and people of mixed race background, and equal levels of distress to African Americans; once SES was added to these regression models, however, non-Hispanic Whites were found to report greater distress at the lowest end of the socioeconomic spectrum than African Americans did. Other research has resulted in similar conclusions (e.g., Ulbrich et al. 1989).

Findings such as these have not yet silenced the important debate about whether poverty is equally or differentially threatening to the maintenance of mental health of both Whites and minority groups. More specifically, scholars are interested in determining whether the effects of poverty are equivalent across racial groups in US society (e.g., an additive model of race and socioeconomic status in predicting psychological distress), or whether poverty is more threatening to minority mental health than to that of White Americans (e.g., a multiplicative model). One problematic issue involves the assertion that the meaning of socioeconomic status itself differs between Whites and minority groups, as minorities are (for various reasons) unable to accumulate comparable levels of overall wealth and status to Whites when absolute income is equal (Williams et al. 1997). Related to this and to other reasons, some studies assert that poverty is actually more damaging to the mental health of minorities than it is to Whites; for example, Kessler and Neighbors (1986) found in a seminal study that the multiplicative model better represented how poverty had a more deleterious impact on minority groups than on Whites (possibly due to additional factors such as racism, discrimination, and other forms of race-related stress; Williams et al. 1997). Similarly, in the Bratter and Eschbach (2005) study, distress levels in non-Hispanic Whites were less negatively impacted by variables such as income, education, and employment than those of Native Americans, Puerto Ricans, and mixed-race individuals. However, other research has contended that the health of individuals of various racial groups are equally effected by poverty (Cockerham 1990; Ostrove et al. 1999), and still other large-scale studies have added to the complexity of the debate by uncovering different findings in different geographic regions of the United States. For example, Schwabe and Kodras (2000) found that the additive and multiplicative models fit data collected from several urban metropolitan areas differently, in the large Epidemiological Catchment Area study. Specifically, poor Whites in Durham, North Carolina, and in Los Angeles were equally likely as poor Blacks to report symptoms of psychological distress, while poor Whites in Baltimore, Maryland were actually more likely than poor Blacks to report being distressed in this study. At the present time, therefore, the data appear to be inconclusive in regard to whether poverty is any more or less damaging to White Americans than to any other racial group. Taken together, it seems most appropriate to identify the experience of poverty as one which, while not at all being exclusive to Whites, certainly is a robust predictor of reduced mental health in this racial group.

Trauma

Large scale epidemiological studies have reported near-identical rates of trauma or slightly lower rates of trauma when comparing Whites to other groups (Breslau et al. 1998, 1995). Studies that find that Whites have equal levels of trauma exposure to minority groups often do not take into account the severity or duration of violence exposure, where Whites often experience less severe or less chronic interpersonal violence. However, a metaanalysis reveals that despite decreased risk for trauma exposure, Whites are at equal or greater risk for developing posttraumatic stress disorder (PTSD; weighted average $r=0.05$; Brewin et al. 2000). This paradox—that Whites experience equal or less trauma but are more likely to experience PTSD—has yet to be explored. Factors related to the development of PTSD in general, and possible explanations for increased risk amongst Whites in particular, are discussed herein.

Across ethnic groups, risk factors for developing PTSD include enhanced distress at the time of the trauma (called *peritraumatic distress*), greater disorientation and cognitive distortion at the time of the trauma (called *peritraumatic dissociation*), weaker perceived social support and greater perceived life threat (Ozer et al. 2003; Brewin et al. 2000), as well as greater trauma severity and life stress (Brewin et al. 2000). It is unclear why Whites may be at increased risk for experiencing PTSD in the aftermath of traumatic events. Perhaps, then, Whites experience other risk factors for PTSD to a greater degree.

One possible explanation for the heightened exposure-to-PTSD ratio in Whites may be the role that social support plays in buffering one from the effects of PTSD. Social support is known to mitigate the likelihood that one will develop PTSD in the aftermath of trauma (Ozer et al. 2003). Several studies have documented differences in the degree and quality of social support received by members of ethnic groups, particularly amongst men. Snowden (2001) found that White men reported being less embedded in social networks and communities than African American men, while Heckman et al. (2000) found that White men living with HIV/AIDS reported less social support from their families than African American men. Similarly, Lincoln et al. (2003) found that social support was a significant buffer against traumatic stress in African Americans, but did not buffer the effects of traumatic stress in Whites. One possible explanation of these data are that the emphasis on social support in minority communities has mitigated the effects of traumatic stress, while Whites may not have as elaborate or developed support networks. An extension of this interpretation may be that Whites may be less likely to disclose traumatic events to people who might provide support for them. Feiring et al. (2001) found that greater abuse severity lead to higher shame amongst Whites but not other groups. Increased shame following traumatic events may prevent disclosure of trauma, therefore blocking access to important social support. Schnurr et al. (2004) note that posttrauma factors, such as social support, are significant predictors of ongoing PTSD symptoms. Hesse and Main (2006) note that in the face of trauma, humans and other primates run toward home, rather than away from danger. Thus, a safe and secure home base is necessary for psychological recovery from distress. If Whites have less social resources for coping with traumatic stress, then it follows that their risk for PTSD would be heightened.

Other studies have focused on the role that one's response during or immediately after a traumatic event plays in the development of subsequent PTSD. Two of these responses, peritraumatic distress and peritraumatic dissociation, are significant predictors of PTSD symptom development. Peritraumatic distress (Brunet et al. 2001) refers to severe emotional reactions to traumatic events that include fear, helplessness, horror, guilt, shame, and physiological reactions including rapid heart beat, perspiration, and loss of bladder control. Peritraumatic dissociation (Marmar et al. 1994) refers to cognitive distortions that may occur during trauma, such as a sense of time speeding up or slowing down, a sense of disconnection from one's body, significant confusion, and amnesia for details of the event. Some studies have indicated that Whites are more likely to experience greater peritraumatic distress and dissociation in the aftermath of trauma. Torres and Han (2000) found that amongst abused women, White women reported greater distress during violence than Hispanic women. Fullerton et al. (2000) found that White survivors of motor vehicle accidents were more likely than other groups to experience dissociation at the time of traumatic events. However, other studies have found that Whites have similar peritraumatic dissociation and distress compared to other groups (e.g., Zatzick et al. 1994).

Taken together, these findings indicate that significantly more research needs to be conducted on how ethnicity impacts the development of PTSD. In particular, it remains unclear how the peritraumatic responses of White trauma survivors impact their later symptom development. Furthermore, it remains unclear what coping mechanisms, including social support, are employed by Whites in the aftermath of trauma that may be recruited to protect this group from the development of PTSD. It is of note, however, that while ethnicity may be a significant filter for traumatic experiences, other factors, such as peritraumatic reactions, may be as important or more important than demographics in determining who develops ongoing symptoms of posttraumatic stress.

Alcohol Abuse

Little contention exists as to the potential damage that the abuse of alcohol can cause to individual physical, psychological, and social functioning (see Tivis et al. 2006, for an overview of a special issue of the *Journal of General Psychology* regarding alcohol's various negative effects). Evidence exists to support the assertion that alcohol abuse appears to be a more common problem among US-born non-Latino Whites than among individuals of other racial groups (with the exception of Native American populations), both in epidemiological studies of nationally representative community samples (Alegria et al. 2006; Harford et al. 2006; Hasin et al. 2007; Huang et al. 2006; Shrout et al. 1992; Zhang and Snowden 1999) and in studies of clinical populations (e.g., Compton et al. 2000; Tercyak et al. 2007). Interestingly, while increasing levels of education are generally thought to buffer against the development of various emotional or behavioral disorders, this may not be the case regarding alcohol abuse. That is, some studies have found that alcohol abuse occurs at higher rates among more educated Whites, while this relationship may not exist for certain racial minority groups (Paschall et al. 2000). Other studies point to possible relationships with income, as higher rates of drinking occur among higher SES groups than low-SES groups (Broman 2007), indicating that the economic advantage enjoyed by Whites in American society may carry with it some threats to well-being. While not all studies "sound the alarm" for Whites being particularly vulnerable to alcohol abuse (e.g., Jackson et al. 2006; Miller et al. 2007), the empirical support for this idea remains strong enough that some widely used abnormal psychology textbooks continue to espouse it (e.g., Hansell and Damour 2005; Sue et al. 2006).

Why might it be the case that European Americans are more likely to engage in problematic drinking behaviors than individuals of African American or Asian American racial background (for example)? The question is a complex one; biological explanations have been offered, for example, which identify Whites as being less likely to be "poor metabolizers" of one compound found in alcohol, leading to fewer undesired effects associated with drinking (Ruiz 2004). Along with biology, one might also speculate that general access to alcohol might also affect consumption; that is, limited economic resources may limit the degree to which members of certain minority groups can afford to use alcohol, compared to Whites. However, these alone cannot be satisfactory explanations when considering general trends in alcohol abuse. Native Americans, for example, appear to lack optimal physiological capacity to metabolize alcohol (Ruiz 2004), and to have the lowest per capita income of racial groups commonly studied (DeNavas-Walt et al. 2007), but members of this group have reported rates of alcohol abuse and dependence that exceed those of Whites (Alegria et al. 2006). In addition, liquor stores and bars are geographically distributed with lower density in areas dominated by non-Hispanic White residents, and at greatest density in areas where greater numbers of racial minorities live (Romley et al. 2007), the reverse of what one would expect if ease of acquisition of alcohol were a major determining factor in consumption. Therefore, other kinds of social and psychological factors must be at play in the relationship between White racial group membership and alcohol abuse.

One intriguing line of research involves investigations of social-cognitive judgments of the appropriateness of specific alcohol-related behaviors, and how those judgments may vary by race. For example, in a study of 1,200 college students on a racial minority-dominated campus, Rice (2006) found that non-Hispanic White students reported consuming an average number of alcoholic drinks at the last drinking session that was more than twice that of Black students in the sample (3.6 vs. 1.6, respectively), a highly statistically significant result. When asked to estimate the average number of drinks consumed by other students in a typical sitting, students of different racial groups did not differ in their average estimates (approximately 5 drinks at a sitting); however, the degree of correlation between each individual student's estimation of his or her own drinking, and his or her estimation of the drinking of others, did vary according to racial group. Specifically, the strongest correlation between own and others' drinking was highest among White students of all the racial groups studied, indicating that White students may have had a different socialization experience in regard to alcohol use than students of other racial groups had (Rice 2006) and therefore make different judgments of appropriate drinking. Other research has shown that increases in the drinking behaviors of both White and minority students, such as African Americans, are associated with more experiences of racial discrimination. However, White students reported far fewer experiences of racial discrimination in this study, while remaining heavier drinkers than Black students in this study (Broman 2007). This lends support to the idea that the motivations to drink among White and Black students may differ considerably from one another.

Strengths Contributing to Mental Health

Increased Access to Mental Health Services

Much evidence exists to suggest that European Americans are more likely than individuals of other racial groups to seek professional assistance for mental health problems (Alegria et al. 2002; Cabassa et al. 2006; Fiscella et al. 2002; Kimerling and Baumrind 2005; Padgett et al. 1994; Razzano et al. 2006; Wells et al. 2001). Lack of access to needed services can result in significantly compromised health, and though generally large numbers of individuals who need services for their mental health problems do not obtain appropriate care (Kimerling and Baumrind 2005), the mental health of White patients appears to be less vulnerable to threat via lack of care than other racial groups (Bloche 2004). Such health disparities may actually be more pronounced in the United States than in other wealthy nations, such as Canada (Lasser et al. 2006). Restricted access can take the form of lacking health insurance which would pay for such services (Alegria et al. 2002; Callahan and Cooper 2004, 2005; Kimerling and Baumrind 2005), which has been widely identified as a significant barrier to the maintenance of mental health for non-White US populations. By extrapolation, then, it seems appropriate to identify generally greater access to acute and long-term mental health services as a factor which contributes to the maintenance of mental health in European American adults (United States Department of Health and Human Services (USDHHS) 2001).

The reasons for this may include the direct results of economic poverty. As stated above, lower proportions of non-Hispanic Whites in the United States have incomes below the poverty level, which translates into larger proportions of this group having adequate insurance coverage which can cover mental health costs (Callahan et al. 2006; DeNavas-Walt et al. 2007). Adequate insurance coverage generally allows access to preventive and maintenance services, while the uninsured often utilize emergency services as "primary care." Consistent with this assertion, individuals identifying as White have been found in some studies to be less likely than Black, Latino, and Asian populations to use emergency mental health services (e.g., psychiatric emergency rooms in medical hospitals) (Chow et al. 2003; Snowden et al. 2006) or to require inpatient hospitalization (Snowden and Cheung 1990; Snowden et al. 2006), probably indicating that European Americans with mental and emotional disorders are more likely to seek assistance for those problems before they progress to the point of needing such intervention. This may be due in part to increased total use of psychiatric medication among Whites, compared to racial minorities (Han and Liu 2005; Miranda and Cooper 2004). In short, lower numbers of individuals forgoing, delaying, or receiving suboptimal mental health care (by choice or necessity) seems to translate into greater overall mental health in European Americans.

Beyond the basic question of overall access to mental health services, data are accumulating which point to the relative advantage that White populations enjoy in access to high-quality, preventive mental health services, even when strict economic factors are taken into account. For example, research has uncovered a greater tendency for low-income White patients (relative to low-income minority patients) to receive (Herbeck et al. 2004; Melfi et al. 1999) and to utilize (Wang et al. 2006) prescriptions for the newest psychopharmacologic therapies with the fewest side effects, which may contribute to greater medication adherence and effectiveness in Whites (and therefore better outcomes) (Herbeck et al. 2004; Mark et al. 2003). Other studies have examined the intersections of race and poverty in the prediction of mental health service usage. For example, in a longitudinal study comparing access to mental health care in economically destitute homeless White and Hispanic patients with severe mental illness, Whites were found to experience greater increases in systemic allocation of mental health resources than Hispanics were (Ortega and Rosenheck 2002). In another study of race differences in service usage within similar economic circumstances, Chow et al. (2003) studied a large sample of residents of high and low-poverty neighborhoods of New York City who had sought any state-supported mental health service during the time of data collection. Their results indicated that Whites living in low-poverty areas were less likely than members of racial minority groups from the same low-poverty neighborhoods to have used inpatient psychiatric services. However, Whites were actually more likely than non-Whites to have used inpatient psychiatric services if they lived in high-poverty areas.

Further, it may be that Whites receiving inpatient care, such as that just described, may be receiving better care than individuals of minority groups who seek inpatient care; that is, the quality of care provided to individuals of different racial groups may differ, even when the level of care provided is the same. For example, Crawford et al. (1998) examined service usage patterns in Massachusetts before and after implementation of large-scale managed-care programs (e.g., programs implemented statewide) to see whether increased financial access to quality mental health care resulted in provision of better care across racial groups. Results indicated that though racial minority groups exhibited a larger shift toward admission to private (as opposed to state-run) psychiatric facilities after program implementation than Whites did, European American patients still were more likely to use private programs both before and after the change in access. As public programs are "generally viewed in the literature to be inferior to privately operated inpatient settings" (p. 102), it appears that Whites remained more likely to receive higher quality care even financial barriers were reduced. Findings such as these have been echoed in other studies of community mental health care for serious mental illness (Kuno and Rothbard 2005), and in similar studies of treatment for substance abuse (Daley 2005), though not all studies have resulted in conclusions consistent with the idea of gross racial disparities (Harman et al. 2004).

Willingness to Utilize the Most Widely Available Mental Health Services When Problems Develop

Beyond economic considerations in access to quality services, differences remain in the frequencies with which members of different racial groups choose to seek treatment, even when able to do so. At this point in time, American mental health care is still largely driven by assumptions about mental health which are most closely associated with European American Western concepts and approaches (Sue et al. 2006). This has been targeted for broad criticism by researchers and providers of mental health services for members of racial minority groups, who (rightly) contend that assumptions about mental health which drive these services may be inappropriate for assisting these clients, for multiple reasons (Cuellar and Panigua 2000). Therefore, it appears that another advantage that Whites have in maintaining their mental health is a system of mental health services which is more closely aligned with their needs, goals, and worldviews than with those of members of minority groups (e.g., with a White racial identity; Burkhard et al. 2003). This "better fit," while not necessarily a conscious factor of advantage in the minds of individual European Americans who seek help from the prevailing mental health system, may have the effect of increasing their general willingness to actively seek services for problems (Ayalon and Young 2005; Cachelin and Striegel-Moore 2007), and to remain engaged with those services over time (Burkhard et al. 2003; though this may vary according to the type of treatment offered; Brown et al. 1999). As research has been mixed in regard to whether general attitudes about mental health treatment vary by race (Gonzales et al. 2005; Schnittker et al. 2000), one might surmise that other attitudinal or experiential factors must be contributing to the final decision whether to seek therapy, or not.

For example, the type of treatment sought may differ among racial groups for various reasons. Screening for mental illness through physicians has been identified as a large-scale intervention for psychopathology, and Whites appear to be more open to undergoing such screenings than minorities are (Rollman et al. 2002). Whites may also be more likely to self-refer to so-called "mainstream" programs (as opposed to "ethnic-specific programs") than are members of minority groups (who more often present for mainstream treatment through referrals from friends, family members, or other service personnel) (Akutsu et al. 1996). This may be due to at least two factors: one, the much greater availability of mainstream programs over ethnic-specific programs to the public, and two, the likelihood of getting services "earlier" in the progression of disorder (before symptoms and dysfunction become obvious enough to others to result in external urging to seek help). In addition, Whites may be advantaged in using mainstream programs, due in part to Whites anticipating fewer experiences of discomfort regarding issues of race during interactions with representatives of the system. For example, White clients may be less likely to evoke feelings of uncertainty in predominantly White therapists, around whether to discuss race as a therapeutic issue (Cardemil and Battle 2003); research has indicated that White therapists may be generally unlikely to discuss race with clients, even in cross-racial therapeutic dyads (Knox et al. 2003). While White consumers of mental health services have been found to consider cultural competency in mental health treatment to be highly important, and (in the case of some specific competencies) equally important as racial minorities do (Fraga et al. 2004), this may be skewed by participant perceptions of "cultural competency" as only relating to the experiences of minorities, and not to themselves as beings with racialized identities. These findings, taken together, may indicate that "Whiteness" is relatively unlikely to become an initial hindrance to the therapy process, as it may be perceived as a shared experience between White clients and their (usually) White therapists. This may contribute to increased anticipation of positive alliance earlier in the therapy process; though client outcomes may not ultimately be improved through this matching (Shin et al. 2005), differences in initial presentation for therapy may be impacted through these various mechanisms to predict greater help-seeking among Whites.

Sense of Control: A Protective Cognitive Variable

A still-developing area of research is examining whether Whites are, on the whole, more likely to feel in control of their lives and destinies than members of other racial groups in the United States are. A strong sense of personal control has been generally viewed for the last few decades as related to more positive experiences of health, including mental health (Rodin 1986). Research specifically examining control-related beliefs in various racial groups seems to indicate that though the majority of American adults report feeling in control of their lives, these beliefs may vary according to demographic factors including race. For example, Bruce and Thornton (2004) examined responses from a large sample of European American and African American adults in the American Changing Lives study (a national probability study conducted at the University of Michigan). While these researchers looked at a large set of demographic and social variables in prediction of perceived control (e.g., gender, income, education, and age), self-identification as being White was among the variables which contributed to greater feelings of personal control. This sense of control, in turn, may contribute to more positive mental health outcomes in Whites. The authors identified these findings as being largely consistent with previous research on this topic (e.g., Shaw and Krause 2001).

Discussion

Applying Strengths to Meet Challenges

The preceding review has illustrated how European Americans already enjoy considerably higher overall chances of accessing and benefiting from the US mental health system, for various reasons. It is deeply unfortunate the beyond the significant obstacles of shame, stigma, and tension within one's immediate social circle that can be associated with addressing one's mental health problems (Hansell and Damour 2004), minority group members appear to experience the additional burdens of decreased economic access to quality services, more inhibitive beliefs and feelings about seeking mental health care, and a decreased sense of control over one's life circumstances. This disparity, however, should not preempt efforts to increase provision of appropriate services to members of all racial groups, including Whites (Kimerling and Baumrind 2005). A considerable share of this effort neces-

Mental health in European American adults: Summary of chapter themes

Demographics	Challenges	Strengths	Recommendations
White (European American) adults, aged 18–64, comprise ~41.9% of US population	Poverty • Higher rates of mental disorder are found among individuals of low SES • Uncertain whether poverty is equally detrimental to the mental health of all racial groups, or whether it is more damaging to certain groups under certain conditions	Access to mental health care • Greater income • Greater health insurance coverage • More frequently offered treatment options which are less distressing (e.g., medications with reduced side effects; less use of restrictive hospitalization)	Allocation of resources • Large numbers of Whites remain unable to access necessary or desired services due to socioeconomic circumstances • Need for increased pursuit of prevention as a critical piece of the continuum of care
Largest single racial x age group in the United States; expected to decrease proportionally over next several decades	Trauma • Risk of exposure to violence is lessened among Whites compared to certain other racial groups • Development of PTSD, however, occurs at equal or even greater rates amongst Whites • Decreased social support, peritraumatic distress, and peritraumatic dissociation may all be involved in this phenomenon	Willingness to use available mental health services • Developed on a Western, European-dominated model • May experience less distrust in helping systems, due to fewer historical experiences of abuse by such systems • May experience less interpersonal discomfort in treatment settings	Future research • Need greater understanding of possible interactions between poverty and racial group status as a factor in mental health • Increasing need to understand racial differences in PTSD development after exposure to violence • Continue to pursue normative beliefs about alcohol use among Whites
Education: Highly educated, with nearly one-third of this group having a Bachelor's degree or higher Income: Generally high, with median income = $ 52,400/year Poverty: Lowest rates of all racial groups (8.2% of US population) but highest by number (16.9 million people)	Alcohol Abuse • Whites are widely found to abuse alcohol at higher rates than other racial groups do • Effect does not appear to be attributable solely to economic factors • May be due in part to physiological capacity for alcohol metabolism • May be due in part to group norms about alcohol impacting individual judgments of appropriate consumption	Control cognitions • Whites may tend to hold stronger beliefs that they are able to determine their own destiny through will and effort • Current definitions of positive mental health are more in line with Western value systems than with non-Western systems	Philosophical approach to White mental health • Resist temptation to see investigation of mental health of Whites as part of an agenda of oppression • Redefine positive and negative mental health as being culture-relative to allow for more open understanding of experiences of all groups

sarily involves changes in public policy and allocation of resources that will assist Whites who are dealing with the challenges of poverty, to access the services they need. This will require changes in prevention efforts, for example. By and large, publicly funded health programs (e.g., Medicaid) result in more extensive preventive coverage for physical illnesses, than they do for mental disorders (Salsberry et al. 2005). Prevention is a critical piece of the continuum of care, and so this failure must be rectified. Given the trends regarding the relative willingness of European Americans to utilize the most common forms of mental health services if they are aware of them, increased preventive efforts are likely to have a strong positive effect on the mental health of these individuals.

Regarding the emerging data on relative tendency to feel in control of their lives, it may be that efforts to persuade European Americans to seek help for their mental disorders could be further strengthened through appeals to this set of cognitions. That is, autonomy, self-determination, and environmental mastery are already considered consonant with the Western model of mental health (e.g., Ryff et al. 2004). Perhaps more broadly publicizing the notion of help-seeking as a way of taking control of one's life (as opposed to an admission of weakness or lack of self-control) could interact with preexisting convictions about personal control, resulting in even greater willingness for European Americans to seek help for mental or emotional issues. As already stated, the actual proportion of the population who choose to seek services is thought to be far lower than the number who need such services, but do not seek them (United States Department of Health and Human Services (USDHHS) 1999). Research in this vein may prove to be very valuable, and significantly improve the mental health of the largest current segment of the US population.

Future Recommendations

As already noted in this chapter and elsewhere in this volume (e.g., Baker et al., this volume), approaching "Whiteness" as an experience shared by many individuals in the European American segment of the United States is still infrequently done in research on mental health issues in various racial/ethnic groups (Burkhard et al. 2003; Knowles and Peng 2005). Research over the last two decades on White racial identity development, while still overcoming significant conceptual and measurement obstacles (Behrens 1997; Knowles and Peng 2005; Leach et al. 2002), may soon offer some promise regarding increased insight into which particular characteristics may make it more likely that Whites with various issues will actually seek help, and from whom (Carter et al. 2004). Given current societal movement toward an increasingly racially pluralistic society, we recommend that examination of White racial identity, and its relation with mental health and disorder, continue unabated. That is, we surmise that the proportional decrease in the US population of Whites will not make Whiteness a less important factor in racial examinations of mental health. Rather, if it is the case that encounters with non-Whites are the major catalyst toward consideration of one's own White racial group membership and identity (Leach et al. 2002) increasing contact between Whites and members of various other racial groups will likely make ongoing study of White racial identity more important over time.

Concluding Comments

This chapter has attempted to present a few of the main challenges that European Americans face in their efforts toward maintaining individual mental health, as well as identifying some of the structural factors which may advantage and protect the mental health of Whites. It is our hope that this review, rather than eliciting a well-intentioned but misguided backlash against "protecting the hierarchical status quo," will highlight how our societal values must allow room for improvement and growth for all individuals. That is, the question is not whether attention should be withdrawn from the needs of one group, and reallocated to address the needs of another—mental health should not be a zero-sum game. Rather, the door of access to what is currently available should be equally open to all Americans, *and* we should make wholehearted efforts to expand our knowledge and resources to benefit members of all groups.

References

Adler, N. E., Epel, E. S., Castellazzo, G., & Ickovics, J. R. (2000). Relationship of subjective and objective social status with psychological and physiological functioning: Preliminary data in healthy White women. *Health Psychology, 19,* 586–592.

Akutsu, P. D., Snowden, L. R., & Organista, K. C. (1996). Referral patterns in ethnic-specific and mainstream programs for ethnic minorities and Whites. *Journal of Counseling Psychology, 43,* 56–64.

Alegria, M., Canino, G., Rios, R., Vera, M., Calderon, J., Rusch, D., & Ortega, A. N. (2002). Inequalities in use of specialty mental health services among Latinos, African Americans, and non-Latino Whites. *Psychiatric Services, 53,* 1547–1555.

Alegria, M., Canino, G., Stinson, F. S., & Grant, B. F. (2006). Nativity and DSM-IV psychiatric disorders among Puerto Ricans, Cuban Americans, and non-Latino Whites in the United States: Results from the National Epidemiologic Survey on Alcohol and Related Conditions. *Journal of Clinical Psychiatry, 67,* 56–65.

Amato, P. R., & Zuo, J. (1992). Rural poverty, urban poverty, and psychological well-being. *Sociological Quarterly, 33,* 229–240.

Ayalon, L., & Young, M. A. (2005). Racial-group differences in help-seeking behaviors. *Journal of Social Psychology, 145,* 391–403.

Bassuk, E. L., Perloff, J. N., & Coll, C. G. (1998). The plight of extremely poor Puerto Ricanand non-Hispanic White single mothers. *Social Psychiatry and Psychiatric Epidemiology, 33,* 326–336.

Behrens, J. T. (1997). Does the White racial identity attitude scale measure racial identity? *Journal of Counseling Psychology, 44,* 3–12.

Bloche, M. G. (2004). Health care disparities: Science, politics, and race. *The New England Journal of Medicine, 350,* 1568–1570.

Boothroid, R. A., Best, K. A., Giard, P. G., Stiles, J. S., Ort, R., & White, R. (2006). Poor and depressed, the tip of the iceberg: The unmet needs of enrollees in an indigent health care plan. *Administration and Policy in Mental Health and Mental Health Services Research, 33*, 172–181. doi:10.1007/s10488-006-0030-x.

Bratter, J. L., & Eschbach, K. (2005). Race/ethnic differences in nonspecific psychological distress: Evidence from the National Health Interview Survey. *Social Science Quarterly, 86,* 620–644.

Breslau, N., & Davis, G. C. (1995). Risk factors for PTSD-related traumatic events: A prospective analysis. *American Journal of Psychiatry, 152,* 529–535.

Breslau, N., Kessler, R. C., Chilcoat, H. D., Schultz, L. R., Davis, G. C., & Andreski, P. (1998). Trauma and posttraumatic stress disorder in the community: The 1996 Detroit area survey of trauma. *Archives of General Psychiatry, 55,* 626–632.

Brewin, C. R., Andrews, B., & Valentine, J. D. (2000). Meta-analysis of risk factors for posttraumatic stress disorder in trauma-exposed adults. *Journal of Consulting and Clinical Psychology, 68,* 748–766.

Broman, C. L. (2007). Perceived discrimination and alcohol use among Black and White college students. *Journal of Alcohol and Drug Education, 51,* 81–86.

Brown, C., Schulberg, H. C., Sacco, D., Perel, J. M., & Houck, P. R. (1999). Effectiveness of treatments for major depression in primary medical care practice: A post hoc analysis of outcomes for African American and White patients. *Journal of Affective Disorders, 53,* 185–192.

Bruce, M. A., & Thornton, M. C. (2004). It's my world? Exploring Black and White perceptions of personal control. *The Sociological Quarterly, 45,* 597–612.

Brunet, A., Weiss, D. S., Metzler, T. J., Best, S. R., Neylan, T. C., Rogers, C., et al. (2001). The peritraumatic distress inventory: A proposed measure of PTSD criterion A2. *American Journal of Psychiatry, 158,* 1480–1485.

Burkhard, A. W., Juarez-Huffaker, M., & Ajmere, K. (2003). White racial identity attitudes as a predictor of client perceptions of cross-cultural working alliances. *Journal of Multicultural Counseling and Development, 31,* 226–244.

Cabassa, L. J., Zayas, L. H., & Hansen, M. C. (2006). Latino adults' access to mental health care: A review of epidemiological studies. *Administration and Policy in Mental Health and Mental Health Services Research, 33,* 316–330.

Cachelin, F. M., & Striegel-Moore, R. H. (2007). Help seeking and barriers to treatment in a community sample of Mexican American and European American women with eating disorders. *International Journal of Eating Disorders, 39,* 154–161.

Callahan, S. T., & Cooper, W. O. (2004). Uninsurance and health care access among young adults in the U.S. *Journal of Adolescent Health, 34,* 112–113.

Callahan, S. T., & Cooper, W. O. (2005). Disparities in usual source and use of health care among young adult Hispanic subgroups in the U.S. *Journal of Adolescent Health, 36*, 99–100.

Callahan, S. T., Hickson, G. B., & Cooper, W. O. (2006). Health care access of Hispanic young adults in the United States. *Journal of Adolescent Health, 39,* 627–633.

Cardemil, E. V., & Battle, C. L. (2003). Guess who's coming to therapy? Getting comfortable with conversations about race and ethnicity in psychotherapy. *Professional Psychology: Research and Practice, 34,* 278–286.

Carter, R. T., Helms, J. E., & Juby, H. L. (2004). The relationship between racism and racial identity for White Americans: A profile analysis. *Journal of Multicultural Counseling and Development, 32,* 2–17.

Chow, J. C.-C., Jaffee, K., & Snowden, L. (2003). Racial/ethnic disparities in the use of mental health services in poverty areas. *American Journal of Public Health, 93,* 792–797.

Cockerham, W. C. (1990). A test of the relationship between race, socioeconomic status, and psychological distress. *Social Science and Medicine, 31,* 1321–1326.

Compton, W. M. III, Cottler, L. B., Abdallah, A. B., Phelps, D. L., Spitznagel, E. L., & Horton, J. C., (2000). Substance dependence and other psychiatric disorders among drug dependent subjects: Race and gender correlates. *The American Journal on Addictions, 9,* 113–125.

Crawford, K., Fisher, W. H., & McDermeit, M. (1998). Racial/ethnic disparities in admissions to public and private psychiatric inpatient settings: The effect of managed care. *Administration and Policy in Mental Health, 26,* 101–109.

Cuellar, I., & Panigua, F. A. (2000). *Handbook of multicultural mental health: Assessment and treatment of diverse populations*. Burlington: Academic.

Daley, M. C. (2005). Race, managed care, and the quality of substance abuse treatment. *Administration and Policy in Mental Health, 32,* 457–476.

DeNavas-Walt, C., Proctor, B. D., & Smith, J. (2007). Income, poverty, and health insurance coverage in the United States. *Current Population Reports, 2007,* 60–233.

Dohrenwend, B. P., & Dohrenwend, B. (1974). Social and cultural influences on psychopathology. *Annual Review of Psychology, 25,* 417–452.

Feiring, C., Coates, D. L., & Taska, L. S. (2001). Ethnic status, stigmatization, support, and symptoms development following sexual abuse. *Journal of Interpersonal Violence, 16,* 1307–1329.

Fiscella, K., Franks, P., Doescher, M. P., & Saver, B. G. (2002). Disparities in health care by race, ethnicity, and language among the insured: Findings from a national sample. *Medical Care, 40,* 52–59.

Fraga, E. D., Atkinson, D. R., & Wampold, B. E. (2004). Ethnic group preferences for multicultural counseling competencies. *Cultural Diversity and Ethnic Minority Psychology, 10,* 53–65.

Gonzales, J. M., Alegria, M., & Prihoda, T. J. (2005). How do attitudes toward mental health treatment vary by age, gender, and ethnicity/race in young adults? *Journal of Community Psychology, 33,* 611–629.

Han, E., & Liu, G. G. (2005). Racial disparities in prescription drug use for mental illness among population in U.S. *Journal of Mental Health Policy and Economics, 8,* 131–143.

Hansell, J., & Damour, L. (2005). *Abnormal psychology*. Hoboken: Wiley.

Harford, T. C., Yi, H.-Y., & Hilton, M. E. (2006). Alcohol abuse and dependence in college and noncollege samples: A ten-year prospective follow-up in a national survey. *Journal of Studies on Alcohol, 67,* 803–809.

Haring, M., Stock, W. A., & Okun, M. A. (1984). A research synthesis of gender and social class as correlates of subjective well-being. *Human Relations, 37,* 645–657.

Harman, J. S., Edlund, M. J., & Fortney, J. C. (2004). Disparities in the adequacy of depression treatment in the United States. *Psychiatric Services, 55,* 1379–1385.

Hasin, D. S., Stinson, F. S., Ogburn, E., & Grant, B. F. (2007). Prevalence, correlates, disability, and comorbidity of DSM-IV alcohol abuse and dependence in the United States: Results from the National Epidemiologic Survey on Alcohol and Related Conditions. *Archives of General Psychiatry, 64,* 830–842.

Heckman, T. G., Kockman, A., Sikkema, K. J., Kalichman, S. C., Masten, J., & Goodkin, K., (2000). Late middle-aged and older men living with HIV/AIDS: Race differences in coping, social support and psychological distress. *Journal of the National Medical Association, 92,* 436–444.

Herbeck, D. M., West, J. C., Riditis, I., Duffy, F. F., Fitek, D. J., & Bell, C. C., Snowden, L. R. (2004). Variations in use of second-generation antipsychotic medication by race among adult psychiatric patients. *Psychiatric Services, 55,* 677–684.

Hesse, E., & Main, M. (2006). Frightened, threatening, and dissociative parental behavior in low-risk samples: Description, discussion, and interpretations. *Development and Psychopathology, 18,* 309–343.

Huang, B., Grant, B. F., Dawson, D. A., Stinson, F. S., Chou, S. P., & Saha, T. D., Goldstein, R. B., Smith, S. M., Ruan, W. J., & Pickering, R. P. (2006). Race-ethnicity and the prevalence and co-occurrence of *Diagnostic and Statistical Manual of Mental Disorders, Fourth Edition*, alcohol and drug use disorders and Axis I and II disorders: United States, 2001–2002. *Comprehensive Psychiatry, 47,* 252–257.

Jackson, K. M., O'Neill, S. E., & Sher, K. M. (2006). Characterizing alcohol dependence: Transitions during young and middle adulthood. *Experimental and Clinical Psychopharmacology, 14,* 228–244.

Kessler, R. C., & Neighbors, H. W. (1986). A new perspective on the relationships among race, social class, and psychological distress. *Journal of Health and Social Behavior, 27,* 107–115.

Kimerling, R., & Baumrind, N. (2005). Access to specialty mental health services among women in California. *Psychiatric Services, 56,* 729–734.

Knowles, E. D., & Peng, K. (2005). White selves: Conceptualizing and measuring a dominant-group identity. *Journal of Personality and Social Psychology, 89,* 223–241.

Knox, S., Burkard, A. W., Johnson, A. J., Suzuki, L. A., & Ponterotto, J. G. (2003). African American and European American therapists' experiences of addressing race in cross-racial psychotherapy dyads. *Journal of Counseling Psychology, 50,* 466–481.

Kuno, E., & Rothbard, A. B. (2005). The effect of income and race on quality of psychiatric care in community mental health centers. *Community Mental Health Journal, 41,* 613–622.

Lasser, K. E., Himmelstein, D. U., & Woolhandler, S. (2006). Access to care, health status, and health disparities in the United States and Canada: Results of a cross-national population-based survey. *American Journal of Public Health, 96,* 1300–1307.

Leach, M. M., Behrens, J. T., & LaFleur, N. K. (2002). White racial identity and White racial consciousness: Similarities, differences, and recommendations. *Journal of Multicultural Counseling and Development, 30,* 66–80.

Lincoln, K. D., Chatters, L. M., & Taylor, R. J. (2003). Psychological distress among Black and White Americans: Differential effects of social support, negative interaction and personal control. *Journal of Health and Social Behavior, 44,* 390–407.

Lorant, V., Deliege, D., Eaton, W., Robert, A., Philippot, P. M., & Ansseau, M. (2003). Socioeconomic inequalities in depression: A meta-analysis. *American Journal of Epidemiology, 157,* 98–112.

Mark, T. L, Palmer, L. A., Russo, P. A., & Vasey, J. (2003). Examination of treatment pattern differences by race. *Mental Health Services Research, 5,* 241–250.

Marmar, C. R., Weiss, D. S., Schlenger, W. E., & Fairbank, J. A. (1994). Peritraumatic dissociation and posttraumatic stress in male Vietnam theater veterans. *American Journal of Psychiatry, 151,* 902–907.

Melfi, C. A., Croghan, T. W., & Hanna, M. P. (1999). Access to treatment for depression in a Medicaid population. *Journal of Health Care for the Poor and Underserved, 10,* 201–215.

Miller, V., Lykens, K., & Quinn, J. (2007). The effects of media exposure on alcohol consumption patterns in African American males. *Substance Abuse, 28,* 41–49.

Miranda, J., & Cooper, L. A. (2004). Disparities in care for depression among primary care patients. *Journal of General Internal Medicine, 19,* 120–126.

Ortega, A. N., & Rosenheck, R. (2002). Hispanic client-case manager-matching: Differences in outcomes and service use in a program for homeless persons with severe mental illness. *The Journal of Nervous and Mental Disease, 190,* 315–323.

Ostrove, J. M., Feldman, P., & Adler, N. E. (1999). Relations among socioeconomic status indicators and health for African-Americans and Whites. *Journal of Health Psychology, 4,* 451–463.

Ozer, E. J., Best, S. R., Lipsey, T. L., & Weiss, D. S. (2003). Predictors of posttraumatic stress disorder and symptoms in adults: A meta-analysis. *Psychological Bulletin, 129,* 52–73.

Padgett, D., Patrick, C., Burns, B., & Schlesinger, H. (1994). Women and outpatient mental health services: Use by Black, Hispanic, and White women in a national insured population. *Journal of Mental Health Administration, 21,* 347–360.

Paschall, M. J., Flewelling, R. L., & Faulkner, D. L. (2000). Alcohol misuse in young adulthood: Effects of race, educational attainment, and social context. *Substance Use and Misuse, 35,* 1485–1506.

Razzano, L. A., Cook, J. A., Hamilton, M. M., Hughes, T. L., & Matthews, A. K. (2006). Predictors of mental health services use among lesbian and heterosexual women. *Psychiatric Rehabilitation Journal, 29,* 289–298.

Rice, C. (2006). Misperceptions of college drinking norms: Ethnic/race differences. *Journal of Human Behavior in the Social Environment, 14,* 17–30.

Rodin, J. (1986). Aging and health: The effects of the sense of control. *Science, 233,* 1271–1276.

Rollman, B. L., Hanusa, B. H., Belnap, B. H., Gardner, W., Cooper, L. A., & Schulberg, H. C. (2002). Race, quality of depression care, and recovery from major depression in a primary care setting. *General Hospital Psychiatry, 24,* 381–390.

Romley, J. A., Cohen, D., Ringel, J., & Sturm, R. (2007). Alcohol and environmental justice: The density of liquor stores and bars in urban neighborhoods in the United States. *Journal of Studies on Alcohol and Drugs, 68,* 48–55.

Ruiz, P. (2004). Addressing culture, race, and ethnicity in psychiatric practice. *Psychiatric Annals, 34,* 526–561.

Ryff, C. D., Keyes, C. L. M., & Hughes, D. L. (2004). Psychological well-being in MIDUS: Profiles of ethnic/racial diversity and life-course uniformity. In O. G. Brim, C. D. Ryff, & R. C. Kessler (Eds.), How healthy are we? A national study of well-being at midlife (pp. 398–422). Chicago: University of Chicago Press.

Salsberry, P. J., Chipps, E., & Kennedy, C. (2005). Use of general medical services among Medicaid patients with severe and persistent mental illness. *Psychiatric Services, 56,* 458–462.

Schnittker, J., Freese, J., & Powell, B. (2000). Nature, nurture, neither, nor: Black-White differences in beliefs about the causes and appropriate treatment of mental illness. *Social Forces, 78,* 1101–1130.

Schnurr, P. P., Lunney, C. A., & Sengupta, A. (2004). Risk factors for the development versus maintenance of Posttraumatic Stress Disorder. *Journal of Traumatic Stress, 17,* 85–95.

Schwabe, A. M., & Kodras, J. E. (2000). Race, class, and psychological distress: Contextual variations across four American communities. *Health (London), 4,* 234–260.

Shaw, B. A., & Krause, N. (2001). Exploring race variations in aging and personal control. *The Journals of Gerontology Series B: Psychological Sciences and Social Sciences, 56,* 119–124.

Shin, S.-M., Chow, C., Camacho-Gonsalves, T., Levy, R. J., Allen, I. E., & Leff, H. S. (2005). A meta-analytic review of racial-ethnic matching for African American and Caucasian American clients and clinicians. *Journal of Counseling Psychology, 52,* 45–56.

Shrout, P. E., Canino, G. J., Bird, H. R., Rubio-Stipec, M., Bravo, M., & Burnam, M. A. (1992). Mental health status among Puerto Ricans, Mexican Americans, and non-Hispanic Whites. *American Journal of Community Psychology, 20,* 729–752.

Snowden, L. R. (2001). Social embeddedness and psychological well-being among African-Americans and Whites. *American Journal of Community Psychology, 29,* 519–536.

Snowden, L. R., & Cheung, F. K. (1990). Use of inpatient mental health services by members of ethnic minority groups. *American Psychologist, 45,* 347–355.

Snowden, L., Masland, M., Ma, Y., & Ciemens, E. (2006). Strategies to improve minority access to public mental health services in California: Description and preliminary evaluation. *Journal of Community Psychology, 34,* 225–235.

Sue, D., Sue, D. W., & Sue, S. (2006). *Understanding abnormal behavior* (8th ed.). Boston: Houghton Mifflin.

Tercyak, K. P., Davis, K. M., & Loffredo, C. A. (2007). Behavioral risk factors among Black and White women newly diagnosed with breast cancer. *Psycho-Oncology, 16,* 224–231.

Tivis, L. J., Chastain, G., & Tivis, R. D. (2006). Alcohol and the human experience: Guest editors' introduction. *Journal of General Psychology, 133,* 325–327.

Torres, S., & Han, H.-R. (2000). Psychological distress in non-Hispanic White and Hispanic abused women. *Archives of Psychiatric Nursing, 14,* 19–29.

Ulbrich, P. M., Warheit, G. J., & Zimmerman, R. S. (1989). Race, socioeconomic status, and psychological distress: An examination of differential vulnerability. *Journal of Health and Social Behavior, 30,* 131–146.

United States Census Bureau, Population Division. (2007a). Table 4: Annual estimates of the White alone not Hispanic population by age and sex for the United States: April 1, 2000 to July 1, 2006. Current population survey, 2007. http://pubdb3.census.gov/macro/032007/perinc/new03_004.htm. Accessed 14 Nov 2007.

United States Census Bureau, Population Division. (2007b). Educational attainment, people 25 years old and over, by total money earnings in 2006, work experience in 2006, age, race, Hispanic origin, and sex. Current population survey, 2007: Annual social and economic supplement. http://pubdb3.census.gov/macro/032007/perinc/new03_004.htm. Accessed 14 Nov 2007.

United States Department of Health and Human Services (USDHHS). (1999). *Mental Health: A Report of the Surgeon General—Executive Summary*. U.S. Department of Health and Human Services, Substance Abuse and Mental Health Services Administration, Center for Mental Health Services, National Institutes of Health, National Institute of Mental Health: Rockville.

United States Department of Health and Human Services (USDHHS). (2001). *Mental health: Culture, race, and ethnicity: A supplement to mental health: A report of the Surgeon General*. U.S. Department of Health and Human Services, Substance Abuse and Mental Health Services Administration, Center for Mental Health Services: Rockville.

Wang, J., Noel, J. M., Zuckerman, I. H., Miller, N. A., Shaya, F. T., & Mullins, C. D. (2006). Disparities in access to essential new prescription drugs between non-Hispanic Whites, non-Hispanic Blacks, and Hispanic Whites. *Medical Care Research and Review, 63,* 742–763.

Wells, K., Klap, R., Koike, A., & Sherbourne, C. (2001). Ethnic disparities in unmet need for alcoholism, drug abuse, and mental health care. *American Journal of Psychiatry, 158*, 2027–2032.

Williams, D. R., Yu, Y., Jackson, J. S., & Anderson, N. B. (1997). Racial differences in physical and mental health: Socio-economic status, stress, and discrimination. *Journal of Health Psychology, 2,* 335–351.

Zatzick, D. F., Marmar, C. R., Weiss, D. S., & Metzler, T. (1994). Does trauma-linked dissociation vary across ethnic groups? *Journal of Nervous and Mental Disease, 182,* 576–582.

Zhang, A. Y., & Snowden, L. R. (1999). Ethnic characteristics of mental disorders in five U.S. communities. *Cultural Diversity and Ethnic Minority Psychology, 5,* 134–146.

Chapter 14
Older White Adults and Mental Health

B. Jan McCulloch, Sara Lassig and Amanda Barnett

This contribution focuses on two primary objectives—outlining mental health in relation to later life and identifying, where appropriate, specific information about the mental health of older White adults. At the heart of such a discussion is the recognition that, with age, regardless of race or ethnicity, individuals demonstrate more diversity and heterogeneity. Therefore, any discussion about elders must recognize that diversity *within* specific groups is expected—in our case, among older Whites.

In his reflections on the Surgeon General's Report of Mental Health, Culture, Race, and Ethnicity, Lopez (2003, p. 419) underscores the message that "culture counts." This report focuses attention on four minority groups: African Americans, American Indians and Alaska Natives, Asian Americans and Pacific Islanders, and Hispanic Americans and emphasizes the heterogeneity within each of these main minority groups. It remains a disservice to Whites if the heterogeneity within this majority group is unrecognized. Wykle and Musil (1993) discuss a number of social and cultural factors that affect the mental health of elders including gender, socioeconomic status, negative life events, physical health, social support, and race and ethnicity. Historical and social contexts also result in significant diversity with all ethnic, racial, and cultural groups including Whites.

The original Surgeon General's Report on Mental Health (1999) was inadequate in that it did not address the importance of culture, race, and ethnicity. In response, a separate report focused on mental health, culture, race, and ethnicity. Lopez (2003) indicates that two tensions remain unresolved:

- Recognition that culture is not static (within a group) but a fluid process—one not constrained by ethnic and racial boundaries; and
- Many individuals, including Whites, are omitted from this examination of mental health, culture, race, and ethnicity—"By practically excluding white folks from our analyses, the considerable diversity within their group and their commonalities with minority groups are not available for consideration" (pp. 425–426).

B. J. McCulloch (✉)
Department of Family Social Science, University of Minnesota, 290 D McNeal Hall,
1985 Buford Avenue, St. Paul, MN 55108, USA
e-mail: jmccullo@umn.edu

E. C. Chang, C. A. Downey (eds.), *Handbook of Race and Development in Mental Health*,
DOI 10.1007/978-1-4614-0424-8_14, © Springer Science+Business Media, LLC 2012

Historically, the mental health of older adults has been a relatively neglected area of scholarship. In fact, public and professional stereotypes of aging frequently associated mental illness with normal aging. More recently, elders' mental health has been recognized as an essential dimension of quality of life. Finch and Tanzi (1997) note that the interplay between genetic risk and lifestyle is an important factor affecting quality of later life.

Early studies examining elders and mental health largely ignored the significance of examining race, culture, and ethnicity. Although most studies consisted of White samples, relatively few studies focused on how majority status might interact with factors influencing specific mental health problems, help-seeking behaviors, or treatment. In short, as we are just beginning to understand how the cultural, social, and historical contexts of minority elders affect their mental health, so too are we beginning to examine these links for White elders.

The Surgeon General's Report on Mental Health (1999) concludes that, throughout the life cycle, continual intellectual, physical, and social activities are important to the maintenance of later life mental health. Rowe and Kahn (1998), in their book on successful aging, also concur. They define successful aging as having three components: a low risk of disease and disease-related disability, high mental and physical functioning, and active engagement with life (p. 38). In addition, multiple factors affect the mental health adjustment of older adults including biological; psychological; and sociological, historical, and cultural determinants (Wykle and Musil 1993).

When mental health is described generally across the life span, older adults have less mental illness as compared to their younger counterparts including less affective, anxiety, and substance disorders. The ways in which older adults experience mental illness also may be different compared with younger adults (Wykle and Musil 1993). Elders have significantly higher rates of severe cognitive impairment including Alzheimer's disease, multi-infarct dementia, and delirium (Rabins 1992; Regier et al. 1988). Jeste et al. (1999) indicate that by 2030, 15 million elders will live with a psychiatric illness. In support, Bartels (2004) states that, by the year 2030, older adults with a major psychiatric illness will more than double. Bartels (2004) also provides prevalence rates for elders with schizophrenia (0.5%), bipolar disorder (0.2%), and major depression (ranging between 1–5%). In addition, others report that between 15–25% of the older adult population living in institutional settings experience incidences of either minor or major depression (National Institutes of Health 1991).

This chapter is divided into four sections. The first section characterizes the older adult population in demographic terms, provides information concerning prevalence and economic costs of mental illness, and concludes with a brief discussion of stigma. The second section highlights information concerning White elders with a focus on adaptability and resilience. The third section presents three mental health issues common for elders, including older Whites—dementia, depression, and anxiety. The final section provides an integrative discussion including recommendations for the future.

Demographic Profile and Economic Consequences

Demographically, the world's population is aging. In 2000, elders represented approximately 7% of the worlds' population or 420 million people (U.S. Census Bureau 2005). In the United States, approximately 12% of the total population is 65 years of age and older (U.S. Census Bureau 2005). Of this group, approximately 83% are classified as White, non-Hispanic (U.S. Census Bureau 2005). In addition, within today's older population, the fastest growing segment of elders are 85 years of age and older. By 2030, this segment of the older population will expand rapidly as the baby boomers move into this age group (U.S. Census Bureau 2005). For US citizens, long life has become an expectation for most. For example, we consider the age of 80 as normative and no longer, particularly for women, consider the age of 90 as exceptional (Zarit 1998).

By 2030, almost 1 in every 5 Americans—72 million people—will be 65 years of age and older (National Institutes of Health 2006). Extrapolating Day's (Day 1996) findings from a decade ago, the White non-Hispanic population is estimated to double over the next 30 years while Latino elders will increase tenfold and African American elders will increase threefold.

In addition to the sheer number of the increasing older population, it remains important to consider the numbers of elders who reside in institutional settings—a characteristic not normative for younger age groups. Approximately 6% of older adults 65 years of age and older live in group quarters, including nursing homes, psychiatric hospitals, and adult group homes. This figure averages the 2% of elders 65–74 years of age as well as 22% for those elders 75 years of age and older (U.S. Census Bureau 2004). Zarit (1998, p. 85) notes that "[N]ursing homes have largely replaced public mental hospitals as the primary treatment setting for all older adults." Of particular relevance here, Gatz and Smyer (1992) estimate that between 43–60% of elders admitted to nursing homes have some type of mental health problem.

We might wish to better understand the older White adults' mental health as a purely academic exercise. However, we are faced with a demographic and economic necessity of understanding and developing appropriate mental health treatments for older adults. Quoting the Surgeon General's Report on Mental Health (1999, p. 381),"[D]isability due to mental illness in individuals 65 years of age and older will become a major public health problem in the near future because of demographic changes." Data are quite limited regarding age-specific costs of mental health care. However, Garske et al. (1999) indicate that when direct and indirect costs of mental illness are combined, the United States spends approximately $150 billion annually. When the use of community-based public health service use was examined among older San Diego County elders, Gilmer et al. (2006) reported that the use of emergency services increased with age while outpatient service use declined.

One cannot address mental health and older adults without brief mention of the role stigma plays in elders' willingness to seek and accept treatment. Gary (2005,

p. 980) defines stigma as "a collection of negative attitudes, beliefs, thoughts, and behaviors that influences the individual, or the general public, to fear, reject, avoid, be prejudiced, and discriminate against people with mental disorders." Sartoruis (2003) notes that examination of stigma, mental illness, and elders remains scant. We suggest that ageist attitudes and negative stereotypes combine with stigma relating to mental illness to create an additional example of *double jeopardy*. Delpa et al. (2005), in their study of stigma among Dutch elders, indicates that stigma results in negative consequences because it undermines elders' self-esteem and psychological well-being, and negatively affects their own behaviors for treatment and social adaptation. They go so far as to state that "stigma may be more damaging to an individual's quality of life than a socially withdrawn existence" (p. 147). Bull (1998), in his examination of mental health and rural elders, also focused on treatment behavior when he noted that elders refused to seek mental health assistance for a number of reasons including identification within their small town network and fear of being labeled "crazy."

Although not specifically associated with stigma, studies have shown that elders are less likely than younger individuals to seek assistance for mental health problems. For example, Burns and Taub (1990) indicate that just less than 8% of older adults living within the community were in need of mental health assistance, but only about 2.5% actually received treatment from mental health professionals with an additional 2.4% receiving assistance from their primary care physicians.

Perhaps the most discouraging aspect about mental health problems among older adults is the false assumption that mental health decline is an inevitable consequence of aging—an assumption that has resulted in inadequate treatment for elders' psychiatric symptoms (Wykle and Musil 1993). For example, persistent bereavement and/or serious depression are not characteristic of later life, should not be considered normal, and should be treated appropriately (Surgeon General's Report on Mental Health 1999). One of the most important breakthroughs in increased attention to the mental health of older adults has been confirmation that, although there are some changes in mental health functioning with age, there is little support for the negative stereotypes that are so commonly associated with the mental health of elders. It is estimated that approximately 20% of individuals 55 years of age and older, however, experience mental disorders that are not part of the normal aging process (Surgeon General's Report on Mental Health 1999).

Elders' Adaptability and Resilience

Although many are not aware of factors that assist older adults with adaptability and resilience, several characteristics have been noted. For example, elders benefit from "stable intellectual functioning, capacity for change, and productive engagement with life" (Surgeon General's Report on Mental Health 1999)—personal characteristics often not associated with later life, but consistently evident among healthy older adults. Rowe and Kahn (1998) also suggest that some human attributes increase with age. The primary of these is wisdom, a valued characteristic that occurs with individuals' accumulation of life experiences. With age, "we become wiser about ourselves and others, about the uncertainties of life, about what is ultimately important and unimportant in people's lives, about things that change and things that do not change in human affairs" (Rowe and Kahn 1998, p. 140).

The importance of education as the foundation for life-long resources also has been shown to significantly affect later life in a number of domains (Rowe and Kahn 1998). Albert et al. (1995) reported that education, assessed by years of schooling, was the strongest of four significant predictors (education, strenuous activity in the home, peak pulmonary flow rate, and self-efficacy) of high cognitive functioning in later life.

We have chosen to include this section on older adult's strengths by briefly outlining findings from a longitudinal study conducted by Johnson and Barer (1997) as a way of highlighting attributes of very late survivorship, an important group in light of the significant increases in elders over the age of 85. We also believe the differences between these very old survivors and much of our understanding of successful aging are important to highlight.

Johnson and Barer reported on a White sample of elders living in the San Francisco area who were 85 years of age and older. These elders, when compared with national statistics on Whites, were similar in that they were predominantly women, widowed, and living alone. About one-third had no children and had witnessed the death of at least one of their children. Even though a large proportion had difficulty functioning, they continued to live a relatively independent life and they viewed their health as good.

Johnson and Barer conducted their study over a six-year period with the goal of examining data on the objective and subjective experiences of adapting to the inevitable challenges of advanced age. They reported that, for the most part, their respondents:

- Emerged as a group with special status because of their long-term survivorship, a status that may be primarily relevant to this cohort of elders.
- Discussed life and experience with a "profound grasp of the practical and philosophical aspects of long-term survivorship."
- Maintained a positive sense of well-being and pride because of their long-term survival status.
- Were different from younger elders because they had outlived their predicted life span (p. 4).

In contrast to discussions of successful aging, Johnson and Barer found that by the age of 85, the majority of White elders in their study experienced some disability and social losses but that their subjective well-being *improved* (italics added). In the face of increasing dependence and loss, these long-term survivors provide us with a more nuanced way of defining what it means to be resilient and adaptable. Significant findings from this study included:

- Elders were active agents in the management of their daily lives which included the mobilization of others if they were incapacitated.
- Elders drew on both cognitive and emotional processes to provide meaning to their daily experiences.
- Elders reconstituted their self-concepts to be in concert with the realities of their lives.
- Very old survivors were different from younger elders in the ways that they adapted to problems of aging:
  - They detached themselves from financial and family worries.
  - They complained less of emotional problems.
  - They felt it less necessary to exert mastery or control over their lives.
  - They faced less outside stressors and hassles—they eliminated some of the sources of their stress as a way of coping.
  - Since others placed fewer demands on them, they "were free to cope with their limitations without distractions" (p. 221).
- When White elders' social relationships were examined, they were described as follows:
  - One-third did not have living children.
  - Some childless elders had strong intergenerational relationships with nieces and nephews.
  - Most reported having as many social relationships as they wanted.
  - Fifty-three percent could identify a close friend even though they spoke of the deaths of friends and family.
  - Although many (about 45%) continued to form new friendships, the definition of friendship was expanded to include those associations made, for example, at church or senior centers.

We have highlighted Johnson and Barer for two primary reasons. First, they provide needed information about how individuals of advanced age interpret their experiences to reframe daily experiences in such a way that most report high subjective well-being. These oldest old do this at a time in their lives when many might judge their existences as lonely, physically challenging, narrowly focused, and lacking in meaning. Second, as more of the population reach these advanced ages, it is important to be aware of the resilience and quality of life among individuals most likely to be at a stage in life where the definition of successful aging is no longer applicable.

Dementia, Depression, Anxiety, and Older Whites

In this, the third section of this chapter, we provide information on three mental health problems commonly associated with later life. This is not to say that the three we have chosen to emphasize are the only mental health issues that affect elders' quality of life; they are, however, the most commonly examined issues appearing in gerontological research on elders and mental health.

Dementia

"Dementia" is a general term meaning the loss of memory and other intellectual abilities (such as thinking, reasoning, and remembering) that is serious enough to interfere with daily life (Alzheimer's Association 2007), and is many elders' most feared diagnosis (Rowe and Kahn 1998). By itself, dementia is not a disease, but instead, a group of symptoms that may accompany certain diseases or conditions (Alzheimer's Association 2007). Symptoms may include disorientation of time and place, lack of judgment, difficulty with abstract thinking, and changes in personality, mood, and behavior. Although dementia is irreversible when caused by disease or injury, it may sometimes be reversible when caused by drugs, alcohol, hormone or vitamin imbalances, or depression (Alzheimer's Association 2007).

The most common form of dementia is Alzheimer's disease, which is a noncurable disease of the brain that causes a steady decline in memory and results in dementia. Providing care to an individual with Alzheimer's disease or a related dementia is a challenging undertaking that brings with it many demands and difficulties for the families of the over five million individuals afflicted with Alzheimer's disease. Because many of these caregivers are elders themselves, the mental health of multiple persons in the family system may be affected by a diagnosis of Alzheimer's disease. Numerous studies have found that caregivers of individuals with Alzheimer's disease or related dementias also are at increased risk for poor mental and physical health outcomes when compared to well-matched noncaregiving controls (e.g., Anthony-Bergstone et al. 1988; Haley et al. 1987).

Dementia cuts across all cultural and racial lines, as demonstrated by the fact that nearly half of persons over the age of 85 have Alzheimer's disease (Alzheimer's Association 2007). Certainly, dementia is not a mental health concern affecting only Whites. By 2050, someone will develop Alzheimer's disease every 33 seconds as compared to every 72 seconds in 2006 (Alzheimer's Association 2007). Prior research has, however, shown that there are differences in the prevalence and etiology of dementia between various races. Weintraub et al. (2000), found that the rate of dementia on admission to nursing homes was higher among Black residents than among White residents, at 77 and 55% respectively. Additionally, Miles et al. (2001) found that African Americans had higher prevalence of vascular dementia and lower prevalence of Parkinsonian dementia than Caucasians. Despite the findings that at least some forms of dementia may be more present in other races than Whites, dementia remains a critical mental health concern for all older adults, including Whites.

In their examination of dementia among three ethnoracial groups, Gurland et al. (1999) reported that across age strata (65–74, 75–84, 85+), Whites had consistently lower prevalence as well as incidence rates of dementia as compared with Latinos and African Americans. In the age strata of 85 and older, prevalence rates were 62.9% for Latinos, 58.6% for African Americans, and 30.2% for Whites (Gurland et al. 1999). The most powerful correlate of lower rates of dementia for Whites was better education.

Elders with low education, regardless of race or ethnicity, have higher than expected rates of dementia (Bachman et al. 1992; Folstein et al. 1991; Gurland et al. 1995; Zhang et al. 1990). Those with less education are also more likely to have multi-infarct dementia (Folstein et al. 1991) dementia relating to alcohol misuse, and unspecified dementias (Fratiglioni et al. 1991). All ethnic and racial groups demonstrate sharp rises in rates of dementia with age.

Each year, the direct and indirect costs of dementias, including Medicare and Medicaid costs and the indirect cost to business of employees who are caregivers to persons with dementia, amount to more than $148 billion. As of 2010, the cost of Medicaid spending for nursing home care for individuals with dementia is estimated to be at $24 billion (Alzheimer's Association 2007).

Depression

Depression, which affects more than 121 million people worldwide, is a common mental disorder that presents with depressed mood, disturbed sleep or appetite, feelings of guilt or low self-worth, loss of interest or pleasure, low energy, and poor concentration (World Health Organization (WHO) 2007). These challenges may become chronic or recurrent and lead to significant impairments in an individual's ability to take care of his or her everyday responsibilities (World Health Organization (WHO) 2007).

In addition, depression can also foretell of other serious illness. Katz (1998) indicates that depression can increase stress, morbidity, and disability. It also can portend increased mortality from heart disease and possibly cancer (Frasure-Smith and Lespérance1995; Penninx et al. 1998). Depression can also lead to suicide, a tragic fatality associated with the loss of about 850,000 thousand lives annually (World Health Organization (WHO) 2007).

Data remain inconclusive regarding age (Kessler et al. 2003; Weissman et al. 1991) as well as racial differences in depressive symptoms (Somervell et al. 1989). However, it would appear that depressive symptomatology among elders is most frequently caused by emotional suffering (Blazer 2003; Cole and Dendukuri 2003) and in the context of physical impairment (Hays et al. 1997). Katz (1998) suggests that the guilt and self-reproach frequently associated with depression among younger adults may be less common among elders while symptoms of a somatic nature may be more common.

In one of the most recent studies examining racial differences among African Americans and Whites, Sachs-Ericsson et al. (2005) concluded that neither being African American nor White was a risk factor in later life depression. Rather, socioeconomic factors were significant in explaining the association between race and depressive symptomatology in both cross-sectional and longitudinal analyses.

Estimates of the rates of depression among the older population are inconsistent. Part of this inconsistency results from how depression is defined (major vs. minor) and whether elders are residing in community or institutional settings. Some suggest prevalence rates for major depression to range from 1–5% (Hybels and Blazer 2003) to as high as 15% for depression (unspecified) among community dwelling elders (National Mental Health Association 2003; Meador and Blazer 1998). Higher rates of depression are estimated for elders receiving health care at home (13.5%) (Bruce et al. 2002), 11.5% of elders residing in hospital settings (Hybels and Blazer 2003), and between 25–30% for persons living in nursing homes (National Mental Health Association 2003; Rovner 1993).

Depression, in addition to being a widely under-treated and under-recognized medical illness (Lyness et al. 1995), is also one of the conditions most commonly associated with suicide in older adults (Conwell and Brent 1995). Although elders comprise 12% of the US population, they account for 16% of all suicide deaths in 2004 (National Institute of Mental Health (NIMH) 2003). Suicide rates increase with age and are highest among Whites, particularly for males (Spicer and Miller 2000). White men, 85 years of age and older, are most likely to die by suicide (U.S. Census Bureau 2005).

In the case of older adults, suicide acts involve lethal methods, including firearms (the most common), drowning, and hanging (Spicer and Miller 2000). Koenig and Blazer (1992) indicate that elders commit approximately 17% of all suicides. For older White males, suicide is a leading cause of death (Wykle et al. 1992). In addition, many older adults who die by suicide, up to 75%, visited a physician within a month before their deaths (Conwell 2001).

White older adults are at an even higher risk for suicide than older adults in general. White men 85 years of age and older have the highest rate of suicide, at 59 suicide deaths per 100,000—five times the national rate of 10.6 (National Institute of Mental Health 2003). Further, White men over the age of 65 have a suicide rate over triple that of the general suicide rate in the United States and are three times more likely to commit suicide than women of the same age group (National Center for Health Statistics, National Health Interview Survey 2005).

The good news is that research has shown elders—even those in institutional settings—respond to active treatment (Katz 1998). Katz makes clear that "major depression is a treatable clinical disorder, not an existential state" (p. 464).

Anxiety

Even though depression is more often discussed as a mental health problem for older adults, it may not be the most common. According to the 1999 Surgeon General's Report on Mental Health, anxiety disorders are the most common form of mental illness among adults 55 years of age and older. Wykle and Musil (1993) suggest that "[A]cross the life span, only substance use disorders in males aged 18–44, affective disorders in women 25–65, and severe cognitive impairment in those 75 years of age and older are more prevalent than anxiety disorders" (p. 7). Among elders, individuals are more than twice as likely to suffer from anxiety as depression. Anxiety disorders such as panic attacks, obsessive-compulsive disorder, and phobias are important but understudied among older adults (Surgeon General's Report on Mental Health 1999). According to estimates presented in this report, during any one year, about 11.4% of adults aged 55 and older have anxiety (Surgeon General's Report on Mental Health 1999). In addition, the likelihood of an older adult developing an anxiety disorder greatly increases if depression is also present. Mehta et al. (2003) found that anxiety symptoms occurred in 15% of older people without depression and 43% of those with depression. Of non-depressed older people, White older women were the most likely to have anxiety symptoms, with 20% prevalence (Mehta et al. 2003).

Some anxiety disorders, receiving little previous study in older adults, are now becoming more prevalent as the need for attention increases. Post Traumatic Stress Disorder (PTSD) is one such example. PTSD, classified by the DSM-IV as a stress disorder type of anxiety disorder, is on the rise in older White males. McFarlane and Yehuda (1996), for example, found that 19 years post combat, 15% of the veteran cohort they examined had PTSD.

The Bigger Picture

Dementia, depression, and anxiety are all significant mental health concerns for White older adults. However, of more importance, are the effects that these three mental health concerns have on older adults' overall quality of life. Certainly, some mental health concerns, such as suicide, are clearly more visible and problematic in older White adults than in non-White older adults. Although conclusions regarding differences in the incidences, etiologies, and treatments of dementia, depression, and anxiety between racial and ethnic groups remain tentative, the fact remains that older adults, in general, remain the most susceptible group facing dementia, depression, or an anxiety disorder.

Discussion

The purpose of this chapter has been the outline of mental health issues for older adults and the provision of specific information where appropriate concerning older Whites. Older adults, regardless of race or ethnicity, generally experience less mental illness as compared to younger adults. However, increasing numbers of elders now and for the future suggest the importance of greater focus on identifying mental illness among elders, insuring access for help-seeking, and developing appropriate clinical treatments. The direct health care costs as well as the indirect costs for delayed or failed treatment are estimated to be in the billions of dollars—a figure that also is estimated to increase in the future.

Although it does appear clear that older White men are significantly more likely to commit suicide than other older males, older females, and younger males, conclusive evidence of striking racial and ethnic differences in mental illness among elders remains elusive. This lack of consensus is likely, in part, due to the availability and empirical validation of culturally specific diagnostic tools. If we are to gain momentum in understanding what race/ethnicity and culture mean in the context of aging and mental health, however, a greater understanding beyond the use of these factors as proxy variables in quantitative analysis must occur. Qualitative studies that provide a more in-depth understanding of the meaning of aging and mental health in the context of race/ethnicity and culture are needed. We wish to make clear that the importance of quantitative studies is not diminished by these recommendations. We recognize that, if we are to have a thorough understanding of how race/ethnicity and culture interface with older adults and their mental health, we cannot do this without a more in-depth understanding.

In addition, our writing of this chapter increased our own awareness regarding how little we know about what it truly means to be a White older adult experiencing aging and, possibly, mental illness. Few studies have focused on the meaning of being a member of specific racial/ethnic and cultural groups. We conclude that little is known about what it means to be "White"—the dominant political race and cultural presence—in the context of aging and mental health. Roedinger (2006) suggests that we are just beginning to develop critical studies of "whiteness." Studies are needed that move beyond proxy explanations; studies that strive to understand how being a member of diverse racial and ethnic groups affects an older adult's interpretation of mental illness, willingness to access service, treatment by professionals and others, and mental health outcomes.

Additional studies also are needed that clearly integrate mental and physical health. Bartels (2004) emphasizes this in his examination of severe mental illness (SMI) and medical comorbidity. He concludes that "[M]edical illness in older adults with SMI is associated with early mortality, disability, reduced functioning, and greater rates of nursing home placement and high-cost emergency services" (p. S255). This recommendation suggests that the time has come to formulate models that capture the complex interface of mental and physical health in the context of race/ethnicity and aging—a daunting task but one that is needed if we are to improve individuals' quality of life—lives that are characterized by such complexity.

Review of Johnson and Barer's study of very late life survivorship provides results that call our attention to the ways in which we often view aging and later life—research and practice focusing on issues and weaknesses rather than on resilience and well-being. As we have increasing numbers of adults reaching advanced age, it seems likely that early assumptions about aging might need re-examining. Studies are needed that critically examine successful aging, quality of life, and subjective well-being to disentangle adaptation and resilience. How are these concepts related to survivorship and healthy aging? What does "healthy aging" mean in the context of advanced old age? If individuals live to advanced old age, should the definitions of successful aging be modified to more clearly define the realities of life at these advanced ages?

Recent studies examining stigma indicate that much work remains if we are to reduce public discrimination and fear of individuals with mental illness (Teachman et al. 2006). A primary governmental and professional goal must be outcomes that increase public mental health literacy. Great strides have been made as increasing numbers of professionals have received training in aging and the needs of older adults. However, for many elders and their families, the primary—and often only—health care professional from whom they seek assistance will be a primary physician, not a mental health professional, let alone a professional with knowledge and experience about older adults.

In the area of clinical treatment, greater general knowledge is needed regarding the positive outcomes for treatment of mental illness for elders. Appropriately treating mental health problems in older adults accrues additional benefits to overall health by improving interest and ability to care for self and increases the likelihood that elders will adhere to care provider advice and direction, particularly regarding compliance with medications (Surgeon General's Report on Mental Health 1999).

When we examine mental illness, elders, including older Whites, remain an under-served and under-diagnosed group. As the population ages, greater numbers of aging individuals will experience mental illness. Greater attention is needed to improve diagnosis, treatment, and assistance in getting appropriate care for these individuals. No statement more clearly underscores this need than that provided in the NIH Consensus Statement regarding depression in later life:

> Many of our senior citizens will live their final years in despair and suffering without any appreciation of their affliction or the understanding and comfort of those most dear to them. Professional help is not often sought or offered, and depression is not likely to be brief. The likely consequences are loss of personal happiness and severe strain on living circumstances. Depression may trigger a shift from home to a nursing facility, or may shift the person from a warm and respected friend or loved one to an isolated individual with lost status. Untreated depression costs money because physical illness requires more medical services, living arrangements become institutional, and employment is lost. These costs should be substantially preventable with presently validated case recognition and treatment techniques (1991, p. 1023).

Acknowledgements The authors would like to acknowledge constructive comments provided by Dr. Barbara Barer, co-author of *Life Beyond 85 Years: The Aura of Survivorship.*

References

Albert, M. S., Jones, K., Savage, C. R., Berkman, L., Seeman, T., Blazer, D., & Rowe, J. W. (1995). Predictors of cognitive change in older persons: MacArthur studies of successful aging. *Psychology and Aging, 10,* 578–589.

Alzheimer's Association. (2007). http://www.alz.org/.

Anthony-Bergstone, C. R., Zarit, S. H., & Gatz, M. (1988). Symptoms of psychological distress among caregivers of dementia patients. *Psychology and Aging, 3,* 245–248.
Bachman, D. L., Wolf, P. A., Linn, R., et al. (1992). Prevalence of dementia and probable senile dementia of the Alzheimer type in the Framingham study. *Neurology, 42,* 115–119.
Bartels, S. J. (2004). Caring for the whole person: Integrated health care for older adults with severe mental illness and medical comorbidity. *Journal of the American Geriatrics Society, 52,* S249–S257.
Blazer, D. G. (2003). Depression in later life: Review and commentary. *Journal of Gerontology: Psychological Sciences & Social Sciences, 58,* 249–265.
Bruce, M. L., McAvay, G. J., Raue, P. J., Brown, E. L., Meyers, B. S., Keohane, D. J., Jagoda, D. R., & Weber, C. W. (2002). Major depression in elderly home health care patients. *American Journal of Psychiatry, 159,* 1367–1374.
Bull, C. N. (1998). Aging in rural communities. *National Forum, 78*(2), 38–41.
Burns, B., & Taub, C. (1990). Mental health services in general medical care and in nursing homes. In B. Fogel, A. Furino, & G. Gottlieb (Eds.), *Mental health policy for older Americans: Protecting minds at risk* (pp. 63–83). Washington: American Psychiatric Press.
Cole, M. G., & Dendukuri, N. (2003). Risk Factors for depression among elderly community subjects: A systemic review and meta-analysis. *American Journal of Psychiatry, 160,* 1147–1156.
Conwell, Y. (2001). Suicide in later life: A review and recommendations for prevention. *Suicide and Life Threatening Behavior, 31*(Supplement), 32–47.
Conwell, Y., & Brent, D. (1995). Suicide and aging 1: Patterns of psychiatric diagnosis. *International Psychogeriatrics, 7,* 53–72.
Day, J. (1996). Population projections of the United States by age, sex, race, and Hispanic origin: 1995 to 2050. *Current Population Report no. P25–1130,* Washington: U.S. Bureau of the Census, U.S. Government Printing Office.
Delpa, M. F. I. A., Graff, R. de, Weeghel, J. van, & Heeren, T. J. (2005). The role of stigma in the quality of life of older adults with severe illness. *International Journal of Geriatric Psychiatry, 20,* 146–153.
Finch, C. E., & Tanzi, R. E. (1997). Genetics of aging. *Science, 278*(5337), 407–411.
Folstein, M. F., Bassett, S. S., Anthony, J. C., et al. (1991). Dementia: A case ascertainment in a community survey. *Journal of Gerontology, 46,* M132–M138.
Frasure-Smith, N., & Lespérance, F. (1995). Depression and coronary heart disease: Complex synergism of mind, body, and environment. *Current Directions in Psychological Science, 14,* 39–43.
Fratiglioni, L., Grut, M., Forsell, Y., et al. (1991). Prevalence of Alzheimer's disease and other dementias in an elderly urban population: Relationship with age, sex, and education. *Neurology, 41,* 1886–1892.
Garske, G. G., Williams, B. T., & Schiro-Geist, C. (1999). The financial costs of severe mental illness. *Journal of Rehabilitation, 65*(4), 39–44.
Gary, F. A. (2005). Stigma: Barrier to mental health care among ethnic minorities. *Issues in Mental Health Nursing, 26,* 979–999.
Gatz, M., & Smyer, M. A. (1992). The mental health system and older adults in the 1990s. *American Psychologist, 47*(6), 741–751.
Gilmer, T., Ojeda, V. D., Folsom, D., et al. (2006). Costs of community-based public mental health services for older adults: Variations related to age and diagnosis. *International Journal of Geriatric Psychiatry, 21,* 1121–1126.
Gurland, B. J., Wilder, D. E., Cross, P., et al. (1995). Relative rates of dementia by multiple case definitions, over two prevalence periods, in three cultural groups. *American Journal of Geriatric Psychiatry, 3,* 6–20.
Gurland, B. J., Wilder, D. E., Lantigua, R., et al. (1999). Rates of dementia in three ethnoracial groups. *International Journal of Geriatric Psychiatry, 14,* 481–493.
Haley, W. E., Levine, E., Brown, L., & Bartolucci, A. (1987). Stress, appraisal, coping, and social supports as mediators of adaptational outcomes among dementia caregivers. *Psychology and Aging, 2,* 323–330.

Hays, J., Saunders, W., Flint, E., & Blazer, D. (1997). Social support and depression as risk factors for loss of physical function in late life. *Aging and Mental Health, 1,* 209–220.

Hybels, C. F., & Blazer, D. G.,(2003). Epidemiology of late-life mental disorders. *Clinics in Geriatric Medicine, 19,* 663–696.

Jeste, D. V., Alexopoulos, G. S., Bartels, S. J., et al. (1999). Consensus statement on the upcoming crisis in geriatric mental health: Research agenda for the next two decades. *Archives of General Psychiatry, 56,* 848–863.

Johnson, C. L., & Barer, B. M. (1997). *Life beyond 85 years: The aura of survivorship.* New York: Springer.

Katz, I. R. (1998). Depression as a pivotal component in secondary aging. In. J. Lomranz (Ed.), *Handbook of aging and mental health: An integrative approach* (pp. 463–482). New York: Plenum.

Kessler, R. C., Berglund, P., Demler, O., Jen, R., Koretz, D., Merikangas, K. R., et al. (2003). The epidemiology of major depressive disorder results from the national comorbidity survey replication (NCS-R). *Journal of the American Medical Association, 289,* 3095–3105.

Koenig, H., & Blazer, D. (1992). Mood disorders and suicide. In J. E. Birren, R. B. Sloan, & G. Cohen (Eds.), *Handbook of mental health and aging* (pp. 379–407). San Diego: Academic.

Lopez, S. R. (2003). Reflections on the Surgeon General's Report on mental health, culture, race, and ethnicity. *Culture, Medicine, and Psychiatry, 27,* 419–434.

Lyness, J. M., Cox, C., Curry, J., et al. (1995). Older age and under-reporting of depressive symptoms. *Journal of the American Geriatrics Society, 43,* 216–221.

McFarlane, A. C., & Yehuda R. (1996). Resilience, vulnerability, and the course of posttraumatic reactions. In B. A. Van der Kalk, A. C. McFarlane, & L. Weisaeth (Eds.), *Traumatic stress: The effects of overwhelming experience on mind, body and society* (pp. 155–181). New York: The Guilford.

Meador, K. G., & Blazer, D. G. (1998). The variability of depression in old age: Narrative as an integrative construct. In J. Lomranz (Ed.), *Handbook of aging and mental health: An integrative approach* (pp. 483–495). New York: Plenum.

Mehta, K. M., Simonsick, E. M., Penninx, B. W. J. H., et al. (2003). Prevalence and correlates of anxiety symptoms in well-functioning older adults: Findings from the health and aging and body composition study. *Journal of the American Geriatrics Society, 51,* 499–504.

Miles, T. P., Froehlich, T. E., Bogardus, S. T., & Inouye, S. K. (2001). Dementia and race: Are there differences between African Americans and Caucasians? *Journal of the American Geriatrics Society, 49*(4), 477–484.

National Center for Health Statistics, National Health Interview Survey. (2003). *Health, United States, 2002, Special excerpt: Trend tables on 65 and older population.* Centers for Disease Control and Prevention/National Center for Health Statistics, Department of Health and Human Services Publication No. 03-1030.

National Institutes of Health. (1991). Diagnosis and treatment of depression in late life. (Reprinted from NIH Consensus Development Conference Consensus Statement, November 4–6, 1991. Washington: NIH, Department of Health and Human Services.

National Institutes of Health. (2006). Dramatic changes in U.S. aging highlighted in new census: Impact of baby boomers anticipated. Washington: NIH, Department of Health and Human Services.

National Institute of Mental Health. (2003). Older adults: Depression and suicide facts. NIH Publication No. 03-4593. Washington: NIH, Department of Health and Human Services.

National Institute of Mental Health (NIMH). (2007). Older adults and mental health. http://www.nimh.nih.gov/health/topics/older-adults-and-mental-health/index.shtml.

National Mental Health Association. (2003). Depression and older Americans. http://secured.nmha.org/ccd/support/factsheet.older.cfm.

Penninx, B. W. J. H., Guralnik, J. M., Pahor, M., et al. (1998). Chronically depressed mood and cancer risk in older persons. *Journal of the National Cancer Institute, 90*(24), 1888–1893.

Rabins, P. (1992). Prevention of mental disorder in the elderly: Current perspectives and future prospects. *Journal of the American Geriatrics Society, 40,* 727–733.

Regier, D., Boyd, J., Burke, J. D., et al. (1988). One-month prevalence of mental disorders in the United States. *Archives of General Psychiatry, 45,* 977–986.
Roedinger, D. R. (2006). Whiteness and it complications. *Chronicle of Higher Education, 52*(45), B6–B8.
Rovner, B. W. (1993). Depression and increased risk of mortality in the nursing home patient. *American Journal of Medicine, 94*(5A), 195–225.
Rowe, J. W., & Kahn, R. L. (1998). *Successful aging.* New York: Pantheon Books.
Sachs-Ericsson, N., Plant, E. A., & Blazer, D. G. (2005). Racial differences in the frequency of depressive symptoms among community dwelling elders: The role of socioeconomic factors. *Aging and Mental Health, 9,* 201–209.
Sartoruis, N. (2003). Introduction: Stigma and discrimination against older people with mental disorders. *International Journal of Geriatric Psychiatry, 18,* 669.
Somervell, P. D., Leaf, P. J., Weissman, M. M., Blazer, D. G., & Bruce, M. L. (1989). The prevalence of major depression in Black and White adults in five United States communities. *American Journal of Epidemiology, 130,* 725–735.
Spicer, R. S., & Miller, T. R. (2000). Suicide acts in 8 states: Incidence and case fatality rates by demographics and method. *American Journal of Public Health, 90,* 1885–1891.
Surgeon General's Report on Mental Health (1999). *Mental health: A report of the Surgeon General.* Washington: U.S. Government.
Teachman, B. A., Wilson, J. G., & Komarovskaya, I. (2006). Implicit and explicit stigma of mental illness in diagnosed and healthy samples. *Journal of Social and Clinical Psychology, 25,* 75–95.
U.S. Census Bureau. (2004). We the people: Aging in the United States. www.Census.gov.
U.S. Census Bureau. (2005a). Population 65 years and over in the United States. 2005 American community survey (No. S0103). www.Census.gov.
U.S. Census Bureau. (2005b). Current population reports, P23–309. 65+ in the United States. www.Census.gov.
Weintraub, D., Raskin, A. Ruskin, P. E., et al. (2000). Racial differences in the prevalence of dementia among patients admitted to nursing homes. *Psychiartric Services, 51,* 1259–1264.
Weissman, M. M., Bruce, M. L., Leaf, P. J., Florio, L. P., & Holzer, C. (1991). Affective disorders. In L. Robins & D. Reiger (Eds.), *Psychiatric disorders in America* (pp. 53–80). New York: Free Press.
World Health Organization (WHO). (2007). Depression. http://www.who.int/mental_health/management/depression/definition/en/.
Wykle, M. L., & Musil, C. M. (1993). Mental health of older persons: Social and cultural factors. *Generations, 17,* 7–12.
Wykle, M. L., Segal, M., & Nagley, S. (1992). Mental health and aging: Hospital care—A nursing perspective. In J. E. Birren, R. B. Sloan, & G. Cohen (Eds.), *Handbook of mental health and aging* (pp. 815–831). San Diego: Academic.
Zarit, S. H. (1998). Very late life: The final frontier. *Aging & Mental Health, 2,* 85–86.
Zhang, M. Y., Katzman, R., Salmon, D., et al. (1990). The prevalence of dementia and Alzheimer's disease in Shanghai, China: Impact of age, gender and education. *Annals of Neurology, 27,* 428–437.

Chapter 15
US Latino Youth

Nancy A. Gonzales, Miguelina Germán and Fairlee C. Fabrett

The Latino population accounted for over 50% of the US population growth between 2000 and 2005 (Pew Hispanic Center 2006) and is expected to continue to increase, from 14.5% currently to more than 25% of the total US population by 2050 (U.S. Census Bureau 2003). A deeper examination of these numbers reveals that a quarter of this Latino population is young, with 11.3 million children and adolescents. These Latino youth are exposed to a number of challenging conditions that place them at increased risk for social, educational, and psychological difficulties. Rates of anxiety, depression, juvenile arrest, substance use, school dropout, and teenage pregnancy are higher for Latino youth when compared to the general population (Gonzales et al. 2002; Jones and Krisberg 1994; National Institute on Drug Abuse (NIDA) 1998; Roberts and Chen 1995; Woodward and Fergusson 2001). Given these demographic trends, greater understanding of risk and protective processes that contribute to these disparities is needed to inform effective intervention strategies for Latino children and adolescents.

Although Latinos are often discussed as if they are one homogenous group, in reality they are characterized by tremendous heterogeneity. Latinos include individuals who can trace their ancestry to 1 of more than 20 Spanish-speaking countries, each possessing a unique culture that has grown out of its own particular social, political, and economic history. Mexico is the country of origin from which the overwhelming majority of US Latinos trace their ancestry followed by Puerto Rico, Cuba, El Salvador, and the Dominican Republic (see Table 15.1). Latinos of various national origins typically have considerable differences in the timing, reasons, and conditions of immigration to the United States, the geographic locations and characteristics of the US communities in which they have settled, demographic factors (e.g., education level, family structure, fertility), and the cultural practices they maintain as a group, as well as their rate of integration with the mainstream US population. Although the bulk of prior research has glossed over such differences and examined Latinos as one monolithic group, some studies that do compare across

N. A. Gonzales (✉)
Department of Psychology, Arizona State University, Box 871104, Tempe, AZ 85287-1104, USA
e-mail: nancy.gonzales@asu.edu

E. C. Chang, C. A. Downey (eds.), *Handbook of Race and Development in Mental Health*,
DOI 10.1007/978-1-4614-0424-8_15,

Table 15.1 Detailed Latino Origin, 2005. (Source: Pew Hispanic Center, September 2006)

	Number	Percent of Latinos
Mexican	26,784,268	63.9
Puerto Rican	3,794,776	9.1
Cuban	1,462,593	3.5
Dominican	1,135,756	2.7
Costa Rican	111,978	0.3
Guatemalan	780,191	1.9
Honduran	466,843	1.1
Nicaraguan	275,126	0.7
Panamanian	141,286	0.3
Salvadoran	1,240,031	3.0
Other Central American	99,422	0.2
Argentinean	189,303	0.5
Bolivian	68,649	0.2
Chilean	105,141	0.3
Colombian	723,596	1.7
Ecuadorian	432,068	1.0
Peruvian	415,352	1.0
Uruguayan	51,646	0.1
Venezuelan	162,762	0.4
Other South American	89,443	0.2
Spaniard	362,424	0.9
All Other Latinos	3,033,648	7.2

Latino subgroups have reported large differences in the prevalence of mental health disorders and other critical outcomes, such as high school completion, substance use, and teenage pregnancy (Alegriaet al. 2006; Delva et al. 2005; U.S. Department of Education 2000; Guilamo-Ramoset al. 2005; Roberts et al. 1997).

Variability across Latino subgroups is not solely explained by country of origin, but is also linked to individuals' birthplace. For example, fertility rates indicate that Latinas born in the United States and who had a birth in the past year are more likely to be unmarried (46.9%) compared to their foreign-born counterparts (31.8%; Pew Hispanic Center 2006). Foreign-born Latino youth also are more likely to live in two-parent homes with more family members, and parents in these families are more likely to be employed, albeit in lower paying jobs, than US-born Latinos (Hernandez et al. 2007). Epidemiological studies also find differences between US- and foreign-born Latino youth in prevalence for mental health and social problems, but these data are inconsistent. Foreign nativity has often been reported as protective against the development of substance use and externalizing problems, a phenomenon which some scholars have dubbed the "immigrant paradox" given the ostensible disadvantages to being foreign born (see Gonzales et al. 2002 for a review). However, other studies find that foreign-born youth have higher rates of behavioral problems and psychiatric illness (Brindis et al. 1995; Weiss et al. 1998).

The tremendous heterogeneity across and within the various Latino populations can create very different challenges in the lives of Latino youth, making it difficult

Table 15.2 Summative table

Cultural-ecological challenges	Cultural strengths
Family and community poverty	Traditional Familism Values
Immigration and acculturation	Ethnic identity
Discrimination and minority status	Bicultural competence

to draw overarching conclusions about which set of circumstances will be most explanatory for any single subgroup. And yet, despite the obvious limitations of ethnic glossing, there are some unique challenges and resources that can potentially promote resilient outcomes across all groups that share common Latino cultural traits. These common risk and protective processes are the focus of the current chapter. Specifically, this chapter presents three conditions (see Table 15.2) that threaten successful adaptation for many Latino youth: poverty and high-risk neighborhood environments, challenges associated with immigration and acculturation, and ethnic discrimination and stereotyping. Following our discussion of these risks and evidence for their role in the psychological adaptation of Latino youth, we discuss how three culturally linked protective resources—traditional familism values, ethnic identity, and bicultural competence—can potentially facilitate positive adaptation and resilient outcomes for Latino youth. Finally, we discuss how our current understanding of these risk and protective processes can be used to inform services, programs, and policies for this population.

Common Challenges for US Latino Youth

Consistent with the goals of this volume, we identified three broad challenges or "unique ecological circumstances" (Garcia-Coll et al. 1996) that research suggests are important for understanding the development and psychological well-being of Latino youth. Our thinking about these issues was guided by a cultural-ecological framework which recognizes the multiple contextual and cultural influences that overlap and interact to shape developmental processes and person–environment transactions over time (Bronfenbrenner 1979; Gonzales and Kim 1997; Szapocznik and Coatsworth 1999). In this framework, developing youth are viewed as influenced by and needing to adapt to multiple social contexts simultaneously, including their families, peers, neighborhoods, and schools. This framework also recognizes the pervasive role of ethnicity and cultural factors, such as immigration and acculturation, in shaping cultural ecologies and adaptive choices. Consistent with this perspective, we identified ecological circumstances that have broad effects on Latino youth because they shape daily experiences, interactions, and psychological outcomes within and across the multiple contexts of their lives. Though these risk conditions are described separately below for clarity, they are interrelated and typically co-occur. Similarly, while these conditions are salient to varying degrees for all Latino subgroups in the United States, and for other ethnic groups as well, there is tremendous diversity of experience within and across groups.

Family and Community Poverty

When compared to the general population, US Latinos have lower educational attainment and hold lower paying, less stable jobs that make it difficult to consistently provide for the needs of their families. Among US-born Latinos under 18 years of age, approximately 36.5% of Puerto Rican families live below the poverty level, followed by 30.1% of Mexican Americans, 26.7% of Central and South Americans, and 18.1% of Cuban Americans. This is compared to only 8.1% of Whites. Consequently, a large proportion of Latino youth, across the different subgroups, encounter a host of barriers and threats to optimal development associated with low socioeconomic status and conditions of poverty. The evidence is overwhelming that children living in poverty are at greatly increased risk for a broad range of emotional, behavioral, and cognitive problems (e.g., Conger and Conger 2002; Duncan and Brooks-Gunn 1997; Luthar et al. 1997; McLoyd 1998). For example, studies consistently find a strong link between family poverty and children's lower cognitive development, special education placement, grade retention, and school dropout (Brooks-Gunn and Duncan 1997; Jimerson et al. 2000). Moreover, across studies, low socioeconomic status is associated with nearly every diagnosed mental disorder (Costello and Angold 1995).

Socioeconomic disadvantage produces a cascade of daily life stressors and a deficit in resources for coping with such conditions. This pattern of increased stress and depleted resources cuts across the contexts of children's lives (Tolan et al. 1997), beginning with the family environment. Research shows when Latino parents are unable to find or maintain stable jobs and a living wage, stress-related disruptions in the personal functioning and relationships of these caregivers have an adverse influence on effective parenting practices and parents' relationships with their children (Barrera et al. 2002; Dumka et al. 1997; Parke et al. 2004). Disrupted parenting includes harsh and inconsistent disciplinary practices, inadequate monitoring of child activities, low involvement in the life of the child, and reduced nurturance or affection toward the child (Dumka et al. 1997; Gonzales et al. 2006; Gorman-Smith and Tolan 1998; Parke et al. 2004). These disrupted parenting practices have all been shown to mediate the relation between economic hardship and Latino youth behavior problems (Gorman-Smith and Tolan 1998; Lindahl and Malik 1999; Parke et al. 2004; Smith and Krohn 1995).

In addition, a majority of Latino families settle in low-income neighborhoods characterized by poverty, transience, high crime rates, and schools with fewer resources. Due to high levels of what Sampson calls social disorganization, economically disadvantaged urban neighborhoods also have low levels of community resources, such as an absence of youth serving organizations that can facilitate positive development, and a lack of community level monitoring of youth activity (Sampson et al. 1997). As a result, unsupervised peer groups and deviant peer activity emerge as serious threats in these neighborhoods (Tolan et al. 1997). Vigil (1999) estimates 4 to 15% (almost as many as 1 in 6) of the urban Latino population are gang members or otherwise gang involved. Association with deviant peers increases risk for the onset of delinquency school dropout, depression, and making "precocious transitions" (e.g., becoming pregnant, and premature independence from parents) in mid-to-late adolescence (Caetano et al. 2005; Krohn et al. 1997; Moffitt and Caspi 2001; Quinton et al. 1993; Stouthamer-Loeber et al. 2002; Vitaro et al. 1997).

The multiple stressors associated with family and community disadvantage also have direct effects on children's coping abilities. Research has shown that active or engaged coping strategies predict better mental health outcomes for low-income youths and provide some protection against the negative effects of stress in an inner city context (Gonzales et al. 2001; Tolan et al. 1997). However, this research also has shown the protective effects of active coping diminish when youth experience extremely high rates of uncontrollable, stressful life events. Moreover, inner city youth are more likely to use avoidant coping when they have been exposed to a lifetime of chronic stressful circumstances over which they have no control, leading to helplessness and increased risk for depression (Deardorff et al. 2003). Similar patterns may be seen for adolescents who reside in rural, low-income communities where resources are limited or when Latino adolescents experience discrimination. In these instances, the choice to avoid the stressor may be more beneficial than to confront it. Despite evidence that avoidant coping may be beneficial in some circumstances, over reliance on avoidance as a general coping style is problematic because it undermines adolescents' sense of mastery, future-orientation, and goal-directed pursuits, all of which are important for optimal youth adjustment.

An additional complicating factor of disadvantaged communities is that adolescents must satisfy basic needs for safety and social connection, and these needs are often more salient than their pursuits of positive future outcomes. For example, when faced with threats of victimization or other pressures from deviant peers, some youths will choose to engage in violence or other deviant acts in order to secure their safety, social status, and a sense of belonging, despite the fact that this choice may lead to serious consequences such as school expulsion or juvenile arrest (Tolan et al. 1997).

Immigration and Cultural Adaptation

Foreign-born youth and children of immigrants typically navigate multiple sets of expectations, values, and norms which can vary substantially across the family, school, and neighborhood contexts in the United States. The learning curve in this adaptation process may be more steep for those youth that have recently immigrated, but also occurs for the children living in Latino families who have been in the United States for many generations. Aspects of the country of origin culture are retained through a process known as *enculturation*, while the process of learning English and US values and norms are typically called *acculturation* (Berry 2003). A growing number of theorists suggest that these acculturative and enculturative processes are separable, each representing a distinct axis of cultural change (Berry 2003; Cuellar et al. 1995; Gonzales et al. 2002; Knight et al. 2007; Zane and Mak 2003), and that individuals can achieve simultaneously high, simultaneously low, or quite different levels of adaptation to mainstream and ethnic cultures (Knight et al. 2007).

The dual processes of acculturation and enculturation can lead to increased opportunities for the development of competence, or increased risk and distress, depending on a number of factors. These variables include the social contexts in which these processes unfold, the degree to which the youth are exposed to culturally linked stressors within these contexts, and the developmental stage of the child. For example, the process of learning English is more difficult for older versus younger immigrant youth, particularly when they attend schools that provide inadequate learning environments for students with limited English proficiency. Language barriers and feelings of marginalization are typically even more pronounced for immigrant parents, particularly those that have limited opportunities to interact within mainstream settings (Garrison et al. 1999). These parents will experience the greatest difficulty linking to their children's schools or accessing other needed services for family members, and their children may be placed in the position of being responsible for negotiating important family matters on their behalf. This phenomenon, known as "cultural brokering" can disrupt normative parent–child roles, place a substantial burden on youth, and negatively impact their ability to invest in their own educational and developmental needs (Cooper et al. 1999). Teachers also may fail to initiate communication with parents because they cannot speak Spanish, do not understand expectations of Latino parents, and view parents as part of the problem in educating children, rather than as a resource (Delgado-Gaitan 1992). Language difficulties, lack of cultural capital relevant to school success, and the obligation to assist the family during times of emotional and financial stress may all help to explain why immigrant youth fail to achieve at the level of their US-born peers despite initially higher educational aspirations (Fuligni and Pederson 2002).

When the dual processes of acculturation and enculturation produce conflicts in cultural values across contexts (e.g., family vs. school; family vs. peer), these cultural clashes may increase risk for psychological distress within Latino youth and between individuals within a family. For example, when family members follow divergent paths in the processes of enculturation and acculturation (e.g., children acculturating faster than parents) some youths may reject their culture of origin, giving rise to parent–child conflict, and adolescents' loss of emotional and social support from their family (Szapocznik et al. 1990). Marital conflicts may be exacerbated as well, owing to shifting cultural values within and between parents (Gonzales et al. 2006; Parke et al. 2004). The combination of intergenerational and intercultural conflicts may exacerbate normative family struggles and disrupt the traditional structure of the family. These processes may contribute to problem behavior, substance use, and suicide attempts among more acculturated youth (Szapocznik and Coatsworth 1999; Zayas 1987).

Research on cultural adaptation has yielded inconsistent results in the prediction of adolescent psychological well-being and mental health. Although the bulk of emerging evidence seems to suggest that more acculturated adolescents display higher rates of problem behaviors, including early age substance use and sexual activity (Gonzales et al. 2002), some studies have failed to find this pattern (Palleja 1987). Evidence also suggests that depression and anxiety may be higher for these youth, but other studies suggest the opposite, with higher levels of acculturation being associated with higher rates of suicide attempts and psychiatric illness (Weiss et al. 1998). An important conclusion to be drawn from this mixed set of findings is that enculturation/acculturation processes produce tremendous variability in outcomes with large group, generational, individual, and contextual differences. For example, although there is some evidence that the initial period following immigration is most difficult, this is likely to depend on the conditions surrounding migration. In one of the few studies that compared two Latino subgroups, Weiss et al. (1998) reported significantly higher rates of internalizing symptoms for youth from Central American compared to those of Mexican ancestry. These differences were attributed to the nature of the immigration process, which was largely involuntary for the Central Americans compared to the Mexican Americans. The majority of Central Americans in their study were refugees or from families who were displaced or forced to flee their countries because of political persecution. Refugees are a subset of immigrants whose typical experiences involve physical and/or psychological trauma, a factor contributing to their high rate of mental health problems for them and their children. Prior research has not adequately accounted for these historical or contextual differences or the way in which one's cultural orientation (enculturation and acculturation) may interact with these broader contextual factors to predict differing outcomes (Birman et al. 2002).

Minority Status and Discrimination

Ethnic or racial discrimination, defined as unfair, differential treatment on the basis of race or ethnicity, is a common experience for members of ethnic minority groups in the United States (Garcia-Coll et al. 1996; Greene et al. 2006). Surveys of minority youth, including Latinos, reveal that 57% report being called a racially insulting name, 31% reported having been threatened by peers because of their race or ethnicity, and 42% believed they had been given a lower grade in school because of their race or ethnicity (Fisher et al. 2000). Latino youth describe discrimination based on English fluency, immigration concerns, negative stereotypes, poverty, and skin color (Edwards and Romero 2008). Stereotypes of Latinos often include expectations of academic incompetence and, for Latino boys, assumptions about the propensity for violence and delinquency (Gibbs 1998; Noguera 2003) that likely lead to more explicit forms of discrimination (e.g., being stopped by policemen, being followed in a store). There is an accumulating literature that suggests Latino youth of Mexican origin also face substantial marginalization in schools—especially related to relationships with teachers—that may contribute to poor academic achievement, persistence, and performance (Valenzuela 1999).

Perceptions of discrimination tend to increase with age (Fisher et al. 2000; Greene et al. 2006; Romero and Roberts 1998; Szalacha et al. 2003) and this is likely due to contextual, cognitive, and identity shifts that occur with normal development. For example, as adolescents' social worlds expand, they have more contact with mainstream culture and more opportunities to experience discrimination, particularly as they attempt to access opportunities in mainstream institutions. As they begin to explore their ethnic identities, they also become increasingly sensitive and attuned to how others treat them, particularly those who are not part of their social groups, and they are increasingly able to discern and reflect upon how their ethnic group is evaluated by the larger society and to anticipate future discrimination (Phinney and Chavira 1992).

Although the prevalence of ethnic and racial discrimination has been well documented in the lives of ethnic minority youth, it is only recently that researchers have begun to explore the implications of discriminatory experiences for development (Garcia-Coll et al. 1996). Research on the effects of racial and ethnic discrimination has shown that it is associated with depression, anxiety, anger, lowered self-esteem, and risky health behaviors for minority youth (Chavez et al. 1997; Greene et al. 2006; Romero et al. 2007; Szalacha et al. 2003; Vega 1995; Wong et al. 2003), and a host of negative physical and mental health outcomes for adults (Kessler et al. 1999). These findings are consistent with social psychological research, which shows that experiences in which one's ethnic group is devalued can lead to negative self-perceptions and increased susceptibility to mental and physical illness (Tajfel 1981). For example, Steele et al. (1995) have demonstrated that when an individual's ethnic identity is attached to a negative stereotype in a testing environment, students underperform academically and suffer from high blood pressure and increased anxiety levels (Blascovich et al. 2001). Perceptions of racial and ethnic discrimination also may reduce adolescents' self-efficacy and foster feelings of helplessness, discouragement, and frustration. These feelings may contribute to the development of depressive symptoms and declines in academic functioning over time (Simons et al. 2002).

However, as with all the contextual challenges discussed in this chapter, there is variability across and within groups, as well as individual variability in adolescents' exposure and vulnerability to the negative effects of discrimination. For example, studies suggest that US-born and more acculturated Latino adolescents are more sensitized to the presence and more vulnerable to the effects of ethnic discrimination against their group (Umaña-Taylor and Updegraff 2007; Vega 1995). Vega and colleagues found that adolescents' perceptions of discrimination and of the United States as a closed society showed a significant relation with behavior problems for US-born but not for foreign-born Latinos. Similarly, Umaña-Taylor and Updegraff (2007) found that Latino youth were more vulnerable to low self-esteem and depressive symptoms as a result of discrimination if they had a strong orientation to the mainstream culture, but not if they had a low mainstream orientation. It is possible that US-born and highly acculturated Latinos are more susceptible to negative ethnic prejudices and stereotypes when they are more invested in the majority culture, and spend significant amounts of time in ethnically heterogeneous or predominantly mainstream social contexts.

The experience and impact of discrimination also varies as a function of an individual's social position. Research has indicated that for those students who are part of an ethnic group who are in the majority in the school or are "high in the [school's] social hierarchy" (Way et al. 2005), the impact of discrimination is less severe compared with students in the numeric minority or less popular. Illustratively, Greene et al. (2006) reported higher rates of perceived peer discrimination by Dominican than Puerto Rican high school students and attributed this difference to the numerical and social dominance of the Puerto Rican students in those schools. In general, there is consensus among scholars that discrimination cannot be examined in isolation as a risk factor because its effects will depend on social status variables, including low socioeconomic status, and whether discrimination occurs in the context of other ecological conditions that challenge the coping capacities of Latino youth.

Cultural Resources That Promote Positive Adaptation

As the foregoing discussion illustrates, Latino youth encounter unique challenges that arise from cultural-ecological circumstances associated with their ethnic group membership and other context defining factors, such as their family's socioeconomic status, history of immigration, integration with mainstream and ethnic communities, and the location of their neighborhoods and schools. These converging cultural-ecological factors expose Latino youth to chronic adversities and cumulative stressors that overwhelm their coping abilities and contribute to the troubling health, educational, and occupational disparities that currently exist. And yet, even when faced with these risks, substantial numbers of both US- and native-born Latino youth adapt quite successfully, succeed in school, and suffer no negative mental health outcomes. We propose that for these children and adolescents, specific cultural-ecological factors combine to offer increased opportunities for development of competencies that enable them to become productive young adults, uniquely prepared for the demands of an increasingly multicultural, global society.

In this section, we discuss three interrelated, culturally linked resources that have been supported in the literature as factors that potentially contribute to positive adaptation of Latino youth and provide some protection against the challenges previously described. Along with our discussion of these cultural protective resources, we describe how they can inform the design of interventions, programs, and policies to better promote psychological well-being and success of Latino youth in the United States.

Traditional Latino Familism Values

Familism, one of the most important culture-specific values of Latinos, describes a strong identification and attachment of individuals with their families (nuclear and extended) and strong feelings of loyalty, reciprocation, and solidarity among members of the same family (e.g., Sabogal et al. 1987). Sabogal et al. (1987) described three facets of familism values: *familial obligations*, defined as the belief that family members have a responsibility to provide economic and emotional support to kin; *perceived support and emotional closeness*, defined as the perception that family members are dependable sources of help should be united and have close relationships; and *family as referent*, the belief that the behavior of an individual is a reflection of the whole family and family members' behaviors should meet with familial expectations. These traditional Latino familism values and the resulting strength of family ties are core features of Latino culture, reflecting perhaps the most significant common thread that cuts across all Latinos subgroups.

Although Latino families become more involved with social systems outside the family as they acculturate, many families maintain their internal patterns of relationships and a strong sense of family loyalty from generation to generation (Rueschenberg and Buriel 1989; Sabogal et al. 1987). A growing body of research suggests that when traditional familism values and behaviors are maintained, they function to promote healthy family interactions and decrease susceptibility to acculturative strains and other negative influences outside the family (Germán et al. 2008; Gil et al. 1994; Szapocznik et al. 1990; Vega et al. 1993). For example, support from family and kinship networks promotes positive adaptation during important life transitions, such as pregnancy and the transition to parenthood, potentially offering some explanation for better birth outcomes consistently reported for low-income Latino women relative to other low-income groups (De la Rosa 2002; Heilemann et al. 2004; Kroelinger and Oths 2000; Laganá 2003; Martinez-Schallmoser et al. 2003; Page 2004; Pearce 1998). The extended family's role in child-rearing following childbirth, and throughout childhood, also may protect children and families from economic hardship (Garcia-Coll et al. 1996). Families who hold these values will be better prepared to deal with financial shortages and will be more likely than others to form alliances with family members and friends to solve economic problems.

In addition to maintaining family unity, traditional family values foster a sense of purpose and motivation for family members to make choices that are centered on the good of the family (Leyendecker and Lamb 1999; Vega 1995), and to prioritize their duty to protect and support the family above individual needs and goals. Perhaps reflecting these cultural values, demographers have noted that Latino families, particularly immigrants, do not fit the profile of low work force participation and high rates of single-parenthood that are associated with other families in poverty (Guendelman and Abrams 1995). A strong family orientation also may motivate parents to meet the difficult demands of the parenting role, despite their economic and personal struggles (Fridrich and Flannery 1995). For example, White et al.

(2009) found that neighborhood disadvantage was associated with disruptions in parenting for Mexican American mothers, but these effects were not significant for those mothers in their sample that endorsed higher levels of familism beliefs (White et al. 2009). Studies also have shown that a sense of family obligation is associated with academic motivation among Latino youth, particularly a belief in the importance and usefulness of education (Fuligni et al. 1999). This "extra" academic motivation may derive from a desire to support and assist the family.

Finally, the value of family as referent can play an important role in fostering the conventional ties and behaviors of Latino youth, through the preservation of strong family bonds and parental authority described above, and through the desire to protect one's family honor. Family honor can inhibit problem behavior because a person will be mindful of the possibility that he or she may bring *verguenza* (shame) to the family through socially disapproved behavior (Zayas and Bryant 1984). These concerns may motivate youth to resist pressures to conform with delinquent peers out of a fear of disappointing significant others (Germán et al. 2008). There is a growing body of empirical research that has supported familism as an important protective factor for Latino youth against a variety of negative outcomes, including substance use (Brook et al. 1998), poor academic performance (Valenzuela and Dornbusch 1994), externalizing behaviors (Gonzales et al. 2008), and the development of deviant attitudes (Gil et al. 2000).

Ethnic Identity

Traditional familism values are but one aspect of enculturation that may be protective for Latino youth. Several authors assert that a strong ethnic identity, another important aspect of enculturation, operates as a protective resource for Latino youth, as well as for other ethnic minority groups (Parra and Guarnaccia 1998; Phinney and Chavira 1992). Ethnic identity refers to the psychological process by which individuals explore their ethnic background, resolve the meaning of their ethnicity, and come to feel positively about their ethnic background (Umaña-Taylor et al. 2004). Phinney (1990) asserts that strong ethnic identity is a key factor in the way immigrants meet the challenges in their new country (Phinney 1990).

Ethnic minority individuals who feel pride in their heritage and have a strong cultural identification have greater self-esteem (Phinney and Chavira 1992) and may be more resilient in coping with stress (Umaña-Taylor et al. 2004). Brook et al. (1998) found ethnic identity buffered the effects of risk factors for substance use, and also increased the potency of other protective factors (Brook et al. 1998). A growing body of evidence also indicates that a strong ethnic identity is a resource for minority youth to counteract the negative effects of discrimination. Strong positive feelings about one's ethnicity can provide a means for Latinos and other minority individuals to focus on the positive aspects of their cultural identity and disavow ethnic and race-based stereotypes of their group. Studies that directly test the protective effects of ethnic identity find a significantly weaker association between perceived discrimination and depression among individuals who report high levels of ethnic identity compared to their counterparts who report lower levels of ethnic identity (Mossakowski 2003; Noh et al. 1999; Romero and Roberts 2003; Sellers et al. 2003; Sellers and Shelton 2003; Wong et al. 2003). This research also suggests, however, that the process of ethnic identity exploration may heighten sensitivity to discrimination by emphasizing one's difference from the dominant culture and escalating the stress of minority status (Greene et al. 2006; Phinney 1990).

Bicultural Competence

Although evidence suggests that a strong orientation to one's ethnic culture may provide important resources for Latino youth in the United States, how they adapt to the overall demands of their bicultural world, including their integration with the mainstream culture, is also important. Although the acculturation process has the potential to increase exposure to a variety of risk processes described above, failure to integrate within the dominant US culture also limits youth adaptation because it can prevent youth from taking advantage of important opportunities and lead to isolation. In fact, Vega found that US-born Latino adolescents with low acculturation levels experienced the highest rate of substance-use initiation and continued experimentation of all the Latino youth in their study. Vega attributes these findings to the "double-jeapordy" situation in which US-born Latino adolescents with low levels of acculturation find themselves. They suffer from the dual risk of language problems and limited life chances experienced by foreign-born Latino adolescents, *and* the perceived discrimination and acculturation conflicts experienced by US-born Latino adolescents.

Emerging research suggests that the most resilient youth may be those that develop strong ties and the ability to interact effectively within both ethnic and mainstream contexts (e.g., LaFromboise et al. 1993; Rogler et al. 1991; Szapocznik et al. 1980). Bicultural individuals benefit from knowledge and participation in the host culture, while retaining the positive, protective factors of their traditional culture. Thus, bicultural youth can navigate successfully multiple cultural contexts, and thus, experience less stress that could result from conflicting cultures. Bicultural individuals appear to benefit from the ability to shift their sociocognitive perceptual schemas in order to fit situational demands. This ability, called cultural frame-switching, is more highly developed in bicultural individuals than it is in their low- or high-acculturated peers, allowing them to handle a wider range of culture-laden situations (Harriatos and Benet-Martinez 2002).

Consistent with this theorizing, biculturalism has been related to a number of indicators of positive adaptation and resilience among Latino youth, including greater self-esteem, ability to socialize in diverse settings, leadership abilities, academic and peer competence, and psychological well-being (Birman et al. 2002; Coatsworth et al. 2005; Parke and Buriel 1998; Szapocznik et al. 1980). Evidence also suggests that biculturalism reduces the risk of substance abuse and problem behaviors and increases school engagement and achievement (Coatsworth et al. 2005; Goldberg and Botvin 1993; Gonzales et al. 2008; Schinkeet al. 1987). For example, although English language ability consistently predicts achievement outcomes, the best academic outcomes are observed for Mexican origin youth that are proficient in English *and* retain Spanish-speaking abilities (Feliciano 2001; Rumberger and Larson 1998). Finally, there is evidence that the whole family unit, including parents and children, benefits from biculturality. Compared to low- and high- acculturated families, bicultural families display lower levels of conflict and demonstrate more commitment and support among family members (Miranda et al. 2000).

Recommendations to Promote Latino Youth Positive Adaptation

Based on the literature we reviewed, we offer four brief recommendations to promote positive outcomes among Latino youth.

1. *Interventions and services should be designed to be compatible with the central role of the family in Latino culture.* The current literature suggests that family-centered interventions are more appealing and effective for Latino youth and families (e.g., Szapocznik et al. 1990), particularly if they are compatible with their language, goals, and core values (Bernal et al. 1995).
2. *Provide opportunities for youth and families to develop a strong ethnic identity and affirm traditional values.* In an effort to build on cultural strengths, intervention strategies have been developed to increase ethnic identity and pride in one's ethnic group. For example, Cuento Therapy (Malgady et al. 1990) used biographical stories of prominent Puerto Ricans in order to expose adolescents to role models of achievement, thereby promoting ethnic pride, a strong sense of ethnic identity, and adaptive ways of coping with poverty and discrimination.
3. *Promote bicultural competence and adaptation.* Aim to increase bicultural competence for all family members to increase coping and resilience of family system and avoid iatrogenic effects (e.g., working solely with youth to better integrate with mainstream might not be beneficial if this approach alienates parents). Family effectiveness training (FET) was designed specifically for Latin American families (primarily of Cuban origin) to restore intergenerational communication, reconstruct traditional hierarchical structures in the family, and have parents and adolescents forge bicultural identities. FET has demonstrated positive effects on family relations and reduction in adolescent antisocial behavior and substance use.
4. *Recognize the multiple contexts that place Latino youth at risk and the need to build competencies across contexts.* Intervention programs must address risk factors across multiple contexts simultaneously. Programs that seek to only change adolescents may be insufficient to effect change, if schools and family contexts are problematic. The Bridges to High School Program is an example of an inter-

vention designed to address four domains critical for Mexican American youth: parent–child relations, youth coping skills, family–school linkages, and culturally linked family interactions and traditions. Ultimately, we believe that interventions that integrate etic (universal) and emic (culture specific) perspectives in the design process have the best rates of participant engagement and attendance and the strongest chance at promoting positive youth outcomes among Latino youth (Griner and Smith 2006).

References

Alegria, M., Canino, G., Stinson, F. S., & Grant, B. F. (2006). Nativity and DSM-IV psychiatric disorders among Puerto Ricans, Cuban Americans, and non-Latino Whites in the United States: Results from the national epidemiological survey on alcohol and related conditions. *Journal of Clinical Psychiatry, 67*(1), 56–65.

Barrera, M. J., Prelow, H. M., Dumka, L. E., Gonzales, N. A., Knight, G. K., Michaels, M. L., et al. (2002). Pathways from family economic conditions to adolescents' distress: Supportive parenting, stressors outside the family, and deviant peers. *Journal of Community Psychology, 30,* 135–152.

Bernal, G., Bonilla, J., & Bellido, C. (1995). Ecological validity and cultural sensitivity for outcome research: Issues for the cultural adaptation and development of psychosocial treatments with Hispanics. *Journal of Abnormal Child Psychology, 23,* 67–83.

Berry, J. W. (2003). Origins of cross-cultural similarities and differences in human behavior: An ecocultural perspective. In Toomela, A. (Ed.), *Cultural guidance in the development of the human mind. Advances in child development within culturally structured environments.* Westport: Ablex.

Birman, D., Trickett, E. J., & Vinokurov, A. (2002). Acculturation and adaptation of Soviet Jewish refugee adolescents: Predictors of adjustment across life domains. *American Journal of Community Psychology, 30*(5), 585–607.

Blascovich, J., Spencer, S. J., Quinn, & D., Steele, C. (2001). African-Americans and high blood pressure: The role of stereotype threat. *Psychological Sciences, 12*(3), 225–229.

Bronfenbrenner, U. (1979). *The ecology of human development: Experiments by nature and design.* Cambridge: Harvard University Press.

Brindis, C., Wolfe, A., McCarter, V., Ball, S., & Starbuck-Morales, S. (1995). The associations between immigrant status and risk-behavior patterns in Latino adolescents. *Journal of Adolescent Health, 17*(2), 99–105.

Brooks-Gunn, J., & Duncan, G. J. (1997). The effects of poverty on children. *The Future of Children, 7,* 55–71.

Brook, J. S., Whiteman, M., Balka, E. B., Win, P. T., & Gursen, M. D. (1998). Drug use among Puerto Ricans: Ethnic identity as a protective factor. *Hispanic Journal of Behavioral Sciences, 20*(2), 241–254.

Caetano, R., Field, C. A., Ramisetty-Mikler, S., & McGrath, C. (2005). The 5-year course of intimate partner violence among White, Black and Hispanic couples in the United States. *Journal of Interpersonal Violence, 20*(9), 1039–1057.

Chavez, D. V., Moran, V. R., Reid, S. L., & Lopez, M. (1997). Acculturative stress in children: A modification of the SAFE scale. *Hispanic Journal of Behavioral Sciences, 19*(1), 34–44.

Coatsworth, J. D., Maldonado-Molina, M., Pantin, H., & Szapocznik, J. (2005). A person centered and ecological investigation of acculturation strategies in Hispanic immigrant youth. *Journal of Community Psychology, 33(2),* 157–174.

Conger, R. D., & Conger, K. J. (2002). Resilience in Midwestern families: Selected findings from the first decade of a prospective, longitudinal study. *Journal of Marriage and Family, 64,* 361–373.

Cooper, C. R., Denner, J., & Lopez, E. M. (1999). Cultural brokers: Helping Latino children on pathways toward success. *Future of Children, 9,* 51–57.

Costello, E. J., & Angold, A. (1995). Developmental epidemiology. In D. Cicchetti & D. Cohen (Eds.), *Developmental psychopathology, Vol 1: Theory and methods* (pp. 23–56). New York: Wiley.

Cuellar, I., Arnold B., & Maldonado, R. (1995). Acculturation rating scale for Mexican Americans—II: A revision of the original ARSMA scale. *Hispanic Journal of Behavioral Science, 17,* 275–304.

De la Rosa, M. (2002). Acculturation and Latino adolescents' substance use: A research agenda for the future. *Substance Use & Misuse, 37*(4), 429–456.

Deardorff, J., Gonzales, N. A., & Sandler, I. N. (2003). Control beliefs as a mediator of the relation between stress and depressive symptoms among inner city adolescents. *Journal of Abnormal Child Psychology, 31*(2), 205–217.

Delgado-Gaitan, C. (1992). School matters in the Mexican American home: Socializing children to education. *American Educational Research Journal, 29,* 495–513.

Delva, J., Wallace, J. M., O'Malley, P. M., Bachman, J. G., Johnston, L. D., & Schulenberg, J. E., et al. (2005). The epidemiology of alcohol, marijuana, and cocaine use among Mexican American, Puerto Rican, Cuban American, and other Latin American eighth-grade students in the United States: 1991-2002. *American Journal of Public Health, 95*(4), 696–702.

Dumka, L. E., Roosa, M. W., & Jackson, K. M. (1997). Risk, conflict, mothers' parenting, and children's adjustment in low-income, Mexican immigrant and Mexican American families. *Journal of Marriage and the Family, 59,* 309–332.

Duncan, G. J., & Brooks-Gunn, J. (1997). *Consequences of growing up poor.* New York: Russell Sage Foundation.

Edwards, L. M., & Romero, A. J. (2008). Coping with discrimination among Mexican descent adolescents. *Hispanic Journal of Behavioral Sciences, 30*(1), 24–39.

Feliciano, C. (2001). The benefits of biculturalism: Exposure to immigrant culture and dropping out of school among Asian and Latino youths. *Social Science Quarterly, 82*(4), 865–879.

Fisher, C., Wallace, S. A., & Fenton, R. E. (2000). Discrimination distress during adolescence. *Journal of Youth and Adolescence, 29*(6), 679–695.

Fuligni, A. J., & Pederson, S. (2002). Family obligation and the transition to young adulthood. *Developmental Psychology, 38*(5), 856–868.

Fuligni, A. J., Tseng, V., & Lam, M. (1999). Attitudes toward family obligations among American adolescents from Asian, Latin American, and European backgrounds. *Child Development, 70,* 1030–1044.

Garcia-Coll, C., Lamberty, G., Jenkins, R., McAdoo, H. P., Crnic, K., Wasik, B., et al.,(1996). An integrative model for the study of developmental competencies in minority children. *Child Development, 67,* 1891–1914.

Garrison, E. G., Roy, I. S., & Azar, V. (1999). Responding to the mental health needs of Latino children and families through school-based services. *Clinical Psychological Review, 19*(2), 199–219.

Germán, M., Gonzales, N. A., & Dumka, L. E. (2008, under review). Familism values as a protective factor for Mexican-origin adolescents exposed to deviant peers. Manuscript submitted for publication.

Gibbs, J. T. (1998). African American adolescents. In J. T. Gibbs & H. L. Nahme (Eds.), Children of color: Psychological interventions with culturally diverse youth (pp. 171–214). San Francisco: Jossey-Bass.

Gil, A. G., Vega, W. A., & Dimas, J. M. (1994). Acculturative stress and personal adjustment among hispanic adolescent boys. *Journal of Community Psychology, 22,* 43–54.

Gil, A. G., Wagner, E. F., & Vega, W. A. (2000). Acculturation, familism, and alcohol use among Latino adolescent males: Longitudinal relations. *Journal of Community Psychology, 28*(4), 443–458.

Goldberg, C. J., & Botvin, G. J. (1993). Assertiveness in hispanic adolescents: Relationship to alcohol use and abuse. *Psychological Reports, 73*(1), 227–238.
Gonzales, N. A., & Kim, L. (1997). Stress and coping in an ethnic minority context: Children's cultural ecologies. In S. A. Wolchik & I. N. Sandler (Eds.), *Children's coping with common stressors: Linking theory, research and interventions* (pp. 481–551). New York: Plenum.
Gonzales, N. A., Tein, J. -Y., Sandler, I.N., & Friedman, R.J. (2001). On the limits of coping: Interactions between stress and coping for inner city adolescents. *Journal of Adolescent Research, 16*, 372–395.
Gonzales, N. A., Knight, G. P., Morgan-Lopez, A., Saenz, D., & Sorolli, A. (2002). Acculturation and the mental health of Latino youths: An integration and critique of the literature. In J. Contreras, A. Neal-Barnett, & K. Kerns (Eds.) *Latino children and families in the United States: Current research and future directions* (pp. 45–74). Westport: Praeger.
Gonzales, N. A., Deardorff, J., Formoso, D., Barr, A., & Barrera, M. (2006). Family mediators of the relation between acculturation and adolescent mental health. *Family Relations, 55*, 318–330.
Gonzales, N. A., Germán, M., Kim, S. Y., George, P. A., Fabrett, F., Millsap, R., Dumka, L., et al. (2008). Mexican American adolescents' cultural orientation, externalizing behavior and academic engagement: The role of traditional cultural values. *American Journal of Community Psychology 31*, 151–164.
Gorman-Smith, D., & Tolan, P. (1998). The role of exposure to community violence and developmental problems among inner city youth. *Development and Psychopathology, 10*, 101–116.
Greene, M. L., Way, N., & Pahl, K. (2006). Trajectories of perceived adult and peer discrimination among Black, Latino and Asian American adolescents: Patterns and psychological correlates. *Developmental Psychology, 42*(2), 218–238.
Griner, D., & Smith, T. B. (2006). Culturally adapted mental health intervention: A meta-analytic review. *Psychotherapy: Theory, Research, Practice, Training, 43*(4), 531–548.
Guendelman, S., & Abrams, B. (1995). Dietary intake among Mexican American women: Generational differences and a comparison with white non-Hispanic women. *American Journal of Public Health, 85*, 20–25.
Guilamo-Ramos, V., Jaccard, J., Pena, J., & Goldberg, V. (2005). Acculturation-related variables, sexual initiation, and subsequent sexual behavior among Puerto Rican, Mexican and Cuban youth. *Health Psychology, 24*(1), 88–95.
Harriatos, J., & Benet-Martinez, V. (2002). Bicultural identities: The interface of cultural, personality, and socio-cognitive processes. *Journal of Research in Personality, 36*, 598–606.
Heilemann, M. S., Frutos, L., Lee, K. A., & Kury, F. S. (2004). Protective strength factors, resources, and risks in relation to depressive symptoms among childbearing women of Mexican descent. *Health Care for Women International, 25*, 88–106.
Hernandez, D. J., Denton, N. A., & Macartney, S. E. (2007). Family circumstances of children in immigrant families: Looking to the future of America. In J. E. Lansford, K. Deater-Deckard, & M. H. Bornstein (Eds.), *Immigrant families in contemporary soceity* (pp. 9–29). New York: Guilford.
Jimerson, S., Egeland, B., Sroufe, L. A., & Carlson, B. (2000). A prospective longitudinal study of high school dropout examining multiple predictors across development. *Journal of School Psychology, 38*(6), 525–549.
Jones, M. A., & Krisberg, B. (1994). *Images and reality: Juvenile crime, youth violence and public policy*. San Francisco: National Council on Crime and Delinquency.
Kessler, R. C., Mickelson, K. D., & Williams, D. R. (1999). The prevalence, distribution, and mental health correlates of perceived discrimination in the United States. *Journal of Health and Social Behavior, 40*(3), 208–230.
Knight, G. P., Jacobson, R. P., Gonzales, N. A., Roosa, M. W., & Saenz, D. S. (2007, in press). An evaluation of the psychological research on acculturation and enculturation processes among recently immigrating populations. In R. L. Dalla, J. DeFrain, J. Johnson, & D. Abbot (Eds.), *Strengths and challenges of new immigrant families: Implications for research, policy, education, and service*. Lanham: Lexington.

Kroelinger, C. D., & Oths, K. S. (2000). Partner support and pregnancy wantedness. *Birth, 27*(2), 112–118.
Krohn, M. D., Lizotte, A. J., & Perez, C. M. (1997). The interrelationship between substance use and precocious transitions to adults statuses. *Journal of Health and Social Behavior, 38,* 87–103.
LaFromboise, T., Coleman, H. L. K., & Gerton, J. (1993). Psychological impact on biculturalism: Evidence and Theory. *Psychological Bulletin, 114,* 395–412.
Laganá, K. (2003). Come bien, camina y no se preocupe— Eat right, walk, and do not worry: Selective biculturalism during pregnancy in a Mexican American community. *Journal of Transcultural Nursing, 14,* 117–124.
Leyendecker, B., & Lamb, M. E. (1999). Latino families. In M. E. Lamb (Ed.), *Parenting and child devlopment in "Nontraditional" families.* Mahwah: Lawrence Erlbaum Associates.
Lindahl, K. M., & Malik, N. M. (1999). Marital conflict, family processes, and boy's externalizing behavior in Hispanic American and European American families. *Journal of Clinical Child Psychology, 28,* 12–24.
Luthar, S. S., Burack, J. A., Cicchetti, D., & Weisz, J. R. (1997). *Developmental psychopathology: Perspectives on adjustment, risk and disorder*. New York: Cambridge University Press.
Malgady, R. G., Rogler, L. H., & Constantino, G. (1990). Culturally sensitive psychotherapy for Puerto Rican children and adolescents: A program of treatment outcome research. *Journal of Consulting and Clinical Psychology, 58*(6), 704–712.
Martinez-Schallmoser, L., Telleen, S., & MacMullen, N. J. (2003). The effect of social support and acculturation on postpartum depression in Mexican-American women. *Journal of Transcultural Nursing, 14,* 329–338.
McLoyd, V. C. (1998). Socioeconomic disadvantage and child development. *The American Psychologist, 52*(2), 185–204.
Miranda, A., Estrada, D., & Firpo-Jimenez, M. (2000). Differences in family cohesion, adaptability, and environment among Latino families in dissimilar stages of acculturation: *The Family Journal: Counseling and Therapy for Couples and Families, 8*(4), 341–350.
Moffitt, T. E., & Caspi, A. (2001). Childhood predictors differentiate life-course persistent and adolescence limited antisocial pathways among males and females. *Development and Psychopathology, 13,* 355–375.
Mossakowski, K. N. (2003). Coping with perceived discrimination: Does ethnic identity protect mental health? *Journal of Health and Social Behavior, 44*(3), 318–331.
National Institute on Drug Abuse (NIDA). (1998). *Drug use among racial/ethnic minorities.* U.S. Department of Health and Human Services. Bethesda: National Institute of Health.
Noguera, P. A. (2003). The trouble with Black boys: The role and influence of environmental and cultural factors on the academic performance of African American males. *Urban Education, 38,* 431–459.
Noh, S., Beiser, M., Kaspar, V., Hou, F., & Rummens, J. (1999). Perceived racial discrimination, depression, and coping: A study of Southeast Asian refugees in Canada. *Journal of Health and Social Behavior, 40,* 193–207.
Page, R. L. (2004). Positive pregnancy outcomes in Mexican immigrants: What can we learn? *Journal of Obstetric, Gynecologic, and Neonatal Nursing, 33,* 783–790.
Palleja, J. (1987). The impact of cultural identification on the behavior of second-generation Puerto Rican adolescents. Unpublished doctoral dissertation, Adelphi University.
Parke, R. D., & Buriel, R. (1998). Socialization in the family: Ecological and ethnic perspectives. In W. Damon (Ed.), *Handbook of child psychology* (Vol. 3, pp. 463–552). New York: Wiley.
Parke, R. D., Coltrane, S., Duffy, S., Buriel, R., Dennis, J., & Powers, J., et al. (2004). Economic stress, parenting, and child adjustment in Mexican American and European American families. *Child Development, 75,* 1632–1656.
Parra, P., & Guarnaccia, P. (1998). Ethnicity, culture, and resiliency in caregivers of a seriously mentally ill family member. In H. McCubbin, E. Thompson, A. Thompson, & J. Fromer (Eds.) Resiliency in native American and immigrant families (pp. 431–450). Thousand Oaks: Sage.

Pearce, C. W. (1998). Seeking a healthy baby: Hispanic women's views of pregnancy and prenatal care. *Clinical Excellence for Nurse Practitioners: the International Journal of NPACE, 2*(6), 352–361.

Pew Hispanic Center. (2006). Pew Hispanic Center Fact Sheet: Statistical portrait of Hispanics in the United States 2006: Summary and chart pack. Los Angeles: University of Southern California Annenberg School for Communication.

Phinney, J. S. (1990). Ethnic identity in adolescents and adults: Review of research. *Psychological Bulletin, 108*(3), 499–514.

Phinney, J., & Chavira V. (1992). Parental ethnic socialization and adolescent outcomes in ethnic minority families. *Journal of Research on Adolescents, 5,* 13–53.

Quinton, D., Pickles, A., Maughan, B., & Rutter, M. (1993). Partners, peers, and pathways: Assortative pairing and continuities in conduct disorder. *Development and Psychopathology, 5,* 763–783.

Roberts, R. E., & Chen, Y. W. (1995). Depressive symptoms and suicidal ideation among Mexican-origin and Anglo adolescents. *Journal of the American Academy of Child and Adolescent Psychiatry, 34,* 81–90.

Roberts, E., Roberts, C. R., & Chen, Y. R. (1997). Ethnocultural differences in prevalence of adolescent depression. *American Journal of Community Psychology, 25,* 95–110.

Rogler, L. H., Cortes, D. E., & Malgady, R. G. (1991). Acculturation and mental health status among hispanics. Convergence and new directions for research. *American Psychologist, 46*(6), 585–597.

Romero, A. J., Carvajal, S. C., Valle, F., & Orduña, M. (2007). Adolescent bicultural stress and its impact on mental well-being among Latinos, Asian Americans and European Americans. *Journal of Community Psychology, 35*(4) 519–534.

Romero, A. J., & Roberts, R. E. (1998). Perception of discrimination and ethnocultural variables in a diverse group of adolescents. *Journal of Adolescence, 21,* 641–656.

Romero, A. J., & Roberts, R. E. (2003). Stress within a bicultural context for adolescents of Mexican descent. *Cultural Diversity and Ethnic Minority Psychology, 9*(2), 171–184.

Rueschenberg, R., & Buriel, R. (1989). Mexican American family functioning and acculturation: A family systems perspective. *Hispanic Journal of Behavioral Sciences, 11*(3), 232–244.

Rumberger, R. W., & Larson, K. A. (1998). Toward explaining differences in educational achievement among Mexican American language minority students. *Sociology of Education, 71,* 68–92.

Sabogal, F., Marin, G., Otero-Sabogal, R., Marin, B. V., & Perez-Stable, E. J. (1987). Hispanic familism and acculturation: What changes and what doesn't? *Hispanic Journal of Behavioral Sciences, 9*(4), 397–412.

Sampson, R. J., Raudenbusch, S. W., & Earls, F. (1997). Neighborhoods and violent crime: A multilevel study of collective efficacy. *Science, 277,* 918–924.

Schinke, S. P., Schilling, R. F., Palleja, J., & Zayas, L. H. (1987). Prevention research among ethnic-racial minority group adolescents. *The Behavior Therapist, 10,* 151–155.

Sellers, R. M., & Shelton, J. N. (2003). The role of racial identity in perceived racial discrimination. *Journal of Personality and Social Psychology, 84*(5), 1079–1092.

Sellers, R. M., Caldwell, C. H., Schmeelk-Cone, K. H., & Zimmerman, M. A. (2003). Racial identity, racial discrimination, perceived stress, and psychological distress among African American young adults. *Journal of Health and Social Behavior, 44*(3), 302–317.

Simons, R. L., Murray, V., McLoyd, V., Lin, K., Cutrona, C., & Conger, R. D. (2002). Discrimination, crime, ethnic identity, and parenting as correlates of depressive symptoms among African American children: A multilevel analysis. *Development and Psychopathology, 14,* 371–393.

Smith, C., & Krohn, M. D. (1995). Delinquency and family life among male adolescents: The role of ethnicity. *Journal of Youth and Adolescence, 24,* 69–93.

Stouthamer-Loeber, M., Loeber, R., Homish, D. L., & Wei, E. (2002). Maltreatment of boys and the development of disruptive and delinquent behavior. *Development and Psychopathology, 13,* 941–955.

Szapocznik, J., & Coatsworth, J. D. (1999). An ecodevelopmental framework for organizing the influences on drug abuse: A developmental model of risk and protection. In M. Glantz & C. Hartel (Eds.), *Drug Abuse: Origins & Interventions* (pp. 331–366). Washington, DC: American Psychological Association.

Szapocznik, J., Kurtines, W. M., & Fernandez, T. (1980). Bicultural involvement and adjustment in Hispanic-American youths. *International Journal of Intercultural Relations, 4,* 353–365.

Szapocznik, J., Kurtines, W., Santisteban, D. A., & Rio, A. T. (1990). Interplay of advances between theory, research, and duplication in treatment interventions aimed at behavior problem children and adolescents. *Journal of Consulting and Clinical Psychology, 58,* 696–703.

Szalacha, L. A., Erkut, S., Garcia-Coll, C., Fields, J. P., Alarcon, O., & Ceder, I., (2003). Perceived discrimination and resilience. In S. S. Luthar (Ed.), *Resilience and vulnerability: Adaptation in the context of childhood adversities* (pp. 414–435). Cambridge: Cambridge University Press.

Tajfel, H. (1981). Human groups and social categories: Studies in social psychology. Cambridge: Cambridge University Press.

Tolan, P. H., Guerra, N. G., & Montaini-Klovdahl, L. R. (1997). Staying out of harm's way: Coping and the development of inner city children. In S. A. Wolchik & I. N. Sandler (Eds.), *Handbook of children's coping: Linking theory, research, and interventions* (pp. 453–479). New York: Plenum

Umaña-Taylor, A. J., & Updegraff, K. A. (2007). Latino adolescents' mental health: Exploring the interrelations among discrimination, ethnic identity, cultural orientation, self-esteem, and depressive symptoms. *Journal of Adolescence, 30,* 549–567.

Umaña-Taylor, A. J., Yazedjian, A., & Bácama-Gomez, M. Y. (2004). Developing the ethnic identity scale using Eriksonian and social identity perspectives. *Identity: An International Journal of Theory and Research, 4,* 9–38.

U.S. Census Bureau. (2003). Facts for features: Hispanic heritage month 2003: Sept15–Oct15 [Online]. Available at http://www.census.gov/Press-Release/www/2003/cb03-ff14.pdf.

U.S. Department of Education. (2000). *Dropout rates in the United States: 1998.* (NCES 2000-022). Washington, DC: U.S. Government Printing Office.

Valenzuela, A. (1999). *Subtractive schooling: U.S.-Mexican youth and the politics of caring.* New York: State University of New York Press.

Valenzuela, A. & Dornbusch, S. M. (1994). Familism and social capital in the academic achievement of Mexican origin and Anglo adolescents. *Social Science Quarterly, 75,* 18–36.

Vega, W. A. (1995). The study of Latino families: A point of departure. In R. E. Zambrana (Ed.), *Understanding Latino families: Scholarship, policy and practice* (pp. 3–17). Thousand Oaks: Sage.

Vega, W. A., Gil, A. G., Warheit, G. J., Zimmerman, R. S., & Apospori, E. (1993). Acculturation and delinquent behavior among Cuban American adolescents: Toward an empirical model. *American Journal of Community Psychology, 21*(1), 113–125.

Vigil, J. D. (1999). Streets and schools: How educators can help Chicano marginalized gang youth. *Harvard Educational Review, 69*(3), 270–288.

Vitaro, F., Tremblay, R. E., Kerr, M., Pagani, L., & Bukowski, W. M. (1997). Disruptiveness, friends' characteristics, and delinquency in early adolescence: A test of two competing models of development. *Child Development, 68*(4), 676–689.

Way, N., Kim, C., & Santos, C. (2005). A contextualized understanding of ethnic identity. Paper presented at the Society for Research on Child Development, Atlanta, GA.

Weiss, S. J., Goebel, P., Page, A., Wilson, P., & Warda, M. (1998). The impact of cultural and familial context on behavioral and emotional problems of preschool Latino children. *Child Psychiatry and Human Development, 29*(4), 287–301.

White, R. M. B., Roosa, M. W., Weaver, S., & Nair, R. L. (2009). Cultural and contextual influences on parenting in Mexican American families. *Journal of Marriage and Family, 71,* 61–79.

Woodward, L. J., & Fergusson, D. M. (2001). Life course outcomes of young people with anxiety disorders in adolescence. *Journal of the American Academy of Child and Adolescent Psychiatry, 40,* 1086–1093.

Wong, C.A., Eccles, J. S., & Sameroff, A. (2003).The influence of ethnic discrimination and ethnic identification on African American adolescents' school and socioemotional environment. *Journal of Personality, 71*(6), 1197–1232.

Zane, N., & Mak, W. (2003). Major approaches to the measurement of acculturation among ethnic minority populations: A content analysis and an alternative empirical strategy. In K. M. Chun, P. Balls Organista, & G. Marín (Eds.), *Acculturation: Advances in theory, measurement, and applied research*. Washington, DC: American Psychological Association:

Zayas, L. H. (1987). Toward an understanding of suicide risks in young Hispanic females. *Journal of Adolescent Research, 2*(1), 1–11.

Zayas, L. H., & Bryant, C. (1984). Culturally sensitive treatment of adolescent Puerto Rican girls and their families. *Child and Adolescent Social Work Journal, 1*, 235–253.

Chapter 16
Psychology of Latino Adults: Challenges and an Agenda for Action

Margarita Alegría, Norah Mulvaney-Day, Meghan Woo and Edna A. Viruell-Fuentes

In 2004, Latinos in the United States numbered 41 million, with 31% under the age of 16. Over the period from 2000 to 2004, Latino population growth represented half the total growth in the United States (The National Academies 2007). Part of this considerable increase includes immigration from Latin America, some who confront major challenges in integrating into the country, such as lack of English proficiency and different norms and lifestyle circumstances (Guarnaccia et al. 2007). These new immigrants also sustain strong ties with their home communities, interacting by phone and email, which contributes to the maintenance of language and culture (Levitt et al. 2003; Viruell-Fuentes 2006). These transnational dynamics pose complex challenges of how best to provide services, given Latinos' circumstances (U.S. Department of Health and Human Services 2001).

Understanding the patterns of mental health needs and effectively planning services for the growing Latino population is paramount, so that communities receiving an influx of Latinos can effectively respond to their distinct service needs. Not only is this group extremely heterogeneous in sociodemographic and contextual characteristics (Guarnaccia et al. 2007), mental health disorder rates and service use profiles tend to vary broadly across immigrant and US-born Latino groups (Alegría et al. 2007a, b). In order to outline the unique strengths and challenges in maintaining and improving mental health for Latino adults, it is necessary to first understand the variability across the population, particularly by gender and nativity, in order to consider how it can inform treatment and service delivery in the United States.

Chapter Focus

This chapter presents information on mental health topics in Latino adults, focusing on socioeconomic factors, and use and access to appropriate mental health services as major challenges to the maintenance of mental health in this group.

M. Alegría (✉)
Harvard Medical School and Center for Multicultural Mental Health Research
Cambridge Health Alliance, 120 Beacon Street, 4th floor, Somerville, MA 02143, USA
e-mail: malegria@charesearch.org

E. C. Chang, C. A. Downey (eds.), *Handbook of Race and Development in Mental Health*,
DOI 10.1007/978-1-4614-0424-8_16, © Springer Science+Business Media, LLC 2012

Family support, biculturalism, bilingualism, and nativity are described as strengths contributing to resilience in this group. We use data from the National Latino and Asian American Study (Alegría et al. 2004) to describe in detail what we already know about Latino adults' mental health and to highlight key themes that this study presents regarding factors that contribute to resilience. We then compare the rates of mental health disorders (depression, anxiety, and substance) of NLAAS Latinos with non-Latino Whites from the National Comorbidity Survey Replication (NCS-R) (Kessler and Merikangas 2004), using a combined dataset of the two studies to illustrate these themes. We conclude with recommended strategies to reduce the risk of mental illness and increase access to mental health services among Latino adults in the United States. We are aware that the present chapter differs substantially from others contained in this volume, in that we describe new analyses of data in addition to a review of the mental health literature in Latino adults. However, the advantage to our deviation from this volume's script is that we are able to offer some of the most recent mental health data on this important and growing segment of US society.

The National Latino and Asian American Study: Focus and Methodological Issues

The National Latino and Asian American Study (NLAAS) is a national psychiatric epidemiologic study estimating the prevalence of psychiatric disorders and mental health service usage in a representative sample of Asians and Latinos. The NLAAS study seeks to assess the role of ethnicity/race, socioeconomic status and environmental context in explaining potential health and service use differences. For this chapter, we limit analyses to the Latino sample of the NLAAS: 2,554 Latinos divided into four subethnic groups (Puerto Rican, Cuban, Mexican, and all other Latinos [mainly from the Dominican Republic, Colombia, El Salvador, Ecuador, Guatemala, Honduras, Peru, Nicaragua]). The NCS-R is a parallel study using overlapping measures and methodology to estimate the prevalence of psychiatric disorders and mental health service use in a national sample of the total US population. Both samples were developed using an integrated methodology as part of the NIMH Collaborative Psychiatric Epidemiology Surveys (CPES) (Colpe et al. 2004), allowing the pooling of data sets. Using an adaptation of a multiple-frame approach to estimation and inference for population characteristics (Hartley 1962, 1974), the CPES allows integration of design-based analysis weights and variance estimation codes to permit analysis of the combined datasets as though they were a single, nationally-representative study. Design and methodological information regarding the combined NLAAS/NCS-R dataset can be found at the CPES website (Interuniversity Consortium for Political and Social Science Research). The NLAAS study was conducted in English and Spanish while the NSC-R interview was conducted only in English. Pooling these samples allows us to contrast how non-Latino Whites and the Latino groups differ, and how they are similar.

Latino Adults in the United States: Demographic and Mental Health Characteristics

Demographic Characteristics of Latinos Adults

The Latino population is expected to swell to nearly a quarter of the total US population in the year 2025 (U.S. Census Bureau 2007). However, this segment is far from homogenous, grouping together individuals of a variety of demographic profiles. Using data from the NLAAS, Table 16.1 illustrates the variability in sociodemographic profile across Latino subgroups. Whereas the age distribution of Latino women does not differ by ethnic subgroup, there are differences among the men, with Mexicans being the youngest of all four groups and Cubans the oldest. Cuban men and women are the most highly-educated and have the lowest rates of poverty. Puerto Ricans have the highest rates of being widowed, separated, or divorced and the highest rates of health insurance coverage. Puerto Rican men have the highest rates of English interview completion, while Cubans have the lowest. The profile for Mexican men differs from Mexican women, with Mexican men demonstrating the highest rates of employment among subgroups, while Mexican women have the lowest. Income does not differ for men across the subgroups, but Mexican women report the lowest income compared to Cuban and Puerto Rican women.

Data from the NLAAS and NCS-R combined datasets show that overall, Latino men and women are younger and have lower levels of education and household income than non-Latino Whites. Latinos are also far more likely to be uninsured and live in the West (see Table 16.2). The differences found in key demographic characteristics of NCS-R non-Latino Whites and NLAAS Latinos parallel ethnic differences found for the general adult population in the United States (U.S. Census Bureau 2000), except in nativity and household income, with more immigrant and lower-income respondents in the NLAAS sample. This is potentially due to Census undercounting of immigrants (Anderson and Fienberg 1999; U.S. General Accounting Office 1998) and non-inclusion of undocumented workers (Margolis 1995). Within the NLAAS Latino sample, US-born Latinos are slightly older than Latino immigrants, but these differences are not statistically significant. However, significant differences in education and income are evident between US-born Latinos and immigrants, with both men and women born in the United States reporting higher income and more education than their immigrant counterparts. Patterns of insurance coverage mirror these findings, with Latino immigrants predictably having higher rates of uninsurance than US-born Latinos.

The patterns for these sociodemographic variables are similar across Latino men and women, with both groups displaying similar nativity differences. For employment status, however, we see less consistent patterns across men and women. Latina women are less likely than non-Latina White women to be employed, whereas Latino males are more likely than non-Latino White males to be employed. The nativity effects for employment illustrate that the patterns of employment for the US-born

Table 16.1 Demographic characteristics of NLAAS Latino females and males across subethnic groups, unadjusted

	Puerto Rican				Cuban				Mexican				Other Latino				p-value-females	p-value-males
	Females		Males		Females		Males		Females		Males		Females		Males			
	$N=282$		$N=213$		$N=301$		$N=276$		$N=470$		$N=398$		$N=374$		$N=240$			
	%	SE	%	SE	%	SE	%	SE	%	SE	%	SE	%	SE	%	SE		
Age																		
18–34	46.3	(4.4)	39.9	(2.8)	46.3	(4.2)	32.2	(2.7)	46.3	(2.7)	54.6	(3.1)	46.3	(3)	52.3	(4.0)	NS	***
35–49	30.2	(3.0)	30.3	(3.2)	30.2	(3.6)	21.2	(2.7)	30.2	(2.5)	30.7	(2.0)	30.2	(2.3)	29.5	(2.7)		
50–64	14.4	(2.2)	20.0	(2.5)	14.4	(1.8)	23.5	(2.1)	14.4	(1.7)	10.2	(1.2)	14.4	(2.2)	12.7	(2.1)		
≥65	9.0	(3.2)	9.9	(4.1)	9.0	(1.8)	23.0	(2.2)	9.0	(1.9)	4.5	(0.9)	9.0	(2.0)	5.5	(2.3)		
Education																		
≤11 years	36.1	(2.4)	32.2	(3.9)	18.7	(3.0)	30.1	(4.0)	53.6	(1.9)	52.4	(3.3)	35.0	(2.4)	32.9	(3.8)	***	***
12 years	27.6	(3.2)	29.6	(2.0)	28.6	(3.3)	24.5	(2.9)	21.9	(1.2)	25.9	(1.9)	23.4	(2.8)	23.8	(3.0)		
13–15 years	25.1	(2.1)	26.1	(3.8)	27.5	(2.8)	20.9	(3.4)	17.4	(2.2)	14.6	(2.7)	26.8	(1.9)	30.6	(3.5)		
≥16 years	11.3	(2.1)	12.0	(1.7)	25.2	(4.0)	24.5	(4.5)	7.1	(1.2)	7.1	(1.3)	14.7	(2.5)	12.7	(2.4)		
Marital status																		
Married	37.1	(3.7)	41.3	(3.1)	54.7	(2.9)	57.3	(3.3)	52.6	(2.8)	61.1	(3.0)	42.0	(2.9)	48.0	(3.6)	**	***
Never married	34.1	(3.6)	36.1	(3.2)	22.2	(2.6)	20.8	(1.9)	25.3	(2.6)	29.9	(2.1)	29.5	(3.1)	37.4	(3.6)		
Widowed/Separated/Divorced	28.8	(3.4)	22.6	(3.4)	23.1	(2.6)	21.9	(3.0)	22.1	(2.1)	9.0	(1.5)	28.4	(2.4)	14.5	(2.4)		
Employment																		
Employed	54.1	(3.3)	62.7	(3.7)	55.6	(2.6)	68.1	(3.7)	45.3	(2.9)	79.1	(2.7)	58.6	(2.2)	73.8	(3.7)	**	*
Out of labor force/other	39.9	(3.6)	29.7	(4.3)	40.2	(2.7)	25.6	(3.8)	46.9	(3.5)	14.8	(2.6)	33.4	(2.4)	16.2	(3.3)		
Unemployed	6.0	(1.5)	7.6	(2.6)	4.2	(1.7)	6.2	(1.7)	7.8	(1.3)	6.1	(1.6)	7.9	(0.8)	10.0	(1.9)		

Table 16.1 (continued)

	Puerto Rican				Cuban				Mexican				Other Latino				p-value-females	p-value-males
	Females		Males		Females		Males		Females		Males		Females		Males			
	$N=282$		$N=213$		$N=301$		$N=276$		$N=470$		$N=398$		$N=374$		$N=240$			
	%	SE	%	SE	%	SE	%	SE	%	SE	%	SE	%	SE	%	SE		
Annual household income																		
≤14,999	31.5	(1.9)	22.6	(2.6)	28.8	(4.0)	22.0	(4.4)	35.6	(4.8)	23.8	(2.5)	26.3	(2.0)	21.2	(3.6)	**	NS
15,000–34,999	20.0	(2.6)	23.9	(2.9)	21.6	(3.4)	25.5	(3.2)	31.5	(2.3)	30.7	(2.7)	30.9	(3.0)	22.5	(4.2)		
35,000–74,999	28.4	(3.5)	30.7	(2.6)	24.9	(3.8)	27.0	(2.6)	23.3	(2.9)	29.2	(3.1)	25.4	(2.6)	35.8	(3.6)		
≥75,000	20.0	(2.4)	22.8	(3.3)	24.8	(5.7)	25.5	(5.0)	9.6	(1.2)	16.2	(2.3)	17.4	(2.5)	20.5	(3.5)		
Poverty ratio	4.0	(0.3)	4.9	(0.5)	4.3	(0.7)	5.5	(1.0)	2.6	(0.2)	3.1	(0.2)	3.8	(0.3)	4.7	(0.5)	***	**
US region																		
Northeast	61.3	(5.9)	55.7	(5.9)	8.5	(4.4)	5.2	(2.3)	2.4	(0.9)	1.9	(0.5)	40.9	(4.2)	36.1	(5.2)	***	***
Midwest	12.6	(5.1)	13.0	(4.7)	0.0	(0.0)	0.0	(0.0)	8.6	(3.6)	10.5	(2.4)	6.3	(1.3)	4.8	(2.0)		
South	18.1	(2.8)	23.1	(3.2)	90.1	(4.6)	92.1	(2.8)	31.5	(10.2)	30.0	(7.1)	22.9	(3.1)	26.1	(5.5)		
West	8.0	(2.2)	8.2	(1.9)	1.4	(1.4)	2.7	(1.7)	57.5	(9.1)	57.6	(6.4)	29.9	(4.2)	33.1	(6.1)		
Language of interview																		
English	57.1	(2.7)	60.0	(2.8)	32.5	(4.7)	24.2	(3.4)	44.6	(6.3)	41.6	(4.5)	46.8	(3.4)	55.2	(4.9)	NS	***
Spanish	42.9	(2.7)	40.0	(2.8)	67.5	(4.7)	75.8	(3.4)	55.4	(6.3)	58.4	(4.5)	53.2	(3.4)	44.8	(4.9)		
Insurance status																		
Private	44.1	(3.4)	51.0	(4.5)	47.6	(3.9)	42.5	(3.2)	29.8	(2.8)	43.4	(3.3)	44.1	(2.9)	56.9	(2.9)	***	***
Public	40.3	(3.7)	26.2	(4.7)	27.0	(3.2)	28.0	(2.7)	26.6	(2.5)	11.7	(1.7)	29.9	(3.5)	9.8	(2.6)		
Uninsurance	13.2	(1.7)	18.6	(2.4)	23.0	(2.9)	27.3	(3.8)	41.3	(3.7)	43.4	(3.6)	23.8	(2.6)	30.0	(3.2)		
Other	2.4	(0.6)	4.2	(1.5)	2.3	(1.1)	2.2	(1.1)	2.3	(0.8)	1.4	(0.6)	2.2	(1.0)	3.3	(1.5)		

NS not significant
$*p<0.05$; $**p<0.01$; $***p<0.001$

Table 16.2 Demographic characteristics of NCS-R non-Latino White and NLAAS Latino females and males, unadjusted

	NCS-R non-Latino White females		NLAAS Latino females			NCS-R non-Latino White males[‡]		NLAAS Latino males			NLAAS US-born Latino females[§]		NLAAS immigrant[†] Latino females			NLAAS US-born Latino males		NLAAS immigrant Latino males		
	$N=2406$		$N=1427$			$N=1816$		$N=1127$			$N=521$		$N=906$			$N=403$		$N=724$		
	%	SE	%	SE	p value	%	SE	%	SE	p value	%	SE	%	SE	p value	%	SE	%	SE	p value
Age																				
18–34	27.1	(1.4)	46.4	(2)	***	28.3	(2.0)	51.5	(2.1)	***	50.5	(3.4)	43.5	(2.1)	NS	55.9	(3.5)	48.4	(2.4)	NS
35–49	28.2	(1.4)	30.1	(1.7)		32.2	(1.7)	29.8	(1.4)		27.4	(2.9)	32.0	(1.5)		27.3	(2.3)	31.6	(1.9)	
50–64	23.5	(1.6)	14.4	(1.2)		22.0	(1.6)	12.4	(0.9)		13.4	(2.1)	15.2	(1.3)		9.9	(1.7)	14.1	(1.1)	
≥65	21.2	(1.6)	9.0	(1.1)		17.4	(1.7)	6.3	(0.9)		8.7	(2.1)	9.2	(1.2)		7.0	(1.8)	5.8	(1.3)	
Education																				
≤11 years	12.2	(1.1)	45.2	(1.7)	***	14.6	(1.4)	45.1	(2.3)	***	29.8	(2.4)	56.3	(2.2)	***	29.7	(2.9)	55.9	(2.3)	***
12 years	32.2	(1.8)	23.4	(1.2)		31.1	(1.9)	25.7	(1.3)		29.1	(2.1)	19.3	(1.4)		32.6	(2.7)	20.9	(1.4)	
13–15 years	30.1	(1.6)	21.1	(1.5)		27.7	(1.5)	19.5	(1.7)		28.5	(2.8)	15.8	(1.4)		26.6	(2.4)	14.5	(2.1)	
≥16 years	25.4	(1.4)	10.2	(1.2)		26.7	(1.7)	9.7	(1.1)		12.5	(1.9)	8.5	(1.5)		11.1	(2.0)	8.7	(1.3)	
Marital status																				
Married	56.1	(1.6)	48.1	(1.9)	***	64.6	(1.8)	56.2	(2.2)	***	40.7	(3.1)	53.4	(2.0)	***	48.7	(3.9)	61.4	(2.7)	*
Never married	16.8	(1.2)	27.5	(1.8)		21.8	(1.7)	31.7	(1.5)		35.2	(3.6)	22.0	(1.5)		37.6	(2.3)	27.6	(2.3)	
Widowed/separated/divorced	27.1	(1.4)	24.4	(1.7)		13.6	(1.2)	12.1	(1.2)		24.1	(2.7)	24.6	(1.5)		13.6	(2.0)	11.1	(1.3)	
Employment																				
Employed	58.5	(1.3)	50.0	(2.1)	***	72.0	(1.4)	75.8	(1.9)	***	54.8	(2.4)	46.6	(2.5)	**	71.1	(2.8)	79.1	(2.3)	*
Out of labor force/other	38.7	(1.3)	42.3	(2.3)		24.5	(1.4)	17.1	(1.7)		34.9	(3.3)	47.6	(2.6)		20.8	(2.5)	14.6	(1.9)	
Unemployed	2.8	(0.5)	7.7	(0.8)		3.5	(0.4)	7.1	(1.2)		10.3	(1.7)	5.8	(0.8)		8.1	(1.6)	6.4	(1.4)	
Annual household income																				
≤14,999	17.9	(1.6)	32.9	(3)	***	9.6	(1.1)	23.1	(1.9)	***	28.2	(3.4)	36.3	(3.3)	***	19.7	(2.1)	25.6	(2.6)	***
15,000–34,999	22.0	(1.2)	29.5	(1.3)		16.9	(1.4)	28.2	(1.8)		25.9	(2.4)	32.1	(1.7)		21.5	(1.7)	32.9	(2.4)	

Table 16.2 (continued)

	NCS-R non-Latino White females		NLAAS Latino females			NCS-R non-Latino White males[ł]		NLAAS Latino males			NLAAS US-born Latino females[§]		NLAAS immigrant[†] Latino females			NLAAS US-born Latino males		NLAAS immigrant Latino males		
	$N=2406$		$N=1427$			$N=1816$		$N=1127$			$N=521$		$N=906$			$N=403$		$N=724$		
	%	SE	%	SE	p value	%	SE	%	SE	p value	%	SE	%	SE	p value	%	SE	%	SE	p value
35,000–74,999	34.3	(1.5)	24.3	(1.9)		38.6	(1.8)	30.6	(2.5)		29.2	(2.2)	20.7	(2.3)		33.7	(3.4)	28.4	(2.6)	
≥75,000	25.8	(1.4)	13.3	(1.3)		34.9	(1.9)	18.1	(1.7)		16.7	(1.8)	10.9	(1.6)		25.1	(3.3)	13.1	(1.7)	
Poverty ratio	4.4	(0.1)	3.1	(0.2)	***	5.6	(0.2)	3.7	(0.2)	***	3.7	(0.3)	2.7	(0.2)	**	4.5	(0.3)	3.2	(0.2)	***
US region																				
Northeast	19.9	(4.0)	19.8	(2.2)	***	21.3	(3.8)	14.7	(1.4)	***	13.4	(2.2)	24.3	(3.3)	*	10.0	(1.7)	18.0	(1.8)	NS
Midwest	26.9	(2.5)	8.4	(2.0)		29.1	(2.8)	9.3	(2.0)		11.6	(4.2)	6.1	(1.4)		12.2	(3.0)	7.3	(2.4)	
South	33.7	(3.2)	30.7	(5.9)		29.8	(2.9)	31.7	(4.1)		27.6	(4.5)	32.9	(7.6)		30.8	(5.1)	32.3	(4.2)	
West	19.5	(3.0)	41.1	(4.8)		19.8	(2.8)	44.3	(4.3)		47.3	(5.5)	36.6	(5.0)		47.1	(5.8)	42.4	(4.4)	
Language of interview																				
English	100.0	(0.0)	45.0	(3.6)	NS	####	(0.0)	45.3	(3.5)	***	83.8	(3.0)	17.1	(2.0)	NS	85.3	(3.1)	17.3	(2.8)	***
Spanish	0.0	(0.0)	55.0	(3.6)		0.0	(0.0)	54.7	(3.5)		16.2	(3.0)	82.9	(2.0)		14.7	(3.1)	82.7	(2.8)	
Insurance status																				
Private	62.0	(1.9)	35.4	(2.5)	***	65.8	(1.4)	47.3	(2.4)	***	43.9	(2.2)	29.4	(3.1)	***	54.1	(3.1)	42.5	(3.0)	***
Public	26.8	(1.7)	29.4	(1.9)		21.1	(1.5)	13.6	(1.3)		31.6	(2.2)	27.8	(2.2)		16.1	(2.2)	11.9	(1.3)	
Uninsurance	9.1	(0.9)	33.0	(2.9)		10.7	(1.1)	37.1	(2.7)		20.9	(2.2)	41.6	(3.1)		26.4	(3.8)	44.6	(3.0)	
Other	2.1	(0.4)	2.2	(0.4)		2.5	(0.5)	2.1	(0.5)		3.5	(1.0)	1.2	(0.3)		3.5	(1.0)	1.1	(0.4)	

NS not significant

*$p<0.05$; **$p<0.01$; ***$p<0.001$

[†] Immigrant Latinos include all people born in Latin America, including the island of Puerto Rico

[§] US-born Latinos include all people of Latin American backgrounds born in the US Mainland

[ł] 1752/1802 (97.2%) of the non-Latino Whites were US born

Table 16.3 Age-adjusted prevalence of lifetime and past-year DSM-IV disorders for NCS-R non-Latino White and NLAAS Latino females

	NSCR non-Latino Whites				NLAAS Latinos			
	Males		Females		Males		Females	
	N=1816		N=2406		N=1127		N=1427	
	%	SE	%	SE	%	SE	%	SE
Lifetime diagnosis								
Any depressive disorder	16.6	(1.2)	25.7	(0.9)	10.4	(1.2)	20.0	(1.3)
Any anxiety	19.4	(1.1)	28.7	(1.1)	12.1	(1.5)	19.8	(1.6)
Any substance	21.4	(1.2)	9.6	(0.5)	17.7	(2.2)	3.7	(0.8)
Any disorder	38.5	(1.8)	42.0	(1.1)	28.8	(2.3)	30.4	(2.1)
Past year diagnosis								
Any depressive disorder	6.6	(0.5)	11.4	(0.6)	6.0	(0.9)	10.8	(1.2)
Any anxiety	11.0	(0.8)	16.9	(0.8)	7.2	(1.1)	11.3	(1.2)
Any substance	5.8	(0.7)	2.3	(0.3)	3.9	(0.5)	0.7	(0.3)
Any disorder	17.6	(1.0)	23.1	(1.0)	12.9	(0.1)	17.6	(1.8)

	NLAAS US-born Latinos				NLAAS immigrant Latinos			
	Males		Females		Males		Females	
	N=403		N=521		N=724		N=906	
	%	SE	%	SE	%	SE	%	SE
Lifetime diagnosis								
Any depressive disorder	10.9	(2.0)	20.8	(2.3)	10.1	(1.4)	19.3	(1.6)
Any anxiety	14.8	(2.7)	21.2	(2.6)	10.0	(1.6)	18.7	(1.4)
Any substance	27.0	(4.2)	7.3	(1.4)	10.6	(1.2)	0.8	(0.4)
Any disorder	37.9	(3.0)	33.5	(3.9)	22.0	(1.8)	27.9	(1.8)
Past year diagnosis								
Any depressive disorder	6.9	(1.4)	10.6	(1.7)	5.4	(1.0)	11.0	(1.2)
Any anxiety	8.2	(1.7)	10.9	(2.1)	3.4	(1.5)	11.6	(1.2)
Any substance	6.0	(1.1)	1.6	(0.6)	2.3	(0.5)	0.0	(0.0)
Any disorder	15.0	(1.6)	18.5	(2.9)	11.3	(1.6)	17.0	(1.5)

	NSC-R non-Latino Whites males vs. NLAAS Latino males	NCS-R non-Latino White males vs. NLAAS US-born Latino males	NLAAS immigrant Latino males vs. NLAAS US-born Latino males
Lifetime diagnosis			
Any depressive disorder	***	*	NS
Any anxiety	**	NS	NS
Any substance	NS	NS	***
Any disorder	**	NS	***
Past year diagnosis			
Any depressive disorder	NS	NS	NS
Any anxiety	*	NS	NS
Any substance	NS	NS	*
Any disorder	*	NS	NS

Table 16.3 (continued)

	NCS-R non-Latino White females vs. NLAAS Latino females	NCS-R non-Latino White females vs. NLAAS US-born Latino females	NLAAS immigrant Latino females vs. NLAAS US-born Latino females
Lifetime diagnosis			
Any depressive disorder	**	NS	NS
Any anxiety	***	*	NS
Any substance	***	NS	***
Any disorder	***	NS	NS
Past year diagnosis			
Any depressive disorder	NS	NS	NS
Any anxiety	***	*	NS
Any substance	**	NS	*
Any disorder	*	NS	NS

NS not significant
*$p<0.05$; **$p<0.01$; ***$p<0.001$

are different across men and women. Whereas US-born Latina women have higher rates of employment than immigrant Latinas, for men the pattern is reversed, with US-born men displaying lower rates of employment than Latino immigrants.

Regarding other socio-contextual variables, we see patterns that suggest more stable family structures for immigrants than for the US born. Despite lower rates of marriage for Latino men and women compared to non-Latinos, when looking only at the Latino groups, immigrant men and women have higher rates of marriage or cohabitation than the US born. Additionally, there is some evidence of greater instability in family structure among US-born Latinos. These patterns could indicate resiliency for immigrant Latinos who have more stable family structures. However, US-born Latinos appear better off socio-economically than their immigrant counterparts, although with lower income and less education than the non-Latino White population. Next, we look more closely at actual rates of mental disorder, and consider potential areas of resiliency and vulnerability for these populations.

Mental Disorders Among Latinos in the United States

Overall, research using the NCS-R dataset has shown higher rates of disorder for non-Latino Whites than Latinos (Kessler and Merikangas 2004). Likewise, when lifetime prevalence estimates of psychiatric disorders are examined for Latinos in aggregate using the NLAAS data, our findings are consistent with this literature. Latinos are at lower risk than non-Latino Whites for all lifetime psychiatric disorders, except agoraphobia without panic (data not shown). In Table 16.3, we see that although lifetime rates of depressive and anxiety disorders for both men and women are higher among NCS-R non-Latino Whites compared to NLAAS Latinos, differences in rates of depression and anxiety between US-born and immigrant Latinos in the NLAAS are not significant once we adjust for age and stratify by gender. However, US-born Latinos in the NLAAS have lower prevalence rates of depression (for men) and anxiety (for women) than NCS-R non-Latino Whites. This suggests that lower rates of lifetime depression and anxiety disorder hold for Latinos as a whole, as contrasted to non-Latino Whites. For 12-month anxiety, we see a similar pattern to the lifetime rates, with NLAAS Latino men and women reporting lower rates compared to NCS-R non-Latino Whites, after age adjustments and stratification by gender. We note that our rates might vary slightly from results presented elsewhere (Alegría et al. 2007a) because we have stratified by gender, and the diagnostic algorithms of the World Mental Health Survey Initiative Version of the Composite International Diagnostic Interview (WMH-CIDI) (Kessler and Ustun 2004) have recently changed.

The Immigrant Paradox

We have also examined the immigrant paradox for Latinos, where foreign nativity seems protective against psychiatric disorders (Burnam et al. 1987), despite the stressful experiences and poverty often associated with immigration. Consistent with the immigrant paradox, US-born Latinos report higher lifetime rates for most disorders than Latino immigrants. Given that the NCS-R did not interview respondents in Spanish, the NLAAS has a much broader sample of immigrant Latinos, enabling us to scrutinize these factors more closely. In fact, when we compare rates of lifetime and 12-month disorders for NCS-R non-Latino Whites with NLAAS Latinos, we see that the protective nativity effect does, in fact, apply in the case of lifetime disorders, most notably substance disorders (see Table 16.3). For lifetime substance disorders, after age adjustments, both US-born men and women have significantly higher rates than Latino immigrants (see Table 16.3). Furthermore, for 12-month disorders, the only differences in prevalence rates between the US-born and immigrant Latinos are for substance disorders. These findings are consistent with other epidemiologic studies that report the immigrant paradox is mainly observed for substance-use patterns among Latinos in the United States (Alegría et al. 2006a). Because most experimentation and heavy use of substances in the United States occurs during the teen and young adult years (Substance Abuse and Mental Health Services Administration 2000), and most disorders start before the age of 24 (Kessler et al. 2005), introduction to US culture during childhood and adolescence may place younger immigrants at particular risk. When childhood development occurs in countries with strong proscriptive norms against illicit drug use, such as in Latin America, and high levels of family stability and cohesiveness, individuals may be protected against substance abuse and dependence when they immigrate as adults.

Although the aforementioned results appear fairly uniform, the NLAAS study has further found that when considering Latinos by nativity and subethnicity, rates of mental disorder vary widely across groups. First, when the Latino population is separated into subgroups, the NLAAS has found variability in the extent to which these rates of disorder apply, with Puerto Ricans approaching the rates of non-Latino Whites (Alegria et al. 2008). In additional analyses not presented in this paper, we find that among Latino subgroups, Puerto Rican men and women have the highest rates of mental disorders, with 39.0% of men and 40.5% of women reporting some lifetime disorder. Puerto Rican men and women report significantly higher risk of anxiety, substance use and any psychiatric disorder when compared to Cubans, Mexicans, and other Latinos. There is less variability in the prevalence of lifetime disorders between Mexicans, Cubans, and other Latinos.

It is important to consider closely the similarities and differences across ethnic subgroups when considering the challenges of effectively providing treatment and prevention services to this population. The similarity in disorder rates between Puerto Ricans and non-Latino Whites could be attributed to the fact that in contrast to the other Latino groups, Puerto Ricans have lived with more than a century of US influence, and are more likely to be bilingual and to have adopted many lifestyle patterns of US society (Guarnaccia et al. 2005). Second, regarding the immigrant paradox, differences by nativity and sub-ethnicity are only evident for depressive and anxiety disorders in Mexicans and for all Latinos except Puerto Ricans for substance abuse disorders. Clearly, understanding the patterns of mental disorder among Latinos involves a nuanced approach to issues of nativity and subethnic group origins. Our data helps to emphasize the importance of not over generalizing the immigrant paradox across all Latino subethnic groups.

These findings suggest two different stories that are important to consider when discussing Latino mental health. On the one hand, the social tensions that US-born Latinos face whereby their socioeconomic profile has improved and yet is inferior to that of the majority culture may lead to increased risk of substance disorders across generations; however, consistently lower rates for many mental health disorders point to sociocultural factors that persist across generational status, supplying a source of resiliency that has the effect of lowering risk of mental disorders for Latino groups. However, the picture is complicated, as more extensive analysis has shown that even this overall nativity effect does not necessarily hold when the sample is broken by subgroups and by other sociocontextual variables, such as time in the United States (Alegria et al. 2007c). In the next section of this chapter, we try to capture the breadth of experience regarding these components of Latino culture. First, we examine challenges to maintaining mental health by detailing areas of vulnerability that specifically affect Latino adults. Then, we describe the strengths that may be protective for Latino mental health, but also the ways in which these protective elements may vary once the heterogeneity of Latino culture is taken into account.

Challenges to Maintaining Latino Adult's Mental Health

Challenge 1: The Role of Socioeconomic Status

Socioeconomic disadvantage has long been associated with increased risk of mental disorder among the mainstream population (Alegría et al. 2000). Many studies have found a positive correlation between poverty and mental disorder (Saraceno and Barbui 1997). However, some studies focused on Latinos have found the opposite (Bird et al. 1988; Costello et al. 2001), particularly among impoverished populations, where traditional SES measures are less predictive than more contextual indicators such as neighborhood violence and rates of female-headed household (Vega and Gil 2007). While socioeconomic disadvantage may be a significant challenge to the mental health of Latinos, the way in which this challenge may be perceived could vary across Latino subgroups. For example, one study using NLAAS data found no relationship between low socioeconomic status and substance use disorder for Latinos (Canino et al. 2008), while another found a decreased likelihood of 12-month anxiety disorders for those with household incomes less than US $ 15,000 compared with those who had household incomes between US $ 35,000 and US $ 74,999 (Alegria et al. 2007a). However, in further analyses, Alegria et al. found that the protective factor of low income disappeared once the analysis was controlled for perceived social standing, suggesting that this income effect may be quite dependent upon subjective views of one's social status in the community.

The relationship between education and risk for mental disorder also presents an intricate story. Whereas lower education has often been associated with higher risk of psychiatric disorders (Patel and Kleinman 2003), some studies have found that among US-born Latinos, it actually appears to be protective (Breslau et al. 2006). Analyses of the NLAAS data suggest this pattern, particularly for women, whereby those who have a high school education have similar odds of any 12-month disorder than those who have completed college, while women with some college have significantly higher odds of mental disorders than those who have completed college. These mixed findings regarding the challenges to mental health evidently due to education require further investigation. One hypothesis is that this is an artifact of how education and nativity influence how individuals endorse symptoms of illness (Alegría and McGuire 2003), a hypothesis we are currently examining.

One potential factor that may interact with socioeconomic status to create challenges for the mental health of Latinos is the level of discrimination and racism that Latinos may encounter in the United States as they achieve higher social status and become more assimilated. Assimilated Latinos may have a greater sensitivity to discrimination than their less-acculturated counterparts. For example, more-acculturated Mexican immigrants have been found to report higher levels of discrimination compared to immigrants who are less acculturated (Finch et al. 2000), suggesting that greater awareness and exposure to the mainstream culture via education and employment may have a commiserate and negative effect by increasing experiences of perceived discrimination. Others also highlight the importance of unraveling the factors that affect integration into US society, suggesting an interaction between socioeconomic standing and exposure to the racialized environment of the United States (Viruell-Fuentes 2007). Looking at the NLAAS, we find that US-born Latinos across all subgroups report discrimination more frequently than immigrants (Perez et al. 2008). As immigrants assimilate, they may have higher expectations for fair treatment—but they may not receive it (Perez et al. 2008). Further, in the NLAAS sample as a whole, Latinos with higher education are more likely to report everyday discrimination, and higher levels of ethnic identity are associated with lower perceived discrimination. Given that Finch et al. (2000) found that perceived discrimination was also related to depression, these relationships may play a role in the protective effect of low socioeconomic status and lower risk for mental disorders found in some studies. These findings also point to one of the challenges for Latino mental health, namely how to encourage the positive effects that increased education and economic resources may provide, while simultaneously maintaining the social and cultural factors that offer a protective influence for mental health.

Challenge 2: Mental Health Service Use

Another critical challenge in supporting mental health for Latinos is the difficulty in engaging many Latinos in entering and remaining in mental health care. Overall, US-born Latinos are less likely to receive mental health services than non-Latino Whites, and immigrants are significantly less likely to receive formal mental health or substance abuse services (see Table 16.4). Cultural factors such as nativity, language, and number of years in the United States have been associated with use of mental health services for Latinos, with those who are US-born, speak English and have the most number of years in the US reporting higher rates of both specialty and any mental health service use (Alegría et al. 2007b). Interestingly, when stratified across those with a DSM-IV diagnosis and those without, these cultural differences only remain for those without a mental health diagnosis. Thus, the area where Latinos appear to be most vulnerable in accessing care falls in preventive or discretionary use of mental health care.

Recent results looking specifically at the use of antidepressant medication among Latinos are consistent with these findings (Hodgkin et al. 2007, data not shown). Not only did the authors find that less than half (43.5%) of those Latinos taking antidepressants had a DSM-IV mental disorder, whether respondents discontinued their antidepressant use was significantly associated with English-language proficiency. Those with good or excellent English proficiency were less likely to discontinue taking antidepressants. In sum, these findings suggest that continued clinical intervention would be beneficial for monolingual Spanish-speaking immigrants who may not yet have full-blown disorder, but are in need of preventive or maintenance treatment.

Table 16.4 Sociodemographic and mental health factors associated with past-year service use (NCS-R non-Latino White and NLAAS Latino, females and males)

	Service type															
	General				Specialty				Human sector				Any service			
	Females		Males		Females		Males		Females		Males		Females		Males	
	$n=544$		$n=220$		$n=482$		$n=251$		$n=229$		$n=108$		$n=935$		$n=435$	
	OR	95% CI	OR	95% CI	OR	95% CI	OR	95% CI	OR	95% CI	OR	95% CI	OR	95% CI	OR	95% CI
Age																
18–34	1.00		1.00		1.00		1.00		1.00		1.00		1.00		1.00	
35–49	1.64	(1.15, 2.34)*	1.89	(1.3, 2.8)*	1.00	(0.72, 1.39)	1.02	(0.6, 1.8)	1.22	(0.72, 2.05)	0.73	(0.4, 1.2)	1.32	(0.99, 1.77)	1.27	(0.8, 2.0)
50–64	1.27	(0.8, 2.02)	2.36	(1.4, 4.0)*	0.58	(0.36, 0.92)*	0.99	(0.5, 2.1)	0.62	(0.26, 1.46)	0.50	(0.2, 1.1)	0.90	(0.6, 1.36)	1.36	(0.8, 2.3)
≥65	0.69	(0.35, 1.34)	0.40	(0.2, 0.9)*	0.06	(0.02, 0.17)*	0.13	(0.0, 0.4)*	0.18	(0.07, 0.45)*	0.04	*	0.24	(0.15, 0.39)*	0.15	(0.1, 0.4)*
Race/ethnicity																
White	1.00		1.00		1.00		1.00		1.00		1.00		1.00		1.00	
Latino US-born	0.71	(0.49, 1.01)	0.71	(0.4, 1.2)	0.50	(0.32, 0.77)*	0.59	(0.3, 1.1)	0.77	(0.39, 1.5)	1.39	(0.8, 2.5)	0.64	(0.47, 0.87)*	0.70	(0.5, 1.1)
Latino immigrant	0.50	(0.31, 0.8)*	0.59	(0.3, 1.1)	0.54	(0.36, 0.8)*	0.37	(0.2, 0.7)	0.75	(0.45, 1.26)	0.74	(0.3, 1.7)	0.47	(0.34, 0.66)*	0.53	(0.4, 0.8)*
Education																
≥16 years	1.00		1.00		1.00		1.00		1.00		1.00		1.00		1.00	
13–15 years	1.41	(0.86, 2.29)	1.30	(0.8, 2.1)	0.47	(0.26, 0.85)*	0.77	(0.5, 1.2)	0.69	(0.31, 1.54)	0.63	(0.3, 1.5)	0.85	(0.54, 1.34)	0.81	(0.5, 1.3)
12 years	1.20	(0.79, 1.83)	1.33	(0.8, 2.2)	0.45	(0.31, 0.65)*	0.66	(0.4, 1.0)*	0.97	(0.45, 2.1)	0.61	(0.3, 1.3)	0.86	(0.6, 1.25)	0.79	(0.5, 1.2)
≤11 years	1.13	(0.81, 1.57)	1.20	(0.6, 2.4)	0.71	0.48, 1.05)	0.69	(0.4, 1.2)	1.04	0.53, 2.07)	0.68	(0.3, 1.8)	0.87	0.64, 1.19)	0.72	(0.4, 1.2)
Marital status																
Married	1.00		1.00		1.00		1.00		1.00		1.00		1.00		1.00	
Never married	1.28	(0.87, 1.89)	0.76	(0.5, 1.3)	1.84	(1.35, 2.5)*	1.41	(0.8, 2.4)	1.10	(0.55, 2.21)	1.43	(0.8, 2.4)	1.51	(1.14, 2.01)*	1.13	(0.8, 1.7)
Widowed/ separated/ divorced	1.34	(0.94, 1.93)	0.91	(0.5, 1.6)	2.20	(1.41, 3.44)*	3.64	(1.9, 7.0)*	1.37	(0.72, 2.61)	2.65	(1.6, 4.5)*	1.73	(1.25, 2.4)*	1.97	(1.3, 3.0)*
Employment status																
Employed	1.00		1.00		1.00		1.00		1.00		1.00		1.00		1.00	
Out of labor force/other	1.35	(1, 1.82)	2.06	(1.1, 3.9)*	1.56	(1.09, 2.23)*	1.80	(1.0, 3.1)*	1.11	(0.75, 1.63)	1.87	(0.8, 4.5)	1.44	(1.12, 1.84)*	1.47	(0.9, 2.4)
Unemployed	0.93	(0.59, 1.46)	2.16	(1.0, 4.7)	1.08	(0.56, 2.09)	1.95	(0.9, 4.2)	1.22	(0.58, 2.55)	1.28	(0.4, 3.7)	1.06	(0.68, 1.63)	2.24	(1.1, 4.5)*

Table 16.4 (continued)

	Service type															
	General				Specialty				Human sector				Any service			
	Females		Males		Females		Males		Females		Males		Females		Males	
	$n=544$		$n=220$		$n=482$		$n=251$		$n=229$		$n=108$		$n=935$		$n=435$	
	OR	95% CI	OR	95% CI	OR	95% CI	OR	95% CI	OR	95% CI	OR	95% CI	OR	95% CI	OR	95% CI
Annual household income																
≥75,000	1.00		1.00		1.00		1.00		1.00		1.00		1.00		1.00	
35,000–74,999	0.68	(0.41, 1.12)	1.03	(0.7, 1.6)	0.76	(0.44, 1.31)	0.70	(0.5, 1.0)	1.67	(0.85, 3.31)	1.62	(0.9, 2.9)	0.88	(0.57, 1.37)	0.93	(0.7, 1.3)
15,000–34,999	0.87	(0.58, 1.32)	1.36	(0.6, 3.1)	0.93	(0.56, 1.56)	0.33	(0.2, 0.7)	1.54	(0.89, 2.66)	0.96	(0.4, 2.1)	0.97	(0.7, 1.36)	0.66	(0.4, 1.2)
≤14,999	0.95	(0.63, 1.42)	0.80	(0.3, 1.8)	0.73	(0.5, 1.07)	0.45	(0.3, 0.8)*	1.30	(0.72, 2.36)	0.90	(0.4, 1.9)	0.95	(0.66, 1.36)	0.57	(0.4, 0.9)*
US region																
Northeast	1.00		1.00		1.00		1.00		1.00		1.00		1.00		1.00	
Midwest	0.95	(0.6, 1.49)	0.72	(0.4, 1.4)	0.70	(0.47, 1.05)	0.58	(0.3,1.1)	1.36	(0.72, 2.57)	1.51	(0.6, 3.8)	1.01	(0.71, 1.45)	0.69	(0.4, 1.2)
South	1.02	(0.64, 1.61)	0.97	(0.6, 1.7)	0.65	(0.46, 0.92)*	0.70	(0.4, 1.3)	0.97	(0.52, 1.82)	1.11	(0.5, 2.7)	0.91	(0.61, 1.35)	0.90	(0.5, 1.5)
West	0.91	(0.6, 1.38)	1.04	(0.6, 2.0)	0.99	(0.74, 1.31)	1.05	(0.6, 2.0)	1.40	(0.73, 2.66)	1.72	(0.7, 4.0)	1.20	(0.83, 1.72)	1.07	(0.6, 1.8)
Insurance status																
Private	1.00		1.00		1.00		1.00		1.00		1.00		1.00		1.00	
Public	1.51	(0.92, 2.48)	1.35	(0.6, 2.9)	2.21	(1.35, 3.63)*	2.84	(1.1, 7.2)	1.35	(0.82, 2.22)	2.02	(0.8, 4.9)	1.87	(1.24, 2.82)*	2.97	(1.4, 6.4)*
Uninsurance	0.87	(0.57, 1.33)	0.38	(0.2, 0.9)*	0.79	(0.43, 1.46)	0.88	(0.4, 1.8)	0.99	(0.53, 1.83)	0.46	(0.2, 1.1)	0.78	(0.56, 1.1)	0.71	(0.4, 1.2)
Other	2.03	(0.78, 5.32)	0.71	*	1.30	(0.71, 2.38)	3.38	(1.0, 11.1)*	0.78	(0.27, 2.23)	0.35	(0.1, 2.0)	1.74	(0.8, 3.78)	2.01	(0.7, 5.4)
Any depression past year																
No	1.00		1.00		1.00		1.00		1.00		1.00		1.00		1.00	
Yes	2.23	(1.39, 3.58)*	1.97	(1.0, 4.0)	1.76	(1.08, 2.88)*	1.55	(0.7, 3.3)	1.66	(0.76, 3.64)	1.81	(0.8, 4.1)	2.02	(1.23, 3.33)*	1.60	(0.9, 2.8)
Any anxiety disorder past year																
No	1.00		1.00		1.00		1.00		1.00		1.00		1.00		1.00	
Yes	1.15	(0.7, 1.9)	0.94	(0.4, 2.1)	0.91	(0.56, 1.5)	1.03	(0.5, 2.1)	1.09	(0.44, 2.74)	1.14	(0.5, 2.5)	0.93	(0.64, 1.35)	0.79	(0.4, 1.7)

Table 16.4 (continued)

	Service type															
	General				Specialty				Human sector				Any service			
	Females		Males		Females		Males		Females		Males		Females		Males	
	$n=544$		$n=220$		$n=482$		$n=251$		$n=229$		$n=108$		$n=935$		$n=435$	
	OR	95% CI	OR	95% CI	OR	95% CI	OR	95% CI	OR	95% CI	OR	95% CI	OR	95% CI	OR	95% CI
Any substance use past year																
No	1.00		1.00		1.00		1.00		1.00		1.00		1.00		1.00	
Yes	0.85	(0.43, 1.66)	0.72	(0.3, 1.7)	1.33	(0.7, 2.51)	1.22	(0.5, 3.2)	0.67	(0.23, 2.01)	2.62	(0.9, 8.0)	0.84	(0.5,.1.4)	0.75	(0.4, 1.5)
Number of disorders past year																
0	1.00		1.00		1.00		1.00		1.00		1.00		1.00		1.00	
1	2.94	(1.57, 5.5)*	5.09	*	3.71	(2.13, 6.47)*	2.04	(1.0, 4.2)	2.47	(1.15, 5.32)*	2.62	(1.2, 5.7)*	3.66	(2.25, 5.97)*	3.81	(1.9, 7.6)*
2	3.33	(1.73, 6.42)*	6.40	(2.1, 19.2)*	3.37	(1.45, 7.86)*	6.33	(2.2, 17.9)*	2.33	(0.54, 9.96)	3.31		3.89	(1.87, 8.08) *	9.83	(3.8, 25.2)*
3+	4.16	(1.67, 10.37)*	7.49	(1.7, 33.8)*	8.58	(3.2, 23.05)*	7.71	(1.8, 33.4)*	3.49	(0.69, 17.68)	0.99	(0.2, 4.6)	7.10	(2.96, 17.05)	10.78	(3.2, 36.2)*

*Significant odds ratio at the $p < 0.05$ level

Challenge 3: Access to Mental Health Care

Access to mental health care among Latinos, particularly recent immigrants, appears to be strongly related to public policy restrictions regarding insurance coverage. Latinos in general are disproportionately uninsured compared to the overall US population, with Mexicans reporting the lowest rates of insurance (Alegría et al. 2006b). Puerto Ricans in general have the highest rates of coverage of all Latino subgroups, as shown in Table 16.1. Interestingly, Latino men and women with public insurance are more likely to access mental health services than those with private insurance (see Table 16.4).

Changes in Medicaid laws require immigrants to be residents of the United States for at least five years before becoming eligible for healthcare benefits. Policy changes in the Personal Work Opportunity and Reconciliation Act of 1996 limit Latino immigrants' ability to access outpatient mental health treatment services. Mental health service provision for minorities may be particularly vulnerable to policy changes and eligibility thresholds. For example, implementation of this five-year rule has not only eliminated enrollment of new immigrants, but enrollment rates also dropped for those who had been in the country for many years and were, in fact, still eligible for the program (Kandula et al. 2004). Language barriers, misunderstandings over requirements, and fears of deportation may influence the take-up of insurance even for eligible immigrants (Capps and Passel 2004).

Understanding the service-use patterns of Latinos and developing policies to address unmet need may be further influenced by the survey methods that are used to collect this information. As noted above, traditional epidemiologic studies such as the NCS-R usually conduct interviews in English only, potentially missing a large portion of respondents who may need services.

Strengths Contributing to Latino Adult Mental Health

Strength 1: Familism

The importance of family ties for Latinos, or familism, is frequently cited as a positive force in promoting lower rates of psychological distress among Latinos (Rivera 2007; Vega et al. 1991). Close-knit family connections have been described as the most distinctive cultural factor of relationship for Latinos (Sabogal et al. 1987). At the same time, family support factors have been associated with decreased likelihood of suicide attempts and ideation (Fortuna et al. 2007), as well as lower likelihood of some mental disorders (Hovey and Magana 2002). The specific mechanisms by which family supports protect Latinos against mental health problems are largely unknown. Recent work suggests that the relationship between family supports and mental health may be intricate. For example, the latest evidence suggests that not only do these relationships vary across Latino subgroups, but for Latinos with high levels of family cultural conflict, close bonds may actually serve to heighten psychological distress. While family cohesion has been found to buffer the effect of family cultural conflict on psychological distress for Cubans, family cohesion has the opposite effect for other Latinos (mainly those from the Dominican Republic, Colombia, El Salvador, Ecuador, Guatemala, Honduras, Peru, Nicaragua), increasing distress for those families experiencing conflict (Rivera et al. 2008).

Strength 2: Latino Biculturalism and Bilingualism

Another factor that appears to influence mental health for Latinos is the way in which the process of becoming part of mainstream US society is balanced with familial obligations and retention of Latino social networks. Emerging evidence of biculturalism and bilingualism as protective factors for Latino mental health point to the importance of how individuals manage the transition between a more traditional Latino home and the demands of the dominant culture (Kim and Ominzo 2006; LaFromboise et al. 1993). Recent research suggests positive effects of bilingualism on mental health (Mulvaney-Day et al. 2007). Language and cultural factors appear to act as a bridge between two worlds, providing a means of negotiating tension between two cultures without being forced to choose one over the other. Moving in mainstream US society might allow more opportunities for social mobility, but retaining social networks and norms from Latino culture might provide a sense of belonging and reciprocity that may shield against hardship. Rates of substance use disorder are lower among Latinos who report more frequent use of Spanish than English with family members (Canino et al. 2008). This suggests that Spanish language use can be a proxy for retaining social networks that maintain Latino norms and lifestyle, even in contexts of elevated drug exposure and crime, which buffers the risk of substance disorders.

Strength 3: Context of Immigration Experience

A further protective factor appears to be the context of the immigration experience for Latinos. As noted above, the influence of nativity on mental health is multifaceted, and differs dramatically across subethnicity and by type of disorder. One study comparing the risk of mental disorder for Latinos who were born in the United States or arrived by age six, versus those who arrived after age six, finds few differences across nativity in risk for depressive or anxiety disorder after adjusting for family stressors, contextual factors and social status factors (Alegria et al. 2007d). This research indicates that nativity does not function as an independent risk factor for mental disorders, but instead sits within a complex framework of other social factors associated with the immigrant experience. For example, family harmony and marital status are central to decreased risk of depressive and anxiety disorders, and perceived neighborhood safety and religious attendance emerge as protective factors for substance-use disorders. Further research has suggested that factors such as age of arrival in the United States and time in the United States also play a significant role in whether nativity factors are protective. The longer Latino immigrants remain in their country of origin, the lower their risk of psychiatric disorders, leading to lower lifetime rates of disorder (Alegría et al. 2007d). Most of this lower risk for psychiatric illness is due to low risk in the country of origin, suggesting that protective familial and cultural values are most salient while in the country of origin and may lose their benefit following immigration to the United States. Once an immigrant arrives in the United States, the risk of onset appears similar to that of US-born Latinos of the same age, probably as a result of the erosion of these protective factors.

Other research has shown that certain specific mental disorders appear to be particularly vulnerable to cultural processes associated with being a US-born Latino. For example, Fortuna et al. (2007) find that the risk of suicidal ideation is higher for US-born Latinos than for immigrants, and for Latinos who report good or excellent English compared to those who have fair or poor English-speaking capabilities. Similarly, risk for substance use disorders is higher for US-born Latinos than immigrants (Canino et al. 2008). Interestingly, in both of these cases, family dynamics are significantly related to the risk for mental health disorder. Higher levels of family cultural conflict are associated with suicidal ideation (Fortuna et al. 2007), and with substance use disorder as well as lower family harmony, family pride and family cohesion (Canino et al. 2008). The quality of family relationships as well as the way in which cultural differences are managed across generations appears to be a significant area of attention for mental health providers working with first- and second-generation Latino families in the United States.

The sum of these changing social and contextual circumstances is often subsumed under the umbrella term of acculturation. Whether acculturation processes per se are a risk factor is obviously a difficult question, given that family relationships, cultural conflict, nativity, and language all combine to create a multifaceted picture of the effects of acculturation. Few empirical studies have actually tested the role of these factors in mitigating the stress of the acculturation experience, and most have been conducted only with Mexicans. Given that Latino subgroups experience unique migratory patterns and social histories that often produce widely varying acculturation experiences (Guarnaccia et al. 2007), it is difficult to assess the relationship between mental health and acculturation for Latinos as an aggregate group. For example, across Cubans, Mexicans, Puerto Ricans, and other Latinos, an analysis of NLAAS data found widely varying experiences of cultural stress in the United States, with Mexicans reporting the highest acculturative distress and Puerto Ricans the lowest (data not shown). However, Puerto Ricans also reported the highest level of family cultural conflict in this study, which has been shown to increase risk for mental disorders (Guarnaccia et al. 2007). Looking at the relationships with mental health using these two related but unique constructs may yield very different findings across subethnic groups. The importance of more discretely considering this variability in measurement of the broad notion of acculturation is only beginning to become clear in recent research, due to limited sample sizes and subethnic composition in previous psychiatric epidemiologic studies (Alegría et al. 2004).

Discussion

Integration of Concepts

An immense gap exists between mental health risks faced by Latinos and our knowledge of how research can be translated to improved mental health services for this underserved population. Latino immigrants represent a particularly complex and vulnerable population due to high rates of poverty, low education, and family separation, and few resources to access care. They often share adjustment stressors such as isolation, hopelessness, socioeconomic disadvantage, and greater intergenerational conflict as well as acculturative stress and language barriers that impact risk for mental disorders. However, despite these many challenges, findings from the NLAAS indicate that many factors inherent to Latino culture may actually be protective against risk of mental disorders. The next challenge for researchers is to determine how best to utilize these strengths to improve Latinos' mental health.

The powerful protective effect of foreign nativity, particularly for substance-use disorders, is one of the more consistent findings across studies. While the exact mechanisms are unknown, it appears that the period immediately after arrival to the United States marks a particularly vulnerable time for Latino immigrants. During this period, exposure to unsafe environments in the United States and low perceived social position, as well being out of the labor force, may increase the risk for substance disorders. Given the protective effect of cultural factors, mental health interventions targeting Latinos should focus on maintaining stable family structures and cohesiveness as well as managing and resolving conflict between the traditional Latino home and the demands of the dominant culture, and dealing with experiences of discrimination and unsafe neighborhoods.

Another powerful finding from the NLAAS is the effect of family harmony, marital status, integration in employment, and self-perception of high social standing as factors that can decrease the risk of depressive and anxiety disorders for Latinos in the United States. These findings indicate the potential to buffer the acculturation process by perceived social mobility and social integration. The potentially negative mental health consequences of the acculturation process may be buffered by maintaining interactions and networks with Spanish-language cultures that help sustain a sense of belonging and family affiliation. On the other hand, Latino social mobility may be linked to bridging with English-speakers and more acculturated Latinos who might offer access to job and educational opportunities. Interventions focused on mediating immigration and acculturation processes may have powerful impacts on mental health outcomes for immigrants who arrive after age six, as well as the US-born. Our data also emphasizes the need to understand how best to cope with experiences of discrimination and marginalization that may be embedded in the assimilation process. Very few approaches in intervention development accommodate diversity or social justice, and how mental illness intersects with experiences of social oppression (Falicov 2003). Developing social interventions that consider structural aspects of marginalization among the US-born may decrease risk for mental health problems. Our findings emphasize the importance of culture and immigration factors on entering and remaining in care, particularly when not experiencing an acute episode of illness. Interventions that facilitate access and recognition of the benefits of preventive care need to be developed for this population.

Future Recommendations

Based on the above findings, several recommendations are offered as potential strategies to reduce risk of mental illness and increase access to mental health services among Latino adults in the United States.

1. Explore policy interventions targeting poverty reduction and augmentation of educational achievement among Latino adults and their families as a way of reducing mental health problems. Examples of potential policy interventions are the expansion of the Earned Income Tax Credit Return in states with high Latino density, and Title 1 programs in schools where poor Latino youth are overrepresented.
2. High levels of unmet need are present across all Latino subethnic groups. Adoption of interventions to improve entry into mental health services should be prioritized for Latinos who do not recognize and attend to their psychiatric illness, but are in need of preventive treatment, before they become disabled or impaired. Public mental health referral campaigns and hotlines may be useful as well as anti-stigma social marketing campaigns.
3. Consider variability in broad notions of acculturation so as to facilitate a receptive environment to help Latinos navigate and anticipate hurdles in US communities.
4. Due to substantial evidence that some of the mechanisms responsible for risk of psychopathology among Latinos may vary by subethnic group as well as disorder (Alegría et al. 2007a), future studies are needed to more directly tailor prevention interventions. Comparing Latinos by subethnicity and nativity is an important way to sort out potential mechanisms involved in increasing or decreasing risk of psychiatric disorder for Latinos living in the United States.
5. The NLAAS data have identified certain vulnerable subgroups within the Latino population, such as Puerto Ricans and monolingual Spanish speakers whose rates of mental disorders are notably higher than other subgroups, and in some cases approach those of non-Latino Whites. Future work should focus on identifying processes linked to risk factors which contribute to high rates of mental disorders, and establishing interventions targeting these subgroups.

6. Our data emphasize the importance of family, contextual, and social status as risk or protective factors for psychiatric disorders. This emphasizes the need for elucidating what in US culture increases the risk of psychiatric disorders.
7. More feasibility studies are needed on how to intervene with US-born Latinos and those who immigrate between birth and age six, since they are at increased likelihood for substance use disorders. Availability of alternative social networks in immigrant enclaves might protect against substance disorders. Researchers should further examine which environmental factors of immigrants' countries of origin contribute to the protective effect found among those who immigrate after age six.
8. Our results point to the importance of conducting longitudinal and qualitative studies that might allow us to better understand the differential risk by age of arrival to the United States, family dynamics, and subethnicity.
9. Risk for psychiatric disorder should be viewed within a developmental context in an effort to determine how different environments protect or reduce risk of psychiatric disorders, particularly during certain age periods.
10. Prospectively, new interventions should incorporate the identified strengths in service delivery.

Concluding Comments

As Latinos continue to gain prominence in the demographic profile of the country, the NLAAS provides a unique opportunity for gaining a deeper understanding of this diverse population and the complex factors that shape Latinos mental health outcomes. Indeed, the analyses presented here provide strong evidence of the importance of disaggregating Latino subgroups. A case in point is earlier research findings, which suggest that Latino immigrants experience a health advantage over their US-born counterparts. In analyses using the NLAAS, this held true in the aggregate for substance use disorders. However, once analyses were disaggregated, it became evident that while the protective effect of nativity applied for most Latinos, it did not hold for Puerto Ricans. Furthermore, in some of the analyses where a protective effect was found, it disappeared after controlling for age, gender, and socio-contextual factors (e.g., family structure and its attendant dynamics). These, as well as other analyses of the NLAAS, highlight the need for undertaking a nuanced approach to Latino mental health outcomes.

In considering the implications of the protective effect of nativity on substance use outcomes among some Latinos, it is important to note that the children of immigrants and immigrant children (the second generation) will constitute the largest component of the Latino population by 2020. To the extent that this segment of the population is at risk for unfavorable substance use outcomes relative to the foreign-born, the absence of effective multi-level interventions that consider broad contextual factors is likely to exacerbate disparities in these outcomes.

Table 16.5 Summary table

Topic	Main findings	Implications for Latino mental health and future research
Sociodemographic factors	Great differences exist in sociodemographic and living circumstances across Latino subgroups in the United States • Mexicans have the youngest age distribution while Cubans have the highest • Cubans are the most highly educated and have the lowest rates of poverty while Mexicans have the lowest levels of education and highest poverty rates • Mexican men have the highest rates of employment while Mexican women have the lowest • Puerto Ricans have the highest rates of English interview completion, while Cubans have the lowest	It is important to understand mental health risks for Latinos taking into account the heterogeneity of the Latino population in the United States, and how the distribution of risk might differ based on sociodemographic factors
Socioeconomic and sociocultural factors	Latino groups experience greater socioeconomic disadvantage compared to the non-Latino White population • Latinos are younger and have lower levels of education and household income compared to non-Latino Whites • Latinos have significantly higher rates of uninsurance than non-Latino Whites A similar pattern exists for US-born Latinos compared to immigrant Latinos, with immigrants having lower SES but more stable social networks • US-born men and women report higher incomes and more education than their immigrant counterparts • Immigrant men and women have higher rates of marriage or cohabitation than US-born Latinos	A primary challenge for Latino mental health is supporting the positive effects of improved SES status that come with increased time in the United States, while also maintaining strong social and cultural connections. Greater family stability may provide resiliency to immigrant Latinos and could prove to be an important area for future intervention work
Psychiatric disorders	Overall, Latinos were less likely to have mental disorders than non-Latino Whites • Latinos are at lower risk than non-Latino Whites for all lifetime psychiatric disorders except agoraphobia without panic In aggregate, differences in the risk for psychiatric disorder are evident between immigrant Latinos and the US-born, particularly for substance disorders. However, when considering Latinos by nativity and sub-ethnicity, rates of mental disorder vary more widely	Given the complexity of the factors related to resiliency and risk for mental disorders across immigrant and US-born Latinos as well as across Latino subgroups, it is important not to over-generalize the effects of the accultura-tive process on risk for disorder. The way in which individuals manage cultural differ-ences across generations is an important

Table 16.5 (continued)

	• US-born Latinos report higher lifetime rates for most disorders than Latino immigrants • Among the specific Latino subgroups, differences by nativity are only evident for depressive and anxiety disorders in Mexicans and for all Latinos expect Puerto Ricans for substance use disorders • Rates of disorder vary substantially across Latino subgroups, with Puerto Ricans having the highest rates of disorders with their rates approaching those of non-Latino Whites	area of attention for mental health clinicians working with these populations. Furthermore, the NLAAS data have identified certain vulnerable subgroups within the Latino population, such as Puerto Ricans. Research efforts should focus on identifying contributing risk factors and developing targeted interventions for these populations
Factors influencing Latino mental health	Familism, or family support factors have been associated with lower rates of psychological distress among Latinos, although recent findings suggest a more complicated relationship • Family support factors have been associated with a decrease in the likelihood of suicide attempts and ideation • Family harmony and marital status are linked to decreased risk of depressive and anxiety disorders • However, among Latino families with high levels of family cultural conflict, close bonds may result in heightened psychological distress, with family cohesion increasing distress for other Latino families experiencing conflict • Those with substance use disorders reported higher family cultural conflict as well as lower family harmony, pride, and cohesion Biculturalism and bilingualism have emerged as protective factors for Latino mental health indicating the importance of how individuals manage the transition between Latino and US culture • Rates of substance use disorders have been found to be lower among Latinos who report more frequent use of Spanish than English with family members Age of immigration and time in the United States have been found to mediate the relationship between nativity and risk of psychiatric disorders	Although nativity is most commonly examined as an independent risk factor for mental disorders among Latinos, our data emphasize the importance of family, contextual, and social status factors as risk or protective factors for Latino mental health. The quality of family relationships, the way in which cultural differences are managed across generations, and the context under which Latinos immigrate appear to be areas of attention for mental health professionals and researchers working with Latinos in the United States

Table 16.5 (continued)

	• The longer Latino immigrants remain in their country of origin, the lower their risk of lifetime psychiatric disorders Contextual factors such as neighborhood environment, particularly neighborhood safety have been found to impact Latino mental health • Perceived neighborhood safety and religious attendance emerge as protective factors for substance use disorders Exposure to discrimination and racism is thought to interact with socioeconomic status resulting in challenges to Latino mental health with Latinos who achieve higher social status experiencing higher rates of discrimination • In the NLAAS, Latinos with higher education were more likely to report everyday discrimination • More acculturated Mexican immigrants have been found to report higher levels of discrimination compared to less acculturated immigrants • Perceived discrimination is related to rates of depression	
Mental health service use	Significant problems still exist in linking Latinos with mental health needs to services and in continued maintenance on anti-depressant medication. Language and cultural factors are strongly associated with use of mental health services • US-born Latinos are less likely to received any mental health service than non-Latino Whites and immigrants are less likely to receive any formal mental health or substance use services • Latinos who are US-born, speak English, and have the most number of years in the United States report higher rates of specialty and mental health service use • Latinos with good/excellent English proficiency were less likely to discontinue taking antidepressants	Improved outreach to monolingual Spanish speakers and Latinos who require preventive mental health care is necessary to help them navigate and anticipate the hurdles in obtaining mental health services

The findings highlighted in this chapter also point to the importance of further unraveling the factors that intertwine in the process of becoming integrated into US society. Analyses of the NLAAS suggest an interaction between socioeconomic standing and exposure to the racialized environment of the United States. This is evidenced, for instance, in findings where US-born Latinos and Latinos with higher levels of education are more likely to report experiences of discrimination. These findings and other findings from the NLAAS suggest the need to expand our conceptual tool kit to include not only measures of nativity and language use but also those related to cultural conflict, discrimination, and perceived social standing (Table 16.5).

References

Alegría, M., Bijl, R., Lin, E., Walters, E., & Kessler, R. (2000). Income differences in persons seeking outpatient treatment for mental disorders: A comparison of the United States with Ontario and the Netherlands. *Archives of General Psychiatry, 57*(4), 383–391.

Alegria, M., Canino, G., Shrout, PE., Woo, M., Duan, N., Vila, D., et al. (2008). Prevalence of mental illness in immigrant and non-immigrant U.S. Latino groups. *American Journal of Psychiatry, 165*(3), 359–369.

Alegría, M., Canino, G., Stinson, F., & Grant, B. (2006a). Nativity and DSM-IV psychiatric disorders among Puerto Ricans, Cuban Americans and non-Latino Whites in the United States: Results from the national epidemiologic survey on alcohol and related conditions. *Journal of Clinical Psychiatry, 67*(1), 56–65.

Alegría, M., Cao, Z., McGuire, T., Ojeda, V., Sribney, W., Woo, M., et al. (2006b). Health insurance coverage for vulnerable populations: Contrasting Asian Americans and Latinos in the U.S. *Inquiry, 43*(Fall), 231–254.

Alegría, M., & McGuire, T. (2003). Rethinking a universalist framework in the psychiatric symptom-disorder relationship. *Journal of Health & Social Behavior, 44*(3), 257–274.

Alegría, M., Mulvaney-Day, N., Torres, M., Polo, A., Cao, Z., & Canino, G. (2007a). Prevalence of psychiatric disorders across Latino subgroups in the United States. *American Journal of Public Health, 97*, 68–75.

Alegría, M., Mulvaney-Day, N., Woo, M., Torres, M., Gao, S., & Oddo, V. (2007b). Correlates of twelve-month mental health service use among Latinos: Results from the National Latino and Asian American study (NLAAS). *American Journal of Public Health, 97*, 76–83.

Alegria, M., Shrout, P., Woo, M., Guarnaccia, P., Sribney, W., Vila, D., et al. (2007c). Understanding differences in past year mental health disorders for Latinos living in the U.S. *Social Science & Medicine, 65*, 214–230.

Alegria, M., Sribney, W., Woo, M., Torres, M., Guarnaccia, P. (2007d). Looking beyond nativity: The relation of age of immigration, length of residence, and birth cohorts to the risk of onset of psychiatric disorders for Latinos. *Research on Human Development, 4*(1–2), 19–47.

Alegría, M., Takeuchi, D., Canino, G., Duan, N., Shrout, P., Meng, X.-L., et al. (2004). Considering context, place and culture: The national Latino and Asian American study. *International Journal of Methods in Psychiatric Research, 13*(4), 208–220.

Anderson, M., & Fienberg, S. E. (1999). *Who counts? The politics of census-taking in contemporary America*. New York: Sage.

Bird, H. R., Canino, G., Rubio-Stipec, M., Gould, M. S., Ribera, J. C., Sesman, M., et al. (1988). Estimates of the prevalence of childhood maladjustment in a community survey in Puerto Rico. *Archives of General Psychiatry, 45*, 1120–1126.

Breslau, J., Aguilar-Gaxiola, S., Kendler, K., Su, M., Williams, D., & Kessler, R. (2006). Specifying race-ethnic differences in risk for psychiatric disorder in a USA national sample. *Psychological Medicine, 36*(1), 57–68.

Burnam, M., Hough, R., Karno, M., Escobar, J., & Telles, C. (1987). Acculturation and lifetime prevalence of psychiatric disorders among Mexican Americans in Los Angeles. *Journal of Health and Social Behavior, 28,* 89–102.

Canino, G., Vega, WA., Sribney, WM., Warner LA., & Alegria, M. (2008). Social relationships, social assimilation, and substance use disorder among adult Latinos in the U.S. *Journal of Drug Issues, 38*(1), 69–101.

Capps, R., & Passel, J. (2004). *Describing immigrant communities (presentation).* Washington, D.C.: The Urban Institute.

Colpe, L., Merikangas, K., Cuthbert, B., & Bourdon, K. (2004). Guest editorial. *International Journal of Methods in Psychiatric Research, 13*(4), 193–194.

Costello, E., Keeler, G., & Angold, A. (2001). Poverty, race/ethnicity, and psychiatric disorder: A study of rural children. *American Journal of Public Health, 91*(9), 1494–1498.

Falicov, C. (2003). Culture in family therapy. In G. Weeks, T. Sexton & M. Robbins (Eds.), *Handbook of family therapy* (pp. 37–57). New York: Routledge.

Finch, B., Kolody, B., & Vega W. (2000). Perceived discrimination and depression among Mexican-origin adults in California. *Journal of Health and Social Behavior, 41,* 295–313.

Fortuna, L., Perez D., Canino G, Sribney W., & Alegria M. (2007). Prevalence and correlates of lifetime suicidal ideation and attempts among Latino subgroups in the United States. *Journal of Clinical Psychiatry, 68*(4), 572–581.

Guarnaccia, P., Martinez, I., Ramirez, R., & Canino, G. (2005). Are ataques de nervios in Puerto Rican children associated with psychiatric disorder? *Journal of the American Academy of Child and Adolescent Psychiatry, 44*(11), 1184–1192.

Guarnaccia, P., Pincay, I., Alegria, M., Shrout, P., Lewis-Fernandez, R., & Canino, G. (2007). Assessing diversity among Latinos: Results from the NLAAS. *Hispanic Journal of Behavioral Sciences, 29*(4), 510–534.

Hartley, H. (1962). Multiple frame surveys. Proceedings of the Social Statistics Section, American Statistical Association, Washington, D.C, 1962, 203–206.

Hartley, H. (1974). Multiple frame methodology and selected applications. *Sankhya, Ser. C, 36*(Part 3), 99–118.

Hodgkin, D., Volpe-Vartanian, J., & Alegria, M. (2007). Discontinuation of antidepressant medication among Latinos in the US. *Journal of Behavioral Health Services and Research, 34*(3), 329–342.

Hovey, J. D., & Magana, C. (2002). Cognitive, affective, and physiological expressions of anxiety symptomatology among Mexican migrant farmworkers: Predictors and generational differences. *Community Mental Health Journal, 38*(3), 223–237.

Interuniversity Consortium for Political and Social Science Research. The Collaborative Psychiatric Epidemiology Surveys: Sample Design. http://www.icpsr.umich.edu/icpsrweb/CPES/about-cpes/sample-design.jsp. Accessed 29 July 2011.

Kandula, N., Kersey, M., & Lurie, N. (2004). Assuring the health of immigrants: What the leading health indicators tell us. *Annual Review of Public Health, 25,* 357–376.

Kessler, R., Berglund, P., Demler, O., Jin, R., & Walters, E. (2005). Lifetime prevalence and age-of-onset distributions of DSM-IV disorders in the national comorbidity survey replication. *Archives of General Psychiatry, 62,* 593–602.

Kessler, R., & Merikangas, K. (2004). The National Comorbidity Survey Replication (NCS–R). *International Journal of Methods in Psychiatric Research, 13*(2), 60–68.

Kessler, R. C., & Ustun, T. B. (2004). The World Mental Health (WMH) survey initiative version of the World Health Organization (WHO) Composite International Diagnostic Interview (CIDI). *International Journal of Methods in Psychiatric Research, 13*(2), 93–121.

Kim, B., & Ominzo, M. (2006). Behavioral acculturation and enculturation and psychological functioning among Asian American college students. *Cultural Diversity & Ethnic Minority Psychology, 12*(2), 245–258.

LaFromboise, T., Coleman, H., & Gerton, J. (1993). Psychological impact of bioculturalism: Evidence and theory. *Psychological Bulletin, 114*(3), 395–412.
Levitt, P., DeWind, J., & Vertovec, S. (2003). International perspectives on transnational migration: An introduction. *International Migration Review, 37*(3), 565–575.
Margolis, M. (1995). Brazilians and the 1990 United States census: Immigrants, ethnicity, and the undercount. *Human Organization, 54*(1), 52–59.
Mulvaney-Day, N., Alegria, M., & Sribney, W. (2007). Social cohesion, social support, and health among Latinos in the United States. *Social Science & Medicine, 64*(2), 477–495.
Patel, V., & Kleinman, A. (2003). Poverty and common mental disorders in developing countries. *Bulletin of the World Health Organization, 81*(8), 609–615.
Perez, DJ., Fortuna, L., & Alegria, M. (2008). Prevalence and correlates of everyday discrimination among U.S. Latinos. *Journal of Community Psychology, 36*(4), 421–433.
Rivera, F. (2007). Contextualizing the experience of young Latino adults: Acculturation, social support and depression. *Journal of Immigrant and Minority Health, 9*(3), 237–244.
Rivera, FI., Guarnaccia, PJ., Mulvaney-Day, N., Lin, JY., Torres, M., & Alegría, M. (2008). Family cohesion and its relationship to psychological distress among Latino groups. *Hispanic Journal of Behavioral Sciences, 30*(3), 357–378.
Sabogal, F., Marin, G., Otero-Sabogal, R., Vanoss, B., & Perez Stable, E. (1987). Familism. *Hispanic Journal of Behavioral Sciences, 9*(4), 307–412.
Saraceno, B., & Barbui, C. (1997). Poverty and mental illness. *Canadian Journal of Psychiatry, 42,* 285–290.
Substance Abuse and Mental Health Services Administration. (2000). National household survey on drug abuse 2000. http://www.samhsa.gov. Accessed 29 July 2011.
The National Academies. (2007). Multiple origins, uncertain destinies: Hispanics and the American future. http://www7.nationalacademies.org/cpop/ADemographicDividend.pdf. Accessed 29 July 2011.
U.S. Census Bureau. (2000). Population profile of the United States: 2000. www.census.gov/population/pop-profile/2000/chap09.pdf. Accessed 22 Nov 2002.
U.S. Census Bureau. (2007). National Population Projections. http://www.census.gov/population/www/pop-profile/natproj.html. Accessed 29 Aug 2007.
U.S. Department of Health and Human Services. (2001). Mental health care for hispanic Americans. In U.S. Department of Health and Human Services, Office of the Surgeon General (Eds.), *Culture, race, and ethnicity: A supplement to mental health a report of the surgeon general* (pp. 129–147). Rockville: U.S.
U.S. General Accounting Office (GAO). (1998). *Decennial census: Overview of historical census issues* (No. GAO/GGD-98-103). Washington, D.C.: U.S. GAO.
Vega, W., & Gil, A. (2007). Alcohol, tobacco and other drugs. In M. Aguirre-Molina, L. Borrell & W. Vega (Eds.), *The health of Latino men: A social and structural analysis*. NewBrunswick: Rutgers University Press.
Vega, W. A., Kolody, B., Valle, R., & Weir, J. (1991). Social networks, social support, and their relationship to depression among immigrant Mexican women. *Human Organization, 50*(2), 154–162.
Viruell-Fuentes, E. (2006). "My heart is always there": The transnational practices of first-generation Mexican immigrant and second-generation Mexican American women. *Identities: Global studies in culture and power, 13*(3), 335–362.
Viruell-Fuentes, E. A. (2007). Beyond acculturation: Immigration, discrimination, and health research among Mexicans in the United States. *Social Science and Medicine, 65*(7), 1524–1535.

Chapter 17
Psychology of Latino American Older Adults: Strengths and Challenges to Mental Health in a Shifting Society

Steven R. Applewhite and John M. Gonzales

Chapter Focus

This chapter presents information on mental health issues in Latino American older adults, focusing on communication difficulties, acculturative stress, and service utilization as major challenges to the maintenance of mental health in this group; family, cultural values, and religion as strengths contributing to resilience in this group; and several issues relevant to bringing the cultural strengths of this group more effectively into the service of increasing their overall mental health.

Introduction

In the last 20 years, there have been dramatic shifts in the age structure of the US population. In the year 2000, there were 35 million Americans (12.4% of the population) ages 65 or older. This population will increase to 40 million by 2010 and 55 million by 2020. Among these older adults are arguably a more educated, politically astute, financially secure, and healthier cohort of older Americans than existed in previous generations. Although many are entering old age as vital, valued, and productive members of society, a segment of this population are ethnic minorities entering old age facing a host of health and mental health problems and with limited resources to handle these problems. Within this population structure are older Latinos whose lifetime contributions to this nation fabric are only eclipsed by a history of social, economic, and political neglect, as well as health and mental health disparities.

Ostensibly, the increase in the older populations and the proportion of older adults will necessitate greater flexibility and advocacy on the part of service provid-

S. R. Applewhite (✉)
Graduate College of Social Work, University of Houston,
110 HA Social Work Building, Houston, TX 77204-4013, USA
e-mail: sapplewhite@uh.edu

E. C. Chang, C. A. Downey (eds.), *Handbook of Race and Development in Mental Health*,
DOI 10.1007/978-1-4614-0424-8_17,

ers and policy makers to effectively address the health and mental health needs of all older adults. Hayes-Bautista (2002) notes that the National Institute of Health Office of Minority Health (1998) concluded that there is "compelling evidence that race and ethnicity correlate with persistent, and often increasing, health disparities among US populations" (Hayes-Bautista et al. p. 18). In its Supplement Report entitled *Mental Health: Culture, Race, and Ethnicity* the Office of the Surgeon General, provides a stark view of mental health issues experienced by racial and ethnic minorities. The report notes that compared to Whites, minorities have less access to mental health services, are less likely to receive needed care, and more likely to receive poorer quality mental health care despite having similar rates of mental disorders. Moreover, OSG rendered it's most substantive finding that "racial and ethnic minorities bear a greater burden from unmet mental health needs and thus suffer a greater loss to their overall mental health and productivity" (USDHHS 2001, p. 3). Against this background, the following demographic profile of contemporary elderly Latino depicts an emerging trend termed the "Browning" of the Graying of America (Henry 1990; Hayes-Bautista et al. 2002).

Demographic Characteristics of US Hispanics/Latinos

Older minorities make up approximately 14% of the nation's elderly population, and 16% of the Medicare population (Henry J. Kaiser Family Foundation 1999). According to the 2000 Census, older Hispanics account for 6% of the older population with estimates reaching 18% by 2050. The U.S. Census distribution of the Latino population was 59.3% Mexican, 9.7% Puerto Rican, 3.5% Cuban, 9.1% Central and South American, 2.3% Dominican, 0.3% Spaniard, and 15.7% "other" Hispanic (Ramirez 2004).

In relation to the total population, Hispanics are a younger population, with a median age of 26.0 years of age, compared to 35.4 for the total US populations. Of the Hispanic population, 4.8% was 65 years and over, compared to 12% of the total population, with older Cubans (18.7%) most likely to be 65 and older. In 2002, older Latinos were mostly concentrated in California (27%), Florida (16%), New York (9%), and Texas (20%) (Ramirez 2004). Mexican-Americans are the largest subgroup in California and Texas due in part to the proximity of the US-Mexican border. Many Hispanics reside in areas they originally immigrated into, forming ethnic enclaves; others reside in geographic areas where their ancestors lived for generations, dating back to turn of the last century. Likewise, Cuban-Americans who fled Cuba during the exodus of the 1950s are concentrated in Florida, whereas Puerto Ricans are concentrated in the Eastern Seaboard and New York.

Statistics on United States versus foreign-born nationality reveal that approximately 60% of Hispanics were born in the United States; more than two in five of foreign-born Hispanics having arrived in the United States in the 1990s. Today the immigrant Latino population has sought residence in virtually every state and city, and the dispersed Latino population contributes to all sectors of the economy and social life. Finally, of the 35 million Hispanics in the United States, more than 75% speak a language other than English at home, and of this population, nearly all (99%) speak Spanish at home (Ramirez 2004).

Education

Despite the overall increase in educational attainment among older Americans, there are still substantial educational differences between older Latinos and the general older population. The 2000 Census indicates that only 52% of all Hispanics completed a high-school education, compared to 80.4% for the total population. The subgroups with the lowest educational attainment are Mexican and Central Americans each with about 46% (U.S. Census Bureau 2000). Older Latinos lag behind in educational attainment, with about 35% of the population having finished high school, compared to 70% of the general older population. In addition, 5.5% of older Latinos had a bachelor's degree or higher, compared to 16.7% of all older persons (Ramirez 2004). From a mental health perspective, the number of years of education completed influence the rate of mental distress among older as noted by Gonzalez et al. (2001), who report that the more education older Mexican-Americans attained, the lower the prevalence of depression.

Insurance

Perhaps no other economic factor is as important to older Americans as the availability of affordable health insurance. Many older Latinos have limited or no insurance and are only minimally insured by Medicaid or Medicare. Likewise, many older Latinos often do not access to health services, even if they have private insurance, due to the prohibitive cost of healthcare and prescription drugs (Collins et al. 2002; Henry J. Kaiser Family Foundation 1999). Hargraves and Hadley (2003) found that Hispanics, when compared to White counterparts, were 22% more likely to report unmet needs, 39% less likely to have a regular healthcare provider, and 38.5% less likely to have visited a doctor in the last year. In addition, even with Medicare insurance, out-of-pocket costs, co-payments, and premiums continue to serve as economic barriers to healthcare.

Poverty/Income

In old age, poverty is a formidable barrier to overcome due to a lifetime of economic, social, and personal factors. According to the U.S. Census Bureau (2004), elderly minorities experience higher levels of poverty or near poverty than their White counterparts. Among the elderly living at or below poverty level, Blacks comprised 34%, compared to 21% for Hispanics and 11% for Whites. For the over-65 age group, Hispanics experienced nearly twice the poverty (19.6%) rate compared to the total elderly population (9.9%). The poverty rate for Latinos aged 75 and over was 22% living at or below the poverty threshold (USDHHS 2003).

Many elderly Latinos have experienced a lifetime of poverty and disenfranchisement due to a host of factors including, but not limited to, language barriers, limited labor force participation, income disparities, limited educational opportunities, prejudice and discrimination, and inadequate social services to name a few. The net result of these factors is that poverty rates are higher for Hispanics 65 and older compared to the total elderly population, with the highest poverty rates experienced by elderly Dominicans (28.6%) and Puerto Ricans (24.4%), and lowest by Spaniards (12.0 %) and South Americans (16.4) (Ramirez 2004).

Poverty is also an enabling factor underlying functional status and debilitating health and social conditions. According to DHHS (Health People 2010), population groups that suffer the worst health status also are those that have the highest poverty rates and the least education. Moreover, disparities in income and education levels are associated with differences in the occurrence of illness, mortality, heart disease, diabetes, obesity, and other chronic conditions. Higher incomes are associated with increased access to medical care, better housing, and safer neighborhoods, leading to increased opportunities for older persons to engage in health-promoting behaviors.

Poverty is the chief factor affecting health and mental health status and care utilization. Gonzalez et al. (2001) reported that older Mexican-Americans with the lowest monthly income had the highest prevalence of depression.

Mental Health Status

Over the last 30 years, the DHHS has published reports on the state of health and mental health in the United States with corresponding goals and objectives to improve the health conditions and opportunities to enhance the well-being of Americans. The initial report, *Healthy People: The Surgeon General's Report on Health Promotion and Disease Prevention* (1979) was followed in 1990 *by Healthy People 2000*, with the latest report *Healthy People 2010* offering national goals and 10-year health objectives. The first goal which recognizes the shift in population aging focuses on increasing the quality and years of healthy life of an aging society. The second goal of particular significance is the elimination of health disparities among segments of the population, including differences that occur by gender, race, or ethnicity, education or income, disability, geographic location, or sexual orientation.

According to the OSG report, between 8–20% of community-dwelling older adults have symptoms of depression (U.S. Department of Health & Human Services [USDHHS] 1999). Reiger and Narrow (as cited in U.S. Department of Health &

Human Services [USDHHS] 1999) reported the best estimates of one-year prevalence rates from the epidemiologic catchment area of those 55 years and older, finding 19.8% having any disorder with 11.4% as having any anxiety disorder and 4.4% having any mood disorder.

Mental illness and depression are equally prevalent in the Hispanic community. In 2001 the Centers for Disease Control and Prevention [CDC] reported that older Hispanics reported the highest prevalence of mental distress, 10% compared to non-Hispanic Whites (5.9%), non-Hispanic Blacks (8.6%), and Asian/Pacific Islanders (2.1%) (Centers for Disease Control and Prevention [CDC] 2004). Dunlop et al. (2003) estimated racial/ethnic differences in rates of depression by using data from the Health and Retirement Survey and found major depression was more prevalent among Hispanics (10.8%) than African-Americans (8.9%) or Whites (7.8%). In addition, depressive disorders for Hispanics was 44% greater than Whites. Factors such as lower education, less income and wealth, lacking private insurance, and employment were associated with higher rates of major depression. Having fewer resources was more common among minority groups than Whites. After adjusting sociodemographic, health, and economic factors, Dunlop et al. found depression was significantly less frequent among Hispanics and Whites. Hispanics with similar sociodemographic and economic profiles as Whites experience depression less frequently and have lower rates of depression. In a study focused on older Mexican-Americans, Gonzalez et al. (2001) reported older Mexican-Americans had a prevalence of depression of 25.4%. By using data from the National Epidemiologic Survey on Alcohol and Related Conditions, Grant et al. (2004) found that rates for any psychiatric disorder for non-Hispanic Whites were nearly twice that for Mexican-Americans: for non-Hispanic Whites the rate was 51.5%; for Mexican-Americans the rate was 36.7%.

To assess the general health status of Americans, the CDC collected data through the Behavioral Risk Factor Surveillance System (BRFSS) and reported significant racial and ethnic disparities in mental health status. Frequent mental disorder (FMD), one measure of status, was defined as having 14 or more days of poor mental health due to stress, depression, or problems with emotions during the previous 30 days. According to the 2004 BRFSS, the prevalence of FMD among elderly Americans over 65 was lowest for non-Hispanic Whites (5.9%) and Asian/Pacific Islanders (6.1), compared to Native American and Alaska Natives (8.4%), non-Hispanic Blacks (9.8%), and highest among Hispanics (11.2%) (Centers for Disease Control and Prevention [CDC] 2004).

Falcon and Tucker (2000) studied older Puerto Ricans, Dominicans, and other Hispanics and found a significantly greater prevalence of high depression scores among Puerto Rican and Dominican elders compared to non-Hispanic Whites. The high depression scores for older Puerto Ricans remained significantly higher even after controlling for a number of social, demographic, and health factors. Other findings include education and income being negatively correlated for older Puerto Ricans and other older Hispanics; the use of English language was inversely related to depression scores for the three Hispanic groups, whereas the number of health problems was significant and positively correlated for all groups. Likewise, in a study to estimate rates of diagnosis of depression and trends in treatment, Crystal et al. (2003) found that receiving no treatment was higher for Hispanics and other ethnic groups, low income, and those with no supplemental insurance. The researchers added that 50.8% of respondents with no supplemental insurance did not receive treatment, concluding that among those diagnosed with depression, Hispanics and other racial minorities were less likely to receive treatment than Whites. Studies found a significant association between depression in older Mexican-Americans and chronic medical conditions. In one study, depression in older Mexican-Americans was found to have a high comorbidity with several medical conditions, including diabetes, cardiovascular disease, hypertension, stroke, cancer, arthritis, urinary incontinence, bowel incontinence, kidney disease, and ulcers (Black et al. 1998).

Challenges to Maintaining Mental Health

Older Latinos face numerous challenges to maintaining optimal health and mental health. Among these challenges are language barriers, lack of appropriate information, a distrust of the delivery system, low income, and low education (Administration on Aging 2001). In addition, being a member of an ethnic minority group places older Latinos in "multiple jeopardy" and at risk for mental distress (Miranda 1991). Three significant challenges that older Latinos face in maintaining their mental health are: (1) communicating with healthcare providers, (2) acculturation and acculturative stress, and (3) access to mental health services.

Communication/Linguistic

Limited English proficiency refers to persons who cannot speak, read, write, or understand English at a level that yields effective communication (Health Care Financing Administration 2000). Latinos with limited English proficiency are at risk for low access to quality care and problems with communicating with their physicians (Collins et al. 2002; Timmins 2002) and mental health providers. Thus, older Latinos with limited English proficiency may experience problems, such as denial or delays of service delivery, and inaccurate diagnosis and assessment. The challenge of communicating with healthcare professional further influences older Latinos' ability to gain knowledge and make informed healthcare choices (Juarbe 1995).

Latinos with limited English language proficiency are more likely to be uninsured and report fair or poor health than English speakers. Moreover, Latinos with fair or poor language proficiency tend to visit their physician significantly less often than English-speaking non-Latino (Derose and Baker 2000). Language proficiency also influences older Latino's ability to express emotions and thoughts, and affects the clinician's interpretation and understanding of older Latino verbal and nonverbal communication (Malgady and Zayas 2001). Morales et al. (1999) examined patient ratings of communication with healthcare providers and noted that Latino Spanish speakers reported more dissatisfaction than Latino English speakers. And both Latino Spanish speakers and Latino English speakers reported more dissatisfaction than Whites. The questions included rating staff on: "*what you say, answers to your questions, explanations about prescribed medications, explanations of medical tests and procedures, and assurance and support of your doctor and the office staff.*" One conclusion drawn from this study is that dissatisfaction with communicating with healthcare providers puts older Latino with limited English proficiency at risk for making poor healthcare choices.

Acculturative Stress

Another challenge for older Latinos is acculturation. *Acculturative stress* refers to the stress that results from the process of acculturation (Berry and Kim 1988; Williams and Berry 1991). It is primarily caused by being marginalized by the mainstream culture, and is influenced by several factors, including a preference for one's language, family cohesiveness, tenure in residency, and coping resources (Smart and Smart 1995; Miranda and Matheny 2000). Acculturative stress has a pervasive, life-long influence on Latinos' psychological adjustment, decision-making abilities, occupational functioning, and physical health (Smart and Smart 1995). A high level of acculturative stress significantly correlates with high levels of depression and is a strong predictor of depression in Mexican immigrants (Hovey 2000).

Studies of nativity and tenure in residency in the United States show differences in the prevalence of mental illness in the Mexican-American population between native born and immigrants. US-born Mexican-Americans have a lifetime prevalence rate of mental illness nearly twice that of foreign-born Mexican-Americans (Grant et al. 2004). Native-born Mexican-Americans and immigrants with a longer tenure in residency are at higher risk of mental illness than those who recently migrated (Grant et al. 2004; Vega et al. 1998). The longer the residency, the more at risk Mexican-Americans become for mental illness.

Service Utilization

Accessing services is a significant challenge for older Latinos who are less likely to receive specialty mental health treatment than African-Americans or Whites, and the likelihood of Latinos receiving any treatment for depression are lower than for White patients (Miranda and Cooper 2004; Padgett et al. 1994). Two additional risk factors that decrease the probability of use for Latino/as are living in a rural area and the availability of psychiatrists (Applewhite & Torres 2003; Freimen and Cunningham 1997).

In addition to the aforementioned obstacles to treatment is the acceptability of services to older Latinos. Choi and Gonzalez (2005b) identified several reasons older minorities drop out of mental health treatment and attributed it to: (1) initial reluctance of treatment, (2) lack of motivation for treatment, (3) sense of shame or stigma related to mental illness, (4) fear of mental health treatment, (5) discomfort with therapy, (6) socioeconomic and cultural distances, (7) lack of support or resistance of adult children, and (8) perception or expectation of a quick cure. Another reason for dropping out or not attending treatment is transportation. When adult children have time constraints or there was a need for transportation, older Latinos are less likely to access services. Older Latinos not only need health and social service information, they also need assistance to access services (Torrez 1998). Deteriorating health exacerbates the need for services and also can be a barrier to accessing services.

When it comes to utilizing mental health services, older Mexican-Americans will first use their general medical provider, followed by other professionals, a mental health specialist, and an informal provider. The more educated older Latinos are, the higher the rate of mental health care utilization. Less educated older Latinos utilized informal providers the most. US-born older Latinos have higher utilization rates for all providers with the exception of informal care (Vega et al. 1999). US-born Mexican-Americans utilize primary care physicians and counselors more than immigrants. Mexican-Americans rely heavily on informal network providers to treat mental illness. When Latinos know where to find a specialty mental health provider and have private insurance, they are more likely to use services (Vega et al. 2001).

There are several enabling factors that influence patient access to mental health services for older minorities, including doctors' referrals; referrals from social workers, churches, and former patients; community outreach; a supportive family; bilingual/bicultural clinicians; dual Medicare/Medicaid eligibility; and transportation (Choi and Gonzalez 2005a). Other contributing factors keeping older minorities in treatment include educating patients at the beginning of treatment on the difference between mental illness and physical illness; educating the respondent, the family, and the community about mental illness and treatment; assurance of confidentiality; bilingual/bicultural counselors; culturally competent therapists; family involvement; and realistic expectations about treatment (Choi and Gonzalez 2005b). In particular, having bilingual/bicultural staff is a key treatment preference for Latinos. Culturally competent care must include verbal and nonverbal communication that is harmonious, humane, respectful, professional, and sensitive. The use of bilingual healthcare professionals' positively affects the content of the interaction during treatment and the patient's recall of the information (Warda 2000).

Strengths Contributing to Mental Health

Older minorities access mental health services for various reasons, but the focus is primarily in loss and adjustment to life changes due to aging. Some common circumstances include retirement, loss of spouse, difficulty adjusting to medical conditions, the loss of independence due to deteriorating health, family conflict, and relationship issues (e.g., role reversal). Older Latinos draw on several strengths for the resilience to cope with these challenges and navigate their environment, including culture, family, community, values, and spirituality.

Resilience has been defined as overcoming adversity, overcoming harmful life stress, or successful adaptation to a challenge (Fraser 1997; Lazarus 1999; Luthar and Ziegler 1991). One definition of resilience that applies well to the experience of older Latinos is overcoming adversity or negotiating life transitions with competence (Greene 2001). Kenyon and Randall (2001) analyzed the elements of life stories and constructed four dimensions of resiliency:

1. The *structural dimension* includes social policies, power relations, and economic conditions.
2. The *sociocultural dimension*, which refers to social meanings associated with aging and the life course.
3. The *interpersonal dimension* includes families and friends.
4. The *personal dimension involves* internal meaning and coherence.

The authors of this chapter have adapted elements of this framework to discuss the significance and centrality of culture and resilience in the lives of older Latinos and Latinas.

Culture

An important strength for older Latinos is their culture. In the OSG's report (U.S. Department of Health & Human Services [USDHHS] 1999), culture is broadly defined as a common heritage or set of beliefs, norms, and values. It refers to the shared, and largely learned, attributes of a group of people. More broadly defined, "Culture is a body of learned beliefs, traditions, principles, and guides for behavior that are commonly shared among members of a particular group. Culture services as a road map for both perceiving and interacting with the world." (Locke 1992, p. 10, cited in Delgado 2007, p. 17). It is these beliefs, values and related attributes that shape the patterns of behavior that define diverse Latino cultures and populations.

Ostensibly, culture and language are critical when accessing treatment services. To the extent that structural barriers have resulted in disparities in mental health services such as lack of culturally competent service providers, many older Latinos demonstrate cultural resiliency by embracing traditional health and mental health beliefs and practices (Applewhite 1995). A familiar scenario is that of the older Latino client explaining his or her symptoms and being misunderstood by the professional. Culture molds the conception and responses to mental illness and can influence interactions with services providers in the mental health system.

Another strength of older Latinos is a *dual perspective*, the notion that people living simultaneously in two cultures, their own and the mainstream culture, have learned to negotiate the values, beliefs, and expectations of each culture or perspective (Norton 1976). This strength has a place in the individual, interpersonal, and structural dimensions of resilience. The dual perspective describes two contrasting systems, a nurturing and a sustaining system. The nurturing environment insulates older Latinos by enhancing their self-esteem, providing cultural resources, and validating those aspects of their life and culture that give meaning to everyday living and relationships. In contrast, the sustaining environment devalues the individual and the cultural dimensions particularly those value, beliefs, norms, language, and behaviors that are outside the mainstream of the dominant culture. Older Latinos derive strength and resilience from a nurturing environment that values older adults and provides a sense of community and peoplehood.

Family

The family is a well-known source of strength for older Latinos and fits within the interpersonal dimension of resilience. The culture of older Latinos consists of the individual, their family, and social networks. The family consists of the nuclear and the extended family, including the *compadrazo* (i.e., godparents) and the nurturing environment commonly referred to as the *barrio* (community, friends and neighbors, clergy, and folk healers). Older Latinos gain meaning through interaction with their family and their social network. The family usually takes care of older Latinos with help from the extended family and community. There is a strong bond for older Latinos involving mental health, well-being, and their health status (Harris 1998.), with the family meeting emotional and psychological needs of older family members who are at the center of the immediate and extended family constellation. Thus, when the elderly experience mental distress, the family experiences mental distress in a symbiotic fashion. Family roles and responsibilities become strained and are changed, and at times reversed. Older Latinos give up the role of primary caregivers and become care receivers. Adult children, frequently the oldest daughter, commonly take on the role of caregiver for their aging parent(s) within the Latino culture. This exchange of caregiving roles which are culturally embedded in the Latino family structure can lead to stress and distress for family members, especially when adult caregiving roles and expectations conflict with traditional norms and responsibilities due to generational differences, economic strains, and acculturation patterns. Stated differently, the presumed automatic guarantees of emotional, financial, and cultural support and insulation do not always prevail in Latino families. Nevertheless, to the extent possible, older Latinos prefer to live with their spouses, live alone, or with extended family, and consider nursing homes or institutions only as a last option.

In rural areas, older Latinos are reluctant to seek formal help and have a strong sense of independence. They often are self-reliant, have a desire to *age in place* in their communities and homes, and are dependent on family support and friends to meet healthcare needs (Angel et al. 1996). Not surprisingly, they prefer to keep medical, mental health, and other problems within the family, which a traditional family norm. This norm, however, is a double-edged sword, because keeping critical health and mental health issues in the family also contributes to their reluctance to take advantage of available healthcare services (Magilvy et al. 2000). Rural elders face challenges that are often intensified due to geographical isolation, the lack of social and caregiving networks, extreme poverty, substandard housing, lack of reliable transportation, environmental hazards, and decreased access and use of social services and health and mental health care facilities. The culture of rural America for older Latinos can be difficult but equally so, a source of strength and lifelong continuity that may be absent in more urban, mobile communities (Applewhite and Torres 2003).

Values and Beliefs

Latinos have values that give meaning to the culture and cultural patterns that contribute to retention in mental health services. These values are strengths in the individual, interpersonal, and sociocultural dimensions of resilience. *Personalismo* and *respeto* are values that older Latinos seek when beginning professional relationships and, at times, are reasons older Latinos accept mental health services. *Personalismo* stresses the significance of personal relationships than institutional relationships (Trevino et al. 1991). This includes the physical space between the patient and the practitioner, appropriate physical contact, and short conversations concerning the family not related to healthcare. This helps in establishing the personal relationship and trust (Flores et al. 2000). *Respeto* ("respect") directs respectful behavior toward others based on age, gender, and authority (Arredondo et al. 1996). Speaking some Spanish, even if not fluent, conveys respect and appreciation for the culture.

Religion

Religion is a critical source of support and strength for older Latinos. It can be placed in more than one dimension of resilience, including individual, interpersonal, and sociocultural strengths. Latinos are mostly Christians, the majority being either Roman Catholic or Protestant. Other religious/spiritual practices among Latinos include *Santeria* and *Espiritismo.* These are the more common religions among Latinos, although other faiths can be found within the Latino population (Vasquez and Clavijo 1995).

One product of Judeo-Christian culture is the permeating construct of fatalism, which leads many Latinos to believe that their future is in the hands of God. When Latinos experience mental distress, symptoms are often interpreted as a deserved punishment God-sent designed for theirs actions and behaviors. The expectation is often stated as "*si Dios quiere*" (if God so wishes). Thus some may come to believe that all they can do is pray in an attempt to modify their present and future situation, predicament, or life circumstances (Carrillo 2001).

Discussion

Complicating Issues in Applying Strengths to Meet Mental Health Challenges

A number of issues make it difficult for clients and providers to correctly assess and diagnose mental health problems in older Latino populations. In addition, the many strengths of this population sometimes go unrecognized, precluding the possibility of harnessing these strengths to buttress well-being in this group. These issues appear to be directly related to how the mental health profession in the United States addresses cultural study and practice. Some of these issues are identified and elaborated upon in greater depth below.

Perceptions of Mental Illness/Culturally Bound Syndromes

Culture sets the stage for how and what people believe; how they behave, solve problems, and communicate; how their identity and interpersonal relationships develop; how they adjust to change, handle stressors, and ultimately cope with mental health problems (Abramson et al. 2002). Culture affects the way older Latinos present symptoms of mental illness, how individuals describe symptoms, the meaning they attach to mental illness, and how they make sense of it (Kleinman 1988). Culture gives meaning to mental illness and treatment in the exchanges individuals have with the professional mental health community.

The Diagnostic and Statistical Manual of Mental Disorders (DSM) (American Psychiatric Association 2000) is used to assess and diagnose mental illness and disorders. This manual uses the language of the profession and presents mental illness in several ways. There are times when Latinos express mental illness as it is described in the *DSM-IV*; at other times they express mental illness in culturally specific ways, and most often without DSM diagnostic equivalents. Addressing this problem, the DSM-IV (2000) provides an Outline for Cultural Formulation and Glossary of Culture-Bound Syndromes to supplement the multiaxial diagnostic assessment and address problems in applying the DSM-IV to diverse populations. Cultural Formulation with its categories "provides a systematic review of an individual's cultural background, the role of the cultural context in the expression and evaluation of symptoms and dysfunction, and the effect that cultural differences may have on the relationship between the individual and the clinician" (pp. 897–898). Five categories that form the basis of the cultural formulation include:

- Cultural identity of the individual;
- Cultural explanation of the individual's illness;
- Cultural factors related to psychosocial environment and levels of functioning;
- Cultural elements of the relationship between the individual and the clinician; and
- Overall assessment for diagnosis and care.

The *DSM-IV* discusses several culture-bound syndromes and defines *culture-bound syndrome* as "recurrent, locality-specific patterns of aberrant behavior and troubling experience that may or may not be linked to a particular DSM-IV diagnostic category … [and] seldom a one-to-one equivalence of any culture-bound syndrome with a DSM-IV entity" (P. 898). The extent to which the practitioner understands the cultural context, arena, and the meaning assigned to sets of experiences of older Latinos, the greater is the likelihood that the clinician will be effective in providing clinical care.

Idioms of distress that are recognized as culture-bound syndromes in Latino culture are *ataque de nervios* (ADN) and *nervios*. Unlike panic attacks (PA) and other psychological disorders, *ataque de nervios* (ADN) include such symptoms as uncontrollable shouting, attacks of crying, etc. It frequently occurs because of a stressful life event resulting in psychological pain and anguish. Descriptions of ADN are similar to panic attacks and presentations of anxiety, mood, dissociative, and somatoform disorders (American Psychiatric Association (APA) 2005).

Latinos may also somatize mental illness. *Somatization* refers to the presence of physical symptoms for which there is no diagnosable physical condition (Kirmayer 1984). Mexican-American families will often describe their family member's schizophrenic symptoms as symptoms of *nervios* and focus on somatic complaints that tend to destigmatize the mental illness (Jenkins 1988). *Nervios* is popularly utilized to refer to a broad and diverse range of distressing emotional states and illness phenomena. In the Latino culture, *nervios* is understood as a condition that often affects adults who are experiencing difficult life conditions. Symptoms of *nervios* include headaches, trembling, heart palpitations, stomach and appetite disturbances, trouble with concentration, sleep problems, and worrying (Guarnaccia and Farias 1988). *Nervios* should be recognized as a "cry for help," as it might be a sign of serious mental and physical dysfunction (Salgado de Snyder et al. 2000).

Adherence

Adherence is the degree to which the individual acts upon treatment advice or recommendations (Chrisman 1977). Culture is important in adherence to medical regimens (Anthsel 2002). With the older Latino culture it is important for healthcare providers to understand who they are, their beliefs, the challenges they face, and how they adhere to their health. The family and the cultural values influence help-seeking behaviors and adherence to medical recommendations. Language is also a factor that affects adherence. In one study, Spanish-speaking clients who required an interpreter had lower adherence rates and poor medical outcomes (Rivadeneyra et al. 2000). The way that services are delivered to older Latinos also impacts adherence and help seeking. *Simpatia* (i.e. lowering conflict and promoting agreement), *familismo* (i.e. primacy of the family), *personalismo* (i.e. relationship building), and *respeto* (i.e. mutual respect) can affect patient adherence to treatment services, as well as health outcomes (Barron et al. 2004).

Older Latinos relationship with their primary care physician is central to adherence to treatment regimens. Latinos are less likely to adhere to treatment recommendations if they distrust their healthcare provider (Christensen 1992). Involving the family in treatment decisions and treatment planning is a way to incorporate *familismo* (Flores et al. 2000). Identifying a primary caregiver from the family and having this person serve as a contact or liaison is also helpful in respecting the family (Antshel 2002), as well as improving adherence to treatment recommendations. Just as the family is positive when it comes to adherence, the family can also get in the way of treatment because of shame and stigma of mental illness (Choi and Gonzalez 2005b). The family may not want their loved one receiving treatment for mental health issues, whether it be a medication for depression or a referral to group therapy.

Psychosocial Interventions

There is evidence that psychosocial interventions are effective with older Latinos. Integrated and collaborative care or case management, in conjunction with cognitive-behavioral therapy, has shown promise in working with older adults and older Latino. Integrated care involves site sharing and a partnership between mental health care and primary care providers (Katon et al. 1997). Older adults are more likely to accept collaborative mental health treatment within primary care settings. Integrated care would improve underutilization of mental health services (Bartels et al. 2004).

Collaborative care or case management as an intervention for older adults with late-life improves physical function more than usual care (Callahan et al. 2005). In a study that compared Spanish speakers with English speakers, case management, along with cognitive-behavioral therapy, is associated with lower dropout rates, greater improvement in depressive symptoms and functioning for Latino. Arean et al. (2005) compared cognitive-behavioral group therapy, clinical case management, and the combination of both to treat low-income older adults with depression. They found that the combination of group therapy and case management resulted in significantly lower depressive symptoms than group therapy alone. The authors concluded that low-income older adults benefit from greater access to social services. Cooper et al. (2003) found that Latinos were less likely to find antidepressant medication acceptable but more likely to find counseling acceptable than Whites.

Researchers concluded that case management improves retention in traditional mental health outpatient care and can improve outcomes for Latinos (Miranda et al. 2003). Case management programs that include cognitive-behavioral therapy have shown improved health outcomes and reduced unmet need for appropriate care among Latino (Wells et al. 2004).

Future Recommendations

In the President's New Freedom Commission on Mental Health (2003), the special mental health needs and strengths of older Latinos are addressed. One of the most studied reasons for Latinos underutilization of mental health services is the lack of linguistically and culturally relevant services (Lopez 2002). Future research should focus on improving mental health services for older Latino. Services will need to address cultural competency and be linguistically appropriate.

One of the most important gaps in the research is on the frequency of mental disorders among Latinos (Marin et al. 2006). Knowing these rates would help improve the identification and treatment of mentally ill Latinos in primary care settings, which is another area of research (Marin et al. 2006). Having better prevalence rates of mental disorders among Latinos will help educate healthcare professionals on the magnitude of the problem. These numbers will also assist primary care physicians in assessing and diagnosing Latinos. Many Latinos have a significant relationship, based on trust, with their primary care physician: this setting needs to be explored.

Another area in which research is needed is how to improve education on mental illness and mental health treatment for the caregivers of older Latinos, their healthcare providers (i.e., their adult children), and the communities in which they reside. Education on mental illness and treatment will help reduce the stigma of mental illness and improve adherence to treatment for older Latinos and Latinos in general (Gonzalez 2006).

The language that research and treatment programs use is another area of research. Professionals and researchers need to understand and learn that Spanish is regional, and exists in different dialects. Latinos come from different regions of the United States and emigrate from different countries. Along with linguistic needs, increasing the number of bilingual/bicultural healthcare providers would improve treatment and research (Gonzalez 2006). In addition, future research should focus on attitudinal barriers to the treatment of depression among ethnic minority patients (Cooper et al. 2003).

Research is needed on access and retention of minority older adults in mental health treatment (Choi and Gonzalez 2005a). The types of services effective in engaging older Latinos and the value of community supports are two areas of research that could strengthen delivery of mental health services to older Latinos (Brennan et al. 2005). To improve the accessibility of services, research is needed on cultur-

Table 17.1 Practice Consideration in Assessing Challenges and Strengths of Older Latino Populations

Demographics	Challenges	Strengths	Recommendations
Hispanic Americans aged 65 or older comprise ~6% of US population; expected to grow to 18% of US population by 2050. 4.8% of Latinos are aged 65 or older (compared to this age group representing 12% of the overall population)	Limited English proficiency (LEP) • Latinos with LEP are more likely to lack insurance coverage, and are less likely to attend physician visits, while reporting poorer health than English speakers • Poor communication with treatment professionals puts this group at risk for inaccurate diagnosis, third-party-payor denial or delay of services, and limited ability to advocate for own health needs	Latino culture • Cultural competence on part of helping professionals improves outcomes • Dual perspective: Receiving appropriate supports when moving fluidly between the values and practices of (at least) two different cultures increases resilience	Improving practice • Clinicians and researchers should utilize cultural formulation and culture-bound syndromes as appropriate • Need for increased recognition of somatization as a less-stigmatizing means of expressing distress • Consider use of integrative/collaborative care approaches to improve adherence
Nationalities represented include Mexican (59.3%), Puerto Rican (9.7%), Cuban (3.5%), Central and South American (9.1%), Dominican (2.3%), Spaniard (0.3%), and "Other" (15.7%)	Acculturative Stress • Stresses associated with marginalization from majority culture are associated with lowered psychological adjustment, decision-making abilities, occupational functioning, and physical health • Risk of mental illness grows among individuals coping with acculturative stress	Family • Social support from family and extended networks validates subjective distress, and protects psychological functioning. However, shared distress can tax family's resources • Desire to take full responsibility for one's own welfare; can lead to greater sense of agency, and/or to exaggerated reluctance to seek help	Future research • Formulate clear guidelines for cultural and linguistic competence with older Latinos, as well as data regarding the effectiveness of specific treatments for specific disorders among members of this group • Great need for epidemiological data regarding mental disorders among Latinos. This data is particularly critical for use in primary care settings • Investigate effects of educating caregivers of older Latinos on common mental health problems in this group

Table 17.1 (continued)

Demographics	Challenges	Strengths	Recommendations
Highly concentrated in select areas (e.g., California, Texas, Florida, New York) Education: ~35% have attained HS diploma (compared to 70% of general older population) Poverty: Rates of poverty among Latino older adults are nearly twice as high as among Whites (19.6% for Hispanics, 9.9% for Whites)	Service Utilization • Older Latinos are less likely to receive specialty mental health services than African Americans or European Americans • Receiving mental health services may be less personally acceptable to older Latinos than to members of other groups • Psychoeducation of patient, family, and community may increase engagement in treatment	Values, Beliefs, Religion • Interpersonal values such as *personalismo* and *respeto* can enhance helping relationships • Religious faith conveys many psychological and social benefits; however, a fatalistic attitude towards one's own well-being may lead to passive coping strategies (e.g., sole reliance on prayer for mental/emotional healing)	

ally competent interventions that are effective with older Latinos (Choi and Gonzalez 2005a; Marin et al. 2006). Studies focused on improving treatment adherence are needed to develop methods for engaging patients (Delgado et al. 2006; Choi and Gonzalez 2005a; Marin et al. 2006).

Concluding Comments

Ultimately, the mental health issues facing older Latinos will soon become a topic of national discussion in research and clinical settings. The population of older adults, 65 years and older, is projected to increase to 40 million by 2010 and to 55 million by 2020! An expansion in population of this type magnifies the existing differential access to social, economic, political, health, and mental health resources on the basis of ethnicity. Furthermore, the correlation of race and ethnicity with persistent and increasing health disparities is evidenced in the reportedly poor access to quality mental health care by minority groups.

Health disparities are experienced by the 14% of the nation's elderly comprised of the US Hispanic/Latino population. Currently, the "Browning" of the Graying of America is mostly seen in California, Florida, New York, and Texas; although the Hispanic elderly reside in every state. Characteristically, the older Latino population exhibits a high degree of resilience. However, in attempting to maintain mental health, aging Hispanics are placed in "multiple jeopardy" and at risk for mental distress. Hope for better outcomes in this group lies in both educating the client and family about mental health treatment and available services, and in providing culturally competent treatment, two factors that would likely be facilitative of the utilization of services by older Latinos.

More research is needed in several areas for this group. Continuing research on prevalence of mental illness among Latinos provides a more accurate means of symptom identification and diagnosis for treatment. It would inform best practices in educating caregivers, providers, and their communities via linguistic and culturally relevant services. Finally, generating evidence-based support of effective interventions can result in increased adherence, access and retention of minority older adults. If such steps are not taken, the differing trajectories which have already been noted in past research can only be expected to widen as this population grows.

References

Abramson, T. A., Trejo, L., & Lai, D. W. L. (2002). Culture and mental health: Providing appropriate services for a diverse older population. *Generations, 26*(1), 21–28.

Administration on Aging. (2001). Cultural competency. www.aoa.gov/may2001/factsheets/Cultural-Competency.html. Accessed February 1, 2002.

Applewhite, S. L. (1995). Curanderismo: Demystifying the health beliefs and practices of elderly Mexican Ameircans. *Health and Social Work, 20*(4), 247–254.

Applewhite, S.L., & Torres, C. (2003). Rural Latino Elders. *Journal of Gerontological Social Work, 41*(1/2), 151–174.

American Psychiatric Association. (2000). *Diagnostic and statistical manual of mental disorders* (4th ed.), Text Revision. Washington: American Psychiatric Association.

American Psychiatric Association. (2003, July). Mental health care and older adults: Facts and policy recommendations. http://www.apa.org/ppo/issues/oldermhfact03.html. Zugegriffen: 21. April 2008.

Angel, J. L., Angel, R. J., McClellan, J. L., & Markides, K. S. (1996). Nativity, declining health, and preferences in living arrangements among elderly Mexican-Americans: Implications for long-term care. *Gerontologist, 36*(4), 464–473.

Antshel, K. M. (2002). Intergrating culture as a means of improving treatment adherence in the Latino population. *Psychology Health & Medicine, 7*(4), 437–438.

Arean, P. A., Gum, A., McCulloch, C. E., Bostrom, A., Gallagher-Thompson, D., & Thompson, L., (2005). Treatment of depression in low-income older adults. *Psychology & Aging, 20*(4), 601–609.

Arredondo, P., Toporek, R., Brown, S. P., Jones, J., Locke, D., Sanchez, J. (1996). Operationalization of the multicultural counseling competencies. *Journal of Multicultural Counseling & Development, 24*(1), 42–78.

Barron, F., Hunter, A., Mayo, & R., Willoughby, D. (2004). Accultration and adherence: Issues for health care providers working with clients of Mexican origin. *Journal of Transcultural Nursing, 15*(4), 331–337.

Bartels, S. J., Coakley, E. H., & Zubritsky, C. (2004). Improving access to geriatric mental health services: A randomized trial comparing treatment engagement with integrated versus enhanced referral care for depression, anxiety, and at-risk alcohol use. *American Journal of Psychiatry, 161*(8), 1455–1462.

Berry, J. W., & Kim, U. (1988). Acculturation and mental health. In P. Dasen, J. W. Berry, & N. Satorius (Eds.), *Health and cross-cultural psychology: Towards application* (pp. 207–236). London: Sage.

Black, S. A., Goodwin, J. S., & Markides, K. S. (1998). The association between chronic diseases and depressive symptomatology in older Mexican-Americans. *Journals of Gerontology: Medical Sciences, 53A*(3), M188–M194.

Brennan, M., Vega, M., Garcia, I., Abad, A., & Friedman, M. B. (2005). Meeting the mental health needs of elderly Latinos affected by depression: Implications for outreach and service provision. *Care Management Journals, 6*(2), 98–106.

Callahan, C. M., Kroenke, K., Counsell, S. R., Hendrie, H. C., Perkins, A. J., Katon, et al. (2005). Treatment of depression improves physical functioning in older adults. *Journal of American Geriatrics Society, 53*(3), 367–373.

Carrillo, E. (2001). Assessment and treatment of the Latino patient. In A. G. Lopez & E. Carrillo (Eds.), *The Latino psychiatric patient: Assessment and treatment.* Washington: American Psychiatric Publishing.

Centers for Disease Control and Prevention [CDC]. (2004). The state of aging and health in America. www.cdc.gov/aging. Accessed June 15, 2007.

Choi, N. G., & Gonzalez, J. M. (2005a). Barriers and contributors to minority older adults' access to mental health treatment: Perceptions of geriatric mental health clinicians. *Journal of Gerontological Social Work, 44*(3/4), 115–135.

Choi, N. G., & Gonzalez, J. M. (2005b). Geriatric mental health clinician's perceptions of barriers and contributors to retention of older minorities in treatment: An exploratory study. *Clinical Gerontologist, 28*(3), 3–25.

Chrisman, N. J. (1977). The health seeking process: An approach to the natural history of illness. *Culture Medicine & Psychiatry, 1,* 351–377.

Christensen, C. (1992). Multicultural competencies in early intervention: training professionals in a pluralistic society. *Infants & Young Children, 4*(3), 49–63.

Collins, K. S., Hughes, D. L., Doty, M. M., Ives, B. L., Edwards, J. N., & Tenney, K., (2002). *Diverse communities, common concerns: Assessing health care quality for minority Americans.*

Findings from the Commonwealth Fund 2001 Health Care Quality Survey. New York: Commonwealth Fund.
Cooper, L. A., Gonzales, J. J., Gallo, J. J., Rost, K. M., Meredith, L. S., Rubenstein, L., et al. (2003). The acceptability of treatment for depression among African-American, Hispanic, and White primary care patients. *Medical Care, 41,* 479–489.
Crystal, S., Sambamoorthi, U., Walkup, J. T., & Akincigil, A. (2003). Diagnosis and treatment of depression in the elderly medicare population: Predictors, disparities, and trends. *Journal of American Geriatrics Society, 51,* 1718–1728.
Delgado, P. L., Alegria, M. Canive, J. M., Diaz, E., Escobar, J. I., & Kopelowicz, A. (2006). Depression and access to treatment among U.S. Hispanics: Review of literature and recommendations for policy and research. *Focus: The Journal of Lifelong Learning in Psychiatry, IV*(1), 38–47.
Delgado, M. (2007). *Social work with Latinos: A cultural assets paradigm*. New York: Oxford University Press.
Derose, K. P., & Baker, D. W. (2000). Limited English proficiency and Latinos' use of physician services. *Medical Care Research & Review, 57*(1), 76–91.
Dunlop. D. D., Song, J., Lyons, J. S., Manheim, L. M., & Rowland, R. W. (2003). Racial/ethnic differences in rates of depression among preretirement adults. *American Journal of Public Health, 93,* 1945–1952.
Falcon, L. M., & Tucker, K. L. (2000). Prevalence and correlates of depressive symptoms among Hispanic elders in Massachusetts. *Journal of Gerontology: Social* Sciences, *55B*(2), S108–S116.
Flores, G., Abreu, M., Schwartz, I., & Hill, M. (2000). The importance of language and culture in pediatric care: Case studies from the Latino community. *Journal of Pediatrics, 137*(6), 842–848.
Fraser, M. (1997). *Risk and resilience in childhood.* Washington, DC: NASW Press.
Freimen, M. P., & Cunningham, P. J. (1997). Use of health care for the treatment of mental problems among racial/ethnic subpopulations. *Medical Care Research & Review, 54,* 80–101.
Gonzalez, J. (2006). Older Latinos and mental health services: Understanding access barriers. *Journal of Human Behavior in the Social Environment, 14*(1/2), 73–93.
Gonzalez, H. M., Haan, M. N., & Hinton, L. (2001). Acculturation and the prevalence of depression in older Mexican-Americans: Baseline results of the Sacramento Area Latino Study on Aging. *Journal of American Geriatrics, 49*(7), 948–953.
Grant, B. F., Stinson, F. S., Hasin, D. S., Dawson, D. A., Chou, S. P., & Anderson, K. (2004). Immigration and lifetime prevalence of DSM-IV psychiatric disorders among Mexican-Americans and non-Hispanic Whites in the United States: Results from the National Epidemiologic Survey on Alcohol and Related Conditions. *Archives of General Psychiatry, 61,* 1226–1233.
Greene, R. R. (2001). *Resiliency: An integrated approach to practice, policy, and research.* Washington, DC: NASW Press.
Guarnaccia, P. J., & Farias, P. (1988). The social meanings of nervios: A case study of a central American woman. *Social Science and Medicine, 26,* 1223–1231.
Hargraves, J. L., & Hadley, J. (2003). The contribution of insurance coverage and community resources to reducing racial/ethnic disparities in access to care. *Health Services Research, 38*(3), 809–829.
Harris, H. L. (1998). Ethnic minority elders: Issues and interventions. *Educational Gerontology, 24*(4), 309–324.
Hayes-Bautista, D. E., Hsu, P. Perez, A., & Gamboa, C. (2002, Fall). The 'browning' of the graying of America: Diversity in the elderly population and policy implications. *Generations, 26*(3), 15–24.
Health Care Financing Administration. (2000). Office for civil rights' policy guidance on limited English proficient persons. http://www.hcfa.gov/medicaid/smd83100.htm. Accessed October 2, 2003.
Henry, J., Kaiser Family Foundation. (1999). The faces of Medicare. http://www.kff.org/medicare/1481-index.cfm. Accessed January 24, 2006.

Hovey, J. D. (2000). Acculturative stress, depression, and suicidal ideation in Mexican Immigrants. *Cultural Diversity & Ethnic Minority Psychology, 6*(2), 134–151. http://www.kff.org/medicare/1481-index.cfm. Accessed January 24, 2002.

Jenkins, J. H. (1988). Ethnopsychiatric interpretations of schizophrenic illness: The problem of nervios within Mexican-American families. *Culture, Medicine, & Psychiatry, 12,* 301–329.

Jenkins, C. L., & Laditka, S. B. (1998). Double jeopardy: The challenge of providing mental health services to older persons. *Administration and Policy in Mental Health, 26*(1), 65–74.

Juarbe, T. (1995). Access to health care for Hispanic women: A primary health care perspective. *Nursing Outlook, 43*(1), 23–28.

Katon, W., Von Korff, M, & Lin, E. (1997) Collaborative management to achieve depression treatment guidelines. *Journal of Clinical Psychiatry, 58*(1), 20–23.

Kenyon, G. M., & Randall, W. (2001). Narrative gerontology: An overview. In G. Kenyon, P. Clark, & B. de Vries (Eds.), *Narrative gerontology*. (pp. 3–18). New York: Springer.

Kirmayer, L. J. (1984). Culture, affect, and somatization, part I. *Transcultural Psychiatric Research Review, 21,* 159–188.

Kleinman, A. (1988). *The illness narratives: Suffering, healing, and the human condition*. New York: Basic Books.

Lazarus, R. S. (1999). *Stress and emotion: A new synthesis.* New York: Springer.

Locke, D. C. (1992). *Increasing multicultural understanding: a comprehensive world.* Newbury Park: Sage.

Lopez, S. R. (2002). Mental health care for Latinos: A research agenda to improve the accessibility and quality of mental health care for Latinos. *Psychiatric Services, 53,* 1569–1573.

Luthar, S., & Ziegler, E. (1991). Vulnerability and competence: A review of research on resilience in childhood. *American Journal of Orthopsychiatry, 61*(1), 7–22.

Magilvy, J. K., Congdon, J. G., Martinez, R. J., Davis, R., & Averill, J. (2000). Caring for our own: Health care experiences of rural Hispanic elders. *Journal of Aging Studies, 14*(2), 171–191.

Malgady, R. G., & Zayas, L. H. (2001). Cultural and linguistic considerations in psychodiagnosis with Hispanics: The need for an empirically informed process model. *Social Work, 46*(1), 39–49.

Marin, H., Escobar, J. L., & Vega, W. A. (2006). Mental illness in Hispanics: A review of the literature. *Focus: The Journal of Lifelong Learning in Psychiatry, IV*(1), 23–37.

Miranda, M. R. (1991). Mental health services and the Hispanic elderly. In M. Sotomayor (Ed.), *Empowering Hispanic families: A critical issue for the 90s*. Milwaukee: Family Service America.

Miranda, J., & Cooper, L. A. (2004). Disparities in care for depression among primary care patients. *Journal of General Internal Medicine, 19,* 120–126.

Miranda, A. O., & Matheny, K. B. (2000). Socio-psychological predictors of acculturative stress among Latino adults. *Journal of Mental Health Counseling, 22*(4), 306–317.

Miranda, J., Azocar, F., Organista, K. C., Dwyer, E., & Areane, P. (2003). Treatment of depression among impoverished primary care patients from ethnic minority groups. *Psychiatric Services, 54*(2), 219–225.

Morales, L. S., Cunningham, W. E., Brown, J. A., Lui, H., & Hays, R. D. (1999). Are Latinos less satisfied with communication by health care providers? *Journal of General Internal Medicine, 14,* 409–417.

National Institute of Heath Office of Minority Heath (1998).

Norton, D. G. (1976). Working with minority populations: The dual perspective. In B. Ross, & S. K. Khinduka (Eds.), *Social work practice* (pp. 134–141). New York: NASW Press.

Padgett, D. K., Patrick, C., Burns, B. J., & Schlesinger, H. J. (1994). Ethnicity and the use of outpatient mental health services in a national insured population. *American Journal of Public Health, 84*(2), 222–226.

President's New Freedom Commission on Mental Health. (2003). *Achieving the promise: Transforming mental health care in America: Final report*. (DHHS Pub. No. SMA-03–3832). Rockville: U.S. Department of Health and Human Services.

Ramirez, R. R. (2004, December). We the people: Hispanics in the United States – U.S. Census Bureau, Census 2000 Special Reports, CENSR-18.

Rivadeneyra, R., Elderkin-Thompson, V., Silver, R. C., & Waitzkin, H. (2000). Patient centeredness in medical encounters requiring an interpreter. *American Journal of Medicine, 108*(6), 470–474.

Salgado de Snyder, V. N., de Jesus Diaz-Perez, M. J., & Ojeda, V. D. (2000). The prevalence of nervios and associated symptomatology among inhabitants of Mexican rural communities. *Culture, Medicine, and Psychiatry, 24,* 453–470.

Smart, J. F., & Smart, D. W. (1995). Acculturative stress: The experience of the Hispanic immigrant. *Counseling Psychologist, 23,* 25–42.

Timmins, C. L. (2002). The impact of language barriers on the health care of Latinos in the United States: A review of the literature and guidelines for practice. *Journal of Midwifery & Women's Health, 47*(2), 80–96.

Torrez, D. J. (1998). Health and social service utilization patterns of Mexican-American older adults. *Journal of Aging Studies, 12*(1), 82–99.

Trevino, F., Moyer, M., Valdez, R., & Stroup-Benham, C. (1991). Health insurance coverage and utilization of health services by Mexican-Americans, mainland Puerto Ricans, and Cuban Americans. *Journal of the American Medical Association, 265*(2), 233–237.

U.S. Census Bureau. (2000). The Hispanic population: Census 2000 Brief. http://www.census.gov/prod/2001pubs/c2kbr01-3.pdf. Accessed July 1, 2005.

U.S. Census Bureau. (2004). 2004 American Community Survey: Population 65 years and over. http://factfinder.census.gov/servlet/STTable?_bm=y&-geo_id=01000US&-qr_name=ACS_2004_EST_G00_S0103&-ds_name=ACS_2004_EST_G00_&-_lang=en&-_caller=geoselect&-state=st&-format=. Accessed June 29, 2007.

U.S. Department of Health & Human Services [USDHHS]. (1999). *Mental health: A report of the Surgeon General.* Rockville: U.S. Department of Health and Human Services, Substance Abuse and Mental Health Services Administration, Center for Mental Health Services, National Institutes of Health, National Institute of Mental Health.

U.S. Department of Health and Human Services. (2000). *Healthy People 2010: Understanding and improving health* (2nd ed.). Washington: U.S. Government Printing Office.

U.S. Department of Health and Human Services. (2001). *Mental health: Culture, race, ethnicity-A Supplement to mental health: A report of the surgeon general.* Rockville, MD: U.S. Department of Health and Human Services, Public Health Service, Office of the Surgeon General.

U.S. Department of Health & Human Services [USDHHS]. (2003). *A statistical profile of Hispanic older Americans aged 65+.* Administration on aging. http://www.aoa.gov/press/fact/pdf/ss_hispanic_elderly.pdf. Accessed July 5, 2007.

Vasquez, C. I., & Clavijo, A. M. (1995). The special needs of minorities: A profile of Hispanics. In B. G. Knight, L. T. Wohlford, & J. Santos (Eds.), *Mental health services for older adults: Implications for training and practice in geropsychology* (pp. 93–99). Washington, DC: American Psychological Association.

Vega, W. A., Kolody, B., & Aguilar-Gaxiola, S. (2001). Help seeking for mental health problems among Mexican-Americans. *Journal of Immigrant Health, 3*(3), 133–140.

Vega, W. A., Kolody, B., Aguilar-Gaxiola, S., Alderate, E., Catalano, R., & Carveo-Anduaga, J. (1998). Lifetime prevalence of DSM-III-R psychiatric disorders among urban and rural Mexican-Americans in California. *Archives of General Psychiatry, 55,* 771–778.

Vega, W. A., Kolody, B., Aguilar-Gaxiola, S., & Catalano, R. (1999). Gaps in service utilization by Mexican-Americans with mental health problems. *American Journal of Psychiatry, 156*(6), 928–934.

Warda, M. (2000). Mexican-Americans' perceptionsof culturally competent care. *Western Journal of Nursing Research, 22*(2), 203–224.

Wells, K., Sherbourne, C., Schoenbaum, M., Ettner, S., Duan, N., Miranda, J., et al. (2004). Five-year impact of quality improvement for depression results of a group-level randomized controlled trial. *Archives of General Psychiatry, 61,* 378–386.

Williams, C. L., & Berry, J. W. (1991). Primary prevention of acculturative stress among refugees: Application of psychological theory and practice. *American Psychologist, 46,* 632–641.

Chapter 18
Race, Age, and Mental Health: Expanding on the Transactional Model of Development to Include the Impact of Racial Group Membership

Christina A. Downey

There should now be little doubt in the thoughtful reader's mind that empirical study of race and ethnicity in relation to mental health has been granted elevated status, particularly in recent years. This seems to reflect a growing and deepening acknowledgement of the variations in experience that members of differing social groups have in American society (Anderson and Nickerson 2005). In particular, the research reviewed throughout the preceding chapters highlighted how greater value is being placed on uncovering differences in typical mental and emotional stability in various groups, and how this topic is receiving increased attention in research and clinical settings. Authors contributing to the present volume collectively reinforced how every major event in the life cycle of mental disorder can be impacted—positively or negatively—by one's racial group status. Specifically, the distribution of risk and protective factors for mental disorders; experience of activating events such as reduced healthcare or trauma exposure; issues involving the diagnostic process; choices made regarding treatment and administration of services; and the quality of relapse prevention care all appear to be moderated, at least in part, by issues of race. In addition, the preceding review illustrated how these differences are already apparent early in the lifespan (e.g., childhood; also see Tamminen 2006 for further discussion) and often persist throughout adulthood and into older age.

In considering the value of approaching the topics of race and age simultaneously in discussions of mental health, I came to more deeply appreciate the dynamic nature of positive and negative mental health in people's lives. Upon reflection, it seemed that it may be enlightening to consider race and age in mental health and illness as important elements in a broadened transactional model of human development (Sameroff 2003). The original transactional model (Sameroff 1975), a highly influential theory of child development, broke away from developmental psychology's long-standing research focus on unidirectional influences on infant and child development (e.g., how mothering behavior shaped children). The trans-

C. A. Downey (✉)
Department of Psychology, Indiana University Kokomo,
2300 S. Washington St., Kokomo, IN 46904, USA
e-mail: downeyca@iuk.edu

E. C. Chang, C. A. Downey (eds.), *Handbook of Race and Development in Mental Health*,
DOI 10.1007/978-1-4614-0424-8_18, © Springer Science+Business Media, LLC 2012

actional model emphasized the need to examine how children—from birth—create or at least contribute to their own experiences of the social world through their own behavioral tendencies, and, simultaneously, how the perceptions and behaviors of caregivers at each stage of this dynamic process create complex social contexts for the child to negotiate. The model's great strength is that it "requires explanations of continuity and discontinuity between adapted and maladapted individuals and between states of adaptation and maladaptation within individuals across time" (Sameroff 2003, p. 613). That is, the way in which any given individual creates and responds to his or her own social-environmental context, determines the degree of adaptation that individual will manifest.

While the model as formulated tends to focus largely on the development of infants, children, and adolescents, I wish to argue in this concluding chapter that this general theme persists throughout the life cycle, and is impacted over the entire life course by one's racial group membership (see Muntaner et al. 2000, for related theoretical discussion). In addition, the significant transactions between individual and context are not only behavioral in nature (e.g., one's behavior creates a situation which one then responds to behaviorally), but also may take place along biological, cognitive, and affective lines. Because there are multiple vectors along which development is occurring, there are multiple pathways which may contribute to positive and negative functioning in any given individual. Individual outcome, in terms of mental health and illness, is the result of the "goodness of fit" between that individual's biological, cognitive, affective, and behavioral characteristics, and the particular environments that he or she encounters and/or selects over the lifespan. By extension, then, any given characteristic cannot be appropriately seen as determining mental health or illness, as I am assuming that the same predisposing factors may contribute to or detract from adaptive functioning depending on external circumstance.

Besides expanding the transactional model to cover the entire lifespan, another important difference to keep in mind between the original transactional model and this reformulated model is the present acknowledgement of how development in the social context (e.g., after birth) is greatly impacted by experiences which occur previous to any true social interaction (e.g., prenatally). That is, Sameroff's (1975) transactional model places less emphasis on prenatal experiences which may lead to changes in behavior upon arrival in the social environment. Without attending to these factors, which tend to vary greatly by race (as well as by other social categories), the individual can be interpreted to be "responsible" for their subsequent development in a way which is different from what I wish to argue. Despite these differences, this proposed model should not be seen as disputing the established transactional model, but rather as applying it more broadly.

I also acknowledge that the complexity of this model is vast; Sameroff (2003) discussed the many difficulties in empirically testing the original transactional model, and adding factors clearly will compound these difficulties. However, it is hoped that by summarizing significant literature regarding each of these identified pathways, I can illustrate that a great deal of scholarship on race and mental health (and illness) can be usefully related to other findings using this model. This discussion leads to a demonstration of how "race isn't everything"; that is, one's group membership (including other groupings, such as gender; Reid 2002) will never be sufficient to explain or predict any individual's functioning, as individual functioning is ultimately the product of the interactions between a unique person with their unique social environment.

The Expanded Transactional Model (ETM) and Race

Biological Influences on Lifelong Development

Biological factors in mental functioning, such as genetics, neurological structure and function, and neurochemical activity are often discussed as predisposing factors, or "setting conditions," which create certain propensities toward adaptation or maladaptation. In regards to mental health and racial group membership, however, a controversial and all-too-sordid history of identifying race itself as a biological—specifically, genetic—phenomenon (Anderson and Nickerson 2005) has plagued efforts to usefully investigate how biological experiences may vary for socially driven reasons. This controversy remains so active and inflammatory that one of the flagship journals of the American Psychological Association, *American Psychologist,* devoted their entire January 2005 issue to articles expounding upon this topic.

Some scholars in this area argue "race" as a means of categorizing people incorrectly but inherently assumes biological difference, as "the commonsense understanding of 'race' correlates certain physical characteristics and lines of descent" (Azoulay 2006, p. 354). This assumption leads to studies of the relations between race and other phenomena (such as health) which—though they may result in findings indicating no clear biological criteria by which to determine race or explain certain other phenomena—result in the current conceptualization of race being inappropriately legitimized (Frank 2007; Smedley and Smedley 2005). Other writers, however, refer to findings from studies of the human genome that indicate that though the vast majority of genetic material present in all humans is identical (>99%), those differences in DNA patterning that do exist can be explained by referring to common geographical ancestry. In short, this conceptualization roughly corresponds to American notions of racial groups (Bonham et al. 2005). Debate along these lines is far from resolved, and it is not our goal to resolve it. Rather, we wish to address biological impacts on psychological functioning that implicate race as a socially constructed phenomenon. Smedley and Smedley (2005) stated the issue bluntly:

> … although the term *race* [author's italics] is not useful as a biological construct … social race remains a significant predictor of which groups have greater access to societal goods and resources and which groups face barriers—both historically and in the contemporary context—to full inclusion. The fact of inequality renders race an important social policy concern (p. 22).

A growing canon of research indicates that certain kinds of biologically significant experiences seem to occur more often among certain racial groups than others, leading to physiological changes in members of these groups that alter development. Means of moderating or alleviating the effects of these experiences also vary by race, completing the cycle of transaction as we are conceptualizing it. Therefore, it is to this literature that we now turn to illuminate these proposed patterns. Findings reported here reflect studies which also considered socioeconomic status in reaching their conclusions about race.

Factors Affecting Development Before Birth

Attention is increasingly being granted to the role that characteristics of the intrauterine environment may play in developmental problems later in the life cycle (Massaro et al. 2006). Critical neurodevelopmental processes initiate within weeks of fertilization and implantation of the zygote. The intricacies of neuronal production and migration during the formative embryonic stage, which are under the control of complex chemical changes initiated by the DNA, are highly vulnerable to disruption by organic and synthetic teratogen exposure (Massaro et al. 2006; Streissguth et al. 1989). Emerging research is also attending to how it is not only protection from damaging factors, but also exposure to positive environmental factors (e.g., nutrients, maternal vocalizations, physical exercise by gestating women, and possibly even music exposure) which may be required to maximize neurobiological development (Massuro et al. 2006). Therefore, the intrauterine environment promotes or detracts from overall physiological development from the first moments of fetal life, and even a fetus which shows no gross abnormalities can sustain damage due to this environment at the neurological level. In addition, it is becoming evident that many aspects of prenatal development differ according to racial group.

Regarding teratogen exposure and neurological damage, studies of compounds such as lead, polychlorinated biphenyls (PCBs), and mercury have revealed their harmful effects on prenatal neurodevelopment and resulting cognitive and behavioral effects (Williams and Ross 2007). Regular exposure to these compounds, most often from exposure to environmental pollution, has been found to be most common among members of non-White racial groups, putting developing fetuses in these groups at greater risk of damage. Researchers and policymakers alike have only recently begun to appreciate the importance of these racial differences (Dilworth-Bart and Moore 2006). More investigations have been made into the neurodevelopmental effects of substances of abuse, such as alcohol and tobacco, due to the fact that this exposure is generally the result of voluntary behavior on the part of pregnant women. Pertinent to discussions of race and alcohol use, Arria et al. (2006) studied a racially diverse sample of 1,632 pregnant women and found that being of White or Hispanic (author's term) racial group was significantly associated with alcohol use during pregnancy. Meschke et al. (2008) found in a large-scale study that Whites were more likely to report prenatal alcohol use than non-Whites, and Perreira and Cortes (2006) found that White women were more likely to report drinking alcohol during pregnancy than Black or Hispanic women (however, some of these differences were attenuated by other factors, such as education). Sadly, a great deal of research has supported an adverse effect of alcohol exposure *in utero* on later development (Williams and Ross 2007). For example, prenatal alcohol exposure has been associated not only with the development of Fetal Alcohol Syndrome (FAS), but also (at lower levels of alcohol exposure) with lowered birth weight (Dew et al. 2007), reduced attentional capacity (Williams and Ross 2007), and reduced IQ among non-FAS children at age four years (Streissguth et al. 1989).

Tobacco use has also been found to be threatening to the fetus and to later childhood development (Williams and Ross 2007). Whites have been found to be more likely to use tobacco during pregnancy (Arria et al. 2006; Perreira and Cortes 2006), and less likely than Hispanics to attempt to quit smoking during pregnancy (Yu et al. 2002). Unfortunately, health outcomes associated with smoking tobacco include low birth weight (Dew et al. 2007), which has been associated with increased risk of mental retardation and cerebral palsy (Collier and Hogue 2007). Other reviews have found that heavy cigarette smoking during pregnancy may be associated with lowered school achievement a decade later (Williams and Ross 2007). Though a direct relationship between maternal smoking and later psychiatric disorder was not found in this study, poor academic achievement may be an indicator of disrupted development that may lead to increased risk of mental disorder later in life. As troubling as these findings are, it may be even more disconcerting to consider how adverse physical and developmental outcomes seem to occur more often among certain racial groups, even controlling for engagement in behaviors that result in teratogenic fetal exposure. For example, infants born to Black women have been found to have a higher risk of preterm birth (Dew et al. 2007) and infant mortality due to various causes (David and Collins 2007) even when patterns of substance use are taken into account. Therefore, race appears to be important to consider even in the most basic of developmental tasks: individual survival.

As stated above, it is not only restricting damaging exposure, but also ensuring sufficient exposure to necessary nutrients and related influences that contributes to optimal neurological development (Massaro et al. 2006). Appropriate prenatal care is widely viewed as a major factor which ensures appropriate fetal access to beneficial substances during gestation; however, much evidence exists that prenatal care access and usage vary greatly according to race. For example, non-White populations have been found to be less likely to utilize several forms of prenatal care services (Martin et al. 2007), even when they had adequate financial access to such services (Gavin et al. 2004). This latter study also found that non-White populations were more likely to receive recommendations for prenatal testing for diseases related to high-risk behaviors, perhaps indicating biased assumptions about the usual behaviors of minority group mothers (Gavin et al. 2004). This is particularly troubling given findings (such as those reviewed above) that non-White populations may actually be less likely to engage in certain high-risk behaviors during pregnancy than Whites. The experience of such stereotyping of non-White mothers may be one factor which deters non-White pregnant women from seeking prenatal care. Non-White populations already report feeling less trust in physicians than White populations do (Armstrong et al. 2007), and physicians actually report more negative ideas about minority group patients than about White patients (van Ryn and Burke 2000). The net result is that the different kinds of neurodevelopmental threats which harm members of different racial groups may or may not be appropriately identified and treated in time to prevent neurological damage to these children, a fact that may lead to different developmental trajectories being established after birth.

Biological Factors in Development After Birth

As people progress through the postnatal stages of development, biological influences continue to support or disrupt the maintenance of mental health. Whether these influences operate at the individual, family, or regional level, racial differences have been uncovered which appear to differentially impact mental health over the lifespan. At the more individual level of analysis, influences such as nutrition have been investigated. A growing number of studies have supported the roles that specific nutrients have in optimal neurological function over the lifespan, making nutrition a natural factor to study in relation to mental disorders (Bodnar and Wisner 2005). Iron and folate appear to be particularly important in this regard. Increased iron and folate in the diet of young children, for example, has been found to be positively associated with IQ scores. Specifically, iron intake was associated with non-verbal IQ scores, while folate was associated with verbal IQ (Arija et al. 2006). Iron deficiency, on the other hand, has been associated with impaired learning, lowered school achievement, and delays in motor development (Brotanek et al. 2007; Gordon 2003). Later in development, dietary folate and iron, as well as omega-3 fatty acids, vitamin B12, zinc, and selenium have been found to be more likely to be deficient among adults with depression than among control groups, and omega-3 deficiency is a risk factor for depression. In addition, folate deficiency appears to be associated with reduced responsiveness to antidepressant medication (Bodnar and Wizner 2005). In the most advanced stages of life, a history of midlife Vitamin B deficiency appears to be associated with increased risk of dementia, while high midlife antioxidant and omega-3 consumption appears to reduce risk for the development of dementia (Donini et al. 2007). Clearly dietary intake has an impact on the stability of lifelong mental health.

Research on racial differences in nutrition has generally found that non-Whites consume diets lower in these important nutrients than Whites do. For example, Hispanic toddlers are more likely to be iron-deficient than Black or White toddlers (Brotanek et al. 2007). In adolescence, Blacks and Hispanics are more likely than Whites to report skipping breakfast, not eating at least two daily servings of fruits or vegetables, and not eating at least two daily servings of dairy products, while Asians were more likely than Whites to eat fruits and vegetables regularly but much less likely to consume dairy products (Videon and Manning 2003). African American girls also appear to be less likely than Whites to increase their fruit and vegetable intake as they progress through adolescence (Striegel-Moore et al. 2006). Similar differences have also been found among adults, with additional differences by race in fiber intake (Bahr 2007). Research has indicated that some of these racial differences cannot be adequately explained by socioeconomic status (Bahr 2007) or other culturally impacted practices, such as parenting style (Cullen et al. 2002). In the absence of vitamin and mineral supplementation, fruits, vegetables, and dairy provide a number of nutrients essential for mental functioning; therefore, it appears that certain differences in mental health-related outcomes may differ due to differences in consumption of these key foods. At the same time, appropriate interventions to increase healthy dietary behavior can be helpful to members of all racial groups (Kirschenbaum et al. 2005).

At the group level, interest in the likelihood of being exposed to the effects of environmental contaminants and pollution has resulted in distressing findings, particularly in regard to race and SES. In addition, knowledge is growing about the specific effects that particular kinds of exposure can have on the development of mental health from infancy to older adulthood. For example, lead exposure has been extensively studied for its adverse cognitive and behavioral consequences in children, and for its negative impact on the cognitive functioning of older adults. Though certain controversies exist as to the appropriate interpretation of longitudinal data in light of various confounding variables, there is general acknowledgment that lead exposure in childhood is associated with reduced cognitive ability, increased behavioral problems such as aggression, and increased problems with inattention. Even with growing public awareness of this threat, risks of lead exposure to non-White children are not abating as rapidly as they are in White populations (Dilworth-Bart and Moore 2006). Unfortunately, non-White populations may face a double threat of poor nutrition and lead exposure, as poorer quality nutrition contributes to higher lead absorption in the central nervous system (Dilworth-Bart and Moore 2006). Other pollutants, such as nitrous oxides, carbon monoxide, and ozone, also may be more present in the living and working environments of minority populations than of Whites, particularly those of lowered SES (Grinesk et al. 2007), with as-yet-undetermined effects on mental and behavioral functioning over the lifespan. Even beyond the direct effects of pollutants on neurological function, believing oneself to be in danger may itself be detrimental to the health of certain racial groups. For example, chronic uncertainty associated with fearing exposure to pollutants is more common among non-White populations than among Whites (Downey and Van Willigen 2005; Johnson 2002; Jones and Rainey 2006). This kind of uncontrollable stressor may have a biological impact, in the form of elevated stress hormone levels on a chronic basis. Elevated stress, of course, has a profound negative influence on psychological and physical health (Taylor 2003).

Application of ETM Principles to Biology and Development

A transactional view of these biological influences (prenatal alcohol and tobacco exposure, nutritious diet, and environmental pollution exposure) and mental health would predict that individuals who have the knowledge and power to make positive changes in their lifestyles and environments would set an adaptive cycle in motion, which would contribute to increased propensity towards mental health. Specifically, abstaining from substance abuse during pregnancy, increased intake of sound nutrition throughout life, and escaping exposure to pollutants (or the fear thereof) should improve the intellectual capacity and executive functioning of individuals, from infancy onward. For example, the mother who abstains from alcohol abuse during pregnancy may not only protect her developing fetus from teratogenic effects, but also may set herself up to be a more engaged and attentive parent when her child is born. These improvements would likely contribute to greater achievement of the child in school and (later) in the workplace, and would likely lead to greater financial stability over the lifespan. These individuals would also be less likely to have extended exposure to stress, and thus experience associated physical and psychological health benefits. Unfortunately, and very importantly, not all of the relevant variables are under equal control for members of differing racial groups. This is a fact that continues to disturb researchers and policymakers alike (Dilworth-Bart and Moore 2006).

Cognitive Factors in Development of Mental Health

Besides examining how cognitive and intellectual ability results from impacts on neurological development, it may also be useful to consider how education-related experiences can impact members of different racial groups in different ways. In addition, varying endorsement of particular beliefs, values, and ideas may affect developmental trajectory in myriad ways among different racial groups, including the development of mental health. Therefore, we next turn to reviewing literature on these kinds of cognitive differences in our discussion of the ETM. As some contributors to the present volume wrote extensively on some of these topics, we encourage the reader to review those chapters as appropriate.

No discussion of cognitive development and race would be complete without reference to the enormous controversy surrounding racial differences in IQ scores (Alderfer 2003; Gottfredson 2005; Rushton and Jensen 2005). Over the past four decades, the debates surrounding these differences in (purported) intellectual ability between (usually) African American, European American, and (sometimes) Asian/Asian American or Latino American samples, have focused on differing total scores on standardized IQ tests. Rushton and Jensen (2005) have published extensively on such studies in regard to the *hereditarian hypothesis*; that is, they see the main question as "whether any significant part of the Black-White IQ difference is genetic rather than purely cultural or environmental in origin" (p. 238). These authors, and some others, have interpreted findings of such studies as supportive of this contention (e.g., Gottfredson 2005; Rushton and Jensen 2006). Other authors, however, have taken a variety of dissenting positions on this argument. For example, it has been argued that inappropriate interpretation of genetic similarities between members of racial groups (e.g., a failure to acknowledge that cultural/historical factors maintained these similarities—they were not evolutionarily or biologically necessary) irreparably confounds the hereditarian hypothesis (Cooper 2005). Other authors have focused in their dissents on the diminishing differences between different racial groups on various measures of intellectual ability since the mid-1960s; the fact that many interventions aimed at increasing testing skills and school preparedness among Black youth appear to be effective; and the fact that academic achievement has not been found to vary with presumed genetic "Whiteness" or "Blackness" (operationalized by skin color, self-reported ancestry, or mixed-race parentage) as evidence that environmental factors are the only plausible explanation for racial differences in IQ scores (Nisbett 2005). Investigations which examined intelligence among adults in the college years have leant further support to the role of experience in intellectual achievement, even beyond the developmental stages of childhood and adolescence (e.g., Myerson et al. 1998).

While this debate may be dismissed by some as irresolvable, it acquires great significance when considered for its transactional implications. In particular, believing members of certain races to be genetically destined to be intellectually inferior to others (or not believing this) immediately evokes discussions of stereotype threat (Aronson 2002; Suzuki and Aronson 2005) within the frame of the ETM. Stereotype threat can be defined as a negative cognitive–affective experience which hinders performance by members of certain groups on particular tasks, if expected performance on those tasks is assumed to be naturally lower for those groups (Aronson 1999, 2002; Gonzales et al. 2002). In the typical scenario regarding intellectual ability, the performance of non-White individuals on standardized intelligence or achievement tests would be hampered if their racial group membership were activated in the context of the testing (e.g., filling in a box indicates one's group membership before taking the test). This would be due to how activation of their racial group membership would also raise their awareness of how their performance might be judged in light of their race. The resulting anxiety, self-focused attention, and devaluation of the task for ego-protective reasons would all serve to reduce performance.

Recent research has revealed that stereotype threat may be a particular impediment to optimal function of working memory (Beilock et al. 2007; Schmader and Johns 2003), and that individuals placed in experimental situations meant to evoke stereotype threat evidence increased stress (evidenced by increased heart rate and respiration during intellectual task performance) (Croizet et al. 2004). While some authors caution against interpreting such findings as indicating that stereotype threat is uniquely responsible for race differences in (for example) IQ scores (Sackett et al. 2004), the effect has appeared consistently in a number of studies and thus appears to be a real phenomenon which is differentially experienced in various racial groups.

The situations where stereotype threat arises differs by racial group, however; for example, Whites have been found to experience stereotype threat when informed that their performance on a math task would be compared to that of Asians, who are assumed to excel on such tasks (Aronson 1999).

The importance of stereotype threat to the ETM lies in how this experience arises in social contexts and in how poor performance may contribute to maintenance of a negative stereotype and continued distress in various kinds of goal pursuit over time. Some of the transactional aspects of this process were discussed by Nussbaum and Steele (2007) in relation to *academic disidentification*. These authors argued that all students enter the academic arena with equal enthusiasm and find education equally rewarding. Over time, however, the differing educational experiences of White and non-White students can cause non-White students to feel that their self-esteem is under greater threat. Therefore, they may progressively devalue educational outcomes, and disconnect their assessments of their own worth from their educational achievement. While the self-esteem of Black youth, for example, has been consistently found to be higher than that of White youth, this may be due to an ultimately maladaptive tendency on the part of Black youth (particularly males) to disengage from education (Cokley 2002). Unfortunately, blatant cues of ability stereotyping are not necessary to impair performance; experimental research has shown that even subtle cues (such as being observed by a majority group member during a task) worsen performance (Stone and McWhinnie 2008).

Even for those non-White students who do not disidentify with academic performance, however, stereotype threat continues to threaten their achievement. Osborne and Walker (2006) found that highly academically identified African American, Latino American, and Native American students, for example, have been found to be at *increased* risk for high school dropout relative to less-identified (and lower achieving) non-White peers. Among European Americans, however, higher academic identification was predictive of lower dropout rates. The authors interpreted these findings as indicating how strong identification with academic achievement actually makes school a more aversive environment for non-Whites, while Whites experience school as more rewarding when they value academic achievement more. Increased high school dropout rates, of course, lowers college admittance rates for non-White students. Stereotype threat may continue to hinder those non-White students who do make it to college, however. Non-White students have been broadly found to achieve lower than Whites in college, with stereotype threat again identified as a possible contributing factor; this experience has also been found to reduce Black college students' performance on the Graduate Record Examination (GRE) (Aronson 2002). Lower scores on this critical part of graduate school entrance requirements may result in lower graduate school admittance rates for African American students, interfering with efforts to attain greater education, income, and social status. The transactional cycle would be completed when the poorer performance of non-Whites would become known to majority culture, maintaining the tendency toward differential, and sometimes discriminatory, behavior toward non-Whites.

Therefore, even if the individual manages to protect their own self-esteem through devaluation of certain kinds of goal pursuits, their likelihood of attaining other kinds of goals might be hampered due to negative stereotypes which would continue to shape their experiences.

Goal pursuit in education and other life domains can also differ between racial groups due to the effects of other cognitive variables. For example, sense of control (Bruce and Thornton 2004), optimism and pessimism (Brown et al. 2005; Chang 1996; Chang et al. 2001, 2003; Heine and Lehman 1995), perfectionism (Chang et al. 2006, 2008; Downey and Chang 2007), and lay ideas about what optimal functioning is (Constantine and Sue 2006; Downey and Chang 2011) may be among the many cognitive variables that can impact developmental trajectory across the lifespan differently in different racial groups.

Application of ETM Principles to Cognition and Mental Health

One of the most widely known pioneers of cognitive theories and mental health, Aaron Beck, asserted that mental disturbance results from negative thinking about oneself, one's circumstances, and one's future (Sue et al. 2006). The mental health of certain individuals may be most influenced by cognitive variables such as those just discussed through a deleterious impact on this cognitive triad, particularly if those individuals connect ideas of individual accomplishment, control, and reward with the kind of fulfilment described by Beck. While it might be expected that all individuals who experience repeated frustration and failure in their life goal pursuit would develop the kinds of depressogenic cognitions that Beck identified as deleterious to mental health, this prediction would be overly simplistic in light of the ETM. Given the preceding discussion of stereotype threat, it seems that we cannot assume that members of all racial groups will subscribe to any given model of mental health equally. For example, poor academic performance may be more closely linked to the development of reduced mental health among European American youth than among minority youth, as minority youth may have engaged in emotional coping strategies which insulated themselves from negative self-evaluations. Similarly, negative thinking may not be equally damaging to members of all racial groups; for example, while Asians have been found to be more pessimistic than European Americans, Asians were no more likely than European Americans to report experiencing negative affect (Chang 1996). It would seem that the development of mental health, or mental dysfunction, may be largely predicated on the model of ideal mental health that one is socialized into over the life course (Constantine and Sue 2006), and how voluntary efforts to attain or maintain that experience are or are not supported by one's environment. If a good fit exists between one's values and one's circumstances and efforts, positive mental health would likely result. However, the inverse would lead to compromised mental health.

Environmental Impacts on Development of Affect Regulation

Affect regulation has been defined as the ability to modulate one's own responses to emotionally valenced internal and external stimuli (Bradley 2000), or the conscious and unacknowledged measures that people take to avoid negative emotion, and maintain positive emotion (Westen et al. 1997). Affect regulation has also been described as encompassing constructs such as emotion regulation, coping, and even some personality traits which involve general tendencies to experience certain emotions (Gross 1998). Affect regulation has been theorized to be of central importance in the development of mental health or illness. In fact, some researchers have gone so far as to hypothesize that dysfunction in the affect regulation system is the primary cause of mental disorder (Bradley 2000). Not surprisingly, biological factors comprise a key component of the development of appropriate affect regulation. However, many environmental experiences may contribute to or detract from appropriate affect regulation, and many of these may differ by racial group in American society.

Relevant to the ETM, the transactional implications of affect regulation are both broad and profound, particularly in connection to differing experiences of various racial groups across the lifespan. For example, individuals exhibiting lower affect regulation may self-select different environments than those with strong affect regulation. Similarly, people with compromised affect regulation may draw out responses from others in the social environment which are more negative. Each of these factors, in turn, may lead to experiences which may increase one's risk of mental disorder. Also key in the ETM is the assumption that interactive cycles are initiated within the context of one's relationships with primary caregivers, with the consequence that threats to these relationships present threats to optimal development of mental health. Therefore, understanding some of the ways in which helpful or harmful experiences contribute to greater or lesser capacities for affect regulation in members of various racial groups is very important. As there is currently no universally accepted method for measuring affect regulation, I take the approach of many authors in this area by focusing on a variety of emotional strategies and outcomes as evidence for the general construct of affect regulation (e.g., Gross 1998).

It has been argued that affect regulation is fundamentally shaped by multiple contextual factors. Specifically, the *functionalist perspective* argues that one's proximal and distal social contexts determine what forms of emotional expression are beneficial or acceptable, and at what times (Zeman and Shipman 1998). Particularly important at the earliest stages of life are social interactions with primary caregivers. For example, one study showed that infants who were being raised by mothers who were more sensitive to their emotions showed a greater capacity for affect regulation, and a greater likelihood of secure attachment to their mothers. In this study, affect regulation mediated the association between mother sensitivity and infant attachment (Braungart-Rieker et al. 2001). In the converse, mothers who experience affective disturbances (e.g., postpartum depression or anxiety) are more likely to have insecure attachments with their infant children (Howell et al. 2006).

These insecure attachments may remain even if symptoms such as those associated depression are effectively treated. For example, mothers depressed postpartum have been found to be less responsive and positive toward their infants than mothers who do not experience postpartum depression, and these tendencies are not improved by alleviating depressive symptoms (Forman et al. 2007).

Similarly, parenting can be impeded by anxiety, in that anxious parents may restrict their own activities, suffer from excessive fears, or even self-medicate with alcohol (Breitkopf et al. 2006). Children raised by mothers debilitated by postpartum depression or anxiety are at increased risk for negative temperament and behavior problems later in development (Civic and Holt 2000; Forbes et al. 2008; Forman et al. 2007). They are also more likely to exhibit behaviors consistent with taking passive emotional regulation strategies (Silk et al. 2006), indications of compromised affect regulation. Given the potentially negative psychological consequences of maternal depression or anxiety to both mother and child, it is important that at-risk mothers and children be identified as early as possible.

The rate of postpartum depression among new mothers has been estimated at approximately 12% of the population (Albright 1993), though some studies have found much higher rates (e.g., approx. 17–23%, Mayberry et al. 2007). Rates have been estimated to be even higher for mothers at the low end of the socioeconomic scale (Rich-Edwards et al. 2006). Regarding experience of postpartum depression among various racial groups, studies have revealed highly contrasting results. For example, Howell et al. (2006) found that non-White racial group membership was positively associated with experiencing symptoms of postpartum depression (anhedonia and/or depressed mood lasting at least two weeks), controlling for age, marital status, SES, type of childbirth (e.g., vaginal vs. surgical delivery), parity, and infant-related role demands (e.g., diapering, feeding, caregiving tasks). Schmidt et al. (2006) also found some race differences in postpartum depression, measured using the Beck Depression Inventory (BDI) in a study of adolescent mothers. In this study, European Americans and Latina Americans were at greatest risk of suffering from moderate to severe postpartum depression, with African Americans appearing to suffer less frequently from this disturbance. In another study of postpartum depressive symptoms, new mothers were surveyed approximately 24–48 hours after delivery, about their experience of depressed mood within the previous two weeks. This study revealed African American mothers to be at greater risk for depressed mood during the end stage of pregnancy, and in the early postpartum period, than White women were, while Latina American mothers appeared to be less vulnerable to this disturbance than Whites (Segre, Losch, and O'Hara, 2006). Interestingly, then, among studies where racial group differences in rates of postpartum depression have been found, different groups have been identified as being most at risk. This may well be the result of how these studies involved samples taken from different geographic areas; that is, inconclusive findings may indicate that members of the same racial group may have very different experiences in different social environments.

Further complicating the picture, however, is the fact that studies resulting in null findings can also be found in the literature. For example, Rich-Edwards et al. (2006)

found in a large-sample study that the differences in postpartum depression they observed between Latina American, African American, and European American mothers were best explained by SES, whether the pregnancy had been intentional or not, and (most significantly) history of major depression prior to pregnancy. Therefore, these researchers, and others, have argued that racial group is not an independent predictor of postpartum depression (Mayberry et al. 2007).

How should these differences in empirical findings be understood? It seems most appropriate at this time to point to methodological differences as a likely explanation for differing results. For example, studies indicating no difference between racial groups in postpartum depression have often used the Edinburgh Postpartum Depression Scale (EDPS; Cox et al. 1987), with a cutoff of 12 or 13 (out of 30 possible points) used to identify women who had "probably" been depressed in the week before administration (Mayberry et al. 2007). Studies finding significant group differences, however, have more often used one-item or two-item scales, focusing on reports of depressed mood or anhedonia as sufficient indicators of postpartum depression. Using these less-stringent criteria, greater proportions of study samples have been identified as clinical groups, perhaps lending greater statistical power to resulting analyses. Also of concern are differences in the timing of instrument administration across studies; measurements were given as soon as 24 hours after delivery in some studies, or as late as 2 years after childbirth in others. This lack of consistency makes it difficult to come to a general conclusion about whether postpartum depression varies in different racial groups; however, enough positive findings exist in the literature to make this question very worthy of further pursuit. This is particularly true given the profound impact that postpartum depression has on quality of life in both mothers and infants, due (at least in part) to its deleterious effects on affect regulation. If racial group differences do exist, it is very important that this be widely recognized so that appropriate preventive steps can be taken (Segre et al. 2006).

Of course, affect regulation as a solely intrapersonal construct lacks useful meaning, as one only is called upon to regulate his or her own emotional responses within environmental contexts. Therefore, it also behooves us to elaborate on how certain emotionally laden experiences may vary as a direct result of one's racial group membership. For example, having experiences which evoke feelings that one's culture has been ignored, degraded, or destroyed are arguably more common among people of non-White racial group membership in the United States, than among White individuals (Sue et al. 2006). While blatant discrimination is no longer openly sanctioned in US society, more covert forms of racism and discrimination continue to exist which negatively impact mental health.

A common means of investigating the possible associations between racism and mental health is to assess the relative effects of perceived racism, which has been conceptualized as a stressor which challenges the individual coping of target individuals (Cassidy et al. 2004). Perception of the unfairness of racism and discrimination has been noted to appear in children as young as preschool age, and some studies have shown that majorities of non-White children report having personally experienced various forms of discrimination by middle childhood (Brown and Bigler 2005). As individuals of various racial groups navigate and develop within the social environment, recurrent negative emotional experiences associated with discrimination can impact different people to different degrees. Theoretically, more frequent and stressful experiences of racism-related stressful events would be associated with more indicators of poor mental health. Indeed, increasing amounts of data indicate this to be likely. For example, Klonoff et al. (1999) found that perceived racism was associated with increased psychopathology, such as anxiety, depression, and symptoms of somatization in a sample of Black adults. Alcohol abuse, another form of psychopathology, is generally more common among Whites than among non-White groups (see Downey and D'Andrea, this volume); however, perceived discrimination has been found to be associated with increased abuse of alcohol in African-American populations (Mays et al. 2007). Williams and Williams-Morris (2000) conducted an extensive review of the literature on the relations between discrimination and mental health among African Americans and select other minority groups, which largely supported the contention that experiences of discrimination can have a detrimental effect on mental health. A more recent review examining general health outcomes associated with discrimination corroborated this conclusion, and warned that health disparities associated with discrimination actually appear to be increasing, rather than decreasing, in recent decades (Mays et al. 2007).

Affect Regulation, Allostatic Load, and the ETM

In connection to affect regulation, which is thought to have its basis in human physiological processes, recent theorizing about the negative effects of discrimination on individual capacity to bear stress may help illuminate the relations between racial group membership and the development of affect regulation. Mays et al. (2007) elaborated a model connecting experiences of racial discrimination to chronic physiological stress, resulting in greater allostatic load for members of oppressed groups. That is, changes in arousal of the body's stress systems, including altered activation of associated brain structures (such as the amygdala and anterior cingulate cortex), lead to accelerated decompensation of physiological stress–response mechanisms. Along with changes to cognitive functioning and immune response, negative impacts to affective stability may result from these abnormalities. Given that the perception and experience of discrimination begins quite early in life, it is possible that allostatic load begins altering the developmental trajectories of certain racial groups from early childhood on. Downstream during adulthood, then, greater susceptibility to mental disorder may result not only from stressful life circumstances endured by one's racial group, but also from experiencing a lifetime of subtle (and not-so-subtle) alterations in physiological and neurohormonal development. Though it may be that members of different cultures or racial groups appear to differ in their conceptions of ideal emotional expression and experience (Tsai et al. 2006), these differences in values may not suffice to protect all members of disadvantaged groups from mental health problems. Indeed, the widely known disparities in various aspects of mental health seem to confirm this.

Behavioral Patterns and the ETM

Given the preceding discussion of biological, cognitive, and affective differences which may emerge between members of various racial groups over the course of the lifespan, it should be unsurprising the differences in behavior would also be evidenced. As a number of authors in the present volume have elaborated upon such differences, particularly in regard to behaviors associated with alleviating experiences of compromised mental health (e.g., help seeking from mental health professionals, indigenous healers, or taking other actions such as prayer), we will not reiterate already-identified tendencies. Rather, we will emphasize the transactional aspects of such decision-making.

The behaviors that one engages in to try to attain or maintain positive mental health are clearly not selected at random. Rather, they are a function of an interaction between several factors: namely, one's learning and value system, which is directly shaped by culture at both the micro and macro levels; the ongoing and changing state of one's decision-making capacity, which varies with the soundness of one's mind, brain, and body; and one's opportunities, which are limited by one's immediate surroundings, access to resources, and general social position (socially, economically, geographically). It is through the action of these multilayered filters that the near-infinite range of the human behavioral repertoire is whittled down to a much smaller set of exhibited behaviors. To the extent that members of the same racial groups are impacted by the same filters, their behaviors will converge. However, the fact that the above equation represents an extremely complex interaction makes it impossible to determine exactly what any given individual will do at any given time.

What we can be certain of is that whatever action an individual takes, it will be perceived and interpreted by others. Those perceptions and interpretations are generally biased toward indicating individual character (e.g., fundamental attribution error), regardless of what obstacles people may experience. Therefore, responses from one's social environment will often reflect this bias (e.g., "You are depressed because *you* are unmotivated, lack talent," etc.), particularly when those responses are driven by attributions about the behaviors of outgroup members (such as members of racial groups different from oneself). Such responses may thus be either very satisfying, or very unsatisfying, depending on whether they accord with one's self-concept. These changes in self-concept, in turn, shift subsequent decision-making. Now, the ways in which we continuously shape one another's behavior certainly demands appreciation at the individual level. However, in the aggregate, it becomes simply dizzying to consider how our individual actions combine into massive social forces, which we may call the stratification of American society.

The Promise of Empiricism: Testing the ETM

The preceding discussion represents just a sampling of the huge literature that could be theoretically related to the ETM. As the reader may have noted, most of the research reviewed here were cross-sectional studies, associating various indicators of health or pathology to various other factors, with race most often representing a grouping variable or predictor in a multiple regression equation. However, the ETM is by nature a developmental theory, which implies a need for longitudinal methods (Singer and Willett 2003). Indeed, as Sameroff and MacKenzie (2003) emphasized in their extensive review of studies emblematic of the transactional approach, cross-sectional research is by definition not adequate to the task of studying dynamic systems. In fact, these authors made it clear that no particular research strategy can do a complete job of documenting transactional systems, as the dynamic nature of mutual influence between the individual and his or her environment across time results in continuous re-organization of perceptions and behavior for the relevant elements of that system.

Despite the unavoidable inadequacies of time-bound assessment of dynamic systems, Sameroff and MacKenzie (2003) praised a number of studies which used sophisticated longitudinal and statistical designs for their efforts at quantifying such changes. Longitudinal approaches were formerly primarily identified with experimental repeated-measures designs. However, over the past several decades these designs have come to be employed with great frequency in many areas of the social and behavioral sciences, whenever human variables are measured at multiple points in time in order to assess change processes (Arnai 2008). The strength of using well-designed longitudinal studies in investigation of the ETM is due to the potential for such studies to track changes in a target (e.g., the developing child) which effect changes in members of his or her transactional system (e.g., the parents), which in turn lead to later changes in the original target. By assessing both 'ends' of the system over time, changes which occur in any member of the system can be empirically linked. That is, the null hypothesis that any assessed changes in the system occurred *independently* of one another, can be tested.

Common statistical approaches employed in longitudinal research include mediator and moderator regression analyses, hierarchical regression analyses, and structural equation modeling (e.g., Rosel and Plewis 2008). These have all been held out as possible tools in the study of transactional processes in development. By statistically controlling for previously assessed levels of mental health or pathology (or any other variables of interest), relations between specific transactional variables and outcomes can be uncovered (Sameroff and MacKenzie 2003). Some researchers have also examined the possibility of viewing development as movement from one categorical stage of functioning to the next, and thus analyzing categorical longitudinal data relative to assessing trends in development (Ato et al. 2005). For example, in this conceptualization, a researcher might assess the development of depression categorically. One category might represent individuals of very high functioning with no symptoms of depression; a second, individuals of high functioning with some symptoms of depression; a third, individuals of moderate functioning with some symptoms of depression; and a fourth, individuals of poor functioning with multiple symptoms of depression (akin to the concept of complete mental health advocated by Keyes 2007). By identifying groups showing similar patterns of movement from category to category in this paradigm, researchers could feasibly search for similarities in their respective transactional systems which might be determining these patterns. The actual statistical techniques employed in longitudinal studies should be chosen carefully, as factors such as the number of observations across time, variability of scaling of the outcome variable(s), and theoretical considerations about appropriate modeling of change (e.g., linear vs. curvilinear, what order of exponential change) all impact results and interpretation (Fraine et al. 2005). [For further reading on statistical approaches with longitudinal data, the reader is referred to Singer and Willett (2003), and to a special January 2008 issue of the journal *Methodology: European Journal of Research Methods for the Behavioral and Social Sciences*.]

To what other kinds of studies could these statistical tools be usefully applied, in order to build evidence for the ETM? Several examples and suggestions have already been provided, and the only things standing between the interested researcher and a host of new empirical insights are sufficient resources, determination, and creativity to accomplish the goal. However, the keys to testing a model such as the ETM lie in (1) gathering sufficient longitudinal data to examine the 'back-and-forth' transformations which may occur between members of a system, and in (2) ensuring that racial/cultural variables are assessed adequately to be included in explanations of results. For example, if a particular researcher is interested in examining the transactional implications of how concerns about environmental pollution may be associated with different mental health trajectories among adults of various racial groups, he or she might first assess diverse samples of adults in areas of similar environmental threat for their level of concern and distress about such threats. At a later time, participants might be assessed again for the degree to which they tried to escape or alleviate the threat, or communicated their concern to civic authorities, and their perceptions of how their concerns were received by these parties. Public data (such as dollars spent on environmental cleanup efforts) could be included as an objective measure of the degree of attention that particular neighborhoods had received in a given time period. Then at yet a later time, mental health outcomes such as depression and anxiety among these participants could be assessed. Various questions might be answered in such a study, including whether the developmental trajectories of members of different racial groups diverged to a degree that was sufficiently strong as to preclude the effects of random chance. In addition, the degree to which these mental health changes corresponded (or did not correspond) to external indicators of responsiveness from the social/civic environment could be investigated. Naturally great attention to the fine details of such a complex study design would be necessary, but the potential benefit is that some examination of how the person and the social environment impact one another could result.

Applying the ETM to Maximize Thriving

Thriving as a Distinct and Desirable Psychological Experience

It has been suggested by many that being mentally healthy requires something more than just not exhibiting signs of mental illness. Indeed, the World Health Organization has defined mental health as involving a subjective sense of well-being, the functional capacity to productively pursue one's own goals, and the wish and ability to contribute to the collective achievement of the goals of one's society (World Health Organization 2004). That is, in a nod to Jerome Wakefield's famous coining of the term ""harmful dysfunction" as a description of abnormal behavior and psychopathology (as cited in Sue et al. 2006), mental health might be described as *advantageous adaptation.* A conceptualization of mental health which evokes this paradigm has been investigated by Keyes (2007), who has shown in several studies that individuals who show no symptoms of mental illness, and who show signs of *flourishing* (which is purported to include such states as positive affect, feeling a sense of purpose in one's life, and feeling integrated into one's community and society) are least likely to be diagnosed with several different mental disorders. Research into lay concepts of health has confirmed that it is not only mental health, but also the idea of health in general, which are frequently defined by laypeople in terms of advantageous adaptation. That is, most people's ideas of what it means to be healthy include concepts of positive mental/emotional functioning, and a sense of life engagement and reward, which are seen as distinct from not becoming ill or disabled (Downey and Chang 2011; Hughner and Kleine 2004). Therefore, it may be that the social and behavioral sciences are only beginning to embrace a conceptualization which has been held by the many for a very long time, presenting a largely untapped wealth of possibilities in human study and intervention (Keyes 2007).

With the growth of positive psychology as a discipline which cuts across many domains of human behavior, it seems clear that the study of human thriving is being seen as an endeavor of increasing worth in American (and global) society. This push toward expansion of work in positive psychology could rightly be seen as forwarding research endeavors relevant to the ETM. While much of the discussion of the present chapter has highlighted the factors and processes which disrupt development across the lifespan (and where race may play a part in those processes), the beauty of a transactional model is how positive intervention results in change not only in a target individual, but also in the system(s) with which that individual interacts (Sameroff and MacKenzie 2003). That is, if the individual and those in his or her social environment are engaged in a continuous dynamic change process, positive change in one party is likely to contribute to positive change in the other party (or parties). Again, however, it is important that racial and cultural factors be attended to in studies of spontaneous or purposeful system shifts, as changes that may arise in (or assist) members of certain racial groups may not have the same impact in members of other racial groups.

For example, interventions aimed at increasing academic success in vulnerable high school students are unlikely to be equally effective for students of all races, as there is a high likelihood that non-White students carry different attitudes and experiences of academics than White students do (e.g., Cokley 2002; Nussbaum and Steele 2007). In this example, it might be well-advised for change agents (e.g., school administrators, guidance counselors, etc.) to take system-targeted actions when trying to reach non-White students and improve their commitment to education. This might involve such unorthodox measures as seeking feedback from, and creating partnerships with, family and community networks when assessing the appropriateness of their own curricula and teaching methods. Likewise, communities served by particular educational institutions could not help but take notice if school authorities sought to learn about, acknowledge, and atone for any role they themselves may have played in undervaluing the strengths and abilities of their non-White students. By putting the "first foot forward" as a positive change agent in a dynamic system which has been on a path of negative outcomes for all members, previously skeptical or embittered non-White students and families might find themselves more invested in making their own changes. Handled correctly, such an action could also provide a valuable opportunity for White students to learn about what modern America requires of its citizens, and the positive outcomes that such change can bring to all. By inviting and supporting the efforts of members of the research community to document the various processes involved in such change, recommendations for further research and application in other settings (e.g., healthcare, mental health treatment, late-life care, care of immigrant, and undocumented populations) would be made possible.

The Current State of the ETM and Recommendations

The preceding discussion was not meant to devalue the many admirable intervention efforts that are currently being conducted within and outside of the United States. Clearly, many millions of citizens dedicate their lives to the effort of providing every individual with a chance to grow and thrive. Rather, in this chapter, I sought to support the efforts of these individuals by showcasing how their many varied efforts could be usefully put into a shared context, with a mutual goal of enhancing quality of mental health—and life—for all. However, three main changes in the status quo of research in mental health would do much to enhance our common efforts.

First, constant and adequate attention must be paid to social contextual factors impacting mental health. Of specific interest in the ETM are race and age, but gender, socioeconomic status, sexual identity and orientation, education, and relevant policy governing participants are just a few of the additional factors that can translate into diverging developmental paths. Accurately describing one's sample in a research study in terms of demographics has generally become normative in published research, but we should move more quickly toward routine empirical examination of whether race (and other factors) makes a reliable difference in observed human experience and behavior (when possible). Null findings in this regard should be esteemed as highly as significant findings uncovering differences—indeed, it would be just as helpful for us to know where race does *not* make a difference in mental health, as when it does. At this time in our history, a growing awareness of the need to examine race as an important factor in mental health requires that we strenuously support such research efforts. The chapters within this volume speak to the many advances made in this regard in recent years, but also make clear how much we do not yet know about race and mental health.

Second, more engagement in longitudinal research in mental health, with the specific characteristics outlined above examining transactional processes, should be pursued. Longitudinal research obviously requires more resources (both temporal and monetary) than cross-sectional research, and requires broader support from research institutions to conduct. For example, academic researchers balance the (sometimes) opposing interests of conducting maximally informative research, and producing an adequate number of research publications to satisfy their various reviewers. While research institutions naturally have full prerogative to set performance expectations of the researchers in their employ, it should fall within the scope of values of these institutions to support their researchers in efforts to conduct the highest quality research possible.

Third, much more money must be made available for investment in research efforts in mental health generally, particularly that which has implications for lifelong development. We have reached a time in our history where medical science allows greater longevity than ever before, but many still face significant obstacles to benefiting from those advances (Keyes 2007). In addition, our intervention efforts are often predicated on correlational or (at best) one-directional longitudinal knowledge about human mental health and pathology. Without knowledge about which systemic factors to anticipate when intervening at the individual, group, community, or policy level, we will find ourselves time and time again being blindsided by variables which were always "there" but which we never thought to account for. It is only by allocating sufficient resources to such research efforts that we will end up saving resources downstream; again, a long-range view will result in the empowerment of all.

Conclusion

This chapter has presented a model of developmental mental health called the Expanded Transactional Model (ETM), which attempts to argue that racial group membership can be significant in biological, cognitive, and affective development over the course of the lifespan. Development is argued (in line with Sameroff 1975) to be transactional in nature, with members of a system involved in a dynamic process of mutual transformation over time. Race is viewed as a likely moderator of many dynamic developmental processes, but individual development is determined by the goodness-of-fit which exists between that person's characteristics and functioning, and their immediate and larger environment and experiences. The model has been shown to have possibilities for both identifying individuals at risk for pathology and for making culturally appropriate, positive individual or systemic interventions to alter the trajectory of development. Research techniques and examples were described, and recommendations for future recommendations and policy were made. The general aim was to challenge researchers and practitioners to consider their work within a larger theoretical context of development, and to encourage further work in this regard.

References

Albright, A. (1993). Postpartum depression: An overview. *Journal of Counseling & Development, 71*, 316–320.

Alderfer, C. P. (2003). The science and nonscience of psychologists' responses to The Bell Curve. *Professional Psychology: Research and Practice, 34*, 287–293.

Anderson, N. B., & Nickerson, K. J. (2005). Genes, race, and psychology in the Genome Era: An introduction. *American Psychologist, 60*, 5–8.

Arija, V., Espara, G., Fernandez-Ballart, J., Murphy, M. M., Biarnas, & E., Canals, J. (2006). Nutritional status and performance in test of verbal and non-verbal intelligence in 6 year old children. *Intelligence, 34*, 141–149.

Armstrong, K., Ravenell, K. L., McMurphy, S., & Putt, M. (2007). Racial/ethnic differences in physician distrust in the United States. *American Journal of Public Health, 97*, 1283–1289.

Arnai, J. (2008). Special issue: Longitudinal approach in psychology and the social sciences. Theoretical and analytical perspectives. *Methodology: European Journal of Research Methods for the Behavioral and Social Sciences, 4*, 1–3.

Aronson, J. J. (1999). When White men can't do math: Necessary and sufficient factors in stereotype threat. *Journal of Experimental Social Psychology, 35*, 29–46.

Aronson, J. J. (2002). Reducing the effects of stereotype threat on African American college students by shaping theories of intelligence. *Journal of Experimental Social Psychology, 38*, 113–125.

Arria, A. M., Derauf, C., LaGasse, L. L., Grant, P., Shah, R., Smith, L., et al. (2006). Methamphetamine and other substance use during pregnancy: Preliminary estimates from the Infant Development, Environment, and Lifestyle (IDEAL) Study. *Maternal & Child Health Journal, 10*, 293–302.

Ato, M., Ato, E., & Gomez, J. (2005). Analyzing change among developmental stages with categorical models. *Quality & Quantity, 39*, 87–108.

Azoulay, K. K. G. (2006). Reflections on race and the biologization of difference. *Patterns of Prejudice, 40*, 353.

Bahr, P. R. (2007). Race and nutrition: An investigation of Black-White differences in health-related nutritional behaviours. *Sociology of Health & Illness, 29*, 831–856.

Beilock, S. L., Rydell, R. J., & McConnell, A. R. (2007). Stereotype threat and working memory: Mechanisms, alleviation, and spillover. *Journal of Experimental Psychology: General, 136*, 256–276.

Bodnar, L. M., & Wisner, K. L. (2005). Nutrition and depression: Implications for improving mental health among childbearing-aged women. *Biological Psychiatry, 58*, 679–685.

Bonham, V. L., Warshauer-Baker, E., & Collins, F. S. (2005). Race and ethnicity in the Genome Era: The complexity of the constructs. *American Psychologist, 60*, 9–15.

Bradley, S. J. (2000). *Affect regulation and the development of psychopathology*. New York: Guilford.

Braungart-Rieker, J. M., Garwood, M. M., Powers, B. P., & Wang, X. (2001). Parental sensitivity, infant affect, and affect regulation: Predictors of later attachment. *Child Development, 72*, 252–270.

Breitkopf, C. R., Primeau, L. A., Levine, R. E., Olson, G. L., Wu, Z. H., & Berenson, A. B. (2006). Anxiety symptoms during pregnancy and postpartum. *Journal of Psychosomatic Obstetrics & Gynecology, 27*, 157–162.

Brotanek, J. M., Gosz, J., Weitzman, M., & Flores, G. (2007). Iron deficiency in early childhood in the United States: Risk factors and racial/ethnic disparities. *Pediatrics, 120*, 568–575.

Brown, C. S., & Bigler, R. S. (2005). Children's perceptions of discrimination: A developmental model. *Child Development, 76*, 533–553.

Brown, C., Matthews, K. A., & Bromberger, J. (2005). How do African American and Caucasian women view themselves at midlife? *Journal of Applied Social Psychology, 35*, 2057–2075.

Bruce, M. A., & Thornton, M. C. (2004). It's my world?: Exploring Black and White perceptions of personal control. *Sociological Quarterly, 45*, 597–612.

Cassidy, C., O'Connor, R. C., Howe, C., Warden, D. (2004). Perceived discrimination and psychological distress: The role of personal and ethnic self-esteem. *Journal of Counseling Psychology, 51*, 329–339.

Chang, E. C. (1996). Evidence for the cultural specificity of pessimism in Asians vs Caucasians: A test of a general negativity hypothesis. *Personality and Individual Differences, 21*, 819–822.

Chang, E. C., Asakawa, K., & Sanna, L. J. (2001). Cultural variations in optimistic and pessimistic bias: Do Easterners really expect the worst and Westerners really expect the best when predicting future life events? *Journal of Personality and Social Psychology, 81*, 476–491.

Chang, E. C., Downey, C. A., Lin, E. Y., & Sanna, L. J. (2006). Pursuing a path to a more perfect future: On causes, correlates, and consequences of perfectionism. In *Judgments over time: The interplay of thoughts, feelings, and behaviors* (pp. 47–65). New York: Oxford University Press.

Chang, E. C., Ivezaj, V., Downey, C. A., Kashima, Y., & Morady, A. R. (2008). Complexities of measuring perfectionism: Three popular perfectionism measures and their relations with eating disturbances and health behaviors in a female college student sample. *Eating Behaviors, 9*, 102–110.

Chang, E. C., Sanna, L. J., & Yang, K. -M. (2003). Optimism, pessimism, affectivity, and psychological adjustment in US and Korea: A test of a mediation model. *Personality and Individual Differences, 34*, 1195–1208.

Civic, D., & Holt, V. L. (2000). Maternal depressive symptoms and child behavior problems in a nationally representative normal birthweight sample. *Maternal & Child Health Journal, 4*, 215.

Cokley, K. O. (2002). Ethnicity, gender and academic self-concept: A preliminary examination of academic disidentification and implications for psychologists. *Cultural Diversity and Ethnic Minority Psychology, 8*, 378–388.

Collier, S. A., & Hogue, C. J. R. (2007). Modifiable risk factors for low birth weight and their effect on cerebral palsy and mental retardation. *Maternal & Child Health Journal, 11*, 65–71.

Constantine, M. G., & Sue, D. W. (2006). Factors contributing to optimal human functioning in people of color in the United States. *Counseling Psychologist, 34*, 228–244.

Cooper, R. S. (2005). Race and IQ: Molecular genetics as deus ex machina. *American Psychologist, 60*, 71–76.

Cox, J. L., Holden, J. M., & Sagovsky, R. (1987). Detection of postnatal depression. Development of the 10-item Edinburgh postnatal depression scale. *The British Journal of Psychiatry: The Journal of Mental Science, 150*, 782–786.

Croizet, J. -C., Despras, G. r., Gauzins, M. -E., Huguet, P., Leyens, J. -P., & Macot, A. (2004). Stereotype threat undermines intellectual performance by triggering a disruptive mental load. *Personality and Social Psychology Bulletin, 30*, 721–731.

Cullen, K. W., Ash, D. M., Warneke, C., & de Moor, C. (2002). Intake of soft drinks, fruit-flavored beverages, and fruits and vegetables by children in grades 4 through 6. *American Journal of Public Health, 92*, 1475–1478.

David, R., & Collins J. Jr. (2007). Disparities in infant mortality: What's genetics got to do with it? *American Journal of Public Health, 97*, 1191–1197.
Dew, P. C., Guillory, V. J., Okah, F. A., Cai, J., & Hoff, G. L. (2007). The effect of health compromising behaviors on preterm births. *Maternal & Child Health Journal, 11*, 227–233.
Dilworth-Bart, J. E., & Moore, C. F. (2006). Mercy mercy me: Social injustice and the prevention of environmental pollutant exposures among ethnic minority and poor children. *Child Development, 77*, 247–265.
Donini, L. M., De Felice, M. R., & Cannella, C. (2007). Nutritional status determinants and cognition in the elderly. *Archives of Gerontology and Geriatrics, 44*, 143–153.
Downey, C. A., & Chang, E. C. (2007). Perfectionism and symptoms of eating disturbances in female college students: Considering the role of negative affect and body dissatisfaction. *Eating Behaviors, 8*, 497–503.
Downey, C. A., & Chang, E. C. (2011). *Assessment of everyday concepts of health: The Lay Theories of Health Inventory.* Manuscript submitted for publication.
Downey, L., & Van Willigen, M. (2005). Environmental stressors: The mental health impacts of living near industrial activity. *Journal of Health and Social Behavior, 46*, 289–305.
Forbes, E. E., Shaw, D. S., Silk, J. S., Feng, X., Cohn, J. F., Fox, N. A., et al. (2008). Children's affect expression and frontal EEG asymmetry: Transactional associations with mothers' depressive symptoms. *Journal of Abnormal Child Psychology, 36*, 207–221.
Forman, D. R., O'Hara, M. W., Stuart, S., Gorman, L. L., Larsen, K. E., & Coy, K. C. (2007). Effective treatment for postpartum depression is not sufficient to improve the developing mother-child relationship. *Development and Psychopathology, 19*, 585–602.
Fraine, B., Landeghem, G., Damme, J., & Onghena, P. (2005). An analysis of well being in secondary school with multilevel growth curve models and multilevel multivariate models. *Quality & Quantity, 39*, 297–316.
Frank, R. R. (2007). What to make of it? The (Re)emergence of a biological conceptualization of race in health disparities research. *Social Science & Medicine, 64*, 1977.
Gavin, N. I., Adams, E. K., Hartmann, K. E., Benedict, M. B., & Chireau, M. (2004). Racial and ethnic disparities in the use of pregnancy-related health care among Medicaid pregnant women. *Maternal & Child Health Journal, 8*, 113–126.
Gonzales, P. M., Blanton, H., & Williams, K. J. (2002).The effects of stereotype threat and double-minority status on the test performance of Latino women. *Personality and Social Psychology Bulletin, 28*, 659–670.
Gottfredson, L. S. (2005). What if the hereditarian hypothesis is true? *Psychology, Public Policy, and Law, 11*, 311–319.
Grineski, S., Bolin, B., & Boone, C. (2007). Criteria air pollution and marginalized populations: Environmental inequity in metropolitan Phoenix, Arizona. *Social Science Quarterly, 88*, 535–554.
Gross, J. J. (1998). The emerging field of emotion regulation: An integrative review. *Review of General Psychology, 2*, 271–299.
Heine, S. J., & Lehman, D. R. (1995). Cultural variation in unrealistic optimism: Does the West feel more vulnerable than the East? *Journal of Personality and Social Psychology, 68*, 595–607.
Howell, E. A., Mora, P., & Leventhal, H. (2006). Correlates of early postpartum depressive symptoms. *Maternal & Child Health Journal, 10*, 149–157.
Hughner, R. S., & Kleine, S. S. (2004). Views of health in the lay sector: a compilation and review of how individuals think about health. *Health: An Interdisciplinary Journal for the Social Study of Health, Illness & Medicine, 8*, 395–422.
Johnson, B. B. (2002). Gender and race in beliefs about outdoor air pollution. *Risk Analysis, 22*(4), 725–738.
Jones, R. E., & Rainey, S. A. (2006). Examining linkages between race, environmental concern, health, and justice in a highly polluted community of color. *Journal of Black Studies, 36*(4), 473–496.
Keyes, C. L. M. (2007). Promoting and protecting mental health as flourishing: A complementary strategy for improving national mental health. *The American Psychologist, 62*(2), 95–108.

Kirschenbaum, D. S., Germann, J. N., & Rich, B. H. (2005). Treatment of morbid obesity in low-income adolescents: Effects of parental self-monitoring. *Obesity Research, 13*(9), 1527–1529.

Klonoff, E. A., Landrine, H., & Ullman, J. B. (1999). Racial discrimination and psychiatric symptoms among Blacks. *Cultural Diversity and Ethnic Minority Psychology, 5*(4), 329–339.

Martin, L. T., McNamara, M. J., Milot, A. S., Halle, T., & Hair, E. C. (2007).The effects of father Involvement during pregnancy on receipt of prenatal care and maternal smoking. *Maternal & Child Health Journal, 11*(6), 595–602.

Massaro, A. N., Rothbaum, R., & Aly, H. (2006). Fetal brain development: The role of maternal nutrition, exposures and behaviors. *Journal of Pediatric Neurology, 4*(1), 1–9.

Mayberry, L. J., Horowitz, J. A., & Declercq, E. (2007). Depression symptom prevalence and demographic risk factors among U.S. women during the first 2 years postpartum. *JOGNN: Journal of Obstetric, Gynecologic, & Neonatal Nursing, 36*(6), 542–549.

Mays, V. M., Cochran, S. D., & Barnes, N. W. (2007). Race, race-based discrimination, and health outcomes among African Americans. *Annual Review Of Psychology, 58,* 201–225.

Meschke, L. L., Hellerstedt, W., Holl, J. A., & Messelt, S. (2008). Correlates of prenatal alcohol use. *Maternal and Child Health Journal, 12,* 442-451. doi: 10.1007/s10995-007-0261-9.

Muntaner, C., Eaton, W. W., & Diala, C. (2000). Social inequalities in mental health: A review of concepts and underlying assumptions. *Health: An Interdisciplinary Journal for the Social Study of Health, Illness & Medicine, 4*(1), 89.

Myerson, J., Rank, M. R., Raines, F. Q., & Schnitzler, M. A. (1998). Race and general cognitive ability: The myth of diminishing returns to education. *Psychological Science, 9*(2), 139–142.

Nisbett, R. E. (2005). Heredity, environment, and race differences in IQ: A commentary on Rushton and Jensen (2005). *Psychology, Public Policy, and Law, 11*(2), 302–310.

Nussbaum, A. D., & Steele, C. M. (2007). Situational disengagement and persistence in the face of adversity. *Journal of Experimental Social Psychology, 43*(1), 127–134.

Osborne, J. W., & Walker, C. (2006). Stereotype threat, identification with academics, and withdrawal from school: Why the most successful students of colour might be most likely to withdraw. *Educational Psychology, 26*(4), 563–577.

Perreira, K. M., & Cortes, K. E. (2006). Race/ethnicity and nativity differences in alcohol and tobacco use during pregnancy. *American Journal of Public Health, 96*(9), 1629–1636.

Reid, P. T. (2002). Multicultural psychology: Bringing together gender and ethnicity. *Cultural Diversity and Ethnic Minority Psychology, 8*(2), 103–114.

Rich-Edwards, J. W., Kleinman, K., Abrams, A., Harlow, B. L., McLaughlin, T. J., Joffe, H., et al. (2006). Sociodemographic predictors of antenatal and postpartum depressive symptoms among women in a medical group practice. *Journal Of Epidemiology And Community Health, 60*(3), 221–227.

Rosel, J. s., & Plewis, I. (2008). Longitudinal data analysis with structural equations. *Methodology: European Journal of Research Methods for the Behavioral and Social Sciences, 4*(1), 37–50.

Rushton, J. P., & Jensen, A. R. (2005). Thirty years of research on race differences in cognitive ability. *Psychology, Public Policy, and Law, 11*(2), 235–294.

Rushton, J. P., & Jensen, A. R. (2006). The totality of available evidence shows the race IQ gap still remains. *Psychological Science, 17*(10), 921–922.

Sackett, P. R., Hardison, C. M., & Cullen, M. J. (2004). On interpreting stereotype threat as accounting for African American-White differences on cognitive tests. *American Psychologist, 59*(1), 7–13.

Sameroff, A. (1975). Transactional models in early social relations. *Human Development, 18*(1), 65–79.

Sameroff, A. J. A. (2003). Research strategies for capturing transactional models of development: The limits of the possible. *Development and Psychopathology, 15*(3), 613.

Sameroff, A. J., & MacKenzie, M. J. (2003). Research strategies for capturing transactional models of development: The limits of the possible. *Development and Psychopathology, 15,* 613–640.

Schmader, T., & Johns, M. (2003). Converging evidence That stereotype threat reduces working memory capacity. *Journal of Personality and Social Psychology, 85*(3), 440–452.

Schmidt, R. M., Wiemann, C. M., Rickert, V. I., & Smith, E. O. B. (2006). Moderate to severe depressive symptoms among adolescent mothers followed four years postpartum. *Journal of Adolescent Health, 38*(6), 712–718.

Segre, L. S., Losch, M. E., & O'Hara, M. W. (2006). Race/ethnicity and perinatal depressed mood. *Journal of Reproductive and Infant Psychology, 24*(2), 99–106.

Silk, J. S., Shaw, D. S., Skuban, E. M., Oland, A. A., & Kovacs, M. (2006). Emotion regulation strategies in offspring of childhood-onset depressed mothers. *Journal Of Child Psychology And Psychiatry, And Allied Disciplines, 47*(1), 69–78.

Singer, J. D., & Willett, J. B. (2003). *Applied longitudinal data analysis: Modeling change and event occurrence*. New York: Oxford University Press.

Smedley, A., & Smedley, B. D. (2005). Race as biology Is fiction, Racism as a social problem Is real: Anthropological and historical perspectives on the social construction of race. *American Psychologist, 60*(1), 16–26.

Stone, J., & McWhinnie, C. (2008). Evidence that blatant versus subtle stereotype threat cues impact performance through dual processes. *Journal of Experimental Social Psychology, 44*(2), 445–452.

Streissguth, A. P., Barr, H. M., Sampson, P. D., Darby, B. L., & Martin, D. C. (1989). IQ at age 4 in relation to maternal alcohol use and smoking during pregnancy. *Developmental Psychology, 25*(1), 3–11.

Striegel-Moore, R. H., Thompson, D. R., Affenito, S. G., Franko, D. L., Barton, B. A., Schreiber, G. B., et al. (2006). Fruit and vegetable intake: Few adolescent girls meet national guidelines. *Preventive Medicine: An International Journal Devoted to Practice and Theory, 42*(3), 223–228.

Sue, D., Sue, D. W., & Sue, S. (2006). *Understanding abnormal behavior* (8th ed.). Boston: Houghton Mifflin.

Suzuki, L., & Aronson, J. (2005).The cultural malleability of intelligence and its impact on the racial/ethnic hierarchy. *Psychology, Public Policy, and Law, 11*(2), 320–327.

Tamminen, T. (2006). How does culture promote the early development of identity? *Infant Mental Health Journal, 27*(6), 603–605.

Taylor, S. E. (2003). *Health psychology* (5th ed.). New York: McGraw-Hill.

Tsai, J. L., Knutson, B., & Fung, H. H. (2006). Cultural variation in affect valuation. *Journal of Personality and Social Psychology, 90*(2), 288–307.

van Ryn, M., & Burke, J. (2000). The effect of patient race and socio-economic status on physicians' perceptions of patients. *Social Science & Medicine, 50*(6), 813.

Videon, T. M., & Manning, C. K. (2003). Influences on adolescent eating patterns: The importance of family meals. *Journal of Adolescent Health, 32*(5), 365–373.

Westen, D., Muderrisoglu, S., Fowler, C., Shedler, J., & Koren, D. (1997). Affect regulation and affective experience: Individual differences, group differences, and measurement using a Q-sort procedure. *Journal of Consulting and Clinical Psychology, 65*(3), 429–439.

Wicherts, J. M., Dolan, C. V., & Hessen, D. J. (2005). Stereotype threat and group differences in test performance: A question of measurement invariance. *Journal of Personality and Social Psychology, 89*(5), 696–716.

Williams, J. H. G., & Ross, L. (2007). Consequences of prenatal toxin exposure for mental health in children and adolescents: A systematic review. *European Child & Adolescent Psychiatry, 16*(4), 243–253.

Williams, D. R., & Williams-Morris, R. (2000). Racism and mental health: The African American experience. *Ethnicity & Health, 5*(3/4), 243–268.

World Health Organization. (2004). Promoting mental health: Concepts, emerging evidence, Practice (Summary Report). Geneva: World Health Organization.

Yu, S. M., Park, C. H., & Schwalberg, R. H. (2002). Factors associated with smoking cessation among U.S. pregnant women. *Maternal & Child Health Journal, 6*(2), 89.

Zeman, J., & Shipman, K. (1998). Influence of social context on children's affect regulation: A functionalist perspective. *Journal of Nonverbal Behavior, 22*(3), 141–165.

Chapter 19
Multidimensional Clinical Competence: Considering Racial Group, Development, and the Positive Psychology Movement in Clinical Practice

Christina A. Downey and Edward C. Chang

The present volume has brought together a wide set of empirical findings from many areas, which are usually (and often quite usefully) considered separately from one another. Specifically, we have endeavored to present a balanced, developmental picture of mental health, and illness in the five most commonly recognized racial groups within the United States. We have encouraged our contributors to offer their expertise on positive and negative psychological functioning in particular subgroups, and to make recommendations for future investigation on each subgroup. We hope that the result of this work is a useful, comprehensive, and informative volume that inspires much future work.

Recurrent themes throughout this text have been several, and have surprised us in their consistency across different research teams. For example, contributors to this volume have voiced broad agreement regarding the need to promote a multicultural perspective on mental health and illness, related to the changing demographics of our nation and known health disparities between groups. However, many authors emphasized how extant knowledge has been developed using an oversimplified definition of what comprises a "race" or "culture." While the racial categories which serve to organize this volume do reflect historical tendencies in broadly categorizing the US population (e.g., a recent review of American youth mental health and race utilized the same categories; Anderson and Mayes 2010), they pose a number of disconcerting problems for present and future work in our field. For example, these categories can complicate research on race, ethnicity, culture, and mental health in a number of ways. At a very basic level, reviewing findings which various researchers agree are applicable to any given group is becoming a more complex endeavor, as terms and labels which are used by some entities, may or may not be used by other entities. The categories here presented have also come under scrutiny (in the present volume and elsewhere; e.g., Stuart 2004) because they may disregard the complex values and histories of unique ethnic and national groups within each

C. A. Downey (✉)
Department of Psychology, Indiana University Kokomo, 2300 S. Washington St., Kokomo, IN 46904, USA
e-mail: downeyca@iuk.edu

E. C. Chang, C. A. Downey (eds.), *Handbook of Race and Development in Mental Health*,
DOI 10.1007/978-1-4614-0424-8_19, © Springer Science+Business Media, LLC 2012

broad category. Almost all authors in this volume presented examples of distinct ethnic/national groups that are often subsumed into the same racial category, despite characteristics which strongly distinguish one subgroup from the others. In addition, it must always be kept in mind that one's group membership is only one aspect of a person's individual identity (Stuart 2004), and therefore group labels must not supersede individual factors that may be contributing to wellness and/or dysfunction. A tension thus exists between breadth and depth in coverage of the kinds of issues addressed in this volume, and in others like it. It seems clear that no single volume could possibly contain the most significant findings on every group and subgroup (and how individuals within those subgroups may differ and why) in the US population—our diversity is simply too great. We remain glad, though, that our contributors repeatedly emphasized the need for researchers to keep within-group diversity in mind when interpreting findings and designing new studies.

Another recurrent theme in this volume involved how level of acculturation is a major factor related to mental health across the lifespan. Level of acculturation appears to be a very significant moderating variable that can impact whether individuals of various groups may thrive or struggle in navigating the daily challenges of living in US society. Authors in this volume did not assume any simple linear relationship between acculturation and well-being, a position supported by recent critiques of the acculturation literature on the whole (Schwartz et al. 2010). Rather, our authors offered a variety of possibilities involving acculturation which may serve to support optimal functioning in each group. For some individuals, increasing familiarity with dominant American culture (including language, societal structures, and sociocultural practices) may be the key to advancing mental health, while for others, maintaining connections to indigenous languages, values, and practices may serve that same goal. For still others, optimum health might involve efforts which combine both increasing skills reflecting acculturation, and maintaining indigenous connectedness. Alongside these possibilities is how the concept of becoming "acculturated" itself may imply the recognition of a status quo, established and maintained by the dominant group—and that in American society, there is a need to critically examine whether diversity of experience and practice is sufficiently permitted within the status quo.

It is our view that an explicit effort should be made to continue to push the boundaries of what culturally informed values and behaviors are now considered "American." This is due to how authors in this volume coalesced around the view that the experiences of minority groups still tend to be underrecognized by the majority group, so acculturation by members of populations newest to US culture often involves a process of struggle and hardship. One goal of questioning current assumptions about "American-ness" would be to release some groups (particularly non-White groups) from the implied need to demonstrate European American values and practices, in order to maintain positive psychological functioning in American society. Many scholars in many places are discussing similar issues elsewhere (e.g., Berry 2008, 2009; Burdick-Will and Gomez 2006; Chirkov 2009; Okigbo et al. 2009), and vehement arguments are being offered by some that interactions between groups may result in more mutual change than is often assumed by current research on acculturation (Berry 2008, 2009). We feel these discussions are needed and productive, and should be pursued empirically as well as theoretically.

Authors in this volume have also embraced the opportunity to explore the two main intended emphases of this text: namely, an equal focus on both strengths and challenges to mental health, and examination of these issues within subscribed age groups across the lifespan. Regarding the strengths that contribute to resilience of members of various groups, our authors repeatedly described feeling challenged to be brief and selective in reviewing this topic. Many recent works on strengths point to the now-classic article on positive psychology by Seligman and Czikszentmihalyi (2000) as a major motivator for research in this area, and we would be remiss to imply that this framework did not contribute to this volume. However, our authors have here summarized findings regarding strengths, protective factors, positive characteristics, and values from each group which have been studied over many decades. Simply put, they could easily have filled an entire volume with these themes alone! Our hope is that by allotting both positive and negative influences on mental health equal platforms in this volume, researchers examining multicultural mental health will see the utility of assessing both positive and negative variables (as both predictors and outcomes) in their future studies. Regarding the other main theme of this text, the lifespan perspective, recent research has shown how discussing unique strengths and needs of individuals at various stages of development is important (e.g., Walsemann et al. 2009), and our authors have clearly embraced this framework. This is not least because ongoing demographic changes in American society will demand that increasing attention be paid to lifespan issues in mental health. That is, the overall age composition of different racial groups continues to shift over time, with some whole groups being younger on average than others (and thus facing different developmental challenges). What these changes will mean for future changes in mental health interventions and policies is yet to be known, but is assured to be significant.

While scholarly interest in the themes raised in this volume is increasing, and associated knowledge is accumulating, there are still many who voice concern that appropriate application of such findings continues to be a challenge for practitioners (Conway Madding 2000; Hays et al. 2010; Law 2007; Orsi et al. 2010; Snowden et al. 2008; Stuart 2004). Of particular note is how progress in applying knowledge about race, culture, and development in the clinical realm does not appear to be moving at similar rates for different groups. The fact that European Americans are more frequently being recognized as one racial group among many in the United States does not change the fact that most of Western psychotherapy grew out of "White" culture (Sue et al. 2007). In addition, the changing demographic picture of the United States is shifting in different ways in different geographic areas, meaning that clinicians training or practicing in some geographic areas may gain more experience with some groups, than they do with others (Green et al. 2009), and the quality of that training can vary widely (Jernigan et al. 2010). Therefore, while knowledge about multicultural practice is growing, there remains much ground to make up on certain fronts.

Despite these caveats, the many valuable points raised by our authors merit consideration in relation to clinical work. Approaching the challenges of the diverse mental health needs of today's society are many. Practical, direct, empirically informed recommendations in this area are therefore warranted. What follows is a brief overview of how multiculturalism, a developmental perspective, and a strengths-based clinical emphasis can shape our approach to various aspects of mental health action. We close our volume with these themes in grateful acknowledgment of those elements of our audience who are seeking to enact these themes in their daily clinical practice.

Enacting Knowledge on Positive and Negative Mental Health in Various Racial Groups Across the Lifespan: Highlights from the Literature

Mental Health Promotion/Mental Illness Prevention

As discussed in an extensive report by the World Health Organization (WHO), mental health promotion "involves actions that support people to adopt and maintain healthy lifestyles and which create supportive living conditions or environments for health" (WHO 2004, p. 6). Naturally for an action to be mental health-promoting, mental health itself must be defined. Mental health according to the WHO is a state centered within the individual, characterized by four features of well-being: being able to express one's abilities, being able to cope with normal stress, experiencing a productive and fruitful work life, and contributing to the larger community (WHO 2001, as cited in WHO 2004). While a number of models of mental health have been offered (Vaillant 2003), the WHO's model has received the endorsement of scholars and government officials from throughout Europe, as well as Australia, Canada, India, New Zealand, South Africa, and the United States (WHO 2004). Part of the reason for this broad endorsement is that it embraces mental health as a positive state, rather than simply the absence of mental illness; promotion, therefore, is action with an inherent goal to enhance positive functioning and capitalize on human strengths. The WHO report also emphasized how supporting positive mental health through promotion, also aims to prevent the onset of future mental illness; this effort was also widely endorsed upon its publication.

Despite this broad support from many areas of the globe, parts of the WHO's (2004) definition of mental health could be critiqued on various grounds, particularly when considered through multicultural and developmental lenses. For example, the WHO's focus on the individual self as primary, and the collective self as secondary or contingent upon the health of the individual self, may not be expected to conceptually connect with members of Asian/Asian American communities (Leong and Lau 2001; Sue et al. 2007). Similarly, some non-White group members may balk at traditional Western clinical efforts to promote mental health at the individual level, rather than at the family or community level (e.g., Johnson and Cameron 2001; Leong and Lau 2001; Vega and Lopez 2001). However, it should be noted that each of the four features of mental health endorsed by the WHO (2004) is inherently and consciously contextual. For example, socioeconomic and environmental factors may all determine these aspects of the mental health of any individual or group (Kenny and Hage 2009); while mental disorder is most commonly diagnosed in individuals (APA 2000), mental health according to WHO (2004) necessarily involves group-level analysis. As the WHO (2004, p. 21) stated in their report, "It is necessary to understand a particular community's concepts of mental health before engaging in mental health promotion.... An understanding of and sensitivity to factors valued by different cultures will increase the relevance and success of potential interventions." This statement clearly does not limit considerations of mental health to the individual level alone.

A more concerning problem with the WHO (2004) approach to mental health promotion is that it appears best suited to describe and impact the mental health of young and middle-aged adults. This appears particularly clear in the definition's references to work and community contribution, as they may limit the utility of this definition when considering children, school-aged youth, adolescents, and adults above standard working age or who experience functional limitations to their productive capacity. Given that developmental level may moderate responses to promotion or prevention efforts (Buhin and Vera 2009; Walsemann et al. 2009), other concepts of mental health may be somewhat more useful to the interested practitioner in promoting mental health among these populations. The individual-level concept of flourishing (reviewed in Keyes 2007) has begun to be explored in youth populations (Keyes 2006) as well as in older adults (Ryff et al. 2003), with significant adjustments made in the construct compared to that which is measured in adults. For example, flourishing in adolescents has been defined in research as experiencing at least one of three possible indicators of emotional well-being (*feeling happy, interested in life,* or *satisfied*) and five of nine possible indicators of psychological or social well-being (*environmental mastery, positive relations with others, personal growth, autonomy, social contribution, social integration, social actualization, social acceptance,* or *social coherence),* as well as not experiencing mental health problems such as depression or conduct problems (Keyes 2007). This two-dimensional assessment of mental health (e.g., presence vs. absence of both mental health, and mental disorder) could be studied and applied to different age groups in ways that reflect their main strengths and challenges. Promotion and prevention would thus go hand-in-hand, as an effort based on supporting flourishing would involve improving functioning on either or both of these dimensions as appropriate.

Another individual-level construct which may be useful for promotion efforts with members of various age groups is psychological flexibility (Kashdan and Rottenberg 2010). This construct is thought to involve those executive regulatory processes which allow for appropriate and functional cognitive, affective, and behavioral responses to immediate and anticipated situations. Psychological flexibility may be a particularly useful construct to emphasize in mental health promotion with various racial and age-defined groups, due to its essentially transactional nature. That is, if situations and challenges encountered by members of different groups tend to differ in important ways, then having the skill of psychological flexibility would tend to equip the individual to respond to those situations effectively and with lessened stress. Effective responses by these individuals would in turn tend to lead to more tolerable future situations—and at those times when the external situation could not be changed directly or easily, the mental health of that individual (and members of his or her social network and community, by extension) would be at least somewhat protected from harm. Concepts such as psychological flexibility, which offer potential for wide applicability to various age-appropriate developmental tasks and personal and social identity development, should be strongly considered for inclusion in mental health promotion efforts.

It is hoped that the reader has a sense of some of the other strengths that may be particularly meaningful and impactful to promote in the groups discussed in this volume. In general, promotion and prevention efforts should consider supporting most of these existing strengths of racial and age groups (remembering of course within-group variability), to the degree that our research has explored and validated those strengths. The natural next question, of course, is what particular forms these promotion and prevention efforts should take. Many possible avenues exist—medical institutions, schools, churches, public campaigns, workplaces, community development programs, and pushes for policy changes at local, state, and federal levels are just some examples (WHO 2004). Clearly the level of intended change should determine the level of implementation. Most interventions identified as promotion or prevention efforts up to this point have focused on individual-level efforts (Hage and Kenny 2009; Nelson and Prilleltensky 2005), where individuals are trained or empowered to cope more effectively with oppressive or stressful environments (Kenny and Hage 2009) or challenging individual symptoms or risk factors (Stice et al. 2009). Still, one theme that we see emerging strongly from the writings of our contributors is that members of various racial groups may respond differently to different formats—and for some groups, the most important promotion or prevention efforts would not take place at the individual level. Therefore, creative efforts to target families, neighborhoods, communities, and community organizations/institutions may glean more positive results with interdependently oriented racial and cultural groups, than the typical individual-level promotion or prevention effort currently does. Groups of scholars, practitioners, and community members should engage in dialogues to determine what flourishing and psychological flexibility (for example) might look like at the group level—how does a family flourish? how does a neighborhood or organization become psychologically flexible?—in hopes that the answers to those questions can lead to concrete promotion/prevention efforts.

Much scholarship has emphasized how high-level social change may be the real key to true promotion of mental health, and prevention of mental illness (Nelson and Prilleltensky 2005). This level of change begins with continuing to examine mental health disparities among and between group members (e.g., Orsi et al. 2010), as well as community, familial, and individual indicators of mental health (e.g., Dumka et al. 1998). Using such data, policymakers, researchers, and practitioners can collaborate to develop targeted actions that impact single or multiple levels of these systems. Issues such as institutionalized poverty, residential and economic segregation, inadequate or inequitable access to education and linguistic support, a lack of understanding in the mental health establishment about group differences in emotional expression or behavioral responses to stress, and the insidious effects of implicit racism on the workings of societal institutions, have all been empirically identified by our contributors and elsewhere as particularly challenging to multiple populations. These are the kinds of environmental/structural factors which are best addressed by continuing examination of the functioning of higher level societal structures. By targeting these entrenched problems through thoughtful policy debate and higher level intervention, conditions will be set for more of the strengths of individuals, groups, and communities to emerge and express themselves through wellness. In turn, promotion and prevention efforts will themselves strengthen the resources of communities under the pressure of social injustice, and function to accelerate the pace of positive social change (Kenny and Hage 2009). Much as the growth and beauty of a flower will be stunted if it is raised in a dark room, the gifts and talents of diverse members of our population are too often obscured and stifled by the miserable circumstances they find themselves in.

Early Intervention

In reviewing the literature on early intervention, it becomes apparent that several reports describing "early intervention" services have examined efforts which have targeted nondiagnosed populations with known risk factors, such as low socioeconomic status. In these interventions, these at-risk populations are generally provided with individual or family-level support services, intended to buffer these populations from developing mental disorders (e.g., see reviews by Calear and Christensen 2009 and Yung et al. 2007) or other conditions known to be associated with mental disorder, such as child maltreatment (Reynolds et al. 2009). However, this kind of intervention resembles the prevention efforts described above, and in fact are sometimes referred to as "selected prevention" (Calear and Christensen 2009; Yung et al. 2007). Having already offered recommendations for mental illness prevention among diverse groups, we will focus this discussion on those early intervention efforts which seek to identify and remedy budding psychopathology at the earliest possible point in the disorder process.

Early intervention efforts for our purposes are those which are targeted at individuals who are showing early symptoms of known disorders (Yung et al. 2007), most of which appear to have been aimed at youth and adolescents. Targeting younger individuals generally makes sense, given broad evidence that first diagnoses of various mental disorders tend to occur by early adulthood (APA 2000), and youth are often situated in environments where early intervention is feasible (e.g., schools and primary care medical facilities). Still, mental disorders can have their first appearance at any point in the lifespan, particularly when excessive environmental stress is present (Hansell and D'Amour 2008), indicating a need to stay informed and attentive to these issues beyond the childhood years (Roberts et al. 2009). Our first recommendation, then, is for increased study of early intervention efforts among community adult and older adult populations. At this time, early intervention for post-traumatic symptoms (Litz and Bryant 2009) and major depression (Goncalves et al. 2009; Le and Boyd 2006) for adults and older adults have received study, but large-scale implementation of empirically supported early intervention efforts has not been consistently initiated. Screening efforts at workplaces (e.g., Kessler et al. 2005; McPherson et al. 2009) and primary care medical offices (Adler et al. 2009) are currently under consideration for various mental health problems, and may assist with identifying individuals who would benefit from early intervention.

This raises another important aspect of early intervention efforts. In order for early intervention to be effective, psychopathology must be validly assessed and diagnosed while symptoms are still relatively mild (Roberts et al. 2009). However, the assessment process itself may fail to accurately identify those individuals; for example, assessment of psychopathology in non-White populations has faced significant scrutiny regarding the reliability and validity of resulting diagnoses (Anderson and Mayes 2010). One significant national study of infant-to-toddler early intervention efforts indicated that non-White children may be more likely to participate in early intervention than White children, possibly related to their more frequent categorization as low income (Scarborough et al. 2004). Though outreaching to diverse communities and families is an important effort, individuals of various racial groups (even those at risk due to economic hardship) may or may not be appropriately identified as developing early symptoms of disorders due to weaknesses in assessment. Of course, identification of need is just the first step; any intervention applied must be shown to reduce symptoms such that development of the full-blown disorder is avoided, in order for an effort to be considered a successful early intervention (Roberts et al. 2009). As already pointed out by several of our contributors, there are many reasons to believe that the effectiveness of the most common intervention efforts may vary in different race and age-defined populations. Therefore, ongoing research must occur in this area, and particular care taken with clinical efforts which utilize assessment of early symptoms.

Another notable feature of early intervention efforts is their focus on dysfunction, rather then wellness. That is, there appears to have been relatively little attention paid in this area to developing positive functioning in target populations (e.g., encouraging and assessing outcomes such as satisfaction with life, social-emotional intelligence, positive life events, or growth of character strengths; Davidson et al. 2006; Vaillant 2003). We see this as problematic for a number of reasons. First, if the populations targeted by these efforts are truly those which are showing only mild symptoms, then logically it follows that their general presentation should be more functional than dysfunctional (e.g., Global Assessment of Functioning (GAF) scores would be expected to be moderately high). Strengths-based clinical approaches would involve capitalizing on these strengths to overcome whatever challenges might be present, and should not be considered an expectable or "throw-away" correlate of recovering from symptoms (Davidson et al. 2006). It could be argued that even when symptoms of psychopathology are not present, a lack of such positive experiences and characteristics might be an early sign of impending mental disorder (Keyes 2007); therefore, a lack of emphasis on positive functioning could be hindering the progress of research and practice in early intervention. Indeed, the effect sizes associated with the reductions of pathology in early intervention conditions may not be very large (Calear and Christensen 2009; Roberts et al. 2009), which might be logical if these efforts are targeting groups where significant pathology is not yet the primary concern. Therefore, our final recommendation regarding early intervention efforts is that they be designed to explicitly include the development of positive mental health, as well as the elimination of emerging symptoms of psychopathology.

Therapeutic Intervention for Psychopathology

A large amount of valuable scholarship has described recommendations for psychosocial intervention with diverse clients. For example, as of early 2010 the popular internet bookstore Amazon (www.amazon.com) lists dozens of scholarly volumes on this topic, with a number focusing on specific therapeutic orientations and/or target populations. Clearly it is impossible to briefly summarize this rapidly expanding literature here, so we will focus on one main theme: Applying certain known strengths of different age and racial groups, to improving functioning in individuals, families, or small groups in the clinical setting. These recommendations are driven directly by points raised by our authors in the chapters in this volume, and are contextualized by some other related research findings. Though points raised in the following sections are organized according to racial grouping, our intent is not to imply that issues or themes raised within one section (e.g., in the discussion of African Americans) do not apply or could not be useful with other groups (e.g., with Asian Americans) or that they will be helpful in treating all members of a particular group. Rather, we believe that certain concepts may be worth further investigation as endeavors to improve positive functioning and reduce psychopathology in diverse individuals continue.

African Americans

High levels of engagement in familial and community relationship building have been frequently noted as a strength of African Americans across the lifespan. Relationship-building occurs in the home, neighborhood, church, and school, and often implicitly or explicitly reinforces a sense of pride in African American identity (Utsey et al. 2003). Individuals can benefit from these strong social bonds from early childhood onward, and these bonds play a particularly significant role in maintaining the mental health and well-being of members of this racial group. Mental health practice with African Americans across the lifespan should work to capitalize on these interlayered bonds to both promote positive well-being and reduce psychological distress. For example, much scholarship has identified the Black church as a strong source of support for African American individuals, families, and communities (Adksion-Bradley et al. 2005; Boyd-Franklin 1989; Queener and Martin 2001), and prayer an important healing practice for disorders as significant as depression (Givens et al. 2007; Loewenthal and Cinnirella 1999; Mitchell and Weatherly 2000), schizophrenia (Loewenthal and Cinnirella 1999), and chemical dependency (Washington and Moxley 2003). The Black church has even been described as the "pulse of the African American community" (Adkison-Bradley et al. 2005, p. 147). Therefore, it is important that clinicians who can anticipate serving African American populations in their practices develop relationships with local Black church leaders, with a goal of true collaboration. That is, mental health professionals and church leaders should view each other as having unique and important skills to share with one another, for the good of the community and its inhabitants.

Mental health professionals seeking to outreach to local churches, as well as to African American individuals and families where pathology may be present, would be well-advised to integrate some of the language of health from African spiritual practices into their work. For example, some therapy approaches which have grown out of African/African American spiritual practice have focused on health as a sense of balance and harmony among different parts of the self, and with the outer world (Queener and Martin 2001). It would seem that clinicians working within a variety of modalities and therapeutic orientations could easily adopt the concept of balance as an organizing principle for various interventions, without having to adopt any particular religious stance. By offering services not as a way to "correct dysfunction," but rather as a way to help "restore inner and outer balance," clinicians of various backgrounds may find their African American clients more receptive to attempting a variety of potentially helpful treatments (whether they involve medication, psychoeducation, psychotherapy, or some other approach). In addition, this framework may be helpful to clinicians who are initially uncomfortable with incorporating spirituality into their clinical practice. This is because the concept of balance can be easily conceptualized as including rewarding spiritual practice, among a number of other positive life practices. Many African American clients may appreciate the helping framework of restoring inner and outer balance, because of its implied acknowledgement of the power of contextual forces on individual and family functioning. The Black church is often viewed by African Americans as a kind of validating and preserving force against an often hostile and inequitable society (Adkison-Bradley et al. 2005). By discussing mental health as inner and outer balance, the clinician is implicitly validating the existence of the hostile and inequitable forces that African American clients may be perceiving or experiencing, which disrupt the balance of their lives. Some authors have gone so far as to state that this kind of acknowledgment of inequity is critical for cross-racial mental health interventions to have any positive effect with African American clients—indeed, this is critical to ensure that the act of intervention itself is not a revictimization of this oppressed group (Stevenson and Renard 1993). Rather than stigmatizing the individual suffering from psychopathology, the "balance" approach empathizes with the sufferer and states a clear positive goal for wellness. This concept also provides an elegant gateway into dialogue with African American youth, adults, older adults, families, and communities regarding what particular intrapersonal and interpersonal balance makes the most sense for that particular person or group.

Asian Americans

Many Asian Americans, particularly from less-acculturated backgrounds and families, may be expected to avoid seeking assistance for psychological, emotional, or social struggles from structures outside the family, such as Western-style mental health establishments. This may be due to a tendency for Asian Americans to view systematized mental health treatment negatively (Atkinson and Gim 1989), perhaps related to an Asian cultural memory of a colonial past which exploited mental health systems to oppress individual and group rights (Deva 2008), or to a history of intrafamilial power structures that tend to strictly dictate public and private behavior (Root 1985; True 1990). While such actions may be viewed as indicative of strong faith in familial bonds and supports, or a sense of cultural self-sufficiency, such choices have a downside: Asian Americans tend to delay seeking needed mental health treatment for themselves or dependent family members until symptoms are quite severe (Kearney et al. 2005; Sue and McKinney 1975; Zane et al. 1994), and members of this group often end treatment prematurely (Sue 1977; Sue et al. 1994). Even for those Asian Americans who seek treatment for themselves or their family members, their therapy outcomes tend to be poorer (Kearney et al. 2005), perhaps related to different client and therapist expectations of what the therapy process itself will involve (Hwang 2006; Kagawa-Singer and Chung 1994; Root 1985; Tseng 2004; Zane et al. 1994), as well as therapist perceptions of Asian American clients' general suitability for treatment (Zane et al. 1994). Therefore, mental health approaches which would attempt to acknowledge these cultural values and differences, and emphasize the most cherished strengths of Asians/Asian Americans, may go furthest to supporting individuals in this group (Kagawa-Singer and Chung 1994; Root 1985; Tseng 2004).

It has been observed that Asian Americans may often be socialized from early childhood to hold the fundamental personhood of themselves and others as manifesting their embeddedness in intricately interwoven social networks, rather differently than European Americans (for example) may be (Markus and Kitayama 1991; Schwartz et al. 2010; Tafarodi and Smith 2001). As has been pointed out that a therapeutic approach will only be seen as credible and valuable if the model of health it espouses "makes sense" in light of the client's cultural values (Root 1985), the individualist–collectivist framework has received some scholarly attention in relation to mental health in Asian American populations. Such expression of collectivist attitudes about personhood are not unique to Asian Americans, nor do all Asian Americans adhere strongly to such a view, but it is possible that attending to the positive aspects of collectivism may resound well with Asian Americans in mental health outreach and intervention. Some research has found that increasing positive social interactions may be associated with greater improvements in mental health symptomology among people of people of Asian cultural heritage, than of European cultural heritage (Tafarodi and Smith 2001). This fact may have clinical implications, in that increasing social skills and positive relationships in the social networks of Asian Americans may be a productive target of intervention. While cognitive approaches have been well-recognized as techniques that can assist social skill-building, dynamic therapies often also include more consideration of the ways that the client–therapist relationship itself can be healing to the client, compared to cognitive approaches (Egan 2009). Individuals who are low in independent self-construal (e.g., conceptually similar to holding a collectivist view of the self) seem to view both cognitive and dynamic therapies as credible approaches to improving mental health (Wong et al. 2003). As research has found low therapist understandability to be an important predictor of low perceived therapist credibility in Asian Americans (Wong et al. 2007), it may be that dynamic approaches which explicitly require the helper to focus on the quality and shared experience of the client–therapist relationship (including whether the client is fully understanding the content and process of the therapy) might be quite appropriate for some Asian American clients.

Findings such as these provide support for the idea that clinicians who focus their outreach and interventions on enhancing younger and older Asian Americans' abilities to interact productively, enjoyably, and with self-control in their social networks, may foster better outcomes with these clients than if they underemphasize these social factors. Outreach efforts to Asian Americans who may be reluctant to present for assistance due to stigma or shame, may be more effective if messages incorporate the social self more prominently (e.g., rather than "Are you feeling depressed? Seek help at _______," a more acceptable message might be "Are your relationships and duties becoming too difficult to bear? Let us support you at _______"). Additionally, clinicians would be wise to remember that they themselves are part of the social network that is indexed by individuals high in collectivism, because the relational experience they foster with their Asian American clients will have deeper implications for these clients' sense of self than is typical with members of some other groups. As many Asian American clients may tend to associate mental health professionals with other health professionals, such as physicians, these clients may expect mental health workers to act in a fairly directive and authoritative manner bespeaking their perceived status (Tseng 2004; Wong 2007). Therefore, it becomes critical for the Asian American client to experience his or her mental health professional as highly competent, nonjudgmental, appropriately authoritative on issues of mental health expertise, respectful, and useful. By recognizing this expectation and seeking to meet it as best as one can, the clinician is setting the stage for productive interpersonal interactions that can allow for goal pursuit outside of the clinical arena.

European Americans

As noted within this volume, European Americans tend to enjoy privileged status in American society. Explicit or implicit discrimination on the basis of race against Whites is relatively rare, socioeconomic status of Whites tends to be relatively high and stable, and lifespan development of White individuals tends to be less disrupted by negative social pressures such as poverty, crime, and incarceration, compared to other racial groups. Therefore, it can be argued that this relative freedom from multiple and interacting social pressures involving race represents a strength of this group that supports the effectiveness of any clinical interventions which may be needed. Still, many individual European Americans suffer from psychopathology, and its various attending life problems. Of particular concern (also noted within this volume) is evidence that European Americans experience higher rates of substance use disorders, such as alcohol dependence, than other racial groups do (Perron et al. 2009). In addition, comorbid diagnoses of other mental illnesses, such as depression, anxiety, schizophrenia, bipolar disorder, and personality disorder (also referred to as dual diagnoses) are highly common among substance abusers (Bender et al. 2006; Cleary et al. 2008; Drake et al. 2008) with roughly half of adult substance abusers falling into this category (Tiet and Mausbach 2007; Veilleux et al. 2010) and up to 90% of adolescent substance abusers showing comorbidity (Bender et al. 2006). Therefore, the present recommendations will focus on interventions for substance use disorders among European Americans, and how awareness of racial issues might relate to treatment of this population.

Though (to our knowledge) treatments for substance use and comorbid disorders have not been designed specifically for different racial groups, particularly European Americans, reviews that have included descriptive information on participant race have revealed that younger and older European Americans are well-represented in existing studies (Bender et al. 2006; Dutra et al. 2008; Perepletchikova et al. 2008). There appears to be data supporting some effectiveness of various treatment modalities, including cognitive behavioral therapy, group therapy, integrated assertive community treatment (ACT), residential programs, and contingency management for adults (Cleary et al. 2008; Drake et al. 2008; Dutra et al. 2008; Horsfall et al. 2009) as well as multisystemic therapy, individual cognitive problem solving, and ecologically based family therapy for adolescents (Bender et al. 2006; Perepletchikova et al. 2008), though effects may vary with substance addictiveness (e.g., studies of opioid dependent individuals show poorer responses to psychosocial treatments than alcohol- or marijuana-dependent individuals; Veilleux et al. 2010). Therefore, it would seem that clinicians have a variety of choices available to them when working with substance abusing or dually diagnosed clients. Still, effects of all of these treatments appear to be modest at best, and strongest in the short-term (Dutra et al. 2008), even when delivered with the high fidelity required in randomized controlled trials.

One treatment approach which merits additional discussion in the present context, due to its particular conceptual correspondence to attitudes associated in the present volume with "Whiteness," is motivational interviewing. Motivational interviewing is a cognitive technique ideally employed in the early stages of treatment for substance use disorders, other mental disorders, and dual diagnoses. It is aimed at increasing the client's awareness of his or her own level of dysfunction associated with substance abuse, and works to identify and capitalize on the strengths of each client to assist him or her in engaging in the treatment process (Horsfall et al. 2009) while actively empathizing with and encouraging the self-efficacy of each client (Perepletchikova et al. 2008). The effectiveness of motivational interviewing, even in the absence of extensive additional treatment, has been demonstrated empirically (Tiet and Mausbach 2007) and appears to retain greater effectiveness over the long-term than other brief interventions (Horsfall et al. 2009), though strong effects have not been found in all studies (Drake et al. 2008). The tenets of motivational interviewing lie in its focus on "personal choice, responsibility, and awareness of the risks and benefits of continued substance use" (Horsfall et al. 2009, p. 27), values which dovetail well with traditional European American beliefs regarding faith in the individual, reduced emphasis on external circumstances as justification for personal actions, and a belief that a strong work ethic coupled with logical decision-making can create profound change in one's experience (Warner and Riviere 2007). As motivational interviewing is relatively simple to integrate into other psychotherapeutic approaches, clinicians should consider receiving training in these techniques and regularly applying them with their White clients. Though aspects of these techniques may not be as well suited to adolescent populations as they are to adults (Perepletchikova et al. 2008), training in these techniques can be relatively straightforward, and the existing evidence in its favor speaks to its potential to enhance other approaches utilized with European Americans. The question of how motivational interviewing can be tailored to better fit the cognitive capabilities of young clients is worth further exploration. Regarding older clients, it should not be assumed that substance abuse or dual diagnosis is a minor problem. The number of older Americans suffering from substance use disorders is projected to double by the year 2020, to 5.7 million (4.3 million of whom will be European American; Han et al. 2009), so clinicians will need to be prepared to apply these techniques to members of various age groups.

Latino Americans

It is estimated that about half of the Latino American population is foreign born (Lanouette et al. 2009; Vega et al. 2007), indicating that issues related to immigration and acculturation are very likely to be salient (whether personally, or via social networks) to Latino American clients in need of mental health treatment (Altarriba and Santiago-Rivera 1994; Anez et al. 2005; Duarte-Velez and Bernal 2007; Miranda et al. 2006). This reality makes it particularly important to attend to cultural strengths that can be tapped for optimal intervention with members of this diverse group. Broadly speaking, Latino American clients approach social relationships, both familial and nonfamilial, in ways which may appear to clinicians in the current mainstream to be more intimate, integrated, trusting, and personal than (for example) European American clients do (Anez et al. 2005; Mezzich et al. 1999). Members of this racial group are often deeply tied to their familial and community networks (Miranda et al. 2006), a reality which can be beneficial or detrimental to client engagement in mental health treatment (Anez et al. 2005; Van Voorhees et al. 2007; Weisman et al. 2005). For clinicians prepared to recognize and view positively the potential benefits of this interpersonal approach, it is likely that clinical engagement and outcomes can be improved over their current levels. For example, it is known that warmth and concern within Latino American families may help buffer children against psychological dysfunction (Duarte-Velez and Bernal 2007; Samaan 2000) and protect adult members with persistent mental health problems against relapse (Vega et al. 2007). In addition, training Latino American families to reduce the frequency of any negative interactions may help reduce pathology in affected members (Vega et al. 2007). In similar ways, clinicians conducting individual psychosocial interventions who learn to express warmth to their Latino American clients, are open to spontaneity and peer-like disclosure with these clients (e.g., "chit-chat"), understand these clients' needs to consult and/or involve their family members in their treatments, and tolerate a relatively deep level of intimacy with these clients without exploiting this closeness, are likely to develop more positive and productive alliances with these clients than if they expect and maintain typical Westernized interpersonal boundaries (Anez et al. 2005; Canive et al. 2001; Van Voorhees et al. 2007).

Once a positive therapeutic alliance has been established with a Latino American client and/or family, various approaches are available to the clinician, including behavior therapy, cognitive therapy, cognitive-behavioral therapy, and various family therapies (Juarez 1985). Behavior therapy, cognitive-behavioral therapy (Juarez 1985; Weisman et al. 2005) and cognitive therapy (Kohn-Wood et al. 2008) may be attractive to clients because they can be applied within relatively few sessions and result in tangible progress within a fairly brief time period. However, family-focused interventions for Latino American clients have received growing empirical attention for their potential to support positive functioning of members of this group (Cannon and Levy 2008; Juarez 1985; Weisman et al. 2005; Willerton et al. 2008). For example, Brief Strategic Family Therapy (BSFT; Muir et al. 2004; Santisteban et al. 2006) has received considerable empirical testing for its efficacy in treating substance abuse among Latino American adolescents, and behavioral and emotional difficulties among Latino American children (as well as African American youth populations). BSFT integrates structural and strategic theories of family therapy, and focuses closely on within-family dynamics to assist families with recovery from these disruptions and stressors. As the therapy works to engage all family members in the process and progress of therapy, rather than just intervening with an individual child or adolescent, interactional patterns are improved and maintained longer than in other therapy approaches (Santisteban et al. 2006; Szapocznik and Williams 2000). Another excellent example of an efficacious family therapy that may resound well with members of diverse, interdependent cultures, such as Latino

Americans, is filial therapy (Garza and Watts 2010). Filial therapy assumes that children in families affected by mental health problems are much more likely to trust and interact in spontaneous emotional ways with their parents, rather than with therapists. By training groups of parents to respond in therapeutic ways to their children during focused play sessions, therapist group trainers work to equip parents with the tools to interact positively and sensitively to their children's thoughts and feelings over the course of their relationship. Filial therapy has been discussed as particularly well-suited to Latino American families, where warmth, trust, interdependence, and intimate involvement are viewed as common strengths, that occur in parallel with strong cultural respect for parental figures and other elders (Garza and Watts 2010). A third approach that not only focuses on the full family system of Latino American clients, but also acknowledges the considerable barriers to care faced by most Latino American families in the United States is medical family therapy (Willerton et al. 2008). In this approach, the medical system becomes the venue for reaching out to families in psychological distress, and aims to become more culturally acceptable to Latino Americans than other therapies through its focus on collaboration between various helpers and client families. These examples should be viewed as an encouragement for researchers and practitioners to continue to explore ways in which the central value of family can be incorporated into various psychosocial interventions, and indeed drive the development of new interventions which view the family is the ideal target and tool for change.

Native Americans

Though Native Americans currently comprise only a very small proportion of the overall population of the United States, there is incredible diversity of cultural traditions, beliefs, practices, and identity within this group (Goldston et al. 2008). It is accepted that certain experiences, such as historical trauma resulting from European colonization and subjugation (Gone 2009), have so permeated the whole of Native culture in North America that it unites these subgroups across tribe or region. However, beyond European colonization there remains important variability in history and practice within the group identified as Native American (or American Indian/Alaska Native/North American Aboriginal, as appropriate or preferred). In addition, there remains a lack of empirical research on cultural influences in the manifestation of psychological distress and illness in Native Americans, and efficacious treatments to resolve these issues (Gone and Alcantara 2007; Sheehan et al. 2007). Still, some important scholarship has been conducted regarding mental health in Native Americans which has revealed some common themes worthy of continued study. These themes, which may be viewed as cultural strengths with potential to improve practice with members of this group, most often center on enculturation (that is, active positive experiences of one's Native identity), commitment to traditional family and community practices, and integrated spirituality of Native Americans (Garrett and Carroll 2000; Goldston et al. 2008; Trimble 2010). Simply put, it appears that Natives who embrace some core values of Native American culture tend to show greater resilience in the face of significant economic, cultural, and historical stress (Manson 2000).

Intriguing work has recently been advanced which has richly explored Native American understandings of health, well-being, and the healing process. Such work manifests how collaborative research efforts with Native American communities are particularly valuable with this highly marginalized, misunderstood, and mischaracterized group (Legaspi and Orr 2007). This work also acknowledges that within contemporary Native communities, current understandings of traditional Native ways have combined with the consequences of experiences such as European colonization, to create unique conceptualizations of health and healing (Gone 2009). For example, Gone (2009) interviewed 19 counselors and clients of a Native healing lodge, regarding the content and process of healing from a centuries-old history of traumatic experiences shared by Native peoples. This study uncovered four main themes describing these individuals' concepts of healing. These four themes were that troubled Native people carry unmanageable emotional burdens associated with historical trauma; that cathartic verbal expression of this pain can be an important part of the healing process; that continuing introspection over time in search of ever-greater self-understanding, is a hallmark of true healing; and that it is therapeutically important to come to an understanding of one's personal struggles within the greater context of cultural loss and trauma suffered by Native peoples. This kind of work is critical to development of effective interventions, as it allows practitioners to achieve greater understanding of the cultural context of diverse clients (Manson 2000; Trimble 2010) as well as to effectively communicate with members of this group regarding information and recommendations (Garrett and Carroll 2000; Kalbfleisch 2009). It has been recommended that efforts to engage Native Americans in therapeutic interactions begin with a gentle, nonconfrontational approach, which should include respectful greeting and hospitality, a gradual and quiet entering into dialogue, and attention to appropriately respectful eye contact (such as averting one's eyes to match any similar show of respect by the client) (Garrett and Carroll 2000). Communication techniques such as storytelling, use of metaphor, and a focus on relationship-building involving relatively intimate levels of helper self-disclosure (Kalbfleisch 2009) can also assist in alliance with Native clients of various ages. By using these processes of communication, practitioners may build stronger levels of trust with their Native clients, which is vitally important to help reduce the understandable hesitance Native American individuals might feel toward engaging with (particularly non-Native) helpers. This effect may be particularly enhanced if the content of interventions explicitly address the themes of family, community, historical trauma, and spirituality that seem to be paramount to positive functioning in this group.

However, the issue of how developmental stage and acculturation/enculturation may interact is important when considering strengths of Native Americans as a group. For example, satisfaction with family interactions appears to support positive functioning in Native adolescents (as might be expected), but greater participation in traditional Native spiritual activities has been associated with poorer psychological and behavior functioning in this age group of Native Americans. This relationship has held even when other influences on adolescent well-being, such as family and peer interactions, have been taken into account (Silmere and Stiffman 2006) and differs from findings with older Natives. This indicates that, similarly to the other broad racial groups of focus in this volume, general recommendations about research or practice must be interpreted cautiously, and not perceived to apply equally (or at all) to all individuals within a racial or age group.

Multidimensional Clinical Competence: Educating Tomorrow's Practitioners About a Strengths-Based, Multicultural, Transactional Developmental Framework

In order to be effective, the recommendations provided above require not only knowledge of various cultural values and practices, but also practical training that leads to clinical competence (Daniel et al. 2004). Contemporary clinical training in American educational institutions has tended to focus on preparing practitioners for a focus on the resolution of psychopathological symptoms within individuals (Maddux 2008). As a graduate instructor in the first author's own (fairly recently completed) clinical program succinctly stated: "Clients come to escape pain, not to build their strengths." There are many problems with such a statement, which relate to themes of this volume. Specifically, while the concepts and constructs which comprise positive psychology, multicultural perspectives, and transactional processes have existed for decades within the discipline of psychology, statements such as these ignore those themes in favor of practice driven by the correction of definable problems. Which "clients," exactly are we referring to? That is, who "counts" as a client, and how much should racial, ethnic, cultural, and developmental considerations impact that definition? What is the nature of the pain experienced? What can we do about pain that arises from circumstances or contexts we have little to no power to ameliorate? Are we safe in assuming that every client will experience treatment as an escape from pain, or might some aspects of our clinical efforts actually alienate or even traumatize certain clients for reasons that we traditionally fail to investigate? What dangers to alliance or progress towards wellness do we hazard if we overlook client strengths? How can we expect those strengths to change and develop over the client's lifespan—that is, does intervening (or not intervening) at one point in time serve to increase or decrease that client's long-term health or vulnerabilities?

We are well aware that these are not new questions—the authors in this volume, and over years of scholarly discourse, prove that to be true—but we are dismayed that clinical training has not yet adequately or consistently incorporated positive psychology, multiculturalism, and lifespan views into its approach to preparing tomorrow's mental health practitioners. To improve this circumstance, training institutions should prioritize these themes explicitly. The American Psychological Association, having published guidelines on the education of practitioners on multiculturalism (APA 2003), has clearly stated multiculturalism to be a priority of research and practice in psychology. However, multiculturalism in mental health practice has not to this point been fundamentally linked to positive psychology or developmental psychology within a clearly defined construction. We therefore offer the concept of *multidimensional clinical competence*, defined as the ability to work collaboratively and constructively with clients of diverse groups, cultures, developmental stages, and levels of functioning, to recognize, utilize, and develop their existing and potential strengths, in the service of reducing existing or potential dysfunction in themselves or within their social systems. We feel that this expansion of the focus of what clinical competence is not only reflects growing values within contemporary psychology, but also will assist in directing the field toward new areas of inquiry and approaches for intervention. The recommendations for practice in the previous section of the present chapter are just part of what can emerge as we continue to explore these themes in the laboratory, clinic, and community.

More is required of us than simply defining the focus of multidimensional clinical competence, however. More importantly (and more difficult) is the need to define specific competencies to be demonstrated by trainees within the multidimensional clinical competence framework. Efforts to define such competencies are often complicated, result in long lists of required skills and knowledge (e.g., Quay et al. 2009) and may be hampered by variance in expert opinion regarding what core skills reflect true competence (Cunningham et al. 2002). While there is understandable hesitation on the part of some to believe that competency as a clinician can be taught at all (e.g., see a fascinating contribution by House 2008, to this discussion), the fact of the current day is that training of clinicians is a widespread effort. As such, it is critical that training includes specific competencies reflecting a strengths-based perspective, multiculturalism, and attention to transactional processes and their interactions with race, culture, and/or ethnicity. In defining such competencies, programs will be able to specifically assess their students' progress on different areas.

Many efforts toward assessing and increasing some competencies related to multidimensional clinical competence have been described. For example, some scholars have recommended that trainees be instructed on cross-cultural empathy, which includes therapist skills at cross-cultural receptivity, cross-cultural understanding, and cross-cultural collaboration (Dyche and Zayas 2001). Roysircar (2004) provided three goals for trainees to pursue throughout their training in multicultural competence: first, that they should expand their self-awareness regarding their values and biases related to culture; second, that they should increase their exposure to and knowledge of differing worldviews; and finally, that they should become highly effective in their interactions across racial, cultural, or developmental lines. Similarly, Stuart (2004) identified 12 suggestions to facilitate multicultural competence, including developing the ability to understand each person's unique cultural outlook, showing skill at uncovering each client's commitment to various cultural identities and values, and approaching assessment in a manner that reflects sensitivity to culture as well as to other client characteristics. These competencies as well as other suggestions can help to develop a specific set of multidimensional clinical competencies for application in training, but must be expanded to manifest an essentially strengths-based perspective (Maddux 2008). At the same time, even as we seek to define specific multidimensional clinical competencies for mental health work, we must be sure not to address such competence is something that can be "achieved" as an end result of training, without a call to enact those skills and philosophy in ongoing clinical and interpersonal practice (Stolle et al. 2005). It is our hope that the trailblazing scholars who have brought multiculturalism, positive psychology, and transactional development to the forefront of our discipline will consider advancing ideas for multidimensional clinical competencies in their future work.

General Conclusion

Over the last several decades, major shifts have occurred in our understanding of what mental health is, what may underlie its growth or decline, and how and when to intervene with another's well-being. For the mental health field in the United States to recognize and legitimize the influence of sociocultural factors, such as race, ethnicity, and socioeconomic status, on individual and group mental health, was really quite revolutionary. To change the locus of wellness or dysfunction from the individual, to the system, was equally striking and resulted in whole new areas of scholarly investigation and clinical treatment. The current active and productive discussion of how constructs from positive psychology can aid in our understanding and response to psychopathology, now holds similar potential to enliven our field. We believe that we are being called to attend carefully to how these perspectives overlap with and enhance one another. This will require a shift from "2-D" to "3-D" thinking; that is, just as the entertainment industry is now bringing Americans ways to view movies and television in greater depth and clarity through computerized three-dimensional technology, we must be reminded to view our theoretical stances, research questions and conclusions, and clinical interventions with appreciation for the diverse and interacting forces that shape what we see and how we see it. The present volume has documented the distance that has been traveled so far, particularly regarding research in these areas. Such efforts must continue, as all people are equally deserving of an opportunity for fulfillment in their lives.

References

Adksion-Bradley, C., Johnson, D., Sanders, J. L., Duncan, L., & Holcomb-McCoy, C. (2005). Forging a collaborative relationship between the Black Church and the counseling profession. *Counseling and Values, 49*, 147–154.

Adksion-Bradley, C., Sanders, J.-A. L., & Lee, C. C. (2006). Counseling African American women and girls. In C. Lee Courtland (Ed.), *Multicultural Issues in Counseling: New Approaches to Diversity* (3rd ed.) (pp. 79–91). Alexandria, VA: American Counseling Association.

Adler, L., Shaw, D., Sitt, D., Maya, E., & Morrill, M. I. (2009). Issues in the diagnosis and treatment of adults ADHD by primary care physicians. *Primary Psychiatry, 16*, 57–63.
Akutsu, P. D., Castillo, E. D., & Snowden, L. R. (2007). Differential referral patterns to ethnic-specific and mainstream mental health programs for four Asian American groups. *American Journal of Orthopsychiatry, 77*, 95–103.
Altarriba, J., & Santiago-Rivera, A. L. (1994). Current perspectives on using linguistic and cultural factors in counseling the Hispanic client. *Professional Psychology: Research and Practice, 25*, 388–397.
American Psychological Association. (2003). Guidelines on multicultural education, training, research, practice, and organizational change for psychologists. *American Psychologist, 58*, 377–402.
Anderson, E. R., & Mayes, L. C. (2010). Race/ethnicity and internalizing disorders in youth: A review. *Clinical Psychology Review, 30*, 338–48.
Anez, L. M., Paris, M., Jr., Bedregal, L. E., Davidson, L., & Grilo, C. M. (2005). Application of cultural constructs in the care of first generation Latino clients in a community mental health setting. *Journal of Psychiatric Practice, 11*, 221–230.
Atkinson, D. R., & Gim, R. H. (1989). Asian-American cultural identity and attitudes toward mental health services. *Journal of Counseling Psychology, 36*, 209–212.
Bagley, C. A., Carroll, J., McCubbin, H. I., Thompson, E. A., Thompson, A. I., & Futrell, J. A. (1998). Healing forces in African-American families. In H. I. McCubbin, E. A. Thompson, A. I. Thompson, & J. E. Fromer (Eds.), *Resiliency in African-American Families* (pp. 117–142). Thousand Oaks, CA: Sage Publications.
Bell-Tolliver, L., Burgess, R., & Brock, L. J. (2009). African American therapists working with African American families: An exploration of the strengths perspective in treatment. *Journal of Marital and Family Therapy, 35*, 293–307.
Bender, K., Springer, D. W., & Kim, J. S. (2006). Treatment effectiveness with dually diagnosed adolescents: A systematic review. *Brief Treatment and Crisis Intervention, 6*, 177–205.
Bernstein, K. S., Lee, J.-S., Park, S.-Y., & Jyoung, J.-P. (2008). Symptom manifestations and expressions among Korean immigrant women suffering with depression. *Journal of Advanced Nursing, 61*, 393–402.
Berry, J. W. (2008). Globalisation and acculturation. *International Journal of Intercultural Relations, 32*, 328–336.
Berry, J. W. (2009). A critique of critical acculturation. *International Journal of Intercultural Relations, 33*, 361–371.
Boyd-Franklin, N. (1989). Five key factors in the treatment of Black families. *Journal of Psychotherapy & the Family, 6*(1–2), 53–69.
Buhin, L., & Vera, E. M. (2009). Preventing racism and promoting social justice: Person-centered and environment-centered interventions. *The Journal of Primary Prevention, 30*, 43–59.
Burdick-Will, J., & Gomez, C. (2006). Assimilation versus multiculturalism: Bilingual education and the Latino challenge. *Journal of Latinos and Education, 5*, 209–231.
Canive, J. M., Castillo, D. T., Tuason, V. B., Tseng, W.-S., & Streltzer, J. (2001). The Hispanic veteran. In W.-S. Tseng & J. Streltzer, *Culture and Psychotherapy: A Guide to Clinical Practice* (pp. 157–172). Arlington, VA: American Psychiatric Publishing.
Calear, A. L., & Christensen, H. (2009). Systematic review of school-based prevention and early intervention programs for depression. *Journal of Adolescence, 33*, 429–438.
Cannon, E., & Levy, M. (2008). Substance-using Hispanic youth and their families: Review of engagement and treatment strategies. *The Family Journal, 16*, 199–203.
Chaudhry, H. R. (2008). Psychiatric care in Asia: Spirituality and religious connotations. *International Review of Psychiatry, 20*, 477–483.
Chazin, R., Kaplan, S., & Terio, S. (2000). The strengths perspective in brief treatment with culturally diverse clients. *Crisis Intervention & Time-Limited Treatment, 6*, 41–50.
Chirkov, V. (2009). Critical psychology of acculturation: What do we study and how do we study it, when we investigate acculturation? *International Journal of Intercultural Relations, 33*, 94–105.

Cleary, M., Hunt, G. E., Matheson, S., & Walter, G. (2008). The association between substance use and the needs of patients with psychiatric disorder, levels of anxiety, and caregiving burden. *Archives of Psychiatric Nursing, 22*, 375–385.

Conway Madding, C. (2000). Maintaining focus on cultural competence in early intervention services to linguistically and culturally diverse families. *Infant-Toddler Intervention, 10*, 9–18.

Cunningham, P. B., Foster, S. L., & Henggeler, S. W. (2002). The elusive concept of cultural competence. *Children's Services: Social Policy, Research, & Practice, 5*, 231–243.

Daniel, J. H., Roysircar, G., Abeles, N., & Boyd, C. (2004). Individual and cultural-diversity competency: Focus on the therapist. *Journal of Clinical Psychology, 60*, 755–770.

Davidson, L., Shahar, G., Lawless, M. S., Sells, D., & Tondora, J. (2006). Play, pleasure, and other positive life events: Non-specific factors in recovery from mental illness? *Psychiatry: Interpersonal and Biological Processes, 69*, 151–163.

DeCarlo, A., & Hockman, E. (2003). RAP Therapy: A group work intervention method for urban adolescents. *Social Work with Groups: A Journal of Community and Clinical Practice, 26*, 45–59.

Deva, M. P. (2008). Bringing changes to Asian mental health. *International Review of Psychiatry, 20*, 484–487.

Dilsaver, S. C., & Akiskal, H. S. (2005). High rate of unrecognized bipolar mixed states among destitute Hispanic adolescents referred for 'major depressive disorder'. *Journal of Affective Disorders, 84*(2–3), 179–186.

Drake, R. E., O'Neal, E. L., & Wallach, M. A. (2008). A systematic review of psychosocial research on psychosocial interventions for people with co-occurring severe mental and substance use disorders. *Journal of Substance Abuse Treatment, 34*, 123–138.

Duarte-Velez, Y. M., & Bernal, G. (2007). Suicide behavior among Latino and Latino adolescents: Conceptual and methodological issues. *Death Studies, 31*, 425–455.

Dumka, L. E., Gonzales, N. A., Wood, J. L., & Formoso, D. (1998). Using qualitative methods to develop contextually relevant measures and preventive interventions: An illustration. *American Journal of Community Psychology, 26*, 605–637.

Dutra, L., Stathopoulou, G., Basden, S. L., Leyro, T. M., Powers, M. B., & Otto, M. W. (2008). A meta-analytic review of psychosocial interventions for substance use disorders. *The American Journal of Psychiatry, 165*, 179–187.

Dyche, L., & Zayas, L. H. (2001). Cross-cultural empathy and training the contemporary psychotherapist. *Clinical Social Work Journal, 29*, 245–258.

Egan, G. (2010). *The Skilled Helper: A Problem-Management and Opportunity-Development Approach to Helping* (9th ed.). Belmont, CA: Brooks/Cole.

Fujisawa, Y., Hamano, T., & Takegawa, S. (2009). Social capital and perceived health in Japan: An ecological and multilevel analysis. *Social Science & Medicine, 69*, 500–505.

Garrett, M. T., & Carroll, J. J. (2000). Mending the broken circle: Treatment of substance dependence among Native Americans. *Journal of Counseling & Development, 78*, 379–388.

Garza, Y., & Watts, R. E. (2010). Filial therapy and Hispanic values: Common ground for culturally sensitive helping. *Journal of Counseling & Development, 88*, 108–113.

Gayles, T. A., Alston, R. J., Staten, D., Harley, D. A., & Dillard, J. M. (2005). Understanding mental illness among African American males: Risk factors and treatment parameters. In D. A. Harley & J. M. Dillard (Eds.), *Contemporary Mental Health Issues Among African Americans* (pp. 49–59). Alexandria, VA: American Counseling Association.

Givens, J. L., Houston, T. K., Van Voorhees, B. W., Ford, D. E., & Cooper, L. A. (2007). Ethnicity and preferences for depression treatment. *General Hospital Psychiatry, 29*, 182–191.

Goldston, D. B., Molock, S. D., Whitbeck, L. B., Murakami, J. L., Zayas, L. H., & Hall, G. C. N. (2008). Cultural considerations in adolescent suicide prevention and psychosocial treatment. *American Psychologist, 63*, 14–31.

Goncalves, D. C., Albuquerque, P. B., Byrne, G. J., & Pachana, N. A. (2009). Assessment of depression in aging contexts: General considerations when working with older adults. *Professional Psychology: Research and Practice, 40*, 609–616.

Gone, J. P. (2009). A community-based treatment for Native American historical trauma: Prospects for evidence-based practice. *Journal of Consulting and Clinical Psychology, 77*, 751–762.

Gone, J. P., & Alcantara, C. (2007). Identifying effective mental health interventions for American Indians and Alaska Natives: A review of the literature. *Cultural Diversity and Ethnic Minority Psychology, 13*, 356–363.

Green, D., Callands, T. A., Radcliffe, A. M., Luebbe, A. M., & Klonoff, E. A. (2009). Clinical psychology students' perceptions of diversity training: A study of exposure and satisfaction. *Journal of Clinical Psychology, 65*, 1056–1070.

Grimmett, M. A., Locke, D. C., Ellis, C. M., & Carlson, J. (2009). Counseling with African Americans. In C. M. Ellis & J. Carlson (Eds.), *Cross Cultural Awareness and Social Justice in Counseling* (pp. 121–146). New York: Routledge/Taylor & Francis Group.

Hage, S. M., & Kenny, M. E. (2009). Promoting a social justice approach to prevention: Future directions for training, practice, and research. *The Journal of Primary Prevention, 30*, 75–87.

Han, B., Gfroerer, J. C., Colliver, J. D., & Penne, M. A. (2009). Substance use disorder among older adults in the United States in 2020. *Addiction, 104*, 88–96.

Hansell, J. H., & Damour, L. K. (2008). *Abnormal Psychology* (2nd ed.). Hoboken, NJ: Wiley.

Hansen, K. K. (1998). Folk remedies and child abuse: A review with emphasis on caida de mollera and its relationship to shaken baby syndrome. *Child Abuse & Neglect, 22*, 117–127.

Harley, D. A., & Dillard, J. M. (2005). The Black Church: A strength-based approach in mental health. In D. A. Harley & J. M. Dillard (Eds.), *Contemporary Mental Health Issues Among African Americans* (pp. 191–203). Alexandria, VA: American Counseling Association.

Hays, D. G., Prosek, E. A., & McLeod, A. L. (2010). A mixed methodological analysis of the role of culture in the clinical decision-making process. *Journal of Counseling & Development, 88*, 114–121.

Hellerstein, D. J., Almeida, G., Devlin, M. J., Mendelsohn, N., Helfand, S., Dragatsi, D., et al. (2007). Assessing obesity and other related health problems of mentally ill Hispanic patients in an urban outpatient setting. *Psychiatric Quarterly, 78*, 171–181.

Horsfall, J., Cleary, M., Hunt, G. E., & Walter, G. (2009). Psychosocial treatments for people with co-occurring severe mental illnesses and substance use disorders (dual diagnosis): A review of empirical evidence. *Harvard Review of Psychiatry, 17*, 24–34.

House, R. (2008). Training and education for therapeutic practitionership: 'Trans-modern' perspectives. *Counselling Psychology Quarterly, 21*, 1–10.

Hsu, L., & Alden, L. E. (2008). Cultural influences on willingness to seek treatment for social anxiety in Chinese- and European-heritage students. *Cultural Diversity and Ethnic Minority Psychology, 14*, 215–223.

Hwang, W.-C. (2006). The psychotherapy adaptation and modification framework: Application to Asian Americans. *American Psychologist, 61*, 702–715.

Ida, D. J. (2007). Cultural competency and recovery within diverse populations. *Psychiatric Rehabilitation Journal, 31*, 49–53.

Ilardi, D. L., & Kaslow, N. J. (2009). Social difficulties influence group psychotherapy adherence in abused, suicidal African American women. *Journal of Clinical Psychology, 65*, 1300–1311.

Jernigan, M. M., Green, C. E., Helms, J. E., Perez-Gualdron, L., & Henze, K. (2010). An examination of people of color supervision dyads: Racial identity matters as much as race. *Training and Education in Professional Psychology, 4*, 62–73.

Johnson, J. L., & Cameron, M. C. (2001). Barriers to providing effective mental health services to American Indians. *Mental Health Services Research, 3*, 215–223.

Jones, L., Brazel, D., Peskind, E. R., Morelli, T., & Raskind, M. A. (2000). Group therapy program for African-American veterans with posttraumatic stress disorder. *Psychiatric Services, 51*, 1177–1179.

Juarez, R. (1985). Core issues in psychotherapy with the Hispanic child. *Psychotherapy: Theory, Research, Practice, and Training, 22*, 441–448.

Kagawa-Singer, M., & Chung, R. C.-Y. (1994). A paradigm for culturally based care in ethnic minority populations. *Journal of Community Psychology, 22*, 192–208.

Kalbfleisch, P. J. (2009). Effective health communication in native populations in North America. *Journal of Language and Social Psychology, 28*, 158–173.
Kashdan, T. B., & Rottenberg, J. (2010). Psychological flexibility as a fundamental aspect of health. *Clinical Psychology Review, 30*, 467–480.
Kearney, L. K., Draper, M., & Baron, A. (2005). Counseling utilization by ethnic minority college students. *Cultural Diversity and Ethnic Minority Psychology, 11*, 272–285.
Kenny, M. E., & Hage, S. M. (2009). The next frontier: Prevention as an instrument of social justice. *The Journal of Primary Prevention, 30*, 1–10.
Kessler, R. C., Adler, L., Ames, M., Barkley, R. A., Birnbaum, H., Greenberg, P., et al. (2005). The prevalence and effects of adult attention deficit/hyperactivity disorder on work performance in a nationally representative sample of workers. *Journal of Occupational and Environmental Medicine, 47*, 565–572.
Keyes, C. L. M. (2006). Mental health in adolescence: Is America's youth flourishing? *American Journal of Orthopsychiatry, 76*, 395–402.
Keyes, C. L. M. (2007). Promoting and protecting mental health as flourishing: A complementary strategy for improving national mental health. *American Psychologist, 62*, 95–108.
Kohn-Wood, L., Hudson, G., Graham, E. T., & Whisman, M. A. (2008). Ethnic minorities. In M. A. Whisman (Ed.), *Adapting Cognitive Therapy for Depression: Managing Complexity and Comorbidity* (pp. 351–372). New York: Guilford Press.
Lanouette, N. M., Folsom, D. P., Sciolla, A., & Jeste, D. V. (2009). Psychotropic medication non-adherence among United States Latinos: A comprehensive literature review. *Psychiatric Services, 60*, 157–174.
Law, S. (2007). The role of a clinical director in developing an innovative assertive community treatment team targeting ethno-racial minority patients. *Psychiatric Quarterly, 78*, 183–192.
Le, H.-N., & Boyd, R. C. (2006). Prevention of major depression: Early detection and early intervention in the general population. *Clinical Neuropsychiatry: Journal of Treatment Evaluation, 3*, 6–22.
Le Meyer, O., Zane, N., Cho, Y. I., & Takeuchi, D. T. (2009). Use of specialty mental health services by Asian Americans with psychiatric disorders. *Journal of Consulting and Clinical Psychology, 77*, 1000–1005.
Lee, S., Juon, H.-S., Martinez, G., Hsu, C. E., Robinson, E. S., Bawa, J., et al. (2009). Model minority at risk: Expressed needs of mental health by Asian American young adults. *Journal of Community Health: The Publication for Health Promotion and Disease Prevention, 34*, 144–152.
Legaspi, A., & Orr, E. (2007). Disseminating research on community health and well-being: A collaboration between Alaska Native villages and the academe. *American Indian & Alaska Native Mental Health Research: The Journal of the National Center, 14*, 24–43.
Leidy, M. S., Guerra, N. G., & Toro, R. I. (2010). A review of family-based programs to prevent youth violence among Latinos. *Hispanic Journal of Behavioral Sciences, 32*, 5–36.
Leong, F. T. L., & Lau, A. S. L. (2001). Barriers to providing effective mental health services to Asian Americans. *Mental Health Services Research, 3*, 201–214.
Litz, B. T., Bryant, R. A., Foa, E. B., Keane, T. M., Friedman, M. J., & Cohen, J. A. (2009). Early cognitive-behavioral interventions for adults. In E. B. Foa, T. M. Keane, & M. J. Friedman (Eds.), *Effective Treatments for PTSD: Practice Guidelines from the International Society for Traumatic Stress Studies* (2nd ed.) (pp. 117–135). New York: Guilford Press.
Loewenthal, K. M., & Cinnirella, M. (1999). Beliefs about the efficacy of religious, medical and psychotherapeutic interventions for depression and schizophrenia among women from different cultural-religious groups in Great Britain. *Transcultural Psychiatry, 36*, 491–504.
Maddux, J. E. (2008). Positive psychology and the illness ideology: Toward a positive clinical psychology. *Applied Psychology: An International Review, 57*, 54–70.
Manson, S. M. (2000). Mental health services for American Indians and Alaska Natives: Need, use, and barriers to effective care. *Canadian Journal of Psychiatry, 45*, 617–626.
Markus, H. R., & Kitayama, S. (1991). Culture and the self: Implications for cognition, emotion, and motivation. *Psychological Review, 98*, 224–253.

Masuda, A., Anderson, P. L., Twohig, M. P., Feinstein, A. B., Chou, Y.-Y., Wendell, J. W., et al. (2009). Help-seeking experiences and attitudes among African American, Asian American, and European American college students. *International Journal for the Advancement of Counseling, 31*, 168–180.

Mays, V. M., Caldwell, C. H., Jackson, J. S., & Neighbors, H. W. (1996). Mental health symptoms and service utilization patterns of help-seeking among African American women. In H. W. Neighbors & J. S. Jackson (Eds.), *Mental Health in Black America* (pp. 161–176). Thousand Oaks, CA: Sage Publications, Inc.

McPherson, T. L., Goplerud, E., Olufokunbi-Sam, D., Jacobus-Kantor, L., Lusby-Treber, K. A., & Walsh, T. (2009). Workplace alcohol screening, brief intervention, and referral to treatment (SBIRT): A survey of employer and vendor practices. *Journal of Workplace Behavioral Health, 24*, 285–306.

McRae, M. B., Thompson, D. A., & Cooper, S. (1999). Black churches as therapeutic groups. *Journal of Multicultural Counseling and Development, 27*, 207–220.

Mezzich, J. E., Ruiz, P., & Munoz, R. A. (1999). Mental health care for Hispanic Americans: A current perspective. *Cultural Diversity and Ethnic Minority Psychology, 5*, 91–102.

Miranda, A. O., Bilot, J. M., Peluso, P. R., Berman, K., & Van Meek, L. G. (2006). Latino families: The relevance of the connection among acculturation, family dynamics, and health for family counseling research and practice. *The Family Journal, 14*, 268–273.

Mitchell, J., & Weatherly, D. (2000). Beyond church attendance: Religiosity and mental health among rural older adults. *Journal of Cross-Cultural Gerontology, 15*, 37–54.

Muir, J. A., Schwartz, S. J., & Szapocznik, J. (2004). A program of research with Hispanic and African American families: Three decades of intervention development and testing influenced by the changing cultural context of Miami. *Journal of Marital and Family Therapy, 30*, 285–303.

Nagai, C. (2007). Culturally based spiritual phenomena: Eastern and Western theories and practices. *Psychoanalytic Social Work, 14*, 1–22.

Nagai, C. (2008). Clinicians' self-assessment of cultural and spiritual competency: Working with Asians and Asian Americans. *Community Mental Health Journal, 44*, 303–309.

Nelson, G., & Prilleltensky, I. (2005). *Community Psychology: In Pursuit of Liberation and Well-Being.* New York: Palgrave Macmillan.

Okigbo, C., Reierson, J., & Stowman, S. (2009). Leveraging acculturation through action research: A case study of refugee and immigrant women in the United States. *Action Research, 7*, 127–142.

Orsi, J. M., Margellos-Anast, H., & Whitman, S. (2010). Black/White health disparities in the United States and Chicago: A 15-year progress analysis. *American Journal of Public Health, 100*, 349–356.

Perepletchikova, F., Krystal, J. H., & Kaufman, J. (2008). Practitioner review: Adolescent alcohol use disorders: Assessment and treatment issues. *Journal of Child Psychology and Psychiatry, 49*, 1131–1154.

Perron, B. E., Mowbray, O. P., Glass, J. E., Delva, J., Vaughn, M. G., & Howard, M. O. (2009). Differences in service utilization and barriers among Blacks, Hispanics, and Whites with drug use disorders (electronic version). *Substance Abuse* Treatment, Prevention, and Policy, 4, no page number given. Retrieved from www.substanceabusepolicy.com/content/4/1/3.

Pole, N., Gone, J. P., & Kulkarni, M. (2008). Posttraumatic stress disorder among ethnoracial minorities in the United States. *Clinical Psychology: Science and Practice, 15*, 35–61.

Quay, H. C., Hogan, A. E., & Donohue, K. E. (2009). Competencies for infant mental health therapists: A survey of expert opinion. *Infant Mental Health Journal, 30*, 180–201.

Queener, J. E., & Martin, J. K. (2001). Providing culturally relevant mental health services: Collaboration between psychology and the African American church. *Journal of Black Psychology, 27*, 112–122.

Reynolds, A. J., Mathieson, L. C., & Topitzes, J. W. (2009). Do early childhood interventions prevent child maltreatment?: A review of research. *Child Maltreatment, 14*, 182–206.

Roberts, N. P., Kitchiner, N. J., Kenardy, J., & Bisson, J. I. (2009). Systematic review and meta-analysis of multiple-session early interventions following traumatic events. *American Journal of Psychiatry, 166*, 293–301.

Root, M. P. P. (1985). Guidelines for facilitating therapy with Asian-American clients. *Psychotherapy: Theory, Research, Practice, and Training, 22*, 349–356.
Rosado, J. W., & Elias, M. J. (1993). Ecological and psychocultural mediators in the delivery of services for urban, culturally diverse Hispanic clients. *Professional Psychology: Research and Practice, 24*, 450–459.
Roysircar, G. (2004). Cultural self-awareness assessment: Practice examples from psychology training. *Professional Psychology: Research and Practice, 35*, 658–666.
Ryff, C. D., Singer, B., Keyes, C. L. M., & Haidt, J. (2003). Flourishing under fire: Resilience as a prototype of challenged thriving. In C. L. M. Keyes & J. Haidt (Eds.), *Flourishing: Positive Psychology and the Life Well-Lived* (pp. 15–36). Washington, DC: American Psychological Association.
Samaan, R. A. (2000). The influences of race, ethnicity, and poverty on the mental health of children. *Journal of Health Care for the Poor and Underserved, 11*, 100–110.
Sanchez, F., & Gaw, A. (2007). Mental health care of Filipino Americans. *Psychiatric Services, 58*, 810–815.
Santisteban, D. A., Suarez-Morales, L., Robbins, M. S., & Szapocznik, J. (2006). Brief strategic family therapy: Lessons learned in efficacy research and challenges to blending research and practice. *Family Process, 45*, 259–271.
Scarborough, A. A., Spiker, D., Mallik, S., Hebbeler, K. M., Bailey, D. B., & Simeonsson, R. J. (2004). A national look at children and families entering early intervention. *Exceptional Children, 70*, 469–483.
Schwartz, S. J., Unger, J. B., Zamboanga, B. L., & Szapocznik, J. (2010). Rethinking the concept of acculturation: Implications for theory and research. *American Psychologist, 65*, 237–251.
Scogin, F., Morthland, M., Kaufman, A., Burgio, L., Chaplin, W., & Kong, G. (2007). Improving quality of life in diverse rural older adults: A randomized trial of a psychological treatment. *Psychology and Aging, 22*, 657–665.
Seligman, M. E. P., & Csikszentmihalyi, M. (2000). Positive psychology: An introduction. *American Psychologist, 55*, 5–14.
Sheehan, A., Walrath-Greene, C., Fisher, S., Crossbear, S., & Walker, J. (2007). Evidence-based practice knowledge use, and factors that influence decisions: Results from an evidence-based practice survey of providers in American Indian/Alaska Native Communities. *American Indian & Alaska Native Mental Health Research: The Journal of the National Center, 14*, 29–48.
Shin, J. K. (2009). Inpatient stays of Asian patients with psychiatric diagnoses in New York City. *Issues in Mental Health Nursing, 30*, 112–121.
Silmere, H., & Stiffman, A. R. (2006). Factors associated with successful functioning in American Indian Youths. *American Indian & Alaska Native Mental Health Research: The Journal of the National Center, 13*, 23–47.
Simpson, S. M., Krishnan, L. L., Kunik, M. E., & Ruiz, P. (2007). Racial disparities in diagnosis and treatment of depression: A literature review. *Psychiatric Quarterly, 78*, 3–14.
Snowden, L. R., Masland, M. C., Libby, A. M., Wallace, N., & Fawley, K. (2008). Racial/ethnic minority children's use of psychiatric emergency care in California's public mental health system. *American Journal of Public Health, 98*, 118–124.
Stevenson, H. C., & Renard, G. (1993). Trusting ole' wise owls: Therapeutic use of cultural strengths in African-American families. *Professional Psychology: Research and Practice, 24*, 433–442.
Stice, E., Shaw, H., Bohon, C., Marti, C. N., & Rohde, P. (2009). A meta-analytic review of depression prevention programs for children and adolescents: Factors that predict magnitude of intervention effects. *Journal of Consulting and Clinical Psychology, 77*, 486–503.
Stolle, D., Hutz, A., & Sommers-Flanagan, J. (2005). The impracticalities of R. B. Stuart's practical multicultural competencies. *Professional Psychology: Research and Practice, 36*, 574–576.
Stuart, R. B. (2004). Twelve practical suggestions for achieving multicultural competence. *Professional Psychology: Research and Practice, 35*, 3–9.

Sue, D. W., Capodilupo, C. M., Torino, G. C., Bucceri, J. M., Holder, A. M. B., Nadal, K. L., et al. (2007). Racial microaggressions in everyday life: Implications for clinical practice. *American Psychologist, 62*, 271–286.
Sue, S. & McKinney, H. (1975). Asian-Americans in the community mental health care system. *American Journal of Orthopsychiatry, 45*, 111–118.
Szapocznik, J., & Williams, R. A. (2000). Brief Strategic Family Therapy: Twenty-five years of interplay among theory, research and practice in adolescent behavior problems and drug abuse. *Clinical Child and Family Psychology Review, 3*, 117–134.
Tafarodi, R. W., & Smith, A. J. (2001). Individualism-collectivism and depressive sensitivity to life events: The case of Malaysian sojourners. *International Journal of Intercultural Relations, 25*, 73–88.
Tiet, Q. Q., & Mausbach, B. (2007). Treatments for patients with dual diagnosis: A review. Alcoholism: *Clinical and Experimental Research, 31*, 513–536.
Ting, J. Y., & Hwang, W.-C. (2009). Cultural influences on help-seeking attitudes in Asian American students. *American Journal of Orthopsychiatry, 79*, 125–132.
Trimble, J. E. (2010). The virtues of cultural resonance, competence, and relational collaboration with Native American Indian communities: A synthesis of the counseling and psychotherapy literature. *The Counseling Psychologist, 38*, 243–256.
True, R. H. (1990). Psychotherapeutic issues with Asian American women. *Sex Roles, 22*, 477–486.
Tseng, W.-S., & Streltzer, J. (2004). Culture and psychotherapy. In W.-S. Tseng & J. Streltzer (Eds.), *Cultural Competence in Clinical Psychiatry* (pp. 181–198). Arlington, VA: American Psychiatric Publishing, Inc.
Utsey, S. O., Howard, A., & Williams, O., III. (2003). Therapeutic group mentoring with African American male adolescents. *Journal of Mental Health Counseling, 25*, 126–139.
Vaillant, G. E. (2003). Mental health. *The American Journal of Psychiatry, 160*, 1373–1384.
Van Voorhees, B. W., Walters, A. E., Prochaska, M., & Quinn, M. T. (2007). Reducing health disparities in depressive disorders outcomes between non-Hispanic whites and ethnic minorities: A call for pragmatic strategies over the life course. *Medical Care Research and Review, 64*, 157S–194 S.
Vega, W. A., Karno, M., Alegria, M., Alvidrez, J., Bernal, G., Escamilla, M., et al. (2007). Research issues for improving treatment of U.S. Hispanics with persistent mental disorders. *Psychiatric Services, 58*, 385–394.
Vega, W. A., & Lopez, S. R. (2001). Priority issues in Latino mental health services research. *Mental Health Services Research, 3*(4), 189–200.
Veilleux, J. C., Colvin, P. J., Anderson, J., York, C., & Heinz, A. J. (2010). A review of opioid dependence treatment: Pharmacological and psychosocial interventions to treat opioid addiction. *Clinical Psychology Review, 30*, 155–166.
Walsemann, K. M., Gee, G. C., & Geronimus, A. T. (2009). Ethnic differences in trajectories of depressive symptoms: Disadvantage in family background, high school experiences, and adult characteristics. *Journal of Health and Social Behavior, 50*, 82–98.
Warner, J., & Riviere, J. (2007). Why abstinence matters to Americans. *Addiction, 102*, 502–505.
Washington, O. G. M., & Moxley, D. P. (2003). Group interventions with low-income African American women recovering from chemical dependency. *Health & Social Work, 28*, 146–156.
Weisman, A., Feldman, G., Gruman, C., Rosenberg, R., Chamorro, R., & Belozersky, I. (2005). Improving mental health services for Latino and Asian immigrant elders. *Professional Psychology: Research and Practice, 36*, 642–648.
Willerton, E., Dankoski, M. E., & Martir, J. F. S. (2008). Medical family therapy: A model for addressing mental health disparities among Latinos. *Families, Systems, & Health, 26*, 196–206.
Wong, E. C., Beutler, L. E., & Zane, N. W. (2007). Using mediators and moderators to test assumptions underlying culturally sensitive therapies: An exploratory example. *Cultural Diversity and Ethnic Minority Psychology, 13*, 169–177.

Wong, E. C., Kim, B. S. K., Zane, N. W. S., Kim, I. J., & Huang, J. S. (2003). Examining culturally based variables associated with ethnicity: Influences on credibility perceptions of empirically supported interventions. *Cultural Diversity and Ethnic Minority Psychology, 9*, 88–96.

World Health Organization. (2004). *Promoting Mental Health: Concepts, Emerging Evidence, Practice: Summary Report* (electronic version). Geneva: World Health Organization, Department of Mental Health and Substance Abuse in collaboration with the Victorian Health Promotion Foundation and the University of Melbourne. Retrieved from www.who.int/mental_health/evidence/en/promoting_mhh.pdf

Xu, K. T., & Farrell, T. W. (2007). The complementarity and substitution between unconventional and mainstream medicine among racial and ethnic groups in the United States. *Health Services Research, 42*, 811–826.

Yung, A. R., Killackey, E., Hetrick, S. E., Parker, A. G., Schultze-Lutter, F., Klosterkoetter, J., et al. (2007). The prevention of schizophrenia. *International Review of Psychiatry, 19*, 633–646.

Zane, N., Enomoto, K., & Chun, C.-A. (1994). Treatment outcomes of Asian- and White-American clients in outpatient therapy. *Journal of Community Psychology, 22*, 177–191.

ERRATUM TO:

Chapter 17
Psychology of Latino American Older Adults: Strengths and Challenges to Mental Health in a Shifting Society

Steven R. Applewhite and John M. Gonzales

S. R. Applewhite
Graduate College of Social Work, University of Houston,
110 HA Social Work Building, Houston, TX 77204-4013, USA
e-mail: sapplewhite@uh.edu

E. C. Chang, C. A. Downey (eds.), *Handbook of Race and Development in Mental Health, pp. 307–328, 2012*. © Springer Science+Business Media, LLC 2012

DOI 10.1007/978-1-4614-0424-8_20

In the original version, the second author's last name is incorrect. The correct name is as follows:

John M. Gonzalez

John M. Gonzalez, Ph.D., LMSW
Assistant Professor
Department of Social Work
The University of Texas - Pan American
1201 West University Drive, HSHE 2.128
Edinburg, Texas 78539
e-mail: gonzalezjm@utpa.edu

The original online version for this chapter can be found at
http://dx.doi.org/10.1007/978-1-4614-0424-8_17

E. C. Chang, C. A. Downey (eds.), *Handbook of Race and Development in Mental Health*,
DOI 10.1007/978-1-4614-0424-8_20, © Springer Science+Business Media, LLC 2012

Index

A
Academic
  achievement, 151
  disidentification, 338
Acculturation, 5, 108, 119, 128, 131, 135, 138, 140, 148, 156–159, 172, 173, 261, 264, 297–299, 312, 313, 316, 368, 371
Acculturation, level of
  assimilated, 113, 117
  bicultural, 113, 117
  marginal, 113, 117
  pan-traditional, 113, 117
  traditional, 113, 117
Acculturation, stress associated with, 172, 173
Adaptability, 138
Adherence, 319
Affect Regulation, Environmental Impacts, 340–343
African American children, psychology of
  maintaining mental health
    maltreatment, 28–30
    mental health services, access to, 30
    punitive parenting, 28–30
    violence, exposure to, 28
  mental health, strengths contribution
    extended social supports, 32
    restrictive parents, 33–35
    robust self-esteem, 35–37
African American community, 36, 77, 364
African Americans, mental health of
  African Americans, demographic characteristics of, 45–47
  racial discrimination
    John Henryism, 55–58
    residential segregation, 49–51
    social support, 52–55
  racism, 48–58
African Americans, service use, 71–74
AI/AN ethnic and cultural identity, 137, 138
AI-SUPERPFP, 129, 139
Alaska Native (AN), 5, 87
Alcohol abuse, 228, 229
Alzheimer's association, 249
American changing lives study, 233
American dream, 212, 213
American Indian (AI), 87, 96
American Indian and Alaska Natives (AI/ANs), 107, 127, 141
American Indian Religious Freedom Act, 116, 119
American Psychiatric Association, 1, 3, 22, 135
American Psychological Association (APA), 1, 15, 18, 47, 134, 331, 359, 361
American psychologist, 331
American society, 110, 223, 228, 329, 340, 344, 356, 367
American-ness, 356
Anthropological, 135
Antipsychotic medications, 5, 70, 78
Anxiety, 251
Asian American adults, psychology of
  maintaining mental health
    acculturation, stress associated with, 172, 173
    discrimination, 170–172
    family conflict, 173, 174
    migration, stress associated with
    prejudice, 170, 172
  mental health, strengths contributing to
    cultural values, 175, 176
    ethnic identity, 178
    familial, religious, and community institutions, 176, 178

E. C. Chang, C. A. Downey (eds.), *Handbook of Race and Development in Mental Health*,
DOI 10.1007/978-1-4614-0424-8, © Springer Science+Business Media, LLC 2012

Asian American children, psychology of
heritage cultural influences, 148, 155
minority experience, 155–158
Asian American older adults, psychology of
maintaining mental health, challenges to
disorders, lack of information and knowledge about, 195, 196
disorders, stigmatization of, 192–195
mental health services, underutilization of, 196–198, 202, 320
mental disorders, prevalence of
mental health, strengths contributing to
familial support, 198, 199
peer support, 200
religion, 199, 200
social networks, 200
spirituality, 199, 200
Asian American Study, 280
Asian Americans, 365, 366
Assertive community treatment (ACT), 367
Association of Black Psychologists (ABPsi), 18–20
Authoritarianism, 35
Avoidant coping, 154, 155

B
Barrio, 316
Balance, 113, 114
Beck Depression Inventory (BDI), 341
Bicultural competence, 7, 261, 270, 271
Biculturalism, 157
Biological models, 2
Biomedical mental health care, 128, 140
Black
church, 364
community members, 13
men, 57
neighborhoods, 51, 60
parents, 34
psychology, 19, 21
students, 13
Black-White IQ, 336
Brief Strategic Family Therapy (BSFT), 369

C
Center for Epidemiological Studies Depression Scale (CES-D), 72–74, 95, 130
Center for Mental Health Services, 90
Centers for Disease Control and Prevention, 68, 87, 95, 311
Child Protective Services (CPS), 29, 30
Citizenship Act, 116
Cognitive-behavioral therapy, 369
Collaborative for Academic, Social and Emotional Learning (CASEL), 216
Community
networks, 5, 128, 139, 140, 348, 369
poverty, 7, 261, 262
Community-based Participatory Research Process (CBPR), 87, 91, 101, 103
Compadrazo, 316
Cross-Cultural Clinical Psychology
North America
deficit model, 16
inferiority model, 13–16
postmodern identities, postwar challenges
culturally deprived model, 18–20
culturally different model, 20
positive psychology model, 21
Culture and child temperament, 149
Culture and Parenting, 150, 152
Cultural adaptation, 263–265
Cultural familiarity, 213
Cultural heritage, 147–162
Cultural relevance, 133, 134, 137, 139, 140
Cultural values, 175, 176
Culturally deprived model, 18–20
Culturally different model, 20
Culture-bound syndromes, 11, 135, 318, 319, 322
Culture-laden situation, 270

D
Deficit model, 13, 16
Dementia, 249
Demographic characteristics
African Americans, 45–47
older African Americans, 67
Latinos adults, 281–287
Latinos, 308
U.S. Hispanics, 308
White American adults, 223
Demographic profile, 245
Depression, 5, 28, 46, 47, 54, 56–60, 68, 71–78, 96, 98–100, 130, 172–175, 191–195, 250, 320, 321, 334, 340–343, 359, 362, 364, 367
Desirable psychological experience, 347
Development
after birth, 334
before birth factors, 332–334
DHHS, 310
Diagnostic and Statistical Manual of Mental Disorders (DSM), 22, 129, 135, 171
Discrimination, 170, 172

DNA, 331
Double jeopardy, 246, 270
Double-Edged Sword, 317
DSM-IV, 252, 286, 291, 318
Dual perspective, 316, 322

E
Economic consequences, 245
Economic disparity, 5, 76, 77, 114, 115
Edinburgh Postpartum Depression Scale (EDPS), 342
Egocentric, 135
Elders' Adaptability, Resilience and, 246–248
Emotional Closeness, 268
Enculturation, 157, 162, 264, 269, 370
Environmental challenges, 131–133, 140
Epidemiologic Catchment Area (ECA), 46
Ethnic identity, 148, 156–162, 169, 175, 178–182, 208, 269
Ethnic media, 195, 202
Ethnic minority, 12, 17, 20, 36, 48
Ethnicity, 3, 12, 14, 22, 38, 56, 58, 72, 109, 137, 209
Ethnophysiology, 134
Eurocentric culture, 71
European American children and youth
  mental health, 215, 216
  well-being, 208–210
European American children, psychology of
  maintaining mental health
    family support, 210
    media exposure, 210, 211
    power and privilege, 211, 212
  mental health
    American dream, 212, 213
    cultural familiarity, 213
    parenting style, 214, 215
    socioeconomic status, 214
    youth, the well-being of, 208–210
European Americans, 367, 368
European American adults, psychology of
  mental health
    alcohol abuse, 228, 229
    poverty, 224–226
    protective cognitive variable, 233
    services, access to, 229–231
    trauma, 226–228
    widely available mental health services, 231–233
  White American adults, demographic characteristics of, 223
European colonization, 370, 371
European subjugation, 370
Evidence-based practice (EBP), 5, 88–90, 92, 94, 100, 103
Expanded Transactional model (ETM)
  affect regulation, 343
  allostatic load, 343
  application, 347–349
  behavioral patterns, 344
  biology principles, 336
  cognition principles, 339
  current state, 348
  development principles, 336
  mental health principles, 339

F
Familial
  obligations, 268, 296
  religious, and community institutions, 176–178
  support, 198, 199, 210
Familism, 268, 295, 302
Familismo, 320
Family as referent, 268
Family conflict, 173, 174
Family effectiveness training (FET), 271
Family heritage, 110
Family issues, 132, 137, 140
Family poverty, 262
Family, 110–112
Fetal alcohol syndrome (FAS), 114, 333
First foot forward, 348
Five-Factor Model (FFM), 2, 3
Functionalist perspective, 340

G
Global Assessment of Functioning (GAF), 362

H
Help seeking, barriers to, 133–137
Hereditarian hypothesis, 336
High-acculturated peers, 270
Historical unresolved grief, 131, 139
Historically Black Colleges and Universities (HBCUs), 12

I
Immigration
  adaptation, 263–265
  experience, 296–298
Indian elders, 112
Indian Health Service (IHS), 118, 121, 122, 127, 129, 130, 132–134
Indian Religious Crimes Code, 116

Intergenerational grief and trauma, 116
Interpersonal dimension, 315
Isolation, 50, 71, 74, 77, 120, 132, 136, 137, 160, 161, 192, 199, 200, 202, 216

J
John Henryism, 55–58
K
Karma, 192, 193

L
Latino Adult Mental Health, 290–293, 295–298
Latino adults, psychology of
  Latino adult mental health
    familism, 295
    immigration experience, 296–298
    Latino biculturalism, bilingualism and, 296
    mental health care, 295
    mental health service use, 291–294
    socioeconomic status, 290
  national Latino, Asian American study, 280
  United States, Latino adults
    demographic characteristics of, 281–287
    immigrant paradox, 288
    mental disorders among Latinos, 287
Latino American older adults, psychology of
  adherence, 319
  complicating issues, 318
  culturally bound syndromes, 318
  demographic characteristics of, 308
  education, 309
  income, 309
  insurance, 309
  maintaining mental health challenges
    acculturative stress, 313
    communication, 312
    linguistic, 312
    service utilization, 313
  mental health status, 310–312
  mental health strengths
    beliefs, 317
    culture, 315
    family, 316
    religion, 317
    values, 317
  mental illness, 318
  poverty, 309
  psychosocial interventions, 320
  U.S. Hispanics, demographic characteristics of, 308
Latino Americans, 368–370
Latino
  biculturalism, 296
  bilingualism, 296
  demographic characteristics of, 308
Linking positive psychology
  ethnicity, 2
  race, 2

M
Ma'ipopole, 11
Maltreatment parenting, 28–30
Matriarchal, 110
Matrilineal, 110
Media exposure, 210, 211
Mental health care, 7, 72, 128, 134, 136, 140, 182, 209, 230, 231, 233, 234, 291, 295, 303, 308, 314, 317, 320, 324
Mental health development cognitive factors, 336–339
Mental disorders, 190–192
Mental health disorders
  lack of information and knowledge about, 195–196
  stigmatization of, 192–195
Mental health promotion, 358–361
Mental health services, 30, 196–198, 229–233
Mental health, Surgeon General's report on, 243–246, 251, 254, 310
Mental illness, perceptions of, 318
Mental illness prevention, 358–361
Migration, stress associated with, 172, 173
Minority
  experience, 147–162
  status and discrimination, 265–267
Mobility, unique costs of, 58, 60
Model minority stereotype, 155, 156, 159, 172
Multidimensional clinical competence
  positive and negative mental health
    African Americans, 363–365
    Asian Americans, 365, 366
    early intervention, 361–363
    European Americans, 367, 368
    Latino Americans, 368–370
    mental health promotion, 358–361
    mental illness prevention, 358–361
    native Americans, 370–372
    psychopathology, 363
  strengths-based, multicultural, transactional developmental framework, 372–374
Multiple jeopardy, 312, 324

N

NAT Self-Assessment Instrument, 94–103
National Comorbidity Study (NCS), 46
National Council of Urban Indian Health, 134
National Indian Child Welfare Association (NICWA), 90, 92
National Indian Council on Aging, 132
National Indian Health Board, 132, 134
National Institute of Disability and Rehabilitation of Research, 90
National Institute of Health (NIH), 207, 244, 254
National Institute of Mental Health (NIMH), 251
National Institute on Drug (NIDA), 259
National Latino and Asian American Study (NLAAS), 8, 281, 284–292, 297–300, 302–304
National Latino Study, 280
National Longitudinal Survey of Youth (NLSY), 210
National Mental Health Association, 251
National Survey of American Life (NSAL), 46
Native American adult lifespan
  facing the winds, challenges
    acculturation, 116, 117
    economic disparity, 115
    education, 115
    health, 114, 115
    intergenerational grief and trauma, 116
  native strengths
    rural native Americans, 122, 123
  native ways, strengths and resilience
    balance, 113, 114
    family, 110, 112
    harmony, 113, 114
    nation, 110
    tribe, 110
    wisdom keepers, 112
  stories, gift of, 123, 124
  understanding the people, 107, 108
Native American populations, 228
Native American Youth and Family Center (NAYA)
  derived outcomes, 100
  goal, 101
  needs, 101
Native Americans
  economically, 116
  psychologically, 116
Native child, 112
Native communities, 112, 113, 119, 122, 130–132, 137–140
Native elder, 112, 123, 124, 127–142
Native nation
  matriarchal, 110
  matrilineal, 110
  patriarchal, 110, 173
  patrilineal, 110
Native strengths, 117–123
Native ways, 108–110
Non-verbal IQ, 334
North America, clinical psychology in, 12–16
National Survey of Black Americans (NSBA), 54

O

Older adults, psychology of
  African Americans, 71–74
  maintaining mental health
    mental health challenges, 70
    socioeconomic status, 68–70
  mental health, strengths contribution
    religiosity, 75
    social support, 74
  older African Americans, 67
Older AI/AN adults, 128–130
Older American Indians and Alaska Natives, psychology of
  maintaining mental health
    environmental challenges, 131–133
    help seeking, barriers to, 133–137
    sociohistorical factors, 131
  mental health, strengths contributing to
    AI/AN ethnic and cultural identity, 137–138
    spirituality, 138, 139
    support systems, 137
  older AI/AN adults, demographic characteristics of, 128–130
Older White adults
  anxiety, 251
  dementia, 249
  demographic profile, 245
  depression, 250
  economic consequences, 245
  elders' adaptability, 246–248
  White older adults, 251
OSG report, 308, 310, 315

P

Parenting style, 214, 215
Patriarchal, 110
Patrilineal, 110
Peer support, 200
Perfectionism, 155
Peritraumatic distress, 226, 234
Personal dimension, 315

Personalismo, 317, 320
Pew Hispanic center, 259
Phenomenology, 134–136
Physical
health, 131, 154, 176, 195, 243, 249, 253, 313, 322, 335
mobility, 132
Polychlorinated biphenyls (PCBs), 332
Positive and negative mental health, 234, 329, 358
Positive psychology, 3
Positive psychology and mental health
ethnicity, 2
race, 2
understanding, 3
value of, 1
Positive psychology model, 21
Postmodern identities, 17–22
Posttraumatic Stress Disorder (PTSD), 28, 129, 226–228, 234, 252
Post-traumatic symptoms, 362
Postwar challenges, 17–22
Poverty, 224–226
Power and privilege, 211, 212
Power moves, 107–124
Practice-based evidence (PBE), 5, 87–91, 101, 103
Practice-based evidence approach
building relationships, 91–94
challenge, 88
culturally appropriate outcome measures, 94
NAT self-assessment instrument, 95–100
NAYA's goals, 101
NAYA's needs, 101
NAYA-derived outcomes, 100
refining plans, 91–94
response, 89–91
Prejudice, 170–172
Primitive
man, 13
people, 13
society, 13
Positive adaptation, 158, 261, 267, 268, 270, 271
Protective cognitive variable, 233
Proven practices, 89
Psychiatric
disorders, 129, 130, 133, 135
distress, 134
epidemiology, 129
issues, 133
symptoms, 130, 133, 135
Psychological
dysfunction, 369
flexibility, 359
Psychological
anthropology, 134
distress, 130, 136, 155, 162, 191, 197, 200, 272
symptoms, 195, 196
Psychopathology, 3, 22, 363
Psychosocial
adaptation, 192
interventions, 320
PTSD, 226–228, 234, 252
Punitive parenting, 4, 27–30, 37

R

Race, 2–4, 6, 12, 16, 20, 59, 60, 67, 72, 217, 243, 244, 280, 308, 310, 331, 349
Race psychology, 15
Racial
discrimination, 5, 48–60, 67
groups, 118, 209–212, 224–226, 228–236
microaggressions, 171
prejudice, 70, 71, 76, 171
stereotype, 155
Racism, 48–58
Randomized Clinical Trials (RCTs), 88–90
Relational World View (RWV), 93, 94
Religion, 199, 200
Residence, place of, 131, 140
Residential segregation, 49–51
Resiliency, 109, 138, 147, 158–160, 175, 176, 209, 210
Respeto, 317, 320
Restrictive parents, 33–35
Robust self-esteem, 35–37
Rural Native Americans, 122, 123

S

Severe mental illness (SMI), 231, 253
Slum and ghetto values, 19
Social acceptance, 359
Social actualization, 359
Social coherence, 359
Social contribution, 359
Social integration, 359
Social networks, 189, 200, 202, 227
Social supports
challenge, 52
extension, 32
serve, 53–55
Sociocentric, 135
Sociocultural dimension, 315, 317

Socioeconomic position (SEP), 50, 53, 56–60
Socioeconomic status (SES), 5–7, 50, 58, 60, 68–70, 76, 78, 116, 190, 209, 214, 217, 224, 225, 228, 234, 243, 262, 267, 280, 290, 301, 303, 332, 335, 341, 342, 348, 361, 367, 374
Sociohistorical factors, 131
Sojourner syndrome, 57–59
Soul loss, 135, 136
Spirituality, 138, 139, 199, 200
Status quo, 236, 348, 356
Structural dimension, 315
Structure and funding, 133, 137, 140
Substance Abuse and Mental Health Services Administration (SAMHSA), 90

T
Traditional Latino familism values, 7, 268
Traditional Native, 110, 123, 136, 138
Transactional model of development
 application of ETM
  desirable psychological experience, 347
  distinct experience, 347
  ETM, current state of, 348
 empiricism, promise of, 345
 Expanded Transactional Model (ETM), race and
  affect regulation, ETM and, 343
  Affect regulation, environmental impacts, 340–343
  allostatic load, ETM and, 343
  behavioral patterns, ETM and, 344
  development after birth biological factors, 334
  development before birth factors, 332–334
  ETM principles to biology, 336
  ETM principles to cognition, 339
  ETM principles to development, 336
  ETM principles to mental health, 339
  lifelong development biological influences, 331
  mental health development cognitive factors, 336–339
Trauma, 226–228
Tribe, 110

U
Understanding the people, 107, 108
United States Census Bureau, 223, 245, 251, 259, 281, 309
United States Department of Health and Human Services (USDHHS), 47, 170, 207, 209, 230, 235, 308
United States, Latino adults, 283–289
U.S. Census Bureau, 45, 128, 133, 169, 170, 189, 208
U.S. Department of Commerce, 128
U.S. Hispanics, 308
U.S. Latino Youth
 common challenges
  family, community poverty and, 262
  immigration, cultural adaptation and, 263–265
  minority status, discrimination and, 265–267
 cultural resources
  bicultural competence, 270
  ethnic identity, 269
  traditional Latino familism values, 268
 promote positive adaptation, recommendations to, 271
U.S. population, 118, 119, 128, 140, 180, 189, 208, 217
U.S. Public Health Service, 30

V
Verbal IQ, 334
Violence, exposure to, 28
Vulnerability, sources of, 154–157

W
Western psychology, 136, 141
White American adults, 223
White older adults, 251
Wisdom keepers, 112
World Health Organization (WHO), 215, 250, 347, 358–360

CPSIA information can be obtained at www.ICGtesting.com
Printed in the USA
LVOW09*1232090913

351618LV00004B/19/P

9 781461 404231